# The Therapist's Handbook

## Treatment Methods of Mental Disorders

# The Therapist's Handbook

## Treatment Methods of Mental Disorders

Edited by
### Benjamin B. Wolman, Ph.D.

In collaboration with

Richard Abrams, M.D.
Michael S. Aronoff, M.D.
Gertrude Blanck, Ph.D.
Ewald W. Busse, M.D.
Morris E. Chafetz, M.D.
Richard D. Chessick, M.D.
James W. Dykens, M.D.
Jack R. Ewalt, M.D.
Patricia L. Ewalt, M.S.W.

Marshal F. Folstein, M.D.
Sanford Goldstone, Ph.D.
Daniel N. Hertz, M.D.
Samuel B. Kutash, Ph.D.
Arnold A. Lazarus, Ph.D.
Sidney Lecker, M.D.
Stanley Lesse, M.D.
Paul R. McHugh, M.D.
G. Donald Niswander, M.D.

R.A. Ramsay, M.D.
Max Rosenbaum, Ph.D.
Dean Schuyler, M.D.
Arthur H. Schwartz, M.D.
Marshall Swartzburg, M.D.
H. Warnes, M.D.
Alan D. Whanger, M.D.
G. Terence Wilson, Ph.D.
E.D. Wittkower, M.D.

Foreword by **Bertram S. Brown, M.D.**

 **VAN NOSTRAND REINHOLD COMPANY**
NEW YORK    CINCINNATI    TORONTO    LONDON    MELBOURNE

Van Nostrand Reinhold Company Regional Offices:
New York  Cincinnati  Chicago  Millbrae  Dallas

Van Nostrand Reinhold Company International Offices:
London  Toronto  Melbourne

Library of Congress Catalog Card Number: 75-28356
ISBN: 0-442-29570-7

Manufactured in the United States of America

Published by Van Nostrand Reinhold Company
450 West 33rd Street, New York, N.Y. 10001

Published simultaneously in Canada by Van Nostrand Reinhold Ltd.

15  14  13  12  11  10  9  8  7  6  5  4  3  2  1


*Library of Congress Cataloging in Publication Data*

Main entry under title:

The Therapist's handbook:  treatment methods of mental
    disorders.
    Bibliography:  p.
    Includes index.
    1.  Psychotherapy - - Addresses, essays, lectures.
I.  Wolman, Benjamin B.  [DNLM:  1.  Psychotherapy.
2.  Mental disorders - - Therapy.  WM420  T398]
RC480.T445  1976  616.8'914  75-28356
ISBN 0-442-29570-7

# Contributors

*Richard Abrams, M.D.* Associate Professor of Psychiatry and Director, University Psychiatric Service, Department of Psychiatry and Behavioral Science, State University of New York at Stony Brook, Stony Brook, New York.

*Michael S. Aronoff, M.D.* Associate in Clinical Psychiatry, Columbia University; Associate Psychiatrist, Presbyterian Hospital; Adjunct Psychiatrist, Lenox Hill Hospital, New York.

*Gertrude Blanck, Ph.D.* Curriculum Director, Institute for the Study of Psychotherapy, New York.

*Ewald W. Busse, M.D., Sc. D.* J.P. Gibbons Professor and Chairman, Department of Psychiatry, Duke University School of Medicine; Founding Director, Duke University Center for the Study of Aging and Human Development, Durham, North Carolina; Past President, American Psychiatric Association.

*Morris E. Chafetz, M.D.* Director, National Institute on Alcohol Abuse and Alcoholism, National Institute of Mental Health, Department of Health, Education and Welfare, Washington, D.C.

*Richard D. Chessick, M.D.* Professor of Psychiatry, Northwestern University Medical School, Evanston, Illinois.

*James W. Dykens, M.D.* Director, State of New Hampshire Division of Mental Health, Concord, New Hampshire.

*Jack R. Ewalt, M.D.* Bullard Professor and Chairman, Executive Committee, Department of Psychiatry, Harvard Medical School, Cambridge, Massachusetts.

*Patricia L. Ewalt, M.S.W.* Assistant Chief, Social Service, Framingham Youth Guidance Center; Clinical Assistant Professor, School of Social Work, Boston University, Boston, Massachusetts.

*Marshal F. Folstein, M.D.*   Assistant Professor of Psychiatry, University of Oregon, Portland, Oregon.

*Sanford Goldstone, Ph.D.*   Professor and Head, Psychology Division, Cornell University Medical College; Head, Community Consultation Services, Payne Whitney Psychiatric Clinic, New York.

*Daniel N. Hertz, M.D.*   Assistant Clinical Professor of Psychiatry, Cornell University Medical College; Attending Psychiatrist, New York Hospital-Cornell Medical Center, and St. Vincent's Hospital, New York.

*Samuel B. Kutash, Ph.D.*   Director, New Jersey Division, New York Center for Psychoanalytic Training.

*Arnold A. Lazarus, Ph.D.*   Professor of Psychology, Graduate School of Applied and Professional Psychology, Rutgers University, Piscataway, New Jersey.

*Sidney Lecker, M.D.*   Assistant Commissioner for Children's Services, State of New York Department of Mental Hygiene, Division of Mental Retardation and Children's Services; Director, Rockland County Mental Health Clinic, Pomona, New York.

*Stanley Lesse, M.D.*   Editor-in-Chief, *American Journal of Psychotherapy;* President, Association for the Advancement of Psychotherapy; Associate Attending Neurologist, Columbia-Presbyterian Medical Center, New York.

*Paul R. McHugh, M.D.*   Professor and Chairman, Department of Psychiatry, University of Oregon Medical School, Portland, Oregon.

*G. Donald Niswander, M.D.*   Director of Psychiatric Education and Research, New Hampshire Hospital.

*R.A. Ramsay, M.D.*   Assistant Professor of Psychiatry, McGill University; Chief, Psychiatric Consultant Service, Royal Victoria Hospital, Montreal, Quebec, Canada.

*Max Rosenbaum, Ph.D.*   Editor-in-Chief, *Group Process;* Lecturer, Department of Psychiatry, New York Medical College, New York.

*Dean Schuyler, M.D.*   Coordinator, Depression Section, Clinical Research Branch, Division of Extramural Research Programs, National Institute of Mental Health, Washington, D.C.

*Arthur H. Schwartz, M.D.*   Associate Professor of Psychiatry, Mount Sinai School of Medicine, New York.

*Marshall Swartzburg, M.D.*   Assistant Professor of Psychiatry, College of Medicine and Dentistry, Rutgers State University, New Brunswick, New Jersey.

*H. Warnes, M.D.*   Associate Professor of Psychiatry, McGill University; Psychiatrist-in-Chief, St. Mary's Hospital, Montreal, Quebec, Canada.

*Alan D. Whanger, M.D.*   Assistant Professor of Psychiatry, Duke University School of Medicine, Durham, North Carolina; Chairman, Geriatric Psychiatry Group, Duke University Medical Center; Consultant in Geropsychiatry, John Umstead, Cherry and Dorothea Dix State Hospitals.

*G. Terence Wilson, Ph. D.* Associate Professor of Psychology, Graduate School of Applied and Professional Psychology, Rutgers University, Piscataway, New Jersey.

*E.D. Wittkower, M.D.* Professor of Psychiatry Emeritus, McGill University; Consulting Psychiatrist, Royal Victoria Hospital, Montreal General Hospital, Reddy Memorial Hospital, Queen Elizabeth Hospital, Montreal, Quebec, Canada.

*Benjamin B. Wolman, Ph. D.* Professor of Psychology, Doctoral Program in Clinical Psychology, Long Island University, Brooklyn, New York; Editor-in-Chief, *International Journal of Group Tensions;* President, International Organization for the Study of Group Tensions; Editor-in-Chief, *International Encyclopedia of Neurology, Psychiatry, Psychoanalysis and Psychology.*

# Foreword

Throughout the remainder of this decade, more than three million individuals in this country will seek the assistance of a mental health professional each year, if current patient episode rate remains the same. The brunt of this national caseload will be borne by the four mental health core disciplines: psychiatry, psychology, psychiatric social work, and psychiatric nursing. Additional vital services will be provided by medical, educational, correctional, pastoral and other human service professionals and paraprofessionals. The multidisciplinary team approach will become increasingly imperative within a diverse population of nearly a quarter billion persons.

Only a century ago, the study of mental health and illness was the stepchild of general medicine and neurology. Prior to that time, "treatment" was found, more often than not, in dungeons, torture, and even exile or death. The era of scientific psychiatry, as we know it today, is a relatively recent phenomenon, founded on an exponentially increasing knowledge of the nature, causes, treatment, and prevention of mental disorder and of the course of normal development.

This volume reflects the major schools of thought and approaches to treating mental illness which comprise the mental health armamentarium today. The distinguished contributors, all authorities in their fields, represent both the traditions and trends in treatment. Such a dynamic approach is inherent to a field where even the definition of our subject is ever open to discussion.

The Handbook represents, also, the interrelationship of research, training, and service which is so essential to continued progress in our field. In any science, but perhaps particularly in ours, a compilation such as this provides fresh insights to evaluative needs and, in turn, to research directed toward the development of refined techniques.

Twenty-five years ago, Freudian psychoanalysis was the most highly developed form of psychosocial treatment. The major somatic treatments were electro-convulsive therapy, insulin "shock," and prefrontal lobotomy. Treatments for central nervous system syphilis and psychosis associated with pellagra were also available. Behavior modification, on the other hand, had not yet emerged from the laboratory. Few psychoactive drugs were known, and these typically were used to manage rather than treat mental patients.

Today, as we see in the first section of this volume, the scene has changed vastly. The full range of mental and emotional disorders is treated by a panoply of techniques ranging from chemotherapy and classical and modified psycho-therapy to behavior therapy and physical manipulation.

Part Two of the Handbook portrays even more strikingly the advancement of our knowledge base over the past quarter century. Specialized treatments for the major and more severe disorders have been made possible through a vastly increased understanding of the biological, biochemical, psychological, and social bases of behavior. Furthermore, chapters on the treatment of antisocial behavior and narcotic and alcohol addictions bring to mind the changing social attitudes with respect to human problems which are more frequently acknowledged to fall within the purview of the mental health practitioner.

Because the contributing authors of this volume need no introduction and because their papers speak well for themselves, I would like to use this space to summarize briefly certain of the events which have led us to these treatment methods and to question where they will lead from here. This overview is based on a major review and analysis by the National Institute of Mental Health of the Institute's contributions to the nation's mental health research effort since passage of the National Mental Health Act in 1946. The full review — *The Report of the Research Task Force: Research in the Service of Mental Health* — is available through the NIMH.

During the first half of the twentieth century, psychotherapeutic treatment, particularly psychoanalysis, was felt to be the only effective form of treatment, and the somatic techniques were held in low esteem. In the late 1940s psycho-analytic emphases were beginning to shift from id to ego psychology and to the study of interpersonal relationships. Rogerian and neoanalytic therapies gained impetus and were supplemented by a number of new adjunctive approaches which included art, music, drama, and play therapy. Also at that time, in part because of the scarcity of trained therapists, a shift in emphasis from individual to group settings was just being explored, a shift that was to de-velop into the most significant modification of psychotherapy during this period.

A major turning point, from any number of perspectives, occurred in the early 1950s with the introduction of psychotropic drugs in the treatment of mental illness. Somatic therapies — based on the recognition that behavior, thought, and feeling are linked to biochemical and neural mechanisms — are, of course, firmly rooted in scientific psychiatry. These include a variety of drug and convulsive therapies. With the development of the psychoactive agents, the treatment of the severe mental disorders has changed dramatically. Whereas schizophrenic patients formerly were likely to spend years in a mental hospital, many are now treated in general hospitals or as outpatients. Patients are discharged into the community to their families, halfway houses, or foster families. Treatment of the affective disorders has been influenced similarly by the new medications. Today, with the usefulness of drugs proven in the control of acute disorders, the researcher's attention is turned toward investigations of the prophylactic action of psychotropic drugs as well as the reduction of drug side effects.

Because the drug-treated patient is more accessible to other forms of treatment, we are also witnessing a resurgence of psychosocial treatment for even the most seriously ill patients. These events have enabled mental hospitals to continue to move from a custodial philosophy to the modern practice of the traditional "moral treatment."

In fact, the psychotherapies — with their focus on treating the "whole person" through verbal and symbolic techniques — have been an area of tremendous growth in recent years. As group therapy qua therapy demonstrated its effectiveness, the way was open for the development and refinement of group approaches applied to such units as the family, the hospital ward, and the community. The number of individual psychotherapies, the variety of techniques, and the number of therapists — both authorized and self-appointed have also grown steadily, matched by the number of consumers — professionally and self-diagnosed. A recent survey of psychosocial modalities revealed more than 130 therapies reported in the literature.

As psychotropic drugs and these concomitant developments were emerging as major forces in the treatment of mental illness, principles of operant and classical conditioning were providing a foundation for the experimental and clinical development of behavior therapy. Essentially a form of psychosocial treatment, behavior therapy has as its goal alteration of principal presenting problems rather than a direct therapeutic focus on personality, character structure, or underlying conflicts. In the view of the behavior therapists, maladaptive responses obey the same laws of learning and conditioning as do "normal" responses and are amenable to change through the application of what is known about learning and behavior modification. Introduced in hospital wards in the 1950s, behavior therapy offered an alternative to orthodox psychotherapeutic techniques. Within ten years, behavior modification techniques were extended from the back wards of institutions to home settings, classrooms, rehabilitation wards, prisons, nursing homes, and other settings. Behavior therapy has become a frequently used treatment, particularly for managing institutional populations and children's behavior problems.

Even this brief summary of highlights serves to distinguish the major categories of treatment — psychosocial, somatic, and behavioral — available to the mental health practitioner. Such a categorization, however, may tend to oversimplify the types of treatments a given client might receive. An individual's behavior is the result of complex interactions involving the biological and physiological bases of behavior, interpersonal relations, and social environment. In selecting a treatment, the therapist must have some conception of what produces, interacts with, aggravates, or sustains the problem to be treated. Does he view the manifest symptomatology as a product of disordered brain function, intrapsychic or interpersonal conflicts, learning deficits, environmental factors, or, as is likely the case, an interaction among all these factors? Overriding considerations must be given to making the treatment fit the unique needs of the individual client. Perhaps in no other branch of medicine are the subjective needs of the patient as paramount as in the treatment of mental and emotional disorders. Thus any of these three major categories of therapy, each with its respective subsets, might be used in succession, in combination, etc.

At the same time that therapeutic approaches are multiplying, "problems of living" are being brought to mental health practitioners in ever-increasing numbers. Consequently, one of the greatest continuing needs of the treatment field is improved therapy evaluation methods. Evaluation is difficult, particularly in the psychosocial area with the many interpersonal variables which must be taken into account. Yet the identification of which therapies are most effective with which groups of patients under what conditions constitutes the matrix from which future therapies will be formulated.

As an immediate result of improved treatment techniques and faster hospital population turnover, we are currently experiencing a need for more effective rehabilitative and follow-up, or maintenance, therapies. Without adequate post-discharge programs — as much an issue of service delivery as treatment efficacy — little is gained in the long run by returning patients to the community.

On a long-range scale, we are witnessing a shift of emphasis, among practitioners and policymakers, from psychological illness to psychological health. In part, this reflects an optimistic attitude toward the possibility of enhancing functioning rather than merely ameliorating distress. This shift is due to both the economics of health care and the realities of effective preventive mental health measures. Continuing research suggests that early identification of emotional problems particularly among children, may permit appropriate intervention, arrest and reversal of processes that could produce serious problems more resistant to change later in life.

The papers presented in this volume provide a base for further modification and revision as we continue to build on our present knowledge and improve our ability to treat mental and emotional disorders.

BERTRAM S. BROWN, M.D.
Director
National Institute of Mental Health

# Preface

There is no general agreement concerning treatment methods of mental disorders. The practitioners, whether they are psychiatrists or clinical psychologists, are divided among themselves, and no one has found the final solution to the multiple therapeutic issues. Follow-up studies and empirical research have offered substantial support to the various therapeutic techniques, but so far no particular approach has won the general approval and no one has the monopoly on truth.

Perhaps no one will ever have. Theoretical physicists have accepted the fact that there are two different theories of light, and psychopathologists will have to live with the fact that there are more than two theories of affective psychosis or schizophrenia. Each theory offers a different rationale for treatment, and even within the same theoretical framework there is room for diverse therapeutic approaches.

The present volume reflects the diversity of viewpoints, and my choice of contributors was based not on communality of approaches. The indisputable competence, experience, and mastery of the relevant material were the sole criterion for the choice of authors for the respective chapters of the Handbook.

The Handbook is divided into two parts. Part One describes the various treatment methods; Part Two is directed to particular psychopathological patterns and describes specific techniques applicable to these patterns. Thus, the professionals who want to know e.g., about chemotherapy in general as applied to the various disorders will seek guidance in the first part of the book, but if they are concerned with chemotherapeutic methods applied to the manic-depressive disorder, they will find the answers in the second part of the book.

Efforts were made to avoid overlapping, but some degree of overlapping and repetition was inevitable, especially between the two parts of the Handbook. For example, the various methods of psychotherapy were described in the first part of this volume, but some repetition was necessary in the second part which describes the application of these methods to particular mental disorders.

In the planning and preparation of this Handbook, I was greatly helped by Drs. Morris Herman, William F. Lhamon and Marvin Stein who offered their time and advice. I am also indebted to Mr. Barry Nathan, Editor, and Mrs. Alberta Gordon, Managing Editor, both of Van Nostrand Reinhold Company. My assistant, Ms. Kathy Mankes, has offered invaluable help in putting this volume together.

BENJAMIN B. WOLMAN

# Contents

# Part One
## General Techniques

# 1 The Process of Treatment

## Benjamin B. Wolman

Any process of treatment, whether it is surgical, dental or psychological, involves two parties, namely the helping professional and the help-seeking public. The patients come to the therapists because they need help. A patient suffers from and is aware of shortcomings or malfunctions of his bodily structure, sensory apparatus, or mental functioning. He looks for somebody qualified and licensed to provide the appropriate treatment for diseases, ills, handicaps and disorders. This patient-therapist relationship, like any other social relationship, can be presented in two dimensions. The first dimension is the dimension of *power;* power being defined as the ability to satisfy needs. People who can satisfy the needs of themselves and others are strong; those who cannot, are weak. The peak of power is omnipotence, and human beings ascribe omnipotent features to their Gods. The bottom of power is the zero point of death; corpses have no power.

The concept of power originates in the physical strength of muscles and jaws, for the primitive man and subhuman species satisfy their fundamental needs such as food, water, shelter, by using their physical strength. With the development of higher nervous functions, the human species has developed and learned to use other elements in order to survive, for survival is the arch-need of all needs.

While the lower levels of power are often activated in the struggle for survival, most human beings have to learn to use other strengths in addition to and in preference to their muscles and jaws. Most human beings procure their food, water, and shelter not through physical fighting, but through work. The use of working tools, technology and the skills for producing, providing, exchanging, shipping and storing goods have become far more important aspects of power than the initial, archaic physical strength.

3

Power, defined as the ability to satisfy needs, applies also to the practitioners in the fields of physical and mental health. The people who have certain innate abilities and have developed these abilities by training and experience, have acquired the power to heal other people's wounds, ills and shortcomings. They are the competent and skilled helpers, called surgeons, dentists, psychiatrists or psychologists, according to their particular training and skill.

Power can be used in more than one direction. Power can be used to help satisfy needs or to prevent their satisfaction. Thus, the interaction between individuals can be presented on quasi-Cartesian ordinates, with the vertical line presenting power, starting with omnipotence at the top and at the bottom, the zero point of power, death. The horizontal line towards the right represents the friendly attitude and towards the left, the hostile attitude. People can be friendly or hostile, friendly meaning willing to satisfy needs, hostile meaning preventing their satisfaction. Let us call these two dimensions of strong-weak and friendly-hostile *power* and *acceptance,* respectively.

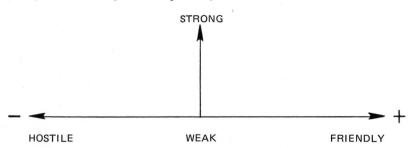

Obviously, when one has a toothache, he looks for somebody who has the *power* to heal his tooth, that is, a competent, skilled and experienced dentist; and at the same time, the patient looks for someone who is *friendly,* or willing to heal him. The dimension of power implies competence; the dimension of acceptance is indicated by integrity, devotion to the profession, and conscientious work with patients.

People interact with one another not on the basis of how things are, but how they *perceive* them. Imagine someone who migrated from another country to the United States. Suppose that in his home country, he was well-known as a highly experienced dentist, and people had flocked to his office, seeking his help. But in the new country, people don't know how good he is and therefore they may not seek his help. The same reasoning applies to the dimension of acceptance. People choose a professional man not on the basis of what he is, but judge him on his reputation, that is, public opinion. When the consensus is that a particular psychiatrist or surgeon or dentist or psychologist is exceptionally gifted and highly competent, then he is believed to be powerful. If he has the reputation of being devoted and conscientious, then he is believed to be friendly and people will seek his help. But such a reputation may or may not correspond to the truth.

## THE RIGHTS OF THE PATIENTS

Suffering people have the right to seek help or to refuse help. There is no way to force anyone to go to a dentist even if one has several rotten teeth. No one forces a man with a broken foot to go into surgery. It is an integral part of civil rights to be free to determine whether one is interested in getting well. Moreover, the patient has the right to decide into whose hands he would put his fate. The patient chooses who is going to be his surgeon or dentist. Of course, the patient may seek advice from a local professional organization if he wishes to do so. He may consult with professionals in the same or related fields about the reputation of the therapist to whom he intends to go, but ultimately, it is the patient who determines *whether* he will seek help and *whom* he will choose as his therapist.

This basic human freedom is not always preserved in the field of mental health. In most countries there are laws which make possible forced hospitalization and, implicitly, permit forced treatment of confined mentally disturbed individuals. This involuntary treatment raises grave moral and legal issues. In my practice, I have had several cases where husbands, wives and relatives insisted on the hospitalization of a member of their family. Their intentions concerning the patient were not necessarily noble. Once I had in treatment, a paranoid schizophrenic woman whose husband had a girlfriend. He wanted to put his hands on a quite substantial inheritance which belonged to his wife. He demanded that I take the necessary steps and hospitalize his wife. In addition to the legal problems, which I could have solved with the help of my colleague psychiatrists and administrators in the hospital where I was the supervisor of psychiatry at the time, the issue presented grave moral problems. This woman undoubtedly *was* a menace to the well-being of her husband. Whether she would go so far as to try to put an end to his life, I wasn't sure, but I could not exclude such a possibility. Moreover, her overt hostility and paranoid accusations impaired her husband's personal freedom and his rights to a minimum of human happiness. What should one do in such a case?

In some cases I had decided to hospitalize the patient. Once, a colleague psychiatrist called me and requested that I see a young woman who developed post-partum psychosis. She was hallucinating and, to the best of his knowledge, suicidal. Since I had been working with schizophrenics for years with some degree of success, he recommended this young woman to me for ambulatory treatment. The young woman was brought to my office by her mother, brother, and husband. The woman was in bad shape; she was incoherent, she hallucinated and her speech was garbled. However, after talking with her for half an hour, I felt that I had a reasonably good chance of successful treatment. Her initial reaction towards me was friendly, and it seemed to me that we could develop good rapport, and I could eventually resolve her emotional conflicts. I called in the mother and told her that although not enthusiastic about it, I was willing to take care of her daughter. In the beginning I had to see the young woman every day, seven days a week; this was a sort of sacrifice on my part for I work five days a week and hate to work on weekends. Moreover, I told her mother that I would be responsible for her daughter for one hour out of every twenty-four hours, and the family must make sure that somebody else would keep an eye on her for the remaining twenty-three hours a day. I explained to the mother that her daughter had strong suicidal tendencies and I must establish a watchdog over her with a sort of hot-line to my office and to my home. The mother replied with a barrage of accusations directed against the ungrateful daughter. She said that because of her daughter, her husband had left her and didn't want to come home. She blamed her daughter for breaking up the family, for causing disorder, grievances and hostility in the family. She resented the fact of the girl's birth, she hated the newborn grandchild, and wished to get rid of both of them.

Certainly, the mother was not the best guardian for this severely sick girl. I invited the brother into my office for a talk while the other members of the family waited in the waiting room. The brother was in worse shape than the patient. He told me hallucinatory stories about his sister. He was apparently a very disturbed young man with a tenuous contact with reality. Certainly, I could not leave this poor girl under the supervision of her brother who needed treatment no less than she did. Finally, I invited the husband. The husband was a youngish looking, charming man in his early thirties. He told me about his studies and his great successes in graduate school. When I asked him about his wife, he told me that she was a little nervous, somewhat quarrelsome and occasionally unpleasant, but otherwise she was all right. He was busy with his studies and did not intend to spend much time with her, especially when she would make a nuisance of herself.

It became obvious that there was no one who could be responsible for the poor girl. I called in all the members of the family to my office and told them that I could not treat her on an outpatient basis and I advised them to take her to a hospital. If they wished so, I could call the director of a private hospital whom I knew and trusted. I suggested that they go straight from my office to the hospital because I wouldn't leave the sick girl with them even for one day. Her husband remarked that she didn't have pajamas and therefore they would not take her to the hospital.

What should be the criterion for involuntary confinement? I recommend confinement only in the case of acute danger of suicide or genocide. But while on the issue of genocide most people would agree with me, on the issue of suicide there is a great deal of controversy.

Thomas Szasz (1971) believes that the individual has the right to his own life and no psychiatrist has the right to "save" one's life against the person's wishes. The moral issue is quite complex because a person may act on impulse; or in a state of severe depression; or he may be unaware of what he is doing; or be unable to use judgment about his situation in life (Shneidman, 1970). But even when a person is a menace to others, the issue is not perfectly clear. What does it mean to be a menace to others? One may recall the case of the young man at the University of Texas who told his psychiatrist, "I feel like killing." According to the newspapers, the psychiatrist told him "Please come next week." Certainly such a conversation makes one doubt whether good judgment could be exercised in regard to all mental cases. There is a country where people are being forcibly hospitalized in mental hospitals whenever they are perceived by the rulers to be "enemies of the people." Many years ago, Henrik Ibsen wrote a play, *The Enemy of the People.* Ibsen described an honest physician who tried to defend the rights of the patients against the greedy fathers of his town. Today, in the Soviet Union, people who disagree with the system and express ideas critical of the leadership are often thrown into mental hospitals and declared insane.

Quite often, in a conversation or an argument, we call neurotic, moron, or insane, those who express opinions contrary to our own. But as long as this is merely a figure of speech, there is no severe threat to the basic human freedoms. But when labeling people as mentally sick becomes a matter for the police, the issue may become quite grave. Certainly in the Soviet Union and, in certain instances, in other countries, some people are forced to undergo treatment which they may not wish to get.

However, even in a democratic society, the issue is far from simple. Should we allow mentally irresponsible people to be at large and jeopardize the lives of others? What should be done in a case when the freedom and the civil rights of one individual clash with the freedom and rights of other individuals?

The question of rights of mental patients hinges upon the definition of mental health.

## THE CONCEPT OF MENTAL HEALTH

A group of psychiatrists and sociologists headed by Dr. Srole undertook a survey of mental health in Manhattan (Srole *et al.,* 1962). They came to the astonishing conclusion that 81.5% of the population is somewhat emotionally disturbed. How then could the 18.5% undisturbed people take care of the 81.5% disturbed ones?

Overinclusions have their spectacular precedent in the Middle Ages when tens of thousands of women were believed to be practicing witchcraft, and witch-hunting was the favorite pastime of monks and theologians. The famous Benedictine abbot Trithemius (believed to be a great scholar and a very gentle person) regretted that there were not enough inquisitors to punish the witches. He wrote the following:

> There is no part in our body that the witches would not injure. Unfortunately, the number of such witches is very great in every province; more than that, there is no locality too small for a witch to find. Yet inquisitors and judges who could avenge these open offenses against God and nature are few and far between. Man and beast die as a result of the evil of these women and no one thinks of the fact that these things are perpetrated by witches.

In 1487, two great theologians, Sprenger and Kraemer, published the book *Malleus Maleficarum* (The Witches' Hammer) in which they recommended, "The witch should be stripped of her clothes, her wounds and marks of torture exposed, her head and genitals shaven so that no devil could conceal himself in her hair, and led into court backwards so that her evil eyes might not rest on the judge and bewitch him " (quoted after Zilboorg and Henry, 1941).

In 1587, the judge Boguet estimated that under King Charles IX, France had 300,000 witches and sorcerers. The witch-hunts continued in Europe well into the eighteenth century, and the last witch was executed in Glarus, Switzerland in June, 1782. Even the more liberal people, such as the British physician Willis, suggested that "Nothing is more necessary and more effective for the recovery of these people than forcing them to respect and fear intimidation. By this method, the mind held back by restraint is induced to give up its arrogance and wild ideas . . . This is why maniacs recover much sooner if they are treated with torture and torments in a hovel instead of with medicaments."

Judging against this background, Dr. Pinel's work was indeed revolutionary. On September 11, 1793, Dr. Pinel was appointed director of the mental asylum of Bicêtre. He declared that the mentally sick, far from being guilty people deserving of punishment, are *sick people* whose miserable state deserves all the consideration that is due to suffering humanity.

Diseases are caused by external forces and one cannot be blamed for being sick. By calling Bicêtre inmates "sick," Pinel gave them a new status – the status of innocent, helpless victims of unknown diseases. There is no doubt that the change from "madman" to mentally "sick" caused a revolution in the treatment of mental disorders. One may torture people without knowing anything about them, but one cannot cure diseases without understanding them. According to Pinel, mental disorders were diseases of the central nervous system caused by heredity and unfortunate experiences.

## THE FIRST PSYCHIATRIC REVOLUTION

Viewing mentally disturbed people as such individuals made them into mental "patients" and as such, exposed them to medical treatment. However, in the vast majority of cases, none of these medical methods worked, and the crossroads of the nineteenth and twentieth century witnessed a growing feeling of skepticism concerning the possibility of curing mental diseases.

Freud's discovery of unconscious motivation opened new vistas in dealing with emotionally disturbed people. Freud maintained that the majority of mental disorders is not of organic origin and thus not related to the nervous system. Although Freud's terminology is rooted in medical phraseology, he strongly objected to the idea that psychoanalysis should ever become a chambermaid to psychiatry.

Small wonder that Freud's ideas met with stern opposition by his contemporaries. Hysteria was believed to be a disease of the uterus (hysterus in Greek) which wandered around the human body in search of moisture. Hysterectomies were often performed on women in order to cure hysteria. When Freud came out with the idea that hysteria is caused by emotional conflicts in childhood and occurs in men also, he was widely criticized and ridiculed.

Whether one subscribed to Freud's ideas concerning disturbed behavior or not, one must admit that the shift of emphasis from the medical model to emotional factors has certainly brought a better understanding of what makes people act in a disturbed manner, thus permitting a more rational approach to the treatment of their irrationality. However, a great many scientists and practitioners, leaning on Freud's ideas, went beyond Freud and discovered additional factors in the so-called mental disorders. The sexual aspects of emotional life are certainly a relevant factor in human behavior but by no means the only one, and possibly not the most important one. While some of Freud's faithful disciples and dissidents have modified his teachings to include other aspects of human life, some experts went even further and rejected the notion of mental disease as such. Dr. Thomas Szasz (1971), R.D. Laing (1973) and I (1973) have introduced new ideas concerning disturbed behavior.

## MENTAL DISEASES OR HUMAN TRAGEDIES

Years of practice, research and teaching in the clinical field make me doubt whether one can draw a sharp dividing line between the so-called normal and abnormal people. There is hardly anyone who could be consistently well-balanced, rational, aware of what to do — in short, always in perfect mental health. Everyone has periods of elation and depression, sociability and alienation, bouncing energy and passivity, thus experiencing periods or moments of irrational behavior.

There are certain cases of clear-cut mental disease in the organic sense of the word. For instance, paresis caused by syphilis, Kirchhoff disease caused by alcoholism, Down syndrome (mongolism) caused by an additional chromosome and so on, are diseases of the nervous or glandular systems. But the vast majority of the so-called mental diseases are *human tragedies* caused by a variety of factors.

The difference between so-called normal and abnormal behavior is a matter of degree. Every human being is occasionally irrational; some people are more often so than others. Some people are so irrational that they need help in adjusting to life.

## THE FOUR CRITERIA

The first criterion of mental health is the relationship between *one's potentialities and achievements.* The inability to actualize one's mental and physical potential is one of the outstanding signs of mental disorder. All other factors being equal, the greater the discrepancy between promise and fulfillment, the more severe is the disorder.

There are, however, cases of gifted individuals who function well in their professional lives as scholars, scientists and creative artists, while unable to act in a balanced and rational manner in their personal lives and interindividual relations. Apparently, their poorly integrated personality structure permits adequate functioning in the conflict-free ego spheres but it fails in conflict-laden areas.

The second criterion of mental health is *emotional balance.* The reactions of healthy individuals are typically in accordance with the nature and magnitude of stimuli. Normally we react with pleasure and joy to situations that enhance our well-being. Happiness is generally attained when one's wishes come true, while grief is the reaction to failure or loss.

Normal emotional reaction is *proportionate* to the stimulus. Let us consider the case of a man who has lost money. Assuming that he is emotionally well-balanced, his reaction will be *appropriate* to the fact of loss and *proportionate* to its magnitude and to the ensuing financial hardship. The more money lost, the greater the degree of upset; if the loss is only a small fraction of his possessions, his worry will be mild and of short duration. A well-balanced individual will do whatever is possible to regain the loss and to prevent the recurrence of losses in the future. A rational, balanced and mentally healthy individual reacts with disappointment to failure — his reaction is proportionate to the damage incurred, and his actions lead to reduction or alleviation of past troubles, and prevention of future ones. In short, normal emotional behavior is *appropriate, proportionate* and *adjustive.*

Disturbed individuals tend to persist in mourning and perpetuating their depressed or aggressive moods instead of compensating for past losses and preventing future misfortunes. Because their emotional balance cannot be easily restored, the depressed or agitated anxiety states are likely to occur again and again. The failure in coping with hardships often leads to increasing irritability, each new frustration adding to the difficulty in restoring emotional balance. It becomes apparent that mental disorder is a dynamic process with a distinct tendency towards deterioration.

The third criterion of mental health is related to the validity of *cognitive functions.* An erroneous perception, an oversight of danger, an inability to distinguish fantasy from reality seriously jeopardize one's existence. A realistic perception of what is going on in the outer world and in one's own life increases one's chances for survival and helps in optional adjustment.

In most mental disorders, the perception of the outer world is disturbed, but not as a result of some malfunction of the sensory organs as is the case in sight or hearing impairments. Nor is the reduced ability to perceive, compare and reason a function of mental deficiency as is true of the retarded. The mental apparatus is, in most cases of mental disorder, fully or partly preserved, but it seems that the mentally disturbed individual is unable to properly utilize his mental capacities because of a malfunction in the realm of feelings.

The more one is disturbed, the poorer is his contact with reality. Everyone makes an occasional perceptual error but, as a rule, we are accurate and capable of correcting our errors. In mentally disturbed individuals, this ability is impaired or nonexistent.

The situation can become quite serious when the picture of the outer world is distorted. An individual who consistently misconstrues or misinterprets what he perceives is said to be *delusional.* For example, when a mentally disturbed individual flees a policeman who simply wants to check his driver's license, in fear that the policeman will arrest him for a noncommitted crime, or when he ascribes hostile feelings to his friends who are loyal and trustworthy, his reality testing is practically nonexistent. Whereas delusions are distorted perceptions, hallucinations are creations out of nothingness. Hallucination is perception without external stimulation, such as seeing ghosts and hearing voices. A hallucinating patient is unable to distinguish his inner fears, wishes and dreams from the outerworld. His ability in reality testing is lost.

The fourth criterion is *social adjustment.* Men live in societies . They interact with one another in cooperation and competition, love and hate, peace and war. The term "social life" denotes both the friendly or cooperative and the hostile or competitive aspects of human interaction.

There are no ideal societies. Every social group has its share of the constructive life-preserving and cooperative factors, as well as the disruptive, destructive and antisocial forces. However, when the forces of hate prevail, life and society perish. No society can afford a free display of hostile and disruptive forces. If these forces are innate in men, they must be checked; if they are learned patterns of behavior, they must be unlearned at least to a point where they do not threaten the survival of men. There is a great diversity in the prohibitive actions of social groups; some are more, some less restrictive; some limit their "thou shalt not kill" restraint to the members of their own group only. The Judeo-Christian civilization believes in the sanctity of human life, but even the most primitive societies did not tolerate unlimited intra-group hatred and belligerence.

The last criterion of mental health is, as stated above, the ability to cooperate with other individuals. Mentally healthy individuals are capable of living on friendly terms with other members of their group. They are capable of cooperation and are willing to enter into social relations based on mutual respect, agreement and responsibility. Normal adults accept and make commitments which they can honor. They may disagree with associates and understand why others may disagree with them. They may occasionally feel hostile, but their actions are generally kept under rational control. They may, however, fight in self-defense and in a manner approved by their cultural group.

## FALLEN ANGELS

The motto of my book *Call No Man Normal* (1973) is "With the exception of organic cases, mental disorder is caused by mismanagement of people (children) by people (their parents)." While not always and not all parents could be blamed for their children's difficulties, I distinguished three patterns of noxious parental interference with the mental health of their children. These patterns are the overdemanding, rejecting and inconsistent parental attitudes. Some parents act as if they were the children who need to be loved, and demand the kind of love and affection from the child that would more properly be expected to come from their own parents. In such families, the parents' attitude toward the child is overdemanding, and the child is forced too early into an overanxious and oversubservient attitude toward his parents. The child, in effect, is robbed of his childhood and forced prematurely to worry about his parents. His parents, disappointed in one another, expect him to compensate for all the love and affection they failed to obtain from each other. The child is not allowed to express his dissatisfaction. Exposed to immature and overdemanding parents, he is expected to become a *model child* who renounces his own desires to please his parents. These model children feel sorry for their parents and feel responsible for their parents' true and imaginary misfortunes. In many instances, this reversal of social roles confuses the child, destroys his self-esteem and deprives him of the ability to become an independent adult. The parents expect the child to act like an angel but there is a limit to how far one can go in suppressing one's own impulses. When the self-controls break down, the angels go berserk and a full-blown schizophrenia develops. Thus, I called schizophrenics "fallen angels."

## INNOCENT CRIMINALS

Children need love and security and, if deprived of both, they may develop the mentality of a hunted animal, a combination of extreme selfishness, hostility and suspicion. They feel that they are alone in a cold and hostile world; it is either devour or be devoured, destroy or be destroyed. Some of these selfish and hostile people come from underprivileged classes and extreme cases of poverty and despair conducive to a "sink or swim" mentality. However, I came across children of upper class families who developed a similar mentality of selfishness, lack of consideration and hostile attitude toward the world. These children received plenty of money but no affection or guidance.

Typically these people are the extreme opposite of the "fallen angels." While schizophrenics are guilt-ridden individuals who fear their own hostility, children of rejection believe that they are innocent even when they exploit and hate other people. In my book *Call no Man Normal,* I called these people "innocent criminals" because they themselves are unaware of their extreme lack of consideration for other people.

## DR. JEKYLL AND MR. HYDE

Individuals with extreme shifts of mood belong to the third category of disturbed people. Traditional psychiatry calls them manic-depressives. I believe that the shifting moods of elation and depression are merely the smoke, while love and hatred are the fire. Some parents reject their child and even hate him, but when the child is seriously ill, the same parents, torn by guilt feelings, shower the child with affection. The prevailing atmosphere of rejection with occasional outbursts of affection makes the child hate and love the rejecting parent and wish to suffer in order to win affection. The moods shift from hatred toward those who don't love him and hatred toward himself (depression) for not being loved, to brief periods of elation when he feels loved by others and therefore loves himself. He becomes a *love-addict*, willing to suffer in order to gain love. In his shifting moods of euphoric love and kindness, he resembles the kind Dr. Jekyll; in the prevailing mood of rejection and depression, he is as full of hatred as Mr. Hyde.

The severity of social maladjustment usually corresponds to the severity of mental disorder, although it is not a simple one-to-one relationship. Uncontrollable hostility is, however, a definite sign of serious disturbance. Social adjustment must not be confused with conformity. The former is the ability for a peaceful and friendly interaction with other individuals, while the latter implies unconditional acceptance of certain social norms and mores. Were conformity identical with social adjustment, all ethnic, religious and political minorities could be considered malajusted. Every inventor, original scientist, creative writer, political reformer and nonconformist, and all pioneers of social, religious or scientific progress could be branded as malajusted.

What then is mental health? Probably a precarious and flexible state of mind when human emotions are somehow balanced and one can relate to himself and others in a wholesome way. When the disbalanced emotions prevail and a person is unable to restore the balance himself, he needs help. Many people occasionally need some help; some people need a prolonged period of help.

## USES AND ABUSES OF POWER

One seeks help from a surgeon or psychotherapist whenever one feels that something is wrong with oneself. When one goes to a dentist, one assumes that the dentist is competent, capable of helping and that he cares, and he is willing to help. The helpers are perceived as being *strong* and *friendly,* and the patient depends on their help. However, outside the treatment hours, one does not necessarily look up to them. If the patient is a broker, the dentist may need the patient's help when he wishes to buy a house. If the patient is a lawyer, his dentist may look up to him if he needs legal advice. Human relations are not a simple hierarchic system in which somebody always looks up to someone else; we need a baker for bread, an accountant for our bills, a dentist to fix our teeth. We look up to them in *their particular capacity,* but they may look up to us whenever *they need* our help.

This relative interdependence does not apply to the treatment of mental disorder. The psychotherapist is not supposed to ever ask the assistance of his patient who is a dentist or a lawyer. The therapist is expected to do more in a particular area; he deals with the patient's total personality. One cannot view his therapist merely as a strong and friendly expert. The psychotherapist has taken the place of the father-confessor, but he is expected to have more power than the priest, rabbi or minister. The patients depend on him in making most vital decisions. The role he plays resembles only one person in one's life; the role of a loving and admired parent.

Treatment of mental disorders often resembles the child-parent relationship. Adult men and women go to someone who is not always wiser nor necessarily better established, more influential, or more powerful than themselves. People seek psychotherapy because they are unhappy and they don't know how to manage their lives. Most of them are unable to adequately cope with their jobs, their families and the whole complexity of life. Some think about quitting life altogether. Many are in despair, practically all are in pain. People usually have valid reasons when they decide to seek help, be it chemotherapy or psychotherapy. They go to someone who they believe can help.

Putting one's faith and fate in the therapist makes one much more dependent than one usually is in regard to one's physician, dentist or lawyer. In the patient-therapist dependency, one necessarily develops an infantile regression, called "transference" by Freud. When one is under stress, one tends to develop regressive moods and to transfer his emotions onto the person who takes care of him. Freud noticed it first, but transference, which is transfer of emotions in a state of regression to infancy, takes place in all kinds of psychotherapy.

This kind of emotional regression creates a patient-doctor relationship unheard of in any other type of treatment. The dependence on the psychotherapist goes to the gut-level. It deals with the deepest human emotions and elicits emotions which are not necessarily related to the here-and-now, factual relationship. I had men and women in treatment who were wiser, more competent, more influential and much richer than I. A dentist asked me how to deal with his patient; an internist consulted me about how to make a diagnosis; a lawyer sought my advice in complex business contracts. It was rather amazing, although not surprising, that these people asked me for advice in areas in which they were far more competent than myself and expected me to give them advice as if they were little children and I was their parent.

Most patients develop affection, admiration, and even love for their doctor. This love has the infantile element of demanding reciprocation — children expect their parents to love them, to care for them and to take care of them. Quite often, this love has sexual undertones, and patients, both male and female, develop heterosexual or homosexual crushes on their therapist. Many a patient, despite the fact that he pays the fees to his doctor in private practice or the society pays the fees in a clinic or hospital, ascribes to himself a position of total dependence and craves the doctor's affectionate attitude. Sometimes transference takes a negative turn and the patient uses his therapist as a target for his hostile feelings. Past grievances against parents and other significant adults are redirected against the therapist who may be unfairly blamed for whatever miseries the patient has experienced in his life.

The patient versus therapist attitude can be presented on two levels. One level is the here-and-now relationship and the patient is aware of the fact that he goes to a doctor whom he pays or who is paid by society, and who is supposed to help him to relieve his tensions and resolve his inner conflicts. But on the other level, a great deal of irrational feelings are directed against the therapist who serves as a target for the patient's emotional onslaughts.

## THE TASK OF THE THERAPIST

Serving as a target for a continuous onslaught of human emotions is a great mental health hazard. Small wonder that psychiatrists have a high incidence of suicide, and some of Freud's early associates, who were inadequately psychoanalyzed, suffered mental breakdowns. It is therefore self-evident that whoever intends to deal with the emotional problems of other people must put his own house in order and undergo his own analysis. In order to save drowning lives, one must be a good swimmer, well-prepared to do the job of lifesaving.

There are three main ingredients that make a good therapist: 1) his own aptitude, 2) his training, and 3) his experience. A therapist's aptitude includes his total personality, because *the total personality is the tool one uses in helping other people.* Psychotherapists, as all other human beings, go through the wear and tear of life; they may fall in love and be disappointed; they may get physically ill or suffer car accidents; they may lose somebody very dear to their hearts; and they may react like all other human beings. However, one expects that even in their personal lives, they are at least as good as the patients they have cured, which means that they act as rational human beings. They should be able to retain rational and self-controlled reactions, irrespective of whatever upheavals they may experience. A therapist who carries his personal troubles to his office does injustice to his patients; thus one of the main criteria for a good therapist is a strong ego, which implies an objective, calm, realistic attitude. Severely disturbed people drown in their unconscious. A good psychotherapist is like a good diver: he should be able to join his patients in their unconscious journey, but he always comes back. He must be able to empathize, that is, be capable of receiving nonverbal messages from his patients.

A good therapist must get involved with his patients without getting involved with them. The psychotherapist must get involved with the patient's cause; he is determined to help his patients. His mind is set on helping people who are in trouble and he is ready to do so. But on the other side, he must not become personally involved with patients nor get caught in the murky waters of morbid countertransference feelings. To be dependable and yet not involved — this is the task of the therapist. Moreover, the therapist's attitude toward his patients is a giving attitude. He must enable them to go through corrective emotional experiences to remedy their past bad experiences and correct their personality deficiencies. However, in order to do that, he must be reasonably independent and serve the needs of the patient and not his own narcissistic needs. If one tries to take a shortcut in defining psychotherapy and asks what its aim is, I guess its aim is to make itself superfluous. A good psychotherapist works in such a way that his work becomes unnecessary. When he helps the patients to grow up, then they don't need him anymore — their dependence on him is terminated while they become more independent in their lives and begin making their own rational decisions.

## THE PITFALLS OF PSYCHOTHERAPY

While the psychotherapeutic situation fosters regression in the patient who looks up to the therapist as if the therapist were his parental figure, the therapist may succumb to the illusion of infantile omnipotence. One of Freud's early associates, Ferenczi (1950) noticed that infants hallucinate omnipotence as their wishes are fulfilled by the loving parents. Quite often, younger colleagues came to me for supervisory sessions with a glowing feeling of success because their patients expressed love and admiration for them. The beginning therapists often take the expression of transference love as a sign of therapeutic success.

Megalomania seems to be the main mental health hazard of psychotherapists. Many a psychiatrist or psychologist develops the illusion of omnipotence because the patients' glowing remarks and admiration can make him believe that he possesses superhuman powers. Such an illusion of omnipotence is certainly a sign of regression, for mature men and women know the limits of their power. In that atmosphere of omnipotence, the therapist may lose some of his professional standards and self-restraint.

Disinhibition is very much in vogue today, and some psychotherapists seem to have fallen prey to the climate of license and decline of self-discipline. Often in meetings of psychiatrists and psychologists, one hears self-praising stories, indicative of an impaired sense of reality. Some psychotherapists seem to believe that their ideas are unquestionably the best ones. This self-righteous attitude represents a violation of the rights of the patients. While the patients come to us in need of help to grow, the imposition of the therapist's ideas on them may prevent growth, and in a way, it unnecessarily perpetuates the infantile dependence of the patient on the therapist.

Sometimes this relaxation of self-discipline and regression into infantile behavior goes quite far. In August 1973, I chaired some sessions at the Congress of Group Psychotherapy in Zurich. Some colleagues reported that they treated patients as "human beings;" they went with them to bars, slept with them, and related to them in an atmosphere of complete freedom. It is my conviction that this kind of freedom is not permitted by professional ethics. People come to us not because they want to drink beer or go to bed, but because they need help. I asked my colleagues in these sessions why sexual relations with somebody with a Ph.d. or M.D. degree who practices psychotherapy is more therapeutic than with somebody who has a Ph.d. or an M.D. in ophthalmology. Moreover, I wondered why the treatment of alcoholism is best conducted in a bar.

I don't believe that psychotherapists, whatever their degrees are, are necessarily superior human beings. Sleeping with a patient comes quite close to statutory rape because patients in psychotherapeutic interaction necessarily regress to an infantile stage and their defenses are lowered; they can be easily carried away by their moods, and they may act as a minor would. Furthermore, since in a transference situation patients tend to see the therapist as a parental substitute, to accept their sexual advances seems tantamount to incestuous behavior.

Unless the psychotherapist exercises a great deal of self-discipline and rational self-control, he is unfit to perform his duties. Unfortunately, not all therapists are properly qualified for their jobs. Some of them act like insecure parents, unable to go through the process of weaning. Insecure therapists unnecessarily prolong the treatment even when the treatment is going nowhere. Quite often I have had referrals of patients by therapists who did not know what to do next with a patient or by the desperate patients themselves, who felt that after five, six or seven years they were still at their starting point.

## REFERENCES

Ferenczi, S. *Selected papers.* Vol. I New York: Basic Books, 1950.
Jahoda, M. *Current concepts of mental health.* New York: Basic Books, 1958.
Laing, R.D. *The politics of experience.* New York: Ballantine Books, 1973.
Shneidman, E.S., *et al. The psychology of suicide.* New York: Science House, 1970.
Szasz, T. *The myth of mental illness.* New York: Harper and Row, 1961.
Szasz, T. The ethics of suicide. *The Antioch Review,* **31,** 1971.
Srole, L., Angner, T.S., Michael, S.T., Opler, M.D., and Rennie, T.A. *Mental health in metropolis.* New York: McGraw-Hill, 1962.
Wolman, B.B. *Call no man normal.* New York: International Universities Press, 1973.
Zilboorg, G. and Henry, G.W. *A history of medical psychology.* New York: Norton, 1941.

# 2 Psychopharmacology and Convulsive Therapy

## Richard Abrams

The biological therapies in psychiatry consist of a variety of pharmacologic, convulsive and other somatic methods. Insulin coma therapy, psychosurgery and convulsive therapy were introduced one after another during the 1930s and provided the first successful and reliable methods for treating patients with major psychoses who, until then, had received only custodial care.

The neuroleptic drugs introduced in the early 1950s provided the first effective chemical therapy for psychiatric patients and were responsible — along with more progressive mental health laws — for the subsequent continued annual decrease in mental hospital populations and for the establishment of an increasing number of acute treatment psychiatric units in general hospitals.

Antidepressant drugs, first used in this country in the late 1950s, were effective in treating many depressed patients in and out of the hospital. These drugs are now well-established in clinical psychiatry although the initial hope that they would replace convulsive therapy in the treatment of depressed patients, remains unfulfilled.

Lithium therapy for manic-depressive illness was made available in this country three years ago and is the first truly prophylactic treatment in psychiatry. Lithium is also the first psychiatric treatment to have been fully tested and demonstrated to be effective prior to its distribution for general clinical use.

In addition to the clinical advances of the biological therapies, the investigation of their mode of action has accelerated progress in neuropharmacology and neurophysiology and provided many hypotheses to be tested concerning the etiology of the major psychoses.

This chapter includes a discussion of psychopharmacologic and convulsive therapies. The more specialized somatic methods, such as psychosurgery and insulin coma therapy, are not available to most practitioners and will not be considered here.

## Psychopharmacology

### GUIDES TO THERAPY

Psychiatry shares with other medical specialties the basic principles of clinical pharmacology. Successful drug therapy results from the administration of active compounds, in sufficient doses, of suitable preparation, by an effective route of administration, and for an adequate period of time.

#### Dose

The correct dose of a psychoactive drug will yield the desired clinical effect without producing excessive side-effects. The dose should be increased rapidly to the desired level or until side-effects supervene. Manufacturers' recommended doses of psychoactive drugs are often inadequate, particularly for the neuroleptics, and one must frequently exceed the "maximum" suggested in order to treat patients successfully.

#### Preparation and Route of Administration

Parenteral administration guarantees drug intake at the most rapid onset of action and the highest blood levels. For orally administered medication the highest blood levels for the greatest duration occur with liquid concentrates which have the added advantage of being difficult for the patient to sequester. Tablets are intermediate in duration of action and "timed-release" capsules least effective in providing adequate blood levels for sustained periods of time. For an adequate absorption, oral preparations should be given one-half hour before or two hours after meals and hospital medication schedules should be arranged accordingly.

#### Duration of Treatment

The duration will vary with the clinical response, diagnosis, severity and chronicity of the illness, and the prior pattern of response to drug therapy. It is unwise to change drugs within the same class in less than two weeks unless side-effects are pronounced or persistent. The necessity for changing drugs can usually be avoided by increasing the dose of the original drug or changing the preparation or route of administration.

In the past, the desirability of long-term administration of neuroleptic drugs had been widely stressed, especially for the treatment of patients diagnosed as having chronic schizophrenia. However, such therapy entails the risk of permanent skin and eye changes and the persistent brain changes underlying tardive dyskinesia, and should be interrupted every 3 – 4 months to be reinstituted only if warranted by the reappearance of symptoms. Diagnoses also require periodic re-evaluation and many patients receiving chronic neuroleptic drug therapy for what was originally diagnosed as a schizophrenic illness will subsequently be found to satisfy criteria for an affective disorder. Lithium therapy, not yet reported to cause permanent skin, eye or brain changes, will then be the appropriate maintenance therapy.

### Side-Effects

Therapeutic doses of active drugs often produce side-effects which prove that the dosage is adequate. If patients show no therapeutic effects or side-effects at doses presumed to be sufficient, they should be suspected of not taking their medication or of being resistant to standard dosages for idiosyncratic reasons. Such patients will often be found to be receiving oral drug preparations, and a change to the parenteral route will usually yield sudden improvement.

### Drug Combinations

In the absence of proven synergism or potentiation, drug combinations generally complicate treatment and multiply unwanted side-effects. There is scant evidence that combinations of neuroleptic drugs are superior to single drugs given in equal doses for the same period of time. Fixed combinations of neuroleptics with tricyclic antidepressants are designated "irrational" by the A.M.A. Council on Drugs as no specific evidence for their efficacy exists.

## NEUROLEPTIC DRUGS

These compounds produce sedation without sleep, emotional quieting and affective indifference. They are all capable of inducing the extrapyramidal syndrome of parkinsonism, dystonia and akathisia, and produce dopamine receptor blockade in various animal species. The two main classes of neuroleptic drugs are the tricyclics and the butyrophenones (Table 2-1). The rauwolfia alkaloids are a third class little used in psychiatry today and will not be further discussed.

### Clinical Indications

Neuroleptic drugs reduce excitement, agitation and overactivity, remove hallucinations and delusions, and restore acutely disorganized thought-processes. Paranoid-hallucinatory syndromes and psychotic excitement states are most rapidly responsive to neuroleptic drug therapy. Such phenomena occur in patients with diagnoses of mania, schizophrenia, paranoid states and a variety of acute

## TABLE 2-1 NEUROLEPTICS.

| Tricyclics | USUAL 24-HOUR DOSAGE RANGE IN MG | | | |
|---|---|---|---|---|
| | *Acute* | | *Maintenance* | |
| Phenothiazines | | | | |
| Chlorpromazine (Thorazine) | 300–2000 | oral | 200–600 | oral |
| | 75–400 | I.M. | | |
| Trifluopromazine (Vesprin) | 100–200 | oral | 50–150 | oral |
| | 60–150 | I.M. | | |
| Acetophenazine (Tindal) | 40–80 | oral | 20–40 | oral |
| Butaperazine (Repoise) | 15–100 | oral | 5–15 | oral |
| Carphenazine (Proketazine) | 25–400 | oral | 25–75 | oral |
| Fluphenazine (Prolixin, Permitil) | 20–60 | oral | 5–20 | oral |
| | 5–30 | I.M. | 25–75 | I.M. |
| | (Hydrochloride) | | (Enanthate, decanoate, weekly/biweekly) | |
| Perphenazine (Trilafon) | 16–80 | oral | 8–16 | oral |
| | 5–30 | I.M. | | |
| Piperacetazine (Quide) | 40–160 | oral | 20–50 | oral |
| Prochlorperazine (Compazine) | 30–150 | oral | 15–75 | oral |
| | 30–100 | I.M. | | |
| Thiopropazate (Dartal) | 30–100 | oral | 15–30 | oral |
| Trifluoperazine (Stelazine) | 10–45 | oral | 5–15 | oral |
| | 6–12 | I.M. | | |
| Thioridazine (Mellaril) | 300–800 | oral | 100–300 | oral |
| Mesoridazine (Serentil) | 50–400 | oral | 25–200 | oral |
| | 25–200 | I.M. | | |
| Thioxanthenes | | | | |
| Chlorprothixene (Taractan) | 100–600 | oral | 50–200 | oral |
| Thiothixene (Navane) | 10–60 | oral | 5–15 | oral |
| | 6–12 | I.M. | | |
| Butyrophenones | | | | |
| Haloperidol (Haldol, Serenace) | 15–80 | oral | 10–40 | oral |
| | 15–40 | I.M. | | |

organic brain syndromes secondary to cerebral arteriosclerosis, intoxications and diverse altered metabolic states.

*Excitement and Overactivity in Acute Mania or Schizophrenia.* Excitement, agitation, restlessness and overactivity are primary indications for neuroleptic drug therapy. During an initial diagnostic observation phase, sodium amobarbital may be temporarily effective and does not fundamentally alter the clinical syndrome. Neuroleptic drug dosages are usually high in psychotic excitement states and parenteral therapy is the rule (e.g., haloperidol, 10-20 mg intramuscular, b.i.d.*). A majority of patients will respond to such a treatment regimen over a 24–72 hour period. If 5–7 days of such high-dose parenteral therapy fails to control an acutely excited patient it is wise to discontinue drugs and initiate convulsive therapy. This is especially the case for those patients who become febrile and dehydrated and present the risk of a fatal outcome in a psychotic exhaustion state.

*Paranoid-Hallucinatory States.* Patients with acute mania, schizophrenia or toxic psychoses may display multiform persecutory delusions often associated with auditory hallucinations and experiences of influence and alienation. If excitement is not marked and patients will accept oral therapy, excellent results can be obtained if treatment is continued for adequate periods of time. A typical regimen might be fluphenazine concentrate increased rapidly to a dose of 40–60 mg/day and maintained at this level for 2–4 weeks. Thought-disorder, whether in the form of flight-of-ideas or acutely fragmented speech ("word-salad"), accompanying such paranoid-hallucinatory states also responds to neuroleptic drugs.

*Emotional Blunting and Formal Thought-Disorder.* These signs occur together in patients who satisfy criteria for "process" or Kraepelinian schizophrenia, who have an extremely poor prognosis with or without treatment. Even prolonged high-dose neuroleptic drug therapy may have only a modest effect in such patients, who often receive the diagnosis of hebephrenia or simple schizophrenia. Their response to convulsive therapy is also poor.

*Catatonic/Stuporous States.* Catatonic posturing, rigidity, mutism and stupor rarely respond satisfactorily to neuroleptic drugs and may occasionally be aggravated by them. Intravenous or intramuscular sodium amobarbital is temporarily useful to differentiate catatonic schizophrenia from manic or depressive stupor or to permit stuporous patients to eat (e.g., sodium amobarbital, 250–500 mg intramuscular, one-half hour before meals). Convulsive therapy rapidly removes the catatonic state, frequently with only one or two treatments, but therapy must be continued with additional convulsive therapy, neuroleptics, or lithium, according to the clinical diagnosis.

## Neuroleptic Drug Selection

Extensive collaborative studies by the Veterans Administration and the National Institute of Mental Health have not revealed important therapeutic differences among the various neuroleptic drugs in the treatment of psychotic patients. Two exceptions are promazine and mepazine which were found less effective than other neuroleptics and are not included in this discussion.

The main criteria for choosing one neuroleptic over another are differences in individual patient tolerance to side-effects, the availability of various preparations

* b.i.d. (twice a day)

and the physician's experience with the different compounds.

### Drug Administration

Patients who are acutely ill require rapid symptom-control which is best achieved with parenteral medication as frequently as every 4 hours. Stepwise dosage increments are needed until clinical improvement occurs or side-effects supervene. For such patients parenteral therapy is best continued for 48 – 72 hours even if their abnormal behavior is earlier controlled, for a rapid change to oral medication frequently results in a relapse. When oral medication is substituted an equal dose of a concentrate should be given in one or two daily divided doses. There is no reason to prescribe tablets for hospitalized patients if a concentrate is available. Extrapyramidal side-effects may first appear when a parenteral is changed to an oral route of administration. This may result from a somewhat different metabolism of oral medication which must first pass through the portal circulation and liver before entering the general circulation and the brain.

### Duration of Therapy

The dose required to achieve full symptom-remission should be continued for two to four weeks and then gradually reduced to a maintenance level. If patients remain symptom-free for three months or so after an acute psychotic illness their medication should be discontinued for an observation period. If symptoms rapidly recur this suggests merely a suppressive action of the neuroleptic drug and a course of convulsive therapy should be considered. Patients who were chronically ill prior to initiation of drug therapy should receive longer courses of treatment, perhaps from six to eight months, but they also deserve a drug-free observation period. Symptoms will recur in about 40% of such patients and therapy ought then be resumed with neuroleptic drugs as convulsive therapy is rarely effective in chronically ill patients.

Indefinite continued administration of neuroleptic drugs not infrequently produces permanent structural brain changes accompanied by involuntary choreiform movements (tardive dyskinesia). The need for such chronic therapy must be clearly demonstrated.

### Side-Effects, Precautions and Contraindications

*Central Nervous System.* The extrapyramidal syndrome of parkinsonism, dystonia and akathisia occurs early in treatment and most frequently with the piperazine tricyclics and haloperidol. The individual components of the syndrome may occur alone or in combination and are a function of the total drug dose and its rate of increase. Patients often adapt to the extrapyramidal syndrome after two or three weeks of treatment, but if it remains distressing or disabling, antiparkinson medication (Table 2-2) or dose reduction will be required. Akathisia

TABLE 2-2   ANTIPARKINSON DRUGS.

| | USUAL 24-HOUR DOSAGE RANGE IN MG | | | |
|---|---|---|---|---|
| *Anticholinergics* | *Acute* | | *Maintenance* | |
| Procyclidine (Kemadrin) | | | 5–30 | oral |
| Biperiden (Akineton) | 2.5–5 | I.M. | 4–8 | oral |
| Cycrimine (Pagitane) | | | 2.5–15 | oral |
| Trihexyphenidyl (Artane) | | | 4–10 | oral |
| *Antihistaminics* | | | | |
| Diphenhydramine (Benadryl) | 25–50 | I.M./I.V. | 50–150 | oral |
| Orphenadrine (Disipal, Norflex) | 15–30 | I.M. | 100–200 | oral |
| *Anticholinergic/antihistaminics* | | | | |
| Benztropine (Cogentin) | 1–2 | I.M./I.V. | 2–6 | oral |
| Ethopropazine (Parsidol) | | | 30–300 | oral |

is most disturbing to the patient and may simulate psychotic agitation or a worsening of the clinical state, leading the physician to erroneously increase rather than decrease the drug dosage. The extrapyramidal syndrome occurs least frequently with thioridazine and chlorprothixene.

Acute dystonia is a dramatic and sometimes alarming occurrence but it carries no morbid risk and responds rapidly to parenteral benztropine, 1–2 mg or diphenhydramine, 25–50 mg. Convulsive seizures may occur with very large doses of neuroleptic drugs (e.g., chlorpromazine in doses over 2,000 mg/day) but these are quite rare and respond to dose-reduction.

About 25–50% of patients receiving long-term neuroleptic drug therapy develop a syndrome of involuntary choreiform movements which persists after the drugs are discontinued (tardive dyskinesia). The symptoms differ from those of the acute extrapyramidal triad and include periodic tongue-protrusion and lip-smacking, puffing and chewing movements of the mouth, athetoid hyper-extension of the fingers and a restless shifting of weight from leg to leg. A comparative study of autopsy material from patients with the syndrome of tardive dyskinesia demonstrated histopathological changes in midbrain structures. The biochemical alterations are believed to be either excessive dopamine accumulation in the basal ganglia, or an increased dopamine receptor sensitivity. The treatment of tardive dyskinesia is unsatisfactory; antiparkinson agents aggravate the syndrome and should not be used. The cerebral amine depleting agent, reserpine, is reported effective in gradually increasing doses to 4 mg/day. Reinstitution of other neuroleptic drugs, particularly the potent dopamine-blocker, haloperidol, also reduces the syndrome, but such therapy is clearly unsatisfactory in the long view.

Tardive dyskinesia has now been reported to occur after only brief courses of neuroleptic drug therapy and for this reason such drugs should probably be reserved for the treatment of severely ill or psychotic patients. Their use in mildly ill or neurotic patients requires re-evaluation as does their use in children and pregnant women.

*Cardiovascular system.* Neuroleptic drugs, especially chlorpromazine, thioridazine and chlorprothixene, produce orthostatic hypotension which is dose-related and occurs more frequently in older patients and with parenteral administration. Adaptation to this phenomenon often occurs over a week or two and patients should be warned to rise slowly from lying or sitting positions. For high-dose parenteral neuroleptic therapy the more potent neuroleptics (e.g., haloperidol, fluphenazine, thiothixene) are preferred as they have little hypotensive effect. Epinephrine should not be used to treat neuroleptic drug-induced hypotensive collapse as the alpha-adrenergic blocking properties of the neuroleptic will leave the hypotensive action of epinephrine unopposed. In such an event, the pressor amine of choice is norepinephrine.

Repolarization abnormalities of the EKG are frequently seen with neuroleptics, particularly thioridazine and mesoridazine. Flattening, notching, splitting and inversion of T-waves, prolongation of P-Q and Q-T intervals, and S-T segment depression may all occur. These EKG changes are related to drug-induced myocardial potassium depletion and are reversed by oral potassium replacement. Neuroleptics should be used cautiously in patients with myocardial disease as there is a suspected relation between the EKG abnormalities and the rare instances of autopsy-negative sudden death in patients receiving these drugs.

*Hematopoietic system.* Agranulocytosis is a rare and dangerous idiosyncratic allergic response to neuroleptic drugs which occurs in the first weeks of therapy at doses exceeding 150 mg/day chlorpromazine or the equivalent. Frequent white cell counts are ineffective in the early detection of this syndrome, which is most successfully prevented by clinical vigilance. Painful oropharyngeal infections and fever are the usual presenting complaint and these may occur within 24 hours of a normal white count. The complaint of sore throat or mouth, or the occurrence of fever in a patient receiving neuroleptics requires that medication be withheld until a white blood cell count is obtained. If there are less than 2,000 neutrophiles per $mm^3$ (40% of a 5,000 total white count) the patient must be seen by a medical consultant without delay. If the white count is adequate, drug therapy may be continued.

*Autonomic nervous system.* The antiadrenergic and anticholinergic properties of the neuroleptic drugs are responsible for their most commonly described side-effects. Dry mouth, stuffed nose, impaired taste, blurred vision, constipation and urinary retention are all dose-related and if severe or persistent respond only to dose-reduction Antiparkinson agents with their own anticholinergic effects merely aggravate these symptoms. Inhibition of ejaculation is an antiadrenergic phenomenon seen most frequently with thioridazine.

*Skin and eye.* Photosensitivity is reported by patients receiving neuroleptics and painful sunburn may result from only brief exposure. Patients should be warned of this possibility and advised to use a suntan preparation to prevent it. Ocular photosensitivity also occurs and can be prevented with sunglasses.

Long-term effects of phenothiazine neuroleptics include a characteristic blue-grey pigmentation of the skin, and the development of stellate lenticular and corneal opacities visible only on slit-lamp examination. These changes have no known clinical sequelae but seem to be permanent. They are a function of the total lifetime dose of medication received and have been reported most often after chlorpromazine therapy.

Pigmentary retinopathy leading to blindness has occurred in patients receiving more than 1,200 mg/day of thioridazine, and no more than 800 mg/day of this drug should be given. For this reason, if high-dose neuroleptic drug therapy is anticipated, thioridazine is a poor initial choice.

*Liver.* Benign intrahepatic cholestatic jaundice occurred during the early years of chlorpromazine use and is now a rare complication of neuroleptic drug therapy. Mildly abnormal liver function tests often occur in patients receiving neuroleptics but their significance is obscure and no untoward results occur if treatment is continued.

*Hormonal changes.* Impaired glucose tolerance with elevated fasting blood sugars often occurs with neuroleptics, more commonly in women than in men. There is no known clinical significance of this and no treatment is recommended. A temporary pseudopregnancy syndrome may also occur in women, with amenorrhea, lactation, breast swelling and false-positive pregnancy tests. Gynecomastia has also been reported in men receiving neuroleptics.

*Fatalities.* Sudden death in patients receiving neuroleptic drugs has various etiologies. Autopsy-negative deaths in psychiatric patients were well-known before the introduction of neuroleptic drugs and patients who died in febrile/dehydrated states were described as having lethal catatonia, "Bell's mania," or manic exhaustion. Altered temperature regulation secondary to the anticholinergic effects of neuroleptics and the oft-prescribed antiparkinson agents has contributed to hyperpyrexic deaths during the hot summer months. Asphyxiation by food bolus has been discovered at autopsy in some patients but these deaths can not readily be attributed to the drug therapy they were receiving. Fluoroscopic examination of patients receiving neuroleptics does show impaired swallowing but not any more so than in chronic patients not receiving drugs. Hypotensive deaths have also been reported, and some deaths have been ascribed to drug-induced cardiac arrhythmias.

*Psychiatric complications.* Depression may occur during or after neuroleptic drug therapy, most commonly when the acute phase of the illness is over. Antidepressant drug therapy or ECT may be required as there is a risk of suicide in such cases. Some of these patients will have been manic during the acute phase and it is unclear whether the depressive state is drug-related or simply that which precedes or follows a manic attack in 50% of patients with or without drug therapy.

*Contraindications.* True contraindications to neuroleptic drugs are rare. Narrow-angle glaucoma is one and pronounced prostatic hypertrophy another. Caution should be employed in prescribing these drugs for pregnant women.

## ANXIOLYTIC DRUGS

These compounds share the sedative, hypnotic, central muscle-relaxant, anticonvulsant, central depressant and addicting properties of the barbiturates. Sudden cessation of these drugs after chronic high-dose administration in man may be followed by convulsive seizures.

Clinically, these drugs are widely prescribed and have replaced barbiturates for anxiety reduction and nighttime sedation in neurotic patients. They are also extensively used in the treatment of delirium tremens, alcoholic hallucinosis, and epilepsy. Anxiety responsive to the action of these drugs occurs in patients with neurotic disorders often with associated phobias, depersonalization, hypochondriasis, neurasthenia, obsessions and depression.

### TABLE 2-3  ANXIOLYTICS.

| | USUAL 24-HOUR DOSAGE RANGE IN MG | | | |
|---|---|---|---|---|
| *Benzodiazepines* | *Acute* | | *Maintenance* | |
| Chlordiazepoxide (Librium) | 30–100 | oral | 10–30 | oral |
| | 150–400 | I.M./I.V. | | |
| Diazepam (Valium) | 15–60 | oral | 10–30 | oral |
| | 15–30 | I.M./I.V. | | |
| Oxazepam (Serax) | 30–120 | oral | 20–60 | oral |
| *Substituted Diols* | | | | |
| Meprobamate (Miltown, Equanil) | 1200–2400 | oral | 600–1200 | oral |
| Tybamate (Tybatran) | 750–3000 | oral | 500–1000 | oral |

Some characteristic drugs, dose ranges and available preparations are given in Table 2-3. There is little hard evidence that one or another of these drugs is to be preferred for any specific clinical use and the choice among them depends on the availability of different preparations and the familiarity of the physician with them.

Oral therapy is the usual mode of administration for anxiolytics and where parenteral therapy is needed as in the treatment of delirium tremens, injectable preparations are available only for the benzodiazepines.    Because tolerance develops rapidly to the antianxiety effects of these drugs they are useful only for short periods of continuous administration.    If unusual circumstances require their administration beyond a 3-4 week period, drug-free intervals may be required to avoid a regular stepwise increase in dosage.    An advantage of the anxiolytics over barbiturate and nonbarbiturate sedatives (e.g., glutethimide) is their lower respiratory depressant effect and consequent diminished lethal potential in suicide attempts.

### Clinical Indications

*Acute anxiety states.*  Patients with diagnoses of anxiety neurosis, hypochondriacal neurosis, hysterical neurosis and other related syndromes are frequently subject to sudden attacks of intense fear or dread, accompanied by shortness of breath, sweating, pressure, pain and pounding in the head and chest, and numbness and tingling of the extremities.  Parenteral anxiolytics are rapidly effective in such attacks and high doses are usually needed (e.g., chlordiazepide, 50-100 mg intramuscular; diazepam, 15 mg intramuscular).  Oral therapy can then be continued with the same agent, as additional injections are rarely required. For subacute anxiety states oral therapy may be used initially to be tapered off and discontinued over 3 - 4 days.

*Chronic anxiety states.*  Patients with chronic, disabling, anxiety may have associated insomnia, depression, phobias, obsessions/compulsions, depersonalization/derealization, hypochondriasis or somatic symptoms and are extremely difficult to treat.  They are often made worse by the neuroleptic drugs or convulsive therapy they receive from physicians who label them "pseudoneurotic schizophrenics," and they frequently abuse alcohol and sedative/ hypnotics. Anxiolytic drugs temporarily relieve their symptoms but adaptation occurs and increasing doses are needed to maintain the *status quo.* Monoamineoxidase inhibiting drugs (MAOI's) although classed as antidepressants are sometimes unusually successful in the treatment of such neurotic patients (see section on antidepressant drugs).

*Delirium tremens.*  This alcohol withdrawal syndrome is characterized by visual and auditory hallucinations, restless agitation, disorientation, shifting consciousness, tremor, vomiting, and a history of recent relative or absolute reduction in alcohol intake. The treatment of choice is parenteral chlordiazepoxide, 100 mg intramuscular/intravenous every 4-6 hours. Neuroleptics such as chlorpromazine or promazine have been recommended in the past but they only increase the morbidity and mortality rate.

The related syndrome of alcoholic hallucinosis is also readily responsive to the benzodiazepines, and these may be given orally as vomiting is usually not a problem.

## Side-Effects, Precautions and Contraindications

Drowsiness, ataxia, confusion and stupor may occur with increasing doses of the anxiolytics, and patients receiving these medications should be warned against driving automobiles or operating complex machinery. The combination of alcohol and an anxiolytic sedative presents a lethal risk for patients who will not refrain from driving.

Transient excitement states may occur when older or extremely agitated patients are treated with low doses of anxiolytics. There is nothing "paradoxical" about these reactions; as for the barbiturates and many other drugs, low doses may be excitatory and high doses inhibitory. If excitement occurs the drug should either be increased or discontinued.

Withdrawal seizures can occur in patients whose long-term high-dose anxiolytic drug therapy is abruptly stopped. As for other addicting drugs, these compounds should be withdrawn gradually.

## LITHIUM

The lithium ion is considered separately as it has no central sedative or tranquilizing properties yet is specifically active in patients with manic-depressive illness. The antimanic action of lithium is more specific than that of neuroleptics or convulsive therapy which are also effective in a variety of other illnesses. About 80% of manic patients achieve full remission or are much improved with lithium therapy, and the prophylactic effect of continued lithium administration against future manic attacks is extremely well-documented. The depressive phase of manic-depressive illness is also less frequent in patients receiving maintenance lithium therapy but here the preventative action is less marked than for mania. An immediate antidepressant effect of lithium has been reported but this is minimal and inferior to that achieved with tricyclic antidepressants.

Lithium is given orally as the carbonate in 300 mg tablets or capsules. The usual starting dose for manic patients is 1,200-1,800 mg/day in three or four divided doses, with weekly monitoring of serum lithium levels during the initial few weeks of therapy. Therapeutic blood levels for acutely ill patients range from 1.0 to 1.5 mEq/L and when this level is stable the lithium dose can usually be reduced to 900-1,200 mg/day assuming a satisfactory therapeutic response.

Serum lithium levels exceeding 2.0 mEq/L are often associated with toxic effects although older patients may become lithium toxic at lower levels. For safety and clinical control lithium serum determinations are usually made at monthly intervals to maintain serum levels of 0.5-1.0 mEq/L.

Manic patients frequently refuse oral medications and there is also a 5-7 day lag before the onset of the antimanic effects of lithium. For these reasons initial therapy with a parenteral neuroleptic or convulsive therapy is often required to control the acute state, after which lithium therapy may be given for its prophylactic action.

## Side-Effects, Precautions and Contraindications

During the initial week or so of therapy, patients may experience a fine tremor, mild fatigue or drowsiness, nausea, abdominal fullness, increased thirst, and polyuria. These symptoms are no indication to reduce dosage and usually remit when stable blood levels are achieved. Vomiting immediately after ingestion of lithium sometimes occurs and can be avoided by instructing patients to take their lithium with food. Genuine toxicity rarely appears below serum lithium levels of 2.0 mEq/L, and is characterized by profuse vomiting or diarrhea, slurred speech, ataxia, coarse tremors, lethargy, myoclonus, stupor and coma. Atypical syndromes may occur with unilateral focal signs mimicking a stroke. Treatment of lithium toxicity is supportive. The drug is stopped and patients may require parenteral fluids, frequent turning in bed to prevent pneumonia, prophylactic antibiotics and airway maintenance. No specific antidote or treatment is yet available for lithium toxicity.

Lithium should be used with extreme caution in patients with impaired renal function, employing low doses (e.g., 150 mg b.i.d. or t.i.d.*) and frequent serum lithium determinations. Caution should be observed in cardiac patients as well, as EKG repolarization abnormalities occur with lithium. This drug should not be prescribed for patients receiving diuretics or a low-sodium diet as severe lithium poisoning may rapidly occur in salt-depleted patients.

About 4% of patients receiving long-term lithium maintenance therapy develop nontoxic goiters which shrink with discontinuation of lithium or the addition of small doses of thyroid hormone. The patients are usually clinically euthyroid but signs of hypothyroidism may occur. The PBI is normal or reduced and there is often an increased uptake of radioactive iodine.

The safe use of lithium in pregnant women is not established and sporadic reports of possible teratogenic effects continue to accumulate. Lithium is excreted in mother's milk and mothers on lithium therapy should bottle-feed their babies. Excessive weight gain and acneiform eruptions are frequent troublesome side-effects of lithium which respond to dose-reduction.

There are no specific guidelines to the duration of lithium maintenance therapy. Patients who have remained well on such a regimen for years may relapse in a week's time when lithium is discontinued. The duration of therapy

* t.i.d. (three times a day)

will depend largely on the number, rate, and severity of prior attacks of illness.

As noted in the section on neuroleptic drugs, manic episodes are frequently followed by depression. This pattern also occurs in patients receiving lithium and it is unclear whether the drug increases the frequency of this pattern. If depression occurs, lithium should be continued and the appropriate antidepressant therapy started (e.g., a tricyclic antidepressant or convulsive therapy).

## ANTIDEPRESSANT DRUGS

There are two main classes of antidepressant drugs, the tricyclics and the monoamine oxidase inhibitors (MAOI's). These drugs have different structures, chemical properties and clinical indications and they will be discussed separately. Psychostimulant drugs such as amphetamines and related compounds have no true antidepressant properties and will not be considered. (An exception is methylphenidate which is used for its enzyme-inhibiting activity as described below.)

### Tricyclic Antidepressants

These drugs are minor chemical modifications of chlorpromazine and were introduced as potential neuroleptics. The prototype drug of this group, imipramine, was immediately found to have antidepressant properties without significant antipsychotic effects. A variety of modifications of the tricyclic prototype have been introduced for the treatment of depressed patients and these are listed in Table 2-4.

## TABLE 2-4   ANTIDEPRESSANTS.

| | USUAL 24-HOUR DOSAGE RANGE IN MG | | | |
|---|---|---|---|---|
| *Tricyclics* | *Acute* | | *Maintenance* | |
| Imipramine (Tofranil) | 150–300 | oral | 100–150 | oral |
| Amitriptyline (Elavil) | 150–300 | oral | 100–150 | oral |
| Desipramine (Norpramine, Pertofrane) | 150–300 | oral | 100–150 | oral |
| Nortriptyline (Aventyl) | 50–100 | oral | 25–75 | oral |
| Protriptyline (Vivactil) | 30–60 | oral | 15–30 | oral |
| Doxepin (Sinequan, Adapin) | 150–300 | oral | 100–150 | oral |
| *MAOI's* | | | | |
| Tranylcypromine (Parnate) | 20–40 | oral | 10–30 | oral |
| Phenelzine (Nardil) | 45–75 | oral | 30–45 | oral |

*Clinical indications and treatment results.*  The best results with tricyclic anti-depressants are obtained in patients with endogenous depressions.  Indeed, the scientific differentiation of endogenous from reactive depression is derived largely from a study of the effects of imipramine in a group of unselected depressed patients.  Imipramine-responders displayed a cluster of symptoms which are now subsumed under the rubric of endogenous depression, and the nonresponders manifested the phenomena associated with reactive depression.  These syndromes are described in more detail in the section on convulsive therapy.  Briefly, the clinical indications for tricyclic antidepressants are the same as for convulsive therapy in depression.

The response rate for patients with endogenous depression to tricyclic drugs is about 60-70%, significantly lower than that for convulsive therapy but usually higher than for placebo.  The presence of hallucinations or delusions in patients with endogenous depression is often associated with an inadequate response to tricyclics or even a worsening of the illness.  It is typically the late-onset unipolar depressive patient who displays such psychotic symptoms and who is often diagnosed as having involutional melancholia or an agitated depression.  Such patients fare poorly with the antidepressants but do well with convulsive therapy.

*Choice of drugs.*  Imipramine and amitripyline are the most widely used  tricyclics and for the most part their effects are interchangeable.  One study showed amitriptyline to be somewhat superior to imipramine for older, agitated depressives, and imipramine more successful in younger, retarded depressives.  Amitriptyline is more sedating than imipramine and may therefore be useful in agitated patients or those with severe insomnia.

The chemical derivatives of imipramine and amitriptyline are widely touted as the active metabolic products of the parent drugs.  However, most studies have shown the parent compounds to be equal or superior to their derivatives in antidepressant activity, with an equal or faster onset of effect.  Side-effects are frequently more pronounced with the desmethylated derivatives and some patients experience insomnia or an unpleasant sense of "activation" with them.  An exception is the amitriptyline congener, doxepin, which is reported to have sedative/anxiolytic properties similar to the benzodiazepines.

*Drug dosage and duration of therapy.*  Adequate dosage is the most important variable for successful tricyclic antidepressant therapy.  For imipramine and amitriptyline the starting dose is 100-150 mg/day which is increased over 3-4 days to 200-300 mg/day.  A daily dosage of either drug below 200 mg/day is often ineffective except in older patients who tolerate poorly the side-effects of higher doses.  For most patients all or the bulk of the dose can be taken at bedtime without increased side-effects and with duration of activity equal to that achieved with multiple daily divided doses.

There is a lag in onset of the therapeutic effects of tricyclic antidepressants and they may not reach their peak clinical effectiveness until after two weeks of continuous administration at the therapeutic level.    Patients who eventually respond to these drugs usually show some improvement at the end of a week, although this may be minimal.    Once symptom-remission has been achieved the drugs should be continued at a maintenance level for one to three months or for the duration of the usual depressive episode if known.    The duration of therapy will also vary with the number and severity of prior attacks.    Continued administration of tricyclic antidepressants beyond that required for the particular episode is not known to prevent future attacks of illness.

The onset of the clinical effects of imipramine and amitriptyline is accelerated by combined therapy with thyroid hormone.    The regimen consists of the addition of 20-40 mg/day of lyothyronine to the tricyclic drug.    The onset of clinical improvement is hastened, and there may also be an improved overall therapeutic effect.    This observation has generally not held true for men.

Methylphenidate has also been used to augment the clinical effects of tricyclic antidepressants, due to its inhibitory effects on hepatic microsomal enzymes. Increased blood levels of imipramine follow methylphenidate administration and there is evidence of a direct relation between blood levels and the therapeutic effects of tricyclic antidepressants.    Side-effects are also related to blood levels and may be increased with such combined therapy.    The usual dose of methylphenidate is 10 mg two or three times a day.

Patients with endogenous depression often require nighttime sedation in addition to tricyclic therapy.    Barbiturates are a poor choice for such sedation as their *enzyme-inducing* properties have been associated with reduced blood levels of tricyclic antidepressants.    Sedatives without enzyme-inducing activity, such as the benzodiazepines, should probably be used instead.

*Side-effects, precautions and contraindications.*    The tricyclic antidepressants share many side-effects of the tricyclic neuroleptic parent drugs, but have more pronounced anticholinergic properties.    Thus, postural hypotension, EKG changes, dry mouth, blurred vision, heartburn, constipation, adynamic ileus and urinary hesitancy and retention all occur.    An extrapyramidal syndrome is absent, however, and there are no reports of tardive dyskinesia consequent to tricyclic antidepressants.    A troublesome, persistent fine tremor does occur, similar to that in thyrotoxicosis.    It is resistant to antiparkinson agents and does not diminish over time.    Dose-reduction may be required, but where this is not advisable, the beta-adrenergic blocking agent propranolol has been used with some success in doses of 10-30 mg/day.

EKG alterations are more frequent with the tricyclic antidepressants than with their parent compounds and there is a significant incidence of unexplained sudden death in cardiac patients receiving these drugs for the treatment of depression.    For this reason convulsive therapy is probably a more conservative method for the treatment of depressed patients with myocardial disease than tricyclic antidepressants.

Hematologic abnormalities also occur with the tricyclics and a case of near-fatal total aplastic anemia has occurred with imipramine. Jaundice is also reported as a rare idiosyncratic response to amitriptyline.

Profuse sweating frequently occurs with the tricyclics, particularly imipramine, a phenomenon not observed with the neuroleptics.

The tricyclics may induce mania in bipolar patients receiving these drugs for depression, a response also observed with convulsive therapy. The occurrence of mania or hypomania in a depressed patient without prior history of such suggests that he suffers from bipolar disease.

Overdosage with tricyclic antidepressants can induce a toxic psychosis. This anticholinergic delirium is characterized by confusion, disorientation, clouding of consciousness, dilated pupils, dry skin, and a history of tricyclic drug ingestion. It is responsive to the cholinesterase-inhibitor physostigmine, 2 mg intravenously, and this may be repeated in 15 minutes and again in half an hour.

Narrow-angle glaucoma and severe prostatic hypertrophy are contraindications to tricyclics. Many consider the recent or continued administration of MAOI's a contraindication to tricyclic antidepressants and this will be discussed more fully.

## Monoamine Oxidase Inhibitors (MAOI's)

These compounds are traditionally listed as antidepressants although most studies show them to be only partially effective in the treatment of patients with endogenous depression. Their activity has always been purportedly greatest in patients with "atypical" depression which usually describes neurotic depressives with associated phobic, obsessional, hypochondriacal or depersonalization symptoms. Until recently little scientific evidence has been adduced in support of these clinical observations. Reports are now accumulating which clearly show that this class of drugs is effective in neurotic patients whose anxiety or depression is associated with the various symptoms noted above and in the section on anxiolytic drugs. Patients with agoraphobia or the "phobic anxiety-depersonalization syndrome" are particularly responsive to MAOI's.

*Choice of drugs.* There are two therapeutically active MAOI's available to American psychiatrists, phenelzine and tranylcypromine. They are structurally similar but the closer resemblance of tranylcypromine to amphetamine is reflected in its initial amphetamine-like stimulating properties, not present in phenelzine. Because of the greater incidence and severity of "cheese reactions" with tranylcypromine this drug is usually reserved for the more severely ill, therapy-resistant patient. Although the manufacturer recommends that tranylcypromine be reserved for hospital use, it is nonetheless well-tolerated by outpatients if they adhere strictly to their dietary proscriptions.

*Clinical indications.* These have been described but not more precisely simply because they are still evolving. Severe neurotic symptoms combined with anxiety or depression and in the absence of a diagnosis of one of the major psychoses constitute the main indication for MAOI's. The diagnosis of "pseudoneurotic" schizophrenia, although purportedly that of a psychosis, often augurs well for a therapeutic response to MAOI's. These severe obsessional patients with multiple neurotic symptoms and anxiety have been more aptly designated "pseudo-schizophrenic" neurotics. If severely crippled by their symptoms, these patients may be referred for psychosurgery, but should always have a full and fair trial with an MAOI before the decision to operate is made.

*Drug dosage and duration of therapy.* The dose of phenelzine is 15 mg three or four times a day, and of tranylcypromine 10 mg two or three times a day. There is a delayed onset of action with both drugs which may be as short as a week and as long as three or four weeks. As most patients referred for MAOI therapy have chronic illnesses which have been unresponsive to other treatments it is wise to continue therapy for four weeks at therapeutic doses before declaring failure. Patients should be warned not to expect any clinical improvement for at least two weeks lest they become discouraged and discontinue treatment prematurely. The initial amphetamine-like stimulation with tranylcypromine may be advantageous in patients whose fatigue and inertia threatens imminent loss of employment. If anxiety is severe the benzodiazepines may be safely prescribed during the initial period before the MAOI's become effective. There appears to be some potentiation of the anxiolytic effect of these compounds and smaller doses are usually required.

The response rates to MAOI's are still poorly defined but perhaps a third to a half of such chronically ill therapy-resistant patients respond to treatment. When a response occurs it may be dramatic and patients characteristically remark that the medication makes them feel "different" than ever before in their lives. Therapy should be continued for two or three months and followed by gradual dose-reduction. For many patients this will result in a recrudescence of symptoms, necessitating resumption of the original dose. Nonetheless it is prudent to attempt dose-reduction at six-month intervals, although for many this will prove unfeasible.

*Side-effects, precautions and contraindications.* The principal side-effect of MAOI's is the dangerous hypertensive crisis which may occur in patients who eat foods with high tyramine content. This "cheese" reaction (so called because ripened cheeses have been associated with a majority of the severe reactions) may range from a sudden, throbbing headache to a paroxysmal hypertensive crisis with subarachnoid hemorrhage and death. It results from failure of the body to metabolize the ingested pressor amine, tyramine, due to the inhibition of monoamine oxidase for which tyramine is a substrate. Treatment of the hypertensive crisis requires an alpha-adrenergic blocking agent, and parenteral phentolamine is the standard (5 mg intravenous). Many physicians provide their patients on MAOI's with 100 mg tablets of chlorpromazine or thioridazine to take immediately for their alpha-adrenergic blocking action, should a "slip" occur in dietary observance.

Foods which have been associated with severe headache or paroxysmal hypertension include cheese (except cottage or cream cheese), pickled herring, liver (especially chicken liver), raw yeast or yeast extracts such as "Bovril" or "Marmite," beer and wine (especially Chianti wine), and Italian broad beans (fava beans). Patients must not take any medications with adrenergic properties, including amphetamines and related compounds, or cocaine. Central nervous system depressants are potentiated by MAOI's and alcohol, opiates and barbiturates should be used with caution. Chlorothiazide diuretics are to be avoided. Patients should be instructed to "clear" any over-the-counter medications with their physician as many such preparations contain pressor amines for their decongestant action. Phenylephrine and ephedrine are contained in many nose-drop preparations and should not be used. If dental procedures are contemplated local anesthetics without epinephrine should be employed.

The ingestion of a tricyclic antidepressant and an MAOI within a two-week period presents a clear risk, although the drugs have been prescribed in combination in the treatment of refractory cases with relative safety in England for years. When considering this point the severity and chronicity of the illness must be taken into account as well as the unfortunate fact that the only remaining procedure is often psychosurgery. For this reason some experienced psychopharmacologists in this country have prescribed combined tricyclic/MAOI therapy in severely ill, therapy-resistant patients with occasional excellent results.

Autonomic side-effects are similar to those of the tricyclics and include postural hypotension, blurred vision, dry mouth, constipation, paralytic ileus and urinary retention. Increased libido is experienced by some, and transient impotence has also occurred in men receiving tranylcypromine. Some patients with personality disorders abuse tranylcypromine because of its amphetamine-like properties. Patients are usually instructed not to take MAOI's within four hours of bedtime as insomnia occasionally results. Increased dreaming has been reported with MAOI's, and some patients complain of frequent nightmares.

Amphetamine-like psychosis can occur with the MAOI's especially tranylcypromine. This toxic psychosis occurs in a clear consciousness, unlike the delirium of tricyclic drug overdosage, and is treated with neuroleptic drugs.

## Convulsive Therapy

In 1935 Meduna first induced therapeutic generalized convulsions with injections of camphor in oil as a treatment for schizophrenia. Based on an erroneous theory of an incompatibility of epilepsy and schizophrenia, and the observation that spontaneous seizures relieved symptoms in mental patients, the treatment was effective. Later observations showed it to be even more effective in patients with depressive illness. The uncertainty of inducing seizures with camphor and the frequent occurrence of repeated seizures led to trials with pentylenetetrazol (Metrazol). These seizures were more dependable although they were associated with intensely unpleasant sensations of impending death just prior to the onset of the convulsion.

In 1938 Cerletti and Bini refined the technique by 'applying alternating current to the temples, inducing instantaneous unconsciousness followed by a grand mal seizure. This method was safe and dependable and became the standard for convulsive therapy.

## CLINICAL INDICATIONS

### The Affective Disorders

The best results with convulsive therapy are obtained in patients with affective disorders, especially the endogenous depressions. This syndrome is characterized by terminal insomnia, inability to cry, depression worse in the morning, guilty ruminations, anorexia, weight-loss, and retardation or agitation. Patients with reactive depressions (depressive neurosis) may fare poorly with convulsive therapy and display initial insomnia, difficulty arising, worsening mood in the evenings, a fluctuating course, emotional reactivity and lability, and self-pity. The terms "endogenous" and "reactive" have no etiological implications and merely define certain clinical syndromes. The presence or absence of a precipitating event does not differentiate the two syndromes.

*Results in depression.* In patients with endogenous depression, improvement with convulsive therapy ranges from 80-100%. A full remission in a psychotically depressed patient is frequently induced with 4–5 seizures but if treatment is terminated at this point relapses commonly occur. For this reason 6–8 seizures are most commonly given. Successful therapeutic outcome may vary inversely with the severity of the depression and patients without hope, preoccupied with ruminations of guilt and worthlessness, and reduced to a depressive stupor often show the best treatment results.

*Compared with drugs.* Convulsive therapy is clearly superior to the antidepressant drugs in the treatment of depressed patients. The older and more psychotic the patient, the less likely he is to respond to drugs. In one study of tricyclic antidepressants there was a group of older, deluded patients who failed with drug treatment only to recover with ECT.

*Combined with drugs.* The use of antidepressant drugs in combination with convulsive therapy has been adovcated in order to shorten the treatment course.

The suggestion has not been objectively studied, but it is worth noting that by the time antidepressants demonstrate clinical effects most depressed patients have already recovered with a course of convulsive therapy.

Patients given maintenance antidepressants following a successful course of convulsive therapy have fewer relapses. Such maintenance therapy is extremely important as the relapse rate following convulsive therapy for depressions ranges from 25–50% within a six-month period. A typical maintenance regimen is amitriptyline 150 mg/q.h.s.* for one or two months.

*Results in mania.* In the treatment of mania, lithium or the neuroleptics are effective and reliable in about 80–90% of patients, and the remaining 10–20% will need convulsive therapy. Acute mania, often characterized by overactivity and psychotic excitement to the point of exhaustion, requires more intensive treatment than depression. Seizures are usually given twice daily for 2–3 days until psychomotor overactivity is controlled. Lithium may then be introduced or the remainder of the treatment course continued with convulsive therapy at the usual rate of three seizures each week.

## Schizophrenia

Convulsive therapy also has an important use in patients with schizophrenia. Although less successful than in the treatment of affective disorders, proper selection of cases will often lead to excellent treatment results.

*Variables related to outcome.* Duration of illness is the most important factor in the selection of schizophrenic patients for convulsive therapy. All studies show an inverse relation between the chronicity of illness and successful therapeutic outcome. The best results are achieved during the first six months of illness. With each succeeding six-month period of continuous illness the therapeutic effect of convulsive therapy dwindles and after a schizophrenic illness has continued for more than two years the results with convulsive therapy do not differ from institutional care alone. Other favorable factors are acute onset, preservation of affect, clouding, confusion or "oneiroid" features, well-adjusted premorbid personality, and a definite precipitating event. These factors are, of course, favorable even without treatment.

*Classification and treatment response.* Paranoid schizophrenia and catatonic excitement have the best prognosis for remission with convulsive therapy. This is undoubtedly related to the favorable prognostic features and affective symptoms often seen in patients diagnosed as having paranoid schizophrenia and to the inclusion in this group of patients of those with acute schizophreniform psychoses with their good prognostic signs and high spontaneous remission rates.

The motor symptoms of catatonic schizophrenia are often dramatically reduced by convulsive therapy and such treatment may be life-saving in excited, dehy-

* q.h.s. (at bedtime)

drated and hyperpyrexic patients. In some patients, however, the relief of stupor reveals persistent formal thought-disorder and emotional blunting which are resistant to further convulsive therapy.

Neither simple nor hebephrenic schizophrenia respond significantly to convulsive therapy. The occasional unexpected remission in a patient with "hebephrenia" probably results from the presence of an incorrectly diagnosed affective illness.

Acute exacerbations in patients with chronic schizophrenia respond to convulsive therapy with results similar to those achieved in acute schizophrenia. The prognosis in such cases depends on the acute features of the current exacerbation and not upon the prior chronic illness course.

*Number of treatments.* More convulsive treatments are required in schizophrenia than in the affective disorders and a course of 10–15 treatments is usual. Even though symptoms may remit after fewer seizures it is advisable to administer a full course or risk relapse within a week of the last treatment.

*Results in schizophrenia.* Improvement rates of 65–80% full and social remissions combined are reported with convulsive therapy in acute schizophrenic patients. Where inadequate treatment is given or where the cases treated are primarily those of chronic schizophrenia the outcome with convulsive therapy is similar to milieu care or sham treatments. An improvement rate of about 70% with convulsive therapy compares favorably with the reported rates of 20–40% in untreated cases.

*Compared with drugs.* Studies comparing ECT with neuroleptic drugs in treating patients with acute schizophrenia reveal similar remission rates and similar relapse rates if follow-up maintenance therapy is used. If maintenance therapy is continued only in the drug-treated cases the relapse rate is higher for ECT; if no maintenance therapy is given at all the relapse rate is reported higher for drug treatment.

*Combined with drugs.* Although some authors recommend combining convulsive therapy with neuroleptic drugs in treating schizophrenia there is no known advantage. It is unsafe to combine reserpine with convulsive therapy because of the hypotensive and respiratory depressant effects, and fatalities have occurred with the combination. The combination of convulsive therapy with phenothiazine neuroleptics is reportedly safer, but unexpected complications and deaths with such therapy have occurred, although rarely. Combined treatment should probably be reserved for the more difficult case.

Organic Psychoses

Of the practical and theoretical interest is the successful use of convulsive therapy in acute organic psychoses such as stupor secondary to head trauma;

bromide psychosis; the delirium of alcohol withdrawal, meningitis, pneumonia, encephalitis, rheumatic fever and uremia; and the dysphoria of epileptic clouded states. The antipsychotic effect of convulsive therapy is here presumed non-specific as the exogenous psychosis may remit without a change in the underlying disorder.

### Neuroses and Character Disorders

Convulsive therapy is of little merit in patients with neuroses and character disorders and may make such patients worse by producing myriad side-effects, real and imagined, which form a nidus for hypochondriacal and obsessional ruminations. The "blurring" effect of the mild organic mental syndrome induced with 2-3 bilateral ECTs is occasionally useful as a temporary palliative measure for patients crippled by intractable obsessive-compulsive neuroses.

### Affective and Paranoid Psychoses of the Senium

Many elderly patients receive the erroneous diagnosis of "organic brain syndrome" when they exhibit affective or paranoid symptoms in association with disorientation and impaired memory. The affective or paranoid coloring is prognostically favorable in such geriatric patients even in the presence of evidence for concurrent arteriosclerosis (e.g., hypertension, angina, retinal changes, diminished pulses). Many of these patients live alone and their personal hygiene and nutritional state deteriorate, yielding a high mortality rate when untreated. These patients with senile pseudodementia may respond dramatically to convulsive therapy, and their poor physical condition is an indication, not a contraindication, for such treatment.

True organic senile or arteriosclerotic psychoses without productive symptoms do not respond well to convulsive therapy. Such patients have characteristic severe cognitive defects and neurological signs of cerebral dysfunction.

## TREATMENT METHODS

The techniques for administering induced seizures are similar and vary principally in the agent of induction, treatment electrode placement and the rate of application.

### General Considerations

*Pretreatment examinations.* No laboratory test is an absolute prerequisite for convulsive therapy and in an emergency treatment may be given immediately. Ordinarily, a medical history and complete physical examination are obtained, and the routine laboratory tests include a urinalysis, hemogram, chest film and an EKG in patients over forty or those with a history of cardiovascular disease.

An EEG, skull films, and dorsal spine films are not routine screening tests.

*Premedication.* Atropine, 0.4 mg subcutaneously is frequently administered 30 minutes prior to treatment to prevent excessive tracheobronchial secretions. If a vagal blocking dose of atropine is needed, as in a patient with a supraventricular arrhythmia, a minimum dose of 1.2 mg is required and this may be given intravenously immediately prior to seizure induction. However, many thousands of treatments are given yearly without atropine premedication and without any unwanted sequelae.

*Anesthesia and muscle-relaxant.* For several patients treated in one session an intravenous infusion is rapid and convenient. The anesthetic and muscle-relaxant are prepared in separate sterile bottles and connected by plastic tubing to a three-way stopcock which, in turn, has a single disposable tube and needle for administering the drugs.

Methohexital (Brevital) is the anesthetic agent of choice and causes fewer cardiac irregularities than the older sodium thiopental (Pentothal). The induction is more rapid, the duration of action shorter, and there is less post-anesthesia confusion as well. A 0.2% (2 mg/ml) solution is given as rapidly as possible until the patient no longer responds to questions (40–80 mg).

Succinylcholine (Anectine, Quelicin, Sucostrin) is the muscle-relaxant of choice. A 0.2% infusion is given rapidly immediately following the methohexital and continued until inhibition of the patellar reflex or until the fasciculations of the first stage of the succinylcholine effect disappear in the muscles of the feet (40–80 mg).

If only one or two patients are to be treated, methohexital may be given by syringe in a 1.0% solution followed immediately by 2.0% succinylcholine through the same needle but using a different syringe. The drug dosages are similar to those noted for the infusion method and it is felt by some physicians that the more concentrated solutions require more caution in their administration.

*Oxygenation.* Ventilation with 100% oxygen is begun when the patient falls asleep and is continued throughout the procedure until spontaneous respirations return. An airway is seldom required. In edentulous patients or those with a full complement of healthy teeth, the jaw is merely held shut at the time the seizure is induced. In patients with poor dentition a rolled-up 4 by 4 gauze sponge should be inserted between the teeth just before treatment is given. Well-fitting dentures or bridges should be left in place but ill-fitting ones must be removed and the sponge used.

*Post-ictal care.* With the return of regular respirations the patient is taken to a recovery area and observed until he awakens and is able to walk. Patients occasionally require tracheal suction or the administration of oxygen and the required equipment should be available.

Emergence deliria occur in about 10% of patients in the immediate post-ictal period. These acute excitement states are extremely difficult to control once they have begun and several staff members are usually required to restrain the patient while the delirium runs its usual 10-15 minute course. Patients who once develop a delirious state usually have it after each treatment and it is readily prevented by an intravenous injection of 5-10 mg of diazepam at the termination of the seizure.

*Ambulatory convulsive therapy.* Outpatient convulsive therapy is useful for patients with low suicide potential, for those who must continue to work during a course of treatment, and for patients who are to receive maintenance treatment. Outpatients are included in the same treatment schedule with inpatients. It is advisable to have a relative or other responsible person take the patient home (about an hour after he awakens) but if this is not possible, patients should remain in a waiting area until examined and cleared for release in their own care by a physician. Relatives should be warned to keep confused or amnesic patients away from friends who might incorrectly assess their mental capacities. Such patients should not enter into business or legal arrangements until amnesia and confusion have disappeared.

Maintenance convulsive therapy is frequently useful in patients who do not tolerate the side-effects of tricyclic antidepressants or who relapse rapidly after treatment in spite of maintenance drug therapy. Such outpatient maintenance convulsive therapy is given at the rate of one or two treatments each month and rarely causes significant memory difficulty. Prophylactic lithium therapy has greatly reduced the number of patients who require maintenance convulsive therapy.

## Specific Techniques

*Bilateral ECT.* This is the standard mode of induction of therapeutic generalized seizures and is the most frequently used method for convulsive therapy. In bilateral ECT a generalized seizure is induced by passing a current between bitemporal electrodes. Treatments are initially given three times a week and reduced to twice a week if amnesia and confusion become prominent. As the post-ECT memory loss with bilateral ECT is directly related to the amount of current delivered it is advisable to use the lowest treatment apparatus setting that will yield a full grand mal seizure.

*Unilateral ECT.* In this method the treatment electrodes are applied to one side of the scalp only, over the nondominant hemisphere, in order to avoid the direct passage of current through the speech and verbal memory areas of the dominant temporal lobe. With adequate current a generalized seizure is obtained. Post-ECT amnesia and confusion do not occur with nondominant unilateral ECT and treatments may be given daily or several times a day without the appearance of these troublesome side-effects. The therapeutic effect of unilateral ECT is also less than that for bilateral ECT and longer courses with unilateral ECT may be required to achieve the usual remission. For some patients 4–6 unilateral ECTs will induce a full remission, but this is infrequent. More often, recovery will not be complete without the addition of 2–3 bilateral ECTs.

*Choice of unilateral or bilateral ECT.* The lack of post-treatment confusion and memory-loss argues in favor of an initial trial with unilateral ECT whenever possible. If there is no clinical urgency such as suicidal risk, overactivity or refusal to eat, unilateral ECT may routinely be given an initial trial of 4–6 treatments, changing to bilateral ECT if significant improvement does not occur. Where time is a factor, as for patients who have a limited number of insurance-paid days in the hospital or who must return to their work by a specific time, it is advisable to initiate treatment with bilateral ECT.

*Flurothyl (Indoklon).* The procedure for inhalant-induced convulsions is similar to that for ECT except that the seizure is induced with 3–4 forced respirations of flurothyl vapor derived from 0.5 ml of liquid flurothyl injected into a vaporization chamber attached to the oxygen bag. There is an initial myoclonic phase, as with pentylenetetrazol, followed by the classic tonic and clonic seizure.

The therapeutic effects of flurothyl convulsive therapy are similar to those of bilateral ECT. Memory-loss and confusion are also similar, with perhaps a bit more immediate post-ictal confusion with flurothyl, and more persistent amnesia with bilateral ECT. As with pentylenetetrazol, many patients develop nausea, vomiting and vertigo during the post-ictal period with flurothyl. Despite this observation, one follow-up study conducted a year after treatment with both methods, reported that patients retrospectively preferred treatments received with flurothyl.

In any case there is little reason to specify flurothyl convulsive therapy for a given patient and as the method is slightly more cumbersome than ECT it is not widely used.

*Regressive ECT.* This technique induces a state of temporary dementia by the administration of 1–3 bilateral ECTs each day until total disorientation, urinary and fecal incontinence, dysarthria and the need for spoon-feeding occur. This acute organic brain syndrome is transient and recovery of cognitive and physiological functioning is complete 2–3 weeks after the final treatment. Therapeutic outcome in the chronic cases treated is asserted to be superior to that achieved with treatments administered at the standard rate. A controlled study did not support this contention, however, and recent clinical trials with this method have not included control groups for comparison. The putative success of regressive ECT may as well be attributed to the increased total number of ECT as to any induced "regression."

## Side-Effects, Precautions and Contraindications

*Memory changes.* The immediate post-ictal confusion is transient and results from the anesthesia, the seizure, and the effects of the seizure-inducing agent (either electric current or the fluorinated ether, flurothyl). For bilateral ECT and flurothyl convulsive therapy there is also an anterograde and a retrograde amnesia, with the retrograde amnesia most pronounced for recently learned items and least for those learned at a more remote time. The retrograde amnesia results from an impairment in the retrieval process and not from interference with stored material. The span of retrograde amnesia shrinks rapidly after a single treatment and is eventually limited to about the 30 seconds immediately prior to the seizures, the "consolidation time" for newly registered material. The antero-grade amnesia is for events subsequent to the seizure and results from faulty registration of new material. For this reason it is permanent and accounts for the frequent statement of patients who have received ECT that their hospital stay is "a complete blank." Permanent alterations of the memory process itself do not, however, occur with convulsive therapy, and this has been amply demonstrated over the past 30 years by a variety of investigators.

Nondominant unilateral ECT does not produce any clinically evident antero-grade or retrograde amnesia, and is followed by a shorter period of post-ictal confusion.

*EEG changes.* Induced convulsions reflect the generalized cerebral seizure discharges occurring during treatment and are followed by EEG changes which persist during the interseizure period. These changes are those of slowing, increased amplitude, and increased rhythmicity. These appear all over the head and are a function of the number and frequency of seizures, the age of the patient, and the location of the treatment electrodes. The EEG abnormalities fade progressively after the final treatment, and are no longer detectable 2–3 months later.

*Other side-effects.* With the introduction of succinylcholine muscle-relaxation, fractures are extremely rare and no special precautions are required. The use of succinylcholine introduces the rare complication of prolonged apnea due to a reduced serum pseudocholinesterase level, probably as a genetic variation. Treat-ment requires continued artificial respiration, usually with intubation, until whatever pseudocholinesterase is present metabolizes the succinylcholine. If apnea is prolonged beyond 30 minutes fresh whole blood can be given to provide exogenous pseudocholinesterase.

Nausea and vomiting in the post-ictal phase can be prevented by 50 mg intra-muscular dimenhydrinate at the termination of the seizure.

Organic psychotic reactions to ECT occasionally occur. These paranoid-con-fusional states arise during the course of treatment and may be misdiagnosed as "uncovered schizophrenia." They usually resolve with continued ECT and are no reason to discontinue treatment. Less commonly, they occur immediately following the last treatment of a series and may then be treated with a brief course of neuroleptics until spontaneous resolution occurs. An EEG taken during the height of these organic paranoid psychoses will show dominant, high-voltage, theta and delta activity.

*Contraindications.* Caution should be observed when combining convulsive therapy and neuroleptic drugs. As noted before, reserpine should not be administered in combination with convulsive therapy and it is best withholding treatment for a week in a patient who has received reserpine or its congeners for the treatment of hypertension.

It is often stated that a brain tumor is a contraindication to convulsive therapy. However, is is unclear why anyone would prescribe ECT for a patient known to have a brain tumor. More correctly, if a patient with a space-occupying lesion of the brain inadvertently receives ECT a rapid clinical deterioration may ensue.

Patients with cardiovascular disease should be treated with caution and their cardiac state carefully defined. The possible deleterious effects of seizures must be weighed against the severe effects of the illness itself in a patient with compromised cardiac status. In such cases the balance will usually weigh in favor of giving ECT. Cardiovascular conditions are thought to be responsible for the mortality rate with convulsive therapy, but this is quite small – probably less than 0.01% of the treatments given. Successful ECT has been reported for patients with recent myocardial infarction, open-heart surgery, and major arterial graft procedures.

Age is no contraindication to treatment and some of the most rewarding results with convulsive therapy are obtained in the elderly debilitated patients described previously, whose primary affective or paranoid disorder masquerades as senile or arteriosclerotic dementia.

When considering indications and contraindications for convulsive therapy the suicidal potential of the patient must be carefully evaluated. This will occasionally take precedence irrespective of the physical condition. A determined patient may commit suicide despite stringent precautions and constant surveillance. Once ECT is started, however, suicide is extremely rare.

# 3 Principles of Psychotherapy

## Michael S. Aronoff and Stanley Lesse

"Psychotherapy," in Western cultures, has many meanings. It usually refers to a strategy or series of strategies, each of which is supported by an explicitly stated, or implicitly implied, theoretical base. The strategies are designed to bring about changes in attitudes, behaviors and life-styles in a group of self-selected people who experience their "life's problems" in the form of recognizable and identifiable emotional reactions. An assumption underlying all forms of psychotherapy is that human behavior is understandable and alterable. Each particular strategy (or "therapy") takes place within a context involving a designated helper, authority or "therapist."

The different technologies represented by different forms of psychotherapy, therefore, are processes by which one may extend his knowledge of himself (in the context of another person's presence), in an attempt to initiate new behaviors and to incorporate them within one's repertoire. Therapists, regardless of their school of thought, listen for expressions of underlying meaning, which are beyond the patient's awareness. These are embodied in symptoms, thought content and associations, fantasy productions, paraverbal and nonverbal cues, and stylistic variations in presentation. That which follows, by way of corrective, explicative, or readjustment maneuvers, depends upon the basic theoretical model of behavior, personality and etiology of behavioral problems, as well as upon the concept of normalcy, held by the particular therapist.

The range and spectrum of psychotherapies is broad and, at superficial glance quite varied. The psychotherapies are categorized according to underlying theory, primary activity undertaken, or any one of a number of specific structural features of the process, goals desired, or types of problems addressed. The spectrum encompasses psychoanalysis, behavior therapies and group therapies. It includes strategies falling under categories such as client-centered therapy, Gestalt therapy, Adlerian and Jungian therapy, transactional analysis, integrity therapy, reality therapy, logotherapy, milieu therapy, primal therapy, hypnotherapy, desensitization. flooding/implosion therapy, aversion therapy, Morita therapy, biofeedback, meditation, psychodrama, dance therapy, occupational therapy, art therapy, poetry therapy, family therapy, conjoint therapy, encounter groups, self-help groups (e.g., Alcoholics Anonymous, Synanon), and so forth (Wolberg, 1967).

The list seems endless and constantly expanding. Each variety of psychotherapy tends to persist once it has been established. The extent to which each persists, however, often depends upon the current vogue and the proselytizing of its advocates.* It seems that although there may be many schools of psychotherapy, the different types of therapy are limited in number and have certain features in common. Each strategy of psychotherapy begins with a procedure of systematic and sequential observation of behavior. The therapist notes historical material and recurring or persistent patterns in the patient's behavior. He then begins an additional interaction with the patient in order to educate the patient and/or redirect certain attitudes or behavior patterns. The therapist, finally, evaluates the apparent effectiveness of his maneuvers to alter the patient's original response pattern. The entire process requires a "working alliance" between the patient and therapist, involving values such as trust, rapport and reality, and based upon a matrix of expectancies (Zetzel, 1956: Greenson, 1965: Goldstein, 1962).

There are, of course, differences among various schools of psychotherapy, based upon the type of technique used, the nature of the goals, and the mutual expectations of both the practitioner and the patient. The goals may be to focus on a specific symptom, or to attempt to increase self-awareness or to reorganize one's life-style. Various schools of therapy propose different goals which, once designated, are then explicated by certain processes. All psychologic problems may be treated, with varying success, by psychotherapeutic processes.

Therapies, depending upon the setting and the nature of the relationship between practitioner and patient, may be brief, time-limited or open-ended. They may vary with different types of patient, depending upon such diverse factors as socioeconomic background, diagnosis, verbal ability, age, sex, etc. They attract different types of practitioners, and may vary in their public appeal. The activities of different schools of psychotherapy are diverse. However, the question is whether the basic principles underlying the techniques utilized are significantly different.

---

*It sometimes appears as if different schools of psychotherapy are in competition for adherents. Unfortunately, the advocates often are not the practitioners but the patients. The different schools then can lend themselves to the politics of personal ambition, professional competition or cultism.

## PROCESSES OCCURRING DURING PSYCHOTHERAPY
## AS SEEN BY DIFFERENT THEORISTS

Strupp states that "a primary purpose of psychotherapy is the acquisition of self-control, mastery, competence, and autonomy . . . inner controls are often guided by central processes, such as beliefs, assumptions about oneself and others. many of which are implicit and highly symbolic. One of the tasks of psychotherapy is to make these symbolic processes explicit." (Strupp, 1973, p. 118.) It might be suggested further that, by making certain processes and representations conscious, they are transformed into less powerful guiding forces that permit the patient greater flexibility in his choice of modes of interaction while attempting to increase his adaptational capacities.

There are, of course, alternative metaphors available for the conceptualization of the processes and goals of psychotherapy. From an adaptational point of view, emotional disorders might be thought of in terms of a disorder in the homeostatic regulation of psychic equilibrium and integration, with faulty feedback loops resulting from distorted central guiding processes or the faulty assimilation of images, affects and thoughts. The goal of psychotherapy, from this vantage point, is the readjustment of the feedback loops. Different methods or processes for obtaining this goal (e.g., insight, imitation, direct retraining) represent possible distinguishing points among the different therapeutic strategies.

Frank (1974) has recently written that the primary function of all psychotherapies is to combat "demoralization." He proposes that anxiety and depression are derivative reactions to this demoralization. Earlier, Frank (1961) was one of the first to emphasize a central role of "persuasion" in all successful psychotherapies. Haley (1963) subsequently emphasized the struggle for control between therapist and patient which is acted out in the communicative interaction between the two, and which the therapist must win for the psychotherapeutic transaction to be successful. Within this framework, the therapist responds to the patient's behavior in a double-binding way, thereby forcing the patient, if he is to continue his relationship with the therapist, to change his mode of interaction.

Orne (1962) also emphasized the importance of the techniques of persuasion and covert coersion in the psychotherapeutic situation — a "persuasion" or control that may be delivered in varying gradations of directness and activity. Bibring and Freud, although they thought that persuasion is a necessary component underlying factors which lead to clinical change in the psychotherapeutic situation, did not believe it to be of so fundamental importance. For, although in psychoanalysis indirect suggestion occurs at all levels of the interaction between patient and practitioner, the resultant insight gained must be applied actively in ongoing situations in the patient's life. In the use of this insight, a new affect is experienced which then offers different controlling properties. What results then, may be a sense of conviction, permitting access to new behaviors, and perhaps, new rewards.

Abroms (1968) takes issue with any theory implying that psychotherapy heals primarily by persuasion. He states that this view does not represent an empirical hypothesis and that neither persuasion nor insight are at the core of healing. Both, instead, provide a stage-setting by means of which new functional linkages can be established which would then lead to the incorporation of behavior changes. For example, in psychoanalysis this is performed via the process of working through, and in certain behavioral therapies via systematic desensitization.

The goal of psychoanalysis is structural personality change. This refers to internal personality change such as the removal of particular defenses, or the conversion of defense mechanisms to coping mechanisms (e.g., intellectualization becoming intellectuality). The goal is not symptomatic change nor the rechanneling of conflicts (e.g., via displacement). Structural change, however, is inferred and not actually experienced as a specific process. This is presumed to be achieved through insight into transferences and resistances, and genetic (or historical) reconstruction of previous inputs to one's behavioral repertoire. Other schools of psychotherapy argue that this type of theory and therapeutic procedure is unnecessary. They believe that a narrower focus of attention can lead to broader gains through stimulus generalization.

The analyst offers himself as a consistent object with a consistent attitude toward the patient. What hopefully results is a secure situation in which the patient has to *tell* rather than *do* things. Then the practitioner can deal with the inherent meanings of the verbal (and nonverbal) presentations. Interpretations are used to further the analytic situation and to stimulate the formation of insight. The analyst neither condemns nor encourages, but highlights certain recurrent patterns. This focusing is thought to encourage insight which then hopefully leads to the desired structural change.

The goals and processes of psychoanalytically-oriented psychotherapy are somewhat different from those of classical psychoanalysis (Rangell, 1954). The assumption that behavioral symptoms are the resultant distillate of an internal conflict remains the same. Here, however, therapeutic tasks include the strengthening of defenses and the clarification of the transference, alerting the patient to individual displacements and classes of misidentifications. The "transference cure" may be the means by which the patient may institute constructive life changes. In this instance, regressive defenses, based on unconscious dependent connections in the form of the so-called magical transference, now substitute for the more pathological defenses previously operative.

Various types of behavior therapy, including logotherapy, employ maneuvers of counter-conditioning using principles of: 1) reciprocal inhibition (the systematic utilization of responses that are inimical to anxiety in the presence of anxiety-producing stimuli), 2) operant conditioning (rewarding the consequences of certain behaviors), and 3) aversive conditioning (punishing the consequences of certain behaviors and thereby attempting to supply a stronger alternative countermotive). "Flooding," as found in implosion therapy, the use of paradoxical intention, and the catharses of psychodrama and primal therapy, operate through the mechanism of sudden and protracted confrontation with an anxiety-provoking stimulus presented in a supportive setting. The suddenness and intensity of the presentation is what distinguishes flooding from desensitization and from the more prolonged procedure of extinction.

Existential therapy offers still another apparently different approach. Existential therapists do not deal with isolated components of behavior. In fact, they do not deal with "health" or "adaptation," but rather with "authenticity." They purportedly take things "as they are" without reducing them to underlying theoretical construction. Gestalt and transactional analysis therapies, in somewhat related traditions, develop tactics to uncover fixed, stereotyped interpersonal interactions ("games") and attempt to free impounded feelings by the use of "play" as an exercise in trying out new roles.

## PROCESSES COMMON TO MOST PSYCHOTHERAPIES

Discussion, explanation, relaxation, exploration, catharsis, support, and drawing connections between internal experiences and external events or responses are techniques employed in different psychotherapies. These interactive techniques are then related to the "nonspecific" effects of the psychotherapies (for instance, mood change) which occur in addition to the general aim of supplying the patient with an organized system for self-understanding and control. How these various processes are conceptualized and utilized leads to the variations involved in the different therapeutic methodologies and their associated descriptive metaphors. While the metaphors associated with the various therapies often reflect the bias of the particular advocate or practitioner, in reality the procedures may not differ significantly from each other. In fact, the stimulus properties of the setting of each form of psychotherapeutic technology may represent variations on a common theme.

One of the factors common to all psychotherapies is the patient's explicit or implicit desire for help. The procedures are conceived of as being voluntary and based on a mutuality of goals. Each form of therapy, in one way or another, explores the beginnings and the extent of the disorder for which the patient seeks help. They all attempt to establish a helping situation with a therapist and, in fact, utilize active processes by which the therapist engages and involves the patient in a working relationship. Thereby, a therapeutic alliance is actively, although perhaps not fully consciously, begun. This is accomplished by history-taking, evaluation, and the completion of a diagnostic process. The therapist then attempts to stimulate the development of new learning and/or a new behavior pattern.

The prerequisites for the establishment of an effective therapeutic setting include a permissive, relaxed sanctuary in which a societally-sanctioned therapist has the trust and confidence of the help-seeker because of his competence and his demonstration of interest and understanding.   The therapist, employing a theoretical construct to explain the patient's problems, determines what therapeutic techniques are to be employed.   He then creates a therapeutic aura which includes positive expectations.   He points out the possibility of a larger spectrum of adaptive options available to the patient, and provides an environment in which "secrets" may be revealed, distorted perceptions may be corrected and symptoms may be ameliorated.   In addition, a sense of mastery and restoration of order may be experienced, new perspectives can be attained, and more mature behavior can be practiced.

Eclectic therapists use different maneuvers at different stages during the evolution of a patient's treatment, and their choice of technologies is guided, in part, by the patient's needs and responsiveness.   Hopefully each strategic variation has a rational basis and is well-directed.   Certainly each strategy is dependent in part upon the cultural role assigned to the various therapies (Frank, 1959) and the mutual expectations held by both the patient and the therapist (Goldstein, 1962; Frank, 1968).   Bromberg (1965) stated that the "underlying precontent premises of the therapist and patient" are the basic part of the therapeutic relationship.   He hypothesized that they preceded the development of transference or countertransference issues within a developing therapeutic situation. With this in mind, the psychotherapies could be viewed as a psychological means of "influence" with a trusting relationship with a designated therapist acting as an impetus for change.

Bibring (1954) has described a hierarchy of operations which the practitioner uses to induce change in the intensive therapies which are designed to restructure mental contents (e.g., altering symbolic frames of reference, freeing impounded affects).   These include suggestion, abreaction, manipulation, and clarification and interpretation.   Transactional therapists hold that what occurs in therapy is the exchange of persuasive messages (i.e., "suggestion" is the common denominator of different therapies).   "Abreaction," in which an affective experience is evoked by proxy (e.g., in encounter groups, primal therapy, child play) has played major roles in some religious cures, aspects of psychodrama and family therapy, aspects of hypnotherapy, and in narcosynthesis previously used in the treatment of war neuroses.   "Manipulation" refers to learning from experience, where a new experience is presented to a patient in order to provide him with a different self- and world perspective.   This is involved in corrective-emotional-experiences, behavioral modification therapy, client-centered and milieu therapies, and group therapies. Learning from experience is not necessarily the agent for change, however, and it remains to be seen to what extent a verbal statement itself may become an agent of change or solution of a problem.   "Clarification" and "interpretation" both represent steps in the explanation to the patient of things about which he is unaware.   Clarification attempts to make the patient aware of how he appears to others.   Interpretation attempts to tie in the forgotten past with the now-clarified present.   The aim of both is to broaden understanding.   They form the basis of therapy which uses insight as a means to change. All five of these operations are used, to a greater or lesser extent, in the treatment of a broad spectrum of patients, with or without the adjunctive use of organic and pharmacologic regimens.

We can say, in summary, that "psychotherapy" is not one particular, unitary process (Strupp, 1973). One determinant of the degree of balance among the various operations within a particular psychotherapeutic strategy, or of the use of that particular form of strategy in the first place, is the evaluation of the role played by intrapsychic defense versus intrapsychic defect (i.e., distortions in cognitive-perceptual systems based on motivational factors versus constitutional factors) in the development and support of a patient's symptom-complex. Every form of psychotherapy seems to have an underlying, at times, unspecified, theory of personality. This theory serves at least two functions. It determines, in part, how the therapist will view the development and integration of behavior. It will also serve as the rationale from which his therapeutic interventions spring. Ideally, his therapy meshes with his theory. Here, we are bypassing the personality-theory matrices in which different psychotherapies are embedded, to look cross-sectionally at the phenomena involved in the structured psychotherapies.

## FACTORS UNDERLYING APPARENT DIFFERENCES AMONG THE VARIOUS PSYCHOTHERAPIES

Differences among what psychotherapists do, within the context of different theoretical approaches, include variations on the themes of: 1) methods (e.g., free association and the interpretation of dreams as compared with systematic relaxation and desensitization); 2) aims (e.g., that of psychoanalysis involving the restructuring of personality via the resolution of the transference neurosis and emphasis on understanding the unconscious determinants of behavior, as compared with focusing more on overt behavior, symptoms and the reality situation of the patient); and 3) kinds of results sought (e.g., reconstructive results as compared with improvement in symptoms, as a measure of progress).

Differences among the different psychotherapies may be more quantitative than qualitative. Emphasis can be directed toward rational or irrational operations, and unconscious factors may be stressed or ignored. Varying degrees of emphasis may be placed upon psychological understanding, ideals, attitudes, or on interpersonal relations. Various aspects of the particular psychotherapeutic procedure (e.g., introduction, engagement, conclusion) may be modified; time commitments, financial arrangements, and the structuring and demand characistics (Orne, 1962) of the therapeutic situation may all be altered and have their own accompanying rationale and putative therapeutic impact. Procedures may be continued beyond the point of symptomatic relief because of belief that: 1) better results will be obtained with the patient then able to resume his own growth; 2) the symptoms *per se* are not the prime problem; and 3) retrogressive displacements, in the form of symptom substitution, will be avoided.

In terms of specific techniques and processes, there are different degrees to which and modes by which different therapists attempt to restructure the cognitive representations of their patients. For instance, emphasis may be placed on the "real" relationships with therapist and on environmental influences, with the explicit encouragement of specific behaviors and a replication of an aspect of the environment for role playing. Alternatively, the transference relationship may be emphasized with the "analysis" of transference and resistance assuming the larger operative role, as opposed to the "use" of the transference solely as a tool. Other examples of different areas where technical focus and thrust may vary among different therapeutic strategies include the extent to which feelings accompanying change are examined, the degree of uncovering done with respect to developmental distortions, and the particular emotional tone chosen to be created within the psychotherapeutic situation. All of these factors are found, however, in the procedures performed by all therapists. Additionally, each therapist evaluates various adjunctive maneuvers for use, based on a number of factors including the following: the interplay among the structural qualities of the particular form of psychotherapy, the patient's expectations, and the patient's ability to use emotionality and verbal communication; the particular area(s) of psychopathology to be worked with; the level of patient sophistication, development and need; and the ability of the patient to work with the therapist at multiple levels, such as real/fantasy, conscious/unconscious, ego-observing/fantasy-participating (G.A.P. Report, 1969). The majority of psychotherapies emphasize the central role of the interpersonal relationship (Snyder, 1961; Murray, 1963) but the specific characteristics of the factors supporting this phenomenon remain to be elucidated.

The differences among the various forms of psychotherapies, with their resultant outcomes, are contingent upon the factors just mentioned, but should also be viewed in terms of the qualities of the patient and the therapist as individuals and as a working, interdigitating team (Singer, 1965; Meltzoff and Kornreich, 1970; Weisskopf-Joelson, 1968). Existentialists such as Buber and Rogers view the therapist as an "authentic presence" in the therapeutic encounter. The role of the therapist in strategies emphasizing learning paradigm is that of a shaper and supervisor. The qualities present in an effective therapist include judgmental and clinical skills, the ability to instill hope, to encourage relaxation, and to provide a warm, tolerant and receptively responsive atmosphere. Most theorists emphasize the importance of the therapist's capacity for empathy and responsiveness (Brady, 1968). A situation is set up whereby the therapist provides a model for imitating as well as participating in the direct retraining or shaping of behavioral responses. But these previously mentioned factors are also very much a part of any doctor-patient relationship.

In its broadest application, psychotherapy refers to an interaction and interrelationship among individual psychodynamics, interactional dynamics, and sociodynamics. In order to be an effective therapist, particularly within a rapidly changing societal matrix, one must be aware of these components and their relationship to each other. One of the thrusts of the administrative strategy called community psychiatry is to make interaction between psychotherapeutic issues of symptom, conflict and ego capacity, on one hand, and environmental inputs on the other, more explicit and substantive in the therapeutic strategy.

## EFFECTIVENESS OF PSYCHOTHERAPY

How then is one to organize one's thinking about the different forms of therapy? How is one to judge the efficacy of differing procedures and the validity of the differing claims of various advocates? Meltzoff and Kornreich (1970), using a broad definition of what constitutes psychotherapy, amply document the effectiveness of such procedures in terms of outcome. However, the criterion of outcome with its subcategories of symptomatic and adjustment improvement, and the relative lack of specificity of patient populations treated, create problems in evaluating different therapeutic regimes. Certainly not all therapists can treat all patients and not all forms of therapy are acceptable to all cultures or subcultures.

Luborsky (1972) has reviewed published studies of the effects of various psychotherapies on adult, mainly nonpsychotic, patients in controlled comparative studies. His findings are as follows: a) in twelve studies comparing individual psychotherapy with group psychotherapy, similar gains were reported for each type: b) seven studies comparing time-limited versus unlimited individual psychotherapy reported similar gains for each; c) in a review of eleven studies evaluating the outcome of psychotherapy as practiced by different traditional schools (e.g., psychoanalysis, client-centered therapy, Adlerian therapy), Luborsky reported that both data and controls in any one category were insufficient to draw conclusions about a particular form of therapy (although there was evidence suggesting that different schools of psychotherapy may provide different benefits for different patients); d) in twelve studies reviewed with respect to the comparison of individual psychotherapy with behavior therapy (excluding treatment of specific "habit" disturbances), if sufficient treatment time was allowed, there seemed to be no significant difference in the benefits to patients between these two forms of therapy. The only exceptions seem to be for mild and circumscribed phobias and agoraphobia, in which desensitization or implosion is better (Bandura, 1971; Boulgouris et al, 1971); e) in thirty-five studies comparing psychotherapy and pharmacotherapy in nonschizophrenic patients, pharmacotherapy was judged better than psychotherapy, and both of them together was better than either psychotherapy or pharmacotherapy alone. The studies with schizophrenic patients show that pharmacotherapy leads to more indicators of improvement than psychotherapy alone; f) in ten studies comparing psychotherapy with other treatments for psychosomatic conditions, all showed overwhelming support for the effectiveness of psychotherapy (with or without attendant medical regimes). Luborsky's conclusions are that; 1) a high proportion of patients who go through therapies make gains (exclusive of psychosomatic conditions and situations utilizing pharmacotherapy); 2) generally, the type of patient probably makes more difference than the type or form of psychotherapy; and 3) although rates of improvement may be similar for different types of therapy, what is considered to be the criteria of improvement may not necessarily be the same.

Exclusive of psychosis, psychosomatic disorders, and perhaps severe character disorders, it would seem that outcome differences for different forms of therapy are more related to the qualities of the therapist and the patient, separately and together. Circumscribed phobias and agoraphobia may be exceptions to this conclusion. In its monograph on psychotherapy (1969), the Group for the Advancement of Psychiatry delineates certain assumptions felt to be implicit in all psychotherapies: a) distress and deviancy can and should be ameliorated; b) learning plays a role in the development of a patient's disturbance; c) this disturbance is amenable to relearning; d) the human relationship, within the therapeutic situation, is an important effector; e) training can improve the necessary abilities of both the therapist and the patient; and f) processes within the therapeutic situation are lawful, however differently they may be conceptualized. They go on to suggest a series of continua along which various processes of the therapeutic operation may be seen to vary when compared cross-sectionally among different strategies of therapy. These are trusting-mistrusting, gratifying-frustrating, revealing-concealing, encouraging fantasy-testing reality, regressing-progressing, and reliving-new experiencing.

Other studies of outcome, as mentioned before, with attendant problems of criteria, control, patient selection and theoretical bias, have reported varying results. Those without a specific cross to bear clearly suggest the effectiveness of psychotherapeutic interventions. We would emphasize that psychotherapy is an effective series of strategies, the specific details of which remain to be delineated. Some theories emphasize the "nonspecific" features of different forms of psychotherapy to account for their effectiveness. Obviously "nonspecific" means not-yet-specifiable or not-yet-particularized. Certainly the subtlety of the interaction and the elusiveness of the factors supporting the interaction do not make the factors involved in psychotherapy "nonspecific."

A further problem in the understanding of the complexity of the factors involved in the psychotherapeutic interaction which may initiate and support behavioral change, is that multiple levels of discourse are used to talk about observed process — from the holistic, man-in-action, I-thou perspectives to the close scrutiny and microdissection of operantly reinforced verbal and nonverbal behaviors. The various approaches to psychotherapy not only offer different specific technologies, but also offer different metaphoric formulations of what might be a similar underlying interpersonal process. In any case, Luborsky's findings provide the basis for looking at similarities and differences cross-sectionally among different psychotherapies and for relating such observations to the empirical evidence, in terms of outcome. It would seem that the "schools" of psychotherapy, *per se,* are not essential features important to outcome. Instead, "outcome" may be related to other factors, alluded to but not as yet sufficiently explained.

## REFERENCES

Abroms, G.M. Persuasion in psychotherapy. *Amer. J. Psychiat.* **124** : 1214 (1968).

Aronson, H. and Weintraub, W. Certain initial variables as predictors of change with classical psychoanalysis. *J. Abn. Psychol.* **74** : 103 (1969).

Bailey, K.G. and Sowder, W.T. Audiotape and videotape self-confrontation in psychotherapy. *Psychol. Bull.* **58** : 143 (1961).

Bandura, A. Psychotherapy as a learning process. *Psychol. Bull.* **58** : 143 (1961).

Bandura, A. Psychotherapy based upon modeling principles. In : Bergin, A.E. and Garfield, S.L. (Eds.), *Handbook of Psychotherapy and Behavior Change,* Wiley, New York, 1971.

Begley, C.E. and Lieberman, L.R. Patients: expectations of therapists' techniques. *J. Clin. Psychol.* **26** : 113 (1970).

Benfari, R.C. Relationship between early dependency training and patient-therapist dyad. *Psychol. Rep.* **25** : 552 (1969).

Bergin, A.E. and Garfield, S.L. (Eds.) *Handbook of Psychotherapy and Behavior Change, An Empirical Analysis.* Wiley, New York, 1971.

Betz, B. Validation of the differential treatment success of "A" and "B" therapists with schizophrenic patients. *Amer. J. Psychiat.* **119** : 883 (1963).

Bibring, E. Psychoanalysis and the dynamic psychotherapies. *J. Amer. Psa. Assoc.* **2** : 745 (1954).

Bierman, R. Dimensions of interpersonal facilitation in psychotherapy and child development. *Psychol. Bull.* **72** : 338 (1969).

Birdwhistell, R.L. *Kinetics and Context: Essays on Body Motion and Communication.* University of Pennsylvania Press, Philadelphia, 1970.

Boulgouris, J.C., Marks, I.M. and Marset, P. Superiority of flooding (implosion) to desensitization for reducing pathological fear. *Behav. Res. Ther.* **9** : 7 (1971).

Boulware, D.W. and Holmes, D.S. Preferences for therapists and related expectancies. *J. Consult. Clin. Psychol.* **35** : 269 (1970).

Brady, J.P. Psychotherapy by a combined behavioral and dynamic approach. *Comp. Psychiat.* **9** : 536 (1968).

Bromberg, W. The nature of psychotherapy. *Trans. N.Y. Acad. Sci.* **28** : 102 (1965).

Bruche, H. Activity in the psychotherapeutic process. *Current Psych. Therapies* **2** : 69 (1962).

Cahoon, D.D. Symptom substitution and the behavior therapies: a reappraisal. *Psychol. Bull.* **69** : 149 (1968).

Caracena, P.F. and Vicory, J.R. Correlates of phenomenological and judged empathy. *J. Couns. Psychol.* **16** : 510 (1969).

Chartier, G.M. A-B therapist variable: real or imagined? *Psychol. Bull.* **75** : 22 (1971).

Chessick, R.D. Psychotherapeutic interaction. *Amer. J. Psychother.* **28** : 243 (1974).

Collingwood, T., Hefele, T.J. Muehlberg, N. and Drasgow, J. Toward identification of the therapeutically facilitative factor. *J. Clin. Psychol.* **26** : 119, (1970).

Cross, H. The outcome of psychotherapy: a selected analysis of research findings. *J. Consult. Psychol.* **28** : 413 (1964).

Dewald, P.A. The clinical assessment of structural change. *J. Amer. Psa. Assoc.* **20** : 302 (1972).

Dyrud, J.E. and Holzman, P.S. The psychotherapy of schizophrenia: does it work? *Amer. J. Psychiat.* **130** : 670 (1973).

Ellis, A. Requisite conditions for basic personality change. *J. Counsel. Psychol.* **23** : 538 (1959).

Eron, L.D. and Callahan, R. (Eds.) *The Relationship of Theory to Practice in Psychotherapy.* Aldine, Chicago, 1970.

Fiedler, F. Factor analyses of psychoanalytic, nondirective and Adlerian therapeutic relationships. *J. Consult. Psychol.* **15** : 32 (1951).

Fiske, D. Strategies in the search for personality changes. *J. Exp. Res. in Personal.* **5** : 323 (1971).

Forizs, L. Some common denominators in psychotherapeutic modalities. *Dis. Nerv. Syst.* **27** : 783 (1966).

Frank, J.D. The dynamics of the psychotherapeutic relationship. *Psychiatry.* **22** : 17 (1959).

Frank, J.D. *Persuasion and Healing: A Comparative Study of Psychotherapy.* Johns-Hopkins Press, Baltimore, 1961.

Frank, J.D. Therapeutic factors in psychotherapy. *Amer. J. Psychiat.* **131** : 271 (1974).

Frank, J.D. Psychotherapy: the restoration of morale. *Amer. J. Psychiat.* **131** : 271 (1974).

Frankl, V.E. Paradoxical intention: a logotherapeutic technique. *Amer. J. Psychother.* **14:** 520 (1960).

Friedman, P. Limitations in the conceptualization of behavior therapists: toward a cognitive-behavioral model of behavior therapy. *Psychol. Rep.* **27** : 175 (1970).

Fromm-Reichman, F. *Principles of Intensive Psychotherapy.* University of Chicago Press, Chicago, 1950.

Gallagher, E., Sharaf, M. and Levinson, D. The influence of patient and therapist in determining the use of psychotherapy in a hospital setting. *Psychiatry.* **28:** 297 (1965).

G.A.P. Report (Group for the Advancement of Psychiatry), Psychotherapy and the dual research tradition, Volume 7 (#73), October, 1969.

Gardner, G.G. The psychotherapeutic relationship. *Psychol. Bull.* **61** : 426 (1964).

Garduk, E.L. and Haggard, E.A. Immediate effects on patients of psychoanalytic interpretations. *Psychol. Issues,* Vol. 7, Monograph 28, 1972.

Garfield, S.L. and Bergin, A.E. Therapeutic conditions and outcome. *J. Abn. Psychol.* **77:** 108 (1971).

Goldman, R.J. and Mendelsohn, G.A.   Psychotherapeutic change and social adjustment:   a report of a national survey of psychotherapists. *J. Abn. Psychol.*  **74** : 164 (1969).

Goldstein, A.P.  *Therapist-Patient Expectancies in Psychotherapy.*  MacMillan, New York, 1962.

Goldstein, A.P.  *Psychotherapeutic Attraction.*  Pergamon Press, Elmsford, N.Y., 1971.

Greenson, R.R.  The working alliance and the transference neurosis. *Psychoanalytic Quart.*  **34** : 155 (1965).

Gunderson, J.C.  Controversies about the psychotherapy of schizophrenia. *Amer. J. Psychiat.*  **130** : 677 (1973).

Haley, J.  *Strategies of Psychotherapy.*  Grune and Stratton, New York, 1963.

Harway, N.I. and Iker, H.P.  Content analysis and psychotherapy. *Psychother. Theory Res. Pract.*  **6** : 97 (1969).

Hertel, R.K.  Application of stochastic process analyses to the study of psychotherapeutic processes. *Psychol. Bull.*  **77** : 421 (1972).

Hill, J.A.  Therapist goals, patient aims and patient satisfaction in psychotherapy. *J. Clin. Psychol.*  **25** : 455 (1969).

Hoehn-Saric, R.,*et al.*  Systematic preparation of patient for psychotherapy:  I and II. *J. Psychiat. Res.*  **2** : 267 (1964).

Honigfeld, G.  Nonspecific factors in treatment. *Dis. Nerv. Syst.*  **25** : 145 (1964).

Houts, P.S., MacIntosh, S. and Moos, R.H.  Patient-therapist interdependence: cognitive and behavioral. *J. Consult. Clin. Psychol.*  **33** : 40 (1969).

Karush, A.  Working through. *Psychoanalyt. Quart.*  **36**:  497 (1967).

Kelley, J., Smits, S.J., Leventhal, R. and Rhodes, R.  Critique of the designs of process and outcome research. *J. Couns. Psychol.*  **17** : 337 (1970).

Kiesler, D.  Some myths of psychotherapy research and the search for a paradigm. *Psychol. Bull.*  **65** : 110 (1966).

Knupfer, G., Jackson, D.D. and Krieger, G.  Personality differences between more and less competent psychotherapists as a function of criteria of competence. *J. Nerv. Ment. Dis.*  **129** : 375 (1959).

Lazarus, A.A.  Behavioral rehearsal vs nondirective therapy vs advice in effecting behavioral change. *Behav. and Ther.*  **4** : 209 (1966).

Lennard, H.L. and Bernstein, A.  *The Anatomy of Psychotherapy.*  Columbia University Press, New York, 1960.

Lorion, R.P.  Socioeconomic status and traditional treatment approaches reconsidered. *Psychol. Bull.*  **79** : 263 (1973).

Lorr, M.,*et al.*  Frequency of treatment and change in psychotherapy. *J. Abn. Soc. Psychol.*  **64** : 281 (1962).

Luborsky, L.  Comparative studies of psychotherapies — is it true that everybody has won and all must have prizes?  Paper presented at 3rd Ann. Mtg. of Soc. for Psychother. Res., June 6, 1972, Nashville.

Luborsky, L., *et al.*  Factors influencing the outcome of psychotherapy: a review of quantitative research. *Psychol. Bull.*  **75** : 145 (1971).

Malan, D.H.  The outcome problem in psychotherapy research. *Arch. Gen. Psychiat.*  **29** : 719 (1973).

Meltzoff, J. and Kornreich, M.  *Research in Psychotherapy.*  Atherton Press, New York, 1970.

Miller, R.L. and Bloomberg, L.I. No therapy as a method of psychotherapy. *Psychother. Theory Res. Pract.* **6** : 49 (1969).

Moos, R.H. and MacIntoch, S. Multivariate study of the patient-therapist system. *J. Consult. Clin. Psychol.* **35** : 298 (1970).

Murray, E.J. Learning theory and psychotherapy: biotropic vs sociotropic approaches. *J. Counsel. Psychol.* **10** : 250 (1963).

Nacht, S. The curative factor in psychoanalysis. *Int. J. Psa.* **43** : 206 (1962).

Nurnberger, J.I. and Hingtgen, J.N. Is symptom substitution an important issue in behavior therapy? *Biol. Psychiat.* **7** : 221 (1973).

Offenkrantz, W. Psychoanalytic psychotherapy. *Arch. Gen. Psychiat.* **30** : 593 (1974).

Orne, M. Implications for psychotherapy as derived from current research on the nature of hypnosis, *Amer. J. Psychiat.* **118** : 1097 (1962).

Parsons, T. On the concept of influence. *Publ. Opin. Quart.* **27** : 44 (1963).

Patton, M.J. Attraction, discrepancy and response to psychological treatment. *J. Couns. Psychol.* **16** : 317 (1969).

Piper, W.E. and Wogan, M. Placebo effect in psychotherapy. *J. Consult. Clin. Psychol.* **34** : 447 (1970).

Rangell, L. Similarities and differences between psychoanalysis and dynamic psychotherapy. *J. Amer. Psa. Assoc.* **2** : 734 (1954).

Sargent, H.D. Intrapsychic change: methodological problems in psychotherapy research. *Psychiatry.* **24** : 93 (1961).

Schacter, S. *The Psychology of Affiliation.* Stanford University Press, Palo Alto, 1959.

Singer, E. *Key Concepts in Psychotherapy.* Random House, New York, 1965,

Snyder, W.U. *The Psychotherapy Relationship.* MacMillan, New York, 1961.

Strupp, H.H. *Psychotherapy, Clinical Research and Clinical Issues.* 1973.

Strupp, H.H. On the technology of psychotherapy. *Arch. Gen. Psychiat.* **26** : 234 (1972).

Strupp, H.H. and Bergin, A.E. Some empirical and conceptual bases for coordinated research in psychotherapy. *Int. J. Psychiat.* **7** : 2 (1969); and critical evaluations of "Some empirical and conceptual bases for coordinated research in psychotherapy." **7** : 3 (1969).

Strupp, H.H. and Williams, J.V. Some determinants of clinical evaluations of different psychiatrists. *Arch. Gen. Psychiat.* **2** : 434 (1966).

Suomi, S.J., Harlow, H.F. and McKinney, W.T. Monkey psychiatrists. *Amer. J. Psychiat.* **128** : 927 (1972).

Tower, L. Countertransference. *J. Amer. Psa. Assoc.* **4** : 224 (1956).

Truax, C.B., *et al.* Effects of therapist persuasive potency in individual psychotherapy. *J. Clin. Psychol.* **24** : 359 (1968).

Wallach, M.S. and Strupp, H.H. Dimensions of psychotherapeutic activity. *J. Consult. Psychol.* **28** : 120 (1964).

Wallerstein, R.S. The problem of assessment of change in psychotherapy. *Int. J. Psa.* **44** : 31 (1963).

Weiss, J. The emergence of new themes: a contribution to the psychoanalytic theory of therapy. *Int. J. Psa.* **52** : 459 (1971).

Weisskopf-Joelson, E. The present crisis in psychotherapy. *J. of Psychol.* **69** : 107 (1968).

Wolberg, L.R. *The Technique of Psychotherapy.* Volumes I and II, Grune and Stratton, New York, 1967.

Wolberg, L.R. Contemporary problems in psychotherapy. *Canad. Psychiat. Assoc. J.* **16** : 387 (1971).

Wolff, H.H. The therapeutic and developmental functions of psychotherapy. *Brit. J. Med. Psychol.* **44** : 117 (1971).

Wolpe, J., Brady, J.P., Serber, M., Agras, W.S. and Liberman, R.P. The current status of systematic desensitization. *Amer. J. Psychiat.* **130** : 961 (1973).

Yeats, A.J. Symptoms and symptom substitution. *Psychol. Rev.* **65** : 371 (1958).

Zetzel, E. Current concepts of transference. *Int. J. Psa.* **37** : 369 (1956).

Zuk, G.H. Family therapy during 1964 – 1970. *Psychother. Theory Res. Pract.* **8** : 90 (1971).

# 4 Psychoanalytic Technique

## Gertrude Blanck

Freud's monumental discoveries have captured the interest of many who hitherto felt baffled by the intricacies of the mind. Some, whose defenses became mobilized, were forced to reject the new science altogether; others first seized upon it as messianic, but later reached a predictable moment when overidealization and grandiose expectation led to disappointment. The former group never accepted psychoanalysis as a science; the latter became its detractors. There remained, fortunately, a third group who welcomed psychoanalysis and who became the hard-working scientists who studied Freud's work the better to be able to extend, elaborate and build upon it. Especially in the current era of theory construction we are indebted to the ego psychologists — Hartmann, Kris, Loewenstein, Anna Freud, Greenacre, Mahler, Jacobson and Spitz — who, as gifted and serious thinkers, ventured beyond the master to explore new ground, thereby providing a body of knowledge unsurpassed as a psychology of normality and pathology.

Psychoanalysis is tripartite — a theory of human behavior, a research tool and a therapy. While this discussion will be restricted to the technique of psychoanalysis, i.e., to that aspect which represents psychoanalysis as a therapy, technique can only exist as a valid treatment procedure when it is solidly based on conceptual ground. To begin, therefore, some historical notes about psychoanalytic theory are in order. Rapaport (1959) divided psychoanalytic theory into four historical eras. "The *first phase* of the history of psychoanalytic ego psychology coincides with Freud's prepsychoanalytic theory; it ends with 1897, the approximate beginning of psychoanalysis proper (Freud, 1887-1902, pp. 215-218). The *second phase,* which ends in 1923, is the development of psychoanalysis proper. The *third phase* begins with the publication of *The Ego and the Id* (1923), and encompasses the development of Freud's psychology, which extends to 1937. The *fourth phase* begins with the crucial writings of Anna Freud (1936), Hartmann (1939), Erikson (1937), Horney (1937), Kardiner (1939), Sullivan (1938,1940) and extends to the present day. The general psychoanalytic psychology of the ego based on the foundations laid by Freud began to evolve in this phase (p. 6)."

This brief historical survey will aid in the understanding of how technique follows theory and will help to indicate which techniques are still pertinent to modern practice, which have been superseded, as well as which have had to be added by the dictates of contemporary theory. The final discussion will show how technique appears on the frontier, that is, as current theory provides rationale for approaches to the formerly baffling pathology of the borderline and narcissistic states. Psychoanalysis as a treatment modality nevertheless remains the treatment of choice for neurosis, and the main burden of this description of technique refers, therefore, to the neuroses.

It is well known that Freud's first technical tool was hypnosis. While he abandoned this technique early, for reasons which shall be explained shortly, it is interesting to observe how some of the "new" nonanalytic procedures involve several which Freudians no longer employ. These include, in addition to hypnosis, suggestion, ventilation, abreaction, and confrontation, among others. They appear and reappear periodically in different guises, such as the variations of conditioning, behavior modification, primal therapy and the like, but in their essence, they represent elaborations on the same themes. Freud began as he did because he thought at first of all pathology as hysteria and of all defense as repression. The ego, in his early definition, was the conscious part of the mental apparatus. Hysteria was the illness resulting from repression of a sexual (usually incestuous) fantasy. He used hypnosis to retrieve the repressed memory in order to make it conscious, that is, to unite it with the rest of the ego, then regarded as already conscious. He later found hypnosis to be ineffective for reasons which only became fully clear when he formulated the structural theory in 1923. By then he knew that not all of the ego is conscious and not all defense is repression. The structural theory explains more fully why hypnosis, suggestion and their modern variations are not theoretically tenable. Simply stated, the theoretical fallacy is that they bypass the ego. The synthetic function (Nunberg, 1931) and the defensive function (A. Freud, 1966) are inoperative in such technique, as are other ego functions. Insight cannot be gained when the ego, the very instrument for its attainment, is bypassed. Without interpretation of defenses they remain intact; countercathexis may even become intensified as behavior is altered; symptoms may take another form and even the character structure may be invaded. Thus, not only is there no cure, but there even exists the danger that pathology may be exacerbated.

These matters are stressed in order to dramatize the importance of the structural theory, the new direction it provided for technique and, particularly, to emphasize that poststructural-theory techniques differ markedly from those which, in the prestructural era, were thought to be effective. The structural theory also provided a new direction for theory building. Its impetus continues to carry theory forward to this day and, predictably, beyond. Shortly after proposing the structural theory, Freud (1959) revised his theory of anxiety, now regarding anxiety as the affective consequence of conflict with which the ego has to deal. This states simply the concept of intersystemic conflict, a theoretical cornerstone upon which traditional psychoanalytic technique is based. Neurosis is, by definition, a pathological solution to the oedipal conflict, arrived at by an ego which employs defenses against anxiety and guilt produced by tension between ego and id or superego and id or superego and ego. Compromise is reached between these conflicting institutions, resulting in symptom formation or, if ego syntonic, in character alteration. Traditionally, therefore, analysis has as its purpose dealing with defense (analysis of resistance) on the one side of the compromise, and uncovering the id wish (making the unconscious conscious) on the other side. The major portion of any psychoanalytic endeavor still pursues this purpose. After the structural theory and the revision of the theory of anxiety, it fell to Freud's heirs to pursue theory construction. Anna Freud (1966) dealt with the defensive function of the ego and contributed immeasurably to technique by pointing out that, since it is clear that defense and resistance are unconscious ego functions, it is as important for the analyst, in listening to the patient's free associations, to concern himself with the functioning of the ego as with the derivatives of the id, formerly regarded as the analyst's sole concern. In fact, it has become a prime tenet of technique that *defense is to be interpreted before content* (Fenichel, 1941). It will later be shown how ego psychological theory modifies still further the prestructural emphasis upon id content alone. The major technical tools of psychoanalysis as they have developed since the structural theory and are practiced today will be described briefly. They are so adequately treated in the standard texts on the technique of psychoanalysis that little would be served in repeating at length what the authors of these texts (Freud, 1958; Glover, 1958; Fenichel, 1941; Sharpe, 1950; Menninger, 1958; Greenson, 1967) have already presented.

*Free association,* while at first devised by Freud to eliminate the analyst's influence upon the direction of the patient's thought, has a broader purpose — that of loosening cathexis of the secondary process so that primary process thought, not ordinarily operative to such a high degree in the waking state of the individual with an intact ego, will, in the analytic process, break through, providing access to the unconscious, especially when resistance is at a low level. Free association is often described as the basic rule of psychoanalysis in that it is the main analytic obligation of the patient.

*Interpretation* is the basic tool of the analyst. For heuristic purposes, Eissler (1953) proposed that an ideal analysis may be conducted using no technique other than interpretation, but he does not extend his argument to insist that, practically, this is possible. Interpretation, formerly regarded as of id content only, may now be of ego as well. On the ego side, one may interpret defense and resistance (A. Freud, 1966) and support may be provided for purposes of strengthening even the intact ego, by interpretation of adaptation (Hartmann, 1958; Blanck, 1966). In its fundamental feature, interpretation disturbs an equilibrium established by the synthetic function (Nunberg, 1931), by introducing a heretofore unconscious element into consciousness, necessitating a new synthesis for the re-establishment of a new equilibrium which now must absorb the added (interpreted) feature. In order to understand the theory of interpretation thoroughly, it is necessary to take into account Waelder's (1936) enunciation of the principle of multiple function in which he enumerated eight aspects of the psyche to be satsified for equilibrium to be maintained. While it would take us too deeply into metapsychology to discuss the principle of multiple function thoroughly here, it is necessary to indicate that theoretical understanding of how interpretation operates in depth adds immeasurably to technical artistry.

At first, theorists of technique (Freud, 1958; Glover, 1958; Fenichel, 1941) cautioned that interpretation is not to be made before the transference neurosis is established and before transference (especially positive transference) becomes resistance. It is now feasible, with the backing of contemporary theory, to begin interpretative work early in analysis. Interpretation is made, not only of resistance, but of the broader and more conscious aspects of the neurosis, paving the way for deeper approach to these same matters later in the analysis. An example is presented here which illustrates both how early interpretation is made and the importance, diagnostically and technically, of the first dream. A woman in analysis with a female analyst dreams that she is in a car with a man who is driving at a dangerous speed and that another woman (understood to represent the analyst, but not yet so interpreted) is in the back seat and tells the man to slow down. This dream informs the analyst that the protection of the pre-oedipal mother is sought against heterosexual anxiety. It indicates the point of fixation and regression and provides the analysis with a direction. The defensive need for the preoedipal mother will have to be analyzed before the positive oedipal conflict may be resolved.

Interpretation is hardly ever a single pronouncement by the analyst. It is to be thought of, rather, as taking place in a series of "incomplete" interpretations (Glover, 1958, pp. 357-358), the totality of which constitutes *the* interpretation. One may envision it as a pyramid with the narrowest, most general, preconscious, partial interpretation beginning at the apex. Intermediary and ever-deepening partial interpretations proceed over many sessions often interspersed with other matters, because free association rather than compulsive analytic zeal propels the treatment. The final, fullest interpretation of the unconscious, completing those that preceded it, constitutes the base of the pyramid. In the case illustrated, the first interpretation was simply, "The woman protects you." The series then proceeds over many sessions in close connection with the patient's associations and leads the patient ever more deeply toward the realization of how she clings to the analyst for protection. For example, she brings her marital problems into the sessions, seeking the analyst's advice about her husband's behavior. When the transference neurosis ensues, the interpretation may be altered to, "You need *me* to protect you." When resistances have been interpreted, such as the attempt to use the analyst in taking sides against the husband, and when genetic material and sexual fantasies have been provided, the interpretation is reduced to the genetic, "You needed your mother to protect you." This is still an incomplete interpretation. The patient is left to wonder why. As associations proceed, she may herself link anxiety about her sexual fantasies to the defense of maintaining a strong libidinal tie to the preoedipal mother. This illustrates not only how interpretation is made in a series of incomplete interpretations, but also how the patient is led to make self-interpretations — how the ego is encouraged to function in the analytic situation. It begins the explanation, to be elaborated upon, of change in technique regarding the division of labor dictated by the theoretical advances in the present era of psychoanalytic theory construction. This description and illustration of the technique of interpretation is also closely related to another technical concept, *working through.* Briefly, working through refers to repeated interpretations from different facets, depending upon the material provided, until the genetic conflict is understood in its entirety. Again, the principle of multiple function is of value in understanding how working through deals with each of the eight aspects of multiple function.

In the United States, *frequency of analytic sessions* is preferably five days a week, minimally four days a week. (Freud saw his patients six days.) The daily succession of sessions propels analytic work because that which is begun in one session is quickly followed up in the next as the stream of associations continues to flow and as the ever-deepening contact with the unconscious is uninterrupted, except for the weekend when the analyst needs to recover his own resources. As an example, a partial (incomplete) interpretation made in a given session may constitute the day residue for a dream that night, which adds new material, so that interpretative work proceeds and deepens. Even without a remembered dream, the unconscious continues its work in the twenty-four hour interval and carries the analytic work forward the next day. Greenacre (1954), in describing the disadvantages of brief therapy and infrequent sessions, shows that long intervals between sessions tend to thicken resistance, allow for re-repression of material already interpreted, and especially permit the negative aspects of transference to be covered over.

The *use of the couch* is misunderstood in unsophisticated quarters because Freud's remark that he did not like to be stared at has been so much overstressed at the expense of the more profound reasons for this procedure. Lying in a relaxed position, without being able to see the analyst, the patient is better able to fantasy and to regress, to project and displace upon the analyst feelings and attitudes toward figures from the past — that is, to form a transference. The supine position also minimizes motor activity, thus encouraging *verbalization* rather than action. Freud (1958) described acting-out as substituting for remembering. Verbalization is now valued, not only because it facilitates remembering, but is understood also to consist of a complex of ego functions which includes symbolization and semantic communication (Spitz, 1957) and is condusive to ego-building, to neutralization and to the establishment of higher levels of object relations. Acting-out, on the other hand, blocks remembering by bypassing the ego, thus lessening opportunity for insight; it permits temporary discharge without therapeutic gain; it obscures the conflict and even reinforces infantile gratification at the risk of rendering the conflict unanalyzable.

There is a form of action on the part of some patients which is to be distinguished from acting-out. This refers to enactment of preverbal affect and experience. Especially from the observational studies (Mahler, 1963, 1965, 1968, 1971; Spitz, 1957, 1965), we have become familiar with the richness of affectivity between mother and child in the early weeks and months of life and of the essential nature of this dyadic relationship for ego development. These studies have also made us aware of the inner life of the child before the acquisition of speech. Spitz (1957) designates 18 months as the average age when speech (semantic communication) begins. But it is not until approximately seven years of age (Piaget, 1955) that capacity for abstract thought develops. Therefore, there is much unsaid in the child's emotional life which results in the adult analysand's relative incapacity to verbalize that which had been experienced outside the verbal realm. One of the newer techniques derived from ego psychological theory is that of enabling the patient to cathect with words those preverbal experiences which otherwise tend to lead to action. Technically, both acting and acting-out, although differently determined, are dealt with by encouraging verbalization; in the instance of acting-out, it is the repressed that is to be verbalized; in acting, we have a more difficult technical task because that which had never been cathected to language must now be cathected retroactively.

*Regression* is facilitated by the use of the couch. Thus regression, primarily a mechanism of defense, becomes secondarily a deliberate part of the technical repertory; regression to the point of fixation leads the analysis to revival of infantile conflict now to be interpreted and resolved. In the present era of psychoanalytic theory-building, it is essential to stress that the intact ego of the analyzable patient rarely regresses unless "in the service of the ego" (Kris, 1952), that is to say, reversibly. Regression is, in the main, along the psychosexual line of maturation only. With little or no danger of ego regression, it is a valid analytic tool; in the psychoanalytically oriented psychotherapy of the less intact ego, regression is to be employed with more caution, if at all. It is this analytic tool that causes many an analyst technical difficulty because misdiagnosis of the structure of the ego, an understandable error made sometimes by even the most experienced diagnostician, leads to the use of regression as a technique when it is contraindicated because the ego, too fragile to tolerate such stress upon it, regresses along with the id. With the loss of ego function, there may be decompensation.

Regression, frequency of attendance and the supine position with freedom to fantasy without the interference of the analyst's appearance in reality, all serve to facilitate the onset of *transference* and *transference neurosis.* Transference is a phenomenon which occurs in everyday life as well as in psychoanalysis. Persons, especially those in positions of authority and nurturing – teachers, doctors, dentists, nurses, policemen, judges, even relatives and friends – are objects of transference. Only the psychoanalyst, however, uses the transference and transference neurosis deliberately and with full awareness of their therapeutic potentialities. Transference neurosis is distinguished from transference in that, when the transference neurosis sets in, there is no longer merely casual repetition of feelings and attitudes from the past displaced and projected onto the person of the analyst, but the totality of the neurosis is revived and relived within the analytic situation. Glover (1958) is very precise about indications that the transference neurosis is beginning to take hold. The drift of associations centers more and more around the analyst's possessions, clothing, office furnishings and, ultimately, upon the analyst himself. Before the transference neurosis proper ensues, that is, in the beginning phase of analysis, the analyst's efforts are devoted to providing the climate within which analysis may best flourish. Along with regression and fantasy formation – in fact, an inherent part of those processes – is promotion of the transference which will lead, shortly after the opening phase, to the transference neurosis. The word *promotion* is not used here in the active sense. The analysand regresses because of his need for the analyst, reviving childhood dependence upon parental guidance and love. There are innumerable instances of such transference dependency being exploited in nonanalytic situations for the advantage of the authority figure. It is one of the proudest features of psychoanalysis that the analyst, conscious of his responsibility for cure, uses the transference entirely for the benefit of the patient. In the contemporary period, Greenacre's (1954, 1959) discussions of the value of guardianship of the patient's autonomy in the transference add an important dimension to the concept of transference as an analytic tool and elaborate on the analyst's responsibility for ensuring that the patient will never become inextricably dependent upon the analyst, although he must become dependent for the purpose of reliving and thereby working through his residual dependency needs to true independence. Greenacre also provides useful clarification of the heretofore black and white consideration of negative and positive transference. She notes that transference shifts and changes, sometimes within the same analytic session. She prefers, therefore, to speak of "active transference-neurotic manifestations" (Greenacre, 1959, p. 486) which describe more fluidly the varying feelings of the analysand toward his primary figures as they shift and change within the transference.

In the contemporary era, distinction is made not only between transference and transference neurosis, but between those phenomena and the real relationship with the analyst. It is now recognized that the analyst cannot altogether constitute the "blank screen" that was earlier thought to be desirable. He has a personality which inevitably reveals itself to the discerning analysand; his office furnishings, clothing, mannerisms and the like give some indication of how he is in reality. His responses to the patient cannot be the same as those of any other person. So, much as he tries to keep personal information at a minimum for the purpose of encouraging fantasy, the patient gains some assessment of him as a person and responds to that. To the extent that he is kind, respectful, empathic and helpful, an alliance is formed which carries the analytic work forward. The patient's contribution to the analytic situation is some capacity to form realistic object relations in the present as well as to transfer from the past. The realistic aspects of his relationship to the analyst have been termed the *therapeutic alliance* by Zetzel (1956) and the *working alliance* by Greenson (1967). Both these rather similar distinctions between transference and a real relationship expand Sterba's (1934) concept of the therapeutic split into an experiencing and an observing ego. In Sterba's terms, the observing ego allies itself with the analyst in their mutual task and goal; the experiencing ego relives in the transference. Usually, except for moments in every analysis when the power of the affective experience causes the ego to lose, temporarily, its capacity to distinguish present from past, the competent ego of the analytic patient is divided in the way that Sterba has described. Reality testing and a good level of object relations lead him not only to ally himself with the analyst in their common goal, but to know that he is a real person. That is not to be relied upon in the treatment of the more disturbed patient. In the analyzable patient, however, his perception of the reality aspects of the analyst as a person increases in value as the analysis proceeds to termination and aids in the dissolution of the transference.

Particularly pertinent to the issue of the capacity to experience the analyst as real as well as an object for transference are the contributions of Jacobson (1971) and Loewald (1962). Jacobson shows how selective identification, normally, is a developmental process. One of the technical implications of her position is that, toward the end of analysis, when distorted self and object representations have been corrected, selective identification with the analyst inevitably takes place. Loewald elaborates on this aspect of the analytic process, describing how termination of analysis involves a mourning process and how identification operates to facilitate giving up the object. Both of these authors move away from the formerly held concept of identification as a defense only (A. Freud, 1966) and point up that it can also be developmental and adaptive. None of the Freudian authors who recognize that there is a real relationship with the analyst in addition to the transferential one implies that this real relationship involves personal friendship or reciprocity in the ordinary sense. They abide by the abstinence rule which is designed to protect the patient from antitherapeutic involvement with the analyst and his personal life.

Transference and transference neurosis were rediscussed at a Panel of the 28th International Congress of Psycho-Analysis held in Paris in July, 1973. At the Panel, Loewald summed up the definition and description of transference by pointing out that it is both interpersonal and intrapsychic and that, by and large, it restructures infantile object relations. Valenstein, another panelist, asserted that the classical definitions of transference and transference neurosis apply to the symptom neuroses only. Currently, he stressed, we are concerned with preoedipal features — that is, the earliest experiences which determine transference. Van der Leeuw added to Valenstein's statement that the narcissistic patient, as contrasted with the neurotic, does not see the analyst as a person in his own right, but only as a need-satisfying object. This follows the theoretical views of Jacobson (1971) and Mahler (1968). Jacobson's formulation that, in the early months of life self and object representations are undifferentiated, coincides with Mahler's observations that, upon emergence from the objectless state of autism, the infant enters into symbiosis with the maternal object. Both these positions lead logically to the conclusion that experiences derived from that period of life cannot be transferred to an object because self and object are one. Arlow, as Chairman of this same Panel, raised questions about the division of transference into positive and negative. It was generally agreed to by the Panel that these are not useful concepts, but surprisingly omitted from that discussion was Greenacre's (1959) proposal that the term *active-neurotic transference manifestations* more accurately describes the fluctuation in feeling that takes place within the transference. Also at the same Panel, Greenson exceeded Fenichel's (1941) parsimonious definition of transference as mistaking the present for the past. Greenson defined transference as a distortion in time. He described the ideal patient as one who is capable of engaging in both transference and a working alliance.

Discussion of transference is not complete without reference to *countertransference*. Orr (1954) dealt with this subject in great detail. Strictly defined, countertransference refers to the unconscious feelings, both libidinal and aggressive, which are incurred by the analyst in reaction to the attitudes and productions of the analysand. Some consider that the only way that the analyst can deal with these feelings is by means of self-analysis. Sharpe (1950), for example, said that it is desirable to analyze one's own dreams about a patient before attempting to deal with the patient in the next session. This does not imply that Sharpe restricted consideration of countertransference to the phenomenon of the dream, but only that she presented this method as an illustration of how to cope with countertransference if it should happen to present itself in the analyst's dream.

Some analysts employ a broader definition of countertransference, including within it not only unconscious but also conscious personal response to the patient. They do not, as do some non-Freudian therapists, advocate using the countertransference in direct interpersonal transaction with the patient. The emphasis is rather upon understanding one's own feelings toward the patient, to engage in self-analysis in order to know why they have occurred, and, if possible, to trace them to their infantile origins and to the analyst's neurotic residua. If countertransference reactions do not yield to self-analysis, or if they are extreme, or if they follow a repetitive pattern, it is desirable for the analyst to seek the help of another analyst. When thoroughly understood by the analyst as not stemming from his own infantile or neurotic responses, countertransference reactions can be useful technical tools.  When the analyst is certain that it is not he who is responding inappropriately, but that the patient is unconsciously stimulating a particular response in him, then it is technically proper to interpret what the patient is doing.  This is perhaps one of the most delicate areas of technique because the analyst must be very well analyzed and must be quite certain that his response is indeed initiated by the patient's unconscious neurotic behavior before he ventures such an interpretation.  Otherwise, it becomes all too easy to "blame" the patient for one's own neurotic responses.  This would constitute a technical error of immeasurable magnitude and, if not corrected, could cause irreparable damage to an analysis.  Such errors may be distinguished qualitatively and quantitatively from the more ordinary, readily correctable errors in interpretation which every analyst makes on occasion.  For example, a misinterpretation of a dream fragment in one session may be corrected in the next session by a new dream or an additional association which informs the analyst that he saw the matter incorrectly in the previous session.  These kinds of ordinary misinterpretations are not even to be regarded in the realm of error and are certainly not of the same magnitude as are persistent misinterpretations based on countertransference.

*Resistance* is defined as the use of defenses in the analytic situation.  Fenichel (1941), among others, cautioned that resistance is always to be interpreted before content.  Analysts have long been familiar with the so-called abuse of free association, whereby a form of pseudo free association takes place without, however, providing interpretable analytic material.  Dreams and memories can also be used in the service of resistance sometimes so subtly that even the most skilled analyst may be temporarily deceived by the patient's unconscious use of defense in this way.  A classic example of resistance in the transference is the presentation of material to intrigue the analyst.  The correct order of interpretation is first of the wish to please, seduce or otherwise interest the analyst, later of the content and of the infantile antecedents.  In order to understand the resistances for interpretative purposes, the analyst listens actively to the associations to determine how to begin to interpret them.  Contrary to logical expectation, resistance does not diminish in consistently descending levels of intensity with interpretation.  Rather, interpretation of resistance leads to new unconscious pathways which the resistance had defended.  This, in turn, touches upon new conflict, which results in intensification of defense against increased anxiety.  Thus, interpretation of resistance does indeed prepare the way for new content, but the experienced analyst is then prepared to deal with ever-intensified resistance until the entire resistant structure crumbles.  In an analysis, the occurrence of increased levels of resistance, although apparently paradoxical, constitutes in fact a confirmation that the analysis is proceeding properly.  That resistance tends to thicken is understandably baffling to the patient whose lack of such technical knowledge leads him to think that the analysis is stalemated when, in fact, progress is good.

In modern technique, although the analyst does still deal interpretatively with the resistances as they occur and, as described, proceeds to deeper layers of conflict, his objective is broadened. No longer is he principally interested in the single resistance or even in the series of deepening levels of resistance which stand in the way of uncovering content. His overall objective is the dissolution of a resistant structure (Kris, 1956), following upon which the patient becomes able to take over his own interpretative work and to approach termination of his need for the analyst. This kind of redistribution of the work of the analysis takes place in the context of employment of the aggressive drive in its neutralized mode in the service of independence. Kris compares this with the unneutralized aggression of the patient who indicates no need for the analyst as a defensive rather than an adaptive measure.

The thrust of the position that countertransference is usually a matter for self-analysis, and is to be revealed to the patient interpretatively only when it is the result of the patient's unconscious instigation (R. Blanck, 1973) leads logically to consideration of the *abstinence rule*. This much misunderstood technical device is, nevertheless, one of the most important in the technical repertory because it is designed to assure that the analysis will be solely in the service of resolving the patient's conflicts. Abstinence means nothing more than that the analyst safeguards the analysis by abstaining from gratifying infantile needs, for the purpose of avoiding reinforcement of fixation. Misunderstandings about abstinence include failure to engage in appropriate human response, maintenance of unnecessary and often cruel silence, and the converse of these — provision of too much gratification and self-revelation in order to prove that one is a "human being." In fact, the analyst is obliged to provide a great deal. Above all, his task is to provide interpretation or to facilitate the patient's capacity for self-interpretation. Human response, if distinguished from neurotic response, self-gratification, and gratification of the patient's infantile wishes, is never contraindicated.

To correct another misconception, the analyst is neither inactive nor silent. His activity consists of maintaining free-floating attention, formulating diagnostic hypotheses, considering when to intervene in the stream of free association, and the like. That he may have to remain silent while this kind of activity is going on is not the equivalent of passivity. He is required also to speak at the appropriate time and with the appropriate wording, and also to think before he speaks. He must actively avoid responding to provocation, seduction and the like except in the manner that will be most helpful to the patient, that is to say, interpretatively. Some regard such procedure as impairing spontaneity. Often this is a rationalization for inappropriate outbursts which gratify the analyst. An analyst who has acquired secondary autonomy (Hartmann, 1958) in his professional role uses himself with pleasurably tinged discipline instead of indulgent self-gratification which would be damaging to the analysis.

A seeming contradiction to this liberal definition of the abstinence rule is posed when the patient, in the throes of the transference neurosis, becomes greatly interested in the analyst as a person. In such circumstances, personal questions are not answered. But neither need they be met with stony silence. After one or two statements such as, "If I answer that question it will impair our work," the competent ego of the analytic patient understands the technical purpose of encouraging fantasy instead of shutting it off with facts about the analyst's personal life. This illustration serves also to illuminate one of the ways in which the therapeutic alliance is called upon and strengthened. Now, patient as well as analyst lend themselves knowledgeably to the same technical purpose without heavy-handed burdening of the patient with technical rules. The analyst has enlisted the patient's reasonable ego in the joint endeavor. This is one of the more important purposes of the abstinence rule — to keep the reasonable ego functioning separate from the experiencing one. Advice-giving also contravenes the abstinence rule because it infantalizes the patient. The analyst's narcissism has to suffer, too, from the fact that analysts are not especially competent in knowing how others should conduct their realistic business. The analyst's expertise lies in the use of a trained (analyzed) personality combined with knowledge of theory and technique to help the patient understand and work through his conflicts. When the ego is relatively freed of conflict, increased adaptive functioning will be available for the patient to employ in arriving at his own reality solutions.

There is some historical justification for the misunderstanding that abstinence is synonymous with silence and, in all fairness, this must be considered. Before contemporary ego psychology, and especially before Kris (1956) made his exceptional contributions to contemporary technique, the division of labor between patient and analyst was thought to be such that the patient was the provider of material and the analyst the interpreter. Under such arrangement, the analyst awaited the emergence of material and the development of the transference neurosis. He was not to interpret the positive transference, nor even other material until transference became resistance (Glover, 1958 ; Fenichel, 1941). Therefore, he was left with not much to say and so silence was, perforce, the practice of that earlier era. The ego psychological approach dictates redistribution of the division of labor. Indeed, it is now thought that the former position encouraged too much dependency upon the analyst as omniscient interpreter and made, ultimately, for difficult termination of analysis. Now active interventions are made at the outset for the deliberate purposes of dealing with initial resistance, promoting transference and transference neurosis, encouraging free association, establishing a therapeutic alliance and allowing regression to proceed along the psychosexual line of maturation to the fixation point.

The concept of *autonomy* also lends itself to misunderstanding. It does not mean that the patient is permitted to do as he pleases, but only that the analyst refrain from usurping ego functions in those areas where the patient's ego is competent — that is, not involved in conflict. In conflict-bound areas, the patient may not have his way because this would result in acting-out, indulgence in infantile gratification, or in errors in judgment. Although we no longer establish, at the outset, a list of rules about what the patient may not do in the course of analysis, neither do we abandon him to the dangers of conflict-bound decisions that would be lastingly disadvantageous. As an example, we might consider that Freud told his single patients not to marry during analysis. But, in those days, analysis was of short duration and long-term engagements were the mores of the times. Now, when analysis can take many years, we do not prohibit marriage. Adult patients in their child-bearing years cannot reasonably be expected to wait until the possibility of having children is over. That we do not prohibit, however, does not mean that we abandon the patient to unwise choices. One might say, for example, if the proposed marriage is not well-enough understood analytically, "If this is going to be a valid marriage, it will be just as valid six months from now. Let us use the time to try to understand more about it." Again, this appeals to the reasonable ego, protects the patient from the omnipotence of the analyst and, simultaneously, from his own conflict-bound ego function of judgment.

The theory, but not necessarily the technique, of *dream interpretation* is based upon Freud's discovery of the construction and meaning of the dream (Freud, 1953). He used his own dreams to describe in detail the nature of the dream work − how the latent content becomes concealed beneath the manifest content. Modern science and instrumentation has made possible experimentation beyond that which was available to Freud in 1899, the year he wrote *The Interpretation of Dreams,* first published in 1900. From recent experimentation (Fisher, 1965) much has been learned about the physiology and psychology of the dream. These experiments tend to confirm Freud's findings in many respects; none refute them. By and large, Freud did not intend the analyses of his own dreams to demonstrate the technique of dream analysis. However, so formidable were his discoveries that few have ventured to write further on dream theory and technique. Among those that did are Sharpe (1937) and, more recently, Altman (1969) and Bergmann (1966). Bergmann adds a new feature to dream theory and especially to the technique of working with the dreams of the so-called borderline or narcissistic personalities. He calls attention to the communicative aspects of the dream, an important consideration in understanding why the patient who is not in analysis proper tells the psychotherapist his dream. In the area of technique, Brenner (1969) has argued that avenues provided by material other than dreams diminish the importance of the dream as the "royal road" to the unconscious. Greenson (1970) has refuted this view, upholding the special position of the dream in the psychoanalytic process. Waldhorn (1967) is spokesman for the widely held position that both dreams and material provided by free association are of equal importance to the analysis; therefore, the analyst's technical interest should be evenly distributed.

It is incontestable that dreams (and parapraxes) can provide quick access to the unconscious. A rather neglected aspect of technique, however, is the question of when and under what circumstances such rapid access is desirable. Following Waldhorn's (1967) view that dream analysis is one aspect of the totality of the analytic process, it is not necessarily the aspect which occupies the analyst's attention at all times. Contemporary modification of technique provides the analyst with even more scope. When uncovering of the unconscious is desirable, one travels the royal road. At other times, however, it may be more pertinent to a particular phase of an analysis to deal with the dream differently. The analyst may choose to work with the ego aspects only, whether these be defense, resistance or adaptation; or he may deem it desirable to deal with the transferential aspects; or he may treat the entire dream as a resistance if, in his judgment, it is proffered unconsciously to that end; or he may decide to bypass the dream altogether because other material is of greater importance at a given phase of the analysis. On the whole, the technique of dream analysis should not follow too literally the method Freud employed in *The Interpretation of Dreams* (Freud, 1953) in associating to each element in an orderly fashion. It has already been indicated that his purpose was the presentation of a dream theory. In the everyday practice of psychoanalysis, one relies upon the patient's random associations to the dream elements, preferably at his selection. Because the associations are free, selection is unconsciously determined. This fact provides leverage for dream analysis in that those elements which are chosen by the patient have a particular significance, probably exceeded, when there is heavy resistance, by the significance of those elements which are overlooked by him.

Symbolism in dreams is, by this time, common knowledge. Yet, there are relatively few reliable standard symbols. The analysis of dreams is far more precise if guided by the unique associations of the patient rather than by the analyst's Procrustean notions about the symbols and even about the dream as a whole. Some dreams, nevertheless, are rather transparent to the experienced analyst, especially if he knows the patient well. In such circumstances, shortcuts may be taken, eliminating the laborious process of seeking associations. Better still, as Kris (1956) has pointed out, it is desirable for the patient to learn to interpret his own dreams with increasing independence from the analyst.

It is already clear that modern technique is influenced by ego psychology. These conceptualizations and the techniques derived therefrom arise from the seminal work of Hartmann (1958) who carried forward the psychology of the ego from Freud's introduction of the structural theory in 1923. The position of the ego as one of a tripartite psychic system and its redefinition as a coherent organization of mental processes (Freud, 1961) led logically to the development of an ego psychology. While Anna Freud (1966) worked on the defensive function of the ego, Hartmann (1958) contributed his theories about the origin and development of the ego and about the adaptive function. His chief contributions are briefly listed here because they constitute the foundation upon which subsequent theorists and technicians proceeded to build. The concept of *primary autonomy* describes what is to be relied upon in each individual in terms of innate equipment; the concepts of the *conflict-free sphere* and of *secondary autonomy* as the result of *change in function* help the analyst distinguish between defense and adaptation; the arrival of the infant with *inborn ego apparatuses* into an *average expectable environment* explains the dyadic relationship and its effect upon structuralization, internalization, and the development of object relations.

Much in the arena of controversy these days is Freud's concept of psychic energy in general and Hartmann's (1952) concept of *neutralization* in particular. Appelgarth (1971), Holt (1965) and others argue that psychoanalytic energic concepts need to be updated in accordance with modern physics and neurophysiology. Parens, on the other hand, has recently (1973) elaborated on the clinical value of the concept of psychic energy in general and of neutralization in particular, with emphasis upon its relevance to aggression. For the clinician, neutralization, which is concerned with transfer of energy from id to ego is indispensable, at least until a better theory is brought forward. Recently, Sandler (27th and 28th International Congresses of Psycho-Analysis, Vienna, 1971, and Paris, 1973) has proposed, in theory, how the concept of neutralization, which he finds merely descriptive, may be eliminated. The technical applicability of Sandler's position and its superiority over that of Hartmann await further clarification.

Hartmann's work, as a whole, was further developed by him in collaboration with Kris (Hartmann and Kris, 1945) and Loewenstein (Hartmann, Kris and Loewenstein, 1946). Contingent upon these important theoretical origins of ego psychology are the further conceptualizations of Jacobson (1971), Mahler (1968) and Spitz (1957, 1965). An integrated presentation of the theories of these major ego psychologists is by Blanck and Blanck (1974). Hartmann is also credited with addition of the concept of intrasystemic conflict to the traditional dynamic view of intersystemic conflict. This has become increasingly useful in dealing with the adaptive function of the ego, whereas the intersystemic concept alone enabled the analyst to deal with dynamic processes only. Examples of intrasystemic conflict are: conflict between two defense mechanisms; between defense and adaptation; between two ego functions, one of which might be more highly developed than the other.

Two papers on ego psychological technique contributed by Kris (1956) alter traditionally held views about some major aspects of technique. He pointed out that we are no longer very interested in the rapid uncovering of the id, but that the patterning of childhood memories and the promotion of the patient's ego capacities in the form of encouraging him in the direction of performing his own analytic tasks now supersede uncovering. His presentation of ego building techniques complements that aspect of Greenacre's (1954, 1959) work which emphasizes guardianship of autonomy. Elaborating upon technique by interrelating it with new theoretical development Kris discusses the value of knowledge about childhood development in understanding the genetic aspect of metapsychology. This came at a time when the observational studies of Mahler (1968) and Spitz (1959, 1965) were providing important insights about preoedipal development.

But it was Hartmann who was the first to write on "The technical Implications of Ego Psychology" (1951). With the accumulation of the ongoing work of the ego psychological theorists, G. Blanck (1966) summarized some of the further implications of ego psychological theory in the treatment of the analyzable patient, pointing up that while a patient with a competent (neurotic) structure may be successfully analyzed in the traditional way, ego building techniques refine and deepen the analysis. In the treatment of borderline structures, where ego building is essential, ego psychological theory and the techniques that are derived from it are indispensable and even make it possible, in some cases, to bring the ego of the borderline or narcissistic patient to the point of analyzability.

On the whole, modern psychoanalytic technique tends more toward promoting growth and independence than did the earlier analytic techniques. Concepts such as the employment of the aggressive drive in the service of ego building (Spitz, 1953; Mahler, 1968; Jacobson, 1964) alter formerly held views about aggression and especially about the resistances of the anal phase when stubbornness, withholding, negativism and the like predominate. The technical problems of this psychosexual stage, coinciding as it does with enormous expansion of the ego, are now surmounted by the understanding that the instinctual drives of the anal phase, when neutralized, serve growth. This is of great technical advantage in dealing with the anal character and with obsessional neurosis. Interpretation of the characteristic resistances of these patients has always been a delicate and sometimes ineffective procedure. If, however, the interpretations are first directed toward the ego building features of the anal phase — the acquisition of the capacity of say "No," (Spitz, 1957) for example, a background is provided for interpretation of the drive aspects and of the defenses against them. That order of interpretation helps the patient understand his aggression not solely as hostility and anal sadism, but rather as aggression in the service of development. This is at once more palatable to the patient, more effective and more correct technically.

Currently, analysts are turning more and more to consideration of the technical problems posed by the so-called borderline and narcissistic patients — that is, those whose ego development has not arrived fully at the level of structuralization where purely neurotic solutions to conflict are possible. When Eissler (1953) introduced his concept of the *parameter,* he still had the analyzable patient in mind. Therefore, he posited four requirements that were to be fulfilled by the parameter. He said (p. 111):

> We formulate tentatively the following general criteria of a parameter if it is to fulfill the conditions which are fundamental to psychoanalysis: (1) A parameter must be introduced only when it is proved that the basic model technique does not suffice; (2) the parameter must never transgress the unavoidable minimum; (3) a parameter is to be used only when it finally leads to its self-elimination; that is to say, the final phase of the treatment must always proceed with a parameter of zero.

To this he added a fourth requisite (p. 115):

> . . . in order to delineate the conditions which a parameter must fulfill if the technique is to remain within the scope of psychoanalysis: the effect

of the parameter on the transference relationship must never be such that it cannot be abolished by interpretation.

By 1954 the psychoanalytic world was becoming more concerned with the less-than-neurotic structures that were presenting for treatment, and a panel on "The Widening Scope of Indications for Psychoanalysis" was held in that year. Much of the trend, to this day, is in the direction of widening the scope of analyzability. Thus, Kohut (1971) has presented a broad theory and technique for treatment of the *narcissistic personality disturbance*. Theoretically, he differs considerably from the ego psychologists whose developmental theories tend to regard narcissism as a normal developmental phase. Jacobson (1964) is particularly informative on this issue. Mahler (1968) believes that the two stages of development that observational discoveries have revealed — autism and symbiosis — are two different levels of narcissism. Her subdivision is of special technical value because it indicates, by its very exposition, that problems having their origin in failure of development in the autistic stage are quite different from problems arising from impaired development in the symbiotic phase. Kohut disagrees sharply with Jacobson and Mahler in theory and also disputes Mahler's methodology. His own view is that narcissism follows two distinctly different developmental lines: (1) from autoerotism to narcissism to object love and (2) from autoerotism to narcissism to higher forms and transformations of narcissism. In the development of the *narcissistic personality disturbance,* a cohesive self has been established and this cohesion distinguishes such patients from the borderline states and renders them analyzable. Thus, Kohut, remaining very much within the theoretical and technical philosophy of "the widening scope" school of thought, believes that analysis of the narcissistic patient proceeds in the traditional way, with deviations only designed to heal the narcissistic fixations.

Kernberg (1967, 1968, 1970, 1971), another contemporary investigator into borderline and narcissistic problems, accepts more readily that these patients are to be treated by psychotherapy as distinguished from psychoanalysis. He differs with Kohut, theoretically as well as technically, employing more of ego psychological theory, especially that of Jacobson, in his schema. His concept of the *borderline personaltiy organization* is that, in these structures, the "good" self and object representations are separated from the "bad" self and object representations by defensive employment of a mechanism of splitting — this for the unconscious purpose of preventing the aggression against the "bad" self-object representations from destroying that as yet undifferentiated unit.

Blanck and Blanck (1974) deal with the "widening scope" issue by asserting that it dilutes psychoanalysis as a technique to extend it to an ever - widening scope of pathology because, in severe pathology, the necessary parameters (Eissler, 1953) reach a point where the least possible deviation from standard technique is, nevertheless, quite large. It is doubtful in such circumstances, whether Eissler's requirement, that the parameter be eliminated before treatment can be successfully terminated, is possible to fulfill. Rather than stretch psychoanalysis to the breaking point, it seems wiser to reserve it for the analyzable neuroses and to devise psychoanalytically oriented psychotherapy, based on the same theory but different in technique from psychoanalysis proper for the borderline and narcissistic states. Since the fixations and regressions of the less structured personalities have their roots in phases of development earlier than the oedipal, and since it is these phases that the combined work of the ego psychologists illuminate so well, an integrated theory of psychoanalytic developmental psychology is indispensable for elaborating techniques for the treatment of these patients. This is especially important because, until the advent of ego psychology, the progression of psychosexual maturation was the only developmental theory available in psychoanalysis. To that may now be added the vast knowledge about structuralization which enables the analyst to devise techniques which are likely to bring success in dealing with preoedipal developmental lesions.

Pathology, in the less structured personality is in essence, pathology of object relations. This vital ego function progresses through graduated stages in its development to the final stage of object constancy. At first, the neonate is objectless; after some weeks, he becomes dimly aware of an "outside" which is experienced as part of the self. Gradually, self and object representations accumulate and then differentiate. The infant moves from the position of regarding the maternal object as part of himself, to viewing her as a gratifier of his needs, to valuing her for her function (Edgecumbe and Burgner, 1973). Ultimately, he acquires the capacity to love and to value the object regardless of his state of need (Hartmann, 1964). Those patients designated as borderline or narcissistic are usually fixated on the object relations developmental line (A. Freud, 1963), at the level of need gratification (Hartmann, 1964). They need therapeutic intervention to help them attain higher levels of object relations. Diagnostic designations of these borderline and narcissistic states still suffer from unclarity, and recent attempts (Kohut, 1971; Kernberg, 1970) at nosological classification of certain clinically presented symptom clusters have not been altogether successful. It leaves more scope, at this stage of our knowledge, to employ description of the various developmental lines as they appear in a given individual to identify pathological areas of development and to know, thereby, where to address treatment. These lines of development are: *psychosexual maturation; taming of the drives* (neutralization, fusion, sublimation); *object relations; levels of anxiety* (from fear of annihilation, to fear of loss of the object, to fear of loss of the object's function, to fear of loss of love and, finally, to fear of the superego). According to Mahler's scheme (1968) they are autism, symbiosis, separation-individuation in four subphases — differentiation, practicing, rapprochement, object constancy. According to Spitz (1965) they are the organizers of the psyche, indicators of which are the smiling response, stranger anxiety, semantic communication; and according to Jacobson (1964), *internalization,* which includes selective identification and superego formation; *defensive organization; adaptive function.*

The borderline and narcissistic personality has failed in some of the early, primitive stages of development, usually along more than simply one or two developmental lines. This suggests that many of the techniques of psychoanalysis proper are not used in these less structured cases, or are used differently qualitatively and in timing. Transference, for example, can only exist when there is sufficient differentiation of self from object representations to make it possible for the patient truly to transfer from a past figure to the analyst. While self and object representations are experienced as undifferentiated, as is the situation in borderline and narcissistic personalities, there can be no transference; therefore, other means of working with the patient who experiences the analyst as part of himself have to be employed. With patients who have experienced excessive, or as Mahler (1968) has termed it, parasitic symbiosis, it is not desirable to enter into a symbiotic transference-like relationship. This is especially so when symbiosis, in the course of development, has been carried on into periods of life later than a phase-specific time. Mahler (1968) has said that the infant needs adequate, phase-specific symbiotic experience in order to proceed into the separation-individuation phase. From that, one can conclude that it is not usually useful to yield to the adult patient's insistence upon continuation of symbiosis because it would seriously impair progress to later developmental phases. In other words, the analyst is constrained to avoid reinforcing fixation. But here one is dealing, not with the better known psychosexual fixations of the pre-ego psychological era, but with fixation in ego development. For the patient who has been severely deprived in phase-specific symbiotic experience, however, there is a need for him to repair some of the shortcomings of that phase in reliving it with the analyst. It is in this regard that Kohut's (1971) technical procedures are of inestimable value because, although there is some controversy about his theoretical formulations, there is no doubt that for some patients, carefully selected diagnostically, there is need for reliving in the therapeutic relationship in order to repair developmental damage. Then development can proceed, this time under the guidance of the growth-producing analyst.

There is also some controversy about whether the relationship with the analyst in such cases can rightfully be regarded as transference. Kohut (1971) believes that it can, but acknowledges that he is extending the definition. No controversy exists, however, about the fact that there usually cannot be transference neurosis in a non-neurotic case. Therefore, by definition, transference neurosis does not often ensue in borderline and narcissistic structures, although it may come about later in treatment, when the ego has been helped to develop to the point where it approaches neurotic structure. In such an eventuality, one deals with the transference neurosis as in the psychoanalysis of neurosis. More likely, but also more dangerous, in impaired or undeveloped structures, is transference psychosis − the belief that the analyst actually *is* the primary object, which comes about by combination of intense need for an undifferentiated partner and of poor reality testing.

Free association is not a "basic rule" in the treatment of the borderline and narcissistic structures because there is danger that too much primary process thinking already exists. Therefore, allowing the patient to speak at random, as in the treatment of neurosis, often means allowing non-therapeutic discharge. It is preferable that the analyst be available for helping the ego structure itself, rather than wander with the patient in the ramblings of the primary process. Therefore, in such type of treatment, the analyst takes a more active role in supplementing ego functions until they can stand on their own.

Interpretation is used, but consists in the main, of interpretation on the ego side, at least until the ego has been strengthened so that it can cope with the drives. Here again, the concept of neutralization is useful. For example, one can offer interpretations such as that the patient experiences the analyst as part of him; that he would like to be understood without words; and similar aspects of nondifferentiation (Jacobson, 1964) or symbiosis (Mahler, 1968). As the patient begins to realize that the analyst is a separate person, he is also likely to become aware that it is his own aggression that causes him to fear his and the analyst's separateness lest they both be destroyed in the process. This, too, can be interpreted for the purpose of encouraging venture in the direction of separation, this time by an aware ego which can take the risk with diminished fear of the destructive consequences of aggressive wishes. When the patient has been informed interpretatively that his aggression is not destructive but can serve growth, neutralization is thereby encouraged and the aggressive drive can more comfortably be employed for growth promoting rather than for destructive purposes. This illustrates how the aggressive drive is used in ego building and how, if approached from the ego side, aggression can be neutralized, that is, transferred to the ego to be used for its benign purposes.

Regarding frequency of therapeutic contact, the less-than-neurotic patient is, by practice, usually seen less frequently than the analytic patient. This, however, is often a matter of convenience and finances rather than a technical decision based upon the sound reasoning that has been established for frequency of contact in the analytic case. Because treatment procedures for the less structured personality are currently in the process of being elaborated (Kernberg, 1968; Blanck and Blanck, 1974), there are, as yet, no hard and fast rules about frequency. Possibly such rules can never be established because the structures of such cases are far more diverse than is neurotic structure. One might, for example, see some such patients as frequently as one would an analytic case; others would be treated on a less frequent schedule; still others would be seen more frequently at times of crisis and less so when the crisis abates. Jacobson (1971) warns against seeing depressed patients too frequently after the suicidal danger has passed, lest continued frequent contact hold out promise of gratifications impossible to fulfill.

The more disturbed patient is usually not treated on the couch because he needs to see the analyst in order to experience reality rather than to lose himself in fantasy. This procedure avoids the already discussed danger of transference psychosis because, in contrast with the better structured ego of the neurotic, these patients do not possess an observing ego to differentiate between fantasy and reality.  Here, too, however, there are no hard and fast rules, and many analysts do use the couch with such patients while exercising careful control to prevent loss of contact with reality.  Contraindicated is the procedure whereby the patient alternates too frequently between chair and couch.  It seems more desirable to keep him seated until one is certain that he can function therapeutically on the couch without danger.  Otherwise one is likely to enter into a jumping jack kind of procedure with the result that neither chair nor couch is used effectively, nor is the patient constrained to stretch his capacity to tolerate frustration and anxiety if change in position offers too ready relief.

Dream analysis, too, differs somewhat from classical psychoanalytic technique when one is treating borderline and narcissistic structures.  This does not imply that dreams are to be avoided.  Usually, if they are approached from the side of the ego, there is no contraindication for their use with the more disturbed patient.  In fact, they may be especially helpful in discovering adaptive processes of which the patient is unaware or does not appreciate.  As an example, a patient may have an anxiety dream of such intensity that, lacking adequate defensive function of the ego, he wakens.  This can be used to point out to him that his ego does function, at least in that he does not allow the dream to proceed to a frightening and disastrous conclusion. This is particularly important because these types of impaired egos lack the capacity to distinguish clearly dream from reality.  This illustration also serves to describe a manner of providing ego support – that is, support of the capacity to function, no matter how limited, so that that functioning can be appreciated and improved upon.

Regression is not usually encouraged because such patients are already severely regressed or fixated and because regression of ego functions is a danger to be avoided in these kinds of structures, as contrasted with the more structured ego of the neurotic patient which rarely regresses irreversibly.  In the borderline states, ego regression can result in decompensation. Therefore, it is of technical importance to prevent regression below the already regressed state of the ego.  Regression along psychosexual lines is equally undesirable because of the ego's incapacity to cope with the drives and the resultant danger that impulses will be acted on without adequate control.

Resistance, too, presents a different problem than in the treatment of neurosis.  It is more likely to take the form of fear of closeness, engulfment, loss of identity.  In other words, fear of closeness is a defense against the wished-for symbiotic merger.  However, there too, the growth promoting features of developmental theory suggest technical devices.  If it is realized that any form of resistance is indicative of an ego that functions to some degree, then this can be turned to technical advantage.  Again, by means of ego interpretation, the ego can be supported by helping the patient to understand the adaptive value of his stance.  Thus, we do not controvert his defenses, but rather support them in a very specific manner.  Specificity is stressed here because it has been found by experience that blanket support is usually ineffective.  Statements such as, "You have done well," have little value now, when we have a theoretical body of knowledge available for understanding exactly how the patient has done well. "You withdrew when you were overwhelmed by your father's rage because that was the best way, at the time, to protect yourself and him from your own anger," is the type of interpretation of adaptation which touches directly upon a specific experience in the patient's life.

Verbalization is most necessary in this type of treatment and must be encouraged to the utmost because it exercises ego function, interposes thought before action and builds object relations. Spitz (1957) designates the acquisition of speech as a crucial organizer of the psyche, requiring of the child that he engage in semantic communication as the vehicle which carries him toward higher levels of object relations. To the normally developing infant, this means that he can no longer enjoy the blissful oneness of being understood without words. For the borderline patient who has not conquered this developmental phase, the analyst, aware that verbalization is essential to growth, assiduously avoids the appearance of intuitive and omniscient understanding. Because of the deeper levels of fixation and regression, these patients tend to act rather than to verbalize. It is necessary, technically, to search out and to help the patient cathect his preverbal experiences with words, especially if they have been traumatic. This is a difficult and slightly risky procedure — difficult because the patient cannot remember, and risky because one can be mistaken and make adultomorphic speculations. When correct, however, the results of such a procedure are likely to be dramatically effective. It is a milestone in the building of object relations when, for example, the patient who never telephones the analyst at times of stress, anxiety or depression, begins to understand that he early gave up crying for relief because none arrived for him.

The foregoing is not an exhaustive itemization of techniques for the treatment of the severe pathologies, but is intended to be illustrative of the trend in technique dictated by the most recent discoveries in ego psychology. These techniques are still in the pioneering stages and only time and experience will indicate whether they are evolving in the right direction. Mahler proposed recently (Pre-Congress Panel of the Association for Child Analysis, Paris, 1973) that the rapprochement subphase of the separation-individuation phase is crucial not only in the etiology of the so-called borderline states, but contributes either favorably or pathogenically, depending upon the nature of the experience at that subphase, to the capacity to deal with the oedipal conflict when that arises. This postulate contains vast and as yet altogether unexplored implications for the treatment of neurosis as well as for borderline and narcissistic states. Thus, a new theoretical frontier appears even before the end of the pioneering era of consolidation of the conceptualizations of the ego psychologists, and also before extrapolation of techniques from these conceptualizations has been completed and tested in large enough sampling to provide as much assurance of their validity as now exists for the classical psychoanalytic techniques. Nevertheless, there is no doubt that we are now in the era when patients formerly regarded as untreatable — those designated by Freud as suffering from "narcissistic neuroses" — are now being treated with a modicum of success with techniques derived from ego psychology. Some reach the level of structuralization which renders them analyzable. However, for the time being, until more refined theory and technique becomes available, it remains accurate to state that the goal of psychoanalysis of the neuroses is that of resolution of the oedipal conflict while the goal of treatment of the borderline and narcissistic structures is resolution of the separation-individuation crisis, with consequent acquisition of identity and object constancy.

## REFERENCES

Altman, L.L. *The Dream in Psychoanalysis.* New York: International Universities Press, 1969.

Appelgarth, A. Comments on aspects of the theory of psychic energy. *Journal of the American Psychoanalytic Association.* **19:** 379–416 (1971).

Bergmann, M.S. The intrapsychic and communicative aspects of the dream. *International Journal of Psycho-Analysis.* **47:** 356–363 (1966).

Blanck, G. Some technical implications of ego psychology. *Internatonal Journal of Psycho-Analysis.* **47:** 6–13 (1966).

Blanck, G. Crossroads in the technique of psychotherapy. *The Psychoanalytic Review.* **56:** 498–510 (1970).

Blanck, G. and Blanck, R. *Marriage and personal development.* New York: Columbia University Press, 1968.

Blanck, G. and Blanck, R. Toward a psychoanalytic developmental psychology. *Journal of the American Psychoanalytic Association.* **20:** 668–710 (1972).

Blanck, G. and Blanck, R. *Ego Psychology: Theory and Practice.* New York: Columbia University Press, 1974.

Blanck, R. Countertransference in the treatment of the borderline patient. *Clinical Social Work Journal.* **I:** 110–117 (1973).

Brenner, C. Some comments on technical precepts in psychoanalysis. *Journal of the American Psychoanalytic Association.* **17:** 333–352 (1969).

Edgecumbe, R. and Burgner, M. Some problems in the conceptualization of early object relationships: Part I. The concepts of need-satisfying relationships. *Psychoanalytic Study of the Child.* **27:** 283–333 (1973).

Eissler, K.R. The effect of the structure of the ego on psychoanalytic technique. *Journal of the American Psychoanalytic Association.* **1:** 104–143 (1953).

Fenichel, O. Problems of psychoanalytic technique. New York: *Psychoanalytic Quarterly,* 1941.

Fisher, C. Psychoanalytic implications of recent research on sleep and dreaming. *Journal of the American Psychoanalytic Association.* **13:** 197–303 (1965).

Freud, A. The ego and the mechanisms of defense. In: *The Writings of Anna Freud,* 2. New York: International Universities Press, 1966.

Freud, A. The concept of developmental lines. In: *The Psychoanalytic Study of the Child,* **28:** 245–265.|New York: International Universities Press, 1963.

Freud, S. *The Standard Edition of the complete psychological works of Sigmund Freud,* J. Strachey *et al.*(Eds.). London: The Hogarth Press, 1953–64.

Freud, S. The interpretation of dreams. *Standard Edition.* **4** and **5:** 339-621 (1953).

Freud, S.   Papers on technique. *Standard Edition.*   **12:**   89-171  (1958).

Freud, S.   The ego and the id. *Standard Edition.*   **19:** 12-59  (1961).

Freud, S.   Inhibitions, symptoms and anxiety. *Standard Edition.*   **20:**   87-156 (1959).

Glover, E.   *The technique of psychoanalysis.*  New York: International Universities Press, 1958.

Greenacre, P.   The role of transference. *Journal of the American Psychoanalytic Association.*   **2:**   671-684  (1954).

Greenacre, P.   Certain technical problems in the transference relationship. *Journal of the American Psychoanalytic Association.*   **7:**   485-502  (1959).

Greenson, R.R.   The exceptional position of the dream in psychoanalytic practice. *The Psychoanalytic Quarterly.*   **29:**  519-549  (1970).

Greenson, R.R.   *The technique and practice of psychoanalysis.*  New York, Hallmark Press, 1967.

Hartmann, H.   *Ego psychology and the problem of adaptation.*  New York: International Universities Press, 1958.

Hartmann, H.   The mutual influences of the development of ego and the id. *The Psychoanalytic Study of the Child.*   **7:** 9-30  (1952).

Hartmann, H.   Notes on a theory of sublimation. *The Psychoanalytic Study of the Child.*   **10:**   9-29  (1955).

Hartmann, H.   Contribution to the metapsychology of schizophrenia. *Essays on Ego Psychology,* pp. 215-240.   New York: International Universities Press, 1964.

Hartmann, H.   Technical implications of ego psychology. *The Psychoanalytic Quarterly.*   **20:**   31-43  (1951).

Hartmann, H. and Kris, E.   The genetic approach in psychoanalysis.   *The Psychoanalytic Study of the Child.*   **1:**   11-30  (1945).

Hartmann, H., Kris, E. and Loewenstein, R.M.   Comments on the formation of psychic structure. *The Psychoanalytic Study of the Child.*   **2:**   11-38  (1946).

Hartmann, H., Kris, E. and Loewenstein, R.M.   Notes on the theory of aggression. *The Psychoanalytic Study of the Child.*   **3** and **4:**   9-36  (1949).

Holt, R.R.   Ego autonomy re-evaluated. *International Journal of Psycho-Analysis.*   **46:**   151-167  (1965).

Jacobson, E.   *The self and the object world.*  New York: International Universities Press, 1964.

Jacobson, E.   *Depression.*   New York:  International Universities Press, 1971.

Kernberg, O.F.   Borderline personality organization. *Journal of the American Psychoanalytic Association.*   **15:**   641-685  (1967).

Kernberg, O.F.   The treatment of patients with borderline personality organization. *International Journal of Psycho-Analysis.*   **49:**  600-619  (1968).

Kernberg, O.F.   Factors in the psychoanalytic treatment of narcissistic personalities. *Journal of the American Psychoanalytic Association.*   **18:**  51-85  (1970).

Kernberg, O.F.   A psychoanalytic classification of character pathology. *Journal of the American Psychoanalytic Association.*   **18:**   800-822  (1970).

Kernberg, O.F.   Prognostic considerations regarding borderline personality organization. *Journal of the American Psychoanalytic Association.*   **19:**   595-635  (1971).

Kohut, H. *The analysis of the self.* New York: International Universities Press, 1971.

Kris, E. *Psychoanalytic explorations in art.* New York: International Universities Press, 1952.

Kris, E. On some vicissitudes of insight in psychoanalysis. *International Journal of Psycho-Analysis.* **37**: 445–455 (1956).

Kris, E. The recovery of childhood memories. *The Psychoanalytic Study of the Child.* **11**: 54–88 (1956).

Loewald, H.W. Internalization, separation, mourning and the superego. *The Psychoanalytic Quarterly.* **31**: 483–504 (1962).

Mahler, M.S. On the significance of the normal separation-individuation phase. In: Schur, M. (Ed.) *Drives, Affects and Behavior,* pp. 161–168. New York: International Universities Press, 1965.

Mahler, M.S. Thoughts about development and individuation. *The Psychoanalytic Study of the Child.* **18**: 307–324 (1963)

Mahler, M.S. *On human symbiosis and the vicissitudes of individuation.* New York: International Universities Press, (1968).

Mahler, M.S. A study of the separation-individuation process:   and its possible application to borderline phenomena in the psychoanalytic situation. *The Psychoanalytic Study of the Child.* **26**: 403–424, (1971).

Menninger, K. *Theory of psychoanalytic technique.* New York: Basic Books, 1958.

Nunberg, H. The synthetic function of the ego. *International Journal of Psycho-Analysis.* **12**: 123–140 (1931).

Orr, I.W. Transference and countertransference: a historical survey. *Journal of the American Psychoanalytic Association.* **2**: 621–670 (1954).

Parens, H. Aggression: a reconsideration. *Journal of the American Psychoanalytic Association.* **21**: 34–60 (1973).

Piaget, J. *The language and thought of the child.* New York: Meridian Books, 1955.

Pre-Congress Meeting of the Association for Child Analysis, Paris, 1973.

Rapaport, D. Introduction to Erikson, E.H. *Identity and the Life Cycle.* Vol. I, pp. 5–17, Monograph number 1 of *Psychological Issues.* New York: International Universities Press, 1959.

Ross, N. An examination of nosology according to psychoanalytic concepts. *Journal of the American Psychoanalytic Association.* **8**: 535–551 (1960).

Sharpe, E.F. *Collected papers on psycho-analysis.* London: The Hogarth Press, 1950.

Sharpe, E.F. *Dream analysis.* London: The Hogarth Press, 1937.

Spitz, R.A. Aggression:   its role in establishment of object relations. In: Loewenstein, R.M. (Ed.), *Drives, Affects, and Behavior.* New York: International Universities Press, 1953.

Spitz, R.A. *No and yes.* New York: International Universities Press, 1957.

Spitz, R.A. *The first year of life.* New York: International Universities Press, 1965.

Spitz, R.A. *A genetic field theory of ego formation.* New York: International Universities Press, 1959.

Sterba, R.   The fate of the ego in analytic therapy.   *International Journal of Psycho-Analysis.*   **15:**   117–126 (1934).

Stone, L.   The widening scope of indications for psychoanalysis.   *Journal of the American Psychoanalytic Association.*   **2:**   567–594 (1954).

Twenty-seventh International Congress of Psycho-Analysis, Vienna, 1971.

Twenty-eighth International Congress of Psycho-Analysis, Paris, 1973.

Waelder, R.   The principle of multiple function.   *The Psychoanalytic Quarterly.*   **5:** 45–62 (1936).

Waldhorn, H.F.   The place of the dream in clinical psychoanalysis.   *Kris Study Group Monograph II,* pp. 96–105 (1967).

Zetzel, E.R.   An approach to the relation between concept and content in psychoanalytic theory.   *The Psychoanalytic Study of the Child.*   **11:**   99–121 (1956).

# 5 Modified Psychoanalytic Therapies

## Samuel B. Kutash

It is a truism that the practice of psychotherapy in the treatment of mental disorders requires the continual modification of the practitioner's systematic approach or methodology in accordance with the needs and problems of each individual patient.  This would imply that the underlying personality theory to which the practitioner subscribes is altered and changed as a result of his practice.  Since this is a *Handbook for Practitioners* we will deal in this chapter with modifications in the *practice* of psychoanalysis and psychoanalytically-oriented psychotherapies.

As experience with patients accumulates, various modified psychoanalytic therapies emerge which have superior usefulness and specific value for the kinds of patients and problems for which they were developed.  The originator of psychoanalysis, Sigmund Freud, developed the classical psychoanalytic method mainly working with patients in Victorian Vienna and particularly with hysterical patients from the upper middle classes. He himself exemplified the readiness to modify his personality theory and methodology as new data emerged with other kinds of patients.  His early clinical experiences with hysterics nevertheless remained central to his treatment. As the editor of this *Handbook* has stated in a recent article (Wolman, 1971), "Freud never hesitated to modify his theory whenever new empirical data suggested that such a modification might be advisable.  Freud never bent facts to fit into a theory; he was never an orthodox Freudian. Must we be?"

To this statement may be added that, above all he never forced patients to fit his system of treatment and his theory but rather discarded treatment techniques that did not "do the job." The prime example of this flexibility was when he discarded hypnosis in favor of free association as a technical tool of psychotherapy.

Freud, however, preserved his *system* of classical psychoanalysis but on an evolving basis while adding to and changing the technical tools of his treatment.

## SYSTEMS AND TECHNICAL TOOLS OF THERAPY

Before describing and discussing the various modifications in psychoanalytic therapies we need to distinguish between systems of psychotherapy and the technical tools or specific techniques which may be used in the framework of some, any, or all of the systems. A given system may have its favorite or preferred technical tools. Thus, the system of Freudian classical psychoanalysis utilizes such technical tools as free association, dream interpretation, use of the couch, analysis of transference and resistance, working through, the abstinence rule, interpretation and construction, and the rule against "acting out."

A complete system of analytic psychotherapy includes, as a minimum, a therapeutic relationship, catharsis or abreaction, insight (both emotional and intellectual), working through and reality testing or the application of the insights and their translation into changed and more effective behavior and living. A system also is based on a well-worked out theory of personality development and of neurosis as well as a *theoretical rationale* for the treatment. These phases of the therapeutic process may be called by different names in the different systems. For example, in classical psychoanalysis and in the most analytically-oriented psychotherapies, the relationship is termed the *transference* while in the Sullivanian system of interpersonal analysis (the "cultural" school) it is referred to and defined as *parataxic distortion.*

Some of the modifications and variations of psychoanalytic therapy represent the development of alternative systems while some consist of the development of different technical tools. In some instances the variation involves the intensive emphasis of one phase of therapy so that it becomes the "complete" therapy in itself (Relationship Therapy, Primal Scream Therapy, Rational Therapy, Reality Therapy). Modifications have also resulted from shifting the emphasis of the focus of the therapy from the id to the ego and superego. We thus have therapeutic methods based on ego psychology as differentiated from the id emphasis of bringing unconscious material into consciousness.

The earliest modifications in technique and treatment resulted from the development of different theoretical systems growing out of ideological and interpersonal disagreements between Freud and his close associates. These included Alfred Adler's system of *individual psychology* (Adler, 1927), Carl Jung's system of *analytical psychology* (Jung, 1920) and Otto Rank's (1945) system of *will therapy.* To these were added the systems of Karen Horney's "holistic" approach (Horney, 1937), Harry Stack Sullivan's (1953) and Erich Fromm's (1955) "Cultural" school, and Wilhelm Reich's (1945) *character analysis.* These are examples of modified psychoanalytic systems of therapy although like E.K. Schwartz (1965) and Lewis (1958) one might question whether the systems of Adler and Jung are basically analytic in the sense of sufficiently recognizing the importance of unconscious processes and the phenomena of transference, the role of infantile sexuality, and the other factors which Freud considered central to his system of psychoanalysis. The basic assumption in this chapter is that the psychoanalytic method of Freud has influenced all subsequent treatment of mental disorders. A variety of the modifications such as the developments in ego psychology and the use of *ego boundary theory* in relation to choice of treatment strategy, and the new orientations toward transference like Heinz Kohut's conceptualizations with reference to the treatment of narcissistic character disorders, represent modifications and extensions of psychoanalytic technique which take into account the cultural changes, changes in life-style and the newest developments in psychodynamic thinking.

Since we are concerned here with the treatment of mental disorders, we will be guided in our presentation of modified psychoanalytic therapies by the practical considerations relating to the treatment of patients rather than a historical review of changes in psychoanalytic thinking. As Harry Guntrip (1973) wrote "to care for people is more important than to care for ideas." We are convinced that each of the systems, methods, and approaches described has made important contributions to the treatment of the kinds of patients for whom they were developed, and in the milieu in which they were elaborated. There is always the question of what is the treatment of choice or variation in technique for the particular patient in his specific circumstances. As Munroe (Munroe, 1955, p. 507) has said, "All good analytic work is actually centered around the patient, not around a theory. The various therapeutic techniques are flexibly applied in accordance with the special requirements of each case and are somewhat modified by each analyst in accordance with his own temperament." The modifications, variations, and modernization of techniques and systems are now so numerous, we must first classify them and then discuss them around the central themes of therapeutic practice. To cover all the variations, individually, would fill a volume in itself. It is hoped that practitioners will be enabled to select those techniques and variations in method that fit best the patient they are treating, and their own skill and temperament.

## CLASSIFICATION OF MODIFICATION IN PSYCHOANALYTIC THERAPY

The modifications and variations of psychoanalytic therapy can best be understood in terms of purpose.

I.   Alternate Systems of Analytic Psychotherapy based on Theoretical or Ideological Differences from Freudian Classical Analysis.

1. The non-Freudian systems
   a. The *individual psychology* of Alfred Adler.
   b. The *analytical psychology* of Carl Jung.
   c. The *Will therapy* of Otto Rank.

        2. Neo-Freudian Systems based on the Cultural Emphasis.
          a. The *holistic* approach of Karen Horney.
          b. The *interpersonal relations* school of Harry Stack Sullivan.
          c. The *cultural* approach of Erich Fromm.

II.    Attempts to Streamline, Abbreviate and Speed Up the Process of Psychoanalytic Therapy.
    1. Stekel's *active analytic* psychotherapy.
    2. Ferenczi's experiments with *active* techniques.
    3. The Chicago school of *brief psychoanalytic therapy.*

III.   Expansions of Freudian Classical Analysis in Various Directions.
    1. The "Object-Relations Approach" of Guntrip, Winnicott, Fairbairn, and the British School.
    2. The "Eight Stages of Man" and Erikson's extension of Freud's theory of character development.
    3. Character Analysis of Wilhelm Reich.
    4. Kohut's approach to the treatment of narcissistic character disorders.

IV.   Modifications Based on the Shift in Emphasis to Ego Psychology.
    1. Federn's ego psychology and the psychotherapy of the ego boundaries.
    2. Wolman's Interactional Psychoanalytic Therapy.

V.    Attempts to Combine Psychoanalytic Therapy With Experimental Psychological Findings.
    1. Mowrer's learning theory approach.
    2. Dollard and Miller's interpretation of learning theory and psychoanalysis.
    3. Ittelson and Kutash's integration of perceptual psychology and psychoanalytic therapy.

VI.   Modernization and Changes in Technical Tools of Psychoanalytic Therapy Applicable to All Systematic Approaches.

VII.  Analytic Group Therapy.

VIII. Analytic Play Therapy.

## CHANGES IN THE ANALYTIC SETTING

The original technical tools of psychoanalysis included the use of the couch with the analyst sitting behind the patient with the lights dimmed so that the patient could concentrate on his inner thoughts and associations with a minimum of distraction. This format has been altered by most of the newer schools of analysis and in insight-oriented psychoanalytic psychotherapy. Most psychotherapy is now conducted on a face-to-face basis and the interaction between patient and therapist receives greater emphasis. Analytic therapy has been extended to a greater variety of patients in addition to the hysterics and obsessive-compulsive neurotics and is now in use with borderline psychotics, character disorders, and people who aim to actualize their unused potentials and develop a richer experience in living.

Frequency of sessions may be geared to the productivity of the patients and no longer do analysts adhere to the tradition of five sessions a week. It is recognized by more therapists that the intensity of and depth of therapy is not necessarily related to the frequency of sessions. For some patients therapy may be on a "superficial" level, four or five times a week, while for others, great depth can be reached in two or three sessions a week. Many patients get good results with visits once a week. The cultural schools generally advocate seeing patients less frequently than four or five times a week.

There are also definite changes in some of the traditional customs of analytic therapy. The previously strict rules about the therapist having no contact with the patient outside the office if he should encounter him by chance have been relaxed. Analysts will now greet their patients and may also, on a selective basis, have communication with members of the patient's family with the patient's consent. This has resulted from a better understanding of the phenomena of transference and countertransference. For example, it is recognized that counter-transference may be present even if the therapist observes all the older rules, and that the overriding consideration is the therapist's awareness of his feelings in relation to the patient and to analyze and be aware of the patient's transference to him as distinguished from the real relationship between patient and therapist which may provide a corrective emotional experience.

Group psychoanalysis and analytic group therapy are now generally accepted as important new additions to the analytically-oriented modalities of treatment. Therapists now more often work with more than one member of a family as in marital therapy and there is a significant new development in working with the entire family in family therapy. (Bell, 1962; Fitzgerald, 1973; Greene, 1965; Rosenbaum and Berger, 1963; Wolf and Schwartz, 1962.)

## CHANGES IN TECHNIQUES

Freud originally adopted the technique of *free association* as a basic method of psychoanalysis and adherence to the fundamental rule was paramount. The rule is now translated into merely requiring that the patient speak freely without censoring or holding back pertinent material. We all know how difficult it is for the patient to achieve truly "free" association. Sullivan questioned early the value of this technique. His patients were, of course, more schizoid and autistic and he felt that patient and therapist tended to indulge in parallel autistic reveries which too often did not meet in truly therapeutic contact (Munroe, 1955). Sullivan, like most of the other neo-Freudians, pointed out the need for and therapeutic value of genuine *communication* between patient and therapist. Free association is now used only occasionally and for a special purpose by many analysts. Horney and Fromm relied more on focused discussion rather than free association.

While all the schools of analysis and most analysts consider dreams to be "the royal road" to unconscious processes, there are marked differences in the interpretive methods and the use made of dreams in the analytic process. Whereas Freud used dreams primarily to help bring unconscious and preconscious material into consciousness in a timely fashion, when the non-Freudians interpret dreams, they do so in relation to the patient's actual current life problems and conflicts. While Freudians use the manifest content to get to the latent content through associations, the neo-Freudians often relate the material to the conflicts and anxieties of the patient in the here and now. A major contribution to more efficient and effective use of dream material has been made by Gutheil (1951) who was a disciple of both Freud and Stekel.

To the major technical tools of free association and dream interpretation, modern analysts and analysts from the non-Freudian and neo-Freudian schools have added and adapted a host of additional techniques some of which are derived from the classical method and many from the modified approaches. The communications from patients do not only consist of verbal free association, the relating of dreams, and the spontaneous expressions or slips of the tongue that were emphasized by Freud. There is now an arsenal of techniques that have been adopted and incorporated into the psychoanalytic therapeutic systems.

Thus, nonverbal communications and behavior within and outside the sessions are now reacted to and taken into account by the analyst. Langs (1973, p. 327) states in his two-volume work *The Technique of Psychoanalytic Psychotherapy,* "Such behavior constitutes a relatively important, although infrequently directly useful, source of data. It includes, for example, in-session rhythmic movements, playing with or pulling hair, biting or picking at fingernails, smoking, getting up from the chair, pacing, sitting away from the therapist, not looking at him, and unusual forms of dress. It may take the form of silences and instances of acting in-disturbed behavior directed toward the therapist. Such matters as requests for matches or Kleenex, leaving the session to go to the bathroom, and the offer of a gift include many nonverbal dimensions, as do many neurotic symptoms."

Attention is also paid to nonverbal cues in the patient's associations. "This includes his tone of voice, mood and affects, phrasing, language and ideas, richness or shallowness of thought, and other such dimensions."

Freud originally treated highly verbal patients who were quite repressed. As experience developed with other varieties of patients, attention to body language, nonverbal communication, and "acting in" behaviors and symptoms as communications began to be incorporated in the psychoanalytic systems of treatment. For example, Adler would ask, "What does the symptom prevent you from doing?" Wilhelm Reich began to analyze "character armor," muscular tension, and character defenses expressed as silence and rigid postures. Rank gave attention to manifestations of will while Ferenczi and Stekel analyzed such phenomena as procrastination and delay. Today, most psychoanalysts utilize all the forms of communication — body language, postures, verbalizations, behavioral communications, etc., within the framework of their system of analytic therapy.

There has developed a large body of techniques for arriving at interpretations and the trend among the neo-Freudians and the eclectic psychoanalysts is to draw from the various technical tools those they consider most applicable to a particular patient. Thus, there is a trend away from the heavy emphasis mostly on past historical material, in the direction of analysis of current events and behaviors which are considered to be representative of the past reaction pattern or what Freud called the repetition compulsion. As Langs (1973, p. 331) says, "References to current events and behavior on the part of the patient and others .... constitute a substantial part of the content of most sessions."

Of course the "depth" analysts working with a patient with sufficient ego strength will search for and bring into focus the latent meaning and this becomes a good source of insight. At the same time, the cathartic discharge takes place in the context of a corrective emotional experience. The analyst helps the patient correlate these insights with reality situations.

In modified psychoanalytic therapy the more flexible individualized interpretation of the significance of acting out has been fostered. Some analysts appraise its significance in terms of whether it does the patient harm or good. Thus, Fine (1971, p. 154) in discussing *acting out* states, "In discussion groups of analysts it frequently becomes apparent that what is acting out for one person is normal release of emotion for another. The meaning of sexuality in the therapist's own life plays a powerful role in his theoretical views on the subject. A decisive question is whether the activity does the person harm or good." In general, the current views range from the original Freudian injunction known as the rule of abstinence while in therapy, to the permissive approach that regards acting out as a communication and piece of behavior that should be analyzed. Acting out can subvert the therapy in some instances but enhance it in others depending on its specific significance. In general, the cultural schools are more likely to work with it in terms of its "here and now" significance.

The concept of acting in is well defined by Langs as "the living out of feelings and fantasies directly toward the therapist in the session, and often has both verbal and nonverbal aspects. It may take the form of direct attempts to seduce or attack the therapist, leaving the session, and pacing about. It usually indicates some kind of neurotic problem, and may convey latent content when viewed in proper context. Such behavior is not uncommon in borderline patients and when disruptive to treatment and the therapeutic alliance, merits prompt exploration and resolution. Nondisruptive forms of this behavior may require both verbal and nonverbal tolerance and response by the therapist."

## THE RELATIONSHIP BETWEEN PATIENT AND THERAPIST

When examining the therapist-patient relationship we must recall that the transference and its utilization as a major agent of the analyst's therapeutic work is one of Freud's most original and creative discoveries. Its crucial importance is recognized by most practicing analysts and psychotherapists but dynamic changes and new developments have taken place in this dimension of analytic treatment. Many modern psychoanalysts have made major contributions to this subject.

Almost every book on the subject deals with this as a major facet of effective therapy.   As an example, we might cite Kohut's discussion of the "mirror" transference in narcissistic patients (Kohut, 1971).

Freud's definition of the transference was a very precise one. He viewed it as a repetition of those attitudes and affects toward the parents that existed during the oedipal period of childhood. This resulted in neurotic patients concerning themselves more with the analyst thus neglecting their problems. Patients sought the analyst's love while others developed a hostile attitude resenting the analyst's authority and becoming competitive.  Freud interpreted these in terms of the oedipal situation which was consistent with his sexual theory of neurosis. Classical analysts and those who adhere to the traditional view still regard the transference as a reliving of the oedipus situation with the analyst.

With the greater use of face-to-face therapy and more direct communication between patient and therapist it became less and less possible for the therapist to conceal his real personal characteristics.  The patient's attitude began to be seen more and more as a blending of transference and realistic appraisal. The unreal and symbolic emphasis became less prominent except in traditional classical couch psychoanalysis. The limitations of the early view and his precise definition of the transference lead Freud to assume that some patients such as narcissistic persons were incapable of transference. Today, Kohut has found that narcissists form a *mirror* transference in which the analyst is seen as a reflection of the patient. This is in line with the patient's self-love.

Freud's concept of transference led to the conclusion at first that only hysterics, obsessive-compulsive neurotics and phobic patients were susceptible to analytic treatment which required ability to form a transference.

All subsequent schools of therapy as they attempted treatment of other varieties of patients extended the concept of transference.  Thus, Reich (1945) extended the idea of transference so that it took into account defensive character traits and repetitive life patterns and applied not only to the libidinous situations of the oedipal period, but to induced long standing habitual patterns of behavior developed in relation to the parents at all other periods particularly the pre-oedipal ones.  He attributed the same irrational quality to these as the other transference phenomena.

Sullivan (1953) began to refer to these phenomena, which now included a variety of distortions, as *parataxic distortions.*   He regarded these as reaction patterns taken from the past and applied indiscriminately to the present situation even though they were no longer appropriate. The therapist's task became one of helping the patient become aware of these as he acts them out, thus learning his true role in his interactions and problems and thus dropping his self-defeating archaic patterns.

Sullivan's great contribution was his therapeutic breakthroughs with psychotic and borderline patients.   He demonstrated that narcissists and pre-genital characters were capable of transference.  As Thompson (1950) has stated, "The indifference or distrust so frequently shown toward the analyst by psychotics is just as truly a repetition of earlier patterns as the hysteric's "love" or "competitiveness."

The neo-Freudian analysts built upon the original idea that the relationship was not one-sided or unilateral and that countertransference was not just an error in treatment, but was always present. The therapist's awareness of his countertransference and the interpersonal transactions enables him to elucidate the patient's problems and to relieve his maladaptive symptoms.

Horney (1939) called attention to the bilateral nature of the analytic interaction. Some analysts, such as Reich (Munroe, 1955) advocated role playing as a means of re-enacting early experiences with the parents and resolving the conflict. The role playing or paradigmatic technique reached its most explicit development in Moreno's technique of *psychodrama* (Moreno, 1946).

One of Horney's major contributions was her novel interpretation of the repetition compulsion. She regarded the phenomena encompassed by this term as more than automatic repetitions of early childhood situations and felt that these did not occur in a compulsive manner. The mother transference was not an exact reproduction of the patient's attitude toward her mother at the age of four. The original basal attitude has been added to and modified in the course of growing up by subsequent experiences with mother figures. The current or final transference is thus the culmination of the accumulated experiences. According to Horney, psychological vicious circles within the person growing out of the neurotic defenses, complicate the transference which then includes a complicated defensive system that must be unwound.

Ferenczi also came to the conclusion that transference is not "a specific type of behavior peculiar to the doctor-patient relationship but, on the contrary, is generally applicable to social intercourse . . . . For Ferenczi, transference is simply a displacement . . . . or as Freud himself put it, 'a wrong connection.' But whereas transference is quite harmless in a healthy person, the neurotic's passion for transference, which prevents him from recognizing objective connections, actually makes him sick" (Wyss, 1973, p. 173).

Of interest as a forerunner of the "here-and-now" analytic therapists are the modifications in technique introduced by Rank. As stated by Thompson (1950, pp. 176-177), "Rank instituted three modifications of technique. The first was, like Jung's and Adler's, placing the chief emphasis on the present situation in the analysis in contrast to Freud's emphasis on the past, while treating reactions to the analytic situation as resistance. For Rank the therapeutic process involves a 'new experiencing,' not merely a re-living of the infantile past." The other modifications were the mother transference emphasis arising out of Rank's stress on the birth trauma, and the setting of a definite time limit for treatment and "considering the patient's reaction to that the most important material to be discussed." Making the analysis a living experience in the present with the analyst is considered Rank's most valuable modification.

Fromm (1947) among his numerous elucidations of analytic therapy, distinguished between rational and irrational authority. Rational authority is based on competence and genuine ability while irrational authority is based on a neurotic need for power. In competent therapy the analyst is a rational authority.

There seem to be as many interpretations and definitions of transference as there are systems of therapy. In the system of Melanie Klein and in terms of object relations theory, "transference is the phenomenon of the patient involving the therapist, who is part of his outer world in the conflicts that constitute his inner world, and its analysis reveals the kind of interaction that is going on between his inner and his outer worlds, mainly by projection and introjection" (Guntrip, 1973, p. 65).

## NEW CONCEPTIONS OF THE ANALYST'S ROLE

Modification in the role of the analyst as conceived by today's psychoanalytic therapists reflect accurately the sweeping sociocultural and historical changes that have taken place. The original "neutral" analyst who tried to preserve anonymity by sitting behind the patient who reclined on the analytic couch on the theory that in this way the relatively uncontaminated transference would manifest itself, has in the modified current approaches, given way to the analyst who faces the patient and recognizes the importance of interactional relatedness and the reality of the therapist's person and characteristics. And as the movement toward more and more revealing and active therapists develops and persists in our activist culture, we begin to have "experiential" therapists who share their feelings and conflicts with the patient. The "experiential" school advocates that the therapist tell the patient how the patient makes him feel and what his concerns are (Whitaker and Malone, 1953). Representative schools of thought that involve greater activity on the part of the therapist are such currently popular techniques and orientations as: *transactional analysis* (Harris, 1973; Berne, 1961, 1964), *Gestalt therapy* (Perls, *et al.,* and Polster and Polster, 1973). *group analytic therapy, group process experiences, and encounter groups* (Bach, 1954; Foulkes and Anthony, 1965; Lieberman, Yalom, and Miles, 1973).

The essential and most relevant problem for the analyst today is how to maintain a suitable and flexible balance between listening, reacting, interacting and control of the process. Flexibility and sensitivity to the patient's needs determine when he reacts and with what mixture of warmth, affects and intellectual resourcefulness. To what extent does the therapist aim to fill the role he is placed in and to what extent is he himself? The view that the analyst must at all costs be himself seems to be appropriate not only with the dictum, "To thine own self be true," but with the current emphasis on "telling it like it is." Truth and reality are stressed by most of the here-and-now approaches. Many modern analysts have adopted and merged in with their system some brand of existentialism. (May, Angel and Ellenberger, 1958). Here, the philosophy of the analyst, his concern with the human condition and the essence of existence, the meaning of life and the promotion of "beingness" become prominent. Some of this can be compared with Adler's, "What life should mean to you" and Maslow's "process of self-actualization."

In non-Freudian methods it is recognized, but in different degrees, that neither the analyst nor the patient can maintain the degree of passivity originally advocated as an ideal by Freud and the classical analysts. As Schwartz (1965) has stated, Tarachow (1963) in presenting the Freudian viewpoint takes the position that, "to the extent that the analyst becomes an object for the patient treatment is not psychoanalytic." Schwartz (1965) goes on to say, "Since it is patently impossible for the patient to remain totally oblivious, totally unaware, and totally unknowing of any reality concerning the analyst, it is futile to hope to attempt ever to achieve such an idealized model for treatment. Analysis in this sense may never occur, may never be experienced." Most non-Freudians of all schools of thought and to a certain extent, the modern Freudian ego psychologists and most notably the object relations school (Guntrip, 1973), regard the analyst as always becoming an "object" for the patient so that they aim at his being a *real being* and along with Adler, Sullivan, etc. emphasize the educational activity of the analyst.

The Freudian ego psychologists such as Erikson (Evans, 1967), Hartmann (1958), Kris (1945), and Lowenstein (1951) certainly emphasize a reality orientation in the therapist's role as does Melanie Klein (1960) in her object relations approach. Hartmann and Kris (1945) developed the concept of the *autonomous ego development* and Hartmann included in his theory of *adaptation* a generalized theory of reality relations which stressed the special role of social relations. It remained for Erikson to build on the theory of reality relationships (1945) and especially to elaborate the theory of the role of social reality (1950) culminating in a *psychosocial* theory of development. This had a far-reaching impact on the analyst's role as did the work of Melanie Klein. The analyst did indeed become an object and in accordance with Erikson's concept of mutuality (1950) an important part of the analytic task is to analyze the ego and promote its strengthening, growth, and healthy development, through restoring healthy object relations. Certainly in helping the patient to resolve such basic conflicts as those involved in patients who have not reached a satisfactory homeostasis in each or in some of the eight stages or phases of the life cycle that Erikson postulates, the anaylst must allow himself to be an object and to analyze the conflicts involved.

Thus, in treating the conflict between *basic trust* and *mistrust* which stems from the earliest Freudian oral stage, the analyst must be capable of being the medium through which the patient can develop the optimal proportion between trust and mistrust. This needs to be accomplished in the *relationship* or *transference* through the analyst's responses and reactions to the patient's unconscious and contrived "tests" of the analyst's reliability. Certainly, this applies to the treatment of those patients whose conflict is between *autonomy* and *shame* and *doubt*.    Autonomy has meaning only in a relationship with another person or people — otherwise it is isolation.   The active role of the therapist in all of the pre-oedipal stages, such as in dealing with the conflict between *initiative* and *guilt* in the patient, is of paramount importance in analysis of the ego.   Kohut (1971) makes the analyst a mirror through which the patient can become aware of himself to the end that he can eventually relate to the therapist as an object.

Most non-Freudian analysts, with the possible exception of Jung, do not aim to promote regression in the patient as part of the analytic process.  This is also related to the change from the couch to the face-to-face treatment.  Yet, Hartmann's concept of regression in the service of the ego has restored some of the values of regression as a reinforcement of the ego as an antidote to the passivity of the patient leading to apathy, isolation, and alienation.  The flexible analyst will work toward helping poorly-controlled, impulse-ridden patients to inhibit so that they can reflect upon and gain a preview of the possible consequences of acting without thinking or feeling.   Thus, with the hysteric or the behavior disorder patient he may encourage looking inward and becoming more aware of inner processes; while with the obsessive patient, the *passive* and *apathetic* patient, and the depressed, he may not only encourage activity, but aim to help them develop the outward look into the world around them and to act decisively and assertively.

An important distinction is often made between the classical psychoanalysts and the neo-Freudian and non-Freudian analysts in terms of *choice of patients.* As recently as 1965, E.K. Schwartz stated, "The more classical analyst justifies his treatment model by restricting psychoanalysis to neurotic patients . . . . The non-Freudians are not so exclusive in the choice of patients, and they treat the more severe neurotics, such as the obsessive, the character-disordered, and the varieties of psychotic patients.  Sullivan, like Fromm-Reichmann, saw schizophrenia as a human process to be understood, participated in, and healed."

The extensions of Freudian theory and practice by the ego psychologists, the child analysts, and the object relations school have, to some extent, enabled Freudian analysts to treat, both through new modifications of classical analysis and through analytic psychotherapy, a greater variety of patients than Freud originally contemplated although he conceived of the possibility of these later developments.  Thus, Guntrip (1973) presents a plausible case for his view that analysis should include a regression beyond the limits called for by the classical Freudian school  He facilitates the patient's regression beyond the oedipal to the pre-genital stages.   "Being accepted and understood in the schizoid position enables the patient to feel hopeful and to be born again" (Witenberg, p. VI, in Guntrip, 1973).

An interesting example of a modern modified psychoanalytic approach to the analyst-patient relationship, is *Interactional Psychoanalytic Psychotherapy,* introduced by Wolman (1965).  Wolman divides all human relations according to the aims of the participants, depending on whether their main purpose is the satisfaction of their own needs (instrumental) or their partner's need (vectorial) or both (mutual or mutual acceptance). A normal or well-adjusted individual is seen as balanced in his social interactions. That is, he is instrumental in the struggle for survival, mutual in relationships with friends and family, and vectorial in regard to children and to those who need help. He is reasonably selfish (instrumental), reasonably mutual, and reasonably vectorial.

Mentally disturbed individuals have difficulty or are unable to preserve this balance. They are either *hyper-instrumental,* displaying infantile selfishness and parasitism as their major mode of relatedness, or they neglect themselves and worry constantly about others in a morbid *hypervectorialism* or they exaggerate in giving and taking in shifting moods of *paramutualism.*

In this conceptualization, the psychotherapeutic process involves an interaction or exchange of cathexes. The analyst's role becomes one of restoring the healthy balance between the three types of relatedness. Wolman (1959), in his work with psychotic patients, regarded transference phenomena as true emotional involvements and as such, used greater caution in treatment. The therapist has the primary attitude of "vectorial" giving to the patient within limits set by the therapeutic situation. There is a resemblance between Wolman's mutual type of relatedness and Erikson's concept of *mutuality* which specifies that there is a crucial mutual coordination between the developing individual and his human (social) environment. Erikson's theory postulates a *cogwheeling of the life cycles.* The representatives of society, the caretaking persons, are coordinated to the developing individual by their specific inborn responsiveness to his needs and by phase-specific needs of their own (Erikson, 1959).

## UNCONSCIOUS VERSUS CONSCIOUS PROCESSES

Classical psychoanalysis had the basic aim of bringing unconscious material into consciousness thus making the previously repressed conflicts available to the ego so that they can be resolved. The techniques utilized are primarily methods of making *unconscious* processes and material *conscious.* Hence, the use of dream interpretation, free association, and slips of the tongue, predominate and are emphasized in the treatment.

The deviations and departures from this basic aim are of several types. One direction is that exemplified by the schools that placed even greater emphasis on the unconscious processes even to the extent of postulating and utilizing the concept of collective unconscious, archetypes, and transcendental ideas (Jung, 1933). More modern derivatives along this line are the various brands of existential analysts and the analysts who utilize the methods of Ferenczi.

At the opposite pole are those analysts and approaches that emphasize the world of outer reality, cultural and environmental influences, and interpersonal transactions and processes. Starting with Adler and Rank, we can also include the adherents of Horney, Sullivan and Fromm. A development within the

Freudian group itself is in the direction of greater emphasis on conscious processes (ego psychology).

Jung extended psychoanalytic principles to subjects with which he was intrigued, namely, the material gathered from myths, legends, fables, stories from the classics, and poetic fantasies. He also demonstrated the resemblance between dream psychology and the psychology of myths, and between the fantasies of the ancients, as expressed in myths and legends, and the thinking of children (Jung, 1920). Eventually Jung discarded Freud's causal approach and felt that mental life could be better understood by adding a *teleological perspective.* Jung thus became the inspiration for the "inspirational" movements in psychotherapy. However, Jung based his approach on a system of psychotherapy with a theoretical rationale as the basis for personality change through treatment. By contrast, the existential analysts whose general philosophical and humanistic values have much in common with Jung, nevertheless stress the phenomenology rather than unconscious processes. This has been labeled "a poorer psychology" with less clear-cut procedures by Wolf and Schwartz (1958, 1959).

Jung's intense preoccupation with the unconscious and his emphasis upon the intrapsychic "led him to the position that, 'Man's unconscious likewise contains all the patterns of life and behavior inherited from his ancestors, so that every human child; prior to consciousness, is possessed of a potential system of adapted psychic functioning (Jung, 1933, p. 184)' " (Schwartz, 1965). Schwartz concludes, "The unconscious perceives, has purposes and intuitions, feels, and thinks as the conscious mind does. Jung claims that there is sufficient evidence for this from psychopathological or clinical experience as well as from the investigation of dream processes. Consciousness is transient, whereas unconscious processes are transcendental or eternal. Reality is not objective or external, but rather internal" (Schwartz, 1965).

The cultural analysts, in contrast to Jung, place much greater emphasis on the conscious processes than he and Freud did. Horney adopted a holistic approach. Her followers deal with the entire activity of the patient, his view and outlook on life, and his conscious existence. Most of the current analysts, Horney, Fromm, Sullivan, and the "here-and-now" schools, consider consciousness to be the central problem of treatment. From this standpoint, the therapist's function has a strong educational aspect. For Adler, and his school in particular, the unconscious was the less understood portion of the personality. Adler emphasized outer reality and social values. He used educational techniques and placed primary emphasis on the role of the ego. He advocated an active attack on the patient's overt difficulties. His method was a didactic one — a form of re-education (Thompson, 1950).

Of particular significance are the changing usages with reference to dreaming and dream interpretation in relation to conscious and unconscious processes. As Green, Ullman and Tauber (1968) have stated, "Freud's self-analysis led to his investigation of his own dreams and childhood memories. His libido theory was based on the ideas he elaborated from these investigations . . .   In the end he focused on the infantile sexuality that he believed was concealed and disguised by the manifest dream content." Freud aimed at discovering and interpreting the latent content of the dream from the patient's associations to the unconscious processes and particularly oral, anal, phallic, and other instinctual strivings.   In classical analysis, the dream, like symptomatic behavior, the communication between analyst and therapist, slips of the tongue, and free associations is used to learn about and bring into consciousness, the *unconscious content* that is not in the patient's awareness.

After withdrawal from the Freudian group, Jung and Adler each developed their distinctive approaches to dreams.   Jung focused on his concern with the collective unconscious and archaic images (Jung, 1933) while Adler used dreams to reveal the "content of his theoretical preoccupation with the social and contemporary strivings of the individual" (Ullman, 1962). Rather than review the individualized contributions to dream interpretation of Rank, Horney, Sullivan, and the experiential and existentialist schools, each of whom use dreams in a manner that fits their theoretical viewpoint, the more recent developments of the "ego psychologists" who focus more on the conscious processes and the *participation of the ego in dreams* and other unconscious processes will be emphasized.   Freud went from the conscious to the unconscious-manifest content to latent content.   The ego psychologists go from the unconscious manifestations to the role of the ego or conscious mind stressing the ego's function of integration and synthesis.

Erik H. Erikson made a startling new addition to Freud's work on dreams within the traditional psychoanalytic school.  He proposed a purposive perspective postulating that a dream may reveal more than a disguised wish fulfillment derived from infantile sources and can even be dreamed *in order to be analyzed* (Erikson, 1954).   Erikson draws attention to the importance of the manifest content of the dream and the way in which the patient reports it verbally.   He shows how the manner and content of the patient's verbalization highlights and makes evident the personal time-space of the dreamer and the nature of his defenses and accomplishments.   However, Green, Ullman and Tauber (1968, p. 148) indicate that "in spite of his attention to the verbal, sensory, spatial, temporal, somatic, interpersonal, and affective aspects of the manifest content, he never abandons the more narrow concept of latent dream material . . . . He goes beyond a concern with psychosexual issues and ego defenses to stress the importance of ego identity and a life plan, thus including much of the neo-Freudian contribution. In a more recent book, *Insight and Responsibility* (1964), Erikson adds a further dimension by assimilating the phenomenological emphasis on immediate subjective experience." Medard Boss (1949), as an existentialist discusses the special quality or mode of existence that is exemplified in dreaming. "He points out that the person who dreams and recalls his dream is identical to the person who continues to function throughout the waking day. *Dreaming characterizes a separate and distinct form of existence for a person as the waking state or non-dreaming state of sleep characterizes another distinct form of human existence for the same identity"* (Green, Ullman and Tauber, 1968, p. 148). Here is the statement of the phenomenal nature of the dream as a form of existence in itself.

Gutheil (1951) utilized the contributions of Adler, Stekel, Jung, Freud, and particularly the *active* school of psychoanalysis and stressed the *past, present,* and *future* reference of the dream. His *Handbook* is perhaps the most practical exposition of dream interpretation.

Bonime (1962) in his handbook, *The Clinical Use of Dreams,* presents the use of dreams, clinically, in the tradition of Horney and Robbins. As Ullman (1962) states in his Foreword, "Like Horney, before him, he writes about analytic data within the context of the actual lives that people lead. In his own words he is interpreting the behavior of people who have dreams rather than engaging in dream interpretation. Horney saw dreams as attempts at solutions of conflicting needs in the organized personality structure. Horney herself, following in the tradition of Adler, saw in dreams a symbolic extension of the problems and adaptive maneuvers characteristic of the waking state.

Sullivan felt that the dream could never be accurately recalled in the waking state and that dreaming mostly takes place in the parataxic mode of experience. He made minimal use of dreams except to reflect back to the dreamer the significant statements to see if it provoked any particular thoughts in the mind of the patient (Sullivan, 1953). Fromm also de-emphasized the dream as a road to the unconscious but instead stressed how the dream illuminates the patient's struggle to avoid responsibility for himself. He also analyzes how the imagery of the dream illuminates "how the patient lives out life in false solutions, idolatrous pursuits, and evasions while it can, at the same time, reveal his hidden potentialities" (Green, Ullman, and Tauber, 1968, p. 150). Gutheil (1951) among others, stressed the problem solving properties of the dream and the proposed solutions inherent in the content.

## EGO PSYCHOLOGY AND DEVELOPMENTAL PROCESSES

The development and functioning of the ego in all the stages of life is now considered, by most non-classical analysts and by the psychoanalytic ego psychologists, to be the most important focus in treatment. Perhaps the greatest impact upon psychoanalysis and psychoanalytic therapies has been made by the advances in ego psychology. Here, the results of the exploration of the family structure and its influence on the sexual and social development of the person must be considered. Significant advances have been made in the intensive study of the pre-genital experiences as the child grows and develops object relations.

In extending the range of applicability of psychoanalysis to children and adults suffering from psychopathology more severe than neurosis, the innovations of Melanie Klein must be cited. She developed methods for psychoanalytically treating many patients previously considered inaccessible to psychoanalysis.

Those analysts who have followed Kleinian techniques are more optimistic about psychoanalysis as a treatment method and may undertake patients suffering from severe character pathology, borderline and psychotic states, and regressed patients (Bychowski, 1952; Kernberg, 1967; Searles, 1965; Winnicott, 1963).

As an example of Bychowski's modification of psychoanalytic procedure for the treatment of borderline patients he stressed, "systematic elaboration of the manifest and latent negative transference without attempting to adhere to full genetic reconstructions on the basis of it, followed by 'deflection' of the manifest negative transference away from the therapeutic interaction through systematic examination of it in the patient's relations with others" and "utilization of environmental structuring conditions, such as hospital, day hospital, foster home, etc., if acting out outside the treatment hours threatens to produce a chronically stable situation of pathological instinctual gratification" and "utilization of the positive transference manifestations for maintenance of the therapeutic alliance, and only partial confrontation of the patient with those defenses that protect the positive transference, etc." (Bychowski, 1952, pp. 257-258).

Klein (1960) worked with the early material influences and the nursing situation as well as the pre-oedipal developmental process. The direct observation of infants (Spitz, 1965) and children and refined considerations of pregenital phases and early narcissism resulted in new emphases in the treatment of regressed or severely disturbed adults. As these findings were applied to therapeutic techniques, new skills were developed to handle the levels of object relations and the early developmental processes.

With greater recognition of the complex intrafamilial influence and the recognition that the key to the treatment of the severely emotionally disturbed person is the understanding of the early maternal environment, it is a natural development to apply analytic principles to the treatment of the family as a group. Today, *analytic family therapy* is increasingly in use (Ackerman, 1958; Ferber, Mendolsohn and Napier, 1972).

Some of the culturist psychoanalysts who have focused on the ego processes have approached these from a combined existential and social interactive point of view. A representative view is that of Rollo May (1967) who speaks of modern man's loss of significance and the difficulties in maintaining personal identity in an "anonymous world." He relates his system to a phenomenological approach to psychotherapy and to existential therapy. Thus, he states, "I should like to make clear at the outset the relation of my views to what is called existential psychology and psychiatry. I am trained in psychoanalysis in the neo-Freudian, interpersonal school, but all my life I have been one to believe that the nature of man himself must be understood as a basis for our science and art of psychotherapy. The existential developments in our culture, whether in literature, art, philosophy or science, have precisely as their *raison d'être* the seeking of this understanding of man" (May, 1967, p. 87).

May's formulation with reference to the focus on consciousness is a clear statement of the current emphasis among the cultural and the existentialist analysts. He states, "I propose that unconscious experience can be understood *only* on the basis of our concept of consciousness. We must posit that the patient comes as a potential unit, no matter how clearly we can see that various neurotic symptoms have been blocked off and thereby have a compulsive effect on him" (May, 1967, p. 97). He goes on to indicate that "unconsciousness consists of the experiences that the person cannot permit himself to actualize. The questions in understanding unconscious phenomena, are, 'how does the individual reject or accept his possibilities for being conscious of himself and his world?' " May also points out the dangers in the relation of existentialism to psychotherapy and re-examines the ego and superego of *freedom* and *responsibility*.

The ego processes and the subject of ego identity and unity serve as the significant point of departure and development of modified technique in the treatment of psychosis, particularly schizophrenia. Most noteworthy in this regard is the work of R.D. Laing (1960) who regards the acute schizophrenic episode as a "metanoic process" in which the patient completely sheds the malfunctioning ego and, if not interfered with by repressive treatments, will grow a new and healthier ego. He likens the therapist to a midwife who presides at the birth of a new ego and whose role is to be with the patient, allay his terror and protect him from his own violence and fears while he is without a fully functioning ego. Laing speaks of the "embodied and unembodied self," the "inner self in the schizoid condition," the "false-self system" and "self-consciousness" (Laing, 1960).

The recapitulation of the developmental process and early relationship with the mother is illustrated in a most innovative approach which extends psychoanalytic treatment systematically to the treatment of *narcissistic personality disorders*. Kohut (1971) has made what may prove to be one of the great breakthroughs in ego psychology and psychoanalysis of the ego. He regards the narcissistic personality disturbance, which Freud felt was almost impossible to treat by psychoanalysis, as a defect in a person's inner cohesion and continuity — "An insufficient consolidation of the self" or ego. His systematic approach may open the door to the successful, rational treatment of one of today's most prevalent disorders.

"These patients establish a specific relationship to the psychoanalyst. They attempt to use him — as does a small child his mother — as a mirror in order to discover themselves and in order to be reflected in his admiration of them. Or they admire the analyst and attempt to experience themselves as part of him, feeling strong and good so long as this experience can be maintained." In the classical tradition such an approach to transference was looked upon as undesirable and as impeding the growth toward realism and maturity. Kohut, however, feels that the therapeutic revival of these unfulfilled childhood needs, "allows the patients to obtain insight into the nature of their psychological imbalance and to gain mastery and control over it." He asserts that "the patients are thus enabled to make two crucial *developmental steps* which they had not been able to make in childhood: they convert their archaic grandiosity into healthy self-esteem, and they transmute external idealized omnipotent figures of their childhood into a set of internal guiding values and ideals."

Perhaps the most succinct summary statement of the contributions of the "ego analysts" such as Anna Freud (1946), Hartmann (1958), Kris (1951), Lowenstein (1955), and Erikson (1950) was made by Wolberg (1967, p. 203) as follows:

1. Behavior is determined by forces other than instinct in the form of response sequences encompassed under the classification of "ego."
2. The ego as an entity has an autonomy separate from both instinct and reality.
3. The ego supports drives for environmental mastery and adaptive learning which are divorced from sexual and aggressive instincts.
4. Female sexuality is an entity on a parity with, rather than inferior to male sexuality.
5. The classical topography does not explain the structure of the psychic apparatus.
6. The therapeutic encounter is more than a means of repeating and working through early traumatic experience; it is an experience in a relationship, containing positive growth potentials that can lead to greater self-actualization.
7. Activity and flexibility in the therapeutic approach are essential; this encourages eclecticism in method.
8. An optimistic, rather than a pessimistic viewpoint is justified regarding man's potentials as a creative, loving, and peaceful being.

## THE IMPACT OF THE EXTERNAL ENVIRONMENT

When Horney wrote her first book, *The Neurotic Personality of Our Time,* she reflected on the effects of her immigration to the United States from Vienna, Austria, the birthplace of psychoanalysis. The change of cultural milieu revamped and changed her thinking and functioning as a psychoanalyst. She pioneered changes with the important aim of adapting psychoanalytic theory and practice to the American culture. Most of the non-Freudian analysts participated in the American "re-organization" of psychoanalysis. The modification included the following considerations: American emphasis on practical results through greater activity stimulated attempts to speed up and abbreviate psychoanalysis leading to less frequent sessions, shorter periods of treatment, and less time-consuming technical tools of psychotherapy. In all fairness, however, attempts to abbreviate psychoanalysis really started with original members of the Freudian inner circle who broke with the founder such as Ferenczi, Stekel, and Rank. Most of the non-Freudian schools moved in this direction. Psychoanalysis a`la Freud was, of course, an original method of empirical clinical research, a theoretical system of personality, and a therapeutic system. It had to start as a time-consuming method.

It was the American influence that, on a massive scale, streamlined and developed variations and abbreviated forms of psychoanalysis and psychotherapy. One who bridged the gap by transferring his activity to the United States was Franz Alexander (Alexander and French, 1946). To what extent abbreviation and streamlining impaired the efficiency, the substance and depth of psychotherapy and analytic treatment is still being debated. Gutheil, who was at one time close to Stekel, pointed out that abbreviating psychotherapy could be compared to altering a father's suit to fit his son. You could not simply cut the length of the sleeves and pants, but you had to alter the whole suit.

Another American influence is definitely cultural. The frontier and open space psychology, the emphasis on personal freedom, ego identity and on activity brought about an amplification of trends toward activity, liveliness, and encounter in therapy. The use of the couch, for example, and the passive attitude of the analyst seems like an "undemocratic" procedure in the current scene. There is now a strong movement toward the extended family form of group analytic therapy, the therapeutic milieu type of treatment, and the growth of community mental health formats of treatment. Thus modified analytic techniques can be brought to bear on current problems of drug abuse, behavior disorders, and similar conditions. More active techniques now abound as do new active technical tools of psychotherapy. The action orientation fed by the American culture is reinforced further by the heavy American emphasis on social realities, equal opportunity, and relatively rapid social change.

The flowering of neo-Freudian and non-Freudian analytic procedures in the United States may certainly be related to strong indigenous social characteristics such as respect for the individual, the emphasis on personal differences and attention to human diversity. As Schwartz (1965) has stated, "The oversimplification and reductionistic systems of orthodoxy seem unacceptable to the American spirit. To treat all individuals and even all groups of individuals in exactly the same way, with the same techniques, is to deny the reality of individual differences and to create a new illusion rather than to cleave to reality. For some of the Freudian analysts, psychoanalytic concepts and principles do not allow modification in techniques."

The single greatest influence on the modification of Freudian psychoanalysis and the most relevant factor in the development of modified psychoanalytic therapies is the significance ascribed to the environment. The analysts of the non-Freudian schools generally place greater emphasis on environmental influences and outer reality than they do on inner processes. The pathogenic environment is given more weight than the instinctual drives, the psychosexual development, and intrapsychic processes as a basis for maladjustment or psychopathological behavior. Thus, the cultural analysts concentrate on the analysis of interpersonal relations and psychosocial factors in the context of societal influences.

A good example of a dynamic cultural approach in psychoanalysis is Erich Fromm's orientation toward treatment. Fromm stresses the value in therapy of uncovering what positive potentialities and healthy aspects of the self have been submerged or obliterated as a consequence of environmental restriction or condemnation. He distinguished between rational and irrational authority and the therapeutic task aims at helping the patient understand his passive compliance with irrational authority and to alter his character structure to relate more assertively and relevantly to the group in a healthy, productive way. Fromm made the task of distinguishing between rational and irrational authority through the patient's relationship with the therapist, the most essential aspect of the process of therapy. If this is correctly handled and achieved, the patient's unused potentialities for self-fulfillment through relationships with other people, can be released and developed.

An examination of most of the non-Freudian approaches shows an increasing emphasis on the analyst's values (Buhler, 1962). This involves such issues as the modeling behavior of the therapist, the question of the relative responsibility for the outcome of the therapy as between patient and therapist, the problem of cultural empathy and culture shock, as well as a host of other issues. Adler, Horney, Fromm, and May place great emphasis on the problems of alienation and the purposefulness of life. This addresses itself in the current scene to the increasing numbers of patients who are "hollow men and women" with symptoms of apathy, alienation from others, drug addiction, extreme passivity and social impotence, and dependency syndromes of one kind or another. College dropouts and executive "copouts" constitute a new group of patients who suffer from "emotional malnutrition." This is an age in which existing value systems are increasingly threatened. More non-Freudian therapies are addressing themselves to these "superego" deficiencies. A good example is Mowrer's *Integrity Therapy*. Many practitioners stress the responsibility of the analyst as well as that of the patient (Schwartz, 1956; Strupp, 1960).

## CHOICE OF PSYCHOANALYTIC TREATMENT MODALITY

The variety of systems of psychoanalysis and the plethora of techniques, approaches, strategies, tactics, and analytically-oriented procedures and therapies, require some attempt to integrate them and to develop a rationale for choosing the strategy and approach best suited to the particular patient. For this purpose the author will utilize Federn's concept of ego boundaries as further developed by Gutheil (1958) and others, such as Zucker (1959), Ivey (1959), and Kutash (1963). We will also draw upon the view that each of the psychoanalytic schools was developed by its originators in response to the problems brought before them by patients who displayed the prevalent neuroses or psychopathological states *of their time and culture.*

We conceive of the ego as developing two major boundaries, one between itself and the outside world of reality and the other between itself and the inner world of the unconscious or id. As Kutash (1965, p. 952) has stated it, "In the psychologically well-functioning individual, these boundaries are optimally cathected and flexible so that the ego functions are properly exercised, including suitable repression and selective admittance into consciousness of primordial and instinctual drives from within and adequate reality testing and cognitive, perceptual experiencing of the external world. The major task of the ego is the successful integration of these pleasure drives and needs from within, with the reality considerations and requirements of the external world." We can thus define the mentally healthy state as even and satisfactory cathexes or homeostasis of the ego boundaries.

As previously stated, Freud developed the pioneering ideas and practices of classical psychoanalysis on a case load which consisted initially of cases of hysteria (Breuer and Freud (1955). In the hysterical personality structure the ego-id boundary is too rigid or over-cathected, reflecting massive repression of instinctual drive in varying degrees and the damming up of libido. This may have resulted from early specific trauma or a chronically traumatic or neurotic early childhood situation in which the major defense of repression was developed and much of the unpleasant, painful material was rendered unconscious. A good share of the libidinal or psychic energy became tied up in maintaining the repressions, leaving an inadequate cathexis of the ego-outer world boundary, which remains too permeable, resulting in such characteristic symptoms as extreme suggestiblity, histrionic acting out, problems of identity, tendencies toward dissociation reactions, emotional displays, and the usual kaleidoscopic array of hysterical symptoms which are acted out.

The rigidity of the inner boundary results in sexual naïvete , belle indifference, lack of drive, and in Freud's day the massive repression resulted also in conversion symptoms like hysterical paralysis, blindness, deafness, hyperesthesias and and anesthesias, etc. The various psychoneurotic reactions like the asthenic, hypochondriacal, conversion, dissociation, and phobic reactions may be thought of as varieties of hysterical personality structure developing under certain specific situations. Phobias may be regarded as symbolic representations of the repressed intrapsychic sources of the original anxiety, which are projected outward or displaced to less threatening objects in the outside world and perceived as external threats. This becomes possible only when the ego-outer world boundary is too fluid or permeable and the ego-id boundary is too rigid. For example, the repression of incestuous wishes and drives may be experienced in anxiety hysteria as a phobic reaction manifested by fear of enclosed places or of tunnels.

With this type of patient, the therapist in the outside world of reality easily makes contact with the patient's ego through the poorly cathected, loose outer boundary. An intense positive transference (described by Freud as "falling in love with the analyst") may be formed which is utilized by the analyst in the therapy to "help bring unconscious material into consciousness through release of repressions" (Kutash, 1965). "This is the classical type of neurosis prevalent in Freud's day as conversion, asthenic, dissociative, and hypochondriacal reactions in relation to which he developed his epoch-making theory and practice of classical psychoanalysis which was aimed at bringing the repressed unconscious material into consciousness, thus releasing libido cathexis from the inner ego boundary and making it available for more optimal cathexis of the outer ego boundary." For this purpose free association, dream interpretation, analysis of transference, the regression to, explanation, and reliving of childhood experiences and the classical techniques of Freudian analysis were useful and effective.

It is when Freud and his disciples and followers began to work with other types of patients such as the *obsessive-compulsive,* that modifications in analytic technique became necessary and began to be introduced.  In the obsessive-compulsive personality structure it is the ego-outer world boundary that is too rigid, not permeable enough or overcathected.  The individual has erected a barrier between himself and the outside world, bolstered by such character defenses as intellectualization, rationalization, isolation of affect, and compulsions.   The inner boundary, by contrast, is too permeable and may be fractured, so that sexual thoughts, unacceptable ideas, and promptings from within continually enter consciousness in the form of obsessions.  These are prevented from being acted out in the environment by the relatively impermeable outer boundary.  This neurotic arrangement sets up the typical symptomatology of the obsessive-compulsive reaction in which "the anxiety is associated with the persistence of unwanted ideas and of repetitive impulses to perform acts which may be considered morbid by the patient" (American Psychiatric Association (1968).   The individual is compelled by pushes from within to carry out his rituals.

A clear explanation of the situation of the obsessive-compulsive neurotic is given by Gutheil (1958, p. 351).

> Although the repressive effectiveness of their ego is reduced, they still must deal with their destructive anti-moral and anti-social tendencies. They are forced to use other means of defense to protect the integrity of the ego, means different from repression or sublimation. In the forefront of the new strategic approach stands magic. From the outset their situation seems desperate. The 'enemy forces' coming from the id, have overrun the weak barricades of repression and have penetrated into the center of the ego fortress. Unable to deal with the enemy at peripheral points, the ego is forced to invoke defenses it has used in its past, such as wishful thinking, feelings of omnipotence, magic formulas, symbolic gestures and compulsive rituals. It resorts to the mechanisms of denial and negation, to various oaths, clauses, and invocations, to ward off the danger of the id invasion.

The reality testing capacity of the obsessive-compulsive is preserved at the expense of rigid defenses around the ego-outer world boundary and its overcathexis.  "Preoccupied as he is with warding off the instinctual forces, he is loath to deal with any influences from the outside world.  He is rigid, incapable of absorbing much that impinges upon him from his environment. His views are extremely conservative since, above all, he is anxious to maintain the existing order" (*ibid,* p. 343).

The treatment of the obsessive-compulsive patient requires an analytic approach that aims at "de-cathecting" or softening the rigid defenses against and denial of external reality. There is a need, for example, for *character analysis* as developed by Wilhelm Reich (Reich, 1945) who worked with the negative transference and analyzed and dissolved the character defenses, rationalizations, denials, intellectualizations, and the compulsive mechanisms, thus releasing energy (libido) for use in sealing up the breaches and strengthening the inner ego boundary.

As stated by Kutash (1965)

> The obsessive-compulsive patient needs to undergo character analysis of the defenses and the rigid character structure since the symptoms are part of character structure and the defenses of rationalization, isolation of affect, etc., need to be penetrated and dissolved, relieving the rigidity of the outer boundary so that the inner boundary can be properly cathected. The obsessions would not be focused on nor would there be a heavy emphasis on bringing more unconscious material into consciousness since the inner boundary is already too vulnerable. The therapist faced by the rigid outer boundary may be confronted with a *negative transference,* hostility, and a host of defenses before he can get through to the patient's ego. The denial mechanisms and attempts at negation will be strong. Treatment not only would not necessarily involve an uncomplicated approach of bringing unconscious material into consciousness, but rather would be directed more toward analyzing the relationships with the outside world and people in it, as in Sullivanian interpersonal therapy (1958) and other neo-Freudian methods (Fromm-Reichmann, 1950: Fromm, 1947).

The Freudian psychoanalytic approach aims at releasing repressions, removing fixations, inhibitions and libidinal blockings. It *also* has the goal of increasing awareness and *insight* concerning inner processes and the unconscious, developing and enriching the ego through its greater awareness and improving its integrative function when its boundaries are in suitable homeostasis and flexibility. Some of the early variants from Freudian technique stressed different approaches to achieving these aims. The classical approach undoubtedly favored techniques for "bringing unconscious material into consciousness." Rank's Will Therapy (1945) aimed at mobilizing the will of the patient through greater awareness of his drives and inner promptings. He also stressed the emergence of these as a form of re-birth and tried to limit the therapy to nine months as a parallel to the gestation period in the birth process. The early abbreviators like Ferenczi, Stekel, and Rank, began the movements toward more streamlined analytic methods for increasing the ego's awareness of inner processes. Stekel (1950), for example, stressed inner conflicts as well as conflicts between anagogic and katagogic drives within the individual.

Freud originally felt that psychoanalysis of the obsessive-compulsive did not work well and encouraged the idea of modifications occasioned by the lack of the development of direct and clear-cut positive transference. Some of the newer schools "cut their teeth" on the character armored and obsessive-compulsive patients whose neurosis did not necessarily develop in the same way as the hysterical cases. According to this view hysteria developed from early traumatic events in the oedipal period or through fixations at various pre-oedipal stages, Such as the oral, urethral, and anal stages. Hysterical character structures showed "heavy loadings of oral, urethral, anal or oedipal influences; hence the emphasis on the past and the first six years of life."

The *obsessive-compulsive* may have weathered the early periods before the age of six without massive repression and become traumatized later by the impact of the outside world of reality. From a more secure, perhaps overprotected early life he developed difficulties in the school years through "traumatic" competitions with siblings and schoolmates. Adler's approach (1932) may be seen as focusing on this type of patient who represents an obsessive-compulsive in *statu nascendi.* The ego attempts to preserve even cathexis of the boundaries by constricting itself for the sake of economy in the distribution of cathexis. Adler thus aimed at overcoming the *inferiority complex* and developing social feeling and interest in the environment. Sibling rivalries were analyzed and ordinal position in the family is stressed as an important behavioral determinant.

With Reich the attention turned to more direct work with the ego-outside world boundary aiming at analyzing the defenses. It was almost inevitable that other therapies would evolve aiming at developing keener *outsight* (awareness of what is really happening in the outside world of people and events). The outward look in therapy leads to a better understanding of the type of lack of awareness referred to as *blind* spots or emotional scotomas (Stekel, 1950) and *selective inattention* (Sullivan, 1953). The inspection of and accurate perception of interpersonal processes and the patient's relationship to others became the major focus of the Sullivanian school and was included in most of the cultural schools. In choosing a therapeutic approach for the obsessive-compulsive patient who in the classical approach could conceivably obsess on the couch for many, many years and receive and verbalize tremendous intellectual insights with no remission of symptoms, but perhaps an increase in the obsessive thoughts that invade the ego, the neo-Freudians would advocate *not* bringing more inner material from the id into consciousness to increase the obsessions, but rather to discard the couch and concentrate on developing sharpness of perception of the outside world. What is really going on in his interpersonal relationships, in the transference, and are his interactions with people flexible and differentiated or based on rules and compulsions?

In the *ambulatory schizophrenic* or *pseudoneurotic schizophrenic* "both ego boundaries are damaged" or "fractured" and there is a danger of schizophrenic decompensation but there are islands of defense in terms of pseudoneurotic symptoms and rigidities in both boundaries, side by side with breaks in the boundaries" (Kutash, 1965). The treatment of the borderline patient has led to the development of a large variety of ego supportive and ego-building methods. Some innovators like Rosen (1953), Laing (1960), and all of the ego psychologists (Guntrip, 1973), have advocated acceptance of the patient in the *schizoid* position and the rebuilding of his ego in a nurturant fashion. Many therapists of the Kleinian school have also developed analytic techniques for repairing egos. Some of the family therapists and group analytic therapists have also made contributions along these lines. Essentially, the treatment of the ambulatory schizophrenic who has patches of rigid defenses and breaks in both ego boundaries requires a careful balance between supportive and uncovering techniques designed to release dammed up energy in the rigid islands of defense so that the cathexis can be available to "seal up the breaks."

In discussing the *depressive neuroses* Kutash (1965) states, "In the *neurotic depressive reaction* the attempt is made to preserve a homeostatic equilibrium in the boundaries by distributing the cathexis evenly through constricting the ego or contracting it. The depressive reaction in this sense may be understood as a defense against the development of actual defect in one of the ego boundaries and obviating the need for compensating in the other boundary in order to preserve equilibrium. In the depressive reaction the circumference of the two boundaries – particularly the outer boundary – become smaller through contraction of the ego, resulting in preservation of accuracy of perception, keen awareness of bodily processes, some hypochondriasis, and preserved and sharpened reality sense. Rather than allow the ego to become impaired, the depressive chooses to depreciate or squelch it until it can be expanded again when the stress or threat is lessened." The treatment of the depressed patient from the analytic point of view has stressed a bifocal approach – measures to expand the ego and its cathexis while lessening the outer or inner stresses by auxiliary measures. Some patients have mood swings and some schools of analysis and innovative techniques have concentrated on interpreting the bright spots when the patient has "black glasses on and everything looks dark" while pointing out the realities and less optimistic aspects when the "rose-colored glasses are on and everything looks rosy." The treatment of depressions have interested all the schools of analytic therapy and these patients have stimulated a large variety of "active" methods such as the *consciousness-raising* techniques and the encounter methods (Rogers, 1970).

The cathexis of the superego in relation to the ego and the ego-superego boundary is another major consideration in modified analytic therapies. Patients with punishing, over-developed superegos and conflicts between "moral" and "anti-moral" forces have been the focus of those of the approaches that have aimed at the clarification of the basic meaning of life, personal being in the world, and a variety of related considerations. Here we must include the *spiritual* emphasis of the Jungian school, the existential analysts and the schools that stress responsibility and committment. Values have become a major focus of the existential schools. Erich Fromm (Coleman, 1960, p. 522), for example, puts forth the thesis that "values are rooted in the very conditions of human existence; hence that our knowledge of these conditions, that is, if the 'human situation' leads us to establishing values which have objective validity; this validity exists, only with regard to the existence of man; outside of him there are no values." The current era presents us with a case load of patients who suffer from identity crises, who doubt the value of their existence, who have difficulty developing a usable system for themselves, and who become apathetic, withdrawn, and ineffectual. It is perhaps not a coincidence that these "new" breeds of neuroses occur in the atomic era when the existence of man as a species is in question since the means for his total self-destruction is available and is not under assured peaceful control. The external existential threat must indeed call forth new adaptive mechanisms to protect the ego and man's awareness.

An overview of the modified psychoanalytic therapies and the continuing new developments in ego psychology and psychoanalytic therapy of the ego raises the question of whether the analytcially oriented therapist can afford to adhere rigidly to a favorite system or school of psychoanalysis and fit the patient into his system or whether there is a need for a rebirth, already under way, of eclecticism in which the therapeutic approach is chosen to fit the particular patient. There is still need for much research and clinical experiences to aid in deciding which is the treatment of choice for whom.

## REFERENCES

Ackerman, N. *The psychodynamics of family life.* New York: Basic Books, 1958.

Adler, A. *Individual psychology and its results in the practice and theory of individual psychology.* New York: Harcourt, Brace, 1932.

Adler, A. *The practice and theory of individual psychology.* Translated by P. Radin. New York: Harcourt, Brace, 1927.

Alexander, F. and French, T.M. *Psychoanalytic therapy: principles and application.* New York: Ronald, 1946.

American Psychiatric Association. *Diagnostic and statistical manual of mental disorders,* Third Edition, 1968.

Bach, G.R. *Intensive group psychotherapy.* New York: Ronald, 1954.

Bell, J.E. Recent advances in family group therapy. *J. Child Psycho. Psychiat.* 1-15 (1962).

Berne, E. *Transactional analysis in psychotherapy.* New York: Grove Press, 1961.

Berne, E. *Games people play.* New York: Grove Press, 1964.

Bonime, W. *The clinical use of dreams.* New York: Basic Books, 1962.

Boss, M. *Meaning and content of sexual perversions.* New York: Grune and Stratton, 1949.

Breuer, J. and Freud, S. (1895). Studies on hysteria. *Standard Edition*, vol. 2. London: Hogarth Press, 1955.

Buhler, C. *Values in psychotherapy.* New York: Free Press of Glencoe, 1962.

Bychowski, G. *Psychotherapy of psychosis.* New York: Grune & Stratton, 1952.

Coleman, J.C. *Personality dynamics and effective behavior.* Palo Alto: Scott, and Foresman and Co., 1960.

Erikson, E.H. Childhood and tradition in two American Indian tribes. *The Psychoanalytic Study of the Child*, I: 319–350. New York: International Universities Press, 1945.

Erikson, E.H. *Childhood and society.* New York: Norton, 1950.

Erikson, E.H. The dream specimen of psychoanalysis. *J. Amer. Psyc. Assoc.* 2: 5–56 (1954).

Erikson, E.H. Identity and the life cycle. *Psychol. Issues.* Mongr. No. 1, 1959.

Erikson, E.H. *Insight and responsibility.* New York: Norton, 1964.

Evans, Richard I. *Dialogue with Erik Erikson.* New York: Harper and Row, 1967.

Ferber, A., Mendelsohn, M. and Napier, A. *The book of family therapy.* New York: Science House, Inc., 1972.

Fine, R. *The healing of the mind.* New York: David McKay Co., 1971.

Fitzgerald, R.V. *Conjoint marital therapy.* New York: Jason Aronson, 1973.

Foulkes, S.H. and Anthony, E.J. *Group Psychology.* London: Penguin Books, 1957.

Freud, A. *The psychoanalytical treatment of children* (1926). New York: International Universities Press, 1946.

Fromm, E. *Man for himself.* New York: Rinehart, 1947.

Fromm, E. *The sane society.* New York: Holt, 1955.

Fromm-Reichmann, F. *Principles of intensive psychotherapy.* Chicago: University of Chicago Press, 1950.

Green, M.R., Ullman, M. and Tauber, E.S. Dreaming and modern dream theory. In: Marmor, J. (Ed.), *Modern psychoanalysis: New directions and perspectives.* New York: Basic Books, Inc., 1968.

Greene, B.L. *The psychotherapies of marital disharmony.* New York: The Free Press, 1965.

Guntrip, H. *Psychoanalytic theory, therapy, and the self.* New York: Basic Books, p. V, 1973.

Gutheil, E.A. *The handbook of dream analysis.* New York: Liveright, 1951.

Gutheil, E.A. Dreams as an aid in evaluating ego strength. *American J. Psychother.* 12: 338–355 (1958).

Harris, T.A. *I'm OK-You're OK.* New York: Avon, 1973.

Hartmann, H. (1939) *Ego psychology and the problem of adaptation.* New York: International Universities Press, 1958.

Hartmann, H. and Kris, E. The genetic approach in psychoanalysis. *The Psychoanalytic Study of the Child.* 1: 11–30. New York: International Universities Press, 1945.

Horney, K. *The neurotic personality of our time.* New York: Norton, 1937.

Horney, K. *New ways in psychoanalysis.* New York: Norton, 1939.

Ivey, E.P. Recent advances in diagnosis and treatment of phobias. *Amer. J. Psychother.* 13: 35–50 (1959).

Jung, C. *Collected papers on analytic psychology.* Translated by C.E. Long. London: Balliere, 1920.

Jung, C.G. *Modern man in search of a soul.* New York: Harcourt, Brace and World, 1933.

Kernberg, O. Borderline personality organization. *J. Amer. Psychoanal. Assoc.* **15**: 641–685 (1967).

Klein, M. *The psychoanalysis of children.* New York: Grove Press, 1960.

Klein, M. *Our adult world and other essays.* New York: Basic Books, 1963.

Kohut, H. *The analysis of the self.* New York: International Universities Press, 1971.

Kris, E. On preconscious mental processes. In: Rapaport, D. (Ed.), *Organization and Pathology of Thought,* pp. 474–493. New York: Columbia University Press, 1951.

Kutash, S.B. Treatment of symptoms, perceptual flexibility, and ego boundaries. Paper read at Eastern Psycholigcal Association, 1963.

Kutash, S.B. Psychoneuroses. In: Wolman, B.B. (Ed.), *Handbook of clinical psychology.* New York: McGraw-Hill, 1965.

Laing, R.I. *The divided self.* New York: Pantheon Books, 1960.

Langs, R.J. *The technique of psychoanalytic psychotherapy,* Vols. 1 and 2. New York: Jason Aronson, 1973, 1974.

Lewis, N.D.C. Historical roots of psychotherapy. In: Masserman, J.H. and Moreno, J.L. (Eds.), *Progress in psychotherapy,* Vol. III, pp. 20–26. New York: Grune & Stratton, 1958.

Lieberman, M.A.; Yolom, I.D. and Miles, M.B. *Encounter Groups: First Facts.* New York: Basic Books, In., 1973.

Lowenstein, R.M. Conflict and autonomous ego development during the phallic phase. *The psychoanalytic study of the child.* **5**: 47–52. New York: International Universities Press, 1950.

May, R. *Psychology and the human dilemma.* New York: Van Nostrand Reinhold, 1967.

May, R., Angel, E. and Ellenberger, H.F. *Existence, a new dimension in psychiatry and psychology.* New York: Basic Books, 1958.

Moreno, J.L. Psychodrama and group psychotherapy, *Sociometry.* **9**: 249–253 (1946).

Munroe, R.L. *Schools of Psychoanalytic Thought.* New York: Dryden Press, 1955.

Perls, F.; Hefferline, R.R. and Goodman, P. *Gestalt therapy.* New York: Julian Press, 1951.

Polster, F. and Polster, M. *Gestalt therapy integrated.* New York: Brunner/ Mazel, 1973.

Rank, Otto, *Will therapy; and truth and reality.* New York: Knopf, 1945.

Reich, W. *Character analysis.* New York: Orgone Institute Press, 1945.

Rogers, C. *Carl Rogers on encounter groups.* New York: Harper and Row, 1970.

Rosen, J.N. *Direct Analysis.* New York: Grune & Stratton, 1953.

Rosenbaum, M. and Berger, M. *Group psychotherapy and group functions: selected readings.* New York: Basic Books, 1963.

Schwartz, E.K. Non-Freudian analytic methods. In: Wolman, B.B. (Ed.), *Handbook of Clinical Psychology.* New York: McGraw-Hill, 1965.

Schwartz, E.R.  Is there need for psychology in psychotherapy?  In:  Krout, M.L. (Ed.) *Psychology, psychiatry and the public interest,* pp. 113–134.    Minneapolis:  University of Minnesota Press (1956).

Searles, H.F.  Positive feelings in the relationships between the schizophrenic and his mother.  *Int. J. Psycho-Anal.*  **39**:  569 (1965).

Spitz, R.A.  Hospitalism.  *The psychoanalytic study of the child,*  Vol. 1:  53–74. New York: International Universities Press, 1965.

Stekel, W.    *Techniques of analytical psychotherapy.*    New York:  Liveright Publishing Corporation, 1950.

Strupp, H.H.  *Psychotherapists in action.*  New York:  Grune & Stratton, 1960.

Sullivan, H.C.  *The interpersonal theory of psychiatry.*  New York:  Norton, 1953.

Sullivan, H.S.  *Conceptions of modern psychiatry,* (second edition.)  New York: Norton, 1953.

Tarachow, S.  *An introduction to psychotherapy.*  New York:  International Universities Press, 1963.

Thompson, C.  *Psychoanalysis, evolution and development.*  New York:  Norton, 1950.

Ullman, M.  Dreaming, life style and physiology: a comment on Adler's view of the dream.  *J. of Individual Psychology.*  **18**:  18–25 (1962).

Whitaker, C.A. and Malone, T.P.    *The roots of psychotherapy.*    New York: Blakiston, 1953.

Winnicott, D.W.  *The maturational processes and the facilitating environment.* New York: International Universities Press, 1963.

Witenberg, E.G.  Foreword.  In:  Guntrip, H., *Psychoanalytic theory, therapy, and the self.*  New York:  Basic Books, 1973.

Wolberg, L.R.  *The technique of psychotherapy,* second edition, Parts I and II. New York: Grune & Stratton, 1967.

Wolf, A. and Schwartz, E.K.  Irrational psychotherapy:  an appear to unreason. *Amer. J. Psychother.*  **12**:  300–314, 508–521, 744–759 (1958).

Wolf, A. and Schwartz, E.K.  Irrational psychotherapy:  an appeal to unreason. *Amer. J. Psychother.*  **13**:  383–400 (1959).

Wolf, A. and Schwartz, E.K.  *Psychoanalysis in groups.*  New York:  Grune & Stratton, 1962

Wolman, B.B.  *Psychotherapy with latent schizophrenics.*  **13**:  343–359 (1959).

Wolman, B.B. (Ed.) *Handbook of clinical psychology.*  New York:  McGraw-Hill, 1965.

Wolman, B.B.  Quo vadis, psychoanalysis?  *J. of Contemporary Psychotherapy.* **4**:  23–26 (1971).

Wyss, D.  *Psychoanalytic schools.*  New York:  Jason Aronson, 1973.

Zucker, L.J.    Ego weakness, ego defenses and ego strengthening.  *Amer. J. Psychother.*  **13**:  614–634 (1959).

# 6 Behavior Modification: Clinical and Experimental Perspectives

## Arnold A. Lazarus and G. Terence Wilson

Before the turn of this century, clinicians devised active and strategic treatments to deal with a wide range of psychopathology. Every student of abnormal psychology is familiar with the pioneering efforts of Mesmer, Braid, Liebeault and Charcot. Their work was characterized by a profound interest in suggestion, "hypnosis," and various forms of social influence. There was also a considerable degree of overlap with some current behavior modification techniques. Apart from these forerunners of modern hypnotherapy and behavior therapy, during the first half of this century many articles appeared, both in America and in Russia, describing the application of conditioning principles to a wide variety of abnormal behaviors. Gesell (1938) listed 57 references of learning and conditioning procedures for overcoming children's clinical problems. Recently Yates (1970) cited a wide range of early conditioning techniques, from Bekhterev's (1923) work with sexual perversions, to Mowrer and Mowrer (1938) and Morgan and Witmer's (1939) treatment of enuresis. In the 1920s and 1930s, considerable work was done using conditioning and deconditioning techniques. Procedures were devised for overcoming children's fears (e.g., Jones, 1924), tics, stuttering and other "bad habits," (e.g., Dunlap, 1932), sexual aberrations (e.g., Kostyleff, 1927; Meignant, 1935), alcoholism (e.g., Ichok, 1934) and even morphine addiction (Rubenstein, 1931).

Under the influence of Rogerian therapy, psychoanalysis, and various other psychodynamic approaches, much of the aforementioned work was considered manipulative, superficial, mechanistic and naive. Active intervention on the part of a therapist was emphatically discouraged. Clinicians were trained to wait for the patient to take the initiative, and to remain passive while doing so. A

judicious interpretation, or a well-timed reflection of the patient's ongoing emotions were the only forms of intervention considered fundamental rather than
palliative. Thus, many effective therapeutic strategies and techniques that were
developing before this century were completely lost. Some were subsequently
rediscovered or reinvented. In recent years, an impressive technology of active
treatment procedures derived from well-controlled clinical and experimental
studies has been developing. *Behavior modification* and the roughly synonymous
term *behavior therapy* is used to describe this applied experimental-clinical trend.

The wave of psychodynamic formulations which dominated psychotherapeutic
attention for the first 50 years of this century tended to eclipse all other points
of view. Thus, Ernest Kretschmer's (1922) text on medical psychology which
described "systematic habituation therapy" and other active techniques had no
influence upon current psychotherapeutic practice. Similarly, books such as
Williams' (1923) *Dreads and Besetting Fears* which regarded "reconditioning as
the foundation of psychotherapy" or Salter's (1949) *Conditioned Reflex Therapy*
also failed to rescind the prevailing Freudian zeitgeist. Clinicians were riveting
their attention to inferred unconscious conflicts. They were preoccupied with
the understanding of underlying "character structures," and intrapsychic processes. Attention was almost entirely deflected away from overt behavior. The
proper study of psychology was said to be aimed at understanding the more
basic unconscious processes.

A schizm developed between academic-experimental psychology and clinical
psychology. The former was essentially behavioristic, mainly following the work
of Thorndike, Pavlov, Watson and Skinner. Clinicians, however, followed a
completely different track. Their domain was replete with subjective tests,
intrapsychic inferences, and speculative theories about the basic motives of
human interaction. Students enrolled in Ph.D. clinical programs often faced a
disconcerting duality. Their academic training was grounded in the experimental
tradition — they learned scientific methods, research designs, statistics, and how
to ferret out data from studies on learning, perception, cognition, and various
social and developmental processes, with a strong emphasis upon laboratory
controls and a high regard for precise and measurable phenomena. In their
predoctoral years of study, however, they served an internship, usually in a
medical setting — a state hospital, a Veterans Administration Center, or a psychiatric clinic — under the auspices of physicians and psychiatrists. In these medical
settings, their academic grounding was, at best, tangential. They learned instead
to apply various medical models and disease analogies in treating "mental illness."
Their mentors and supervisors were usually psychiatrists heavily invested in
psychodynamic thought and theory, often scornful of non-medical practitioners
and quite ignorant of matters derived from experimental psychology. After
immersing themselves for at least a year in this environment, students would
return to their universities to conduct research for a dissertation. Now they
were required to suspend all that they had learned about putative repressed
complexes and how to burrow deep into the interstices of the unconscious.

Once again they were required to conceptualize psychological matters in precise, quantifiable terms, and to switch from fanciful inferences, to the accumulation of data that was subject to verification and replication.

In part, the behavior modification "movement" may be seen as an attempt to remedy the aforementioned state of affairs — to bridge the gap between the laboratory and the clinic. This is being accomplished *not* as some therapists insist (e.g., Sloane, 1969; Woody, 1971; Feather and Rhoads, 1972; Birk, 1973) by marrying learning principles to psychodynamic formulations. As Lazarus (1973) has underscored, an amalgam of behavioral and psychoanalytic formulations in an eclectic psychobehavioral union produces syncretistic muddles that obscure critical differences between the respective models. Nor does one have to insist upon a scientist-practitioner model. Nevertheless, a fruitful dialogue between laboratory scientists and practicing clinicians is entirely feasible. As Lazarus and Davison (1971, pp. 196–197) pointed out:

> Laboratory scientists and practicing clinicians can each offer unique contributions in their own right and can conceivably open hitherto new and unsuspected clinical-experimental dimensions for research and practice. Ideas tested in the laboratory may be applied by the practitioner who, in turn, may discover important individual nuances that remain hidden from the laboratory scientist simply because the tight environment of the experimental testing ground makes it impossible for certain behaviors to occur or for certain observations to be made. Conversely, ideas formulated in the clinic, provided that they are amenable to verification or disproof, can send scientists scurrying off into laboratories to subject the claims of efficacy to controlled tests.

In recent years it has become increasingly apparent that sophisticated behavior modifiers have been incorporating empirically validated clinical observations into their basic repertoires. Thus, in contrast with early stimulus-response formulations which attempted to reduce nearly all clinical complexities to phobic anxieties (e.g., Wolpe, 1958; Eysenck, 1960) the present-day behavior modifier draws on a wide range of social learning theories and techniques. Although some radical behaviorists still insist that overt behavior is the only respectable realm of scientific inquiry, and that introspective reports are totally inadmissible, these constitute a decided minority. Indeed, the field of behavior modification is now cognizant of "private events," the fundamental significance of cognitive mediation and the relevance of covert processes and self-regulatory mechanisms (Bandura, 1969).

## CONTEMPORARY ORIGINS OF BEHAVIOR MODIFICATION

Ebbinghaus's much quoted observation that "psychology has a long past but a short history" is particularly true of behavior modification. While the major historical roots of behavior modification are imbedded in the animal laboratories of Pavlov, Bekhterev, Thorndike and early Skinner, current behavioral practices owe their impetus to work conducted no earlier than 1950. In England, Shapiro (1951) described the application of experimental psychology to the single case and contrasted it with the traditional approach in clinical psychology. Eysenck (1959) defined behavior therapy as the application of "modern learning theory" to emotional disorders, and together with his students and associates exercised a powerful influence on early developments.

In America, Lindsley and Skinner (1954) conducted laboratory studies to demonstrate that the behavior of severely disturbed persons followed the same learning principles as that of normal persons. Like the English behavior therapists, Skinnerians also focused their attention upon the experimental study of the single case — although Skinner *et al.* worked mainly with psychotic patients. Their operant conditioning procedures were predicated upon the assumption that behavior is a function of its consequences. Whereas the English workers made use of hypothetical constructs to explain their findings, American behavior modifiers followed Skinner's eschewal of all mediating constructs. The broad application of operant conditioning to the whole range of psychiatric problems was underscored by Ullmann and Krasner (1965).

The term "behavior therapy" first appeared in the literature when Lazarus (1958) used it to describe Wolpe's (1954) objective psychotherapy procedures. This work was carried out in South Africa, and was independent of the English and American efforts previously alluded to. Wolpe's (1958) book on "reciprocal inhibition" contained many of the points of emphasis that were first documented by Jones (1924), Dunlap (1932), Guthrie (1935), Herzberg (1941) and Salter (1949). It constitutes one of the significant landmarks in the development of behavior therapy, and despite conceptual shortcomings, was vigorously promoted by Eysenck (1960) who hailed its publication as "the coming of age of behavior therapy as an independent and practically applicable discipline," (Eysenck, 1960, p. xi). Besides, there was a widespread dissatisfaction among mental health workers with traditional approaches to psychodiagnosis and psychotherapy and by the time Wolpe's (1958) book appeared many were ready to examine alternative methods of treatment. Clinical psychologists were growing especially dissatisfied with their futile exercises in administering and scoring batteries of projective and other routine tests lacking in reliability and validity.

Behavior modification and therapy gained enormous momentum from 1963 to 1970. Four new journals devoted to behavior modification or behavior therapy were launched during this time period: *Behaviour Research and Therapy* was started in 1963, the *Journal of Applied Behavior Analysis* in 1968, and *Behavior Therapy* and the *Journal of Behavior Therapy and Experimental Psychiatry* in 1970. These four journals alone publish over 200 articles on behavior modification each year. The number of additional articles, books, monographs, published symposia and edited anthologies is quite overwhelming.

A task force report on the field of behavior modification conducted under the auspices of the American Psychiatric Association concluded that "behavioral principles employed in the analysis of clinical phenomena have reached a stage of development where they now unquestionably have much to offer informed clinicians in the service of modern clinical and social psychiatry," (Birk *et al.,* 1973, p. 64). It would seem that behavior modification has "come of age" and can no longer be regarded as a passing fad.

## BEHAVIORAL ASSESSMENT AND DIAGNOSIS

Criticisms of conventional psychiatric diagnoses are by no means confined to behaviorally-oriented clinicians, but widespread dissatisfaction has been expressed about the nosological inadequacies, low reliability and limited prognostic value of traditional diagnostic labels. A valid and reliable diagnosis should lead to logical and specific forms of treatment. It has become clearly evident that terms like "schizophrenia," "neurosis," "anxiety-hysteria," "psychosis," "character disorder," and similar labels usually suffer from internal inconsistency, imprecision, and lack the specificity for generating meaningful treatment interventions. A useful diagnosis should specify salient etiological antecedents (i.e., those that have current therapeutic relevance) and provide reasonable prognostic indications.

It has also become increasingly evident that medical analogies and the entire concept of illness and disease may have little to do with those problems of living we call "psychopathology." And conversely, even in clear-cut somatic diseases, physicians have come to realize that social and psychological influences, including various expectations and particular behavior patterns cannot be ignored. In behavior modification, the diagnostic process (usually referred to as the "functional analysis" or a procedure of "problem identification") endeavors to describe the patient's complaints in objective terms, while searching for antecedent and maintaining factors, and the probable means by which each problem area can be resolved.

In behavioral assessments, presenting complaints are usually divided into *behavioral excesses* (e.g., exhibitionism, compulsive checking, frequent rage reactions, overeating, and so forth), and/or *behavioral deficits* (e.g., impotence, social withdrawal, timid and unassertive reaction patterns, etc.). In essence, the behavior modifier endeavors to increase and/or decrease the frequency of specific behaviors, depending upon their social context. A diligent search is conducted to uncover and clarify the variables in the patient's biological, psychological and sociological systems that maintain the current problem behaviors. Kanfer and Saslow (1969) have provided a comprehensive description of the functional analysis of behavior. Their schema incorporates the patient's areas of adequate and optimal functioning into the analysis, and stresses that these assets are important for planning treatment strategies. The behavioral analysis is continually modified and refined as more information about the patient is gained. Wherever possible, an attempt is made to quantify the behavioral descriptions.

Frequency distributions are compiled — how many aggressive outbursts, how many avoidance responses, how many negative self-statements, how many delusional remarks did the patient emit? Self-monitoring is also highly recommended, especially for well-motivated patients who can count their own positive and negative responses to a wide variety of stimuli.

In the practical details of his day-to-day work, the behavioral clinician, like any well-trained therapist, attempts to understand his patients' personal constructs, their presenting complaints, the factors that gave rise to their difficulties, their conflicts, perceptual distortions, and idiosyncrasies. Thus, history-taking, assessment and evaluation combine to yield an accurate portrait of the patient in a unique network of social interactions. But unlike the general psychiatric anamnesis, no less attention is paid to overt behavior than to verbal reports of feelings, thoughts and fantasies. Secondly, as already mentioned, behavior modifiers do not regard the task of diagnosis as that of assigning the patient to a category, and then applying the treatments that are considered to be best for members of that category. The behavior modifier seldom asks *why* questions — Why do you become so anxious in crowded places? Why are you punishing yourself? Questions starting with how, when, where, what and who are found to be more productive for eliciting the significant personal and situational variables that cause and maintain emotional disturbances. (How did you respond at the time? What were you doing? Who was with you? When did this happen? Where was your husband?) The upshot of a functional analysis is a detailed and specific range of hypersensitivities, shortcomings, avoidance behaviors, and social inadequacies for each patient. Specificity is the hallmark of behavior therapy. Where a traditional therapist may speak of a patient as "an obsessive-compulsive personality with passive-aggressive tendencies," behavior therapists would say, "Mr. Smith washes his hands on an average of 96 times a day; he is inhibited with most authority figures, although he is inclined to over-assert his authority with subordinates; he avoids intimate contacts with women which he attributes to his premature ejaculation; he is hypersensitive to criticism, rejection, and disapproval." Each of the foregoing problem areas would then be even more clearly articulated, with special emphasis being devoted to eliciting and maintaining conditions.

Lazarus (1973a) has proposed a more detailed and systematic assessment process. During diagnostic interviews and throughout the course of therapy, his *multimodal* orientation examines seven interactive modalities: overt behavior, affective responses, sensory reactions, emotive imagery, cognitive processes, interpersonal relationships and a "medical modality" especially characterized by indications and contraindications for the use of drugs or medication. The acronym BASIC ID (derived from Behavior, Affect, Sensation, Imagery, Cognition, Interpersonal and Drugs) provides a useful mnemonic for remembering the separate yet interrelated modalities. Although *overt behavior* (e.g., compulsive rituals, tics, blushing, tremors, crying spells, stuttering, delusional speech, etc.) and *interpersonal responses* (e.g., arguments, discussions, affectionate gestures, etc.) are amenable to direct observation, the other modalities depend upon verbal reports. Affect, imagery, sensation and cognitive processes are hypothetical constructs — "off limits" to radical behaviorists, but clinically crucial to behaviorally-oriented therapists. The application of various sensory exercises is clearly behavioral, however (e.g., the prescribed use of tactile interchanges along a graded series of intimate encounters for overcoming sexual inhibitions). But the statement, "I have an image of my late mother's funeral" is, strictly speaking, verbal behavior. Yet within the multimodal framework, it is assumed that associated "verbal operants" involving interrelated "affective responses," "cognitions," and "subjective sensations," can be elicited. "The image makes me feel sad and sorry for myself, as I keep thinking that I am to blame for her premature death, which, in turn, makes me feel tense all over." In terms of this framework, a multimodal behavior therapist would then pursue the following types of interventions:

*Behavior:*    Increase the number of positive-reinforcing activities in which the patient participates.

*Affect:*    Teach the patient to express anger in an assertive manner instead of lapsing into self-pity.

*Sensation:*    Use deep muscle relaxation to overcome generalized tension.

*Imagery:*    Show the patient how to dwell on pleasant memories instead of focusing on negative elements.

*Cognition:*    Try to alter negative self-talk by disputing internalized guilt-inducing sentences.

*Interpersonal:*  Be sure that nobody is maintaining the self-denigrating behaviors by inappropriately offering sympathy and warmth.

*Drugs:*    If "sadness " or "depression" persists or becomes more intense, medication may be indicated.

Thus the aforementioned assessment-therapy approach takes each problem area and endeavors to institute corrective procedures across significant objective and subjective parameters. In the light of this multifaceted orientation, the misleading impression created by Eysenck's (1959) unfortunate slogan *"Get rid of the symptom and you have eliminated the neurosis"* is readily apparent. As a result of this type of statement, it has been alleged that behavior therapy is a superficial mode of treatment which ignores the "real" underlying causes of behavioral disorders, and which is therefore likely to result in "symptom substitution." However, the multimodal behavior therapy approach does focus on *all* the relevant antecedent, mediational and maintaining factors which contribute to each one of the client's problems. Far from being an incomplete or superficial therapeutic approach, multimodal behavior therapy is perhaps the most comprehensive and flexible treatment approach to the entire range of child and adult behavioral disorders.

## Special Clinical Considerations

The ardent behavioral clinician will from time to time encounter certain difficulties and therapeutic paradoxes. His systematic manipulation of environmental contingencies may alter people's responses to stimuli in remarkable ways, and yet in other instances zero progress will ensue. Echolalic children may learn coherent speech, back-ward schizophrenics may become more productive human beings, and chronically anxious, obsessive and depressive individuals may embrace a fulfilling and assertive *modus vivendi*. In more precise cases, such as the elimination of certain tics, temper tantrums, compulsive rituals, sexual deviations, and withdrawal tendencies, the behavior modifier may even be able to employ A-B-A designs to demonstrate that his interventions were indeed the active ingredients of the observed changes. But the paradox to which we referred may enter suddenly when a seemingly simple encopretic child continues to soil himself despite ingenious modifications in various rewarding and punishing contingencies. Or perhaps a client consistently "forgets" to practice her relaxation exercises as a precursor to desensitization therapy. Or an impotent man instructed to avoid coital demands and to comply with a graded series of intimate exchanges suddenly reports that his potency is fully restored.

It is easy to offer various post hoc explanations according to learning principles, but the utility of so doing in terms of their predictive value is obviously useless. When examining therapeutic failures, to insist that target behaviors did not shift in a desired direction because the maintaining conditions and requisite reinforcements were inadequately manipulated, may be true in many instances, but this reasoning becomes tautological when consistently invoked as an explanatory principle. Social learning theory may be called upon to investigate and to add information regarding interpersonal expectancies that lead to various paradoxes in communication. The foregoing has been well documented from a different clinical perspective (e.g., Haley, 1973). To cite a specific case in point, it is often reported that by "prescribing the symptom" a rapid diminution of "symptomatic behavior" may ensue. We have already alluded to the fact that certain impotent men may "defy" their therapists and become fully potent when instructed to refrain from sexual intercourse. Similarly, one of us found, in treating a seemingly refractory case of anorexia nervosa, that the woman gradually resumed normal eating patterns upon being told to try to lose another 10–15 pounds.

To point out that the behavior changed because the therapist altered the reinforcers that maintained her non-eating behavior begs the question. It is difficult to account for the fact that other shifts in reinforcement failed to achieve the desired end (e.g., selective inattention, withdrawal of privileges, and time out procedures). It is also difficult to predict when a "paradoxical intervention" may exacerbate the situation. To prescribe a 10–15 pound weight loss is hardly a "cure" for anorexia nervosa! We are merely re-emphasizing the fact that existing principles of learning cannot readily account for many of the phenomena that the practicing clinician encounters. The crucial question — as yet unanswered — is what combination of techniques will prove most effective with what types of problems, delivered by which therapists to what patients?

## SIGNIFICANT BEHAVIOR MODIFICATION
## TECHNIQUES AND DIRECTIONS

Wolpe (1958) outlined 14 behavior therapy techniques: assertive responses, sexual responses, relaxation responses, systematic desensitization based on relaxation, conditioned avoidance responses, anxiety-relief responses, aversion therapy, feeding responses, respiratory responses, interview-induced emotional responses, abreaction, correcting misconceptions, thought stopping, and the use of drugs. Lazarus (1971) added the desert island fantasy technique, the inner circle strategy, cognitive restructuring, group methods, emotive imagery, time projection, the "blow-up" technique, and a variety of ancillary procedures. Combined with various operant training methods such as contingency contracting, the deliberate use of modeling, positive and negative reinforcement, time-out procedures, and so forth, there are probably more than 24 basic behavior modification techniques. The remainder of this chapter will outline and review some of the important directions and procedures in the field.

### Systematic Desensitization

The basic assumption behind desensitization procedures is that the fear evoked by subjectively threatening situations can be reduced by a graded and progressive exposure to a hierarchy of anxiety-generating situations. The client is taught to employ various "anti-anxiety" responses (e.g., deep muscle relaxation, pleasant imagery, or rational self-assurance) and thereby systematically extinguish each level of anxiety. The most effective desensitization procedures appear to require actual exposure to real-life situations (Sherman, 1972) although imaginal desensitization (i.e., counterposing through relaxation the tensions and fears that arise while vividly picturing distressing events) has also proved effective in many instances (Paul, 1969, pp. 105-159).

Over the past decade, the range of experiments and case studies on the applications of systematic desensitization has been astoundingly widespread and numerous. As far as process mechanisms are concerned, data from both animal and human studies have discredited Wolpe's (1958) original reciprocal inhibition hypothesis, and have indicated that the necessary conditions for the successful desensitization of fear/avoidance behavior are nonreinforced exposure to the fear-producing situation (Davison and Wilson, 1973; Wilson and Davison, 1971). In actual clinical practice, desensitization probably also involves important attitudinal and expectancy components, demand characteristics, and cognitive relabeling.

It is extremely laborious to construct intricate anxiety hierarchies, to present items over and over again to deeply relaxed clients, and to proceed in this piecemeal fashion each session. Fortunately, when desensitization seems clearly indicated, most clients are capable of benefiting from the procedure as part of a self-management program (Goldfried, 1971). The client usually plays cassette recordings of relaxation exercises in his own home at his own convenience, and then pictures a range of distressing scenes and/or systematically exposes himself to actual life situations under conditions of relaxation. The therapist's role is to prompt, encourage and supervise the process by discussing various options for overcoming trouble spots, by facilitating the use of gradual rather than abrupt sequences of anxiety-provoking scenes, and by offering support at each stage of the proceedings. In terms of increased cost-effectiveness and the hours saved for therapist time to be devoted to more crucial activities (e.g., behavior rehearsal, modeling, family intervention, and cognitive restructuring) self-control and self-management procedures are of inestimable value.

## Flooding

Flooding refers to a procedure which involves prolonged, high intensity exposure to phobic stimuli. Contrary to Wolpe's (1969) admonition that "exposure, and prolonged exposure in particular can seriously enhance phobic sensitivity" (p. 127), protracted nonreinforced exposure to fearful stimuli does reliably result in a reduction of autonomic arousal and the extinction of avoidance behavior (cf. Wilson and Davison, 1971). Although the findings from analogous laboratory studies on flooding are often inconsistent (Morganstern, 1973), impressive evidence of the efficacy of the technique comes from a study on psychiatric patients by Marks, Boulougouris, and Marset (1971). In fact, they found flooding to be more successful than desensitization, particularly in cases of generalized, more severe phobic complaints. It is highly probable that much of the conflicting evidence on flooding is due to procedural variations in its use. A crucial consideration when employing flooding techniques is to ensure that the duration of each fear-producing trial is prolonged to produce a clear-cut diminution of anxiety. Since flooding entails the use of high intensity anxiety, it carries some risk. Before employing flooding procedures, it is important to establish that the client can safely experience the discomfort entailed, and the ends justify the means.

Flooding *in vivo* has also proved to be superior to a placebo control treatment in eliminating chronic obsessive-compulsive behaviors that had failed to respond to previous psychiatric treatment (Rachman, Hodgson, and Marks, 1971). Preventing compulsive patients from carrying out their rituals (i.e., a "reality-testing" process) appears to be the decisive element in producing extinction of these cases. Mills, Agras, Barlow, and Mills (1973) treated five compulsive patients using them as their own controls and demonstrated that response prevention is a necessary condition for the elimination of rituals. An important clinical caution is that these procedures often have to be extended to the home situation of the patient. Family members have to be instructed in how to avoid reinforcing inappropriate responses and in precise ways of rewarding more constructive behaviors incompatible with compulsive tendencies. Lastly, it must be pointed out that flooding differs from the technique of implosion. The success achieved with flooding has been accomplished without the inclusion of the psychodynamic component which Stampfl and Levis (1967) have argued is a vital part of "implosion therapy," and this reaffirms our conclusions, stated earlier, that integrating psychodynamic and behavioral techniques is not only logically inadmissible, but without any scientifically acceptable evidence.

## Behavior Rehearsal

Lazarus (1966) introduced the term "behavior rehearsal" into the literature and described it as "a specific procedure which aims to replace deficient or inadequate social or interpersonal responses by efficient and effective behavior patterns. The patient achieves this by practicing the desired forms of behavior under the direction and supervision of the therapist" (p. 209). Role-playing and role-reversal procedures are important components of behavior rehearsal. The therapist assumes the role of significant people in the client's life, and progressive series of important encounters are enacted. Feedback from videotapes or tape recordings is often useful in monitoring the client's mode of expression, verbal content, inflection, tone of voice, resonance, and for removing needless apologies, hesitations or querulous overtones. Nonverbal behavior, such as posture, facial expression, gait, and eye contact is also shaped. Behavior rehearsal, unlike other forms of role-playing such as "psychodrama," (Moreno, 1946) focuses primarily on modifying current maladaptive behavior patterns rather than "working through" symbolic conflicts.

Perhaps the most frequent application of behavior rehearsal is within the context of assertion training, i.e., for overcoming situations where clients complain that they are at a loss for words, exploited by others, timid and inhibited, or unable to express love, affection and other positive feelings. Clinical reports documenting the value of behavior rehearsal abound, but research studies are only beginning to appear in the literature. McFall and Marston (1970) and McFall and Lillesand (1971) have demonstrated that even a rudimentary form of behavior rehearsal is significantly more effective than a placebo in eliminating unassertive behavior.

## Aversion Therapy

Historically, aversive conditioning methods have been a major part of the total behavioral management of various problems, including alcoholism and drug addiction, cigarette smoking, obesity, and maladaptive sexual deviation. In an exemplary application of aversion therapy to the treatment of sexual deviations Marks and Gelder (1967) shocked transvestites and fetishists contingent on their imagined performance of deviant behaviors, after which the patients were similarly shocked for engaging in these activities in reality. Multidimensional response measurement of sexual arousal within the context of a multiple baseline design showed that deviant sexual arousal was extinguished only after a response had been specifically punished. The deviant behavior, which was of long-standing origin, was completely suppressed at the end of treatment, without any interference with normal heterosexual imagery and behavior. A two-year follow-up of an expanded sample of 24 sexual deviates indicated that this form of aversion therapy was very successful in modifying the inappropriate behavior of transvestites, fetishists, and sadomasochists. Transsexuals, however, showed little or no response to treatment. (Marks, Gelder, and Bancroft, 1970). Evans (1967) has described the successful treatment of exhibitionists along similar lines.

The differential response to aversion therapy by transvestites and transsexuals may be attributed to the fact that aversion therapy appears to be helpful mainly in those cases in which the client has available alternative sources of sexual gratification. The transsexual's problem is one of overall gender-role reversal rather than specific maladaptive sexual desires (cf. Pauly, 1969), such that aversive conditioning alone is, at best, incomplete treatment. Barlow, Reynolds, and Agras (1973) have recently described the first successful attempt to change gender identity in a 17-year-old male transsexual using a multifaceted social learning treatment regimen. Following the initial failure of aversive conditioning to modify transsexual patterns of behavior, Barlow *et. al.* shaped up masculine behavior patterns and vocal characteristics, and developed heterosexual fantasies in a graduated sequential manner. At this point, they were able to change the client's transsexual patterns of arousal using aversive conditioning which had failed earlier. This innovative case report is an outstanding instance of how single-subject methodology can be used to demonstrate that the behavioral procedures employed were responsible for the alteration of behavior.

Homosexuality has been extensively treated by behavior therapy and is the only area of unconventional sexual behavior in which group outcome studies have been conducted. The preferred method of treatment has been Feldman and MacCulloch's (1971) anticipatory avoidance (AA) technique. Attractive male slides are presented followed by painful electric shock that can be avoided if the client responds within a given period of time to remove the male slide from view and substitute a female picture. Feldman and MacCulloch have claimed approximately 58% success in eliminating homosexual behavior at a one year follow-up, and have found this AA technique to be superior to time-limited psychotherapy. Franks and Wilson (1973) have pointed out that several methodological problems with their design preclude an unequivocal interpretation of these results. However, Birk, Huddleston, Miller and Cohler (1971) have demonstrated the efficacy of the AA technique in a well-controlled experiment in which homosexual patients received aversive conditioning treatment and showed significantly greater heterosexual responsiveness than control patients treated by a convincing attention-placebo procedure.

Methods based on aversive imagery, such as "covert sensitization," have also been experimentally demonstrated to decrease inappropriate sexual arousal in homosexuals and pedophiles (e.g., Callahan and Leitenberg, 1973). For instance, real or imaginal deviant sexual stimuli (e.g., "You're alone with a sexy-looking 10-year-old girl.") are repeatedly paired with symbolically induced feelings of intense disgust or revulsion (e.g., "Imagine vomiting all over yourself.") so as to decondition the arousal properties of the undesirable erotic scenes.

In a critical evaluation of behavioral treatment of homosexuality, Wilson and Davison (1974) have questioned the almost exclusive reliance on aversive conditioning methods. Homosexuality has been too narrowly conceptualized, and behavioral assessment has often been inadequate in identifying the complex factors controlling homosexual behavior. A broader social learning approach is advocated, emphasizing the reduction of heterosexual anxiety and the development of heterosexual responsiveness. Direct and specific techniques for increasing heterosexual arousal include orgasmic reconditioning, the use of classical conditioning in which sexual arousal to female stimuli is achieved by repeatedly pairing them with erotic slides of males, and instrumentally reinforcing penile erection to heterosexual fantasy and external stimuli (cf. Barlow, 1973; Wilson and Davison, 1974).

Of major importance with respect to the ethics of aversive control and behavior change has been the reconsideration of heterosexuality as always the desirable therapeutic objective in the treatment of the homosexual client. Unlike Freudian theory, behavior modification does not automatically regard deviations from conventional heterosexual behavior as "abnormal." Rather, homosexuality is assumed to be acquired, maintained, and modified by a variety of social reinforcements, and it is the client who makes the decision in selecting the goal of therapy (Bandura, 1969). Indeed, recent behavioral case reports have described how homosexual clients were helped to adjust more satisfactorily to a permanent homosexual identity. Fensterheim (1972) successfully treated impotent homosexual males with systematic desensitization and Kohlenberg (1974) used a modified Masters and Johnson approach in helping a homosexual pedophile to become attracted to other adult homosexuals. Behavior therapy need not necessarily impose society's values on unwilling homosexual participants (Davison and Wilson, 1973b). Moreover, Davison (1973) has raised the question as to whether any behavioral change can be imposed upon a reluctant client who would seem to have at his disposal a number of counter-control devices to nullify the intended effects of even the most powerful behavior modification techniques.

As in the case of sexual deviations, aversion therapy has been the preferred behavioral approach in treating alcoholics and drug addicts. Conventional classical aversive conditioning procedures utilizing electric shock have been found to be ineffective despite earlier claims to the contrary (Miller, Hersen, Eisler, and Hemphill, 1973; Wilson, Leaf and Nathan, 1975). Compelling theoretical considerations and strongly suggestive clinical reports indicate that aversive methods based on chemically-induced nausea might be more successful in suppressing excessive drinking in alcoholics (Wilson and Davison, 1969). In the treatment of habitual cigarette smokers, for example, Lichtenstein, Harris, Birchler, Wahl, and Schmahl (1973) have shown that an aversive conditioning procedure based upon nausea-inducing rapid smoking is significantly more effective than placebo therapy in achieving a long-term reduction in the rate of smoking. Another useful aversive self-management procedure is to have the client enter into a contingency contract which specifies penalties for violating mutually agreed upon behavioral limits. Boudin (1972), for example, treated a black woman who was addicted to amphetamines by having her arrange to have a check, that for her constituted a substantial sum of money, automatically sent to the Ku Klux Klan should she revert to any drug use.

While non-aversive forms of treatment are probably preferable, given equal efficacy, the very necessary role of appropriate, informed aversive control in behavior modification must be realized. Whenever it is important for a person *not* to make a specific response (e.g., *not* to engage in self-injurious behavior as seen in certain autistic children), it is possibly more effective to punish the occurrence of the behavior than to reward its absence. Therapists called upon to eliminate behavior such as head-banging, tongue-biting, eye-gouging, or chronic ruminative vomiting, will find that such behavior can usually be eliminated with a brief application of a strong aversive stimulus immediately after the person begins to perform the maladaptive behavior (Lang and Melamed, 1969; Risley, 1968). To augment the aversion therapy, it is also useful to withdraw any social reinforcement for the self-injurious behavior, and include deliberate positive reinforcement of responses that compete with self-destructive behaviors. The life-threatening nature of some of the foregoing problems calls for powerful interventions.

To conclude this section, we re-emphasize the point that the practitioner cannot view aversive control as necessary and sufficient for therapeutic change. Used with great caution, and with the client's freely given informed consent, it may, on occasion, be extremely useful as part of a broad-spectrum behavioral approach which has recently been shown to be effective with complex problems such as alcoholism and drug addiction — problems that hitherto have remained resistant to practically all forms of psychotherapeutic intervention (cf. Copeman, 1973; O'Brien, Raynes and Patch, 1972; Sobell and Sobell, 1973).

## Behavioral Self-Control

In contrast to the earlier stages of development of behavior therapy in which the sole emphasis was on the control of behavior by the external environment, recently the concern has turned to the role of *self-regulation* of behavior (Bandura, 1969). Behavioral conceptions of self-control range from the extreme operant position which maintains that self-control "really refers to certain forms of environmental control of behavior" (Rachlin, 1971), to more cognitive approaches in which self-regulatory mechanisms are said to mediate behavior by supplementing the effects of direct environmental control (Thoresen and Mahoney, 1974). Kanfer and Karoly (1972) have defined self-control as those processes by which an individual maintains or alters a pattern of behavior in the absence of immediate external supports; and they have identified three component parts. Self-monitoring refers to the systematic observation of one's own behavior, e.g., the number of calories consumed on a daily basis. The person then self-evaluates his behavior, that is, judges the adequacy of his performance in terms of some standard or comparison criterion, e.g., a caloric intake in excess of 1500 calories per day. Depending on whether the behavior matches the standard or not, the person then either applies self-reinforcement or self-punishment, covertly or in reality, e.g., watching a favorite T.V. show contingent on appropriate eating habits.

The way in which self-control is conceptualized in behavioral terms is less important to the practitioner than the application of specific self-control strategies to different problem disorders. The following are some examples of clinical self-control techniques. Self-instructional training is a procedure in which clients are explicitly trained to monitor irrational, self-defeating thoughts; realize how these thoughts or self-verbalizations are responsible for generating emotional turmoil; and learn constructive self-statements which are incompatible with anxiety (cf. Meichenbaum and Cameron, 1973). The assumption is that these covert processes obey the same psychological laws as do overt behaviors, and can be modified by the same techniques of modeling, reinforcement, and aversive consequences. Controlled studies have indicated that self-instructional training is as effective as systematic desensitization in reducing irrational anxieties, and that it can even be used to significantly improve the thought processes, attention span, and abstract behavior of schizophrenics. The similarity of Meichenbaum's and Cameron's self-instructional training methods to Ellis's (1962) system of rational-emotive therapy should be obvious. Ellis's ideas have for the most part existed outside the mainstream of behavior therapy until the more recent recognition of the important influence of mediating cognitive activities on behavior (Franks and Wilson, 1973; Lazarus, 1971).

Among the best known self-control methods for regulating problem behaviors have been the procedures originally described by Ferster, Nurnberger and Levitt (1962) for treating obesity, and which have since been extended to a variety of problems, including cigarette smoking, alcoholism, and improving study habits. In the typical weight reduction program, for instance, the client is initially taught to keep detailed observations of the behavior to be controlled, i.e., excessive eating. This is followed by the modification and control of the discriminatory stimuli which govern eating. The client is instructed to narrow the number of stimuli associated with the act of eating by having his food in one place, with distinctive markings (e.g., a purple tablecloth), and to eat only at a specific time. Eating while engaging in any other activity such as watching T.V. or reading is strictly discouraged. Procedures are then introduced to disrupt and control the actual act of eating. Number of mouthfuls of food have to be counted, eating utensils have to be placed on the table in-between bites, all food has to be chewed slowly and completely swallowed before the next bite, and so on. Finally, explicit sources of reinforcement are arranged to support behavior that delays or controls eating. These may be provided by supportive family members, or, even more practically, be self-administered. Several well-controlled studies attest to the efficacy of these self-control procedures in producing lasting weight loss (Stuart, 1967; Levitz and Stunkard, 1974; Mahoney, 1974; Roman-czyk, Tracey, Wilson and Thorpe, 1973).

Self-monitoring and self-evaluation strategies have been implicit in virtually all forms of behavior therapy, and are increasingly being investigated as important behavior change methods in and of themselves. The use of self-evaluation by disruptive children, for example, is discussed in the section on token reinforcement programs. In fact, most behavioral techniques are being viewed within the context of the self-management of behavior. Goldfried (1971) has characterized systematic desensitization as a self-control procedure, and Bandura (1969) has concluded that the aversion therapies such as covert sensitization are best con-strued as self-control methods in which the client cognitively recreates the aversive consequences in order to control undesirable behavior. Inappropriate feelings and behavior are not automatically deconditioned by the application of learning methods. The extension and refinement of the theoretical underpinnings and clinical implications of the self-regulation of behavior will undoubtedly constitute one of the most important and productive developments in behavior modification over the next few years.

## Overcoming Sexual Inadequacy

The direct use of sexual responses for eliminating anxiety-associated cues attached to sexual participation was described by Wolpe and Lazarus (1966). People suffering from sexual inadequacies (e.g., impotent men, or non-orgasmic women) often display a performance-oriented anticipatory anxiety — "Am I going to obtain an erection?" "Will I have an orgasm?" "Will he consider me good in bed?" "How will I compare to her previous lover?" Fundamentally, discharges of the autonomic nervous system determine the character and quality of sexual performance. Anticipatory anxiety elicits predominantly sympathetic autonomic discharges which inhibit sexual arousal and/or performance. The basic strategy for overcoming sexual anxiety is for the client to approach his/her partner only as far as pleasurable feelings predominate. It is emphasized that one must never explicitly or implicitly press beyond the point at which sexual arousal remains in the ascendant over anxiety. A gradual and progressive *in vivo* sexual retraining occurs. The cooperation of a helpful and willing partner is often essential. The therapist briefs the partner beforehand concerning his or her role in the re-educative and desensitization process.

In many cases it helps simply to remove the onus of an expected level of performance by stressing that there are several ways of achieving orgasmic satisfaction and sexual fulfillment without penile-vaginal stimulation. The client is then instructed in the relevant oral, manual and digital manipulations. These activities generally provide powerful sources of sexual arousal, but they also distract attention from the sufferer's own problem through focusing on pleasures bestowed on the other person.

The foregoing retraining sequence has been elaborated upon by Masters and Johnson (1970) whose intensive program of sexual re-education is well-known. O'Leary and Wilson (1975) have provided a detailed analysis of the Masters and Johnson program within the framework of social learning. In brief, of 790 individuals treated, only 18.9% had not been fully restored to effective sexual functioning at the end of the two-week therapy program. These improvements were maintained at a five-year follow-up evaluation, and represent a conservative estimate of success. Despite the highly select and selected nature of the population treated by Masters and Johnson, the evidential value of their findings is considerable, especially when it is remembered that over 50% of their patients had previously failed to derive any relief from psychotherapy, which has never been shown to be effective in overcoming sexual dysfunction. The convincing nature of Masters and Johnson's (1970) results is reinforced by Hartman and Fithian's (1972) report of comparable success using similar therapeutic procedures, and the clinical findings of Brady (1971), Lobitz and LoPiccolo (1972), and Wolpe and Lazarus (1966).

The formal Masters and Johnson program insists upon certain elements that many behavior therapists have found to be unnecessary (e.g., the need for both a male and female therapist to treat a husband and wife unit) and omits certain procedures that we have found to be essential in certain cases. Systematic desensitization is often necessary for overcoming nonsexual fears that nevertheless inhibit sexual performance, such as irrational fears of blood, of assault, of control, and some claustrophobic reactions.

Another important imagery technique is *orgasmic reconditioning.* In applying this technique to a woman with vaginismus, the following sequence would be recommended. The woman would be instructed to masturbate in the privacy of her home, and immediately prior to achieving orgasm, she would vividly imagine penile insertion into her vagina. The image seldom interferes with arousal or orgasmic intensity. Thereafter, the client repeatedly imagines the intromission scene earlier in the masturbatory sequence, until the image of penile insertion can initiate sexual arousal. Upon completing the procedure in imagery, the next step is to repeat the process in actual behavior. Wilson (1973) described the successful use of orgasmic reconditioning in treating a severe case of vaginismus which had previously failed to respond to both graded sexual responses and systematic desensitization.

Lobitz and LoPiccolo (1972) have described the use of several additional techniques within the context of a modified Masters and Johnson program. These techniques include agreements in which money deposits are refunded to the client on the basis of cooperation with the therapist's instructions, the use of role-playing to increase interpersonal skills while disinhibiting feelings of shame, and graduated masturbation exercises for women, particularly in case of primary orgasmic dysfunction.

In cases of premature ejaculation, the use of Semans' (1956) method of controlled partner-induced manual stimulation has proved effective. "This consists of controlled acts of manual stimulation of the penis by the wife which lead to a progressive increase in the amount of tactile stimulation needed to bring about ejaculation . . . When the husband feels a sensation which is, for him, premonitory to ejaculation, he informs his wife and removes her hand until the sensation disappears. Stimulation is begun again and interrupted by the husband when the premonitory sensation returns," (Wolpe and Lazarus, 1966, p. 106). Masters and Johnson (1970) recommend a "squeeze technique" in which the woman applies pressure to the penis before withdrawing contact. In some instances, a breakdown of sexual responsiveness is often one clear-cut manifestation of a larger interpersonal problem involving anger, resentment and hostility. Hence, as with all behavior disorders, the need for adequate, multimodal assessment cannot be overemphasized. While many of the behavioral retraining procedures have a mechanistic overtone, the actual implementation of these procedures is within a context of affection, tender consideration, emotional warmth and mutual caring.

## Group Methods

Lazarus (1961) described the use of group desensitization and compared it to more traditional group methods in treating phobic disorders. Paul and Shannon (1966) conducted a rather elaborate study on "chronically anxious clients" and demonstrated the therapeutic value of employing group desensitization plus group discussion with re-educative goals. Lazarus (1968, 1971) described an additional range of group behavioral techniques in groups (e.g., combined use of sexual responses and desensitization, as well as assertion training groups). More recently Lazarus (1975) has described the use of multimodal behavior therapy in groups.

In the past few years, the number of reports on behavioral group therapy has been increasing (e.g., Fensterheim, 1972; Franks and Wilson, 1973). A distinction needs to be made between behavior therapy in groups (where individuals receive therapy in a group, such as relaxing and picturing individual scenes for desensitization purposes) and group behavior therapy (in which the group process is employed to produce behavioral change, such as the use of social rewards for nondeviant responses). Kass, Silvers and Abroms (1972) described behavior therapy *through* the explicit use of a group by employing broad-spectrum group behavior therapy with a hysterical patient population. Lazarus emphasized that "the reason for practicing behavior therapy in groups is not merely that it provides a saving in therapists' time and effort, but because in many instances, learning, relearning and unlearning seem to be facilitated greatly in group settings " (Lazarus, 1968, p. 150). Behavioral groups facilitate the process of discrimination training by enabling clients to sample a range of experiences that highlight similarities and differences between people. Decrements in subjective feelings of isolation often seem to follow group participation. And a helpful "cooperative-competitive" atmosphere is fostered which enables the therapist to reach hitherto "unmotivated" group members.

There are several important differences between behavioral groups and traditional psychotherapy groups, T-groups, encounter groups and the various sensitivity-training procedures that abound. In the first place, the main objective of behavioral groups is to modify deviant and aberrant behaviors on a long-term basis. Whereas weekend marathon encounters often lead to short-lived joie de vivre, the purpose of group behavior therapy is to promote lifelong adaptive habits, to enhance social and interpersonal skills, and to extinguish maladaptive responses, especially those that interfere with congenial and assertive person-to-person interactions.

In behavioral groups, relatively little time is spent on "process material" within the group. When friction between group members is an impediment to effective behavior change, process variables will be examined and more facilitative responses will be modelled (Lazarus, 1973a). But in general, there is little evidence that group interactions inevitably capture the essence of each member's style of communication, or that the group becomes a microcosm of each client's significant personal interactions. Groups may frequently elicit situation specific behaviors that are by no means prototypical of the individual's other intra- and interpersonal responses (cf. Mischel, 1968).

The main focus in behavioral groups is upon the clients' meaningful and significant encounters outside of the group. Each member brings to the group his or her own problems of adjustment outside of the group. The group medium then functions as a platform and springboard for training, rehearsing and equipping the participants to cope with life's problems *in vivo*. Special attention is taken to ensure that gains achieved within the group will transfer and generalize outside the protective confines of the group meetings. Thus, specific homework assignments figure prominently at the end of each behavioral group meeting.

## THE OPERANT APPROACH IN BEHAVIOR MODIFICATION

It is becoming increasingly arbitrary to discriminate between behavioral methods as being based either on classical or operant conditioning approaches. However, there is a body of procedures which are customarily identified as operant conditioning approaches, and which are distinguished by certain common features of operant methodology. These characteristics have been summarized by Krasner (1971, p. 613) as "the intensive study of individual subjects, the control of the experimental environment, the control of individual behavior, the emphasis on objective observation and recording of behavior, the importance of consequences of behavior, the empirical nature of the approach, and the intense involvement of most of its proponents." Of special importance has been the single-case methodology of the operant approach. The ingenious use of reversal (ABA), multiple baseline, and multiple-schedule designs have added immeasurably to our knowledge of the controlling influences on different forms of behavioral disorders (cf. Leitenberg, 1973).

Since the early laboratory studies of Skinner on psychotic behavior, operant procedures have been progressively applied to a diverse array of psychiatric disorders. Indeed, Ullmann and Krasner (1969) have written an influential textbook on abnormal psychology which conceptualizes the development, maintenance, and modification of all forms of abnormal behavior primarily in operant conditioning terms. Any synopsis of the massive literature explosion in this field is necessarily selective, and we have chosen to focus on current developments in token economy programs, biofeedback procedures, and treatment approaches to children's disorders as illustrative of the general developments within this burgeoning area of behavior modification.

## Token Economy Programs

Perhaps the most impressive application of operant conditioning principles has been the behavior modification of entire groups of individuals through the use of token economy programs. Since the pioneering introduction of a token economy program on a psychiatric hospital back ward for chronic psychotic patients by Ayllon and Michael (1959) and Ayllon and Azrin (1965), token reinforcement programs have multiplied to the point where Atthowe (1973) has recently concluded that "most treatment, rehabilitative, correctional and educational settings use some form of contingent contracting." Token programs have been instituted with an extraordinarily wide range of different behaviors in diverse populations, including psychiatric inpatients and outpatients, retarded and autistic children, delinquent youths, normal and disturbed children in classroom settings and even low-income families in a community-improvement program (cf. Kazdin and Bootzin, 1972; Rickard, 1971). The successful implementation of these group-oriented reinforcement contingency systems has far-reaching implications not only for the practice of behavior therapy, but also as Krasner and Krasner (1973) point out, for economic planning and the design of whole social systems.

Although the procedures and goals of the many procedures subsumed under the rubric of token economy programs may vary, they all share the following common defining characteristics. First, the specific behaviors which are to be modified or developed have to be identified and operationally defined. Typical target behaviors would include self-hate behaviors in psychotic patients or improved academic performance in children. Secondly, the available reinforcers in the environment have to be determined. Reinforcers are the "good things in life" which people are willing to work for. In the case of the hospital patient these might range from such fundamental privileges as watching T.V., a private room, or cigarettes, to more idiosyncratic activities such as feeding kittens or receiving mail order catalogue items. For the child in the classroom a reinforcer might be candy, toys, or extra recess time. Decisions about which behaviors to reinforce, and what reinforcers to employ often raise important questions concerning social values and legal constraints which are discussed below. Thirdly, there are the tokens themselves. The token is a compound discriminative and secondary reinforcer which stands for the back-up reinforcers. The advantages of using tokens as reinforcers are that they bridge the gap between the target behavior and the back-up reinforcers, they permit the reinforcement of any response at any time, and they provide the same reward for patients who have different preferences in back-up reinforcers. The token itself might be a tangible item such as a poker chip or a plastic card, or else it might be a checkmark on a piece of paper. Finally, there are the exchange rules of the program, that is, how tokens may be earned and the cost of the back-up reinforcers. These exchange rules involve complex relationships which have been analyzed in terms of, and compared to, the economic principles governing real-life society outside of the immediate token economy environment (Winkler, 1972). Although token economy procedures have often been described in oversimplified reinforcement terms, Krasner (1971) has stressed that they incorporate many social influence processes including operant and classical conditioning, social reinforcement, modeling, and expectancy of success. Within this general social influence context the specific token reinforcement contingencies play the decisive role in regulating behavior change.

Contrary to the frequently expressed criticism that token programs are simplistic, impersonal, and mechanistic, their successful implementation demands a wide range of clinical skills, including flexibility, creativity, perseverance, and "canny know-how" on the part of the behavior therapist. Perhaps the most formidable task involves staff training. The operation of the token program, and indeed all operant-based behavior modification procedures, can best be understood in terms of Tharp and Wetzel's (1969) triadic model of treatment intervention. According to this model, the therapist functions as a *consultant* who possesses the necessary knowledge of how to formulate and plan behavior change programs. These plans are then implemented by the *mediators,* those people who have the closest contact with the *target* — anyone who has a problem to be modified. Mediators may be parents, teachers, peers, nurses, attendants, or employers — in fact, anyone who is in the position to control the important reinforcement contingencies in the target's environment.

Mediators have to be taught to systematically observe and reward behavior. Nurses and teachers, for example, have to be assured that this will facilitate their own job of managing patients or children rather than overburden them with additional responsibility. They have to feel that they are part of a worthwhile program and their suggestions about how the program might be improved or revised should be encouraged. It is imperative that the personnel who dispense the reinforcers must themselves be rewarded for appropriate behavior. Controlled studies have shown that psychiatric aides and schoolteachers typically show low rates of positive reinforcement for appropriate patient or student behavior. Merely instructing aides about how to implement behavior modification procedures has scant effect on the targets. However, providing aides with regular feedback about the improvement of specific patients and awarding them monetary bonuses contingent upon changes in the patients' behavior, produces significantly more appropriate behavior on the part of the aides (Pomerleau, Bobrove and Smith, 1973). Similarly, rewarding increases in aide-dispensed reinforcement directly results in greater behavioral improvement in patients (Katz, Johnson and Gelfand, 1972).

## Outcome and Evaluation

In a major review of operant conditioning treatment approaches in institutional settings, Davison (1969) concluded that while they showed promise, they had not yet been proven to be effective in changing the hospitalized patient to the point where he could function "normally" again in society. Based as they are on the application of social learning principles within an interpersonal context, the efficacy of behavioral treatment techniques cannot be evaluated in terms of medically-based concepts of "cure" and "spontaneous remission." Whereas the latter concepts are appropriate in describing the treatment of physical diseases, they are conceptually irrelevant to the assessment of the modification of abnormal behavior which is extensively controlled by social variables. As Bandura (1969) points out, it is important to distinguish between the induction of therapeutic change in a specific set of problem behaviors, the generalization of these changes to situations in the real world outside of the institution, and the long-term maintenance of improvement. The induction, generalization, and maintenance of therapeutic behavior change might be controlled by different factors, and might require different modification strategies. For example, the fact that token economy programs produce changes within the institutional setting where they are administered but which do not transfer to nontherapeutic situations is not necessarily a reflection of the inadequacy of token economies. The outcome of reinforcement methods depends both on the induction of treatment changes *and* on the nature of the post-treatment environment. If the environment is unchanged from the conditions which originally generated the patient's problems, then there is a very high probability that the problem behaviors will reappear. Deliberate steps have to be taken to ensure the generalization of therapeutic changes to the natural environment and to arrange for appropriate maintenance conditions.

The majority of token economy programs which have been reported were concerned primarily with inducing behavior change within institutional settings. Initially the emphasis was simply on establishing that the group application of operant conditioning principles could produce behavior change. This demonstration was followed by studies showing that there is a causal relationship between the introduction of specific operant procedures and behavior change.

Ayllon and Azrin (1965) provided an excellent example of a token economy program which employed the within-subject ABAB or reversal design in demonstrating that the behaviors of chronic back ward schizophrenics could be systematically modified using operant conditioning principles. In this ABAB design, the target behavior is alternately reinforced, not reinforced, and then reinforced again in consecutive phases of the study. The target behaviors chosen by Ayllon and Azrin were primarily work assignments both on and off the ward, and self-care behaviors. The back-up reinforcers were selected on the basis of the Premack principle, which states that any high probability behavior can be used to strengthen any other behavior occurring at a lower probability. The importance of this principle is that it greatly extends the range of otherwise restricted reinforcers which can be used with chronic psychiatric patients who display little interest in their immediate environment. Ayllon and Azrin (1965) convincingly showed that increases in the target behaviors were a function of the response-reinforcement contingencies. Behavior increased only when contingently rewarded, and decreased markedly when the tokens were either withdrawn completely or distributed to the patients on a noncontingent basis. Withdrawing all tokens and making back-up reinforcers freely available to patients irrespective of how they behaved resulted in their job performance deteriorating to less than one-fourth of its rate when contingently rewarded with tokens. Atthowe and Krasner (1968) similarly documented that self-care behaviors and social responsiveness toward other people could be increased with the framework of a token economy which encompassed virtually every aspect of ward and hospital life.

Other studies have shown that token economy programs produce significantly greater change than control groups receiving alternative forms of treatment. Fairweather (1964) found that rewarding small groups of hospitalized patients for improvements in problem-solving and self-management abilities resulted in significantly greater social interaction, decreased pathological behavior, and enhanced communication than a control group which received the conventional hospital therapeutic program. Maley, Feldman and Ruskin (1973) showed that chronic psychotic patients in a token economy were better oriented, more cooperative and communicative, displayed greater social interaction, and exhibited less psychotic behavior than closely matched subjects receiving a conventional treatment program.

The aim of these studies — to improve behavior within the hospital — was clearly accomplished. These changes are far from trivial. Operant procedures can successfully reverse the debilitating effects of institutionalization which is often iatrogenic in nature (Goffman, 1961; Rosenhan, 1973; Ullmann and Krasner, 1969). Token economies which result in greater self-management and social involvement mean a happier, more productive, and more dignified life for patients — even if they remain hospitalized. The fact that the morale of the the nurses and attendants on a successful token economy are greatly improved (cf. Atthowe and Krasner, 1968) has obvious indirect benefits for the patients who are then regarded as fellow human beings capable of improvement, rather than impersonal, faceless figures who are irreversibly "sick" and who have only to be kept clean and quiet (Rosenhan, 1973). Moreover, the very behaviors which have been shown to be so successfully modified by these token economy programs have often prolonged the psychotic patient's length of hospitalization, and the statistics indicate that the longer a patient remains in a psychiatric hospital the less likelihood there is of ever returning him to the community (Fairweather, Simon, Gebhard, Weingarten, Holland, Sanders, Stone and Reahl, 1960; Ullmann, 1967).

Given the limited yet important aims of these studies it is not surprising that they have failed to accomplish the goal for which they were not designed, namely, returning patients to the community on a long term basis. Although the Atthowe and Krasner (1968) program led to a doubling of the rate of discharge of patients, 11 of the 24 released patients returned to the hospital within nine months. Similarly, the recidivism rates for patients discharged from Fairweather's (1964) program were about equal irrespective of the type of therapy they received. Fifty-five percent of all patients who had been hospitalized longer than two years had relapsed at a six-month follow-up.

A similar pattern of results has been duplicated with token economy programs in other settings such as the classroom and in a community-based center for pre-delinquent boys (O'Leary and O'Leary, 1972; Phillips, Phillips, Fixsen and Wolf, 1971). While token reinforcement procedures have resulted in substantial increase in academic performance and appropriate social behavior with normal and emotionally disturbed children and with delinquents, demonstrations of the long-range efficacy of these methods are lacking. Almost inevitably it has been found that treatment gains in social behaviors deteriorate once the reinforcement procedures are withdrawn. Nor have behavior modifiers been particularly successful in demonstrating generalization of the beneficial effects of token procedures to periods during which no token and back-up reinforcers are available to the children.

### Extending the Token Economy into the Natural Environment

Even the most comprehensive token economy programs, such as Fairweather's (1964) which taught patients the socially relevant skills of decision-making and problem-solving, have failed to reverse the discouragingly high recidivism rate. This indicates that rehabilitation procedures have to be extended from the hospital setting to the natural environment to which the ex-patient returns so as to ensure the generalization and maintenance of improvement. Indeed, Anthony, Buell, Sharratt, and Althoff (1972) have suggested that the adjustment of the ex-patient after being discharged is a function of the post-hospital environment and is unrelated to the type of treatment he received irrespective of whether it was psychotherapy or drug treatment.

Despite Baer's, Wolf's, and Risley's (1968) injunction that "generalization should be programmed, rather than expected or lamented," it is clear that behavior modifiers have as yet paid insufficient attention to the problems of generalizing behavioral improvement from the institutional setting to the community (cf. Atthowe, 1973). However, some recent studies have demonstrated how this formidable task might be accomplished. In an extension of his previous treatment program, Fairweather transferred mental hospital patients to a semi-autonomous lodge located within the community as soon as they were functioning adequately on the hospital ward (Fairweather, Sanders, Maynard, and Cressler, 1969). Under professional supervision, the patients took responsibility for operating the lodge, organizing employment, and earning money by running a janitorial service which they themselves managed. All income was distributed among the lodge members according to each person's contribution to the lodge's functioning. Periodically, some patients were readmitted to the hospital for brief periods of booster treatment sessions. The lodge became fully autonomous after 33 months and a follow-up evaluation was made of the patients' status 40 months after their discharge from hospital. Compared to a control group which received the traditional assistance and outpatient therapy available to most hospital patients upon their discharge, patients who lived and worked together in the community fared significantly better in resuming a meaningful role in society. The median percent of time lodge members had spent in the community was 75% compared to 15% for the control group, while the figures for time of employment were 40% and only 1%, respectively.

In a similar rehabilitation program which focused on the *gradual* reintroduction of the ex-hospital patient into the community, Atthowe and McDonough (1969) moved patients from a token economy on the ward, through a self-managed, self-help ward, to rented houses in the community. These patients worked in special projects which the program coordinated, such as operating gas stations and renovating houses. Some patients left the shelter of the program completely and obtained similar jobs in the community. A follow-up period of up to one year showed a recidivism rate of about 12% and an employment record of 100%. The impressive magnitude of these findings can be gauged from the fact that recidivism rates among most institutional populations within the first year range from 65 to 80%.

Achievement Place in Kansas is a community-based, family style behavior modification center for pre-delinquent children. The program operates on the basis of an elaborete set of token reinforcement procedures in which the youths progress from a system of immediate, concrete rewards to more delayed, natural reinforcers as they acquire more desirable behavior patterns. While at the center, the youth moves from earning privileges on a daily point system, to a weekly point system, and then to a merit system in which all privileges are free and prosocial behavior maintained solely by praise and approval. Following four weeks of success on the merit system, the youth enters the homeward bound system in which he is returned to his home. The parents are trained in behavior management skills, and meetings between the parents and Achievement Place staff are gradually diminished until terminated completely after six months to one year unless problems recur.

Fixen, Phillips and Wolf (1973) have reported follow-up findings on 16 boys discharged from Achievement Place. Compared to data from 15 boys committed to a state institution in Kansas, and to 13 boys who had been placed on formal probation, the boys who were a product of the Achievement Place system showed strikingly lower recidivism rates, significantly greater school attendance, and far fewer offenses than the others. Moreover, the annual operating cost of Achievement Place is considerably less (more than 50%) than the costs of an institution or state school.

Both the Fairweather *et al.* (1969) and the Atthowe and McDonough (1969) programs involved restructuring the post-hospital environment in which the patient lived. Reinforcement contingencies were arranged to continue to support the behavioral improvement which was initiated in the hospital. Another strategy for producing generalization and maintenance of behavior is to train individuals to regulate their own behavior.

Drabman, Spitalnik, and O'Leary (1973) have shown how the effects of a token reinforcement program with disruptive children in the classroom can be generalized to situations and times when no tokens or back-up reinforcers are available, by teaching self-control to the children. Pupils were taught that they could earn tokens for matching their teacher's evaluation of their academic performance and social behavior. The checking of their self-evaluations was *gradually* eliminated until there was no reinforcement consequence or inaccurate self-evaluations. The teacher did, however, continue to praise the boys for matching the teacher's evaluation of their behavior. In other words, although the children could misbehave and still be rewarded, they maintained low levels of disruptive behavior and high rates of academic output. Drabman *et al.* (1973) suggest that the children's self-evaluations became both conditioned reinforcers and cues which served as mediational statements which guided appropriate classroom behavior. Furthermore, this improvement transferred to other classroom periods during which the token economy was not in effect. Walker and Buckley (1972) demonstrated the generalization and maintenance of the treatment effects of a token economy classroom across time and situations by reprogramming the problem child's peer group to support improved academic and social functioning.

To summarize this discussion, O'Leary and Drabman (1971) have outlined ten procedures which have been shown to increase the probability of promoting generalization and maintenance. These include the following: Provide a good academic program to remedy deficient academic repertoires; give the child the expectation that he is capable of doing well; involve the children in the specification of contingencies; teach the children to evaluate their own behavior; involve the parents; and gradually introduce more and more natural reinforcers that exist within the classroom setting, such as privileges.

## Social, Ethical and Legal Considerations

In his role of consultant, planning behavior change programs on a group basis, reorganizing institutional practices, and extending broadly conceived reinforcement principles into the community setting, the behavior modifier is acting as the architect of large-scale social change. This entails a tremendous responsibility. If the environment is to be restructured to maximize the availability of positive reinforcement for appropriate behavior, then the behavior modifier "must be knowledgeable of and influence the power and economic structures of the environment in which he operates . . . he must deal with those individuals in power who have the resources to make changes in the social system. He must become aware of the overt and covert leaders and the reinforcers and contingencies that hold a community together . . ." (Atthowe, 1973, p. 37). An example of this expanded social influence role of the behavior modifier is seen in the Atthowe and McDonough (1969) rehabilitation program which required the joint planning and mutual cooperation of trade unions, the local housing authority, and the residential community. In like fashion, at Achievement Place, the community-based behavior modification center for pre-delinquent boys, leaders of the local community have been actively involved in the determination of the program's goals since the boys' behavior directly affects the community (Fixen et al., 1973).

As we have already commented, specifying the target behaviors in a token reinforcement program represents a value judgment about what behaviors are desirable. Winett and Winkler (1972) echoed the sentiments of many critics by alleging that behavior modifiers have devoted themselves to maintaining a system of education in the classroom which values order, silence, and obedience above creativity and individual academic growth. O'Leary (1972) has shown this analysis to be misleading, but underscores the importance of considering the nature of the behaviors therapists are asked to modify. Behavior modification is a system of principles and techniques about how to change behavior; it does not assert which behaviors should be changed by whom, or when. O'Leary (1972), for example, points out that behavior modification procedures are quite compatible with either the open classroom concept or the more traditional structured learning arrangements.

While the behavioral literature is replete with numerous outstanding examples of the enormously beneficial and humanitarian application of token reinforcement procedures, the abuse to which "behavior modification" is open is regrettably illustrated by a paper by an American psychiatrist, Cotter (1967), entitled "Operant Conditioning in a Vietnamese Mental Hospital." Krasner (1971) has commendably denounced Cotter's characterization of his cruel and oppressive methods as having little to do with behavior modification. We especially repudiate the reporting of this deplorable paper in a collection of behavior modification studies by Ulrich, Stachnik, and Mabry (1970).

Recently enacted and additional pending legislation threaten to disallow both some of the target behaviors and the types of reinforcement which have often been used in token economy programs with hospitalized patients (cf. Wexler, 1973). According to one such legal decision, working on institutional jobs can no longer be required by making rewards contingent on satisfactory work performance (e.g., Ayllon and Azrin, 1968). Furthermore, any work performed by patients within an institution must be "rewarded" by minimum wage levels, which would make such programs prohibitively costly.    Of even greater significance to behavior modification procedures has been the trend in legal thinking toward guaranteeing the absolute rights of mental hospital patients. These rights would include personal privileges, privacy, access to T.V., cigarettes, and ground privileges, among others, which are routinely used as contingent reinforcers in many operant token reinforcement programs.

Increasing societal concern for the rights of mental hospital patients is not inconsistent with the informed application of behavior modification (Goldiamond, 1974).    Behavior modifiers themselves have been moving away from a reliance on basic reinforcers such as food and personal privacy toward more diversified and idiosyncratic reinforcers.    Resorting to drastic forms of back-up reinforcers is not always necessary.    Fairweather et al. (1969) achieved their impressive results without depriving patients of any basic rights. The reinforcers they used were money incentives, passes to leave the hospital, and social reinforcement developed in small group settings.    Moreover, all patients received a minimum monetary allowance and one pass per week regardless of whether or not they displayed behavioral improvement.

Regrettably, abuses of behavior modification in institutions like mental hospitals and prisons have been reported.    As with any other body of knowledge, behavior modification can be misused, and it is imperative that safeguards for the protection of all individuals' dignity and civil rights be developed.    An important step in this direction has been taken by the American Psychological Association in constituting a special Commission on Behavior Modification. Representing diverse professional and lay interests, its function is to recommend guidelines for the ethical and legal application of behavioral techniques.

### Generalization and Maintenance of Behavior Change

The preceding sections have emphasized the necessity for designing specific procedures to program generalization and maintenance of behavior change produced by token economy programs, and discussed several practical steps which can be taken to achieve this objective.    The same considerations apply to all behavioral treatment methods, and O'Leary and Wilson (1975) have pointed out how the successful long-term treatment of different behavioral disorders by behavior therapy has involved definite attempts at ensuring maintenance of therapeutic progress.

One of the erstwhile prescriptions for producing persistence of behavior change after the formal treatment program has been terminated has been to use intermittent schedules of reinforcement and a sufficient number of conditioning trials to ensure overlearning (cf. Eysenck and Rachman, 1965). However, as both Bandura (1969) and Lazarus (1971) have pointed out, the solution to the question of maintenance of treatment effects is more a function of the scope of the therapy program rather than the technical niceties of the conditioning paradigm employed.    Behavioral disorders are usually controlled by several factors.    To the degree to which a behavioral treatment program is not multifaceted and does not focus on all the relevant maintaining variables its chances of effecting lasting relief are dubious.    Mahoney (1974) similarly observes that a broad-spectrum behavioral approach can enhance trans-situational as well as trans-behavioral generalization by equipping the client with broad problem-solving abilities which transcend a narrow therapeutic focus.

Several post-therapy strategies have been shown to be effective in reducing the problem of relapse.   Lemere and Voegtlin (1950) found that alcoholics who were participants in post-therapy booster sessions of aversive conditioning to alcohol showed strikingly few reversions to drinking compared to the typically high relapse rate associated with the treatment of alcoholism.   Booster treatment sessions within the year following therapy have similarly facilitated lasting improvement in sexual adequacy (e.g., Masters and Johnson, 1970), psychotic patients (e.g., Fairweather et al., 1969), and enuresis (e.g., Baker, 1969). Other successful outcome studies of behavior therapy have employed explicit maintenance strategies for providing social support and reinforcement for the continuation of treatment gains and newly acquired self-control skills.   The efficacy of these maintenance methods is reflected in the impressive superiority of behavioral treatment programs over traditional therapy procedures in the long-term reduction of alcoholism at six months and two years respectively (Hunt and Azrin, 1973; Sobell and Sobell, 1973); in Stuart's (1967) unprecedented success in maintaining clinically significant weight loss in obese patients over a one-year period; and in the rare accomplishment of the persistence of a greatly decreased rate of cigarette-smoking in habitual smokers at a six-month follow-up evaluation (Chapman, Smith and Layden, 1971; Lichtenstein, Harris, Birchler, Wahl and Schmal, 1973).   Maintenance procedures will often necessarily require training family members or other important figures in the client's natural environment in the skills of reinforcing appropriate behavior and eliminating previous modes of social interaction which might have contributed significantly to the development of the original problem.   Illustrative examples include the training of the parents and teachers of problem children (Patterson, 1971) and the families of obsessive-compulsive patients (Hodgson, Rachman, and Marks, 1972).

Biofeedback

One of the most interesting recent developments in behavior modification has been biofeedback — the application of operant principles to a variety of different physical and psychophysiological disorders. Until a few years ago it was believed that the autonomic nervous system could only be influenced by classical conditioning procedures, and that operant conditioning was only effective in modifying skeletal responses. The dramatic demonstration that autonomic functioning could be brought under operant control has not only provided a model in terms of which the diversity and persistence of visceral functioning can be explained, but also suggests that psychosomatic problems might be eliminated directly by the therapeutic use of operant-feedback procedures.

The paradigmatic experiment which demonstrates the instrumental regulation of visceral responses in rats is one in which spontaneous fluctuations in a response such as heart rate, are accurately measured and followed by reinforcing consequences if they are in the appropriate direction. The desired response is shaped by gradually requiring increasingly greater changes in heart rate in order to be reinforced. The rat is curarized in these experiments and rewarded by means of direct electrical stimulation of rewarding centers in the brain. Consequently, the changes in heart rate which are obtained cannot be attributed to the indirect effects of skeletal activity or altered patterns of respiration. Using these procedures rats have been trained to either increase or decrease their heart rate while other autonomic responses, e.g., intestinal contractions, remain unaltered. Conversely, intestinal contractions can be modified by operant-feedback procedures without producing any change in heart rate. The specificity of this control shows that it is the operant conditioning procedure which causes the change and not any other uncontrolled factor such as general autonomic arousal.

Similar findings have been obtained with human subjects, although the magnitude of the changes have generally been smaller and it has been more difficult to rule out alternative explanations of the results in terms of indirect mediating influences caused by changes in respiration and other skeletal responses. Nonetheless, volunteer subjects have been trained to produce changes in an impressive range of physiological functions including heart rate speeding, slowing, and stabilization; electrodermal activity; systolic and diastolic blood pressure; skin temperature; peripheral vasomotor responses; EEG rhythms; and penile erections (cf. Barber, DiCara, Kamiya, Miller, Shapiro, and Stoyva, 1971; Stoyva, Barber, DiCara, Kamiya, Miller and Shapiro, 1972). The therapeutic promise of biofeedback procedures can be illustrated by reference to their application in the treatment of different cardiovascular disorders. Benson, Shapiro, Tursky and Schwartz (1971) produced clinically significant decreases in blood pressure in five of seven hypertensive patients after extensive biofeedback treatment. Briefly, their procedure entailed giving the patients both visual and auditory feedback contingent upon an appropriate response, i.e., a small blood pressure change in the direction away from a specified criterion blood pressure value on each heartbeat. In addition patients were reinforced on a fixed-ratio schedule with interesting slides or indications of small financial rewards as their blood pressure began to decrease. Unfortunately, there is no evidence of the stability of these changes when the feedback was withdrawn; nor do we know the degree to which these changes transferred to situations outside the laboratory. Furthermore, it is not possible to determine whether the biofeedback or the additional rewards, or both, were responsible for the modification of blood pressure.

Migraine is a psychosomatic disorder which is mediated through the autonomic nervous system and which has been treated with biofeedback. Following a serendipitous finding in a research subject whose migraine disappeared spontaneously after a rise in temperature of 10 degrees Fahrenheit in her hands, Sargent, Green and Walters (1972) systematically trained migraine sufferers to increase their hand temperature, which is directly related to increased peripheral blood flow. Specifically, patients were given feedback of their skin temperatures so that they increased their finger heat relative to that of their forehead. The patients also received autogenic training, a form of relaxation produced by concentrating on phrases such as "I feel quite relaxed." Initially weekly or biweekly sessions were given until the patients could generate and recognize warmth in their hands. Thereafter training sessions were reduced to a monthly basis. Measures of the efficacy of this procedure consisted of a global clinical rating of the patients' improvement and independent assessments of patients' daily ratings of the severity of headaches and the potency of analgesic drugs required to relieve headache pain. Pre- and post-treatment data are available for 32 patients who were followed-up for periods ranging from 1 to 22 months. Ninety percent were judged to be improved on the basis of clinical interviews with an internist, as compared to an average independent assessment of the patients' daily ratings of 74% improvement. This discrepancy is not surprising, since global clinical and specific behavioral ratings seldom correlate very highly (Bandura, 1969).

Shapiro and Schwartz (1972) report the treatment of two patients with Reynaud's disease by providing feedback for increased blood volume in the toe and hand, respectively. The first patient responded favorably with increases in blood flow and reports of less pain and more warmth in his toes and feet. Fifteen months later he complained that his cold feet had returned and requested further treatment. The second patient appeared to derive no benefits at all.

Biofeedback has received a phenomenal amount of publicity, and its application to humans has been widely heralded as a kind of "autonomic behavior therapy," and a means of finally achieving conscious control over involuntary bodily functions. Regrettably, the exaggerated publicity has far exceeded its currently demonstrable scientific value (Miller, 1973). O'Leary and Wilson (1975) have issued several caveats in evaluating the therapeutic potential of biofeedback procedures. Most of the research with humans has involved "normal" volunteer subjects, and with few exceptions the results have been statistically significant but too small to have much substantive or clinical significance (Blanchard and Young, 1973). And where preliminary applications have been made to the clinical population, the results, while encouraging, have in no sense established the therapeutic efficacy of operant-feedback procedures. It has not been adequately demonstrated that the results obtained in the highly artificial laboratory situation will generalize to the natural environment. Systematic studies controlling for subject expectancies and placebo effects have yet to be carried out. An alternative explanation of the results obtained with biofeedback in terms of placebo effects is very plausible in view of the enormous public interest in this area. Finally, comparative outcome studies are necessary to show that alternative treatment methods, which might require less in the way of expensive and highly sophisticated physiological apparatus, are not equally effective. For example, Blanchard and Young (1973) have suggested that cardiac functioning may be as effectively controlled by muscle relaxation training as by biofeedback.

The most successful example of the therapeutic potential of operant-feedback methods involves the modification of cardiac arrhythmias. Weiss and Engel (1971) treated eight patients with irregular heartbeats, or premature ventricular contractions (PVCs), which increase the probability of other heart problems and sudden death. Hospitalized patients were given feedback about beat-by-beat changes in heart rate. A visual signal indicated when their heart was responding according to the particular training schedule being used — speeding or slowing heart rate, alternating speeding and slowing, and maintaining heart rate within a certain range. The latter condition provided the patients with feedback about the occurrence of PVCs.

All eight patients achieved some control over their heart rate, even after external feedback had been gradually *faded out,* indicating that true self-control had been acquired. Four of the patients showed lasting and generalized reductions in PVCs at follow-up 3 to 21 months after treatment, while a fifth patient was able to recognize their occurrence and control them by resting at home. Subsequent examination revealed that two of the patients who did not respond favorably had extremely diseased hearts, suggesting that a body organ cannot be too damaged if operant-feedback is to have any ameliorative effects. It was discovered that the third unsuccessful patient feared an improvement in his heart problem since this would entail his losing disability benefits and returning to work. It is very probable that this patient actively sabotaged the treatment program, which raises an important clinical issue. Even if biofeedback can modify important physiological activities, it would be most successful as part of a multifaceted behavioral treatment program which would take into account other relevant maintaining variables such as the advantage to the patient of being either physically or psychologically disabled.

## Behavior Modification with Children

Bijou and Redd (in press) have recently indexed the increasing popularity of behavioral treatment methods for children by noting that the current behavior therapy literature consists of well over a thousand titles, whereas 20 years ago a review of the child therapies showed that nearly all the techniques in use were some variant of child psychoanalysis and client-centered play therapy. The tremendous attention child behavior therapy has received is not only due to its more scientific nature than the traditional psychodynamic techniques with which therapists have become disaffected, but also to its applicability to children with a wide range of different problems and disorders, many of which were essentially untreatable by conventional methods (e.g., autism and severe language deficiencies). And, most of all, compelling evidence exists as to the efficacy of behavioral intervention across these diverse problems.

Bijou and Redd (in press) discussed behavior therapy with children in terms of four major therapeutic procedures:    a) weakening aversive behavior and strengthening desirable behavior; b) modifying shy, withdrawn and phobic behavior; c) establishing new behavioral repertoires; and d) bringing behavior under appropriate prosocial stimulus control.    O'Leary and Wilson (1975) organized their coverage of the behavioral approach to the etiology and treatment of children's disorders by focusing on specific problem areas such as fears and phobias, autism and childhood schizophrenia, enuresis and encopresis, mental retardation, academic and social problems, and delinquency.    The remainder of this section provides an evaluation and description of representative behavioral strategies within some of the children's disorders listed above.

The process of developing new behavior repertoires is well illustrated in the treatment of academic and social problems.    The successful use of token reinforcement programs in this respect has been referred to in preceding sections of this chapter (e.g., Drabman et al., 1973; Walker and Buckley, 1972).    Other multifaceted treatment approaches have demonstrated even greater efficacy. Following the discovery that economically deprived children who had been in Head Start programs initially showed improvement on measures of academic and social skills but at a two year follow-up were indistinguishable from children who did not participate in Head Start programs, the federal government established Follow Through, a kindergarten, first and second grade program for children in Head Start in an effort to maintain the initial gains made in Head Start programs.

Approximately 25 different approaches to Head Start and Follow Through have been funded by the federal government and are being evaluated for their efficacy in overcoming academic failure and social maladjustment. In brief, the two programs utilize behaviorally trained teacher aides in a highly structured classroom situation with individualized program instruction, and employ behavioral principles to enhance the efficiency and efficacy of the different teaching methods.    An interim progress report revealed that of all the programs, the two behavioral programs ranked first and second in order of success.    Becker (in press) has reported the results of one of these two programs in schools located throughout the country.    An improvement in reading of 4.8 grade levels from prekindergarten to post-third grade was obtained.    The overall gain from pre-first grade to post-third grade was 4.1 grade levels.    These gains are not only superior to the expected gain for economically disadvantaged children of .6 grade levels per year, but also are more than that expected for the average child in the nation.

A well-controlled study by O'Leary and Kent (1973) compared the broad behavioral treatment of 15 inattentive, aggressive, and disruptive children who were also lacking in motivation, to 16 non-treated, matched control children.

Four behavior therapists each treated four children, spending a total of 20 hours of consultation over a four-week period training the parents and teachers of the children in behavioral management skills for social and academic problems. A one year follow-up shows that the treated children were significantly superior to controls on teacher ratings of academic and social behavior and systematic observational measures of disruptive classroom behavior. There were no differences between the groups on standardized achievement tests. Walter and Gilmore (1973) compared a behavioral program to a stringent attention-placebo condition in the treatment of children with conduct problems and found that the behavior modification program produced significant decreases in deviant behavior whereas the control group showed increases in deviant behavior. Lastly, a six month follow-up evaluation of children displaying various problems including social withdrawal, delinquent acts, immaturity, academic retardation, temper tantrums and phobias, and who were treated with behavior modification by psychological interns at the State University of New York at Stony Brook, revealed that both parents and therapists rated over 80% of all problems improved. The correlation between therapists' judgments and the independently assessed parental ratings of success was highly significant. These findings are significantly superior to similar estimates of the success of traditional child psychotherapy (e.g., Levitt, 1963). Of greatest interest, perhaps, in view of the frequent criticisms of behavior therapists as impersonal purveyors of inflexible and mechanistic behavior control manipulations, was the finding that 96% of the parents liked their therapists. The personal attributes of the therapists which were most frequently noted by the parents were warmth, understanding, and sincere interest in the client.

Infantile autism is a very serious childhood disorder with which behavior modification has been shown to produce definite improvement where all other forms of therapy have proven ineffective (Rimland, 1964). The early application of operant conditioning procedures to autistic children by Ferster and DeMeyer (1961) and Lovaas (1966) and his colleagues represents one of the best known landmarks in the development of behavior modification. In view of the considerable attention Lovaas's work has received over the years and the difficulty of the disorder he has attempted to remedy, the recent long-term evaluation of the results of his treatment program with 20 autistic children is of particular significance (cf. Lovaas, Koegel, Simmons and Long, 1973). The treatment procedures used by Lovaas are a classic example of establishing appropriate stimulus control over behavior, i.e., training the children to attend and respond to aspects of their environment which they had previously ignored.

Once severe self-destructive and tantrum behaviors are eliminated, the major objective of treatment is language acquisition, since effective social interaction and learning is mainly mediated through the use of language. This goal is accomplished by a combined treatment procedure of modeling and reinforced guided performance. The therapist models increasingly more complex forms of verbal behavior and the child is contingently rewarded for imitating the modeled responses. The verbal prompts are gradually faded out until the child can accurately label different features of his environment.  Abstract functions are taught in a similar manner.  Primary reinforcers such as food, as well as social sources of reinforcement such as expressions of affection are made contingent upon appropriate behavior.  The withdrawal of the therapist's attention, or placing the child in an isolation room for brief periods (time out), or even a slap on the thigh or a strong electric shock, are used to eliminate bizarre or psychotic behavior.

Initially the treatment was conducted on an inpatient basis, with children receiving as much as eight hours of treatment per day, six to seven days a week. In the later stages of the program the children were seen as outpatients and the parents were trained to implement the necessary behavioral methods.  The number of weekly treatment sessions was then gradually reduced until the child was discharged from therapy.   For the first few months thereafter, the therapist visited the home.  These visits were then terminated and the parents were intermittently contacted by phone.

All the children treated had been diagnosed as autistic by at least one agency not associated with Lovaas's program, and had previously failed to respond to alternative forms of therapy.  Follow-up evaluations made from one to four years after the end of therapy showed that those autistic children who had been discharged to a state hospital had lost the gains they had made and had increased their psychotic behavior, whereas children who remained with their parents maintained their gains or improved even further.  Those parents who were most successful in modifying their children's inappropriate behavior were characterized by their willingness to be directive and use strong consequences, such as food and spankings; to treat their child as though he were "normal" and to commit a major portion of their lives to implementing the necessary contingency management procedures.  Changes in I.Q. scores were recorded for 19 of the 20 children evaluated.  Originally they were untestable but after treatment they functioned at the moderately retarded level.  Significant positive changes in social behavior as measured by the Vineland Scale were also obtained.

An even more dramatic illustration of the potential efficacy of behavioral treatment of at least some autistic children is provided by the case of Dicky. Wolf, Risley, and Mees (1964) originally reported successfully treating a 3 1/2-year-old autistic boy, Dicky, by eliminating self-destructive behavior and tantrums, teaching him speech and appropriate social behaviors, and preventing loss of his eyesight by training him to wear glasses. Nedelman and Salsbacher (1972) have recently reported on the boy's status as a 13-year-old.  As a result of continued behavioral treatment he progressed to the point where he was able to attend classes in elementary school, and has a verbal I.Q. of 106. At 3 years he had been untestable, and at 5 years he had an I.Q. of only 50.

Behavior modification with children has been predominantly characterized by the use of procedures derived from operant conditioning.  However, the entire range of social learning principles is applicable to children's disorders, and several studies and clinical reports have indicated the advantages of a multifaceted treatment approach. Modeling, which is often implicitly incorporated into operant strategies, and which was a prominent feature of Lovaas's treatment program, appears to be a particularly powerful method of modifying behavior. It has been used to eliminate phobic behavior, facilitate the expression of inhibited response patterns, and transmit new patterns of behavior (cf. Bandura, 1971). The influence of modeling on all three of these classes of psychological functioning is illustrated in O'Connor's (1972) study which reported the treatment of extreme social withdrawal in a six-year-old boy by a method combining modeling and guided participation. The extension of these procedures to the broad range of developmental problems in children is strongly recommended, and are to be preferred to the use of imaginal desensitization, which does not appear to be very successful in treating phobic children (cf. Miller, Barrett, Hampe and Noble, 1972).

In addition to modeling principles, Meichenbaum and Cameron (1973) have indicated that impulsive children can be trained to use self-instructions to control their disordered behavior. Other studies have demonstrated the potential role of self-monitoring and self-evaluation of behavior by children (e.g. Drabman, *et al.,* 1973), and the more extensive use of a variety of self-control procedures seems to offer considerable promise in increasing the efficacy of behavior therapy and facilitating the generalization and maintenance of treatment effects.

The clinical behavior therapist endeavors to maximize his therapeutic effects by deliberately combining several strategies and techniques. Lazarus (1959) made combined use of operant and respondent strategies in treating a child who was afraid of traveling in moving vehicles. The child was given chocolate as a reinforcer for the operant behavior of talking about cars, then for sitting in cars, and finally for riding in cars. In the same manner, various stimuli such as toy cars and proximity to actual vehicles were paired with the pleasant unconditioned stimuli of eating chocolate. Similarly, Lazarus, Davison and Polefka (1965) applied classical and operant strategies in overcoming a school phobia in a nine-year-old boy. The first phase of therapy was largely an *in vivo* desensitization, but as the boy grew less fearful, the therapist's warmth and attention became contingent upon various approximations to the eventual goal of normal school attendance. The technique of *emotive imagery* (Lazarus and Abramovitz, 1962) has been especially useful in overcoming children's fears. In essence, this technique involves the presentation of stronger and stronger phobic images which are woven into more powerful positive and enjoyable fantasies. While vividly imagining the fear-producing situations, the child is told a story that arouses his feelings of pride, mirth, serenity, or his sense of adventure.

Despite the considerable success of behavior modification methods with children's disorders, objections to the direct treatment of such problems have continued to reflect doctrinaire and misinformed convictions about the spectre of "symptom substitution." The control of a common childhood complaint like enuresis is a case in point. Salk (1972) has recently restated an opposition to the use of automatic conditioning devices such as the bell and pad on account of the fact that they will "affect the child's personality" and result in sexual impotence later in life. Yet careful follow-up evaluations of the results of the treatment of enuresis by behavioral means has unequivocally shown not only a significant decrement in bed-wetting, but also a generalized improvement in the child's functioning both in the school and at home as measured by behavioral ratings and projective tests (Baker, 1969; DeLeon and Sacks, 1972). There is still no empirical evidence that behavior therapy results in "symptom substitution," which, as we pointed out earlier in this chapter, is totally inconsistent with a conceptualization of behavior therapy as multifaceted treatment in which all the maintaining variables of problem behaviors are taken into account in planning therapeutic interventions.

## A Concluding Comment

Considerations of space have prevented us from presenting anything more than brief and highly selective illustrations of current developments within the field of behavior modification. Indeed, the proliferation of ideas within the boundaries of behavior modification has been so vigorous that it has come to mean different things to different individuals. There seems to be no universally accepted definition, no consensus as to goals, concepts or underlying philosophy, no agreement as to its purview, no monolithic point of view, no overriding strategy or core technique, no single founding father, no general agreement about matters of training, and there is no single profession to which primary allegiance is declared (cf. Franks and Wilson, 1973).

Yet there does seem to be one common level to which nearly all behavior modifiers would subscribe — that the strength of behavior modification lies not so much in its measured successes as in the unique combination of social learning theory and scientific method which the well-trained behavior modifier brings to the clinical scene.

The skill of the behavior therapist lies in adapting the data and methodology of the scientist generated in the laboratory, to the more complex and less structured gray world of the clinic and the natural environment. While retaining his experimental rigor, the effective behavior modifier is able to allow his clinical acumen to temper the need for experimental purity with the more compelling need to help his patients in the here and now. This is the ideal to which we may aspire. While we sing of our successes, it is salutary to take a long, sober, hard look at our accomplishments in terms of all of these variables, at our failures as well as our successes, at our conceptual rigidity as well as at our flexibility of thought. To be truly dynamic, behavior modification must somehow combine scientific rigor — with its emphasis upon careful observation, data, testing of hypotheses and subsequent feedback — with an open-minded spirit of inquiry which holds nothing sacrosanct, which has no disciples and which is ever open to self-correction on the basis of empirically derived data.

## REFERENCES

Anthony, W.A., Buel, G.J., Sharrat, S. and Althoff, M.E. Efficacy of psychiatric rehabilitation. *Psychological Bulletin.* **78**: 447–456 (1972).

Atthowe, J.M. Behavior innovation and persistence. *American Psychologist.* **28**: 34–41 (1973).

Atthowe, J.M. and Krasner, L. A preliminary report on the application of contingent reinforcement procedures (token economy) on a "chronic" psychiatric ward. *Journal of Abnormal Psychology.* **73**: 37–43 (1968).

Atthowe, J.M. and McDonough, J.M. *Operations re-entry.* (Film of Veterans Administration Hospital, Palo Alto, California. Released by Indiana University.) Washington, D.C.: United States Department of Health, Education, and Welfare, Social and Rehabilitation Services, 1969.

Ayllon, T. and Azrin, N.H. The measurement and reinforcement of behavior of psychotics. *Journal of the Experimental Analysis of Behavior.* **8**: 357–383 (1965).

Ayllon, T. and Azrin, N.H. *The token economy.* New York: Appleton-Century-Crofts, 1968.

Ayllon, T. and Michael, J. The psychiatric nurse as a behavioral engineer. *Journal of the Experimental Analysis of Behavior.* **2**: 323–334 (1959).

Baer, D.M., Wolf, M.M. and Risley, T.R. Some current dimensions of applied behavior analysis. *Journal of Applied Behavior Analysis.* **1**: 91–97 (1968).

Baker, B.L. Symptom treatment and symptom substitution in enuresis. *Journal of Abnormal Psychology.* **74**: 42–49 (1969).

Bandura, A. *Principles of behavior modification.* New York: Holt, Rinehart and Winston, 1969.

Bandura, A. Psychotherapy based upon modeling principles. In: Bergin, A.E. and Garfield, S.L. (Eds.), *Handbook of psychotherapy and behavior change,* pp. 653–708. New York: Wiley, 1971.

Barber, T., DiCara, L.V., Kamiya, J., Miller, N.E., Shapiro, D. and Stoyva, J. (Eds.) *Biofeedback and self-control: An Aldine Reader on the regulation of bodily processes and consciousness.* Chicago. Aldine-Atherton, 1971.

Barlow, D.H. Increasing heterosexual responsiveness in the treatment of sexual deviation: A review of the clinical and experimental literature. *Behavior Therapy.* **4**: 655–671 (1973).

Barlow, D.H., Reynolds, E.J. and Agras, W.S. Gender identity change in a transsexual. *Archives of General Psychiatry.* **28**: 569–579 (1973).

Becker, W.C. Some effects of direct instruction methods in teaching disadvantaged children in Project Follow-Through. *Proceedings of the International Symposium on Behavior Therapy.* Minneapolis: Appleton-Century-Crofts, in press.

Bekhterev, V.M. Die perversitaten und inversitaten vom standpunkt der reflexologie. *Archives Psychiatrie Nervenkrankheiten.* **68**: 100–213 (1923).

Benson, H., Shapiro, D., Tursky, B. and Schwartz, G.E. Decreased systolic blood pressure through operant conditioning techniques in patients with essential hypertension. *Science.* **173**: 740 (1971).

Bijou, S.W. and Redd, W.H. Child behavior therapy. *American handbook of psychiatry,* in press.

Birk, L.   Psychoanalysis and behavioral analysis:  Natural resonance and comple-
mentarity.  *International Journal of Psychiatry.*  **11:**   160–166 (1973).

Birk, L., Huddleston, W., Miller, E. and Cohler, B.   Avoidance conditioning for
homosexuality.  *Archives of General Psychiatry.*   **25:**   314–323 (1971).

Birk, L., Stolz, S.B., Brady, J.P., Brady, J.V., Lazarus, A.A., Lynch, J.J., Rosenthal,
A.J., Skelton, W.D., Stevens, J.B. and Thomas, E.J.  *Behavior therapy in
psychiatry.*  Task Force Report, American Psychiatry Association, Washington,
D.C., 1973.

Blanchard, E.B. and Young, L.D.   Self-control of cardiac functioning:  A promise
as yet unfulfilled.  *Psychological Bulletin.*  **79:**  145–163 (1973).

Boudin, H.M.   Contingency contracting as a therapeutic tool in the deceleration
of amphetamine use.  *Behavior Therapy.*  **3:**  604–608 (1972).

Brady, J.P.   Brevital-aided systematic desensitization.   In:  Rubin, R.D., Fensterheim, H., Lazarus, A.A., and Franks, C.M.  (Eds.), *Advances in behavior
therapy.*   New York:  Academic Press, 1971.

Callahan, E.J. and Leitenberg, H.  Aversion therapy for sexual deviation:  Contingent shock and covert sensitization.  *Journal of Abnormal Psychology.*  **31:**
60–73 (1973).

Chapman, R.F., Smith, J.W. and Layden, L.A.   Elimination of cigarette smoking
by punishment and self-management training.  *Behaviour Research and Therapy.*  **9:**  255–264 (1971).

Copeman, C.D.  Aversive counter conditioning and social retraining:  a learning
theory approach to drug rehabilitation.   Unpublished doctoral dissertation,
State University of New York at Stony Brook, 1973.

Cotter, L.H.  Operant conditioning in a Vietnamese mental hospital.  *American
Journal of Psychiatry.*  **124:**  23–28 (1967).

Davison, G.C.   Behavior modification techniques in institutional settings.  In:
Franks, C.M.  (Ed.), *Behavior therapy:  Appraisal and status.*  New York:
McGraw-Hill, 1969.

Davison, G.C.   Counter-control in behavior modification.  In:  Hamerlynck, L.A.,
Handy, L.C. and Mash, E.J. (Eds.)  *Behavior change:  methodology, concepts,
and practice,* pp. 153–167. Champaign, Illinois:  Research Press, 1973.

Davison, G.C. and Wilson, G.T.   Processes of fear-reduction in systematic
desensitization:   Cognitive and social reinforcement factors in humans.
*Behavior Therapy.*  **4:**  1–21 (1973a).

Davison, G.C. and Wilson, G.T.   A survey of the attitudes of behavior therapists
toward homosexuality. *Behavior Therapy.*  **4:**  686–696 (1973b).

DeLeon, G. and Sacks, S.   Conditioning functional enuresis:  A four year follow-
up.  *Journal of Consulting and Clinical Psychology.*  **39:**  299–300 (1972).

Drabman, R., Spitalnik, R. and O'Leary, K.D.   Teaching self-control to disruptive
children. *Journal of Abnormal Psychology.*  **82:**  10–16 (1973).

Dunlap, K.  *Habits:  Their making and unmaking.*  New York: Liveright, 1932.

Ellis, A.  *Reason and emotion in psychotherapy.*  New York:  Lyle Stuart, 1962.

Evans, D.R.  An exploratory study into the treatment of exhibitionism by means
of emotive imagery and aversive conditioning.  *Canadian Psychologist.*  **8:**  162
(1967).

Eysenck, H.J.   Learning theory and behaviour therapy.   *Journal of Mental
Sciences.*  **105:**  61–75 (1959).

Eysenck, H.J. *Behaviour therapy and the neuroses.* New York: Pergamon Press, 1960.

Eysenck, H.J. *Experiments in behaviour therapy.* New York: Pergamon Press, 1964.

Eysenck, H.J. and Rachman, S. *Causes and cures of neurosis.* London: Routledge and Kegan, Paul, 1965.

Fairweather, G.W. *Social psychology in treating mental illness: An experimental approach.* New York: Wiley, 1964.

Fairweather, G.W., Sanders, D.H., Maynard, H. and Cressler, D.L. *Community life for the mentally ill: An alternative to institutional care.* Chicago: Aldine, 1969.

Fairweather, G.W., Simon, R., Gebhard, M.E., Weingarten, E., Holland, J.I., Sanders, R., Stone, G.B. and Reahl, J.E. Relative effectiveness of psychotherapeutic programs: A multicriteria comparison of four programs for three different patient groups. *Psychological Monographs.* **74:** (5, Whole No. 492) (1960).

Feather, B.W. and Rhoads, J.M. Psychodynamic behavior therapy: Theory and rationale. *Archives of General Psychiatry.* **26:** 496–511 (1972).

Feldman, M.P. and MacCulloch, M.J. *Homosexual behavior: Therapy and assessment.* Oxford: Pergamon Press, 1971.

Fensterheim, H. The initial interview. In: Lazarus, A.A. (Ed.), *Clinical behavior therapy,* pp. 22–40. New York: Brunner/Mazel, 1972.

Fensterheim, H. Behavior therapy: Assertive training in groups. In: Sager, C.J. and Kaplan, H.S. (Eds.), *Progress in group and family therapy.* New York: Brunner/Mazel, 1972.

Ferster, C.B. and DeMyer, M.K. The development of performance in autistic children in an automatically controlled environment. *Journal of Chronic Diseases.* **13:** 312–345 (1961).

Ferster, C.B., Nurnberger, J.I. and Levitt, E.B. The control of eating. *Journal of Mathetics,* **1:** 87–109 (1962).

Fixen, D.L., Phillips, E.L. and Wolf, M.M. Achievement Place: Experiments in self-government with pre-delinquents. *Journal of Applied Behavior Analysis.* **6:** 31–48 (1973).

Franks, C.M. and Wilson, G.T. *Annual review of behavior therapy: theory and practice.* New York: Brunner/Mazel, 1973.

Gesell, A. The conditioned reflex and the psychiatry of infancy. *American Journal of Orthopsychiatry.* **8:** 19–30 (1938).

Goffman, E. *Asylums.* New York: Anchor, 1961.

Goldfried, M.R. Systematic desensitization as training in self-control. *Journal of Consulting and Clinical Psychology.* **37:** 228–235 (1971).

Goldiamond, I. Toward a constructional approach to social problems: Ethical and constitutional issues raised by applied behavior analysis. *Behaviorism.* **2:** 1–84 (1974).

Guthrie, E.R. *The psychology of learning.* New York: Harper and Row, 1925.

Haley, J. *Uncommon therapy: The psychiatric techniques of Milton H. Erickson, M.D.* New York: Norton, 1973.

Hartman, W.E. and Fithian, M.A. *Treatment of sexual dysfunction.* California: Center for Marital and Sexual Studies, 1972.

Herzberg, A. *Active psychotherapy.* London: Research Books, 1941.

Hodgson, R., Rachman, S. and Marks, I. The treatment of chronic obsessive-compulsive neurosis: Follow-up and further findings. *Behaviour Research and Therapy.* **10:** 181–189 (1972).

Hunt, G.M. and Azrin, N.H. A community reinforcement approach to aclohol-ism. *Behaviour Research and Therapy.* **11:** 91–104 (1973).

Ichok, G. Les reflexes conditonnels et le traitement de l'alcoolique. *Progress in Medicine* (Paris). **2:** 1742–1745 (1934).

Jones, H.G. The application of conditioning and learning techniques to the treatment of a psychiatric patient. *Journal of Abnormal and Social Psychology.* **52:** 414–420 (1956).

Jones, M.C. The elimination of children's fears. *Journal of Experimental Psychology.* **1:** 382–390 (1924).

Kanfer, F.H. and Karoly, P. Self-control: A behavioristic excursion into the lion's den. *Behavior Therapy.* **3:** 398–416 (1972).

Kanfer, F.H. and Saslow, G. Behavioral diagnosis. In: Franks, C.M. (Ed.), *Behavior therapy: appraisal and status.* New York: McGraw-Hill, 1969.

Kass, D.J. Silvers, F.M. and Abroms, G.M. Behavioral group treatment of hysteria. *Archives of General Psychiatry.* **26:** 42–50 (1972).

Katz, R.C., Johnson, C.A. and Gelfand, S. Modifying the dispensing of reinforcers: some implications for behavior modification with hospitalized patients. *Behavior Therapy.* **3:** 579–588 (1972).

Kazdin, A.E. and Bootzin, R.R. The token economy: An evaluative review. *Journal of Applied Behavior Analysis.* **5:** 343–372 (1972).

Kohlenberg, R.J. Treatment of a homosexual pedophiliac using in vivo desensitiation. *Journal of Abnormal Psychology.* **83:** 192–195 (1974).

Kostyleff, N. L'inversion sexuelle expliquee par la reflexologie. *Psycholgie et vie.* **1:** 8–12 (1927).

Krasner, L. The operant approach in behavior therapy. In: Bergin, A.E. and Garfield, S.L. (Eds.), *Handbook of psychotherapy and behavior change,* pp. 612–652. New York: Wiley, 1971.

Krasner, L. and Krasner, M. Token economies and other planned environments. In: *Behavior modification 1973.* Chicago: The National Society for the Study of Education, 1973.

Kretschmer, E. *Kretschmer's textbook of medical psychology.* (E.B. Strauss, trans.) London: Oxford University Press, 1934. (1st German edition 1922).

Lang, P.J. and Melamed, B. Case report: Avoidance conditioning therapy of an infant with chronic ruminative vomiting. *Journal of Abnormal Psychology.* **74:** 1–8 (1969).

Lazarus, A.A. New methods in psychotherapy: A case study. *South African Medical Journal.* **32:** 660–664 (1958).

Lazarus, A.A. The elimination of children's phobias by deconditioning. *Medical Proceedings (South Africa).* **5:** 261–265 (1959).

Lazarus, A.A. Group therapy of phobic disorders by systematic desensitization. *Journal of Abnormal and Social Psychology* **63:** 505–510 (1961).

Lazarus, A.A. Behaviour rehearsal vs. non-directive therapy vs. advice in effecting behaviour change. *Behaviour Research and Therapy.* **4:** 209–212 (1966).

Lazarus, A.A.  Behavior therapy in groups.  In:  Gazda, G.M. (Ed.), *Basic approaches to group psychotherapy and group counseling.*  Springfield: Charles C. Thomas, 1968.

Lazarus, A.A. *Behavior therapy and beyond.* New York: McGraw-Hill, 1971.

Lazarus, A.A.  Avoid the paradigm clash. *International Journal of Psychiatry.* **11:** 157–159 (1973).

Lazarus, A.A.  Multimodal behavior therapy:  Treating the "BASIC ID." *Journal of Nervous and Mental Disease.* **156:** 404–411 (1973a).

Lazarus, A.A.  Understanding and modifying aggression in behavioral groups. In:  Jacobs, A. and Spradlin, W. (Eds.), *The group as agent of change.* New York: Behavioral Publications, 1973b.

Lazarus, A.A.  Multimodal behavior therapy in groups.  In:  Gazda, G.M. (Ed.), *Basic approaches to group psychotherapy and group counseling,* (rev. ed.). Springfield:  Charles C. Thomas, 1975.

Lazarus, A.A. and Abramovitz, A.  The use of "emotive imagery" in the treatment of children's phobias. *Journal of Mental Science,* **108:** 191–195(1962).

Lazarus, A.A., Davison, G.C. and Polefka, D.A.  Classical and operant factors in the treatment of a school phobia. *Journal of Abnormal Psychology.* **70:** 225–229 (1965).

Lazarus, A.A. and Davison, G.C.  Clinical innovation in research and practice. In:  Bergin, A.E. and Garfield, S.L. (Eds.), *Handbook of psychotherapy and behavior change,* pp. 196–213. New York:  Wiley, 1971.

Leitenberg, H.  The use of single case methodology in psychotherapy research. *Journal of Abnormal Psychology.* **82:** 87–101 (1973).

Lemere, F. and Voegtlin, W.L.  An evaluation of the aversion treatment of alcoholism. *Quarterly Journal of Studies on Alcoholism.* **11:** 199–204 (1950).

Levitt, E.E.  Psychotherapy with children. A further evaluation. *Behaviour Research and Therapy.* **1:** 45–51 (1963).

Levitz, L.S. and Stunkard, A.J.  A therapeutic coalition for obesity:  Behavior modification and patient self-help. *American Journal of Psychiatry.* **131:** 424–427 (1974).

Lichtenstein, E., Harris, D.E., Birchler, G.R., Wahl, J.M. and Schmahl, D.P. Comparison of rapid smoking, warm smoky air, and attention placebo in the modification of smoking behavior. *Journal of Consulting and Clinical Psychology.* **40:** 92–98 (1973).

Lindsley, O.R. and Skinner, B.F.  A method for the experimental analysis of the behavior of psychotic patients. *American Psychologist.* **9:** 419–420 (1954).

Lobitz, W.C. and LoPiccolo, J.  New Methods in the behavioral treatment of sexual dysfunction. *Journal of Behavior Therapy and Experimental Psychiatry.* **3:** 265–272 (1972).

Lovaas, O.I.  A program for the establishment of speech in psychotic children. In:  Wing, J.K. (Ed.), *Early childhood autism.* Oxford:  Pergamon Press, 1966.

Lovaas, O.I., Koegel, R., Simmons, J.Q. and Long, J.S.  Some generalization and follow-up measures on autistic children in behavior therapy. *Journal of Applied Behavior Analysis.* **6:** 131–166 (1973).

Mahoney, M.J.  Self-reward and self-monitoring techniques for weight control. *Behavior Therapy.* **5:** 48–57 (1974a).

Mahoney, M.J. *Cognition and behavior modification*. Cambridge: Ballinger, 1974b.

Maley, R.F., Feldman, G.L. and Ruskin, R.S. Evaluation of patient improvement in a token economy treatment program. *Journal of Abnormal Psychology* 82: 141-144 (1973).

Marks, I., Boulougouris, J. and Marsit, P. Flooding versus desensitization in the treatment of phobic patients: A crossover study. *British Journal of Psychiatry*. 119: 353-375, (1971).

Marks, I.M. and Gelder, M.G. Transvestism and fetishism: Clinical and psychological changes during faradic aversion. *British Journal of Psychiatry*. 113: 711-729 (1967).

Marks, I.M., Gelder, M.G. and Bancroft, J. Sexual deviants two years after electrical aversion. *British Journal of Psychiatry*. 117: 73-85 (1970).

Masters, W.H. and Johnson, V.E. *Human sexual inadequacy*. Boston: Little, Brown, 1970.

McFall, R.M. and Lillesand, D.B. Behavior rehearsal with modeling and coaching in assertion training. *Journal of Abnormal Psychology*. 77: 313-323 (1971).

McFall, R.M. and Marston, A.R. An experimental investigation of behavior rehearsal in assertive training. *Journal of Abnormal Psychology*. 76: 295-303 (1970).

Meichenbaum, D. and Cameron, R. Training schizophrenics to talk to themselves: A means of developing attentional controls. *Behavior Therapy*. 4: 515-534 (1973).

Meignant, P. Reflexes conditonnels et psycho-pathologie: Quelques remarques concernant les perversions et les anomalies sexuelles. *Gazette of French Medicine*, pp. 327-332, 1935.

Meyer, V. The treatment of two phobic patients on the basic of learning principles. *Journal of Abnormal and Social Psychology*. 55: 262-266 (1957).

Miller, L.C., Barret, L.L., Hampe, E. and Noble, H. Comparison of reciprocal inhibition, psychotherapy, and waiting list control for phobic children. *Journal of Abnormal Psychology*. 79: 269-279 (1972).

Miller, N.E. Interactions between learned and physical factors in mental illness. In: Franks, C.M. and Wilson, G.T. (Eds.), *Annual review of behavior therapy: Theory and practice*, pp. 645-668. New York: Brunner/Mazel, 1973.

Miller, P.M., Hersen, M., Eisler, R.M. and Hemphill, D.P. Effects of faradic aversion therapy in drinking by alcoholics. *Behaviour Research and Therapy*. 11: 491-498 (1973).

Mills, H.L., Agras, W.S., Barlow, D.H. and Mills, J.R. Compulsive rituals treated by response prevention. *Archives of General Psychiatry*. 28: 524-529 (1973).

Mischel, W. *Personality and assessment*. New York: Wiley, 1968.

Moreno, J.L. *Psychodrama*. New York: Beacon, 1946.

Morgan, J.J.B. and Witmer, F.J. The treatment of enuresis by the conditioned reaction technique. *Journal of Genetic Psychology*. 55: 59-65 (1939).

Morganstern, K.P. Implosive therapy and flooding procedures: A critical review. *Psychological Bulletin*. 79: 318-334 (1973).

Mowrer, O.H. and Mowrer, W.A. Enuresis: A method for its study and treatment. *American Journal of Orthopsychiatry*. 8: 436-447 (1938).

Nedelman, D. and Salzbacher, S.I.  Dicky, at 13 years of age:  A long-term success following early application of operant conditioning procedures.  In: Semb, G. (Ed.), *Behavior analysis and education, 1972.*  Laurence:  Follow-through Project, 1972.

O'Brien, J.S., Raynes, A.E. and Patch, V.D.  Treatment of heroin addiction with aversion therapy, relaxation training and systematic desensitization.  *Behaviour Research and Therapy.*  **10:**  77–80 (1972).

O'Connor, R.D.  Relative efficacy of modeling, shaping, and the combined procedures for modification of social withdrawal.  *Journal of Abnormal Psychology.*  **79:**  327–334 (1972).

O'Leary, K.D.  Behavior modification in the classroom:  A rejoinder to Witnett and Winkler.  *Journal of Applied Behavior Analysis.*  **5:**  505–511 (1972).

O'Leary, K.D. and Drabman, R.  Token reinforcement programs in the classroom:  A review.  *Psychological Bulletin.*  **75:**  379–398 (1971).

O'Leary, K.D. and Kent, R.N.  Behavior modification for social action:  Research tactics and problems.  In:  Hammerlynck, L.A., Davidson, P.O. and Acker, L.E. (Eds.), *Proceedings of the Fourth Banff International Conference on Behavior Modification,* pp. 69–96.  Champaign, Illinois:  Research Press, 1973.

O'Leary, K.D. and O'Leary, S.  *Classroom management:  The successful use of behavior modification.*  New York:  Pergamon Press, 1972.

O'Leary, K.D. and Wilson, G.T.  *Behavior therapy: Application and outcome.*  Englewood Cliffs, New Jersey:  Prentice-Hall, 1975.

Patterson, G.R.  Behavioral intervention procedures in the classroom and in the home.  In: Bergin, A.E. and Garfield, S.L. (Eds.), *Handbook of psychotherapy and behavior change,* pp. 751–775.  New York:  Wiley, 1971.

Paul, G.L.  Outcome of systematic desensitization, II.  In:  Franks, C.M. (Ed.), *Behavior therapy: Appraisal and status,* pp. 105–159.  New York:  McGraw-Hill, 1969.

Paul, G.L. and Shannon, D.T.  Treatment of anxiety through systematic desensitization in therapy groups.  *Journal of Abnormal Psychology.*  **71:**  124–135 (1966).

Pauly, I.B.  Adult manifestations of male transsexualism.  In:  Green, R. and Money, J. (Eds.), *Transsexualism and sex reassignment,* pp. 37–58.  Baltimore:  John's Hopkins Press, 1969.

Phillips, E.L., Phillips, E.A., Fixsen, D.L. and Wolf, M.M.  Achievement Place:  Modification of the behaviors of predelinquent boys within a token economy.  *Journal of Applied Behavior of Analysis.*  **4:**  45–59 (1971).

Pomerleau, O.F., Bobrove, P.H. and Smith, R.H.  Rewarding psychiatric aides for the behavioral improvement of assigned patients.  *Journal of Applied Behavior Analysis.*  **6:**  383–390 (1973).

Rachlin, H.  *Introduction to modern behaviorism.*  San Francisco:  Freeman, 1970.

Rachman, S., Hodgson, R. and Marks, I.M.  The treatment of chronic obsessive-compulsive neurosis.  *Behaviour Research and Therapy.*  **9**  237–247  (1971).

Rickard, H.C.  *Behavioral intervention in human problems.*  New York:  Pergamon Press, 1971.

Rimland, B.  *Infantile autism.*  New York:  Appleton-Century-Crofts, 1964.

Risley, T.R.  The effects and side effects of punishing the autistic behaviors of a deviant child. *Journal of Applied Behavior Analysis.*  **1:**   253–262 (1968).

Romanczyk, R.G., Tracey, D.A., Wilson, G.T. and Thorpe, G.L.  Behavioral techniques in the treatment of obesity: A comparative analysis. *Behaviour Research and Therapy.*  **11:**  629–640 (1973).

Rosenhan, D.L.  On being sane in insane places. *Science.*  **179:**  250–258 (1973).

Rubenstein, C.  The treatment of morphine addiction in tuberculosis by Pavlov's conditioning method. *American Review of Tuberculosis.*  **24:**  682–685 (1931).

Salk, L.  *What every child would like his parents to know.*  New York:  David McKay, 1972.

Salter, A.  *Conditioned reflex therapy.*  New York:  Farrar, Strauss, 1949.

Sargent, J.D., Green, E.E. and Walters, E.D.  Preliminary report on the use of autogenic feedback training in the treatment of migraine and tension headaches. *Psychosomatic Medicine.*  **35:**  129–135 (1973).

Semans, J.H.  Premature ejaculation: A new approach. *Southern Medical Journal.*  **49:**  353–361 (1956).

Shapiro, D. and Schwartz, S.E.  Biofeedback and visceral learning:  Clinical application. *Seminars in Psychiatry.*  **4:**  171–184 (1972).

Shapiro, M.B.  An experimental approach to diagnostic psychological testing *Journal of Mental Science.*  **97:**  748–764 (1951).

Sherman, A.R.  Real-life exposure as a primary therapeutic factor in the desensitization treatment of fear. *Journal of Abnormal Psychology.*  **79:**  19–28 (1972).

Sloane, R.B.  The converging paths of behavior therapy and psychotherapy. *International Journal of Psychiatry.*  **7:**  493–503 (1969).

Sobell, M.B. and Sobell, L.C.  Individualized behavior therapy for alcoholics. *Behavior Therapy.*  **4:**  49–72 (1973).

Stampfl, T.G. and Levis, D.J.  Essentials of implosive therapy: A learning-based psychodynamic behavioral therapy. *Journal of Abnormal Psychology.*  **72:**  496–503 (1967).

Stoyva, J., Barber, T., DiCara, L.V., Kamiya, J., Miller, N.E. and Shapiro, D. (Eds.) *Biofeedback and self-control: An Aldine Annual on the regulation of bodily processes and consciousness.*  Chicago:  Aldine-Atherton, 1972.

Stuart, R.B.  Behavioral control of over-eating. *Behaviour Research and Therapy.*  **5:**  357–365 (1967).

Tharp, R.G. and Wetzel, R.J.  *Behavior modification in the natural environment.*  New York:  Academic Press, 1969.

Thoresen, C.E., and Mahoney, M.J.  *Behavioral self-control.*  New York:  Holt, Rinehart and Winston, 1974.

Ullmann, L.P.  *Institution and outcome.*  New York:  Pergamon Press, 1967.

Ullmann, L.P. and Krasner, L.  *Case studies in behavior modification.*  New York:  Holt, Rinehart and Winston, 1965.

Ullmann, L.P. and Krasner, L.  *A psychological approach to abnormal behavior.*  Englewood Cliffs, New Jersey:  Prentice-Hall, 1969.

Ulrich, R., Stachnik, T. and Mabry, J.  *Control of human behavior.*  Glenview, Illinois:  Scott, Foresman and Company, 1970.

Walker, H.M. and Buckley, N.K.  Programming generalization and maintenance of treatment effects across time and across settings. *Journal of Applied Behavior Analysis.* **5**:  209–224 (1972).

Walter, H.I. and Gilmore, S.K.  Placebo versus social learning effects in parent training procedures designed to alter the behavior of aggressive boys. *Behavior Therapy.* **4**:  361–377 (1973).

Weiss, T. and Engel, B.T.  Operant conditioning of heart rate in patients with premature ventricular contractions. *Psychosomatic Medicine.* **33**:  301–321 (1971).

Wexler, D.B.  Token and taboo:  Behavior modification, token economies, and the law. *California Law Review.* **61**:  81–109 (1973).

Williams, T.A.  *Dreads and besetting fears.*  Boston:  Little, Brown, 1923.

Wilson, G.T.  Innovations in the modification of phobic behaviors in two clinical cases. *Behavior Therapy.* **4**:  426–430 (1973).

Wilson, G.T. and Davison, G.C.  Aversion techniques in behavior therapy:  Some theoretical and meta-theoretical considerations. *Journal of Consulting and Clinical Psychology.* **33**:  327–329 (1969).

Wilson, G.T. and Davison, G.C.  Processes of fear reduction in systematic desensitization:  Animal studies. *Psychological Bulletin.* **76**:  1–14 (1971).

Wilson, G.T. and Davison, G.C.  Behavior therapy and homosexuality:  A critical perspective. *Behavior Therapy.* **5**:  16–28 (1974).

Wilson, G.T., Leaf, R. and Nathan, P.E.  The aversive control of excessive alcohol consumption by chronic alcoholics in a controlled laboratory setting. *Journal of Applied Behavior Analysis.* **8**:  13–26 (1975).

Winett, R.A. and Winkler, R.C.  Current behavior modification in the classroom:  Be still, be quiet, be docile. *Journal of Applied Behavior Analysis.* **5**:  499–504 (1972).

Winkler, R.C.  A theory of equilibrium in token economies. *Journal of Abnormal Psychology.* **79**:  169–173 (1972).

Wolf, M.M., Risley, T. and Mees, H.  Application of operant conditioning procedures to the behavior problems of an autistic child. *Behaviour Research and Therapy.* **1**:  305–312 (1964).

Wolpe, J.  Reciprocal inhibition as the main basis of psychotherapeutic effects. *Archives of Neurology and Psychiatry.* **92**:  205–226 (1954).

Wolpe, J.  *Psychotherapy by reciprocal inhibition.*  Stanford:  Stanford University Press, 1958.

Wolpe, J.  *The practice of behavior therapy.*  New York:  Pergamon Press, 1969.

Wolpe, J. and Lazarus, A.A.  *Behavior therapy techniques.*  New York:  Pergamon Press, 1966.

Woody, R.H.  *Psychobehavioral counseling and therapy: Integrating behavioral and insight therapies.*  New York:  Appleton-Century-Crofts, 1971.

Yates, A.J.  The application of learning theory to the treatment of tics. *Journal of Abnormal and Social Psychology.* **56**:  175–182 (1958).

Yates, A.J.  *Behavior therapy.*  New York:  Wiley, 1970.

# 7 Group Psychotherapies

## Max Rosenbaum

Clinical practitioners may be overwhelmed by the proliferation of group techniques that are grouped under the rubric of group therapy. There has been a tremendous surge in the field of group psychotherapy and this growth has been in the nature of a geometric progression, as validated by the amount of articles published in the field. The overwhelming majority of the articles are clinical in their presentation. The theoretic contributions are rather barren and the preponderance of material is testimonial in nature. Unfortunately, as one observes the entire field of treatment, there is no evidence that any school which has followed and developed a particular approach to psychotherapy, has agreed to disband because the approach simply did not work. Each school of psychotherapy continues to remain in existence and the adherents to a particular approach continue to cling to the concepts and techniques that they believe effective. While their loyalty is to be applauded, systematic research is ignored.

There is a plethora of techniques and maneuvers, all of which are labeled as group psychotherapy. A conference held in 1972 put the following under the rubric of group psychotherapy: encounter, sensitivity training, Gestalt therapy, bio-energetics, family therapy, consciousness-raising, transactional analysis, interactional analysis, psychosynthesis, theatre of encounter, group games, movement in depth, fantasy imagery, alexander techniques, rolfing. Probably as the reader is studying this list there are other terms being devised. There are many misconceptions about group psychotherapy and it is important to differentiate group psychotherapy from the many group endeavors that psychiatrists, psychologists, social workers, counselors, pastoral counselors, and paraprofessionals of a kind are engaged in (Mullan and Rosenbaum, 1962). I (Mullan and Rosenbaum, 1962) have defined group psychotherapy in my text on group therapy and have described the continuum of group psychotherapy. This ranges from the reparative and supportive approaches which are directed to strengthening weak defenses to the reconstructive approach which aims for deep-seated personality change. There are many people who mistakenly assume, that every gathering of three or more persons who meet at the same time and in the same place and talk about their problems is a form of group psychotherapy. This is a distortion. In the broadest sense, there is some kind of release at work and probably some kind of therapy, but it is generally unplanned and may be called group interaction of a nontherapeutic nature. The emphasis here is not on personality change but minimal personality alteration (not as in the practice of intensive group psychotherapy). People have joined groups to advance causes or interest since the beginning of recorded time. There are some who claim that they can validate group interaction experiences as far back as the early Egyptian civilization. In the Western culture, the Old and New Testament give us detailed pictures of people working together in groups to advance or promote a variety of causes. Certainly if people sit down and face one another's problems in open discussion there is the real possibility of serious communication. Generally, many distortions about one another come to the surface and there is relief brought to the participants. There is more sharing of responsibility as the process of communication develops. Distortions are lessened as a result. Optimally this results in a change in the culture and climate of the industry, school or institution — or wherever the group meeting is taking place. These groups are *human relations groups,* described by some people as meetings where "rap sessions" take place. The members of such groups are able to set goals that are comfortable for group participants. Decisions can be made without resorting to parliamentary rules of procedure and legalisms. It is at this point that the small nontherapeutic group comes to an end. Communication has been enhanced and promoted. The institution within which the group was organized can function as an integrated setting and serve its community and goals more realistically. But there is a difference between the small nontherapeutic group and group psychotherapy. I favor a psychoanalytic approach to group psychotherapy, although other approaches will be described and discussed in this chapter.

The intensive psychotherapeutic group is generally made up of seven to ten patients. The group meets two or more times each week, although some psychotherapists prefer to meet with group members once or more individually and then see them in the group once a week. This is referred to as combined psychotherapy. The interaction in the group is verbal as opposed to recreational or other motor methods. Nonverbal communication, such as body posture, facial mannerisms, seating arrangements (where the group member sits; is he or she part of the circle of patients or sitting on the outside; does he or she always take the same seat, etc.) are all noted by the group leader. The group members rarely know one another before they meet in the group. In smaller communities, some patients are concerned about meeting someone they know in other settings before they are placed in the group. They are encouraged to explore this fear or, if it is too uncomfortable, they are given the option of leaving the group. I prefer the consistent use of the group method when patients are placed in the group. Therefore, patients are encouraged to discuss all problems within the group and are not encouraged to meet with the psychotherapist individually. The individual therapy setting is often used by patients as an opportunity to avoid material that may be more profitably explored in the group. Very dependent personalities, ambulatory psychotics, patients who have had very deprived childhood experiences with little contact with a stable parent figure or a parent surrogate may need continued individual meetings with the therapist even after they have joined the group. While it is true that the group experience may be *diluted* by these individual meetings, it is also true that the experience of the group therapy may create enormous pressure upon such a patient — pressure which he is unable to bear without the support of additional individual therapy sessions.

The group therapy setting is in contrast to discussion groups or groups that discuss events of the day. Structure and an agenda are kept to a minimum by the group therapist, who has prepared and selected patients for the group experience. The therapist who works with a group fosters interaction and the deep expression of emotion. Patients are encouraged to engage in continuous and deep exploration of childhood experiences. The interpersonal and intrapsychic problems of the present and past are discussed. Relationships that are based on transference are fostered, explored by continuous contact and "worked through." Toward the end of intensive group psychotherapy, transferences are markedly reduced and people are seen as they are. The therapist who leads a group should have training in individual psychotherapy, psychopathology and psychodynamics and therefore be able to recognize and interpret transference phenomena. Unless he is unusually gifted, the untrained group leader cannot do this job. Through the model of the group therapist, members of the group are sensitized and become aware of transference phenomena. These transference distortions are then "worked through" in group setting.

There has been some distortion of what the term *transference* means. In its simplest form the patient seeks, mostly on an unconscious level, to relieve or relive in the relationship with the therapist, his gratifying but usually traumatic experiences with significant figures from his earlier years. As a result of this working through in therapy, the patient's self-awareness is enhanced. He begins to recognize the roots of his patterns of interacting with other people in the therapy group. He begins to recognize his patterns of interaction with the group leader. Some practitioners become confused and do not realize that other group techniques which foster socialization, interaction and a feeling of belonging are not group psychotherapy of an intensive nature. Basic to intensive psychoanalytic group psychotherapy is the recognition of transference and countertransference phenomena. *Countertransference,* a term that is often distorted, means that the therapist uses his own distorting and restrictive defenses against a clear perception of and response to the material that the patient brings up either in the group or in individual meetings. The therapist usually uses these defenses because he has learned them as a way of avoiding the experiencing of his own anxiety and guilt. It should be noted that a large group which has too many participants precludes member-to-member interaction and the goal of deep-seated characterological change is blocked or thwarted.

When the student of group therapy is confronted with the variety of techniques which profess to be group psychotherapy it is valuable to have some guidelines or structure, or else the entire field appears to be in a state of chaos. I suggest that the reader constantly keep in mind as the reference point that group therapy should be conceived of as a continuum rather than compartmentalizing the "systems" of group treatment. As noted earlier, the continuum ranges from the repressive-inspirational to the regressive-reconstructive which reflect the two extremes in the goal of effecting personality change. Between these two extremes are the reparative and supportive types of therapy. The reparative approaches are directed toward the strengthening of weak defenses.

In earlier writings I have discussed in detail the history of group psychotherapy in the USA (Mullan and Rosenbaum, 1962; Rosenbaum, 1962). The field has grown to the point where there are many competitors for the term "founder." As far as I can observe Pratt, a Boston internist, introduced the use of group procedures in his work around the turn of the twentieth century. It is worth mentioning that group psychotherapy evolved in Boston, the heartland of American democracy. Indeed, it is a technique which stresses peer relationships and the "wellness" of the patient rather than the "illness." Many of its origins were pragmatic and practice usually ran far ahead of systematic theory. It is certainly true that group therapy can be practiced very authoritatively, but this is not recommended if one wants to make optimum use of the potentials lying dormant when a group of patients assembles together to engage in group therapy. Some writers have described Freud as a *basic figure* in group psychotherapy. In my opinion it is inaccurate to attribute this type of importance to Freud. While Freud did outline a concept of group psychology in 1921 (Freud, 1957), his focus was on individual psychodynamics. Freud spoke of a "group of two" but he does not appear to have incorporated any concept of group dynamics or cultural anthropology other than the early writings of Le Bon, the French sociologist who was concerned with the mob. Possibly Freud's interest in the group was "turned off" by his personal difficulties with Adler and Jung, both of whom appear to have been more involved with the idea of group psychology. In this respect, Jung looked for a rather mystical or religious significance in his approach to the group. Adler, very interested in the political concepts of socialism, was always attracted to the idea of working with community groups as well as with working class patients. Many of his students became involved in work with groups early in the history of group psychotherapy. None of what has been written should minimize Freud's contribution to social psychology and ego psychology. While many students have emphasized that Freud based his theories on instinct, Freud never ignored the relationships of people to one another. In my opinion he overemphasized psychoanalysis as a basis for social psychology. Freud's major conclusion with regard to groups is as follows: In the group, the individual surrenders his own ego ideal and replaces it with the group ideal of the leader of the group. The process is unconscious. Freud's major points concern the significance of the superego in the behavior of the group: the importance of the group leader and the libidinal ties between group members which are at work in the formation of a group. Many of the "new" techniques that proliferate almost daily can be traced back quite easily to early pioneers in the fields of individual psychotherapy and group therapy. Unfortunately, many of the "new pioneers" — if indeed one can call them pioneers — have not done their homework. A trip to the library will quickly indicate the history of the "newly discovered approach." For example, many contemporary psychotherapists feel that they have originated something truly innovative in using techniques of self-disclosure where the therapist shares feelings or problems with the group members. Yet Paul Schilder, an early figure in the field of psychotherapy, who based his work on psychoanalytic concepts and who had a great genius for grasping psychological and physiological concepts, was carrying out experimental projects in group psychotherapy with low income patients at Bellevue Hospital in New York City as far back as the early 1930s. At that time he was quite forthright in expressing his value systems with the group he was working with. He was quite outspoken in defense of his value system and made no effort to obscure or conceal his feelings (Schilder, 1939, 1940).

The reader should keep in mind that group psychotherapy is a field that is expanding geometrically. Group psychotherapy practice has always been considerably in advance of conceptual clarity and theoretical understanding. Those who treat people in groups stem from every school of individual psychotherapy; and every major school has attempted to apply its theoretic orientation to group psychotherapy with resultant confusion. On occasion there is a breakdown in communication because there is no common language. For example, in academia there is a group known as *social learning* theorists. In psychoanalysis, there is a group known as *object relations* theorists. There are some marked theory differences between the two groups but there is a tremendous similarity. Both groups believe that behavior patterns can be radically modified by the effect of one person upon another. Both groups agree that the infant's and young child's personality is especially vulnerable to behavior modification which is permanent in nature. This confusion in language and possibly theory puzzles the student of group psychotherapy, but one should remember that the relief of suffering is primary for the practitioner who cannot wait for theory to catch up to practice. The majority of practitioners who work with groups and who come from training that is psychoanalytic in nature or influenced by the concepts of psychoanalysis, attempt to explain group psychotherapy in terms of individual dynamics. Some have struggled beyond Freud's speculations, expressed in his book, *Group Psychology and the Analysis of the Ego* (1957).

As noted before, Freud was highly influenced by the concepts of Le Bon, the French sociologist who described the group as a collective entity — a distinct being. From this, Freud deduced that the group is held together by common identification with a leader and in his book Freud described what he called the *primary group*. Freud's speculations, which is what they actually were, have been adopted by many group psychotherapists as fact and as a theoretic rationale for their work in group psychotherapy. Freud stated: "The indestructible strength of the family as a natural group formation rests upon the fact that this necessary presupposition of the father's equal love can have a real application to the family." Therefore, to extend this concept, the therapist's love for the patient and the patient's positive feeling for the therapist sustains the individual patient in the move to the psychotherapy group.

The greatest strides in group treatment appear to have been made in the United States but there was a great deal of activity going on in Great Britain at the same time. Most of this activity was stimulated during World War II.

During the 1930s patient groups were formed in and out of mental hospitals in the United States. The purpose of this repressive inspirational approach was to foster a sense of group identification. A.A. Low, a Chicago-based psychiatrist, organized a movement called Recovery, Incorporated (Low, 1950). His groups were generally large and self-directed and he called his method "will training" since he rejected psychoanalysis as a therapeutic technique and philosophy. His first group began in 1937 and was composed of patients who had been in Illinois psychiatric hospitals and who had received shock treatments or physical therapies. The emphasis in Recovery, Incorporated groups is upon self-help with much attention paid to group camaraderie. It is questionable as to whether Low ever researched the literature when he began to work with his groups. Interestingly enough, Pratt (1953), the pioneer in group therapy in the United States, and a whole group of therapists after him, also made much use of group camaraderie. All of these people with the exception of Pratt, without being aware of it, were following the precept of Dejerine, the French psychiatrist who at the turn of the twentieth century wrote in a book: "Psychotherapy depends wholly and exclusively upon the beneficial influence of one person upon another." (Dejerine and Gauckler, 1913). Many therapists, as noted earlier, are quick to label their techniques as new discoveries but these discoveries seem to vanish very quickly. In 1957 Corsini tried to identify and label more than 25 different methods of group psychotherapy by name. Many of the methods that he listed and labeled have disappeared from the literature which supports the point made earlier — practice has been way ahead of theory.

The earliest group treatment techniques used in state mental hospitals consisted of groups of patients organized with a leader presenting the material that was to be used for guided discussion. This is a *directive-didactic* approach and is still used in many mental hospitals. The stress is verbal-intellectual and the technique is very applicable to regressed, psychotic patients in hospital settings. The emphasis is upon conditioning and pedagogy and the technique is also helpful in prisons, where group members evidence marked social distortion patterns. This technique is also used with paroled convicts or juvenile offenders in penal settings. The therapist serves as a leader in this approach. He may deliver talks or lectures and these have to be well planned so that there is maximum structure for group members. Often the materials are printed in a kind of book and there is a logical and planned sequence. On occasion a group member will be encouraged to bring up a problem which is then used for general discussion. It is believed that the planned presentation of material both stimulates and controls the associations, as the group members gradually begin to participate in the lectures and group discussion. The technique is helpful in a hospital where there is a staff turnover. Since the program is carefully planned another group leader may take over rather easily. The idea of the printed word is not too unlike a Bible reading group and the book format carries additional weight. The lecture and discussion approach discourages silence which is not helpful when one works with psychotics. This is far different from a group leader's experience with a group of neurotics where silence in the group might indicate reflection or introspection about a particular issue. The *directive-didactic approach* does not pressure the group participant. The group leader may stop his presentation at any time or return to material that has been presented previously. Some hospitals with the help of creative library staffs, have organized programs of bibliotherapy with assigned selected readings. Recently there has been an interest in poetry therapy where poetry is used as a bibliotherapy technique. The approach described has been effective in working with a variety of regressed patients. It makes maximum use of personnel who are encouraged to follow the planned program (Klapman, 1950, 1952). The work of behavior therapists (see Chapter 6) falls into the broad category of directive-didactic approaches since specific symptoms are treated with an intellectual approach. In one study patients in a group who suffered from phobic disorders were exposed to group desensitization. The group leader constructed a hierarchy of anxiety stimuli and patients were exposed to training in muscle relaxation. The group leader then introduced stronger anxiety stimuli while at the same time encouraging muscular relaxation. It should be noted that such techniques work with homogeneous groups — patients all suffering from comparable symptomatology. There have been very positive results presented with groups composed of people who feared airplane travel. The stress in the behavioral approach is upon relief of symptoms. It is believed that relief of symptoms will lead to relief of anxiety and that is the goal of treatment. Since the beginning of the practice of group therapy in the United States there have been many advocates of the *repressive-inspirational approach*. In this approach the emphasis is upon fostering a sense of group identification (Marsh, 1931; Kotkov, 1950). The group that is formed is strongly supportive and a subculture of support is set up. The leader's enthusiasm or charisma plays a major part in the success or failure of such a group. Many group movements such as Synanon (the drug addicts treatment approach), Alcoholics Anonymous, the Christian Science religious movement, Weight Watchers, are all part of the repressive-inspiration approach. The members of the group realize that they are "all in the same boat" and this realization leads to a tremendous sense of relief for group participants and serves as a stimulus to move forward. For the practitioner of the repressive-inspirational approach the following mechanisms are at work and may be utilized at any time: esprit de corps, communal feeling, an environment that is friendly, group status, group identification, socialization of the group, loss of isolation, ego support. The sharing of experiences and reassurance are of major importance as well as the testimony and example of others.

There are three major forces at work in group psychotherapy: an approach which stresses *action;* an approach which stresses the *emotional;* an approach which stresses the *intellect.* The action approach and the emotional approach are imbedded in the repressive-inspirational psychotherapy method.

## PSYCHODRAMA

Jacob L. Moreno introduced psychodrama into the United States in 1925. Prior to this he had worked in Vienna with a theatre of spontaneity based on action methods. He claims that he devised the terms group therapy and group psychotherapy to emphasize the importance of the group in the treatment of the individual. In his theatre of spontaneity he began to use play and role-playing techniques. His original Theatre of Spontaneity was located near the Vienna Opera which may have influenced his entire approach. Moreno, who died in 1974, himself, was an outgoing, dynamic man – and like a performer in grand opera would appear to be larger than life. His techniques reflect his approach to human behavior. He was very charismatic and his personality which may have been abrasive to some psychiatrists, has obscured his outstanding contribution to the field of group psychotherapy.

Since Moreno introduced psychodrama, he has developed modifications of the method such as sociodrama, role-playing, sociometry and axiodrama. He states that five instruments are used in his method of psychodrama:

*The first instrument – the stage.* The stage is intended to be an extension of life and is beyond the reality of life. It provides the patient with a "space for living." The earliest American psychodrama theatre was built with three stage levels, with the top stage, the balcony, used for superego figures. A circular stage may be seen as the aspiration levels of the patient on stage, as he moves from one circle to another.

*The second instrument – the patient or subject.* The patient is requested to be himself on stage. He is encouraged to share his thoughts and feelings and this is where the skill of the psychodrama director becomes very important. According to Moreno the patient is NOT to perform but to respond as things come to his mind. This is related to the theory of spontaneity and Moreno states that spontaneity operates in the present. He distinguishes between creativity related to the act itself — and spontaneity, which is related to the readiness for the act. Whether many of these definitions appear to be playing with language is debatable, but the reader should attempt to look further as to what Moreno is striving for — freedom of expression. Once the patient expresses himself a process of enactment occurs where the patient may present a current problem, or discuss his concerns about a future problem or engage in role-playing to clarify his fears or anxieties. The stress is upon the *actional* and *emotional* and the patient in psychodrama is actively discouraged from performing but encouraged to be what he is. Terms have been invented to describe the techniques that are used: mirror techniques, reversal of roles, double ego, auxiliary ego, and others that are too numerous to list. Some of the techniques that Moreno has listed seem to obscure rather than clarify but some terms have been incorporated into the language of everyday life. A very popular technique in psychodrama is role reversal. A father and son who are constantly bickering or overtly hostile to one another are encouraged to reverse roles — the father takes the part of the son and the son the part of the father. They are encouraged to feel, think and experience the behavior of the person whom they are role-playing and role reversing. Auxiliary ego represents the absent people or ideals, delusions or hallucinations.

*The third instrument — the psychodrama director.* The director is a *psychotherapist;* he may attack, joke or laugh with the patient. He may decide to be passive or active or feel that it is wiser for the patient to dominate the psychodrama session.

The director, a *producer,* keeps the action going. Through all this he maintains rapport with the audience which is always an integral part of the psychodrama.

The director is an *analyst;* he integrates into his interpretation of the psychodrama information that he has obtained from the patient's family, friends or neighbors. He also integrates and interprets the responses of members of the audience who are watching the psychodrama.

*The fourth instrument — the auxiliary egos.* The use of auxiliary egos (staff of therapeutic aides) aids the director, for this group of people serves as an extension of the director. The auxiliary egos are important since they serve as therapeutic actors and represent in the patient's world ideals, delusions or absent people.

*The fifth instrument — the audience watching the psychodrama.* The patient may help audience participants as he re-enacts all of the combined problems of the members of the audience. The audience is very important because it serves as a sounding board for the patient. The audience is a mixed group and this heterogeneity elicits spontaneous responses from both audience and patient.

Moreno believes that an isolated patient who lives in a world of hallucinations and delusions will be helped by an understanding and accepting audience. To this writer's knowledge there is no record of a hostile audience that was destructive to the patient.

According to Moreno, Freud was either ignorant of or did not understand the valuable therapeutic implications of the Greek drama. He also states that he has rediscovered the Greek drama and brought it up-to-date. With his usual expansiveness he has overlooked the fact that Freud was concerned with different approaches to human behavior. It is extremely unlikely that Freud was either ignorant of or unaware of the Greek drama and its value, particularly when one observes Freud's interest in antiquities.

In the psychodramatic approach to group therapy Moreno has effected mental catharsis by concentrating on the initial phase rather than the end phase of the drama. He believes catharsis to be embodied in every form of human activity and states that his technique and theory is devoted to finding both the different forms of catharsis and what catharsis means. He states that spontaneity is the principle behind catharsis. He also claims that he placed the psyche itself on the psychodramatic stage. According to his theory, the psyche originally came from the group — was transformed into a stage performance by an actor on the stage — and now is returned to the group in the form of psychodrama.

Psychodrama as a treatment modality and theory has gone through many ups and downs. It has never really caught on as part of the mainstream of psychotherapeutic practice. Moreno has constantly struggled to spread his concepts in the field of psychiatry, psychology, social work and education. His books have been translated into many languages and he has informed me that his technique has been used in Russia and .in Shanghai, China. The techniques he has pioneered are embodied in many so-called avant-garde techniques. His approach has found its way into many industrial counseling settings and possibly with the resurgence of interest in the use of paraprofessionals in psychiatric settings there may be a marked renewal of interest in psychodrama (Moreno, 1953, 1969).

Recovery, Incorporated was discussed earlier. In England there were also psychiatrists concerned about methods of reaching large groups of psychiatric patients. During the late 1940s there were professional papers presented that indicated that many varieties of group psychotherapy were being practiced in England. One of the important techniques promoted by a British psychiatrist, Joshua Bierer (1948) is the *therapeutic social club*. This technique is particularly directed toward the promotion of social participation skills among patients who have just left a closed mental hospital setting. In these clubs the therapist plays a largely passive role and minimizes his presence. Bierer began his work in England in 1938 and the first club was formed at Runwell Mental Hospital. The patients were and still are encouraged to organize the social clubs along parliamentary lines and to follow rules of parliamentary procedure. It is clear that there is considerable social skill and awareness that is required. In fact, what Bierer may have proposed without being aware of it was a form of modeling behavior, since patients learn from others as they are encouraged to collect dues, arrange their own social activities and care for the premises where they hold their meetings. This group of experiences is an introduction to the stresses of the "world outside" the mental hospital, and the acquisition of a behavioral repertoire helps patients deal with the "culture shock" as they leave the protected mental hospital. Even today, with the so-called open mental hospital, there remain many institutional settings where patients begin to lose the skill of social participation. The day hospital that gained favor in the 1950s is very much along the lines of Bierer's original orientation, although Bierer did not originate it. Another outgrowth of the therapeutic social club is the "halfway house" where patients often reside as they move from the mental hospital to the stresses of the community.

While Maxwell Jones (1953), the exponent of the therapeutic community concept, has not based his work upon Bierer's experiences, his entire effort to promote parity amongst professionals and patients and break down the caste structure and hierarchies which exist in mental hospitals is all part of a concept which encourages patients to stress their strengths rather than their pathology. There are probably mental hospitals and outpatient clinics which do not encourage or promote equalitarian structures because of many unresolved status needs of the professional personnel. However, study of the early history of therapeutic social clubs indicates that long before World War II there have been efforts made to encourage mental patients to rely more upon their own resources.

## ACTIVITY GROUP THERAPY AND GROUP PSYCHOTHERAPY WITH CHILDREN AND ADOLESCENTS

In the treatment of children the effort is made to support the child's ego growth. During this period the child learns to cope with his inner chaos, the emotions that almost or on occasion do overwhelm him. This child finally achieves an adequate interaction with the world and the community he lives in. The group experience provides a family-like setting. This setting leads to corrective emotional experiences. The group therapist guides by clarifying verbally, directs and restrains protectively.

In 1896 Witmer, an American psychologist, established the first psycho-educational clinic for emotionally disturbed children who manifested evidence of their confusion in the school setting. There was no substantive work done in a psychodynamic approach to treatment of children in groups until 1934 when Slavson began working with groups of children at the Jewish Board of Guardians in New York City. He described his concepts as stemming from group work, progressive education, and psychoanalysis. It is interesting that Slavson's social philosophy was that of a Socialist and he was very interested in reaching groups of people. He described his approach as therapy *by* the group rather than therapy *in* the group. By the time he reported his work at a conference in 1943 he had treated 800 children in 63 different groups. He described his treatment as "interpersonal therapy" and he treated children who ranged in age from 8 to 15 years. His emphasis was on *activity* rather than *interview* and that is why his approach is called *"activity group therapy."* Children were placed in a structured situation and the group leader planned his actions according to a theory. This approach is not to be confused with a variety of recreational approaches to children.

In the controlled group the leader sets up a permissive environment for the children. He does not offer interpretations but permits the children to act out conflicts and emotions. He sets the ground rules and there are specific limits. Slavson formulated his approach as he observed that children communicate largely through motor activity and the use of play gives them an opportunity to work out fantasy life and tensions. This can easily be observed as one watches children at play. They do not need an automobile to create and fantasy the driving experience. His goal was and is the control and education of the emotions of the child.

Generally the setting for activity group therapy is work in arts and crafts. The activity group lasts for about an hour and a half — a time span which does not unduly fatigue either the child or the group leader. The group leader then provides a meal for the children and they all work together in this task. The meal preparation, eating together, cleaning the utensils and dishes is all part of the sharing experience. The group leader gratifies the orality of the child and functions as a benign parent surrogate. There may be planned picnics or swim parties but all of this is within the theory of educating and controlling the emotions of the child. The warm, accepting, and giving group leader has set up a positive transference and the therapy is situational in nature. Gradually, it is believed that insight develops as the child is accepted. The group leader studies the interaction of the children and obtains a comprehensive picture of the child's conflicts and behavior problems. An activity group is composed of eight children of the same age. Careful structuring is necessary to achieve a balance. For example, the group leader might place in the same group a motoric, aggressive child to counter the passive, withdrawn child.

Many of Slavson's ideas were quickly adopted in outpatient clinics, hospitals and social agencies. Modifications of his approach are used with children of preschool age, and this is an extension of activity group therapy. The emphasis here is particularly on play. The very infantile and demanding child is able to express his enormous needs for mothering through the use of play materials. But unlike individual play therapy the child has to share and cannot have the group leader to himself. When the age range moves up to adolescence there is more emphasis on the *discussion* group but there is still attention paid to meal planning, feeding, etc., activities which would generally be discouraged in the adult therapy group (Godenne, 1964).

In low income, ghetto-type community settings the patient population may stem from such disordered home settings that there is a great need for a stable parent surrogate who serves as a model and provides a benign and accepting climate. By means of this model, early adolescents learn to move from infantile impulse behavior to a more *real* appreciation of the *real* world's demands. In this case the group, based on activity group therapy, meets a specific need and is much more effective than the intellectual approach, which may work with adolescents who come from middle-class settings where there is a more stable family structure and more attention is paid to the resolution of emotional problems through verbal interaction.

There are arguments amongst practitioners of activity group therapy as to the wisdom or inadvisability of placing only adolescents of the same sex in the same group. There are reports of mixed groupings but much of this seems related to the therapist's own personality, the supply of patients and treatment goals. More recently there has been work in groups with psychotic children and adolescents (Sobel and Geller, 1964; Speers and Lansing, 1964, 1968).

There are few follow-up studies of group therapy with children and adolescents and the studies that have been carried out do not control for time and other factors. But one can fairly say that group therapy for children and adolescents helps them feel unconditionally accepted by group members and the group leader. This in turn helps trigger off the child's or adolescent's own growth possibilities.

In a culture where basic values are constantly being challenged and re-evaluated, where the very concept of the family as a social unit is being attacked, the need for a planned group therapy for children and adolescents would seem more than ever a critical need in psychotherapy — especially when the suicide rate for adolescents is increasing.

As an additional note of caution to the practitioner, Slavson (1964) has cautioned against the use of traditional psychoanalytic psychotherapy with adolescents. He states:

> The essentiality of groups in the treatment of the young lies more than it does with adults in corrective relationships in the living situation, and all that it implies, in addition to reweighing of psychic forces.

In the treatment of adolescents in groups there should be an emphasis on the functioning of the ego. Consequently, the approach will combine education, guidance and psychotherapy. The group should have a minimum of a didactic approach. The actuality of the here and now problem should be emphasized in the group meetings rather than unconscious material. The group leader should use every opportunity, without becoming pedantic, to encourage psychological awareness in group members. Slavson called this the stimulation of psychological literacy.

For some period of time, *activity group psychotherapy* was eagerly used by professionals and then began to fall into a period of disuse. It is now being used again as the treatment modality for emotional problems of latency. It appears to be the best method for primary behavior disorders. One report (Beard, Goertzel and Pearce, 1958) even reported its use with regressed adult psychotics. The practitioner should remember that *activity group therapy* was the first method of group treatment of children with a theoretic design. It is basic to activity-interview group psychotherapy, therapeutic play groups in schools as well as play group therapy. While interpretations of behavior are not advanced, the principles and practices of these therapy approaches are rooted in psychoanalytic concepts which are based upon Freud's writings. The practitioner should always remember that the basic concept in activity group therapy is that behavioral problems of children and personality problems that result are to be attributed to experience. Further, these experiences can be modified by corrective experiences in a conditioned environment. This is NOT behaviorism, since the approach is based upon psychoanalytic concepts.

At this time, the field of adolescent group psychotherapy is weak with respect to theoretic models. The emphasis is upon techniques which may be effective, such as: confrontational techniques, encounter techniques, marathon groups, peer groups. Many of the current models are borrowed from work with adults and add nothing to our understanding of the uniqueness of adolescence.

Psychoanalytic group therapy has been covered earlier in this chapter. The more specific approaches have been detailed in other writings (Mullan and Rosenbaum, 1962; Yalom, 1970). Currently there are other modifications of this basic approach. The "newer approaches" appear to be a reaction to the more rigid application of psychoanalytic concepts. Possibly they reflect the disenchantment of some practitioners who had hoped for a much quicker solution to the emotional difficulties of patients. Indeed, Berne, the founder of transactional analysis (Rosenbaum and Berger, 1975) looked forward to the time when patients would be "cured" after one meeting with a group therapist. It is a dream worth pursuing, but I remain skeptical as to whether it is feasible. Two approaches that are "au courant" are the Gestalt therapy approach with groups and the transactional analysis approach to groups.

## GESTALT THERAPY AND ITS USE IN GROUP THERAPY

Frederick S. Perls, known as Fritz Perls, was born in Germany and stated that he was trained in psychoanalysis with some of its outstanding teachers. He moved to South Africa and there developed his concepts of Gestalt therapy. The term gestalt stems from the classic work of psychologists in Germany who used the word to describe the holistic quality of the human organism. It is extremely doubtful as to whether they envisioned its use in the way Perls decided to employ the term. Gestalt therapy encompasses a highly flexible approach to intensive psychotherapy and Perls believed it to be a theory of personality. Some of his students use the term to describe an entire approach to life. Perls moved to New

York City, where with his then wife he trained many therapists. He moved to Miami, Florida; Cleveland, Ohio; Carmel, California (Esalen); and just before his death to Vancouver, British Columbia. In each place he trained younger therapists and they became his enthusiastic followers.

Perls was a brilliant and charismatic therapist. He was remarkably intuitive but could become easily bored with a patient. He did not hesitate to express his boredom and simply dismiss a patient. He believed that individual therapy had outlived its usefulness. While his students describe his work as group therapy he actually conducted one-to-one therapy in a group setting. He would be seated next to an empty chair. This empty chair was called the "hot seat" and Perls would work with the patient who was seated in it. He would vary in his approach. He placed great value on dreams, but he might respond to posture, voice patterns or a problem that the patient presented. For the most part, the entire responsibility for participation was placed upon the patient who was part of the group. There was no encouragement to participate. Perhaps Perls felt that observation of others was therapeutic. He stressed the immediate and many of his techniques were and are related to psychodrama although he never acknowledged this specifically. He attempted to evoke intense emotional responses by asking the patient to take on different roles: he might encourage the patient to role-play the experience of being dominated as a child, although he would not use terms such as role-play. He was able to evoke very intense emotional responses and memories. In his approach to dreams he stated that each part of the dream, objects as well as human beings, represented a part of the self of the patient who presented the dream. This he called a part of the individual dreamer's gestalt. The patient was urged to express each of the dream symbols. Again, this is very closely related to psychodrama. The stress in the Gestalt therapy approach is upon catharsis which is very dramatic and which Perls believed would lead to basic change in personality. Perls theorized about the neurosis as follows. There are five layers. The first is the layer of social behavior. This he believed to be meaningless and consisting of trite or stereotyped behavior. The second is role-playing, which is dependent upon which stereotyped piece of behavior is to be examined. Third is impasse – when the therapist refuses to accept this stereotyped behavior. The patient then experiences enormous fear and a sense of emptiness. Fourth is implosion. The opposing forces within the patient are in battle and the patient may often describe this as terrifying. Perls felt that this was a fear of death. The fifth layer is an explosion, which may express itself in enormous joy, anger or grief. While there has been distortion of Perls's viewpoint, he was too aware a therapist to settle for abreaction *per se.* Toward the end of his life he was quite blunt in attacking the practitioners who espouse instant joy or instant cure. He called them "phoney therapists."

His techniques, while stimulating, appear to be more a reaction to group therapists who become too static and too intellectual in their approach. He discouraged free group interaction and was definitely in control of the group. Since he was a gifted therapist he may have justified this type of control as necessary in order to achieve his goals. Perls treated any comments made by other group members as interference. Many participants in the groups that Perls conducted state that they were helped by a process of empathic identification. Perls stressed simple terms and used vernacular expressions. His approach has been modified by students of his who maintain a longer involvement with patients who come for treatment. Of course, there are others who are more fascinated by the "gimmickry" his approach may foster. It is reasonable to ask what happens to the resistant or rather detached patient who is exposed to Gestalt group therapy. In my opinion such a patient would get lost. Perls's work, like many contemporary approaches, may reflect a certain impatience with a more introspective approach and is probably very feasible with patients who desire much more interaction with the therapist. Also, being the center of attention, in "the hot seat", may be very important for some patients. (Perls, 1969 a and b; Perls, Hefferline and Goodman, 1961; Fagan and Shepherd, 1970; Polster and Polster, 1973.)

## TRANSACTIONAL ANALYSIS AND ITS USE IN GROUP THERAPY

Eric Berne, a psychiatrist, originally from Montreal, Canada, began training in psychoanalysis in New York City and finally moved to San Francisco, California. While Berne stated that he was trained as a psychoanalyst, neither of the institutes he attended will attest that he was accredited by them. However, Berne began work on his ideas as early as 1949 when he published articles on intuition. He was concerned with the capacities of the ego and stated that the child ego state was the most valuable part of the personality. Transactional analysis, the technique that Berne developed, began to be used actively in about 1954. He organized a group of professionals in the San Francisco Bay area and they met with Berne from 1958 until his sudden death in 1970. Since then, his students have organized themselves into formal societies where they offer courses of training with accreditation.

Transactional analysis postulates three forms of ego function: the parent, the adult, and the child. According to Berne, these are observable states, unlike the abstract superego, ego and id. The *child* ego state is indicated by the fact that a person behaves the way he did as a child. Since society frowns upon *child* behavior, there is not much of it to be observed except at parties or sports events where "highjinks" are accepted. People who are locked into the *child* ego state use *child* expressions such as "gee whiz" or "golly" or "jiminy;" or they may walk like children or sit like children or act in a "wide-eyed" fashion. The *adult* ego state is rational but divorced from feelings. It is data-gathering and very arbitrary. The *parent* ego state is basic to civilization's survival. It is modeled after the parent figures or authority figures who served as parent surrogates. People are believed to live with ego states working at the same time but very quickly. Sometimes people successfully obscure ego states, acting like an *adult* while actually being the *child*. An individual may have learned to verbalize the arbitrary and capricious behavior of a *child* in reasonable *adult*-like language patterns. What has been presented is a very concise picture of the theory. In many ways Berne, without being aware of it, has reformulated the role theory of many social psychologists. For example, can one be a father, husband, lover all at the same time, or what intervening processes are involved?

As far as group therapy is concerned, a patient's behavior is understood in terms of ego states. The behavior that exists between two people should be examined in terms of a transaction. The transactional analysis at work is the transaction that occurs in the ego states (*child, adult, parent*) within one person rather than transactions among people. According to Berne, people's lives can be seen as a series of games which are endlessly repeated. He has described these games in detail and states that they are something more than what Freud called the repetition-compulsion. He stated that while the repetition-compulsion is the re-enactment of past life experiences which have never been resolved, his concept of games looks both forward and back. From this, Berne has described his concept of the script where games follow a predetermined way, based on decisions that the patient made in early childhood, when he was too young to make such a serious decision. People then, make decisions in early childhood that become the blueprint for life and, seeing life as a movie or stage script, they function according to the plan.

In clinical practice the transactional analyst observes the transaction, discovers the games of the patient, and works out the script that the patient is following. The group of patients is very heterogeneous and Berne did not believe in or encourage selection procedures. He did restrict certain patients, however, such as those in the manic phase, hysterics, phobics, and obsessionals. It is interesting to note he recommended they be treated psychoanalytically. Today, many psychoanalysts recommend that phobias are best treated by behavior therapists. When one observes the patients he excluded, in spite of his declared position of "no selection," he seems to have settled for very verbal and very motivated patients. The goal in transactional analysis is "cure" – a very elusive term. It is stated by the transactional therapist that there is a contractual statement where patients agree to meet in a group setting, and the patients often decide with the therapist what material is irrelevant or meaningless. It is questionable whether this goal is as simply achieved as Berne believed. A transactional approach to group therapy is very much leader-oriented. The leader is very much in control and this is not too unlike Gestalt therapy. The leader works with each group member in turn. Therapy is conducted, according to Berne, *in* a group rather than *with* the group. The therapist exercises strong leadership and he does not abdicate this role. Once he does, the treatment group becomes a "party." Transactional analysis is very pragmatic and yet is effective amongst patients who need a very structured setting and a strong leadership. (Berne, 1949, 1963, 1964, 1966).

The techniques of Gestalt therapy and transactional analysis have their antecedents in the work of Wilhelm Reich (1949), who has had a renaissance in contemporary psychotherapy with interest in "body language" and "body armor." Perls, a contemporary of Reich, was probably much more aware of what he took from Reich's work. Berne may have been aware but never expressed his indebtedness. One thing is clear. Many of the innovators have never really studied the history of psychotherapy.

Recently, there has been an interest in the use of video tape techniques in work with groups. There is a great deal of interest in the use of confrontation and the immediate replay of behavior that has occurred in the group. While there is a great deal of excitement about video tape approaches, it is too early to say whether the approaches will withstand the scrutiny of time (Rosenbaum, 1970).

Over the past five years there has been an interest in the marathon group meeting. This is a time-extended group where the group members agree to meet for a long time period — ranging from 12 to 48 hours. The group meets continuously and food is served. Occasionally either group members or the group leader take a short nap. According to its proponents the physical exhaustion induced by the prolonged time span as well as the intense psychological contact between group members who are "locked in" with one another leads to very accelerated group movement and interaction. The intensity is supposed to dissolve long established defenses. In fact, the group quickly attacks such defense mechanisms and simply will not tolerate them. The proponents of such an approach feel that the honesty and intensity and confrontation more than justify the abrasiveness and wear and tear that occurs. The question is whether patients need time intervals between therapy sessions to digest and assimilate the awareness and insights they have gained. Advocates of the marathon approach to group therapy deny this significance.

The practitioner who approaches group therapy may often find what appears to be chaos but this is not so. What is at work is a field in ferment. The growth of the population, the demand for services in mental health, the exigencies of training and the all too eager adherence to a theoretical position by some group therapists, contribute to the sense of confusion. There are conflicting statements presented between those who espouse a psychoanalytic position and those who take a sociological stance. This conflict appears in approaches to marital therapy, family therapy and couples therapy. There are differences between those who stress a group approach to group therapy and those who focus on the individual in group therapy. The term group therapy covers a great range of activities and many of these activities are aimed at different goals. The goal of each practitioner influences in profound ways the style and approach that is used. In addition, different approaches often reflect different personalities. A more motoric psychotherapist will often stress a different approach than a quieter and more reflective group therapist. There is no single approach and technique that is effective in the treatment of emotional problems.

Currently there is some degree of excitement about the use of encounter techniques in group psychotherapy. The entire encounter movement appears to have "crested" but some of the experiential and encounter approaches will probably persist in group psychotherapy. If encounter techniques are used selectively and used at the appropriate time, they may stimulate a transient experience of regression which in turn permits a degree of affect to emerge. Of course, the trained leader knows what to do at this point. The untrained leader will simply promote abreaction. For those patients who are very intellectual in their defense mechanisms, the regressive experience that is promoted through encounter techniques may work effectively. For other patients, the techniques are merely experienced as brutal intervention and confrontation. The reports of destructive experiences that patients undergo with encounter techniques are beginning to accumulate. Perhaps this is more an expression of poorly trained group leaders than of the techniques. We shall have to await further research. But we must move carefully in this regard.

There are definite indications that group therapy is often the therapy of choice and not a therapy that is used because of a shortage of personnel or an effort to "bail out" the waiting list in a clinic or hospital. The climate of a group that is led by a trained professional moves toward a peer relationship. A climate is encouraged which taps the "best" in the patient. Individual therapy often encourages hanging on to pathology. When a democratic atmosphere is provided in the group the person begins to experience different ethical systems and different social models. The therapist is finally seen more realistically and not as an idealized parent. The integration into a culture is promoted and the patient begins to experience life as a person. At this time, there are some group psychotherapists who are attempting to utilize general systems theory in order to gain a broader perspective in work with groups (Bertalanffy, 1968). There is some effort made to stress the use of positive feedback in establishing change in group members. This work is in very early stages and its advocates are struggling for answers. But all this bodes well, for it indicates that group psychotherapy is alive and well and growing.

## REFERENCES

Beard, J.H., Goertzel, V. and Pearce, A.J. The effectiveness of activity group therapy with chronically regressed adult schizophrenics. *International Journal of Psychoanalysis.* **8**: 123-136 (1958).

Berne, E. The nature of intuition. *Psychiatric Quarterly.* **23**: 203-218 (1949).

Berne, E. *The structure and dynamics of organizations and groups.* New York: J.B. Lippincott, 1963.

Berne, E. *Games people play.* New York: Grove Press, 1964.

Berne, E. *Principles of group treatment.* New York: Oxford University Press, 1966.

Bertalanffy, L. von. *General systems theory – foundations, development, applications.* New York: Braziller, 1968.

Bierer, J. (Ed.) *Therapeutic social clubs.* London: H.K. Lewis, 1948.

Corsini, R.J. *Methods of group psychotherapy.* New York: McGraw-Hill, 1957.

Dejerine, J And Gauckler, E. *The psychoneuroses and their treatment.* Philadelphia: Lippincott, 1913.

Fagan, J. and Shepherd, I.L. (Eds.) *Gestalt therapy now: theory, techniques, applications.* Palo Alto, California: Science and Behavior Books, 1970.

Freud, S. Group psychology and the analysis of the Ego (1921). In: *Standard Edition of the Complete Psychological Works of Sigmund Freud, Vol. 18.* London: Hogarth Press, 1957.

Godenne, G.D. Outpatient adolescent group psychotherapy. I. Review of the literature of use of co-therapist, psychodrama and parent group therapy. *American Journal of Psychotherapy.* **18:** 584-593 (1964).

Jones, M. *The therapeutic community: a new treatment method in psychiatry.* New York: Basic Books, 1953.

Klapman, J.W. The case for didactic group psychotherapy. *Diseases of the Nervous System.* **11:** (2): 35-41 (1950).

Klapman, J.W. and Lundin, W.H. Objective appraisal of textbook mediated group psychotherapy with psychotics. *International Journal of Group Psychotherapy.* **3:** 116-126 (1952).

Kotkov, B. Bibliography of group therapy. *Journal of Clinical Psychology.* **6:** 77-91 (1950).

Low, A.A. *Mental Health through will-training.* Boston: Christopher, 1950.

Marsh, L.C. Group therapy of the psychoses by the psychological equivalent of the revival. *Mental Hygiene.* **15:** 328-349 (1931).

Moreno, J.L. *Who shall survive?* New York: Beacon House, 1953.

Moreno, J.L. The Viennese origins of the encounter movement, paving the way for existentialism, group psychotherapy and psychodrama. *Group Pscyhotherapy.* **22:** (1-2): 7-16 (1969).

Mullan, H. and Rosenbaum, M. *Group psychotherapy: Theory and practice.* New York: Free Press – Macmillan, 1962.

Perls, F.S. *In and out of the garbage pail.* Lafayette, California: Real People Press, 1969a.

Perls, F.S. *Gestalt therapy verbatim.* Lafayette, California: Real People Press, 1969b.

Perls, F.S., Hefferline, R.F. and Goodman, P. *Gestalt therapy.* New York: Julian Press, 1961.

Polster, E. and Polster, M. *Gestalt therapy integrated: contours of theory and practice.* New York: Brunner/Mazel, 1973.

Pratt, J.H. The use of Dejerine's methods in the treatment of the common neuroses by group psychotherapy. *Bulletin New England Medical Center.* **15:** 1-9 (1953).

Reich, W. *Character analysis.* New York: Orgone Institute Press, 1949.

Rosenbaum, M. In: Wolman, B. (Ed.), *Handbook of Clinical Psychology.* New York: McGraw-Hill, 1962.

Rosenbaum, M. The issue of privacy and privileged communication. In: Berger, M.M. (Ed.), *Videotape techniques in psychiatric training and treatment,* pp. 198-206. New York: Brunner/Mazel, 1970.

Rosenbaum, M. and Berger, M.M. *Group psychotherapy and group function,* (rev. ed.). New York: Basic Books, 1975.

Schilder, P.    Results and problems of group psychotherapy in severe neurosis. *Mental Hygiene.* **23:** 87-98 (1939).

Schilder, P.    The current of criminals and the prevention of crime, *Journal of Criminal Psychopathology.* 149-161 (1940).

Slavson, S.R.    *An introduction to group therapy.* New York: Commonwealth Fund, 1943.

Slavson, S.R.    Para-analytic group psychotherapy.    In:    *Pathways in Child Guidance.* Vol. 6, No. 1, 1964.

Sobel, D. and Geller, J.J.    A type of group psychotherapy in the children's unit of a mental hospital. *Psychiatric Quarterly.* **38:** 262-270 (1964).

Speers, R.W. and Lansing, C.    Group psychotherapy with preschool psychotic children and collateral group therapy of their parents:    a preliminary report of the first two years.    *American Journal of Orthopsychiatry.*    **34:**    659-666 (1964).

Speers, R.W. and Lansing, C.    Some genetic dynamic considerations of childhood symbiotic psychosis. *Journal of the American Academy of Child Psychiatry.* **7:** 329-349 (1968).

Yalom, I.D.    *The theory and practice of group psychotherapy.* New York: Basic Books, 1970.

# 8 Family Therapies

## Sidney Lecker

As the field of family therapy has grown over the past decade to include thera-pists of diverse backgrounds, theroretical positions that range from social learning theory through psychoanalysis, time frames for therapy that go from intensive "crash" weekends to long-term (several years) durations, and techniques that in-clude conventional verbal interaction, family sculpting, and videofeedback etc., it has become apparent that the term "family therapy" might elude agreeable definition.  To those who both practice it and also observe the therapy of their colleagues who profess radically different approaches, the apparent range is con-siderably narrowed.  Most practitioners' work is quite similar in an operational sense despite differences in background theory and "gimmicks" employed to accentuate aspects of the mainstream process.  In this chapter, I will stress what is common to most family therapies and then discuss one theoretical framework that underlies my own work.

Any therapy may be usefully analyzed from the following points of view:

1. The therapeutic person

2. The therapeutic modality

3. The therapeutic context

All therapies (*modalities*) are influenced by the characteristics of their prac-titioners (the therapeutic *person*) and the *context* in which the therapy is practiced.

The best overview of who currently practices family therapy and from which theoretical backgrounds they come, is the G.A.P. report (March, 1970).  That monograph is worth reading as an orientation to the field, perhaps even before

the reader goes on with the reading of this chapter. As people, family therapists are more exhibitionistic than other therapists, using observed interviews
(live or on video tape) far more than any other school of psychotherapy. They
are happy exhibitionists, however, communicating freely with their students,
confessing their own mistakes openly to patients and transmitting an enthusiasm
about their work that succeeds in winning converts to the field in ever-increasing
numbers. Family therapists tend to be more surgical than analytical although
the latter, as in all good "surgery," is not forgotten. In family therapy, the
therapeutic "person" is often a couple, as the vogue of cotherapy has been
spreading in the field recently. The cotherapy phenomenon has been theorized
about at length in direct proportion to growth of the practice. It is more
common in teaching settings than in private practice, in my experience, for simple
economic and human reasons — few private patients can afford double fees, and
if they could, the private therapy fee scale for a solo therapist would probably
soon rise to that level. Cotherapy is expensive (but who cares when on a
University or clinic salary). Its practice is growing probably because the stress
of the session is diluted in cotherapy, the feedback from one's cotherapist is
growth-promoting and often, the therapists enjoy sharing the marital-parental
role in which they are cast by the family.

The *therapeutic context* of family therapy is most likely to influence its
practice and for reasons extraneous to the modality itself. In a Mental Health
Center Crisis Unit the focus is more likely to be short-term, partly due to the
nature of the client population but most heavily influenced by pressures of
waiting lists, the length of the psychiatric resident's rotation on the unit, the treatment philosophy of the unit chief and perhaps even his political philosophy which
may dictate that his unit distribute its resources to the largest number of clients
possible. In private practice, the therapist, his values, and the economics of the
situation may sway the therapy into a long-term model. In psychoanalytically
dominated settings, short-term family therapy may be tolerated as long as its
practitioners leave long-term work to the orthodox practitioners who wield the
power.

As the object of this chapter is to transmit information that will be useful in
the practice of family therapy, the remainder of this text will focus on the
*therapeutic modality* itself.

What family therapists have in common is the regard for the family as a
*planning unit.* Within the universe thus defined, there are some therapists who
see the family as the "patient" and will refuse to proceed with treatment unless
all family members are present. Others see the family as a system that has been
highly influential in the development of the personalities of the member children;
as the major arena for the working out or acting out of internal conflicts; and as
an immense reservoir of therapeutic and growth-promoting potential. These
therapists may see whatever part of a family that chooses to come to the session
or they may select a part of the family system to work with at a given point
with the goal of eventually constructing or reshaping the family into a viable,

problem-solving and gratifying personal environment for its members. If that goal is approached, at some point the members will be able and will desire to come to the therapy sessions together as a "final phase" of therapy. These therapists, although preferring to work with the total family, see that possibility as part of a continuum of their work in bringing a family group from "sick" to "healthy" family functioning.

What most distinguishes family therapy techniques from individual therapy is the use in family therapy of interpersonal interventions based on "live" here-and-now data, or historical data to illustrate the here-and-now phenomena, as contrasted with the reliance on transference phenomena in individual therapy. In order for the transference to develop in a therapeutically useful way, the one-to-one therapist must be a "blank screen" for the projection by the patient of disruptive conflicts and aspects or relationships from his past. The therapist receives attributions by the patient which come from the latter's experiences with significant figures in his past and current life. Realizing that the therapist has added little to these projections, the patient who authored them is made curious and encouraged by his therapist to seek the roots of these projections. Making these repressed influences conscious and thus accessible to reexamination by the patient and therapist is a major instrument of change in individual therapy.

In family therapy, the significant adults in the children's lives are right there in the room. The roles and role relationships that influenced the parents' personality are also alive and acted out in the parents' handling of their family roles. A father in a family, remembering his "son" role in his family of origin, treats his son with reference to and very often strongly influenced by his "son" experience and his perception of his father's actions which influenced him as a son. The family therapist cannot use transference as a tool but need not in order to be effective. He has before him a set of interpersonal relationships that are *directly* available for analysis and change without reference to how they may lead to transference projections and distortions. The energies available for change in family therapy are not limited to those liberated as defenses are weakened (as in individual therapy) but are the total energies of the family members — their collective strength — which can be focused on the sum of the problems encountered by them. Where one family member has a "blind spot" another can see; where one family member is fearful of experiencing pleasure another can show him that enjoyment is not dangerous; where one family member is mute for certain emotions another member can articulate these. The process of the therapy is to facilitate each member's functioning through recruiting strengths from the therapeutic family system (family members plus therapist(s)).

One may ask at this point, "If families have so much collective strength that can be shared, why isn't that done by them without the aid of a therapist?" The answer to this, in my opinion, is only partially available in each family studied, but the data obtained in a complete family history usually strongly suggests why family members in the "sick" family have evolved their functions in such a way as to cancel out each other's strengths rather than contribute their resources to a common family reservoir upon which all members can draw. The way in which this data is gathered, the theoretical framework in which it is interpreted and the way in which the family is encouraged to study their own functioning in the light of the preceding is the substance and technique of family therapy. In individual therapy, the therapist waits for sufficient "material" to emerge before making an interpretation. In play therapy, the emergence of that "material" is eased by the therapist patiently employing toys and drawings which are familiar forms of expression to a child and which also have symbolic value. Given enough time, the child will communicate bit-by-bit his perception of his life and problems through the play medium. In family therapy, the experience of the therapist is at the opposite extreme in terms of the rate of flow of "material." The therapist is deluged by family interactions and his problem is how to order those perceptions and how to set priorities as to which of many concurrent themes he should interpret. Individual analytic therapy is a "slow-motion" version of life. Family therapy is in "real time" with no "instant replays." Given the blinding speed at which events transpire in the family session, various schools of therapists have developed techniques to order and/or select the data that is emerging. Of all the family therapy professional groups or "clans" that have elaborated techniques for analyzing family functioning, the group at the Institute of Family and Community Psychiatry at the Jewish General Hospital in Montreal led by Nathan Epstein has developed the most comprehensive and useful tool I have seen (Epstein, Sigal and Rakoff, unpublished). With some modifications, the strategies and content of my approach to family functioning parallels and follows theirs.

The family therapist must operate with a troubled family at two levels simultaneously. An illustrative analogy of that bimodal approach would be the approach of an owner to his automobile having mechanical troubles. When one experiences car trouble, the universal reaction is to look for a good mechanic. But a mechanic may not know more than the rudiments about the principles and problems of design of an internal combustion engine. The real expert in that field is the automotive engineer. Why isn't he sought out (even by the rich) when the car is acting up? The mechanic has a standard set of tools and operating procedures. When there is a squeak in the left front area he looks for several possible causes. If he finds that a bearing needs grease he applies it, etc. The automotive engineer could possibly design a squeak-free car or a silent-squeaker. Why isn't he consulted? The answer is that the objective of the owner is to do the best with what he has — to repair his car and that's all! And for that task, the mechanic with his part-reflex, part cognitive approach to the problem is best equipped to supply a remedy. If the object of the exercise was to redesign the car to reduce or eliminate squeaks, the automotive engineer would be the proper man to consult.

In family therapy, the therapist must have a standard set of tools of analysis and intervention to set right the major and obvious defects in the way families operate. In that way he is a mechanic or technician. He must also understand the principles behind the functioning of a family unit so that he may create new tools as needed and help redesign the family structure so that it is more trouble-free or, more accurately, more effective in expressing and solving its own problems.

There are six useful categories by which to analyze family functioning in the "mechanic" style of approach. These are as follows:

1. *Relationship patterns.* If you have done a sociogram of a group (a diagrammatic representation of affinities and divisions between group members) you may also analyze families in the same manner. In fact, if you prearrange the chairs in the therapy rooms in a random fashion and say to the family, "Why don't you go in and have a seat — I'll be with you in a few minutes," upon entering the room you are likely to find that the seating arrangement is a living sociogram of family relationships. The identified patient — family scapegoat — may be seated removed from the family, possibly even out of their line of sight, slightly behind the group. Parents in a silent "emotional divorce" are seated at opposite ends of the group or with the identified patient — battleground of their disagreements — seated between them. A mother may be seen seated partially draped over her symbiotic child partner who is willingly or numbly so enfolded.

The relationship patterns become clearer and the quality of the relationships more richly illustrated by observing the timing of remarks, eye-contacts, affective exchanges etc., between members.

Having observed the relationship patterns, these can be portrayed by the therapist to the family. For example, one might say, "I noticed that throughout the session Jimmy (the identified patient) was seated away from the rest of you as if he wasn't a member of the family. No one invited him to move closer and, in fact, whenever he started to speak, he was interrupted or criticized by the whole family just after talking. It appears that Jimmy has no room for himself in the family and nobody is going to allow him or help him to get any when he tries for some."

Even in the absence of complete knowledge of the family dynamics which might lead to re-engineering of the family, temporary repair of a family defect can be made by an intervention which follows from the observation of a "sick" relationship pattern. Of course, any change in family functioning as a result of an isolated observation of a family pattern would probably spontaneously revert outside of the therapy. However, the persistence of the therapist, in this case in countering the exclusion of the child, can lead to an examination of the dynamics behind it as the temporary re-entry of the child into the family economy under the sway of the therapists' direction may stir up phenomena which reveal the dynamics behind the child's exclusion.

2. *Affective expression* may be clear/marked, direct/displaced, verbal/nonverbal. No key to a family's functioning is more useful than emotions which are hidden in some ways by the members individually or the group as a whole. Emotions

may be masked instead of clearly expressed. For example, a mother may say, "I'm disappointed" rather than "I'm angry" when expressing her feelings about her teen-age daughter for fear that her husband would side with his daughter against an attack by her mother; but the mother's expectation, based on experience, is that he would side with his wife if she took a "disappointed" stand. This conversion from clear to masked emotional expression on the part of the mother might reveal a whole complex of relationships between father, mother and daughter which may even reach back to the grandparents and their relationships with the parents. The small clear/masked conversion of affect should be expressed by the therapist. He may have to push his observation somewhat against the mother's resistance but may find support for the accuracy of his observation from other family members or from data which emerges later as a result of his observation.

Similarly, if the therapist observes that a mother, rather than talk about her annoyance at her husband's inadequate financial support of the family, stresses her son's poor school performance, he may remark how she is *displacing* from husband to son. Affect may also be hidden by denial and repression and in spite of these defenses be expressed *nonverbally*. In this case the therapist should verbalize what is being nonverbally expressed, seeking corroboration if necessary from the family. Often, the therapist may need to authorize the expression of an emotion by such a typical remark as, "I notice when your father cut you off while you were talking you clenched your fist but remained silent. If I was in your place, I too might have felt angry like I noticed you did. However, for some reason, you didn't tell your father you were angry at being interrupted. (To the father) "Do you want your son to tell you when he's angry at you?"

The uncovering of affect that has not been dealt with by the family invariably leads to revelations of the traumatic events which interfered with the development of a member's or the group's capacity to deal with that affect. Bringing such events to light allows the total family's strength to cope with the often long buried but still influential memories. A family that collectively has learned to deny depression because of the unresolved grief of a parent over some loss may through this "protective" device severely constrict their functioning and the growth of each member. By opening the system up so that the support of the other members can flow to the grieving parent, the mourning process may finally be completed.

3. *Modes of behavioral control.* These range from rigid to flexible to chaotic, and may be consistent or inconsistent. The noxious aspects of behavioral control modalities in a family may be the persistence, for example, of rigidity or chaos; or an inconsistency between all modes leading to an unpredictability in a member's mind as to what behaviors are functional or dysfunctional in that family environment.

These patterns of behavioral control may also lead to the uncovering of important family dynamics. A family may severely constrain one member's freedom when he is an effective "spokesman" for the group in highlighting the parents' marital difficulties. Once silent, the therapist may notice that restrictions on the "spokesman" ease. This unconscious group attempt to silence the spokesman may reflect the family's ambivalence about the marriage, seeing aspects which they wish preserved and untouched — hence the need to silence the spokesman who may "rock the boat." Yet other aspects of the marriage may be causing pain for all members, hence the need for the "spokesman." Undoing the controls on the expression of the painful issues can open the way for family solutions to the problems.

4. *Family roles.* Each family member exists within a role cluster. This aggregate may include "normal" roles such as parent, spouse, breadwinner, and "idiosyncratic" roles that are so varied that they are best depicted in the creative language of each family observer. Some idiosyncratic roles are common such as, "the scapegoat," or "the patient" or "the ideal one." Very often, existing in the role itself is pathological for the individual such as the, "scapegoat" or the "black sheep" roles. Sometimes roles within the cluster are pathologically meshed such as, "spokesman" and "scapegoat." Very often, the fact that one family member sees and expresses things clearly singles him out for the family's hostility. Sometimes two members carry conflicting roles such as when both parents struggle to win the "confidant" role of one child. Often, a role is age-inappropriate such as when a child is used to supply the affection missed from the spouse. Where roles are pathological, intervention is called for. Sometimes it must be surgical in style, such as when a child is being mercilessly victimized in which case the therapist should proscribe such behavior clearly, and firmly apprise the parents of the price in pathology such victimization will exact.

What is important to remember is that a role, although acted out by one member, is group-determined, not member-determined. One cannot be a "victim" if no one will victimize him. One cannot be a "leader" if no one will follow. When a family presents a member's role as "the problem," as for example: "Our problem is that Jimmy is a 'devil.' He's always getting into trouble at school etc.," the therapist should pursue a line of questioning as follows: "How did he get to be that way? When was it better — it couldn't have always been that way? Why did it change?" In other words, the therapist looks for the *group's needs* or *pressures* for Jimmy to act that way. The family will often try to convince the therapist that Jimmy indeed merits the label of "devil" or "problem" by running down the list of his offenses. They should be sharply deflected from such a course as the willingness of the therapist to hear the list of "charges" reinforces the labeling process. His efforts should direct the family to understanding "how Jimmy got to be the way he is." That is, the therapist should help the family to see what they contribute to the problem behavior of each other and how they, as a group use certain aberrant behaviors to fulfill group needs that may be better satisfied in other more productive ways. Very often the language of the family will imprison a member in his role such as when the "devil" is told by all what it is they don't want him to do but never what they would like of him or feel he may fulfill in them. The therapist in such cases may have to be a translator for the family, converting a complaint and restriction such as, "Jimmy always criticizes and attacks me – I hate him – I don't want him to talk to me anymore" into "I want Jimmy to approve of me or at least to criticize me in a way that shows me how I might improve myself. When he insults me it hurts, because deep down I value his opinion and need his approval."

Role-changing is always difficult, as Banton has described (Banton, 1965). The degree of difficulty is related to the increment of change and the number of people who meet the person in both new and old roles. The solution to facilitating role changes in most cultures is to cermonialize the change. In this way the individual feels lifted out of the context of the old role and changed in some way. His associates make a parallel reorientation by confronting the person in this new role at the ceremony. This function is basic to rites of passage ceremonies in all societies.

In family therapy, role transitions from adolescence into adulthood, from patienthood into health, etc., are facilitated by the "ceremony" of the therapy in which the therapist regards the identified patient in a different way than is customary in the family setting. In fact, all family members see their roles differently in the new context of the therapist's demand that they examine what positive contribution they can make to the family. The parents are seen by their children not only as parents but more clearly as husband and wife. And through the process of examining the parents' family of origin and how it influences their roles as parent and spouse, they are seen by their own children and themselves as children-in-the-past who shared the same needs and fears as their children are now experiencing. Through this process, role relationships become reoriented and often significantly improved through the mutual understanding engendered by such sharing.

5. *Family rules* are covert or overt. Every family operates within the framework of a complex set of rules, some of which are openly stated, most of which are in force with varying degrees of awareness among members as to their existence, ranging to certain rules that are so buried that there exist covert rules against discussing those other covert rules. If laws are cast with the intention of assuring equality among those subject to the laws, then an operating principle in that system of justice must be that there be "publicity" with regard to the statutes (Rawls, 1971). Relationships are most equitable when all the rules are known to each member of the social group. As Rawls (1971, p. 3) has said, "Justice is the first virtue of social institutions, as truth is of systems of thought".

Many families have covert statutes which restrict the expression of certain frustrations at the expense of the interest of one or more members in order to preserve a pathological but stable family social order. Family therapy, in exposing and publicizing to all members the existence of covert rules, allows for their challenge and for the establishment of equality for the members who must live within their framework.

For example, one child knows that to provoke an argument with her parent leads to a typical sequence in which the anger is followed by parental guilt and compensatory leniency. Another child in the same family, less equipped for or inclined to aggression, suffers severe restrictions in silence. In addition there is a rule that the members must not discuss the above situation openly as this would stir things up and cause trouble with the more aggressive child. Exposing the rule of silence as well as the rule that parental guilt is the key to leniency allows for a modification of family functioning to provide equality for both children and more constructive behavior by all.

6. *Anxieties, defenses, and their interpersonal demand counterparts.* Each family member brings to the family a set of anxieties and defenses against these anxieties which constitute his neurosis and/or personality structure. In family therapy we are interested in the interpersonal expression of personality structure and conflict and do not attempt to directly effect change in an individual's internal economy — although frequently this is a consequence of family system alteration. This aspect of the work of family therapy is by far the most controversial, as it is the center of the struggle between those who practice analytic individual therapy and those, even of the same background and training, who work with families. The criticisms of family therapy are that it, "Opens things up too quickly," or that it, "Removes defenses too rapidly without the advantage of a strong therapeutic alliance (as in individual therapy) which would facilitate constructive work with the anxieties uncovered," or, "It exposes children to the problems of their parents before they are old enough to integrate them." All these criticisms are accurate pictures of what goes on in family therapy and also, therefore, of what goes on in disturbed families as well! They are criticisms of the process of a sick family whose operation is revealed and remedied by the family therapist. The sick family does indeed load problems daily onto the weakest members, often the children; the family therapy reveals and relieves this pattern. It is true that a person's defenses and anxieties are discussed openly in family therapy, but ingrained conflicts and defenses cannot magically be dissolved by discussion. Anyone who has done one-to-one treatment knows the real dimensions and tenacity of resistance. The family therapist knows these features of personality well and is preoccupied with the *impact they have on other family members.* He is interested in what interpersonal demands are made on a developing infant by a compulsive mother. He may need to point out the need for an infant to deal with messes while recognizing, based on the mother's history as revealed in the family sessions, why she is so sensitive to messes of all kinds. He may remark on her need to keep things orderly much of which behavior is adaptive, and yet he might encourage her, based on her knowledge of the child's needs as "taught" to her by the therapist, to allow the child to mess and to learn his own way to clean up his mess with gentle guidance by elders.

The family therapist may also recruit the help of another family member in this process saying, "You know how your wife is sensitive about messes, emotionally and generally. You also know your child needs to play at home with some freedom in order to develop his personality and intelligence. Given the fact that your wife is so sensitive to these messes that she frequently forgets herself and gets terribly upset about it, do you think you might remind her when you see that trend developing or take over the situation at that time?" (To the wife) "Do you want your husband's help in this problem?" No lasting change is ever intended in the woman's defense by such an intervention, but it is aimed at dissociating her compulsivity from certain aspects of the child-rearing. As she sees the child messing and also learning to clean, or getting into emotional messes and being helped to express and resolve the underlying conflicts by other family members, she herself may become less anxious and the compulsive defenses less prominent in her life and especially in her interpersonal relationships. The goal of the family therapy is to acquaint each member with the impact their anxieties and defenses have on other members as well as to indicate to each member what they might contribute to the family system that might reduce the noxious impact certain anxieties and defenses may have on all members.

Up until this point we have considered six different aspects of family functioning that may be observed and changed in a mechanistic way. Where the therapist finds "masked affect" he attempts to convert it into "clear affect;" where he sees a private "family rule" he gives it publicity for the sake of distributive justice, and so on. At this level he needn't know family dynamics *per se* but makes adjustments to the end-products of those dynamics. He can change the consequences of bad design but cannot redesign the family structure. In order to do the latter he must move from the position of "mechanic" as in the automotive analogy described earlier, and assume the role of "automotive engineer" whose goal is to move beyond the basic set of repair tools and objectives of the mechanic and to redesign the engine itself so as to make it more trouble-free. At this point, each family therapist peels off in his own behavioral science direction since there is broad disagreement among family theorists as to what makes families what they are – what makes them tick. To a large degree the disagreements among theorists do not influence their function as therapists as most family therapy work is of the "mechanic" type which differs little from school to school. That portion of the work that is influenced by theoretical background does lead to different gimmicks, styles, or devices employed by the different schools of family therapy. I will not review and explain each of these in this chapter as the best advocate of any position is a "believer." I do not write contracts with my clients as some family therapists do because I believe that reward and punishment contingencies are only a fraction of the way behavior is determined. I don't focus exclusively on communication between members as the "systems" school advocates because there is more to families than the "how" of their functioning – I ·am concerned also with the "why" and "where" of their behavior. As to the latter, any therapy is severely constrained by the limits imposed by the therapeutic environment. People behave differently in an office than they do at home, work, school, in an amusement park, etc. The family therapist must remember this and inquire about aspects of behavior he sees in the office context, soliciting comparisons to other environments in which the members also find themselves. To a man who, in his family setting, is browbeaten by his adolescent children and henpecked by his wife he might ask, "How are things for you at work? How is it you can supervise three employees there but in your family you act like you need people hounding you and so they do?"

The "why" or meaning of behavior is my particular bias in family therapy and, to my mind, basic to the other approaches as well. A particular behavior has roots in the person's earlier experiences that have determined its form and impact on that person. How I regard loss, depression, weeping, and sharing all of this with others is based on my experience with similar events in the past in relation to the significant people then in my life. If I use a particular style of communication when I am sad it is because of the complex of memories that sadness provokes in me. If loss has an exaggerated punishment aspect for me it is because of what my previous experiences with loss have taught me. To re-examine these lessons of the past and how they have shaped the present is more important than writing contracts to change the present or merely changing the way in which the realities of the present are communicated. This, in my opinion, is where the "mechanic" hands things over to the "automotive engineer." This is where short-term family therapy ends and long-term family therapy begins. This is how "superficial" and "deep" approaches to family therapy are distinguished. In order to discuss the meaning of behavior and how it is dealt with in the family setting I must recapitulate the history of psychoanalytic thinking which guides my understanding. This will probably be the worst summary of the thinking of the psychoanalytic movement in its entire history, but it will also be the shortest and least boring.

Freudian theory viewed behavior as determined by drives that have biological roots which collide with social reality, and out of this confrontation an executive apparatus is born and shaped (the ego and superego). The ego psychology school (Anna Freud, Hartmann, Kris, Lowenstein and others) shifted emphasis to the ego with a variety of theoretical and therapeutic consequences. The ego was now viewed as having autonomy in the absence of conflict — it capacities of motility, perception, memory, etc., — not born out of conflict (having primary autonomy) but being susceptible to enslavement by conflict. Where conflict does operate to produce a defensive behavior pattern, that pattern might long outlive the conflict because of its adaptive utility (secondary ego autonomy). Therapeutically, the ego psychologists were able to view behaviors in new and useful ways. A child masturbating was seen as not only expressing a biologically-based drive but also, from an ego psychology frame of reference, viewed as expressing independence from his parents by assuring himself that he possessed the capacity to gratify himself in the absence of a parental contribution. With this emphasis on understanding behavior, therapists began to stress healthy aspects of all behaviors, even psychotic delusions.

Melanie Klein and her disciples saw the psyche as shaped out of a series of transactions between the infant and his mother. At first there is no boundary between the infant's concepts of self and mother. They both occupy a limitless and timeless terrain whose only points of reference are those events and body parts that generate pain and pleasure. The infant's perception of the good breast that feeds him forms the basis and shapes an aspect of his inner universe — his "good object" — by introjection.

Similarly the infant perceives externally frustrating, pain-inducing aspects of life which resonate with inner felt pain or anxiety. The infant tends to project onto the external object his inner discomfort converting a previously "good" mother into a "persecutory" mother against which he needs to aggress. The succession of fluid projections and introjections leads to many distortions as the external object is "taken in" carrying along with it the projections that the child has made onto it. Reality testing brings internal and external object images closer together in concept. From this splitting into *good* and *bad* objects a first ordering of experiences occurs. As time sense and memory begin to emerge, the child perceives in the same external object within the same time frame the currently experienced "bad" attributes and the remembered "good" attributes. This ameliorates the effect of the "bad" experience on the child and allows him to dispense with or reduce the splitting and projection/introjection techniques. He can hang onto and tolerate anxiety and pain by remembering pleasure; he can tolerate an apparently threatening-frustrating mother by remembering her good attributes. He then can develop a more defined boundary between himself and others as the inner and outer splitting is reduced. All this process requires in order to occur is that there is a preponderance of good over bad experiences. Under circumstances of stress, all of us have a tendency to revert to the earlier infantile mechanisms of splitting, projection and introjection.

W.R.D. Fairbairn and H. Guntrip (1969) in their object-relations theory brought the theory of interpersonal relationships a step further. They postulated that an infant internalizes a complex of frustrating experiences in which there was antecedent excitation by an exciting (but not gratifying) object leading to the internal formation of a libidinal ego. The frustration and consequent rejection the infant experiences is at the hands of a rejecting object leading to the formation internally of an anitlibidinal ego. The more emotionally neutral aspects of life lead to the internal formation of a central ego. Repression takes place at two levels according to Fairbairn and Guntrip. First there is repression of the libidinal and antilibidinal egos by the central ego, the ego of daily living. Second, there is a deeper repression of the libidinal ego by the antilibidinal ego. In summary and explanation, the internal desire for a gratifying object (libidinal ego) is killed off or repressed by another inner force which warns that "only frustration can come of such a desire." That function is performed by the antilibidinal ego.

The Kleinian and Fairbairnian advances of theory made it possible to understand how influential relationships are in the formation of personality. Henry V. Dicks (1967) translated this theory into an approach to the therapy of couples. The marital combination, in my opinion, is the keystone of family structure and must be understood if there is to be understanding of and change in the core family structure of disturbed families. I would like to greatly simplify Klein's and Fairbairn's concepts for a moment for the purpose of illustrating the point that the marital combination is central to family functioning.

Let us consider the psyche of man as composed of two aggregates of identity that are called the "good" and "bad" internal objects respectively. According to Fairbairn, there are four basic modes by which people deal with these:

1. *The Paranoid Technique.* In this mode, the person retains and identifies with the good object but projects the bad object into the outer world. He sees and condemns in others what he hates in himself.

2. *The Hysteric Technique.* This mode is opposite to the paranoid one. Here, the person retains the bad object internally and projects the good object into someone in his world. He idolizes in others what he feels he lacks, and feels internally persecuted by his somatic or psychic pain.

3. *The Obsessional Technique.* In this mode the person recognizes both good and bad objects as residing within himself and sees them as in a constant struggle. He sides with the good object by identification in an attempt to overcome or eradicate the bad object.

4. *The Phobic Technique.* In this mode, the person projects both good and bad objects and is in constant flight from the bad object which he sees as ubiquitous or in hot pursuit of him. He seeks shelter with those in the world upon whom he has projected his good object — that is, those in whom he has found strength or in whom he needs to see strength.

The use of the terms paranoid, phobic, etc., are meant to depict the four modes of dealing with internal objects and are not used here to describe clinical diagnostic categories in which the terms originated. We are all, under some circumstances, inclined to use all of these modes as are our patients. Shaped by their early object-relations, certain individuals gravitate toward the use of one or the other of these modes more frequently.

Let us consider some of the possible marital combinations that may exist between people tending toward these four types or modes of handling internal objects.

*Paranoid-Hysteric.* This combination might make for quite a stable couple. One partner searches in the other for just those attributes which the other seeks to retain and identify in himself. The hysteric wants to find strength — the paranoid can recognize only his own good internal object. The paranoid seeks weakness in others — the hysteric is eager to confess to weakness.

*Paranoid-Paranoid.* This combination might be explosive. Each partner seeks to rid himself of the bad object and find it in the other one who will become infuriated at such fault-finding. Warfare might scar and disrupt and even destroy such a marriage. However, the introduction of a child into the situation may stabilize things. The child can serve as a repository for the bad objects of both members and become, at a later date, the identified patient in a troubled family.

The paranoid-hysteric couple who were stable without a child may begin to battle with the arrival of progeny as one parent needs to idealize and the other parent needs to depreciate others. Each parent will then be antagonized when his projections onto the child are contradicted by his spouse. Frequently this problem is resolved when a second child arrives with one child taking the scapegoat (bad object) role and the other being idealized (good object).

The permutations and combinations between people with these four modes leads to a typology of marriages by means of which one can understand the core structure of troubled families — the neurotic marital combination. The children, in completing the family, serve as repositories for the parental projections. Tracing the parents' histories to their families of origin allows one to understand how the parents were used as repositories for projections of their parents' internal objects. The transactions between parents and grandparents and the resultant internalized objects in the parents explain the family's current dynamic functioning in all cases. The ultimate aim of long-term, deep family therapy is to explore the three-generational interactions and to relieve the members of the necessity of utilizing projection to an extreme degree. When this happens, they will be able to look for strength in others without neglecting to value their own strength. They will be able to tolerate their own aggression enough to recognize it in themselves without having to attribute it to others. They will be able to call for a halt to what is provoking their anger without forgetting to or fearing to ask for the love and support of the other members.

The family therapist in his dual role of "mechanic" and "automotive engineer" must first get the parts of the family working again which he does by clarifying communications, challenging stifling family rules, helping members out of crippling roles, etc. When this is accomplished he may go beyond that objective and explore how the family got to be the way they were when treatment was begun and attempt to redesign a family more capable of mutual satisfaction and problem-solving. This he does by burying old introjects in the past where they belong. This in turn reduces the tendency for family members to project onto one another and allows them instead to see each other and themselves as they really are.

# REFERENCES

Banton, Michael. *Roles: An Introduction to the Study of Social Relations,* pp. 93-94. Basic Books, New York, 1965.
Dicks, Henry V. *Marital Tensions,* p. 71. Basic Books, New York, 1967.
Epstein, N.B., Sigal, J.J. and Rakoff, V. "Family Categories Schema." Unpublished.
The Field of Family Therapy. Group for the Advancement of Psychiatry, Vol. VII, Report No. 78, March, 1970.
Guntrip, H. *Schizoid Phenomena, Object Relations and the Self.* International Universities Press, Inc., New York, 1969.
Rawls, J. *A Theory of Justice,* p. 133. The Belknap Press of Harvard University Press, Cambridge, Mass. 1971.
Ibid, p. 3.

# 9 Hospital Care

## Arthur H. Schwartz
## and
## Marshall Swartzburg

## SCOPE OF THE PROBLEM

Large numbers of patients require hospital care for the treatment of mental illness each year, reflecting the importance of this problem for the health of the nation. In 1971, there were 1,269,000 admissions to inpatient services in the United States (Mental Health Statistics, NIMH, in press). Inpatient admissions accounted for 43% of all admissions to psychiatric services as compared with 77% in 1955, reflecting a shift to ambulatory care for the mentally ill. Patients residing in mental hospitals at the end of a year fell from 633,500 in 1955 to 391,000 in 1970. However, more than 1.7 million people were hospitalized for mental illness at some point during 1971, while in 1955 only 1.3 million people were treated in mental hospitals.

Currently, the inpatient admission rate is approximately 600 individuals per 100,000 population. Males have a higher admission rate to mental hospitals than females, with the figures being 696 per 100,000 and 512 per 100,000 respectively. Of the patients admitted, schizophrenics account for 27%, depressives for 22 1/2%, alcoholics and drug abusers for 21% and organic brain syndromes for 6%.

By 1972 there were 1,917 inpatient services and 989 day treatment services in the United States. More than one-third of these inpatient services are located in general hospitals, one-fourth in purely psychiatric hospitals, almost one-fifth in residential treatment centers for emotionally disturbed children and almost one-sixth in community mental health centers. While state and county mental hospitals account for only 17% of the total number of inpatient facilities in the nation, they receive 32% of the admissions and house 78% of all the patients in mental hospitals at any one time.

## INDICATIONS FOR PSYCHIATRIC HOSPITALIZATION

Broadly speaking, patients are admitted to psychiatric hospitals for the same purposes for which they are admitted to general medical services. Hospitalization may be considered in the face of difficult diagnostic questions, when it is necessary to give specialized treatment, and when it is necessary to protect the patient and society from the effects of the illness.

A patient may be hospitalized for diagnostic purposes when extended and close observation of his behavior and mode of relating to others or special diagnostic procedures are indicated.

Certain therapeutic interventions, particularly those that carry a substantial risk of morbidity, should often be undertaken in a setting where response and reaction to treatment can be conveniently monitored. For example, such procedures as electroconvulsive therapy, withdrawal of drug dependent individuals, the use of psychopharmacological agents at therapeutic dose levels in patients whose physical condition is compromised usually require an inpatient setting. Psychiatric hospitals also provide a structured setting within which psychotherapeutic interventions are possible for disturbed patients whose illness precludes their use on an ambulatory basis.

The supports provided by a multidisciplinary professional staff on a 24-hour basis make it possible for anxiety laden material to be dealt with more rapidly and effectively than could ever be possible if the patient were not hospitalized. In addition, the psychiatric hospital can provide a complete milieu within which the patient's interactions with others and with authority figures can be directed and utilized, so as to become the major focus of treatment. In a sense, the total life pattern of the patient can be examined and treated within the "small society" created in the psychiatric hospital.

Hospitalization also provides an opportunity to interrupt the deleterious psychosocial interactions that patients may have been experiencing in their family, work or social environment. Such an interregnum enables the patient to reassess his position and his relationships, so that pathological interactions may be changed. Hopefully, new adaptive patterns are then developed so that vital relationships may be preserved and situational crises mastered.

Some patient's adaptive skills are so poor that only long term residential treatment centers can provide a setting within which these skills may be developed and vital maturational tasks, such as education, can be accomplished. Such centers also provide viable living situations for individuals whose home environments are so pathological that no amount of outpatient treatment could hope to insure normal growth and development.

Finally, it may be necessary to hospitalize a patient, even against his will, to protect him and society from suicidal, homicidal, or assaultive behavior. Extremely regressive behavior, during which the patient essentially becomes incapable of functioning on an independent basis, may also force hospitalization. In fact, it is such an inability to function effectively in any nonstructured setting that accounts for most of the patients who are hospitalized for prolonged periods of time, often on a custodial basis after having received either inadequate or unsuccessful treatment.

The Group for the Advancement of Psychiatry (G.A.P. Report, 1969) in discussing the use of the psychiatric hospital stressed the fact that "there are positive reasons for hospital care." In their view, hospitalization was not to be undertaken as a last resort, but rather as a positive step toward health when that health could be best achieved within a hospital setting.

To accommodate changing concepts of care and to take into account advances in treatment techniques, hospitals have been evolving slowly for almost two hundred years, with rapid change occurring in the last two decades.

## THE DEVELOPMENT OF THE MODERN INPATIENT UNIT

In 1793, Philippe Pinel removed the chains confining patients at the Bicêtre, a hospital for the mentally ill in Paris, and began a new era in the treatment of the mentally ill. Anton Muller, in Germany, Vincenzo Chiarugi, in Italy, and William Tuke, in England, were pioneers in their countries in the development of the "moral treatment" of the mentally ill. In the United States, Dorothea Dix successfully crusaded for the development of new psychiatric hospitals. However, the ideals of Pinel and Dix were lost in the rapid population growth and urban industrialization which characterized the first decades of the twentieth century.

By the 1930's, the typical mental hospital was a large public institution, isolated in a rural setting, away from the patient's family and home. Instead of a pleasant, restful setting, where warm and kind attention could be paid to the patient, the institution had become an overcrowded prison-like environment where custodial care alone was available. The less disturbed patients could work in housekeeping and ground tending activities, but for a large number of patients, not even labor was available to break the monotony of confinement in barren wards. Staffing was usually inadequate. With the exception of a few "interesting" patients seen in psychotherapy, an atmosphere of therapeutic nihilism pervaded the hospitals. The introduction of insulin coma and electroconvulsive therapy in the late 1930's generated some therapeutic enthusiasm but did not change the basic atmosphere. It was not until theroretical principles elucidated by the growing disciplines of social psychology and anthropology and reinforced by practical experiences from World War II, led to a rethinking of the basic concepts of hospital care, that change began to appear.

The necessity of administering large numbers of men during the war and the need to maintain effective leadership and good morale led to an increased awareness of the importance of social factors in human life and institutions. When these principles were applied to mental hospitals it was gradually realized that the way a mental hospital was organized had something to do with the behavior of the patients within it and the outcome of their illness. (Rowland, 1938; Bateman and Dunham, 1948; Dunham and Weinberg, 1960.) Goffman (1961) vividly described the devastating effects of the mental hospital as an organized institution upon the patients. Bellnap (1956) documented how the culture of a mental hospital was carried on by its infrastructure of nurses, aides, and long-term patients and was impervious to reform from the top. That a different approach to patient care was possible was demonstrated during and immediately after the war when the necessity to treat large numbers of psychiatric disorders led to the use of rapid and intensive treatment and manpower saving devices such as group therapy and patients assisting each other.

Perhaps the greatest jolt to the status quo came from the study of Stanton and Schwartz (1954) in which they described a hospital as a total culture in which staff and patients interact within a single social system where events in one area affect all others. They described how covert conflicts between two staff members could have an adverse effect on patients and pointed out that when such disagreements were brought out into the open and resolved, not only the patients' behavior, but, also, the mental health of the staff would improve. Caudill (1958) described in detail, the processes that characterized hospital life. To understand life within a hospital it was necessary to take into account not only the individual attributes of a group of patients and staff members, but also their relative positions in the status and role structure of the hospital.

At the same time that social scientists were documenting the structure and processes of the mental hospital, an effort was being made by mental health professionals to develop new models of patient care. If the social structure was capable of exerting a profound antitherapeutic effect upon patients, then by utilizing the principles developed by the social scientists, a social structure could be created which would have a therapeutic effect upon patients. This came to be known as a therapeutic milieu or community.

Maxwell Jones (1962), a pioneer in the field, described the therapeutic community as an attempt to utilize the institution's total resources, especially the nurses, aides, and other patients in an attempt to help the sick individual. To accomplish this it was deemed necessary to establish open communications and to eliminate the hierarchical system of authority so that patients and staff could examine what they were doing and how it affected them and others. These principles proved to be successful in a variety of settings including state, military, and general hospitals (Greenblatt, York and Brown, 1955; Artiss, 1962; Kaufman, 1965). The role of the psychiatric administrator both on the hospital and single ward level became increasingly important (Wessen, 1961; Clark, 1964).

It should be noted, however, that during the decade from 1955 to 1965, great advances were made in the field of psychopharmacology, with the development of the phenothiazines and the antidepressants. These drugs made it possible to manage disturbed patients in an open setting and by reducing agitation enabled the patient to participate in the milieu. By making fundamental changes in the course of a patient's illness, they allowed for fundamental changes in the hospital setting.

Developments in ego psychology provided a further theoretical base for milieu therapy (Cumming and Cumming, 1967). Cumming conceived of patients as individuals with impaired ego function and postulated that ego growth occurs through crisis resolution. Milieu therapy was seen as offering a patient a structured and protected environment in which the individual could solve a series of graded problems in adaptation. The patient could thus master the role behavior necessary to be a participating member of society. Traditional psychotherapeutic techniques could be interwoven with milieu therapy making both more meaningful and effective (Edelson, 1964).

The importance of the individual being returned to the community as a functioning member of society was emphasized in *Action for Mental Health,* the report published by the Joint Commission on Mental Illness and Health in 1961. This report noted that the innovative developments in hospital care in the previous decade had made such a goal possible and recommended that mental health services be provided on a local community level. The Community Mental Health Center Act of 1963 was passed to implement this concept and mandated inpatient units as one of the five essential services of a community mental health center. The need to develop new inpatient units in centers whose needs and facilities varied greatly has led to further innovations in models of hospital care which use the principles of milieu therapy as the prime therapeutic modality or as an adjunct to other forms of treatment.

## MILIEU THERAPY AND THE THERAPEUTIC COMMUNITY

Programs emphasizing milieu therapy with a therapeutic community model as their core have been developed throughout the country. Although these programs have been established in diverse settings including state hospitals, veterans' hospitals, military hospitals, general hospitals, mental health centers, and private psychiatric centers, they share many features in common.

Ideally, the ward should avoid an institutional appearance and should be so designed that small group interactions and a sense of community are fostered (Osmond, 1957; Lebensohn, 1965). An open door policy is usually considered to be an important element of a therapeutic community (Schwartz, Mako and Smith, 1972; Stern, 1957; Rubin and Goldberg, 1963). Its purpose is to foster a sense of self-reliance in the patient and to discourage tendencies toward regression. The message to the patient is that he must assume at least a partial responsibility for his behavior and functioning even in the face of very real psychopathology. It should be stressed that the feasibility of having an open door on wards treating acutely disturbed patients could not have been considered prior to the advent of psychotropic medications and other somatic therapies.

Prior to the development of chemotherapy, locked wards and seclusion rooms were the rule whenever acutely disturbed individuals were hospitalized. Hopefully, the appeal to the so-called "healthy part of the patient's ego" enhances dignity and promotes trust and a sense of collaboration between patients and staff.

In a well functioning milieu program, patients are introduced to the expectations of the ward culture by both staff and other patients at the time they enter. The patient is quickly taught that open communication is valued. Secrets between patients and other patients or staff members are discouraged so that decisions may be made in an open forum with the full participation of the entire community.

Patients are urged to assume responsibility not only for themselves but also for their fellow patients and may be asked to aid in the care of more disorganized individuals. Such an emphasis leads to group interaction and a tendency for peer assessment. Patients are encouraged to comment on each others' behavior, pathology and life difficulties, even though the assumption of such familiarity would be somewhat inappropriate in the world at large. Such activity further enhances the sense of community. All events and interactions that take place on the ward are discussible and become grist for the treatment process. The usual arenas for such discussions are the so-called patient-staff or community meetings and patient government meetings (Kaufman, 1970; Williams, 1970; Gerhardt, 1968).

In theory, the closer the actual functioning of a particular milieu approaches its stated value system, the more effectively these values can be used in treating patients. These values usually include free and open communication, analysis of all events in terms of individual and interpersonal dynamics, examination of each individual's role and how it affects others, and a flattening of hierarchical layers of authority so that power and responsibility may be shared.

Some inpatient units attempt to achieve these values by creating a therapeutic milieu program consisting of group centered activities such as group therapy programs, psychodrama, and an active ward activity and recreational program. Others go further and attempt to build therapeutic communities with an emphasis on patient government. The stumbling blocks to an actualization of any ideal model are difficulties concerning the sharing of power between staff and patients and problems relating to role definitions amongst the staff (Rubenstein and Lasswell, 1966; Greenley, 1973). Sharing of power varies from systems in which patients make virtually all of the decisions affecting their lives, including which patients may be discharged or placed in seclusion (Schwartz and Farmer, 1968), to systems in which patients have an advisory function but no real authority. The more disturbed the patient body, the more critical the decisions, and the more rapid the patient turnover, the less is it possible for the staff to share authority and control with patients. However, as Maxwell Jones (1962) has pointed out, there is no one model of a therapeutic community.

Recently, attempts have been made to study the atmosphere actually achieved in therapeutic communities and to elucidate the processes by which values are transmitted to patients and staff (Moos and Houts, 1968; Jackson, 1969; Marohn, 1970; Pierce, Truckett and Moos, 1972). Findings suggest that factors such as pleasant ward atmosphere, adequate physical facilities, and a high degree of patient motility and freedom to leave the ward unattended, reflect humanistic concern but are not crucial to therapeutic effectiveness. Small hospital size, high ratios of nurses and attendants, frequent staff-patient inter-action, and a high degree of patient involvement in treatment programs appear to be the important determinants of hospital effectiveness (Linn, 1970). In-creasing the size of the ward or decreasing the staff ratios tends to lead to a more rigid structure with greater staff control and decreased patient responsibility. Interactions between staff and patients become not only less frequent but also less spontaneous, supporting, and understanding. Even with adequate staffing there is a tendency toward less well developed treatment programs and greater cultural disorganization on large wards (Moos, 1972). The division of staff and patients into separate teams has been one approach to solving this problem on large wards.

The process by which a ward culture is achieved and maintained has also been studied (Almond, Keniston and Boltax, 1968, 1969 a and b). It has been shown that the therapeutic ideology of the staff is transmitted to the patients only through the social structure of the ward. Regardless of how frequently staff val-ues are articulated, they will have minimal impact unless the ward culture inte-grates these expectations with the patients' role in the particular setting. In order to maintain a stable ward ethos constant reinforcement by the senior leadership, of the values felt to be essential to the milieu, must be carried out within the staff as well as with the patients. New additions to the staff, as well as new patients, must be carefully initiated into the predominant value system.

Almond and his co-workers studying a typical acute psychiatric ward or-ganized as a therapeutic community found that while patient acceptance of the prevalent value system within the ward setting correlated with staff assessments of patient improvement, these assessments had no critical relationship in actual fact to how a patient fared behaviorally during or after hospitalization. They found that the maintainance of the ward value system was really of importance not to the health of any particular patient but rather to the health of the milieu itself. The milieu, in turn provided the social controls necessary for an acutely disturbed patient to be maintained in an active treatment program. However, they questioned whether some patients, depending upon their age, severity of illness, or expectations for care, might not fare just as well or better in alternate settings.

In addition to their proponents, therapeutic communities have generated a fair amount of criticism. They have been criticized for holding to a unitary con-cept of the treatment of the patient, regardless of the clinical problem, with a resulting loss in the diveristy and flexibility needed for a varied patient population (Fisher and Weinstein, 1971). Problems of role blurring and role confusion have been noted (Herz, Wilensky and Earle, 1966). The ability of disorganized acute schizophrenics to participate meaningfully in group interaction has been questioned (Herz, 1972; Spadoni and Smith, 1969). It has also been suggested that many patients might prefer a more traditional hospital setting (Linn, 1969; Levinson and Gallagher, 1964). Advocates of traditional psychotherapeutic approaches complain about the increasing shift in the treatment focus within the therapeutic community from intrapsychic factors to the interpersonal and socially disruptive aspects of a patient's illness. On the opposite side of the philosophic spectrum, therapeutic communities have been criticized for encouraging prolonged hospitalization for patients who could have been treated just as adequately in crisis intervention or brief treatment wards. Other criticism has focused on such issues as permissiveness, lack of lockable doors, avoidance of ECT, and the practice of consensus medicine. In fact, however, these criticisms are unrelated to the presence or absence of a therapeutic milieu and focus on issues which might arise in any hospital setting.

## MILIEU ON INTERMEDIATE AND ACUTE TREATMENT SERVICES

With the advent of psychotropic medication, halfway houses and rehabilitation programs in recent years, there has been a sharp trend toward a shorter period of hospitalization for each index episode. The trend toward shorter periods of inpatient care has been accelerated by the limited benefits provided by insurance companies, the increased cost of a hospital stay, and the community mental health center movement which has committed limited resources to the care of large numbers of potential patients. There has, therefore, been a shift from the reconstruction of the individual patient while he is still hospitalized to the suppression of acute symptomatology and the development of outpatient aftercare programs that are available to the patient upon discharge.

As a result of the above mentioned trends and policy shifts, the percentage of acutely upset patients in psychiatric hospitals has increased. Patients now tend to enter hospitals when upset for the first time or when they suffer exacerbation of an on-going illness. This population shift has made it necessary for hospital wards to seek a way to establish an orderly and systematic treatment approach in the face of potential chaos.

From the moment a disturbed patient arrives on the ward he is told that aberrant behavior is not permissible and will not be tolerated. At first glance such a statement appears bizarre. After all, has the patient not already received such admonitions from friends, family and society at large prior to his entrance into the hospital? Was it not because of his inability to adhere to ordinary patterns of behavior that he was admitted? The reasons for the success of such an approach in the hospital, despite earlier failures, are complex. In the first instance, somatic therapies are available. In the second instance, the ward setting makes it possible for the patient to receive assistance in what becomes a joint endeavor. Before hospitalization, the patient was asked by angry contacts to cease and desist. In the hospital, people genuinely interested in his well-being and, usually, without rancor offer their assistance and help the patient modify his behavior. This is most effective when other patients participate in the process. A disturbed patient can be taught, for example, that an alternative to assaultive behavior when upset is to ask for medication. A patient who becomes agitated after a visit with relatives can be taught that talking to other members of the community often affords an alternative to intensification of a psychotic process. Most importantly, skilled personnel help the patient recognize the apparent reasons and situations that trigger bizarre behavior. The establishment of a working alliance between the patient and other patients and staff contributes significantly to the amelioration of disturbed patterns of interaction. Psychotropic medication helps the psychotic patient control his behavior, while at the same time community supports help him reflect upon and modify his behavior.

The skilled staff is able to break into the upsetting behavior patterns by sifting out, contacting and utilizing those aspects of the patient's ego which have remained intact. Crucial to the functioning of an acute unit is the confidence that staff and patients have that upsetting behavior can be controlled and, in fact, often has been controlled in the past with substantial benefit to other patients. Patients who have lived through such interactions themselves are invaluable in insuring the success of a milieu approach. Without this sense of cohesiveness and common purpose, acute wards disintegrate either into chaos or a collection of over medicated and somnolent individuals.

Regardless of how effective such a setting may be, there are times when the social structure begins to fall apart. Sudden, rapid turnover of patients or staff, a particularly disturbed group of patients, or evidence of malfunctioning within the system, such as a suicide on the service, may all lead to a crisis of confidence in the system.

At such times it is essential for the staff to rebuild the sense of community. This can be accomplished in many ways. One approach follows the principles elucidated by Almond, Keniston and Boltax (1968, 1969a and b). Maintenance of the ward milieu assumes paramount importance. All other activities are subordinated to this overriding need. The door, if open, may be shut. Patients may be prohibited from going on pass, regardless of their individual state of progress. Individual psychotherapy, if present, ceases and is replaced by group meetings. The purpose of these activities is to focus the attention of staff and patients onto the community itself, and the focus does not shift until the milieu is re-established.

The shortening of the period of hospitalization has made it necessary for psychiatrists to continually keep one eye, if not both, firmly fixed on the factors that will make it possible for the patient to survive as soon as possible in the community at large. This necessitates an active involvement of the patient's family in the treatment process, as well as possible intervention in the patient's work situation.   Work with the families of patients is necessary not only to alter maladaptive patterns, but to make the family more accommodating to the patient and his symptomatology.   Schwartz, Myers and Astrachan (manuscript in preparation) have shown that families are much more satisfied with the results of the patients' treatment, and thus more receptive toward maintaining him at home if they have been actively involved in the treatment process.   Depending upon the resources at a particular institution's disposal, family involvement can be quite intense and include individual work with various members of the family, as well as a focus on the whole family, or it may be limited to so-called "family nights" where families of patients come into the hospital and meet with the patients and staff.   The purpose of the latter procedure is to at least insure a feeling of involvement and avoid the development of a feeling of isolation on the part of the patient.

The treatment approaches subsumed under the therapeutic community concept have had their greatest impact on patients for whom a 6-week to a 6-month hospitalization is both indicated and possible.   While all diagnostic categories have been treated in such settings, they have proven particularly useful for the treatment of acute schizophrenics, patients suffering from affective disorders, and patients with an acting-out proclivity triggered by marital or familial conflict.   During the first 2-4 weeks of the hospitalization, the acute symptoms which prevent the patient from fully participating in the life of the community as a responsible member are actively treated with medication and community support.   The effectiveness of such an approach is enhanced by the fact that the patient is removed from most of his external stresses.   These will not be reintroduced until such time as it is felt the patient can begin to cope with them without decompensation.   After the acute symptomatology, e.g., delusions, hallucinations, confusion, extreme agitation, psychomotor retardation, etc., has abated, the focus of treatment shifts to the prominent causes that precipitated the hospitalization.   It is at this point that marital conflicts, difficulties between parents and adolescents, and other adaptational difficulties that patients have had are dealt with.   The chronic pattern of maladaptive behavior, no longer hidden by the gross presenting symptomatology, becomes the focus of work within the ward setting.   Non-psychotic patients, who exhibit acting-out behavior which could not be tolerated within their social setting, often spend the first few weeks testing the limits of how much disruption the ward will tolerate. Like psychotic behavior this, often provocative behavior must be dealt with as it appears, in order to allow these patients to begin to deal in a reflective way with the causes of their difficulties in the outside world.   Some of these patients have what might be termed an initial "honeymoon" with the hospital staff, during which none of their maladaptive behavior patterns are manifested. This period of quiescence usually passes within a few weeks as the intense relationships developed within a therapeutic community setting effectively mirror difficulties that these patients have had in other close relationships.   During the latter phases of their hospitalization patients become models for more recent admissions and are able to help the staff care for disturbed patients. The ability to function in a responsible manner enhances patients' dignity and self-esteem.

The process of discharge involves a step-by-step assumption by the patient of the responsibilities that he will be expected to assume in the outside world. Passes to home, work or school and social activities are approved and monitored by the entire community of patients and staff. There are times when the community must prod a reluctant or regressed patient into moving forward and times when the community must rein in overeager but underprepared members. Wherever possible, arrangements for outpatient therapy should be made before discharge and preliminary contacts should have taken place. Stabilization of the patient on his maintenance medication dose, which usually involves a reduction from the levels required initially, should be accomplished well before discharge. It is not advisable to reduce medication just as the patient is being discharged. Ideally, the principle that only one major change at a time is allowed, is followed.

The supportive care and warmth engendered by the hospital setting as well as the intense involvement that patients have with one another and the staff in a therapeutic community is very difficult for the patient to relinquish. The outside world is usually not as solicitous as the hospital and it is often possible to ease the discharge process by gradually extending the period of time that a patient is outside of the hospital prior to total discharge. Meetings in the hospital which recently discharged patients routinely attend serve the dual purpose of providing supportive contact to the discharged patient and by discussing the problems of re-entry into the community, preparing other patients for their discharge.

Intense involvement within a ward means that successes and failures are deeply felt. Patients who do not respond to treatment, who leave against medical advice, suicide or who have to be transferred to other hospitals for prolonged care have a major impact upon the community. This is best handled by frank discussion between staff and patients. Without such discussions morale may be expected to fall and it will be hard to maintain a sense of community.

There are, of course, some patients who have the need to grow in a structured and protected environment over a prolonged period of time. Finances are usually a determining factor in whether or not such a treatment approach can be initiated. Currently, such well known long-term residential intensive treatment facilities as Austin Riggs and the Yale Psychiatric Institute charge in the neighborhood of $30,000 per year. Should such funds be available, this treatment is of particular value for disturbed adolescents whose families are in chaos and where a resolution of this chaos is not possible. It is also of great value in the treatment of patients whose pathology is such that community facilities, e.g., schools or the home environment cannot tolerate the particular individual and it is not felt that the particular difficulties are as yet so established that they cannot be altered by intensive treatment.

## THE 3-6 WEEK SERVICE

Increasingly, general hospitals are opening wards devoted to the care of psychologically disturbed patients. These wards, as a result of insurance policies and hospital costs, as well as the need to serve large numbers of disturbed patients seeking help, have tended to focus their attention on patients who can benefit from a 3-6 week period of hospitalization. Such wards have also tended to become the standard in the burgeoning community mental health centers and those general hospitals which formerly took patients for longer periods of time are tending to follow this emerging pattern of care as well. This shortening of the period during which patients are hospitalized for acute illness necessitates the structuring of a unit in a somewhat different fashion than has been described for wards in which patients stay for longer periods of time. Differential goal setting is also mandated.

Psychotic patients hospitalized on 3- to 6-week services spend a larger proportion of their hospital time in severely disturbed states than they do in longer term settings and they are not able to serve as models for incoming patients. As a result, such wards tend to have a high ratio of acutely disturbed patients receiving care at any one time. Either the ward has a high staff-patient ratio or it must limit the number of psychotic patients who can be admitted at any particular time. Biological and physical methods of dealing with disturbed behavior must take precedence over social interventions if large numbers of acutely disturbed patients are to be treated. The staff must become actively involved in the details of the patient's problem, since there is little time or opportunity for intense community relationships to emerge. Without such interpersonal and social controls it becomes considerably more difficult to maintain a so-called "open-door policy" on short-term wards.

It has been pointed out that maintaining an open door does not in and of itself constitute good patient care and in short-term settings an insistence upon holding to an open door at all costs may limit the type of patient who can be treated or actually compromise patient care (Abroms, 1973). Open doors have been said to limit regressive proclivities and to focus the patient's attention on the world to which he must return. However, the tendencies toward regression are weaker in settings in which patients know that they must receive a very time limited treatment and in which patients are discharged almost as soon as their acute symptomatology has begun to abate.

The open door cannot, therefore, be made a goal in and of itself. A balance must be struck between the amount of physical, biological and social controls that can be achieved in such settings. The dangers of rigidly insisitng that an open door must be maintained are that patients may be refused admission if they are considered disruptive, overmedicated to the point of somnolence if admitted, or placed in seclusion rooms keeping them isolated from social experiences for a longer period of time than might be considered desirable.

An example of how such a balance can be achieved follows:  An agitated psychotic patient is admitted to such a service.  Initially he requires medication at high levels and may be kept in a quiet room, if such a room exists, for a period of 2-3 days.  At the end of that time, if it is possible to keep the door to the ward closed, he can join the other patients on the ward.  When his judgment has improved even further, the door may be opened.  Such considerations play a role on longer term services, but because of a higher rate of turnover on shorter term services, decisions as to the "state of the door" come up more frequently and require constant assessment of the ward atmosphere as well as the clinical functioning of the patients currently being housed.

Short periods of stay influence the type and frequency of treatment that may be given to patients. ECT, for example, may be used for the treatment of severe depression as opposed to medications which take longer to act.  The guiding principle is the suppression of acute symptomatology as rapidly as possible.  The brief period of time available between the accomplishment of this task and discharge must be used to focus on reentry into the community.  As opposed to longer term settings, patients are often discharged on high doses of medication, with reduction to maintenance levels becoming possible only after the patient is reintegrated into the community.

There is little opportunity to use the therapeutic milieu to enhance the dignity and self-esteem of patients by encouraging them to assume responsibility within the hospital setting.  Assumption of responsibility must occur outside the hospital and in some cases must be deferred until after discharge.  Step-by-step assumption of life responsibilities from within the hospital is not possible and patients who require such a procedure do not fare well in such brief settings.  Patients who can return to a reasonably functioning state following a brief hospitalization or those who can return home and use outpatient therapy to accomplish this task are, indeed, benefited.

In a setting where milieu therapy is emphasized, the patient is given the message that he is in the hospital to work on his problems, without much relief.  On some 3-6 week units the concept of an interregnum is applicable.  The medical model in which patients are quickly treated and allowed to recuperate is more closely approximated.  Such settings place a premium on there being effective outpatient follow-up resources available within the community.  Indeed, this is a cornerstone principle of the community mental health center movement.  Without such follow-up resources, short-term wards are doomed to failure in the treatment of many patients, especially schizophrenics, and tend to become revolving door facilities with patients periodically entering hospitals and then decompensating upon their return to the community.

The concept of a patient as a member of a group within the hospital setting is muted on a short-term ward.  There is substantially less role blurring and a tendency for staff-patient distinction to be maintained.  After all, patients are less involved with each other and it is left to the staff to structure the social milieu.

Occupational and recreational therapy as a mode of rehabilitation and as a means of helping patients to deal with inner conflicts become less meaningful as hospital stay diminishes. If such professionals are part of the hospital staff, they must become expert in job finding, occupational testing and many of these functions must be shifted to the outpatient follow-up sphere. Following hospitalization they can effectively aid in the rehabilitation and resocializing of the patient.

It is very difficult during a 3-6 week hospitalization to intervene in a patient's chronic maladaptive patterns and long standing intrapsychic conflicts. Therapeutic interventions focus on the "here and now" and attempts are made to restructure parts of the environment. Contacts between the staff and patients tend to be supportive in nature and there is usually little, if any, attempt to engage in explorative psychotherapy unless it is anticipated that such intervention will be continued upon discharge.

## CRISIS INTERVENTION UNITS

One of the more recent innovations in inpatient care has been the development of crisis oriented brief treatment units, spurred by the practical needs of community mental health centers mandated to provide comprehensive care to a given population and by the growing popularity of crisis intervention as a treatment technique. Crisis theory as originally postulated by Lindemann (1944) and elaborated and popularized by Caplan (1964) states that rapid and appropriate intervention in a time of a hazardous life situation can prevent the development of maladaptive coping mechanisms which may lead to regression into illness. By preventing the effects of adaptational failure and the resulting disability, crisis intervention is supposed to avoid the need for more extensive treatment at a later time. In addition, it is postulated that resolution of the crisis can promote psychological growth and healthier adaptive patterns in the future. Ideally, crisis intervention should be done on an outpatient basis, but since seriously disturbed or suicidal patients necessitate hospitalization, it became necessary to develop a new model of inpatient treatment which could utilize the principles of crisis intervention.

While the exact format varies from unit to unit, most crisis oriented brief treatment wards share the same treatment principles. Every effort is made to prevent the patient from adopting the identity of a hospitalized psychiatric patient. The length of hospitalization is made as brief as possible, varying from 24 hours to a week. The patient is urged from the first day to begin to plan for discharge and often is told that he will not be allowed to stay on the unit beyond a fixed period of time. Treatment is intensive and psychiatric symptoms are suppressed with medication as rapidly as possible. Family, friends, and appropriate social agencies are immediately involved in the patient's care to re-establish the supports necessary for the patient to be discharged. Treatment goals are formulated as soon as possible and are limited in their scope. Therapy is focused on the "immediate precipitating issue." Every effort is made to correct those factors which made it impossible for the patient to function in his usual role and thus necessitated hospitalization.

Brief treatment units are characterized by a high degree of flexibility. Scheduled ward activities are usually held to a minimum. A daily patient and staff meeting to plan the day's activities and to review progress is often the only ward meeting in crisis units. Work passes, home visits, and day or night hospitalization programs are tailored to fit the needs of the individual patient. The patient is continually encouraged to assume as much of his usual role in society as possible.

Discharge takes place when the acute symptomatology improves and a social network in which the patient will be able to survive is established. Patients who are unable to be discharged are referred for further hospitalization. Outpatient follow-up is often provided by the staff of the crisis unit for a period of time to provide continuity of care during the critical period immediately following discharge from the hospital. The patient is later referred to other outpatient facilities or discharged from treatment. The more risks a unit is willing to run in its discharge policy, the more crucial close follow-up becomes since significant numbers of patients will be unable to tolerate discharge and will have to be readmitted.

Patient care on brief treatment units is by its very nature intensive, demanding, and stressful work requiring rapid assessment and decision making. For this reason the team format is often used so that the stresses and anxieties may be shared among team members who can mutually support each other. One team may be working with the patient, a second with the patient's family, and a third with social agencies. Because of the short duration of the patient's stay, many clinical activities must take place in the evening hours and during weekends and thus more staff members become involved in the patient's treatment. This further magnifies the need for careful coordination and good working relationships among team members.

In one setting which utilized a 3-5 day hospitalization format, 63% of all patients admitted were able to be discharged without further hospitalization during a follow-up period of one year. Of those patients with a schizophrenic diagnosis, 50% were able to be discharged without the need for further hospitalization (Weisman, Feirstein and Thomas, 1969). Similar results have been reported by other units (Rhine and Mayerson, 1971).

Brief treatment units are ineffective in treating illnesses where no amount of social intervention can significantly shorten the course of the illness. Patients with severe psychotic depressions, full blown manic attacks, severe schizophrenic reactions, and certain organic states rarely can recover sufficiently to be discharged within one week. However, brief treatment units are often very successful in treating chronic schizophrenics who have adjusted their lives to the limitations imposed by their illness, but who have had a mild to moderate exacerbation of their symptoms because of some life stress. Patients with mild hypomanic episodes often can be started on medication and safely discharged within a week. The protective setting of a hospital and the facilities for rapid intervention in the social field make brief treatment units especially useful in the treatment of patients with neurotic depressions, with suicidal ideation, or those who have made a suicide gesture.

Crisis intervention units have been criticized on both theoretical and practical grounds. Crisis reactions are varied and unclassified. In a strict sense a "crisis" refers to a life event or circumstance which brings about a disruption of adaptation in which the usual modes of coping no longer work. Used in its loosest sense, crisis becomes almost synonymous with the concept of precipitating event and almost any patient can then be designated a "crisis patient."

It has been questioned whether crisis theory in its strictest sense is in fact applicable to many of the patients admitted to crisis intervention wards. Schizophrenic patients have been shown to decompensate in life situations that are not particularly hazardous and schizophrenia as an illness does not fit the crisis model of rapid resolution (Beck and Worthen, 1972). There is also a growing awareness that many other patients who appear to be in an acute crisis have long standing characterological problems and ego weaknesses that make the psychological growth and long-term therapeutic gain that theoretically should follow crisis resolution highly unlikely. In general, it can be said that the ability of crisis intervention techniques to promote growth and to facilitate more effective coping in the future is far from proven (Langsley, 1972).

Brief treatment units have also been criticized for taking too many risks with disturbed and suicidal patients, for forcing patients to make important life decisions before the implications are fully understood by either staff or patients, and for giving patients the sense that they are being hurried out of the hospital. At times there is a tendency to over concentrate on the life events that precipitated the patient's entrance into the hospital and to pay inadequate attention to the psychopathology of the underlying illness. When prevention of hospitalization to avoid regression is seen as an end in and of itself, clinicians may become reluctant to refer the patient for further hospitalization despite the clinical indications for such a referral.

Although brief treatment units have many theoretical shortcomings and practical problems, the popularity of these units continues to grow. Large numbers of patients are presenting themselves for treatment at the emergency rooms of hospitals or at the walk-in clinics of mental health centers. Many require inpatient treatment. The advantage of brief treatment units is that they enable hospitals to treat large numbers of patients and provide at least symptomatic relief. Brief treatment units are a relatively new development and they are still in a period of evolution. While crisis theory provided the initial rationale for these units, the theory is not crucial to the functioning of these units especially as they become integrated into systems of services and facilities that can provide comprehensive mental health care. Pragmatic and empirical considerations and observations must take precedence. Brief treatment should be applied where it can work and crisis intervention is only one brief treatment model.

In addition to brief treatment, these units can serve as highly sophisticated admission units where skilled evaluation can be done and appropriate dispositions, either to further inpatient or outpatient treatment, can be made. In a system of mental health care that is becoming more varied and complex this task has assumed increasing importance.

## THE STATE HOSPITAL AND PROBLEMS OF CHRONICITY

It was initially believed by some mental health administrators that new techniques of treatment combined with the increasing availability of community mental health facilities would allow state hospitals to be gradually phased out (Stewart, LaFare, Grunberg and Herjanic, 1968; Hecker, 1970). This hope was given some credence by a steadily falling census since new medications, expanded ward treatment programs, and increased community facilities allowed patients to be discharged from state hospitals to their families or to convalescent homes, halfway houses and boarding houses (Lamb, 1968). However, not all patients could be discharged and, many who were, returned to the state hospital after short periods of residence in the community. It has become apparent that while the typical state hospital may be changing, reports of its imminent demise were premature.

Among the new developments at state hospitals, as well as V.A. hospitals, has been the use of behavior modification techniques. Behavior therapy has been used to treat patients with severe regression manifested by such symptoms as mutism, eating disorders or deviant behavior (Ayllon and Michael, 1959; Ayllon, 1963; Ayllon and Azrin, 1964). Verbal conditioning has been used to convert irrational and delusional speech into more appropriate communications (Rickard, Dignam and Horner, 1960; Ullmann, Krasner and Collins, 1961; Meichenbaum, 1966a and b). The theoretical basis of these techniques has been questioned as well as the amount of generalization, resulting in the improvement of other areas of the patient's behavior that occurs (Greenspoon, 1962; Davidson, 1969). While it is yet to be shown that patients can improve sufficiently to be discharged with the use of these techniques alone, they may be used to ease problems of ward management and allow the patient to participate in other treatment approaches.

Behavior modification techniques have also been used to organize wards as token economies. In a token economy, patients are given tokens for desired behavior. The rewarded behavior can be anything from a simple activity such as self-care in the case of a regressed patient, to more difficult accomplishments such as satisfactory job performance in the case of a patient approaching discharge. The tokens, in turn, can be exchanged for simple privileges such as watching T.V., to more significant rewards such as obtaining a more desirable job within the hospital. In state and V.A. hospitals where a shortage of personnel often exists, these programs are especially useful in dealing with chronic patients whose discharge is prevented, not by acute psychiatric symptomatology, but rather by decreased social skills and motivation. This is especially true in V.A. hospitals where patients with service connected disabilities are literally paid for remaining sick and hospitalized. How effective token economies are in producing an increased discharge rate is still uncertain. In one study, following the establishment of a token economy, twice as many men were discharged from the hospital compared with the previous year. However, half of the discharged patients returned in nine months (Atthowe and Crasner, 1968).

Despite the recent advances in the treatment of chronic patients it has become apparent that there is a hard core of patients who are refractory to treatment and cannot be discharged (Lamb and Goertzel, 1972). One group of hard core patients consists of those who cannot manage outside a hospital setting. Such patients include assaultive patients, extremely regressed patients, patients with severe organic pathology and patients with antisocial proclivities such as fire setting or deviant sexual behavior. Another group consists of those patients who are determined to lead an institutional existence and who will defeat any attempt to maintain them outside of a hospital setting.

It is also being recognized that the placement of patients in the community does not guarantee an existence preferable to a hospital (Lamb and Goertzel, 1971). An individual can lead an institutionalized existence in a boarding house as well as in a state hospital and in many instances a hospital environment may be more humane (Aviram and Segal, 1973).

In addition to long-term patients, the state hospital must serve new patients who continue to enter. Despite the expansion of the community mental health center system, many communities have inadequate or no facilities. In other cases, efforts on the part of community hospitals to achieve open wards result in the referral of severely agitated patients to state hospitals. Difficult to treat patients such as alcoholics, drug addicts, and patients with organic pathology are often selectively referred to state hospitals. Modern treatment techniques have resulted in a progressively shorter length of stay in the hospital but inadequate follow-up often results in the revolving door phenomenon where patients are discharged only to return again and again to the hospital. Significantly, more patients released without referral are rehospitalized compared to those referred for outpatient care (Zolik, Lantz and Sommers, 1968). Even when adequate referral resources are available, the referral process may be subverted. Hostile and belligerent demands for release on the part of the patient or his family may lead to inadequate discharge planning. In other instances the staff may feel that the patient will not follow through and hence make only a half-hearted effort to arrange a proper disposition. If the lag time between discharge and the first outpatient visits exceeds two weeks, an inordinately high rehospitalization rate results (Zolik, Lantz and Sommers, 1968). It is very common to see schizophrenics, who stop their medication as soon as the supply issued to them at discharge by the hospital runs out, re-enter the hospital with a recurrence of psychotic symptoms.

In an effort to provide continuity of care, many state hospitals have adopted a program of regionalization in which a given unit of the state hospital serves a particular geographic catchment area. (Greenblatt, Sharaf and Stone, 1971). Follow-up services may also be provided by this unit and close linkages can be developed between a catchmented unit and community resources in their area.

It has also been suggested that the previously mentioned policy of early discharge may not be the wisest course for many patients. Kris, Schiff and McLaughlin, (1971) have noted that many chronic patients do not begin their chronic hospitalization with their first hospitalization but are discharged only to return and then become chronic hospital patients. This is especially true of adolescents who may require a more substantial in-hospital effort to master developmental tasks prior to discharge if rehospitalization and chronicity are to be avoided.

While many state hospital systems have made marked progress in improving the quality of care offered to mentally ill patients, recent court decisions applying the concept of "right to treatment" have tended to prod laggard systems into modernizing and upgrading their programs. Courts have held that patients who are involuntarily hospitalized have a right to treatment and merely offering custodial care does not satisfy this right (Bazelon, 1969). In some cases, the courts have gone so far as to decree the number and qualifications of mental health professionals required to provide adequate care for a given patient population (Robitscher, 1972). These mandates, however, ignore the hard reality that there are some patients and conditions which, given the present state of the art, often do not respond to even the most intensive treatment approaches (Twerski, 1971). The resolution of this conflict may lie in the development of objective standards of patient care which would allow the care offered by an institution to be evaluated and compared with other facilities.

## PARTIAL HOSPITALIZATION

The first modern psychiatric day hospital was begun by Dzhagarov in Moscow in 1933. However, it was not until after World War II that such hospitals were established in the western world. (Bierer, 1951; Cameron, 1947). Between 1958 and 1963 the number of day and night treatment centers increased from 8 to 141 (*APA Proceedings,* 1958; Conwell, Rosen, Hench and Bahn, 1964). Partial hospitalization peaked in popularity during the 1960s with the development of community mental health centers, since it was one of the five mandated services qualifying a center for public support (Kramer, 1962).

In recent years the popularity of day hospitals declined as it became possible to specify more clearly the various tasks that day hospitals had performed and to compare the efficacy and efficiency of the day hospital and other treatment settings with respect to these functions (Astrachan, Flynn, Geller and Harvey, 1970).

Day hospitals can perform three basic functions. They can function as an alternative to full-time hospitalization, as a stepping stone from full hospitalization to outpatient treatment, and as a setting for the rehabilitation of the chronically ill.

Day hospitals, as an alternative to inpatient wards, can be organized as free standing units not attached to an inpatient service. The purpose of such an arrangement is to keep the patient involved at least partially, with his family and his community. Treatment techniques that have been found useful on inpatient wards, e.g., milieu, are applied in similar fashion in these settings. While day hospitals can be organized in many different ways they lend themselves particularly well to a team structure. In such settings a particular group of staff members become expert in the problems of a specific group of patients. Since patients leave the hospital each day, inter-team difficulties are minimized.

Therapeutic activities in the day setting have included group, individual and family therapy, occupational and recreational therapy, psychodrama and, where indicated, somatic therapies including electroshock therapy. A typical feature in most day settings is a "wrap-up" meeting at the end of each day to assess each patient's progress and to evaluate whether or not each individual may return to the community for the night. The more disturbed the patient population, the more vital such a wrap-up becomes.

A variety of clinical conditions can be treated in a day hospital setting. Such conditions include schizophrenia, depression and character disorders. In general, schizophrenics treated in day hospital settings are less confused, show fewer cognitive disturbances and have a greater degree of social competence than those treated in inpatient settings. Depressed patients in day hospitals tend to be more similar to those found on inpatient wards (Hogarty, Dennis, Guy and Gross, 1968). Unless no other treatment facilities are available, acutely suicidal, homicidal or confused patients are not ordinarily accepted into day hospitals.

With the development of comprehensive mental health services the range of patients referred to day hospitals as an alternative to inpatient hospitalization has narrowed. Severely disturbed patients are sent to inpatient units; acute patients, with a potential for rapid recompensation, are referred to crisis intervention units. Patients without gross disturbances are, increasingly, being treated on an outpatient basis, which has been made increasingly possible by advances in psychopharmacology. As a result there is a tendency for day hospitals, established as alternatives to inpatient units, to concentrate their efforts on patients who tend to be more chronic, and who see active treatment as a threat to longstanding regressive needs and patterns of dependency. Such patients tend to stay in day hospitals for prolonged periods of time, exceeding in average stay the amount of time more acute patients have to spend on inpatient units.

While the popularity of the free-standing day hospital has, for the above mentioned reasons, declined in recent years, it has left an impact on the care of hospitalized patients. It is now recognized that the use of day status is a valuable tool in facilitating a patient's re-entry to his home, community or work after a period of hospitalization. Day hospitals fulfilling this transition function are best associated with an inpatient service so that continuity of care may be preserved. This has further tended to limit the utilization of free-standing day hospitals for the care of patients. Day hospitals associated with inpatient services function best if patients are first admitted to the inpatient service. This allows each patient to become a part of the total program. If patients are directly admitted to day status they may view themselves as "better," more privileged and less sick than the inpatients. Alternatively, they may feel deprived, less cared for and barred from "real" treatment.

While not as common as day hospitalization, night hospitalization offers specific advantages, especially for the male patient, over traditional hospitalization (Beigel and Feder, 1970). A patient may continue to work, while at the same time being protected from stresses in his home environment. Concentrated hospital treatment is possible without jeopardizing the patient's job. Its main use is as a transition from inpatient care when it is important to determine if patients who work can function on the job.

At present, day settings can play a major role in the rehabilitation, re-education and resocialization of the chronically ill, particularly those patients with reduced social skills who cannot be expected to achieve a consistently high level of functioning. In such settings, therapy would ideally be more supportive and conducted over a longer period of time than on acute services or in free-standing day hospitals. Social and vocational rehabilitation, geared to the specific potential of each patient, become more important than therapies focusing on intrapsychic conflicts. The service may be geared to psychotic patients, neurotic patients or both (Jones, Cormack and Bow, 1963; Freeman, 1962).

It has been suggested that chronic patients who cannot tolerate the total push of acute services and who drop out of such services will do better in a less stressful day care setting (Beigel and Feder, 1970). These day care centers, as opposed to the earlier day hospital models, may have treatment programs conducted primarily by social workers, occupational and recreational therapists and community mental health workers. They may be located outside of hospital settings and within the community they are supposed to serve. In this way, they can become a part of the total rehabilitative programs operant in a particular region including sheltered workshops and halfway houses. They can also operate on a flexible schedule providing a range of care for those who need to be seen weekly or less for socialization and/or medication and for those patients who require daily care.

## EVOLVING PATTERNS OF HOSPITAL STAFFING

The rapid expansion of facilities for the care and treatment of the mentally ill that occurred during the past decade highlighted the necessity for adopting a multiprofessional approach to treatment.  With limited personnel, it was necessary to expand the role of psychiatric nurses, aides and social workers, to encompass tasks that had formerly been reserved for psychiatrists and psychologists.  Simultaneously with the breakdown of a system that rigidly defined professional role, psychiatrists and hospital administrators became increasingly cognizant of the important tasks that had been performed by aides and nurses and the tremendous influence that such interventions had on patients.  Once this became apparent, upgrading of skills and in-service education programs became imperative and commonplace. The increasing value placed upon paraprofessionals is reflected in the evolution of terms that have been used to designate them.  Orderlies became psychiatric aides, who then became mental health workers.  Career ladders have been established within the civil service system to allow for career progression within this latter category.

The assumption of increased responsibility by mental health workers created an increased sense of professionalism which led to enhanced morale, a feeling of professional self-worth, and an insistence that an egalitarian social system be established on hospital wards.  The psychiatrist has abandoned his earlier position of total command and authority and has become, instead, the leader of a team composed of nurses, social workers and aides (Bauer, 1970).  While usually the best educated and informed member of the team, the psychiatrist has learned to share decision making power with his colleagues and to function as a "coach, consultant and teacher."  The team is ideally able to bring differential expertise to bear on individual patients or particular problems.  In addition, it provides a vehicle for coordinating the efforts of all staff involved in particular cases and for providing vital exchanges of information about each case.  Each member need not have identical skills or similar needs to know everything about each patient.  Every contribution made by each member is not necessarily valid or acceptable.

Teams get into difficulty because of problems that arise within each team as well as those that result when various teams function in a single setting.  Patients live in a ward or hospital setting and they interact with other patients and many staff members, irrespective of team boundaries.  Should interactions between patients on different teams take place, the team member involved may neglect to look at the total picture, focusing only on the patient who is the team's responsibility.  Disruptive behavior may be inadequately handled or ignored if another "team's patient" is involved.  On the other hand, interventions on the part of one team's staff with another team's patients may be viewed with disfavor by the patient's team.  To avoid such chaos it is essential that teams interact with one another and the unity of the total setting be preserved.  Such problems are markedly diminished in day hospital settings because patients can more easily be separated according to team assignment, and this accounts for the popularity of the team approach in such settings (Astrachan, Flynn, Geller and Harvey, 1970).

Regardless of the setting, intrateam difficulties may arise. The structure of the team may lead to diffusion of responsibility. The concept that everyone is responsible can lead in practice to no one's being responsible. Attempts to practice democracy can lead to decisions being made by consensus, with expertise having to yield to less qualified opinion. Individual team members are often loathe to act independently when necessary for a patient's benefit, choosing the safer course of waiting for team meetings to thoroughly consider each issue. The close working relationships between staff members engendered by the team setting may lead to a tendency for team members to protect each other and team cohesiveness at the expense of patient care. Team members may be reluctant to challenge a staff member's work with patients, rather than risk the ire of the criticized person. Patients may be labeled as difficult to work with by the team rather than acknowledging that certain team members have difficulty working with certain patients. Such difficulties are not unique to teams, but the degree of cooperation demanded in team settings fosters such behavior unless the teams are acutely aware of this tendency.

Nurses and aides have, increasingly, been called upon to assume new responsibilities and duties, e.g., history taking, mental status examination, group leadership, and team coordination. They have, also, in various settings, (Cline and Rouzer, 1971; Stern, Beck and Mack, 1972) become the primary therapist for patients, assuming responsibility for the patient's psychotherapy. As a result of these new role definitions, aspects of patient care formerly associated with the nursing role have tended to become devalued and the newer roles, felt to have more prestige, are the only ones seen as capable of giving work satisfaction. What was formerly perceived as excellent nursing care may now be viewed as pill pushing and mere drudgery, left over from an antiquated medical model. The once highly prized ability to provide intimate and constant contact with very disturbed patients, still a clinical necessity, is viewed as custodial care. Battles between hospital administrators and nurses over whether street clothes or traditional uniforms will be worn are the tip of the iceberg in nursing's push for recognition, prestige and work satisfaction (Klein, Pillsbury, Bushey and Snell, 1972). While uniforms may not be the issue, there is a real need in mental hospitals for traditional nursing care.

## CONCLUSION

Until recent years psychiatric hospitals were considered to be the most traditional and stable setting for the care of the mentally ill. Today the field of hospital care is in ferment. Basic issues, e.g., what is psychiatric illness, who is sick, who needs hospitalization, what is good hospital care, who is capable of treating mentally ill patients, what is recovery, when should a patient be discharged, have become hotly debated and remain unresolved. The continuum of opinion ranges from those people who feel that hospitalization should be avoided whenever not absolutely necessary (Decker and Stubblebine, 1972) to those who feel that prolonged hospitalization offers a patient the best possibility for restructuring his personality and recovering from his illness. Scarce resources, time limits dictated by third party payments, and the need to provide care for large numbers of patients have required innovative solutions and procedures. Hospital treatment today includes crisis intervention units, intensive milieu units with emphasis on group interaction, behavior modification wards, day hospitals and long-term settings with emphasis on individual psychotherapy. Within each setting, hospitals vary according to who treats patients, with what modality of treatment, and according to which theoretical framework. In some settings, only psychiatrists do traditional psychotherapy, while in others, members of other disciplines or generic mental health workers also serve as psychotherapists. In large cities, mental health workers with little formal training, but with knowledge of the patients' cultural origins and familiarity with the patients' language are often called upon to take major treatment responsibilities. Such trends are upsetting to some professionals, welcomed by others, and are a matter of indifference to a third group who believe that medication and removal of the patient from his conflictual environment is all that can be accomplished in a hospitalization, especially a brief one.

While pioneer studies in evaluation research (Schwartz, Myers and Astrachan, 1973; Riedel, Brauer, Brenner, Goldblatt, Schwartz, Myers and Klerman, 1971; May 1968) and nascent studies in utilization review may eventually help us determine the answer to some of the preceding questions, as well as establish good and accepted standards of care, at the present time decisions as to what kind of hospital is appropriate for which patient, with which syndrome, rest in the hands of the referring clinician.

## REFERENCES

Abroms, G.M. The open-door policy: a rational use of controls. *Hospital and Community Psychiatry.* 24: 81-84 (February, 1973).

Almond, R., Keniston, K. and Boltax, S. The value system of a milieu therapy unit. *Archives of General Psychiatry.* 19: 545-561 (November, 1968).

Almond, R., Keniston, K. and Boltax, S. Value change in milieu therapy. *Archives of General Psychiatry.* 20: 339-351 (March, 1969a).

Almond, R., Keniston, K. and Boltax, S. Milieu therapeutic process. *Archives of General Psychiatry.* 21: 431-442 (October, 1969b).

American Psychiatric Association Proceedings, 1958. Day Hospital Conference, Washington, D.C., 1958.

Artiss, K.L. *Milieu Therapy in Schizophrenia.* Grune & Stratton, New York, 1962.

Astrachan, B.M., Flynn, H.R., Geller, J.D. and Harvey, H.H. Systems approach to day hospitalization. *Archives of General Psychiatry.* 22: 550-559 (1970).

Atthowe, J.M., Jr. and Crasner, L. A preliminary report on the application of contingent reinforcement procedures (token economy) on a "chronic" psychiatric ward. *Journal of Abnormal Psychology.* 73: 37-43 (1968).

Aviram, U. and Segal, S.P.  Exclusion of the mentally ill.  *Archives of General Psychiatry.*  **29:**  126-133 (July, 1973).

Ayllon, T., Intensive treatment of psychotic behavior by stimulus satiation and food reinforcement.  *Behavior Research and Therapy.*  **1:**  53-61 (May, 1963).

Ayllon, T. and Azrin, N.H.   Reinforcement and instructions with mental patients.  *Journal of Experimental Analysis Behavior.*  **7:**  327-331 (July, 1964).

Ayllon, T. and Michael, J.   The psychiatric nurse as a behavioral engineer.  *Journal of. Experimental Analysis Behavior.*  **2:**  323-334 (October, 1959).

Bateman, J. and Dunham, H.W.   The state mental hospital as a specialized community experience.  *American Journal of Psychiatry.*  **105:**  445-448 (1948).

Bauer, W.   Recent developments in mental health manpower.  *Hospital and community psychiatry.*  **21:**  11-17 (January, 1970).

Bazelon, D.  The right to treatment: the courts role.  *Hospital and Community Psychiatry.*  **20:**  129-135 (May, 1969).

Beck, J.C. and Worthen, K.  Precipitating stress, crisis theory, and hospitalization in schizophrenia and depression.  *Archives of General Psychiatry.*  **26:**  123-129 (1972).

Beigel, A. and Feder, S.L.  A night hospital program.  *Hospital and Community Psychiatry.*  **21:**  26-29 (1970).

Beigel, A. and Feder, S.L.  Patterns of utilization in partial hospitalization.  *American Journal of Psychiatry.*  **126:**  101-108 (1970).

Bellnap, I.  *Human Problems of a State Mental Hospital.*  McGraw-Hill, New York, 1956.

Bierer, J.   *The Day Hospital:   An Experiment in Social Psychiatry and Syntoanalytic Psychotherapy.*   Lewis, London, 1951.

Cameron, D.E.  The day hospital. *Modern Hospital.* **69:** 60-62 (1947).

Caplan, G.  *Principles of Preventive Psychiatry.*  Basic Books, New York, 1964.

Caudill, W.  *The Psychiatric Hospital as a Small Society.*  Harvard University Press, Cambridge, Mass., 1958.

Clark, D.H.  *Administrative Therapy.*  Tavistock Publications, London, 1964.

Cline, D.W. and Rouzer, D.L.  The physician as primary therapist in hospital psychiatry.  *American Journal of Psychiatry.*  **128:**  407-411 (October, 1971).

Conwell, M., Rosen, B., Hench, C. and Bahn, A.K.  The first national survey of psychiatric day-night services.  In:   R.L. Epps and Hanes, L.D. (Eds.),  *Day Care of Psychiatric Patients,* pp. 91-105.  Charles C. Thomas, Springfield, Illinois, 1964.

Cumming, J. and Cumming, E.   *Ego and Milieu:   Theory and Practice of Environmental Therapy.*  Atherton Press, New York, 1962.

Davidson, G.C.  *Appraisal of Behavior Modification Techniques with Adults in Institutional Setting in Behavior Therapy,* pp. 220-278.  C.M. Franks (Ed.) McGraw-Hill, New York, 1969.

Decker, J.B. and Stubblebine, J.M.   Crisis intervention and prevention of psychiatric disability. *American Journal of Psychiatry.* **129:** 725-729 (1972).

Dunham, H.W. and Weinberg, S.K. *The Culture of the State Mental Hospital.* Wayne State University Press, Detroit, 1960.

Edelson, M., *Ego Psychology, Group Dynamics and the Therapeutic Community.* Grune & Stratton, New York, 1964.

Fisher, A. and Weinstein, M.R. Mental hospitals, prestige, and the image of enlightenment. *Archives of General Psychiatry.* **25**: 41-48 (July, 1971).

Freeman, P. Treatment of chronic schizophrenia in a day center. *Archives of General Psychiatry.* **7**: 259-265 (1962).

Gerhardt, S. The evaluation of a patient government. *Hospital and Community Psychiatry.* **19**: 329-330 (1968).

Goffman, E. *Asylums.* Doubleday, New York, 1961.

Greenblatt, M., York, R. and Brown, E.L. *From Custodial to Therapeutic Care in a Mental Hospital.* Russell Sage Foundation, New York, 1955.

Greenblatt, M., Sharaf, M. and Stone, E. *Dynamics of Institutional Change.* University of Pittsburgh, 1971.

Greenley, J.R. Power processes and patient behaviors. *Archives of General Psychiatry.* **28**: 683-688 (May, 1973).

Greenspoon, J. Verbal conditioning and clinical psychology. In: Backrack, A.J. (Ed.), *Experimental Foundations of Clinical Psychology,* pp. 510-553. Basic Books, New York, 1962.

Group for the Advancement of Psychiatry: *Crisis in Psychiatric Hospitalizations,* Report #72, 1969.

Hecker, A.O. The demise of large state hospitals. *Hospital and Community Psychiatry.* **21**: 261-263 (1970).

Herz, M.I. The therapeutic community: a critique. *Hospital and Community Psychiatry.* **23**: 69-71 (March, 1972).

Herz, M.I., Wilensky, H. and Earle, A. Problems of role dysfunction in the therapeutic community. *Archives of General Psychiatry.* **14**: 270-276 (March, 1966).

Hogarty, G.E., Dennis, H., Guy, W. and Gross, G.M. "Who goes there?" – A critical evaluation of admissions to a psychiatric day hospital. *American Journal of Psychiatry.* **124**: 934-944 (1968).

Jackson, J. Factors of the treatment environment. *Archives of General Psychiatry.* **21**: 39-45 (1969).

Joint Commission on Mental Illness and Health, *Action for Mental Health.* Basic Books, New York, 1961.

Jones, A.L., Cormack, G. and Bow, L. Within the day hospital. *American Journal of Psychiatry.* **119**: 973-977 (1963).

Jones, M. *The Therapeutic Community.* Basic Books, New York, 1962.

Kaufman, A. The role of the staff advisor in patient government. *Hospital and Community Psychiatry.* **21**: 298-300 (1970).

Kaufman, M.R. *The Psychiatric Unit in a General Hospital.* International University Press, Inc., New York, 1965.

Klein, R.H., Pillsbury, J., Bushey, M. and Shell, S. Psychiatric staff: uniforms or street clothes. *Archives of General Psychiatry.* **26**: 19-22 (January, 1972).

Kramer, B.M. *Day Hospital.* Grune & Stratton, New York, 1962.

Kris, A., Schiff, L. and McLaughlin, R. Susceptibility to chronic hospitalization relative to age at first admission. *Archives of General Psychiatry.* **24**: 346-352 (April, 1971).

Lamb, H.R. Release of chronic psychiatric patients into the Community. *Archives of General Psychiatry.* **19**: 38-44 (July, 1968).

Lamb, H.R. and Goertzel, V. Discharged mental patients – are they really in the community. *Archives of General Psychiatry.* **24**: 29-34 (January, 1971).

Lamb, H.R. and Goertzel, V. The demise of the state hospital – a premature obituary. *Archives of General Psychiatry.* **26**: 489-495 (June, 1972).

Langsley, D.G. Crisis intervention. *American Journal of Psychiatry.* **129**: 734-736 (1972).

Lebensohn, Z.M. *Facilities and Organization in the Psychiatric Unit in a General Hospital,* Kaufman, M.R. (Ed.) International University Press, Inc., New York, 1965.

Levinson, D.J. and Gallagher, E.B. *Patienthood in the Mental Hospital.* Houghton Mifflin Company, Boston, 1964.

Lindemann, E. Symptomatology and management of acute grief. *American Journal of Psychiatry.* **101**: 141-148 (1944).

Linn, L.S. Social characteristics and patient expectations toward mental hospitalization. *Archives of General Psychiatry.* **20**: 457-469 (April, 1969).

Linn, L.S. State hospital environment and rates of patient discharge. *Archives of General Psychiatry.* **23**: 346-351 (October, 1970).

Marohn, R.C. The therapeutic milieu as an open system. *Archives of General Psychiatry.* **22**: 360-364 (1970).

May, P.R.A. *The Treatment of Schizophrenia.* Science House, New York, 1968.

Meichenbaum, D.H. The effects of social reinforcement on the level of abstraction in schizophrenics. *Journal of Abnormal Psychology.* **71**: 354-362 (1966a).

Meichenbaum, D.H. The effects of instructions and reinforcement on thinking and language behaviors of schizophrenics. Unpublished Doctoral Dissertation, University of Illinois, 1966b.

Mental Health Statistics, NIMH: The Utilization of Mental Health Facilities – 1971. Series B, Number 5, in Press.

Moos, R. Size, staffing, and psychiatric ward treatment environments. *Archives of General Psychiatry.* **26**: 414-418 (May, 1972).

Moos, R. and Houts, P. Assessment of the social atmosphere of psychiatric wards. *Journal of Abnormal Psychology.* **73**: 595-604 (1968).

Osmond, H. Function as the basis of psychiatric ward design. *Mental Hospitals.* **8**: 23-30 (1957).

Pierce, W.D., Truckett, E.J. and Moos, R.H. Changing ward atmosphere through staff discussion of the perceived ward environment. *Archives of General Psychiatry.* **26**: 35-41 (1972).

Rhine, M.W. and Mayerson, P. Crisis hospitalization within a psychiatric emergency service. *American Journal of Psychiatry.* **127**: 1386-1391 (1971).

Rickard, H.C., Dignam, P.J. and Horner, R.F. Verbal manipulation in a psychotherapeutic relationship. *Journal of Clinical Psychology.* **16**: 93 (1960).

Riedel, D.C., Brauer, L., Brenner, M.H. Goldblatt, P., Schwartz, C., Myers, J.K. and Klerman, G. Developing a system for utilization, review and evaluation in community mental health centers. *Hospital and Community Psychiatry.* 22: 229-232 (1971).

Robitscher, J. Courts, state hospitals, and the right to treatment. *American Journal of Psychiatry.* 129: 298-303 (September, 1972).

Rowland, H. Interaction processes in the state mental hospital. *Psychiatry.* 1: 323-328 (1938).

Rubenstein, R. and Lasswell, H.D. *The Sharing of Power in a Psychiatric Hospital.* Yale University Press, New Haven, 1966.

Rubin, B. and Goldberg, A. An investigation of openness in the psychiatric hospital. *Archives of General Psychiatry.* 8: 264-276 (March, 1963).

Schwartz, A.H. and Farmer, R.G. Providing milieu treatment in a military setting. *Hospital and Community Psychiatry.* 19: 271-276 (1968).

Schwartz, C., Myers, J.K. and Astrachan, B.M. The outcome study in psychiatric evaluation research. *Archives of General Psychiatry.* 29: 98-102 (1973).

Schwartz, C., Myers, J.K. and Astrachan, B.M. Concordance of multiple assessments of the outcome of schizophrenia. Manuscript in preparation, 1973.

Schwartz, R.A., Mako, A.E. and Smith, Q. Patient management in a 100% open hospital. *Hospital and Community Psychiatry.* 23: 85-87 (March, 1972).

Spadoni, A.J. and Smith, J.A. Milieu therapy in schizophrenia. *Archives of General Psychiatry.* 20: 547-551 (May, 1969).

Stanton, A. and Schwartz, M. *The Mental Hospital.* Basic Books, New York, 1954.

Stern, E.S. *Operation Sesame. Lancet.* 1: 577-578 (March, 1957).

Stern, M.J., Beck, J.C. and Mack, J.E. Training nurses to be therapists on a psychiatric inpatient service. *Hospital and Community Psychiatry.* 23: 218-221 (July, 1972).

Stewart, A., LaFare, H.G., Grunberg, F. and Herjanic, M. Problems in phasing out a large public psychiatric hospital. *American Journal of Psychiatry.* 125: 82-88 (July, 1968).

Twerski, A.D. Treating the untreatable. *Hospital and Community Psychiatry.* 22: 261-264 (September, 1971).

Ullmann, L.P., Krasner, L. and Collins, B.J., Modifications of behavior through verbal conditioning: effects in group therapy. *Journal of Abnormal and Social Psychology.* 62: 128-132 (1961).

Weisman, G., Feirstein, A. and Thomas C., Three day hospitalization — A model for intensive intervention. *Archives of General Psychiatry.* 21: 620-629 (1969).

Wessen, A.F. *The Psychiatric Hospital as a Social System.* Springfield, Illinois, Charles C. Thomas, 1964.

Williams, E.W. Advanced levels of patient government. *Hospital and Community Psychiatry.* 21: 300-301 (1970).

Zolik, E.S., Lantz, E.M. and Sommers, R. Hospital return rates and prerelease referrals. *Archives of General Psychiatry.* 18: 712-717 (June, 1968).

# 10 Aftercare
Daniel N. Hertz

## INTRODUCTION

Aftercare, which had been the stepchild of mental health services, has become the focus of world attention since 1955, when the tremendous increase in mental hospital discharge rates forced the spotlight onto this previously neglected area. With the advent of tranquilizing drugs and antidepressants, more active and innovative treatment modalities, and an optimistic treatment climate, hospitalizations are now shorter and chronic patients remarkably fewer, despite the increasing admission rates. A great many long-hospitalized patients have been released to the community. Yet along with this trend has been an alarmingly high readmission rate, a "revolving door" syndrome of discharge and readmission. In New York State, statistics show that 28% of patients discharged from state mental hospitals in recent years have been readmitted within six months of their release, and up to 50% are expected to be readmitted eventually (Wren, 1973). Clearly, something is wrong.

The pendulum of concern for the rights of mental patients has shifted along with the trend to ready discharge. Dr. Robert Reich, Director of Psychiatry for the New York City Department of Social Services, eloquently expressed his concern (1973, pp. 911-912):

> Newspapers and psychiatric journals have in recent months featured stories about the great strides in the treatment of severe chronic mental illness . . . . But what has happened to these chronically ill patients . . . . Few have families of their own and many are too mentally dysfunctional to live within a normal family setting. Confused and delusional, they turn

to welfare departments to look after them . . . In New York City the Department of Social Services attempts to place these patients in whatever settings are available. The aged are referred to nursing homes, where they receive little psychiatric care and no real therapy . . . (C)hronically mentally ill persons (occupy proprietary home beds) . . . There are no day programs, little recreation, and nobody to check into the physical well being of the occupants. There people, many of whom have been in state institutions for fifteen years or more, rarely leave the building. They sit and stare into space, and regress as if in the back wards of state hospitals . . . . Most of the mentally ill are referred to cheap single-room occupancy hotels and rooming houses . . . They share this space with prostitutes, discharged prisoners and drug addicts.

Alarmed, Dr. Reich (p. 912) concludes that "our policy of discharging helpless human beings to a hostile community is immoral and inhuman." The development of satisfactory aftercare facilities is a moral imperative.

The demand for better aftercare facilities is echoed by relatives of discharged patients. A group of relatives of patients at Manhatten State Hospital accused the New York State Department of Mental Hygiene of "callous indifference" to the plight of released patients. The group demanded that the authorities rescind directives designed to empty state mental hospitals until there were decent facilities in the community for those released. "To assert the noble principle of 'community treatment' without making adequate provision for proper housing, follow-up care and treatment, rehabilitation and job training . . . is an immoral and malicious mockery of these helpless and ill people" (Wren, 1973).

As the concerns of officials and relatives alike have shown, there are many basic unanswered questions concerning aftercare. What happens to those discharged patients for whom no special treatment provisions are made? How many stay out of the hospital, and for how long? If they remain out, how well do they function, and what is the course of their illness? For those who decompensate, are there any high risk periods? Why do they decompensate? Does aftercare influence the course of the illness or the chance of readmission? If so, are there any aftercare programs that are particularly effective? Which are not? Unless there are answers to these and other questions, post-hospital treatment will remain a morass of well-meaning guesswork. This chapter will examine the evidence currently available, attempting to form a more coherent picture from the great mass of scattered data. Specific programs for children, drug addicts, alcoholics and offenders will not be covered.

A clarification about the use of the studies covered by this chapter is in order. "Aftercare" is used in the psychiatric literature to describe the *total* treatment program for the psychiatric patient after his discharge from the hospital. It encompasses all patients and all programs; it includes predischarge readiness and planning, post-hospital residential arrangements, resocialization techniques, vocational rehabilitation and professional care for all patients released from a psychiatric hospital, regardless of diagnosis. Statistics quickly reveal the wide variety of patients loosely lumped together as "discharged mental patients" for whom aftercare is sought. In New York State, excluding facilities for narcotics addicts, there were 41,531 patients discharged from state mental hospitals in the year ending March 31, 1971. Diagnostic categories were (Weinstein, DiPasquale and Winsor, 1973):

|  | % |
|---|---|
| Schizophrenia | 40.6 |
| Alcohol-related conditions | 17 |
| Other and undiagnosed | 14 |
| Psychosis of old-age | 5.6 |
| Affective disorders | 4 |
| Personality and behavior disorders | 3.8 |
| Organic brain syndrome | 2.9 |
| Drug-related conditions | 2.4 |
| Other psychoses | 2 |
| Mental retardation | 1.3 |

All these categories are included in the patient population lumped together in most studies of "aftercare." It must be kept in mind that this breadth creates built-in limitations for such studies. Because of them, general studies of aftercare are limited to espousing broad treatment principles; yet treatment programs, to be effective, must be tailored to the needs of the individual patient.

In an excellent detailed study of those patients discharged from New York State mental hospitals from 1966-1971, (Weinstein, DiPasquale and Winsor, 1973), it was found that of those admitted during 1971, 35.3% left the hospital alive within 1 month, 55.9% within 2 months, and 85.1% within 9 months. Their median stay was 1.5 months; for those admitted in 1954, it had been 8 months. In terms of readmission of those released during 1971, 11.0% returned within 1 month, 15.8% within 2 months, 28% within 6 months and 32.8% within 9 months of their release. Readmission rates of those patients discharged in the earlier years of the study follow a similar curve, and gradually rise to about 50% in 4 years. The highest rates of return within 6 months (re-entry) were found among the mentally retarded (35.2%), those with alcohol-related conditions (31.5%) and those with schizophrenia (30.9%). The lowest re-entry rates were among those diagnosed with other psychoses (19.1%) and psychoneuroses (21.6%). There was a strong relationship between the number of previous admissions and the length of time out of the hospital: For those with no previous admissions, only 16.3% returned within 6 months; for those with one previous admission, the comparable rate was 26.3%, and the rate increased with each additional previous stay, reaching 69.7% for those with eight or more. There was very little association between the length of hospitalization and the re-entry rate. The six-year trend in the exit rate (discharge rate per time period) showed a pronounced upward movement, from 34.0% in 1966 to 55.9% in 1971. The re-entry rate also increased during the six-year period, from 20.4% in 1966, to 28.5% in 1970, and dropped slightly to 27.7% in 1971.

The Illinois Department of Mental Health reports similar hospital trends (Levy, 1971). They believe that the high readmission rate reflects the need for further work in the development of community resources to maintain patients in the community after discharge.

In a study of 229 male patients discharged from mental hospitals in the London area, all of whom had been in the hospital for two or more years, 68% remained out of the hospital for at least one year (Brown, Carstairs and Topping, 1958). Of those who relapsed during the six years of the study, 74% of the schizophrenic patients did so in the first year, compared to only 58% of the non-schizophrenics.

Prediction of post-hospital success or failure is extremely difficult. With the multitude of illnesses and symptoms represented by the mental hospital population, specific personality or symptom criteria do not statistically hold up. Yet with the schizophrenic patients, premorbid factors rather than age at hospitalization are crucial in determining post-hospital adjustment (Pollack, Levenstein and Klein, 1968). Premorbid asocial schizophrenics have a poorer chance for a favorable outcome (Gittelman-Klein and Klein, 1969), with withdrawal being the most important single measure in predicting success-failure when all variables are considered collectively (Sherman, Moseley, Ging and Bookbinder, 1964).

In an interesting ten-year follow-up study of female ex-mental patients and matched "normal" neighbors, interviews with the women and their husbands elicited data on domestic performance, social participation, expectations of performance, psychological functioning, and marital and family adjustment. It was found that 45% of the ex-patients were treated for psychiatric problems in the ten-year period, compared to 11% of the controls. The Langner Psychiatric Screening Scale indicated poorer functioning for patients and their husbands than for controls and their husbands. Controls were much better adjusted and happier in their marriages than the ex-patient couples. The children of ex-patients tended to be more poorly adjusted in school, at home and in the community than the children of the controls. Ex-patients centered more of their social activities around home and family, whereas controls were more likely to hold jobs (Molholm and Dinitz, 1972).

## BACKGROUND

Aftercare has been with us for hundreds of years in many forms. The family placement programs in Geel, Belgium, for instance, date back to the seventeenth century. Yet it has only been since 1955, with hundreds of thousands of patients being discharged to their home communities, that there occurred a worldwide shift in treatment emphasis from hospital to community (Ryan, 1969). Prior to that, with long-term hospitalization the rule, patients were not uncommonly hospitalized to the end of their lives. Understandably, community facilities for released patients were rare.

From a historical overview the shift in treatment emphasis seems also a shift from private to public concern, voluntary to legislative, remedial to preventive. In England, the Mental Health Act of 1959 stressed the need for preventive and aftercare facilities and sheltered workshops in the community (Sharpe, 1972). The Federal Community Mental Health Centers Act of 1963 in the U.S. stressed the return of treatment responsibility to the local communities (McGarry and Kaplan, 1973).

The need for community aftercare facilities is now recognized worldwide. In England, Sharpe (1972) noted advances in treatment methods necessitated by the change from custodial to progressive patient care. Therapeutic communities, preventive therapy and resocialization techniques are being actively pursued in Italy (Scarzella, 1970). There are aftercare programs in Poland (Tretor, 1972) and in Russia (Babayan, 1969). All "Developed" countries have some aftercare services, and many "developing" countries have experimental programs (Lin, 1968).

Yet, despite the need, aftercare facilities have developed slowly. In 1961, the Final Report of the Joint Commission on Mental Illness and Health reported that "(a)ftercare services for the mentally ill are in a primitive state of development almost everywhere." In the U.S., the report noted, there were at that time only nine halfway houses, less than two dozen day hospitals, eight rehabilitation centers, seventy ex-patient clubs, and foster-home services for discharged patients in less than one-quarter of all the states. We will survey what has happened since then.

## PRE-DISCHARGE PLANNING

The hospitalized patient commonly develops a dependence on the hospital and his doctor, and a sense of security associated with the hospital setting. Thus he feels ambivalent about leaving. Unless his conflict is resolved, chances for successful rehabilitation are diminished. Helping the patient develop an expectation of rehabilitation and a positive attitude toward it is therefore an important step toward achieving that goal. Ideally, such planning should begin as soon as the patient enters the hospital.

The programs developed to meet this challenge have been varied. Establishing small groups of patients to discuss problems of daily living while increasing their personal responsibility in order to simulate normal life as closely as possible is one method which has been used to ease the transition (Ritchey, 1971). Where possible, involving family in the treatment program and post-discharge planning seems advisable. The V.A. hospital at Perry Point, Maryland prepares chronically ill psychiatric patients for discharge through use of social group techniques, early and continued involvement with the patient's family, and direct contact with the community through the use of the services of selected, supervised volunteers. The program has worked well as a means of breaking through the patient's fears of new situations and leaving the security of the hospital (McGriff, 1965). To help the patient adjust to the post-hospital social situations he'll encounter and make use of the community facilities and programs available, Rosenberg and Colthoff (1967) took a group of patients and had *them* "volunteer" to serve as helpers or assistant group leaders in program areas at local community centers. Each volunteer contributed four hours of service each week and attended all volunteer conferences. This introduction to community facilities through active rather than passive participation seems to have been of significant and lasting value. Follow-up studies indicated that almost all of the patients continued to use the community centers in various ways after their discharge from the hospital.

The chronic patient who has spent much time in a hospital setting presents a special challenge in pre-discharge planning. He has been rewarded repeatedly in the hospital environment for being compliant, passive and uninterested in changing his behavior. Now he must be taught new habits and given new directions: improving his appearance, working at a job, social interaction. Liberman (1971) adapted behavior modification techniques to these goals at the Laboratory of Human Behavior at St. Elizabeth's Hospital in Washington, D.C. He attempted to structure the hospital setting in such a way as to make it more like the world outside the hospital, theorizing that if the patient is to learn behaviors which will enable him to adjust to the community, he must have the opportunity to practice these behaviors prior to release.

A coordinated transition between hospital and aftercare is extremely important to the successful adjustment of the patient once out of the hospital. If the same therapist can continue treatment, the continuity can be an important bridge. Unfortunately, particularly when hospital training programs are involved, I have noted from my own experience that artificial criteria are often established separating the staffs treating inpatient and outpatient groups. Both patient and therapist suffer under this arrangement.

The transition from hospital to community is the key point in successful aftercare. Yet it is currently the weakest link in the aftercare chain. Without active and imaginative programs to familiarize patients with community treatment facilities, discharged patients are largely lost to aftercare. Pre-discharge planning is a vital first step in assuring patients the benefits of available aftercare programs. Personal contact is vital; simply instructing a patient that after discharge he must contact his local outpatient department is largely ineffectual. Without help, only the well-motivated and better-functioning patient is likely to reach the aftercare facilities so much needed by the very patient who is unable or unwilling to seek them on his own. Without appropriate pre-discharge planning and aggressive follow-up techniques, aftercare becomes a public relations word rather than an effective post-hospital program, and the stage is set for the cycle of rehospitalization.

Statistical studies demonstrate the value of specific pre-discharge planning. One such study analyzed the correlation between readmissions and types of discharge referrals.    Some 4,376 discharged patients, representing the entire patient population discharged from four Virginia state hospitals between 1963 and 1964, and 2,122 readmitted patients were studied.  Significantly, the largest percentage of readmissions was in the patient group which had no   specific referral to an aftercare facility at the time of discharge.  Of these patients, 56.4% were readmitted.  Of those referred to mental health services, only 32.8% were readmitted; the rates dropped further with those referred to supportive agencies (26.9% readmitted) and to family care or nursing homes (17.8% readmitted) (Zolik, Sommers and Lantz, 1967).

Studies of readmission rates of patients not in specific aftercare programs generally show 1- to 5-year readmission rates of 35-50% (Charalampous, 1963; Gaviria and Lund, 1967; Kris, 1965; Pollack, Levenstein and Klein, 1968; Sherman, Moseley, Ging and Bookbinder, 1964; Silverman, 1971; Zolik, 1967). High as they are, these figures may reflect a significant underestimation of psychiatric hospital readmissions. Other studies show rates which soar as high as 90% (Burvill and Mittelman, 1971; *Lifeline: Aftercare*, 1962; *Medical World News*, 1969).   By defining readmission so as to exclude prior hospitalization at other institutions, inadequate search to uncover prior inpatient experience elsewhere, breakdown of communications between the office doing the statistical reporting and the staff members eliciting this information, and premature submission of statistics, reported rates may underemphasize the "revolving door syndrome." One study of 1,137 admissions to the Cleveland Psychiatric Institute showed that two out of five readmissions had been misclassified as first admissions (Friedman, Lundstedt, Von Mering and Hinko, 1964).

Effective aftercare programs can and do significantly affect the functioning and readmission rates of discharged patients.  In a seven-year follow-up study, Kris has shown that the ratio of rehospitalization can be reduced to 10% or less with a thorough and aggressive follow-up program.  In this program, patients were started in a special research aftercare clinic on the day immediately following their release from the hospital, and were seen weekly during the first two or three months and, when necessary, more often.  In cases of recurrence of severely disturbed behavior and reappearence of overt psychotic symptoms, control of the relapse was brought about by treating such patients in a day hospital established in conjunction with the clinic.  This aftercare research unit maintained close contact with the patient's family and friends, and used aggressive follow-up techniques if the patients failed to keep an appointment.  Within 24 hours there would be a phone call, followed by a letter.  If a second appointment was broken there would be a home visit.  Maintenance pharmocotherapy was required with most patients, especially chronic schizophrenics.  Drug therapy was considered safe; there were minimal complications.  Families were indoctrinated and educated to appreciate the patient's need for prolonged medication, like a diabetic's need for insulin. Thirty-five percent found jobs on their own, and only 10% needed vocational rehabilitation.  Outstanding factors causing failure to readjust in the community were friction in the family, isolation and inadequacy of pharmacotherapy.

In Georgia, a special aftercare clinic, emphasizing group therapy, reduced the one year rehospitalization rate to 11.4% with a patient group of 25% alcoholics (Fleurant, Hicks, Norris, Gouge and McKay, 1972). From Houston, Charalampous reports that 35-50% of the patients generally are readmitted within a year. He feels that poor results at rehabilitation facilities are possibly caused by their emphasis on milieu therapy and psychotherapy, which he feels are of limited usefulness for patients with chronic functional psychoses. Many chronic mental patients can be maintained in the community if properly kept on ataractic drugs. An aftercare clinic was set up in the Houston State Psychiatric Institute where patients with chronic functional psychoses are followed and maintained on drugs after discharge. The author reports that the attrition rate is less than 10%, and fewer than 5% of the patients have to return to inpatient care (Charalampous, 1963).

In another study (Caffey, Jones, Diamond, Burton and Bowen, 1969), patients were divided into three groups. Group A received normal hospital care with discharge at the physician's discretion and normal aftercare for a year. Group B received brief intensive treatment aimed at discharge in three weeks with a special schedule of aftercare visits and outpatient treatment. Group C received normal hospital care with discharge at the physician's discretion and a special schedule of aftercare visits and outpatient treatment. Group C produced the lowest number of readmissions; Group B was next. The authors' conclusion was that an intensive aftercare program seems to play an important role in reducing or preventing readmissions.

Many other studies, using a variety of techniques and approaches, give support to the value of aftercare programs (Brooks, 1961; David, 1971; Ellsworth, 1968; Myers and Bean, 1968; Nol and Fuller, 1972; Rutman and Loeb, 1970). Dissenting findings are few and far between.

Lamb and Goertzel (1972) randomly assigned long-term ex-state hospital patients to high or low expectation community programs. The high expectation group had pre-release group sessions at the state hospital. Focus was on problems the patients might encounter in the community and their ambivalence about ending hospital dependency. They were taken to visit family and friends, halfway houses and day treatment centers. Group methods and resocialization were emphasized, and vocational rehabilitation was available. The low expectation group had little pre-discharge assistance; they were released primarily to family care or boarding homes, where little was required of them. The results of Lamb and Goertzel's study showed that the high expectation program was superior not so much in keeping patients out of the hospital longer as in increasing their level of social and vocational functioning. There was no significant difference in how long the patients remained in the community either in the early months or after two years.

The other recent major study with negative results (Lagey, 1972) states that a ten-year follow-up survey of former mental hospital patients in an experimental program showed no significant differences among four treatment groups in hospital recidivism five and ten years after the termination of the project. The four groups were treated as follows: the first group received the routine services both in the hospital and in the community following discharge from the hospital; the second group received at least 30 days of intense pre-discharge planning and preparation for discharge in the hospital, and the routine services in the community. The third group received the routine hospital services and special professional and community help. The fourth group received the special treatments both in the hospital and in the community. All four groups spent about three of the ten years since the termination of the original project in accumulated hospital recidivism.

Despite these two largely negative studies, the preponderance of evidence supports the hypothesis that most aftercare programs do help patients function well and remain well. Clinical experiences would also indicate that, with most patients still partially symptomatic at the time of discharge and affected by residuals of their illness, access to total professional care, good living arrangements, socialization and vocational help can only improve the situation. Though some illnesses have an etiology and pathogenesis not yet understood, which may be tied into physiological, anatomical and/or genetic pathology, their liability is lessened when the patient functions in a healthier environment. While there may be some patients with a progressive intractable illness that present treatment methods do not effectively reach, the great majority of patients do respond to the psychological, social and biochemical resources that we have available to offer.

Let us, therefore, attempt to determine what we have to offer in aftercare programs that *can* make a difference.

## RESIDENTIAL ARRANGEMENTS

The right living climate can be a major factor in creating an environment for successful rehabilitation. An appropriate residential setting can provide the ex-patient with not only a healthy climate and an atmosphere conducive to growth, but also with an opportunity for developing skill in social interaction and and the ability to care for himself and move out into the world. The availability of appropriate residential facilities is often a major determinant in the decision to discharge the psychiatric patient. In a 1968 study of chronic schizophrenic patients, Hogarty concluded that discharge was more a function of hospital and community resources than of patient condition. Pokorny and Frazier (1968) concluded that 25% of the entire patient population at seven Texas mental hospitals could be discharged immediately if suitable living facilities were available.

The family unit has been the traditional focus of discharge planning, and still remains the first resource which should be considered. However, the family setting is not always a satisfactory answer to the problem of a healthy living climate even when the patient has family available with whom he could live;

often, pathological interactions make return to the family setting inadvisable. Further, an increasing number of patients have no family unit to return to. Must they be released to the isolation of a lonely room?

If the ex-patient has family willing and able to have him return, a decision as to the advisability of such placement is required. The only specific data available for guidance concerns schizophrenics. In an article entitled "Some Data Concerning readmission of Discharged Schizophrenic Patients," Cropley and Gazan (1969) report a two-year follow-up study of chronic schizophrenic patients to determine whether living with one's own family after discharge is a significant variable affecting retention of released schizophrenics in the community. The subjects were classified as members of either an immediate family group, a foster home group or a living alone group. Tabulating the number of readmissions to the hospital and total length of rehospitalizations, results failed to show a significant difference among groups. However, when the two sexes were considered separately, there was a tendency for foster home females to do better than the other two groups of females.

Although there are many comments in the literature about negative effects of schizophrenics' returning to live with their families, this conclusion is not supported by exacting studies. Possibly there is no valid generalization. In each specific case, the clinician must exercise his judgment as to what role the family pathology is playing in the individual's illness.

## HALFWAY HOUSES

One creative solution to the problem of providing a healthful living environment for released patients has been the establishment of supervised residences, the so-called psychiatric halfway houses. Dr. Richard Budson (1973), in a thorough review, states:

> The entire delivery of care to troubled and needy people is in a period of rapid change. Throughout the fabric of a variety of care-delivery systems, one constant pattern emerges — diminishing importance of the large institution and strong augmentation of small community-based residential facilities commonly known as half-way houses or community residences. These facilities are being established in great numbers, not only for the emotionally troubled, but also for the mentally retarded, the drug dependent and alcoholic, youths from broken homes, and youthful and adult offenders and other handicapped people (p. 64).

Their numbers have grown rapidly — from 7 in 1961, to 40 in 1964, to 148 in 1969. Now they number in the thousands. Budson believes that the rationale for this new movement was four basic deficiencies of the traditional institution. First, its large size and limited staff lead to a social breakdown syndrome, an "iatrogenically induced withdrawal from interpersonal exchange." Second, the patient was considered sick 24 hours a day, the passive recipient of care, which reinforced his image as defective and helplessly dependent on the hospital staff. Third, the closed society of the hospital, with its harsh rules and codes of punishment, induced compliance to the power system and reduced patient initiatives toward health. Fourth, the patient was isolated from the community.

The halfway house provides an antidote for many of the deficiencies of the traditional institution. The typical community residence is small, usually limited to 10 to 25 residents in a family-like atmosphere. Ideally, the occupants are considered residents, not patients. The house is in an open setting, part of a neighborhood, responsive to general social codes and mores, and integrated within the community. Supervision is provided by houseparents, managers and/or social workers.

The goals and philosophy of the supervising body and the make-up and degree of disability of the resident group influence the structure and model of the many halfway houses. Some require the residents to be admitted directly from a psychiatric hospital; others require only that the resident suffer from an emotional illness and anticipate benefit from the residence. Many have a maximum period of residence, commonly in the six-month to one-year range. Those that don't are finding their places increasingly occupied by those residents who can function in a halfway house but can't make the transition beyond. Some halfway houses require their residents to work or attend school with a short time of arrival; others require all residents to be in psychotherapy. Most, but not all, have live-in staff, commonly referred to as houseparents. Some have daytime staffing; some none at all. Consultant social workers, psychologists and psychiatrists are available to most. Cooking, shopping and housecleaning may be done by staff or residents, or by some combination. Generally at this time most programs want house managers who have personal stability, integrity, common sense, warmth, and a commitment to helping people, instead of formal training.

Community residences are still in the early stages of development and much experimentation is in process. Wilder, Kessel and Caulfield (1968) reported their experience after one year with the Overing Apartments, a "high expectation" halfway house supervised by the Albert Einstein College of Medicine. Overing Apartments was designed to provide a temporary, sheltered, homelike environment for ex-patients who either had no home or whose home was not conducive to recovery. Clinically, the residents had severe psychiatric disorders, with 77% diagnosed as schizophrenic reaction. To emphasize healthy aspects of their personalities, the rent was lowered if the tenant worked or studied. Tenants could come and go as they wished, and had full responsibility for their own personal care, meals and maintenance of apartments. Originally there was a six-month time limit on residence; it was later changed to nine months. Tenants were rated during residence and for six months afterward in clinical, social, and vocational areas. At their six-month follow-up, 41% of the females and 50% of the males were living on their own. The study concluded that the older, better motivated, more employable tenant did best in this setting, while the adolescents required a separate, more structured, nurturing program.

The high expectation approach is also reported from England, with some variations.   Darley and Kenny (1971), analyzing the low success rates of traditional day treatment centers for psychiatric patients, found that former patients were generally not accepted by the community as recovered, but assigned a new and damaging role as citizens-on-probation. They called this expectation of failure the "Queequeg Syndrome." To counteract the progressive deterioration in self-respect and confidence they felt was caused by this systematic undervaluing of the ex-patient's ability, they designed a rehabilitation program aimed at relearning the ability to cope with normality in all its forms and limitations, and regaining the ability to accept unpleasant emotions as normal.   The new program set up a therapeutic community in which all responsibility was shared by the staff and members equally.   Darley and Kenny concluded that this experience of self-direction in a group setting eliminated the feeling of chronic disability.

Other creative efforts to solve the problem of a healthful environment for ex-patients have varied the halfway house approach. Undergraduates of Harvard and Radcliffe established a cooperative halfway house in which the eager and intense students live together with ex- "chronic patients" Additional schools in the Boston area have joined the program, with encouraging results (Greenblatt and Kantor, 1962). In Fort Worth a study project used the YMCA as a transitional facility for rehabilitating chronic psychiatric patients. It was found to be an excellent alternative to the conventional halfway house, producing excellent results at less cost (Baganz, Smith, Goldstein and Pou, 1971). Cooperative apartments are another variation. One such program in Brookline, Massachusetts was set up by the MHA with a social worker as apartment coordinator. Residents paid a weekly fee and were responsible for general maintenance, shopping and cooking (Stein and Sorenson, 1972).

The halfway house has also been used as a pre-discharge program. Brooklyn State Hospital established its own halfway house on the grounds of the hospital. Harmony House is used for patients who no longer require intensive psychiatric care, to eliminate their hospital dependency and prepare them for self-sufficiency in the community (Klein, 1972). Three major programs are provided: a prevocational evaluation and exploration program to develop work potential and work habits; a personal adjustment training program for learning socially acceptable behavior and attitudes; and a homemaking program to develop independent community living and self-sufficiency. These adjustments are thus included as a part of the institutional treatment, before discharge into the community and the possibility of loss of the patients to aftercare.

To meet the problem of the resident who is unable to move from the halfway house into totally independent living, the El Camino House in California has developed a satellite housing program. Residents who are able to care for themselves but need some continued supervision are discharged to live in scattered apartments, usually with one or more roommates who are discharged at the same time. The apartment occupants must agree to attend a meeting of apartment residents at least twice a month and to remain in treatment. Follow-up services include a social club. The satellite program has reduced the length of stay at El Camino House; it is hoped it will reduce rehospitalization (Richmond, 1970).

It is difficult to make valid comparisons between programs of different halfway houses. Because of their small size, their samples are small and statistically unreliable. Furthermore, some programs take only carefully selected patients with predictably better prognosis. Others serve primarily schizophrenic patients who probably present a high risk of hospital readmission, the most common criteria used in rating program "success." General evaulation of the trend of development of such facilities is more feasible. Glasscote, Gudeman and Elpers published a comprehensive review of the programs of eleven halfway houses in 1971. Their conclusions, and the tone that pervades the literature, indicate that halfway houses represent a major step forward in rehabilitation.

## FAMILY CARE PLACEMENT

Another residential alternative is family care placement. By moving patients into the homes of relatively healthy families in the community, the family setting can be utilized as a positive therapeutic milieu. The ex-patient can thus spend most of his time in the context of normal family life rather than in an institutional environment, while avoiding returning to the setting which originally fostered his illness.

The oldest family care program is the famous one in Geel, Belgium. The Geel program and two others, in Beilen, the Netherlands, and Lierneux, Belgium, are described by Kernodle (1972). Surveying the legendary and historical origins of the Geel program, Kernodle concludes that in Geel the "practice of adopting the mentally ill and retarded into their homes and providing them with love and understanding is an ancient tradition." In 1952, the colony became a state institution, and the families that "adopt" patients are now paid by the government.

Currently there are 1,600 patients in foster care in Geel, of whom 65% are mentally retarded. About one-eighth of the households in the village have patients in foster care, with a maximum of two patients allowed in one family. The family placement program is an adjunct of the colony hospital, which has a yearly admission rate of 500 selected patients, 100 of whom are sent to foster care. Placement procedures are often informal, as the staff reside in the community and know many of the families personally. After family placement, the hospital is used mainly as a back-up resource, and the staff continue to provide any professional services necessary. However, psychotherapy tends to be minimal after placement. Many patients remain as permanent family members after their release from the program. The programs at Lierneux and Beilen are similar.

The most important factor in the success of the family placement programs seems to be the prestige bestowed on the family who adopts patients. However, the program is presently threatened by encroaching urbanization.

In *The Case for Family Care of the Mentally Ill,* Morrissey (1967) has reviewed the history of family care. He notes that research findings vary considerably and are at times contradictory. Perceptions of family care vary from extensions of the custodial hospital to dynamic selective treatment resources. According to Morrissey, the most important factor in family care treatment and rehabilitation is its acceptance as a valuable therapeutic resource, which he strongly feels it is. His study shows that considerably fewer patients are rehospitalized with family care placements than with regular home visits to their families. However, this may be due to more careful selection of patients placed in family care or to a more contrived environment and more careful supervision. Morrissey believes that schizophrenia, in particular, can be treated more effectively in a family care home than in a hospital.

Family care programs have been met with resistance in the U.S., possibly due to ignorance concerning mental illness. One study in New Haven, Missouri strove to overcome this resistance by establishing the positive involvement of the townspeople in the development of a program to integrate released psychiatric patients back into the community, with some success (Keskiner, Ruppert and Ulett, 1970). It seems clear that the underutilization of family care placement as a resource for placement of ex-patients will be reversed only by further education of both professionals and the community.

## OTHER LIVING ARRANGEMENTS

Many patients are not discharged to supervised residences or well-meaning families, but go to some form of licensed community boarding home. This is largely a stop-gap measure used when other more desirable placements are unavailable. A major problem with such placements is keeping the residents active enough to prevent apathy and regression. Few boarding home operators have enough training or experience to conduct activity programs. Many have no inclination to do so, and feel they lack the time. In an attempt to overcome the problem, Simon (1972) describes one-day workshops for boarding home operators where instruction is given in simple activities. Professional participants included the total range of hospital personnel, with the chaplain not forgotten.

A more successful integration of non-professionals in providing alternative living arrangements for ex-patients was achieved in a Boston Hospital program of landlord-supervised cooperative apartments, described by Chien and Cole (1973). From the program's inception in December, 1967, 35 apartments have been established in the area around Boston State Hospital. The landlords, who were not initially a part of the mental heatlh team or trained for mental health work, are screened by the hospital staff. They serve as paid houseparents, doing more at first and less as time goes on. The program is closely supervised by a hospital team. Results have been encouraging; the readmission rate has been a low 18% and the program is enthusiastically endorsed by most patients. Chien and Cole quote an annual cost of $2,183 per patient per year and believe that this program is financially and logistically superior to other residences.

The problem of patients who need long-term, possibly permanent care but can function away from the hospital under drug therapy was solved at Graylongwell Hospital in England by the establishment of a group home away from the hospital for these patients. Capstick and Kirby (1970) found this a successful alternative to long-term hospital stay.

## DAY AND NIGHT HOSPITALS

Partial hospitalization has become an important alternative to full-time hospital care and an essential element in the new community mental health centers. As defined by NIMH, "a psychiatric day-night service is one having an organized staff whose primary purpose is to provide a planned program of milieu therapy and other treatment modalities. The service is designed for patients with mental or emotional disorders who spend only a part of a 24-hour period in the program."

The first day care facility in the U.S. dates back to 1935, when Dr. J.M. Woodall admitted day patients to Adams House Sanitarium in Boston. The first organized day hospital in the western hemisphere was reported in 1946 at Allan Memorial Institute of Psychiatry in Montreal, Canada. Yale Psychiatric Clinic began one in 1948, the Menninger Clinic, one in 1949. By the early 1970s they were numerous, some affiliated with psychiatric hospitals, others with a clinic or general hospital.

A typical day care program runs from 9 A.M. to 5 P.M. and offers individual and/or group psychotherapy, patient-staff meetings, recreational, social and vocational activities. The programs tend to be flexible, and geared to the needs of the individual. Those that offer children's programs allow for family participation; the child is not totally separated from his family, the parents have a respite during the day and special teaching or training can be provided.

Night hospitals typically run from evening until work or school in the morning, and benefit those patients who can handle their job during the day but are unable to deal with their family or other home situation at night.

Kalmans (1970) describes a day treatment center at the Arlington Mental Health Center which offers individualized treatment plans for three categories: people in crisis who might otherwise be hospitalized; former patients who need a bridge to the outside world; and outpatients whose problems cannot be dealt with in once-a-week therapy. The majority of the patients are schizophrenics, often with overt psychotic symptoms. Many of the patients would have to be hospitalized if the center did not exist. Four-fifths of the patients are women; to facilitate their attendance, a nursery class and playroom for their preschool children is provided. Family members are encouraged to keep in touch with the staff for assistance with both personal and practical problems concerning the patient. The program offers individual, group and family psychotherapy, work therapy, psychodrama, art and dance therapy, community meetings and adult education.   Kalmans concludes that the program has successfully encouraged patients to accept responsibility for their own destiny.

The Fort Logan Mental Health Center in Denver has a large day hospital program, described by Bonn (1972). The day center is only one part of a coordinated mental health center which also includes inpatient services, crisis intervention, outpatient follow-up care, and various types of sheltered residential facilities and vocational rehabilitation. The Fort Logan day hospital program is able to service a large number of patients. Three reasons are cited by Bonn. First, satellite day centers were established, eliminating problems of transportation and serving patients in preferred familiar community surroundings. Second, day care is used for a wide spectrum of patients. The clinical criteria used for admission is the patient's need for ego-supportive activities for a fairly extended time. The presence of suicidal or homicidal tendencies or confusion does not automatically contraindicate day care. Third, the administrative structure facilitates the use of day care. All treatment modalities are available within each unit; thus patients are easily moved into different intensities of treatment. The day program offers large and small group therapy, psychodrama, family therapy, marital counseling, crisis intervention, activity therapies, medication follow-up, and training to improve self-care, social skills and interpersonal relationships. Some centers also offer vocational rehabilitation. Bonn concludes that all diagnostic categories benefited from the program.

Table 10-1 shows the use of day care in fiscal 1970-1971 by all divisions of Fort Logan:

TABLE 10-1.

| | Total Patients | No. Patients Using Day Care | No. Days in Day Care | No. Patients Using Only Day Care |
|---|---|---|---|---|
| Adult psychiatry | 1,902 | 624 | 48,042 | 103 |
| Alcoholism | 1,251 | 251 | 3,214 | 22 |
| Geriatrics | 251 | 10 | 947 | 1 |
| Crisis | 391 | 22 | 1,205 | 2 |
| Child psychiatry | 170 | 30 | 3,027 | 7 |
| Adolescent psychiatry | 125 | 25 | 681 | 5 |
| Total | 4,090 | 962 | 57,116 | 140 |

(Bonn, 1972, p. 159.)

As professionals are gaining more experience with the part-time hospital, its use has been extended beyond its original role as a purely transitional facility. It is being found to be an effective primary treatment method for many types of patients, regardless of diagnosis or socioeconomic background. Nevertheless, it is still underutilized for this purpose. Feder (1971), in "The Indications and Techniques of Partial Hospitalization," states that the sustained underutilization of the part-time hospital may be due to an incomplete understanding of the concept by patients, families, and the professional community. When partial hospitalization is seen not as a reduction of inpatient care but rather as an extension of outpatient care, it may then become the logical portal of entry to treatment for any patient for whom hospitalization is being considered.

There are many day care results published (Carney, Ferguson and Sheffield, 1970; Kris, 1962; Shammas, 1971; and Thomson, 1968 are examples) including one from the USSR (Kutin, 1971). They are uniformly enthusiastic and optimistic about day care programs. Results show shorter hospitalizations, less likelihood of readmission, better employment records of ex-patients, and better results generally. The overall success of the programs seems logically to militate a future trend toward greater expanded part-time hospital facilities.

The one major problem encountered to date has nothing to do with the clinical efficacy of the programs. Although the cost is much less than that of full hospitalization, to date most private insurance plans do not cover partial hospitalization. Thus, for economic reasons, part-time hospitalization is only available to the rich or indigent. Until this nonsensical situation is remedied, partial hospitalization will remain underutilized.

## PROFESSIONAL CARE

Professional post-hospital treatment of the psychiatric patient, like other phases of aftercare, is an area in which the choice of treatment is dependent both on the individual patient and on the disorder from which he is suffering. There are, however, numerous studies indicating that psychotherapeutic contact in aftercare does lower readmission rates (Prince, Ackerman and Barksdale, 1973; Donlon, Rada and Knight, 1973; Fleurant, Hicks, Norris, Gouge and McKay, 1972; Lamb and Goertzel, 1972; Langsley and Kaplan, 1970; Lurie and Ron, 1971; Pittman, Flomenhaft and Langley, 1971; Racklin, 1972; Safirstein, 1969). Most of the studies cover the total population of ex-hospital patients; the statistics reported present an impressive indication of the value of psychotherapy as part of the total treatment program in aftercare.

Prince, Ackerman and Barksdale (1973) collected data for patients diagnosed as functional psychotics who were released from the South Carolina State Hospital from February, 1970 through January, 1972 (see Table 10-2). Before release, patients from the 22 counties served by the project took part in a pre-release group and were given specific appointments for follow-up group treatment in the clinic nearest their home. Patients who came from the other 24 counties generally received the more traditional individual follow-up treatment, with the majority seen once monthly by a psychiatrist for a brief medication check and supportive psychotherapy. All patients were allowed the choice of a mental health clinic or a private physician (not necessarily a psychiatrist). The form of treatment group varied with the clinic. The most common approach was a monthly group meeting lasting 60 to 90 minutes in which between 10 and 20 patients were seen jointly by a psychiatrist and a nonmedical staff member. Problems were discussed and ideas shared for most of the session, after which medications were reviewed.

TABLE 10-2  FOLLOW-UP DATA ON 1,182 DISCHARGED CHRONIC PSYCHOTIC PATIENTS.

| Method of Treatment | No. of Patients | Returned During Year | In Hospital at End of Year |
|---|---|---|---|
| Referred to mental health center but never reported | 328 | 49% | 43% |
| Referred to mental health center and treated (all methods) | 690 | 37% | 23% |
| Referred to private physician but never reported | 91 | 46% | 41% |
| Referred to private physician and treated | 73 | 26% | 22% |

(Prince, Ackerman and Barksdale, 1973, p. 931.)

In analyzing those cases treated at the mental health center clinics, interesting statistics emerged (see Table 10-3).

TABLE 10-3  BREAKDOWN OF MENTAL HEALTH CLINIC TREATMENT CASES.

| Method of Treatment | No. of Patients | Returned During Year | In Hospital at End of Year |
|---|---|---|---|
| Group follow-up with medication (special group) | 216 | 25% | 14% |
| Individual medical checks | 258 | 44% | 30% |
| Other: intensive psychotherapy, family therapy, or combination | 216 | 40% | 24% |
| Total | 690 | | |

(Prince, Ackerman and Barksdale, 1973, p. 932)

Thus only 14% of the patients seen in groups were in the hospital on the anniversary of their release, compared with 30% and 24% treated in other ways. Their conclusion is that group methods are quite practical for the treatment of large numbers of chronic psychotic patients, and may well be the preferred treatment.

The group of schizophrenias is the largest diagnostic category among aftercare patients.  The value of psychotherapy in treating schizophrenia remains an open question. In the excellent article *"The Psychotherapy of Schizophrenia: Does it Work?"* Dyrud and Holzman (1973) state: "Empirical studies of the treatment of schizophrenia show the unequivocal ameliorative effects of psychoactive drugs. No comparable effects have been claimed for psychotherapy. As a result, psychotherapy has tended to be negated as a viable therapeutic factor in the treatment of schizophrenia." Dyrud and Holzman suggest, however, that the conclusion is invalid, and has been based on inadequate and misleading data. Among the criticisms which they aim at the studies are charges of serious methodological errors, inappropriate outcome criteria, inadequate assessment procedures to measure change, unsound selection of therapists, and unclear diagnostic appraisals. They point out that the heterogenous nature of psychotherapeutic intervention clouds the issue further; there is no "dose" of psychotherapy, and the term itself covers a vast range of methods, techniques and goals.

Schizophrenia itself encompases a heterogeneity of conditions, including "the clear-cut process schizophrenias, insidious in their onset in early adolescence and proceeding ever more malignantly into dementia; the oscillating, phasic schizophrenic conditions; the rigid, litigious paranoid schizophrenic processes that appear in the third and fourth decades of life; and the acute schizophreniform psychotic episodes, from which some patients apparently recover completely . . . . There are nonpsychotic conditions, too, that we label schizophrenic: the so-called latent schizophrenias, incipient schizophrenia, ambulatory schizophrenias and even remitted schizophrenias" (Dyrud and Holzman, 1973, p. 671). The authors emphasize that a crucial diagnostic task is the assessment of the relative contributions of familial, genetic, conflict, biochemical, psychological and sociocultural factors in order to be able to aim a treatment program at its proper target. Many therapeutic methods could be used. Evaluation of the benefits of psychotherapy should include a measurement of the patient's level of functioning and other more sophisticated criteria, not just discharge or readmission rates.

Presently our research armamentarium lacks sensitive instruments to detect the myriad intrapersonal changes that occur with and without psychotherapeutic intervention. Many acutely schizophrenic patients improve dramatically regardless of what we do; some remain psychotic in spite of what we do, but there is the large group of patients for whom it can matter very much what we do. The proper function of psychotherapeutic intervention in "what we do" is clearly not settled; the question remains open as to what treatment is appropriate and adequate for which patients.

A major factor in the success of aftercare programs depends on keeping patients on enough medication for a long enough time. The literature is filled with emphasis on the importance of medication in the treatment of previously psychotic patients. Kris (1962, 1963, 1965) documents this thoroughly in her detailed aftercare studies. Other U.S. studies agree (Capstick, 1970; Chalalampous, 1963; Cole and Davis, 1968; Ehrhardt, 1967; Lamb and Goertzel, 1972; Varsamis, 1970); foreign studies echo this conclusion (Heinrich and Baer, 1969 in Germany; Kruglova, 1970 in the USSR; Roder, 1970 in Denmark).

The large majority of hospitalized patients have had psychotic illnesses. The aforementioned studies clearly show the importance of drug treatment in their aftercare. Phenothiazines are most commonly used with schizophrenic patients; there is a newer trend toward using long-acting intramuscular phenothiazines for those patients who are undependable medication takers. The treatment of manic-depressive disorders now emphasizes pharmacotherapy, with the use of lithium being a major breakthrough. The involutional disorders are usually treated with pharmacotherapy and/or ECT in addition to psychotherapy. No effective drug treatment is available for the organic psychoses associated with the aging process, but research with RNA and hyperbaric oxygen is in its early stage.

Lamb and Goertzel (1972) found that patients often do not understand the goals of treatment, and that educating them is important. It must be brought home to the patients that their illness does not stop the day they leave the hospital, and that, for some, medication will be necessary indefinitely. The patient must be helped to overcome the common tendency to equate the need for medication with the concept that he is "still sick."

A small percentage of ex-hospital patients are diagnosed as neurotic or as having character disorders. For these patients the prevalent treatment is psychotherapy, with anti-anxiety drugs used when indicated. There is growing use of behavior therapies for some of these disorders.

The studies in the literature present overwhelming evidence that patients who remain in aftercare treatment programs do much better than those who do not. Yet there are many patients who never get started in aftercare treatment, some because of the failure of pre-discharge planning. More drop out after starting. Raskin and Dyson (1968) conducted a study to delineate the reasons for the failure of the aftercare facilities to prevent rehospitalizations. They found that the majority of readmitted patients are not in treatment at the time of their rehospitalization, and postulated three reasons for this finding: first, patients with an impulsive and stormy life-style persistently fail to keep their aftercare appointments; second, occasionally patients are discharged from aftercare because the chronicity of their illness is not recognized; third, patients drop out of aftercare because of increasing hopelessness about the chronic difficulties of their lives. This last problem was largely prevented during follow-up by the therapists' activity in keeping the patient in treatment and by the use of family therapy and vocational rehabilitation to lessen the patient's hopelessness.

Readmissions of patients who remain in treatment were found by Raskin and Dyson to occur for two main reasons: first, there are patients who require hospitalization whenever they experience a change of therapists; and second, there are patients who are so lonely within the community that they cannot be maintained there despite aftercare.

Huessy (1963) emphasizes the benefits of involving the family physician, who often is the only treatment modality in rural areas. From Japan, Hiraoka (1969) points out that patients often live far from aftercare facilities, and do not attend because of transportation difficulties.

Aftercare programs utilize a wide range of professional and paraprofessional personnel. Psychiatric nurses can play a valuable role (Nickerson, 1972).

## SOCIAL CLUBS

Social clubs for ex-patients have sprung out of a recognition that a frequent contributing cause of hospital readmission is a recurrence of withdrawal from society and a breakdown in the area of communication with other people. Since 1938 when the first social club was founded in Great Britain by Dr. Joshua Bierer, they have grown in number, membership and variety. The social club movement in the U.S. began in California in the 1950s.

In "Psychiatric Social Clubs Come of Age," Grob (1970) lists the common elements of social clubs: they are community-based, noninstitutional, intrinsically social, democratic in emphasis, exhibit a preference for horizontal ordering of staff, use volunteers, and concentrate on group activity. A typical social club program includes such unstructured activities as games, picnics, movies, exhibits and coffee klatches, and such structured activities as discussion groups, hobby groups, classes and sports.

For many, social clubs have become an important part of their rehabilitation program, the main weapon in learning social techniques. A conference on social clubs reported in *Social Clubs, Yes* (1963), stated the purpose of the social club:

> to help its members achieve and maintain positive social and vocational adjustments in the community by providing opportunities, situations, and experiences calculated to help prevent both social isolation and further social disability. Under qualified leadership, the social club can achieve its purpose by providing activities in the community which combine social interaction, recreation, personal development, and ego support.

This conference felt that patients should be professionally referred, and concluded that the director is the key figure in success, with volunteers essential. It seemed vital to the conferees that the social club develop and maintain good relationships with physicians, hospitals and clinics, day and night hospitals, government agencies (DVR, state employment agencies, welfare departments) and private and volunteer agencies (family service, MHA's community and volunteer services).

There is a diversity of opinion whether ex-patients should remain members of a social club indefinitely. Regardless, the social club should certainly be used as a stepping-stone toward regular community resources and services.

A controlled, experimental study to evaluate the effects of a social rehabilitative program showed that patients involved in such programs were rehospitalized less and functioned better in the community (Wolkon, Karmen, and Tanaka, 1971). Hillside Hospital (Lurie and Ron, 1972) developed a socialization program for younger patients using multiple family group therapy, activity group therapy, task-centered groups, individual and family counseling, and vocational counseling. Alumni Group Therapy, a program developed for the aftercare of chronic schizophrenics at the Chicago State Hospital, may have been responsible for a drop from 55% to 37.5% rehospitalization during the first year after discharge (Craig, 1971).

Winston, Papernik, Breslin and Trembath (1972) report about an ex-patient club from Kings County Hospital in Brooklyn, N.Y. They found that earlier ex-patient clubs had run into six principal problems:

1) There was a lack of professional involvement.
2) The clubs were often a long distance from the member's homes.
3) The more socially adequate patients joined, and those patients most in need were not members.
4) The more competent members left the club.
5) The hard core of sick persons remaining repelled others from joining.
6) Some were reluctant to have anything to do with reminders of their having been psychiatric patients.

The new Kings County club was designed to provide a structure for the continuation of relationships formed in the inpatient therapeutic community. It was necessary because "(t)hose patients with severe ego deficits in the area of object relations tended to return to withdrawal and isolation after discharge, despite the fact that while in the hospital they were able to interact with other patients and gain gratification from these relationships." It was expected that club membership be transitory rather than an ongoing experience. The authors believe the club was a success primarily because it was an extension of common inpatient experiences for all members, and the staff members' involvement provided organizational benefits as well as a link with therapeutic facilities.

In 1937, Dr. Abraham A. Low, a psychiatrist, founded the group called Recovery, Inc., in Chicago. It is now a nationwide organization, with many members. Its purpose is to prevent chronicity in new patients and relapses in former mental patients. The organization is managed and controlled by former patients.

The recovery method consists of reading the writings of Dr. Low, attending meetings, and putting the method to work in daily life. The Recovery meetings have five steps. First, members gather around a table and introduce each other by first names. Following this, they read aloud from Dr. Low's writings. Examples from daily life are then followed by a question and answer period, and mutual aid. Recovery members discover that their suffering is not unique and that life consists mainly of trivialities. There is mutual support and encouragement.

Lee (1971) used Recovery meetings at the Camarillo State Hospital in California to help bridge the gap between hospital and community. Self-help was an active concept in Lee's program. He felt Recovery was a useful aid and, used flexibly, supported other therapeutic efforts.

## VOCATIONAL REHABILITATION

Vocational rehabilitation is based on the premise that work is good for mental health.  For many patients who have been family breadwinners, economic necessity militates that they return to a level of functioning where they can again work.  For many who have never learned a vocational skill, the feeling of competence and productivity resulting from the mastery of a trade produces positive psychological reinforcement.  It can enhance self-respect, increase feelings of maturity and responsibility, lead to a feeling of independence, and increase the patient's standard of living.

Aftercare vocational rehabilitation was an outgrowth of the "industrial therapy" initiated in British psychiatric hospitals in the 1920s — simple contract assembly work for patients to perform.  In the U.S., the nation's first paid work program for the mentally ill was inaugerated at the Northampton (Massachusetts) V.A. Hospital in 1947.  Vocational rehabilitation then evolved into a program outside the hospital and began to include vocational testing, counseling, vocational training, sheltered job learning situations, sheltered work programs, and job placement.  It was only in 1954 that psychiatric patients were included in the Federal Vocational Rehabilitation Act.  Formal "industrial therapy" organizations developed as a result, such as the Altro Workshops and the V.A.'s CHIRP program (Black and Benney, 1969).

In an article "Spinning Straw into Gold," Durie, Gardner and Matthews (1972) describe the program of Forward House in Montreal where that social rehabilitation center set up a vocational rehabilitation program.  Over a three-year period 266 patients were referred.  Approximately half of this group, those whom the staff felt they could relate to and work with, were accepted.  At first, four programs were set up:  small business; domestic; transitional employment placement; and remotivation sessions.  Later a Forward House store was added which served as an outlet for Forward House handicrafts and took consignments from other communities and hospitals.  The authors concluded that:  patients are best referred during a period of active treatment; there should be a close liaison between the hospital and the rehabilitation center; diagnostic categories have little predictive value of success or failure; group leaders should be autonomous, and the staff flexible; individually tailored programs are desirable; and follow-up of successful placements in the community is desirable.  They felt the program was of definite benefit to many patients.

A novel program was instituted at the Westboro State Hospital in Massachusetts (Grimberg, 1970).  Patients were diverted from a noncompetitive system, where everything is given free, to a competitive situation where everything is earned.  A monetary system was set up and patients were paid 1.5 tokens per hour for working in hospital industrial placement or in a voluntary work program.  From wages earned, patients were expected to pay for room, board, medication and therapy.  A hierarchy of dining areas and sleeping quarters meant that a patient had to acquire a "better paying" job if he wished better facilities.

Eighteen months was the maximum time allowed in the program. During the final months the work program varied between a sheltered workshop placement and actual job placement in the community. Employed by community industry, the patient leaves the hospital and enters a halfway house where follow up and therapy are provided. Grimberg feels that an inhospital competitive society has proven more effective than the institution regulated society in preparing patients for jobs in the community and complete discharge from the hospital.

The literature abounds with the assumption that work is therapeutic, with little attempt to validate this hypothesis. Many studies used work rehabilitation as an index of "treatment success" or "recovery," so that work and successful treatment of mental illness become synonymous and a self-fulfilling prophesy. Micek and Miles (1969) attempted to evaluate the rehabilitative and therapeutic value of work for psychiatric patients. The subjects were assigned to groups where work therapy was either compulsory or forbidden. Follow-up information was obtained at 3- and 12-month intervals after discharge or transfer to low intensity treatment. At the time of transfer, the staff gave clinical ratings of response to treatment, and at the follow-up the patients were asked to rate individual therapy methods as most or least helpful. The staff ratings showed no significant differences between subjects in work therapy and those in other therapies. When the patients subjectively rated helpfulness of the various therapies, however, work therapy was frequently listed as "most helpful" and seldom as "least helpful."

Else Kris (1962), in her extensive experience at the Research Unit of the New York State Department of Mental Hygiene Aftercare Clinic, found that about 35% of the patients referred to the clinic were able to find gainful employment on their own, and only about 10% needed some form of vocational rehabilitation, either to learn new skills, to brush up on old skills, or to develop work tolerance.

Ryan (1969) conducted a survey for the National Association for Mental Health which adds a wry note. Studying the problems facing patients leaving mental hospitals in their search for work, he reports tentative indications that their return to the labor force is not as much of a problem as might have been expected. Ironically, they are finding difficulty not so much with prospective employers as with those statutory agencies which are specifically designed to help them.

## SUMMARY

Aftercare, a previously neglected area of psychiatric treatment, is now getting major emphasis. It encompasses pre-discharge planning, professional care, residential arrangements, socialization techniques and vocational rehabilitation. It is effective in improving patient functioning out of the hospital and decreasing readmission rates. Dynamic programs are necessary to keep patients in aftercare programs. Continuing psychotherapy and maintaining long-term pharmacotherapy are essential. We must provide these necessary treatments. "Freedom to be sick, helpless, and isolated is not freedom" (Reich, 1973, p. 912).

## REFERENCES

*Action for Mental Health.* Final Report of the Joint Commission on Mental Illness and Health. New York: Basic Books, 1961.

Aged long-term hospital patients show "restorative potential." *Frontiers of Hospital Psychiatry.* 5: 1, 2, 11 (1968).

Angrist, S., Dinitz, S., Lefton, M. and Pasamanick, B. Rehospitalization of female mental patients. Social and psychological factors. *Archives of General Psychiatry.* 4: 363-370 (1961).

Arthur, G., Ellsworth, R.B. and Kroeker, D. Readmission of released mental patients: a research study. *Social Work.* 13: 78-84 (1968).

Babyan, E.A. Zakondatel'stvo SSSR i nekotorykh zarubezhnykh stran po psikhiatrii. *Zhurnal Nevropatologii I Psikhatrii Imeni S.S. Korsakova.* 69: 1617-1623 (1969).

Baganz, P.C., Smith, A.E., Goldstein, R. and Pou, N.K. The YMCA as a halfway facility. *Hospital and Community Psychiatry.* 22: 156-159 (1971).

Bass, R. *A method for measuring continuity of care in a community mental health center.* Mental Health Statistics, Series C., No. 4. Rockville, MD: NIMH, 1972.

Bentinck, C. Opinions about mental illness held by patients and relatives. *Family Process.* 6: 193-207 (1967).

Bey, D.R., Chapman, R.E. and Tornquist, J. A lithium clinic. *American Journal of Psychiatry.* 129: 468-470 (1972).

Black, B.J. Industrial therapy in the United States. In: Black, B. *Principles of industrial therapy for the mentally ill,* pp. 60-120. New York: Grune & Stratton, 1970.

Black, B.J. and Benney, C. Rehabilitation. In: Bellak, L. (Ed.), *The Schizophrenic syndrome,* pp. 735-756. New York: Grune & Stratton, 1969.

Bok, M. and Bourestom, N. Age, patients: desires, residential facility and community tenure among chronic elderly mental patients. *Gerontologist.* 8: 35 (1968).

Bonn, E.M. Day care: a vital link in services. *Hospital and Community Psychiatry.* 23: 157-159 (1972).

Boriskov, V.P. Vliyaniye podderzhivayushchey terapii neyroleptikami na prisposoblyaemost k trudu bolnykh shizofreniyey. In: Vosstanov. *Terapiya I sots-trudov readapt bol'nykh ner-psikh zabolevanyami,* pp. 66-70. Leningrad: Nauch-issled psikhonevrolog inst vm bekhtereva, 1965.

Brooks, G.W. Effective use of ancillary personnel in rehabilitating the mentally ill. *Texas State Journal of Medicine.* 57: 341-347 (1961).

Brooks, G.W., Deane, W.N. and Ansbacker, H.L. Rehabilitation of chronic schizophrenic patients for social living. *Journal of Individual Psychology.* 16: 189-196 (1960).

Brown, B.S. Pathways and detours to and from the mental hospital. *Missouri Medicine.* 60: 253-256 (1963).

Brown, G.W., Carstairs, G.M. and Topping, G. Post-hospital adjustment of chronic mental patients. *Lancet,* pp. 685-689. September 27, 1958.

Brown, J.K. Mental patients work back into society. *Manpower.* 2: 23–25 (1970).

Bryant, J. and Sandford, F. Psychiatric nursing in the community. *Nursing Mirror and Midwives Journal.* 134: 37-39 (1972).

Budson, R.D. The psychiatric halfway house. *Psychiatric Annals.* 4: 64-83 (1973).

Burvill, P.W. and Mittelman, M. A follow-up study of chronic mental hospital patients, 1959-1969. *Social Psychiatry.* 6: 167-171 (1971).

Caffey, E.M., Jr., Galbrecht, C.R. and Klett, C.J. Brief Hospitalization and aftercare in the treatment of schizophrenia. *Cooperative Studies in Psychiatry.* 78: 1-17 (1969).

Caffey, E.M., Jones, R.D., Diamond, L.S., Burton, E. and Bowen, W.T. Brief hospital treatment of schizophrenia: Early results of multiple-hospital study. *Psychiatry Digest.* 30: 62 (1969).

Capstick, N. Long-acting drug treatment in overall psychiatric management. *Diseases of the Nervous System.* Supplement 31: 15-17 (1970).

Capstick, N. and Kirby, J. A group home project. *Lancet,* pp. 516-518. September 5, 1970.

Carney, M.W.P., Ferguson, R.S. and Sheffield, B.F. Psychiatric day hospital and community. *Lancet.* 7658: 1218-1220 (1970).

Charalampous, K.D. The long-term care of the chronic mentally ill patient, a medical approach. *Medical Record and Annals.* 56: 257-258 (1963).

Cheadle, J. The psychiatric nurse as a social worker. *Nursing Times.* 66: 1520-1522 (1970).

Cheney, T.M. and Kish, G.B. Job development in a veterans administration hospital. *Vocational Guidance Quarterly.* 19: 61-65 (1970).

Ch'en, C.C. An examination of social resources in the rehabilitation of the mentally ill. *Mental Health Bulletin.* 14: 11–12 (1969).

Chien, C. and Cole, J.O. Landlord-supervised cooperative apartments: a new modality for community-based treatment. *American Journal of Psychiatry.* 130: 156-159 (1973).

Clark, M.C. Alpine House. *Provo Papers.* 7: 68-70 (1963).

Cohen, E.S. and Kraft, A.C. The restorative potential of elderly long-term residents of mental hospitals. *Gerontologist.* 8: 264-268 (1968).

Cohen, P.H. Sheltered industry in psychiatric rehabilitation. *Medical Journal of Australia.* 2: 200-203 (1967).

Cohen, S., Leonard, C.V., Farberow, N.L. and Shneidman, E.S. Tranquilizers and suicide in the schizophrenic patient. *Archives of General Psychiatry.* 11: 312-321 (1964).

Cole, J.O. and Davis, J.M. Clinical efficacy of the phenothiazines as antipsychotic drugs. In: Efron, D.(Ed.), *Psychopharmacology: A review of progress 1957-1967* #1836, pp. 1057-1063. Washington, D.C.: USPHS 1968.

Coleman, J.V. and Arafeh, M.K. The Connecticut cooperative care project. *Current Psychiatric Therapies.* 9: 234-240 (1969).

Coohan, J.P. A lot more of the usual – community mental health in Manitoba. *SK & F Psychiatric Reporter.* 35: 13-16 (1967).

Craig, R.J. Alumni group therapy for chronic schizophrenic outpatients. Hospital and Community Psychiatry. **22**: 204-205 (1971).

Cropley, A.J. and Gazan, A. Some data concerning readmission of discharged schizophrenic patients. *British Journal of Social and Clinical Psychology.* **8**: 286-289 (1969).

Crow, N. The multifaceted role of the community mental health nurse. *Journal of Psychiatric Nursing and Mental Health Services.* **9**: 28-31 (1971).

Daniel, G.R. and Freeman, H.L. *The treatment of mental disorders in the community.* Baltimore: Williams & Wilkins, 1968.

Darley, P.J. and Kenny, W.T. Community care and the "Queequeg syndrome": A phenomenological evaluation of methods of rehabilitation for psychotic patients. *American Journal of Psychiatry.* **127**: 1333-1338 (1971).

David, A.C. Effective low cost aftercare. *Mental Hygiene.* **55**: 351-357 (1971).

Denber, H.C.B. and Rajotte, P. Problems and theoretical considerations of work therapy for psychiatric patients. *Canadian Psychiatric Association Journal.* **7**: 25-33 (1962).

Dignity sounds the keynote. *Medical World News.* **10**: 34L-34M (1969).

Donlon, P.T., Rada, R.T. and Knight, S.W. A therapeutic aftercare setting for "Refractory" chronic schizophrenic patients. *American Journal of Psychiatry.* **130**: 682-684 (1973).

Driemen, P.M. and Minard, C.C. Pre-leave planning: effect upon rehospitalization. *California Mental Health Research Digest.* **8**: 196-197 (1970).

Durie, M., Gardner, R.V. and Matthews, C.J. Spinning straw into gold. *Mental Hygiene.* **56**: 39-42 (1972).

Dyrud, J.E. and Holzman, P.S. The psychotherapy of schizophrenia: Does it work? *American Journal of Psychiatry.* **130**: 670-673 (1973).

Ehrhardt, H. Medikamentose Voraussetzungen einer erfolgreichen rehabilitation bei endogen psychosen. *Psychotherapy and Psychosomatics.* **15**: 17 (1967).

Elder, M.E. and Weinberger, P.E. A family centered project in a state mental hospital. *California Mental Health Research Digest.* **8**: 189-190 (1970).

Ellsworth, R.B. Community measures of treatment effectiveness of released patients. In: *Nonprofessionals in psychiatric rehabilitation,* pp. 129-165. New York: Appleton-Century-Crofts, 1968.

Elosuo, R., Hagglund, V. Paakkinen, E. and Alanen, Y.O. Development of outpatient services in psychiatric departments: a study of the activities of an after-care clinic. *Social Psychiatry.* **4**: 82-84 (1969).

Evans, A.S. and Bullard, D.M., Jr. The family as a potential resource in the rehabilitation of the chronic schizophrenic patient. *Mental Hygiene.* **44**: 64-73 (1960).

Evje, M.C., Bellander, I., Gibby, M. and Palmer, I.S. Evaluating protected hospital employment of chronic psychiatric patients. *Hospital and Community Psychiatry.* **23**: 204-208 (1972).

Feder, S.L. The indications and techniques of partial hospitalization. In: Masserman, J. (Ed.), *Current Psychiatric Therapies,* pp. 167-174. New York: Grune & Stratton, 1971.

Fleurant, L., Hicks, E., Norris, M., Gouge, R. and McKay, A. A twelve-month review of the aftercare clinic activities in Barrow and Walton counties. *Journal of the Medical Association of Georgia.* **61**: 352-354 (1972).

Flomenhaft, K. and Langsley, D.G.   After the crisis.  *Mental Hygiene.*  **55**: 473-477 (1971).

Flynn, J.P.  The team approach:  A possible control for the single service schism, an exploratory study. *Gerontologist.*  **10**:  119-124 (1970).

Freeman, H.E. and Simmons, B.G.  *The mental patient comes home.* New York: John Wiley & Sons, 1963.

Friedman, I., Lundstedt, S., Von Mering, O. and Hinko, E.N.  Systematic underestimation in reported mental hospital readmission rates. *American Journal of Psychiatry.*  **121**:  148-152 (1964).

Furst, W. Daycare:   Comprehensive management of the mentally ill patient in the community. *Sandoz Panorama.*  **8**:  26-28 (1970).

Gardner, R.A. Community work therapy in a mental hospital setting. *American Archives of Rehabilitation Therapy.*  **17**:  29-34 (1969).

Gaviria, B. and Lund, R.D.  Fort Logan patients two years later:  A pilot study. *Journal of the Fort Logan Mental Health Center.*  **4**:   163-176 (1967).

Gittelman-Klein, R. and Klein, D.F.  Premorbid asocial adjustment and prognosis in schizophrenia.  *Journal of Psychiatric Research.*  **7**:  35-53 (1969).

Glasscote, R.M., Gudeman, J.E. and Elpers, R.  *Halfway houses for the mentally ill:  A study of programs and problems.* Washington: The Joint Information Service, 1971.

Gottesman, L.E.  Extended care of the aged:  Psychosocial aspects. *Journal of Geriatric Psychiatry.*  **2**:  220–249 (1969).

Greenblatt, M.  *The prevention of hospitalization:  treatment without admission for psychiatric patients.* New York: Grune & Stratton, 1963.

Greenblatt, M. and Kantor, D.  Student volunteer movement and the manpower shortage. *American Journal of Psychiatry.*  **118**:  809-814 (1962).

Grimberg, M. The surrogate society: A new approach to rehabilitation. *Journal of Rehabilitation.*  **36**: 34-35 (1970).

Grinspoon, L., Ewalt, J.R. and Shader, R.  Psychotherapy and pharmacotherapy. **125**: 124 (1968).

Grob, S.  Psychiatric social clubs come of age. *Mental Hygiene.*  **54**:  129-136 (1970).

Harms, E. Aftercare of the psychiatric patient: an 1847 view. *American Journal of Psychiatry.*  **125**:  694-695 (1968).

Harrison, E.  Mental aftercare. *Assignment for the 60's.* New York:  Public Affairs Pamphlets, 1961.

Heinrich, K. and Baer, R.  Zur depot-neuroleptischen therapie schizophrener in der klinischen ambulanz. In:  Heinrich, K. (Ed.), *Neurolept, Dauer-Und Depottherapie in der Psychiatrie,* pp. 77-83. Constance, Germany:  Schnetztor, 1969.

Herz, M.I.  Crisis unresolved. *International Journal of Psychiatry.*  **9**:  586-591 (1970).

Hiraoka, E.   The health center's view of a community issue – previously institutionalized schizophrenics. *Community Psychiatry.*  **4**:  37-40 (1969).

Hogarty, G.E.   Hospital differences in the release of discharge ready chronic schizophrenics. *Archives of General Psychiatry.*  **18**:  367-372 (1968).

Hogarty, G.E. and Goldberg, S.  Drug and sociotherapy in the post-hospital maintenance of schizophrenia. *Archives of General Psychiatry.*  **24**:  54-64 (1973).

Howard, B.F.   An optimistic report on total rehabilitative potential of chronic schizophrenics. *Archives of General Psychiatry.* **3:** 345-356 (1960).

Huessy, H.R.   Increased use of the family physician in the aftercare of state hospital patients. *American Journal of Public Health.* **53:** 603-608 (1963).

Jansen, E.   The role of the halfway house in community mental health programs in the United Kingdom and America. *American Journal of Psychiatry.* **126:** 1498-1504 (1970).

Jones, M.   *The therapeutic community: A new treatment method in psychiatry.* New York: Basic Books, 1953.

Kalmans, E.T.   Low-cost individualized treatment in a day center. *Hospital and Community Psychiatry.* **21:** 394-397 (1970).

Kelley, F.E. and Walker, R.   A follow-up evaluation of a paid hospital activity program. *Newsletter for Research in Psychology.* **11:**   32-33 (1969).

Kernodle, R.W.   Three family placement programs in Belgium and the Netherlands. *Hospital and Community Psychiatry.* **23:** 339-345 (1972).

Keskiner, A., Ruppert, E. and Ulett, G.A.   The New Haven project. Development of a foster community for mental patients. *Attitude.* **1:**   14-17 (1970).

Kiev, A.   Community psychiatry: Observations of recent English developments. *Comprehensive Psychiatry.* **4:** 291-298 (1963).

Kiev, A.   Some background factors in recent English psychiatric progress. *American Journal of Psychiatry.* pp. 851-856 (1963).

Kinross-Wright, J. and Charalampous, K.D.   A recent development in the chemotherapy of schizophrenia. *Medical Records and Annals.* **56:** 224-225 (1963).

Kirby, J.H.   The discharged mentally ill patient:   Aftercare and maintenance in the community. *Medical Times.* **97:** 127-132 (1969).

Klein, L.E.   The hospital halfway house. *Mental Hygiene.* **56:** 30-33 (1972).

Kobrynski, B. and Miller, A.D.   The role of the state hospital in the care of the elderly. *Journal of the American Geriatrics Society.* **18:** 210-219 (1970).

Kramer, B.M.   *Day hospital – A study of partial hospitalization in psychiatry.* New York: Grune & Stratton, 1962.

Kramer, M.   Problems in psychiatric epidemiology. *Proceedings of the Royal Society of Medicine.* **63:** 553-562 (1970).

Kris, E.B.   Effects of pharmacotherapy on work and learning ability – a five year follow-up study. *Recent Advances in Biological Psychiatry.* **3:** 30-34 (1961).

Kris, E.B.   Five-year community follow-up of patients discharged from a mental hospital. *Current Therapeutic Research.* **5:** 451-462 (1963).

Kris, E.B.   Five years' experience with the use of drugs and psychotherapy in a community aftercare clinic. *American Journal of Public Health.* **52:**   (Part 2) 9-12 (1962).

Kris, E.B.   Post-hospital care of patients in their community. *Current Therapeutic Research.* **4:** (Supp.):   200-205 (1962).

Kris, E.B.   The role of the day hospital in the rehabilitation of mental patients. In: *Proceedings of the Institute on Rehabilitation of the Mentally Ill,* pp. 33-36. New York: Altro Health and Rehabilitation Services, 1962.

Kris, E.B.   The value of a psychiatric aftercare clinic. *Physician's Panorama,* pp. 19-23. November, 1965.

Kruglova, L.I.  Dinamika sotsial 'no-trudovogo prisposobliniia bol'nykh shizofreniei v sviazi s shirokim primeniniem psikhotropnykh sredstv. In: Efimovich, N. (Klin.), *Patogenez I Lechenie Nervno-psikh. zabolevanii*, pp. 223-228. Moscow: Soviet Ministrov RSFSR, 1970.

Kutin, V.P.  Rezhim Dnevnogo Statsionara I Problema Readaptatsii v psikhiatricheskikh bol'nitsakh. *Zhurnal Nevropatologii I Psikhiatrii Imeni S.S. Korsakova.* **71**: 1249-1250 (1971).

Lagey, J.C.  *The Minnesota follow-up study ten years later.* New York: New York University, 1972.

Lamb, H.R. and Goertzel, V.  Discharged mental patients – Are they really in the community? *Archives of General Psychiatry.* **24**: 29-34 (1971).

Lamb, H.R. and Goertzel, V.  Evaluating aftercare for former day treatment center patients. *International Journal of Social Psychiatry.* **18**: 67-77 (1972).

Lamb, H.R. and Goertzel, V.  High expectations of long-term ex-state hospital patients. *American Journal of Psychiatry.* **129**: 471-475 (1972).

Langsley, D.G. and Kaplan, D.M.  Project summary: The family concept in comprehensive psychiatric care. *Final Report, NIMH Grants,* 1970.

Lear, T.E., Bhattacharyya, A., Corrigan, G., Elliott, J., Gordon, J. and Pitt-Aitkens, T.  Sharing the care of the elderly between community and hospital. *Lancet.* **7634**: 1349-1353 (1969).

Ledvinka, J. and Denner, B.  The limits of success. *Mental Hygiene.* **56**: 30-35 (1972).

Lee, D.T.  Recovery, Inc.: Aid in the transition from hospital to community. *Mental Hygiene.* **55**: 194-198 (1971).

Leopoldt, H.  Industrial therapy in psychiatric hospitals. *Nursing Mirror and Midwives Journal.* **128**: 16-18 (1969).

Levy, L.  An evaluation of a mental health program by use of selected operating statistics. *American Journal of Public Health.* **61**: 2038-2045 (1971).

Liberman, R.P.  Behavior modification with chronic mental patients. *Journal of Chronic Diseases.* **23**: 803-812 (1971).

*Lifeline: Aftercare.*  Philadelphia: Smith Kline & French Laboratories, 1962.

Lin, T.  Community mental health services: a world view. In: *Com. mental health, an international perspective,* pp. 3-17. San Francisco: Jossey-Bass Inc., 1968.

Ludwig, A.M.  Responsibility and chronicity: new treatment models for the chronic schizophrenic. In: Abroms, G. *The New Hospital Psychiatry.* pp. 237-260. New York: Academic Press, 1971.

Lurie, A. and Ron, H.  Socialization program as part of aftercare planning. *Canadian Psychiatric Association Journal.* **17** (Special Supp. 2): 157-162 (1972).

Lurie, A. and Ron, H.  Multiple family group counseling of discharged schizophrenic young adults and their parents. *Social Psychiatry.* **6**: 88-92 (1971).

Lyashko, G.A.  K Voprosu O Povtornykh Postupleniyakh V Psikhonevrologicheskiye Bol'nitsy Leningrada. *Voprosy Psikhiatrii I Nevropatologii.* **7**: 403-408 (1961).

Maeda, E. and Rothwell, N.  *Discussion, listing and bibliography of psychiatric halfway houses in the U.S.* American Psychiatric Association. Psychiatric Studies and Projects, No. 9, 1963.

Manizade, A.   The county mental health center and its role in community psychiatry. *Maryland State Medical Journal.* **16**: 49-51 (1967).

May, P.R.A. *Treatment of schizophrenia: A comparative study of five treatment methods.* New York: Science House, 1968.

McGarry, L. and Kaplan, H. Overview: Current trends in mental health law. *American Journal of Psychiatry,* pp. 621-630. **130**: 6 (June 1973).

McGriff, D.   A co-ordinated approach to discharge planning. *Social Work.* **10**: 45-50 (1965).

*Medical World News,* 1969.

Mental Health Authority.   Residential Services: Reports (Psychiatric and Informal Hospitals). In: *Report of the Mental Health Authority,* 1970, pp. 33-50. Melbourne: Government Printer, 1971.

Mental health hostels. *British Medical Journal.* **5709**: 552-553 (1970).

Micek, L.A. and Miles, D.G. Perspectives on work therapy. *Current Psychiatric Therapies.* **9**: 202-208 (1969).

Miller, A.   The Lobotomy patient — a decade later: A follow-up study of a research project started in 1948. *Canadian Medical Association Journal.* **96**: 1095-1103 (1967).

Molholm, L.H. and Dinitz, S. Female mental patients and their normal controls: A restudy ten years later. *Archives of General Psychiatry.* **27**: 606-610 (1972).

Morrissey, J.R. *The case for family care of the mentally ill.* New York: Behavioral Publications, 1967.

Myers, J.K. and Bean, L.L. Final considerations. In: *A decade later: A follow-up of social class and mental illness,* pp. 201-222. New York: John Wiley, 1968.

Myers, J.K. and Bean, L.L. Social class and the treatment process. In: *A decade later: A follow-up of social class and mental illness,* pp. 80-111. New York: John Wiley, 1968.

Nickerson, A. Psychiatric community nurses in Edinburgh. *Nursing Times.* **68**: 289-291 (1972).

Nol, E.A. and Fuller, W. Perspectives on psychiatric aftercare in the community. *Michigan Medicine.* **71**: 1009-1013 (1972).

Odegard, O.   The pattern of discharge and readmission in Norwegian mental hospitals, 1936-63. *American Journal of Psychiatry.* **125**: 333-340 (1968).

Olshansky, S.   The vocational rehabilitation of ex-psychiatric patients. *Mental Hygiene.* **52**: 556-561 (1968).

Oltman, J. and Friedman, S.   Results at a "half-way house." *Diseases of the Nervous System,* pp. 317-318 (1964).

Over 65. *Medical World News.* **11**: 300 (1970).

Palmer, M. *The Social Club.* New York: National Association for Mental Health, 1966.

*Partial hospitalization.* U.S.P.H.S. Publication #1449. Bethesda, Md.: National Institute of Mental Health, 1966.

Pattison, E.M. Group psychotherapy and group methods in community mental health programs. *International Journal of Group Psychotherapy.* **20**: 516-539 (1970).

Payne, J. New Scope for industrial therapy. *Mental Health.* Winter 42-43 (1969).
Perkins, M.E. and Bluestone, H. Hospital and community psychiatric approaches. In: Bellak, L. (Ed.), *The schizophrenic syndrome,* pp. 667-713. New York: Grune & Stratton, 1969.
Pittman, F.S., III, Langsley, D.G., Flomenhaft, K., DeYoung, C.D., Machotka, P. and Kaplan, D.M. Therapy techniques of the family treatment unit. In: Haley, J. (Ed.), *Changing families: A family therapy reader,* pp. 259-271. NewYork: Grune & Stratton, 1971.
Pokorny, A.D. and Frazier, S.H. Local care would benefit many state psychiatric patients. *Texas Medicine.* **63**: 37-38 (1967).
Pokorny, A.D. and Frazier, S.H. Texas surveys its mental hospital population. *Hospital and Community Psychiatry.* **19**: 88-89 (1968).
Pollack, M. Levenstein, S. and Klein, D.F. A three-year post-hospital follow-up of adolescent and adult schizophrenics. *American Journal of Orthopsychiatry.* **38**: 94-109 (1968).
Prince, R.M., Jr., Ackerman, R.E. and Barksdale, B.S. Collaborative provision of aftercare services. *American Journal of Psychiatry.* **130**: 930-932 (1973).
Psychiatrisches Rehabilitationszentrum in Zurich. *Praktische Psychiatrie.* **49**: 78-80 (1970).
Racklin, S. Adolescent psychiatry in a foster care residence: Future directions. *Mt. Sinai Journal of Medicine.* **39**: 586-591 (1972).
Raskin, M. and Dyson, W.L. Treatment problems leading to readmissions of schizophrenic patients. *Archives of General Psychiatry.* **19**: 356-360 (1968).
Raush, Harold L. and Raush, C.L. *The halfway house movement: A search for sanity.* New York: Appleton-Century-Crofts, 1968.
Rawls, J.R. Toward the identification of readmissions and non-readmissions to mental hospitals. *Social Psychiatry.* **6**: 58-61 (1971).
Recovery, Inc., Chicago, Illinois: National Headquarters, Recovery, Inc., 1967.
Reich, R. Care of the chronically mentally ill – a national disgrace. *American Journal of Psychiatry.* **130**: 911-12 (1973).
Rene, A.D., Rice, R.G. and Ghertner, S. Assessing patient needs for counseling and rehabilitation services in hospital setting. *Newsletter for Research in Psychology.* **14**: 33-35 (1972).
Richmond, C. Expanding the concepts of the halfway house: A satellite housing program. *International Journal of Social Psychiatry.* **16**: 96-102 (1970).
Ritchey, R.E. Activity Groups help long-term patients solve everyday problems. *Hospital and Community Psychiatry.* **22**: 335-336 (1971).
Roder, E. A prognostic investigation of female schizophrenic patients discharged from Sct Hans Hospital, Department D, during the decade 1951-1960. *Acta Psychiatrica Scandinavica.* **46**: 50-63 (1970).
Romme, M.A.J. Organisatie gezondheidszorg en langerdurende psychiatrische opneming. *Tijdschrift Voor Sociale Geneeskunde.* **48**: 402-406 (1970).
Rosenberg, G. and Colthoff, P. A community participation program for the hospitalized mental patient. *Journal of Jewish Communal Service.* **43**: 253-259 (1967).
Roth, J.A. and Eddy, E.M. Where do they go from Rahab? In: Roth, J. (Ed.), *Rehabilitation for the unwanted,* pp. 144-167 New York: Atherton Press, 1967.

Rutman, I.D. and Loeb, A. *Comprehensive, Community-based rehabilitation services for the psychiatrically disabled.* Springfield, Virginia, NTIS, 1970.

Ryan, G. Back on the market. *Mental Health.* Winter, 8-9 (1969).

Ryan, W. *Community care in historical perspective.* Canada's Mental Health Supplement #60. Ottawa, Canada: Department of National Health and Welfare, 1969.

Safirstein, S.L. A system of secondary prevention in a psychiatric aftercare clinic of a general hospital. *Diseases of the Nervous System.* **30**: (supplement) 122-125 (1969).

Safirstein, S.L. Psychiatric aftercare including home visits. *New York State Journal of Medicine.* **71**: 2441-2445 (1971).

Salvesen, C. Treatment of suicidal patients in outpatient/aftercare department. *Tidsskrift for den Norske Laegeforening.* **92**: 1193-1194 (1972).

Scarzella, R. Attivita clinico-scientifica nell'ospedale civile di Ivrea.-II. Proposte per la realizzazione del servizo psichiatrico extraospedaliero nel settore psichiatrico del canavese. *Minerva Media.* **61**: 2731-2736 (1970).

Schuerman, J.R. Marital interaction and posthospital adjustment. *Social Casework.* **53**: 163-172 (1972).

Schwartzberg, A.Z. The older psychiatric patient and the community. *Geriatrics.* **22**: 182-186 (1967).

Scoles, P. The chronic mental patient: Aftercare and rehabilitation. In: Berlatsky, E. (Ed.), *Social work practice,* 1969. New York: Columbia University Press, 1969. pp. 61–75.

Searle, D.J. The psychogeriatric services. *Nursing Mirror and Midwives Journal.* **131**: 10-11 (1970).

Shammas, E. Day care centers in Rhode Island state hospitals. *Rhode Island Medical Journal.* **54**: 541-545 (1971).

Sharpe, D. Things have changed. *Nursing Mirror and Midwives Journal.* **134**: 21-23 (1972).

Sherman, L.J., Moseley, E.C., Ging, R. and Bookbinder, L.J. Prognosis in schizophrenia. A follow-up study of 588 patients. *Archives of General Psychiatry.* **10**: 123-130 (1964).

Shot in the Arm for psychotherapy. *Medical World News.* **9**: 62-63 (1968).

Siegle, A. Pioneer at work. SK & F *Psychiatric Reporter.* **37**: 16-17 (1968).

Silverman, M. Comprehensive department of psychological medicine: Three-year review of inpatients referred for aftercare visits. *British Medical Journal.* **3**: 99-101 (1971).

Silverstein, M. *Psychiatric aftercare: Planning for community mental health services.* Philadelphia: University of Pennsylvania Press, 1968.

Simon, C.S. Boarding Home Operators Participate in workshop. *Hospital and Community Psychiatry.* **23**: 1972.

Smith, C.M. Experiment in psychiatric home care. *Canada's Mental Health.* **13**: 8-13 (1965).

*Social Clubs . . . Yes. Report of a Consultation on Social Clubs.* New York: National Association for Mental Health, 1963.

Solomon, N. and Gorwitz, K. *Mental Hygiene Statistics Newsletter-x-12.* Maryland Department of Health and Mental Hygiene, December 10, 1969.

Spilken, A.Z. *The relationship of patient personality to dropout from psychotherapy.* Ann Arbor, Michigan: Univ. M-Films, No. 71-26488.

Stein, E. and Sorensen, K.D.  A cooperative apartment for transitional patients. *Mental Hygiene.* **56**: 68-74 (1972).

Steiner, J. and Kaplan, S.R.  Outpatient Group "Work-For-Pay" activity for chronic schizophrenic patients. *American Journal of Psychotherapy.* **23**: 452-462 (1969).

Taylor, I.  The third life:  Rehabilitation of a long-stay patient. *Nursing Times.* **66**: 956 (1970).

Thompson, P. *Bound for Broadmoor.*  London:  Hodder & Stoughton, Ltd., 1972.

Thomson, C.P.  Developing a day program at the Royal Edinburgh Hospital. *Hospital and Community Psychiatry.* **19**: 14-17 (1968).

Tiffany, D.W., Cowan, J., Eddy, W., Glad, D. and Woll, S.  Introduction.  In: *Work inhibition and rehabilitation, Part I,* pp. 1-8.   Kansas City, Missouri: Institute for Community Studies, 1967.

Treter, A.  Z Zagadnien rehabilititacji psychiatrycznej. *Psychiatria Polska.* **6**: 203-207 (1972).

U.S. National Institute of Mental Health, Office of Program Planning and Evaluation.  Bringing mental health services to the community.  In:  NIMH. *Mental health of urban America,* pp. 73-95.  Washington:  U.S. Government Printing Office, 1969.

University of Indiana Audiovisual Center. *Fountain House.*  Bloomington, Indiana:  (16MM Film), 1969.

Varsamis, J.  Antipsychotic drugs:  an essential tool of community psychiatry. *Canadian Journal of Public Health.* **61**: 432-435 (1970).

Wallis, R.R. and Katf, N.Y.  The 50-mile bridge:   consultation between state hospital and community mental health center staffs. *Hospital and Community Psychiatry.* **23**: 21-24 (1972).

Watt, N.F.  Five-year follow-up of geriatric chronically ill mental patients in foster home care. *Journal of the American Geriatrics Society.* **18**: 310-316 (1970).

Wechsler, H.  Halfway houses for mental patients:  A survey. *Journal of Social Issues.* **16**: 21-22 (1960).

Weinstein, A.S., Di Pasquale, D. and Winsor, F.  Relationships between length of stay in and out of the New York State mental hospitals. *American Journal of Psychiatry.* **130**: 904-909 (1973).

Weinstein, G.G.  Pilot programs in day care. *Mental Hospitals.* **11**: 9-11 (1960).

Weiss, J. and Schaie, K.W.  Factors in patients' failure to return to a psychiatric clinic. *Diseases of the Nervous System.* **19**: 429-430 (1958).

Whitehorn, J.C. and Betz, B.J.  A study of psychotherapeutic relationships between physicians and schizophrenic patients. *American Journal of Psychiatry.* **111**: 321-331 (1954).

Widdowson, R.K. and Griffiths, K.A.  A voluntary work program for outpatients. *Hospital and Community Psychiatry.* **22**: 151-153 (1971).

Wierig, G.J., Jr. and Robertson, R.J.  Social connectedness and community adjustment. *Journal of Clinical Psychology.* **28**: 30–31 (1972).

Wiesel, B.  Flexibility:  Key to planning of hospital psychiatric services and facilities. *Journal of the American Hospital Association.* **41**: 65-68 (1967).

Wijffels, A.J.A.M.   A psychiatric center in the Netherlands. *Hospital and Community Psychiatry.* **23**: 186-188 (1972).

Wilder, J.F., Kessel, M. and Caulfield, S.C.   Follow-up of a "high expectations" halfway house. *American Journal of Psychiatry.* **124**: 1085-1091 (1968).

Wilder, J.F., Levin, G. and Zwerling, I.   A two-year follow-up evaluation of acute psychotic patients treated in a day hospital. *American Journal of Psychiatry.* **122**: 1095-1101 (1966).

Williams, M.A.   Social Worker and counsellor in vocational rehabilitation. *Canada's Mental Health.* **19**: 20-24 (1971).

Winick, W.   An automated system for reviewing patient care. *Hospital and Community Psychiatry.* **23**: 27-29 (1972).

Winkler, W.T.   Das Moderne Psychiatrische Krankenhaus. *Hippokrates.* **40**: 107-114 (1969).

Winkler, W.T., Kruger, H., Zumpe, V. and Veltin, A.   Ergebnisse soziodiagnosticher und soziotherapeutischer massnahmen bei langjahrig hospitalisierten schizophrenen. *Psychotherapy and Psychosomatics.* **17**: 1-9 (1969).

Winston, A., Papernik, D., Breslin, L. and Trembath, P.   Therapeutic club for formerly hospitalized psychiatric patients. *New York State Journal of Medicine.* **72**: 3027-3029 (1972).

Witkin, H., Lewis, H.B. and Weil, E.   Affective reactions and patient-therapist interactions among more differentiated and less differentiated patients early in therapy. *Journal of Nervous and Mental Disorders.* **146**: 193-208 (1968).

Wolkon, G.H., Karmen, M. and Tanaka, H.T.   Evaluation of a social rehabilitation program for recently released psychiatric patients. *Community Mental Health Journal.* **7**: 312-322 (1971).

Wolkon, G.G. and Tanaka, H.T.   Professional's views on the need for psychiatric aftercare services. *Community Mental Health Journal.* **1**: 262-270 (1965).

Woodruff, C.R.   Pastoral care of the discharged psychiatric patient. *Pastoral Psychology.* **21**: 21-26, 28-29 (1970).

Wren, C.S.   28% of state's mental patients return within 6 months after being released. *The New York Times,* p. 43, July 12, 1973.

*Yolles, S.F. and Kramer, M.   Vital statistics.* In: Bellak, L. (Ed.), *The schizophrenic syndrome,* pp. 66-113. New York: Grune & Stratton, 1969.

Zolik, E.S., Sommers, R. and Lantz, E.M.   Hospital return rates and prerelease referrals. *Virginia Medical Monthly.* **94**: 549-552 (1967).

# 11 Preventive Methods and Mental Health Programs

## Jack R. Ewalt and Patricia L. Ewalt

*"A strategy for health improvement should include personal health care, environmental control measures and measures of influencing health related behavior." (Breslow, 1973)*

### Preventive Methods

This section will present primary and secondary preventive methods only, since tertiary prevention is a public health term for the treatment and rehabilitation of illness which will be covered by other authors.

### PRIMARY PREVENTION

Primary preventive methods will be discussed under two headings: (a) those methods which alter the individual through some biologic or metabolic manipulation within the body; (b) those methods which alter the environment. To be effective, a primary method must reasonably insure that the condition to be prevented will not occur when the person (or population) is exposed to the causal element.

The prevention of psychological or social behavior that is unacceptable to the individual or others requires an understanding of the complexity of the determinants of human behavior. Ewalt and Farnsworth (1963) discuss this as do Lindsley and Reisen (1968, p. 273):

Behavior is the end point in a series of consequences and interactions which begin with the genetic history of an organism, be it microbe or man. Growth, maturation, and development of an organism are embodied not only in the form and function with which it is endowed, but also in the modifications of these imposed by environmental influences. The chemical composition of its genes, as well as its subsequent soma, are important in the determination of the form and function of the organism, but perhaps no less so than intra- and extra-cellular exchange, intra- and extra-organismic relations, or physical, mental, and social interactions among organisms.

## Manipulation of Immune or Metabolic Factors in the Body

Among the most successful methods of primary prevention under this category is the vaccination which prevents the development of smallpox due to an alteration in the body's immune capacities.

A rare but devastating form of mental retardation is prevented by routine examination of the urine of newborn infants to detect abnormalities in phenylalanine metabolism. Failure to detect these in the newborn state results in disastrous problems in growth and development. Detection of these abnormalities in phenylalanine metabolism and the maintenance of infants on a diet free of phenylalanine, enables them to develop normally. At about age six they may then go on a normal diet, free of the pathology which would have resulted in severe impairment in mental growth and development had they been given an ordinary infant diet.

Beri-beri, once a common mental disorder accompanied by severe physical illness and death, is known to be due to dietary deficiencies, particularly the inadequacy of the "B" vitamin factors. An adequate diet maintains the body's nutrition and the illness does not develop.

In the long view, hope for the primary prevention of schizophrenia and the manic depressive disorders, is in genetic, biochemical, and social and psychological investigations. Most people now believe that genetic predisposition is a necessary but not sufficient cause of schizophrenia. Just how this predisposition is manifested in the organism is unknown and we therefore cannot at this time pretest patients for susceptibility to schizophrenia as we can, for example, in the phenylalanine cases.

Investigation of the enzymatic and transmittor substances in the brain, particularly the catecholamine metabolism studies, lend hope that eventually the metabolic disorder of whatever origin may be discovered and perhaps corrective products or diets may effectively prevent the development of the symptomatology. Unfortunately, at the moment these are only hopes which should spur further research but should not lead to false claims of known preventive methods or specific therapies, even though such are offered from time to time. Genetic counseling which may offer opportunities for primary prevention must await more specific understanding of the genetic predisposition. At the moment some studies indicate that the predisposition may not be for schizophrenia *per se* but for more general psychopathology — the socioenvironmental and developmental factors determining which form of psychopathology becomes manifest. In the manic depressive disorders, genetic studies are fewer but perhaps a bit more specific than in the schizophrenic disorders. This may be so in part because the symptomatology of the manic depressive illness is a bit more specific and does not present the differential diagnostic problems sometimes seen in schizophrenias. Substantial progress has been made by Schildkraut (1973) and others to demonstrate with at least reasonable certainty a definite biochemical abnormality in catecholamine metabolism, probably genetically determined, in patients suffering from depressions. Unfortunately to date no biochemical or other test for an imminent attack of depression or mania has been developed although prodromal symtomatology has been fairly well established. Some patients live their whole lives in a mildly hypomanic state or in a mildly depressive state without showing either social or mental decompensation.

Patients with recurring manic attacks placed on lithium maintenance therapy are in most instances protected against further attacks. In a sense this is primary prevention, but some might call it follow-up therapy and rehabilitation. There is evidence that lithium therapy in bipolar manic-depressive patients prevents the depressive swings; and there is still other evidence, although less impressive, that unipolar recurring depressions of the depressive psychotic type may be prevented by lithium. While it is definitely known that the lithium replaces sodium ions, just how this acts to prevent the recurrence of manic attacks and how it acts to control manic symptoms is unknown at this time.

Environmental Manipulation

As examples of primary prevention owing to environmental manipulation, it is well known that malaria can be prevented by mosquito control in the environment and that typhus can be prevented by rat and lice control.

In the mental health field it is known that lead poisoning can cause certain forms of mental retardation and other pathology in infants and children. Lead poisoning can be prevented by environmental control such as insisting on the use of lead-free paint, cleaning up old premises with peeling lead-content paint, and checking air pollution for lead additives.

At the moment there is hope that environmental manipulation, particularly the improvement of family relationships and socio-economic conditions, will prevent at least the more serious manifestations of schizophrenia and manic depressive psychosis in persons congenitally predisposed to these disorders, and perhaps will cut down on the incidence of neuroses, character disorders, and other behavior decompensations thought to be principally due to psychological stresses.

From a historical perspective, however, one tends to be cautious in expecting an elimination of mental disorder through environmental manipulation. A premise of the "mental hygiene movement" — a precursor of "community mental health" at the beginning of this century — was that correction of the environment would contribute to the prevention of mental disorders. This hope accounts for the naming of the movement and of one of its products, the child guidance or "habit" clinics. Mental health consultation with courts, schools and employers was described at that time.  Exposure of medical students to mental illness and its treatment with the purpose of increasing their ability to detect and refer "incipient cases" was begun.  Classroom techniques devised by Ryan (1938), Prescott (1938) and others, have influenced teaching in regular classrooms and special classes for the emotionally disturbed.  Although many of these techniques have been more systematically formulated, or at least differently formulated recently, none of them are new.  Their influence over the years may be judged by the reader.

Even though the prevention of serious antisocial behavior and psychopathology has not occurred as was hoped, pessimism seems unwarranted in that the theory and the interventions were frequently too limited reasonably to expect success.  It seems unlikely that any single genetic, chemical, psychologic, or social factor could cause diverse and serious problems in growth and development or that correction of any one could prevent illness.  The view of Kahn (1970) seems a better approach to research on primary prevention:

> the conditions of life experienced by people of lower social class position tend to impair their ability to deal resourcefully with the problematic and the stressful.  Such impairment would be unfortunate for all who suffer it, but would not in itself result in schizophrenia.  In conjunction with a genetic vulnerability to schizophrenia and the experience of great stress, however, such impairment could be disabling.

A number of methods are now thought to aid in normal growth and development in the mental health aspects of behavior and are believed by some actually to prevent the development of serious pathology.  A number of studies seem to show that emotional deprivation in infancy and early childhood can have serious long-term effects on the mental health and behavior of children.  Anna Freud and Dorothy Burlingham (1943, 1944), and Spitz (1959) observed that infants deprived of adequate mothering failed to thrive either mentally or physically.  These observations sparked a series of investigations on early development of children that continue to the present, but only the more recent studies will be mentioned (see La Veek, 1968 for a good review of recent work and Soddy for a presentation circa 1956).

In a ten-year follow-up study of several hundred consecutive births, Werner *et al.* reported in 1968 that "More than 10 times as many children were affected by deprived environment than by perinatal stress, indicating the need to refocus emphasis about diagnosis and remediation from 'reproductive casualties' to 'environmental casualties.' "

In a long-term study, Skeels (1966) demonstrated that children removed from an institutional environment to adoptive homes, when examined in adult life, had made significant gains in health and achievement as compared to a similar group who stayed in the institution.

As we have previously mentioned, it is likely that the course of schizophrenia is greatly affected by qualities of the environment, even though the condition is most probably genetically based. Similarly, it is likely that many other conditions, including those more common and benign than schizophrenia, are multiply influenced. For example, the studies of Bell (1968) and of Graham, Rutter and George (1973) suggest a cyclical interaction of genetic and environmental factors — the child's innate characteristics evoking certain behavior in parent figures, and they in turn evoking certain behavior, favorable or unfavorable, in the child.

Owing to observations of this nature, some recent preventive programs have attempted a broad impact on the very young child's environment. Since previous efforts may have failed through treating one aspect and ignoring others, several aspects of the preschool child's life situation have been taken into account. For example, Pavenstedt (1967) and associates described a program of multiple therapeutic and educational inputs for preschool children and their families.

On a national scale, Head Start programs also attempted to coordinate multiple services, both to remedy and to enhance physical, social, and educational capacities of preschool children. Head Start exemplifies the difficulty of demonstrating that primary or even secondary prevention has occurred. The program explicitly attempted to counteract multiple environmental influences previously shown to hinder learning and social adjustment of school-age children — factors such as lack of verbal and visual stimulation, poor health care, lack of social skills customary in classrooms, or alienation of parents from the educational system if not the social system as a whole. Yet despite a coordinated effort to deal with previously identified deficits and thus to prevent disability, substantiation of accomplishments achieved by the program has been strongly questioned. The Skeels study provides the most supportive evidence known to us that alteration of environment may be expected to alter individual functioning over time.

In summary, owing to the current difficulty, if not impossibility, of specifying either the incidence, the causes, or the results of most mental conditions in most individuals, it seems wise to be very cautious in use of the term primary prevention of mental illness. Continued support of research to identify causes and preventive methodologies is highly desirable precisely because so little is yet known. Diversion of mental health resources, as such, predominantly into environmental manipulation is not yet justified by scientific findings. However, even though improvement of the social and physical environment does not prevent mental disorder, it may not be necessary so to justify improvement of the quality of human experience.

## SECONDARY PREVENTION

Secondary prevention is usually defined as early detection, early intervention, or early treatment.

There is abundant evidence to indicate that early detection and treatment of schizophrenia yields better results than similar efforts expended on patients allowed to become chronic. Patients with schizophrenia who start treatment within the first twelve months of their illness have a much better prognosis than those who are ill two or more years. There is also evidence that detection and treatment of problem drinking before it reaches a state of compulsive alcoholism is more effective than the treatment of the full-blown problem which tends to become a chronic recurring illness.

Aside from these relatively specific conditions, however, the *for whom, when,* and *how* of early detection and early treatment become unclear.

There is a grey zone of definition between those with mild forms or the beginning phases of mental illness and those who are anxious, angry, or depressed over real life situations. For example, to say that people from a ghetto are mentally ill because they are worried, depressed, or somewhat paranoid is not sound. Yet these people may need and want mental health services for such problems even though they are not mentally ill. Secondly, there are people who, owing to either environmental or personal deficits, are incapable of taking a customary amount of responsibility for themselves and their families. Many of these people would object to being considered mentally ill and yet others in the same circumstances may seek to obtain, and professional persons may seek to provide, the extra assistance that becomes available if their problems *are* considered mental illness. Examples from daily practice are numerous:   the dependent, anxious, or improvident person who cannot work becomes defined as ill and eligible for disability payments if a physician gives him some diagnosis.

Shuval, Atonovsky, and Davis (1973) have shown that "Helping people cope with failure is a stable function of medical authorities and is likely to persist in the face of possible changes in the structure of professional roles." The physician thus has granting authority to make incapacity legitimate by naming it illness. Shuval, *et al.* think it unlikely that an equally attractive alternative will develop. Similarly, the alcoholic is ill by legislative act in some states, and in others the recidivist criminal and delinquent are defined as medical problems. Society has not really decided how to handle the so-called "sociopath" and other persons with antisocial characteristics. There is an increasing tendency to regard them as "sick" (Shuval *et al.,* 1973) and to refer them to various mental health agencies. Unfortunately many mental health agencies are not equipped in either staff or clinic and bed space to cope successfully with them. Not all of the tendency to define these people as mentally ill comes from within the mental health professions. The inability of the correctional system to rehabilitate any substantial number of offenders causes people, more in desperation than in firm belief in the "sick" theory, to look elsewhere. This rather confusing picture can be reduced to one simple fact. No matter how we categorize the extremely incapable or sociopathic persons, they are coming to mental health agencies, and it behooves us, as I (J.R. Ewalt) said in my APA Presidential Address in 1964, to learn how to cope with them.

Most secondary prevention will be done at the point of first contact with the caring professions, with family physicians, clergymen, school counselors, industrial health services, family service agencies, visiting nurses, and others who have contact with people who are under stress, troubled, or perhaps having mild somatic disturbances. A survey of the non-institutionalized U.S. population (Gurin, Veroff and Feld, 1960) revealed that one in four had been so troubled they feared a "nervous breakdown," and one in seven had sought help from a clergyman, family physician, or a psychiatrist, in that order of frequency of use. The education of family physicians in primary detection and intervention in early disorder, and the staffing of industrial and school programs, and pediatric, general medical, and surgical clinics with mental health consulting personnel, are well-established for the purpose of secondary prevention and need no documentation. When psychiatric services, as well as other medical services are made available in multi-service centers within neighborhoods, a number of people come forward for treatment who had apparently not been seen in the more formally established hospital clinics and private practitioners' offices. That satellite services reach an additional group of patients can be illustrated in almost any neighborhood health center. Where multi-services are available, patients seem to come earlier, and some patients who would have avoided going to a formal mental health clinic will in some instances come to a multi-service center. A preliminary survey in Massachusetts, as well as surveys in other states, shows that catchment areas with well-staffed mental health centers refer very few patients to state mental hospitals. As of 1972, there were within the United States, 295 community mental health centers, and an even larger number of psychiatric clinics and general hospital psychiatric units in addition to private, municipal, county, state, federal mental hospitals.

There is evidence, although not very substantial, that intervention at the court clinic level, can be of assistance to some types of offenders. The experience of the Legal Medicine Department in Massachusetts has also shown that incarcerated offenders treated in individual or group therapy during their sentence and after parole or discharge, have a lower recidivism rate than those who were not so treated. Unfortunately, one cannot generalize from the encouraging statistics to all prisoners because the prisoners involved are a self-selected group who have volunteered for therapy and may therefore represent those with a better prognosis.

Experience with "client-operated" drop-in centers has shown that young people on drugs or with general health problems such as venereal disease and malnutrition, come because these centers are thought to be non-establishment centers. In such settings properly oriented physicians and social service personnel may offer care and attention which otherwise would not have been sought.

In Boston, schools for children with special educational problems are better patronized by the people in the community if they are operated outside of hospital settings (Casey, unpublished).

Confrontation groups for treatment of drug abuse operated by non-professional people, frequently recovered addicts, are found in all parts of the country. They vary in style and technique: some have contact with a physician or hospital for withdrawal from the drug, others do not. The Joint Information

Service study on the effectiveness of these groups was somewhat discouraging (Glasscote, Sussex, Jaffe, Ball, Brill, 1972), but the validity of their data has been challenged by some. At the time of this writing, there seems to be some decrease in heroin use, and increase in cocaine and "downers," but it is a bit early to discover what effect, if any, this change in drug preference will have on the confrontation group movement. Some of the early groups (e.g., Synanon) have moved away from drug dependent cases and have now become communal living arrangements. Despite the discouraging results from the Joint Information study (Glasscote, Sussex, Jaffe, Ball, Brill, 1972) it seems reasonable to continue support and study the effectiveness of the confrontation method because of the undoubted success of Alcoholics Anonymous in treating severe alcohol addiction.

Owing to the variety of settings now accepted as providing early detection and intervention, it may be worthwhile to re-emphasize the importance of early and thorough evaluation of the nature of the problems encountered. A careful history and mental examination with an investigation of the milieu from which the patient comes are essential. Depending on the nature of the information obtained in the preliminary history-taking and examination process, psychological tests may or may not be helpful as well as a detailed neurological examination, EEG's and other lab tests. One's attitude toward the patient should be investigative as well as supportive during the early phases of management, and a flexible attitude as to the possible ultimate diagnosis should be maintained. By such procedures, one will avoid declaring an autistic child retarded, or considering a patient who is responding with hysterical symptoms to somatic disease either neurotic without giving attention to his somatic disease, or physically ill without attention to the neurotic aspects. The therapist at the secondary intervention level should take responsibility to select the modality of treatment most needed by the patient, not allowing dispositions to be confined to those with which he himself is most confortable.

## Community Mental Health

Since the chronological development of the community mental health legislation and implementation has so frequently been described, it will not be discussed here. Instead, some implications of the concept *community mental health* will be mentioned including emphases and problems which have evolved from the concept.

### ENLARGEMENT OF THE COMMUNITY OF CONCERN

Following World War II a number of developments caused civilian problems with mental illness and mental retardation to become a national concern rather than solely the problem of the separate states and private agencies. A century before, Dorothea Dix had exposed the abuses of mental patients to state legislatures in order to make mental illness a responsibility of the states rather than cities, towns, or families. Similarly, during the late forties, journalists, especially Gorman and Deutch, described the extent of the problem of public neglect of mental illness. In addition, during World War II many became familiar with public mental hospitals as attendants during their alternative to military service, and those who did serve in the military had observed the rather common occurrence of emotional breakdown in previously "normal" persons under extreme stress. All of these occurrences, plus the very large number of draftees who had to be turned away owing to emotional disability, impressed a large number of previously uninformed persons with the extent of mental illness, the inadequacy or absence of treatment, and the enormous human waste involved.

## AVAILABILITY OF SERVICES TO THE TOTAL COMMUNITY

During the same period of increase in public concern with mental problems, there was increasing scrutiny within the mental health professions of the distribution of services. Even though there has been criticism of some of its aspects, *Social Class and Mental Illness* by Hollingshead and Redlich (1958) raised questions that have had enormous influence on subsequent practice and research. These studies sought to describe subgroups of the population to be served and to question in what ways services rendered might differ for one subgroup or another. Specifically, they questioned whether wealthier, better educated people were likely to obtain what was thought to be better service than poorer, less well educated people.

Related to these were the earlier studies of Faris and Dunham (1939) on the greater occurrence of serious mental illness in the central areas of the cities. This resulted in a series of studies espousing the "drift" hypothesis versus the "causal" effect of ghetto life. These have been reviewed with new insights by Kahn (1973). (Perhaps it is worthy to note that no study has demonstrated any advantage to being born in the ghetto, although there is evidence that such areas offer a haven for decompensating alcoholics and other derelicts.) Taken as a whole, such studies imply that characteristics of the clients and the care-givers may, but should not be permitted, to interfere with the provision of service to segments of the community. Experience suggests that preoccupation with ethnic, racial, and socioeconomic differences is useful up to a point, and then may become destructive to the implementation of a spectrum of services. That is, too often a superficial interpretation of sociological data leads to categorization of types of service supposedly needed or not needed by types of people, ignoring the range of individual variations within groups. For example, statements are heard to the effect that poor people should have short-term treatment because they are incapable of awaiting delayed gratification or that mothers on welfare want money and not casework. A small but verbal minority may, by use of such statements limit or eliminate treatment facilities for an entire neighborhood.

When one considers the concept of mental health services for the total community, goals become ever more complex. What services in particular shall be considered *mental health?* One of the purposes of Dorothea Dix's compaign for state responsibility for mental patients in the mid-nineteenth century was to eliminate confusion of disturbed persons with offenders and paupers in prisons and poorhouses where their physical and mental problems were ignored. Similarly, a goal in the establishment of the psychopathic hospitals early in the twentieth century was more appropriate treatment of mentally ill persons who were often jailed. The proper place for treating or incarcerating an intoxicated person was an extremely lively issue in professional journals and the press then as it is now. Thus from the very establishment of public care-giving institutions in this country, there has been a consistent confusion in conceptualizing those who are to be considered poor, sick, criminal and/or mentally ill. There has also been a consistent tendency increasingly to classify all of these categories as problems of mental health (see also Shuval *et al.,* 1973). Therefore, in espousing the concept of an obligation to provide mental health services to all segments of the community, one is concerned not only with the quality of service to people with diverse socioeconomic conditions but to people with an ever-increasing diversity of what once had been considered social and legal problems.

Moreover, not only have the number of conditions considered appropriate for mental health services greatly increased, but the concept of what constitutes *services* has itself become enlarged. The conditions entitled to treatment are also considered causes or aggravators of further mental health problems. That is, criminal behavior in a certain individual may be considered to require direct treatment of that person. If, in addition, the prevalence of criminal behavior in a neighborhood is high, many feel that the causes of this criminality should be sought out and treated, and that this is also, or even predominantly, a mental health task. Hence, the concept of mental health service to total communities has produced a complexity and diversity of activity at least partly related to enlarged notions of what constitutes mental health's domain and of what constitutes service to this domain. As we have suggested in the earlier discussion of prevention, the all-inclusiveness of such goals contributes to the difficulty of evaluating the effectiveness of mental health services. The broadening of goals to such an extent, however desirable, may suggest the curability of conditions which we are far from precisely describing, let alone treating.

## UTILIZING STRENGTHS OF THE COMMUNITY

Community mental health has included the idea that diverse elements of the community may be helpful as well as harmful to health maintenance and restoration. This idea, though it sounds self-evident, had not been emphasized nearly as much during the pre-World War II period. The formal responsibility for psychiatric treatment rested with highly specialized personnel treating people in institutions, often at a physical distance from the community. Even when outpatient treatment was used, the therapist-patient relationship was considered the curing agent with far less emphasis placed on the patient's family, social, and vocational circumstances than is currently common. One of the major assets of the mental health volunteer movement of the 1950s was thought to be their "bridging the gap" between the community and the mental hospitals, including both the patients and the professional persons therein. In those days, development of transitional settings such as halfway houses, sheltered workshops, foster home care for adult patients, then day and night hospitals, was considered a considerable advance in re-introducing patients to the community. Many thought, however, that it would be far better never to remove patients from the community, or if so, very briefly and not far. At the present time, some feel that a problem of an opposite nature has been created: whereas formerly there was a reluctance to retain any mentally ill persons or criminal offenders in the community, there is now a reluctance to exclude any of these individuals from it. Although such a view has high regard for the rights of the individual who might have been excluded, serious problems may occur for the spouses and children of these persons and for other community members. Neither is independent residence in the community necessarily the provision of choice for the disturbed individuals themselves. They may and sometimes do become isolated from sources of treatment and from other people altogether, re-introducing the situation prevailing when Dorothea Dix urged assumption of state and national responsibility for treatment of mentally ill persons. Alternative forms of residence may be necessary considering the rights and needs of both disturbed persons and others. Unfortunately no well-organized research information is currently available to suggest what alternatives would be more effective in improving the quality of life for the chronic patient.

## COMMUNITY PARTICIPATION IN MENTAL HEALTH PLANNING

In addition to the expectation that citizens will tolerate and assist disturbed persons within the community, it is expected that community representatives will participate in selecting and planning the services to be offered. Citizen influence on the provision of psychiatric services has been prominent since the beginning of the mental hygiene movement, and while citizen influence has continued in the separate structure of national, state, and local mental health associations, it has been institutionalized in a second hierarchical structure representing area, regional, state, and national levels. These structures are too well-known to require further explanation. However, their involvement, despite the intra-professional and professional-citizen tensions thus created, seems essential in some form for at least two reasons: (1) it was observed from the beginning of the child guidance movement that community-based mental health services tended to die out unless local citizens provided both financial and advisory support; (2) the enormous diversity of activities under the rubric "mental health," whose influence we have emphasized throughout, again has its effects — it is necessary to select among all the possible objectives those which each community finds most urgent and is most willing to support. For several years the individualizing tendencies of local communities have been balanced by the stand-ard-setting influence of the federal government through the grant-giving power of the Institutes of Health and Mental Health and eligibility standards for Medicare and Medicaid payments. Even though some felt that federal standards were too arbitrary, with the withdrawal of categorical federal money, neglect of certain segments of communities is again a danger.

## MANPOWER ADAPTATIONS

Once the range of disorders which is now called mental illness is considered, together with the range of preventive and/or therapeutic measures which is thought capable of affecting these disorders, it should be no surprise that the numbers and kinds of persons considered to be "mental health workers" have grown immensely. Not only have the numbers increased but the nature of train-ing for the traditional professions has changed. There has been more emphasis on work with allied professions, and individuals and groups without professional training have been added to the "mental health team."

If one considers mental health practitioners to be charged with the study and treatment (prevention and/or therapy) of individuals, groups, and communities, then all of these activities have grown in recent years. In all the major mental health professions, despite the addition of many other possible emphases, the practice of individual psychotherapy has continued to increase. In both psychiatry and social work in which the treatment of individuals was a major emphasis even before World War II, the absolute number of persons primarily practicing psychotherapy or casework has grown although relative to the total number in these two disciplines the proportion of persons in this form of prac-tice has diminished somewhat. The training of clinical psychologists since World War II has increasingly emphasized psychotherapy. The training of nurse therapists at the master and doctoral level has developed even more recently, and in occupational therapy, emphasis on psychodynamics and treatment of individ-uals has also increased in some programs.

In addition to individual practice, however, there has been vastly renewed interest in both the biological and social aspects of mental illness. Since the definition of mental problems is so vague and the influences upon these problems very poorly understood, the boundaries of professional responsibility for study and treatment of social problems have become very obscure. As a result, a great many persons who believe that the alteration of communities in some way or other is necessary for prevention of mental illness are occupied in ways that a great many other people consider having little to do with emotional problems. Such arguments are entirely unresolved at this time, and are unlikely to be resolved until the complexities of social influences on individuals are better understood and conceptualized (Kahn, 1973).

The question of where resources should be placed in practice is reflected in questions about emphases in training. While the majority in the various professions have felt that curricula should reflect the broader approach to mental health, the extent to which various areas should be incorporated into the curriculum is unsettled. Various approaches have been used to resolve the dilemma: specialization by group to be served, e.g., geriatrics, children; specialization by modality, e.g., behavior modification; generalization, e.g., a little of the biological, sociological, psychological, political, legal, etc. Although there have been many adaptations, there is little agreement with respect to core curriculum needs. Several newer disciplines have also been added to the mental health professions in recent years, defining areas of specialization within older professions. These include pastoral counselors, special class teachers, tutors of emotionally disturbed children, and child care counselors.

In addition to the traditional and newer mental health disciplines, individuals and groups without professional education have come to be considered mental health resources. While citizens have long been represented in policy-making and service-giving as volunteers, here we speak of persons or groups who are paid by individuals or communities for services thought to aid in mental health. These include sensitivity groups, drug rehabilitation centers, and indigenous non-professional workers. This development is a logical extension of the concept that "the community" is a major ally in the prevention, care, and rehabilitation of those with emotional problems. If it is, many think, let the community be organized and represented formally on the treatment team or resource referral list. Some think that untrained persons from the poverty areas are capable of better understanding poor patients and of being better accepted by them. This movement has partly been fostered by lay persons who believe professional persons do not understand, or worse, are hostile or harmful. It has also been promoted by professional persons who believe that additional forms of help could thus be provided; that a bridge could be formed between estranged groups and "establishment" resources; and the indigenous, non-professional helpers might themselves be helped by becoming active in others' behalf. It is interesting that the bridge-building which was formerly thought needed between the severely ill and the rest of the community is now thought needed between one segment of the community and another, irrespective of the extent of illness. Unfortunately, as time has gone on the claim by professionals that untrained persons could be helpful in mental health activities came to be interpreted by politicians, among others, as meaning that untrained people could do everything as well as trained people. Some professionals seem to think this as well. There is an even more delicate issue among professional persons as to whether the various trained disciplines are interchangeable. These personnel issues may well become clearer when the objectives for each person to be served and for the mental health field more generally become clearer. When it is obscure whether a person's mental health is to be treated by giving him money, cleaning his neighborhood, prescribing him medicine, improving his marital relations, or straightening out his head, then it is no wonder that there is confusion over who can best help him.

Finally, there is a combining of trained and untrained mental health personnel, with professions who serve the emotionally disturbed but whose primary function is defined otherwise. The most significant example of this collaboration has been the growth of psychiatric units in general hospitals. More community mental health center programs are organized using general hospitals than mental hospitals as their resource for hospitalization. For the past several years, there have been more admissions for mental disturbance to general hospitals than to mental hospitals. In addition to the advantage of providing hospitalization in a setting usually more acceptable to patients and families than mental hospitals, the inclusion of psychiatric units in general hospitals promotes interaction between psychiatric and general medical personnel. Other forms of collaboration between psychiatric facilities and schools, social agencies, health resources, and so on, are no longer "pilot programs" but in most places common.

Such collaboration is becoming formalized in consortia of the various health, education, and welfare services at the local level and administrative hierarchies organized so as to foster integration of services. Often called multi-service centers, family life centers, or some even more euphemistic name, they offer a place where a troubled person or a person in trouble, can come with an expectation of immediate help. If more extended or definitive help or treatment is needed, the agent of the multiple-service center can function as the patient's ombudsman in the hospital, welfare office, rehabilitation center, school department, or probation office, to list only a few.

There are many organizational, administrative, and financial problems to be solved as these agencies expand the number and kind of people they serve. The curtailment of federal funds for those in low income sections has slowed the growth of such services, but that neighborhood response to this problem is aiding in finding solutions is substantial evidence of the usefulness of the neighborhood family life center concept. These consortia seem to represent the current structural response to the vast proliferation of concerns which have come to be considered community mental health.

## REFERENCES

Bell, R. A reinterpretation of the direction of effects in studies of socialization. *Psychological Review.* **75**: 81-95 (1968).

Breslow, L. Research in a strategy for health improvement. *International Journal of Health Services.* Vol. 3, No. 1, p. 7 (1973).

Casey, A. Unpublished data — special education. Division of Massachusetts Department of Education.

Ewalt, J.R. Presidential Address, A.P.A., *Journal of the American Psychiatric Association,* Vol. 121, June, 1964.

Ewalt, J.R. and Farnsworth, D.L. *Text book of psychiatry,* p. 14. McGraw-Hill, New York, 1963.

Faris, E.E. and Dunham, H.W. *Mental disorders in urban areas.* University of Chicago Press, Chicago, 1939.

Freud, A. and Burlingham, D. *War and children.* International Universities Press, New York, 1943.

Freud, A. and Burlingham, D. *Infants without families.* International Universities Press, New York, 1944.

Glasscote, R., Sussex, J.N., Jaffe, J.A., Ball, J. and Brill, L. *The treatment of drug abuse.* Joint Information Service. American Psychiatric Association and National Association for Mental Health. Washington, D.C., 1972.

Graham, P., Rutter, M. and George, S. Temperamental characteristics as predictors of behavior disorders in children. *American Journal of Orthopyschiatry.* **43**, No. 3: 328-339 (April, 1973).

Gurin, G., Veroff, J. and Feld, E. *Americans view their mental health.* Basic Books, New York. (A Joint Comm. Mono.), 1960.

Hollingshead, A.B. and Redlich, F.C. *Social class and mental illness.* John Wiley & Sons, New York, 1958.

Kahn, M.L. Social class and schizophrenia: A critical review and a reformulation. *Schizophrenia Bulletin,* p. 60. N.I.M.H. Issue #7, Winter, 1973.

LaVeek, G.D. (Ed.) *Perspectives on human deprivation: biological, psychological and sociological.* National Institute of Child Health and Human Development, U.S.P.H.S. - U.S. Dept. H.E.W., Washington, D.C., 1968.

Lindsley, D. and Reisen, A. *Biological substrates of development and behavior — in perspectives on human deprivation.* H.E.W., National Institute of Child Health and Human Development, Washington, D.C., 1968.

Pavenstedt, E. (Ed.) *The drifters: children of disorganized lower-class families.* Little, Brown & Co., Boston, 1967.

Prescott, D.A. *Emotion and the educative process.* American Council on Education, Washington, D.C., 1938.

Ryan, W.C. *Mental health through education.* Commonwealth Fund, New York, 1938.

Schildkraut, J. Norepinephrine metabolites as biochemical criteria for classifying depressive disorders and predicting responses to treatment. Preliminary findings. *American Journal of Psychiatry.* **130** (6): 695 (June 1973).

Shuval, J.T., Atonovsky, A. and Davis, A.M. Illness, a mechanism for coping with failure. *Social Science and Medicine.* **7**: 259 (1973).

Skeels, H.M. Adult status of children with contrasting early life experiences. Monograph Society for Research in Child Development. **31**: Serial #105 (1966).

Soddy, K. (Ed.) *Mental health and infant development,* 2 vols. Basic Books, New York, 1956.

Spitz, R.A. *A genetic field theory of ego formation.* International Universities Press, New York, 1959.

Werner, E., Bierman, V.M., French, F.E., Simonian, K., Connor, A, Smith, R.S. and Campbell, M. Reproductive and environmental casualties: A report on the 1-year follow-up of the children of the Kauai Pregnancy Study. *Pediatrics.* Vol. 42, No. 1, p. 123 (July, 1968).

# Part Two
## Specialized Techniques

# 12 Phenomenological Approach to the Treatment of "Organic" Psychiatric Syndromes

## M.F. Folstein and P.R. McHugh

### INTRODUCTION

Discussions of the treatment of so-called organic brain syndromes often reveal an Achilles heel in psychiatric thinking: confusion in relating the principles of empirical diagnosis and those of empathic understanding to the treatment of an individual patient. This confusion probably derives from the continuing internecine ware of psychiatrists who have tended to divide into one camp called "dynamic," marching under an empathic banner, and another "biological," flying the flag of empiricism.

We believe that methods espoused by both camps contribute to the care of patients and certainly of patients with brain disease, but their principles can be applied only after any patient's condition has been defined and his individual mental disposition appreciated. Diagnosis in this dual sense brings out the skills available for the two aspects of treatment: 1) The empirically discovered remedies for the particular class of disorder and 2) the empathical management of the difficulties emerging for this particular patient from his disabilities in his particular life situation and his individual nature.

In this chapter it will be demonstrated that the classical tradition of psychiatric phenomenology (Jaspers, 1963) that emphasizes an assessment of the forms of mental symptoms as much as their content in deriving a treatment of dementia and delirium is effective and comprehensive while avoiding the distraction of theroetical divisions. We will review briefly the definition of the particular syndrome being discussed, describe its actual clinical presentation with pertinent phenomenology and thus demonstrate that knowledge of these characteristics is required for a treatment plan that considers both the issues of the category of illness and the individual patient's human responses.

## DELIRIUM

*Definition.* By delirium we mean that mental disorder characterized by a disturbance of varying severity in consciousness: that aspect of mental function defined as a continuum from fully awake to coma. With it there is disruption of cognitive functions recognizable in disturbances of thinking and perception. The syndrome of delirium is the common outcome of any number of pathological physical conditions disrupting cerebral function without destroying cerebral tissue such as toxicity from chemicals and vital organ failure (Curran and Wolff, 1935). This definition can encompass the categories listed in several previous classifications (Kraepelin, 1968; Bleuler, 1924; D.S.M. II, 1968). For the historical development of the definition of delirium, see Lipowski (1967).

*Presentation.* A delirious patient can present in a variety of ways that can bewilder the observer. He may be restless or drowsy, anxious or aggressive, fearful or unpredictable. His behavior may fluctuate during the day; the patient may be alert at times or stuporous and groggy at other times.

The doctors are often faced with a puzzling amount of information and misinformation. The patient is complaining of uncertainty and insecurity. His family notices him change and they may report symptoms of hallucinations and delusions. Nurses reporting patients' inconsistencies may suggest he is exaggerating his problems or is purposely uncooperative. Diagnoses suggested by these features could include schizophrenia, hysteria, anxiety state or mania. Patient "E" appeared completely dressed in the middle of the night in December saying that she had heard it was time to go swimming. She was inattentive and over-talkative, pacing up and down. Her mental state improved after antibiotic treatment and drainage of an abscess of the foot. Patient "H" became drowsy and assaultive when nurses tried to undress her. On examination she was disoriented with poor concentration and felt she was being poisoned. Her mental state improved when her polymyalgia was treated with Prednisone.

*Phenomenology.* These patients are usually comprehended only if a doctor conducts a methodical examination. Then he will be impressed first by the difficulty in gaining the patient's attention and holding it focused in the interview. The patient seems distractible, vague, falling back to sleep; and the doctor must repeat himself, sometimes shaking the patient to gain an answer and holding him in order to accomplish the simplest task of communicating. For all this, the patient may be easily distracted by extraneous events and become angry as the doctors try to force him to attend. It is apparent that the patients have great difficulty in sustaining the thinking process and in fact report that it is an effort. Usually though, the examination reveals that he is disoriented, sometimes simply in time and place but perhaps to a degree that he does not appreciate whether he is standing or lying, dressed or undressed, indoors or outdoors. He may have some insight into his difficulties and may react with emotional feelings. The talk of some patients is jumbled and confused as is their thought with one idea poorly linked to another. This may prompt some to think of a schizophrenic thought disorder. Patients experience hallucinations, usually of a vivid, visual kind but changing and multiple. Similarly delusions that are constantly changing and developing in response to environmental stimuli are common.

It is though, the recognition that the patient is beclouded in consciousness and can focus attention only with great difficulty that best explains his emotional distress and the confused variety of responses that he displays.

In addition to these mental experiences certain performances of the delirious patient are noteworthy. Complex motor functions such as writing a sentence or drawing an abstract design are frequently impaired. Disturbances of posture and coordination manifested by asterixis, ataxia and nystagmus are sometimes present as is an increase in undirected motor activity manifested by senseless picking at bed clothes or by the restlessness and agitation best seen in delirium tremens. The disturbance in cerebral physiology can be documented by a slowing of the EEG frequencies in most cases of delirium — an extremely useful diagnostic sign in some patients (Engel and Romano, 1944). Once the recognition of the syndrome of delirium is established on the basis of morbid mental phenomena, disturbed behavior and EEG changes, the search for its cause can begin.

Delirium is usually the result of a toxic or metabolic disturbance caused by either pathology of body organs or ingested poisons including drugs. The reversibility of the delirium will depend on the reversibility of the metabolic disturbance and its irreversible pathological cause, i.e., toxic chemicals that are eliminated in a few days or kidney failure will produce similar mental disturbances but different prognoses. The onset of a delirium, sudden or insidious as well as the duration, days to months, will also rest with the nature of the pathological lesion. Thus, delirium can be reversible or irreversible, acute or chronic, depending on its cause. For a classification of the causes of delirium see Posner (1971).

Rational treatment will be directed aganist the causal process — removal of the poison. However, while the search for etiology and hence rational treatment is in progess, empirical psychiatric treatments and empathetic management techniques are helpful. These general principles will be described later.

## DEMENTIA SYNDROME

*Definition.* By dementia we mean that psychopathological syndrome characterized by a deterioration of intellectual capacity occurring in clear consciousness. The deterioration of intellect is manifest by a change of personality, amnesia, disorientation and the failure in performance of tasks involving language, calculation and construction. This global disturbance should be distinguished from the selective disturbances in either memory or language as found in Korsakov's and aphasic syndromes, respectively. It is further to be distinguished from mental retardation or mental defect which is a condition of limited intellect present from birth.

*Presentation.* Patients suffering from dementia syndromes present with a variety of experiences which are often of more concern to the family and friends than to the patient. Presenting symptoms are varied and will depend as much on the social situation and previous personality of the patient as on the extent of the neuropathology.

Patient "A" was brought to the attention of the physician when on a trip to Israel with his wife he left the tour party in a remote desert area and returned to his hotel without informing them. A minor manhunt was begun by his wife. Several years later he developed amnesia and disorientation and progressively, dementia. Patient "B" a conscientious, corporate attorney was reading and writing a complex contract in his law firm when a friend noticed his stained tie and wrinkled suit, a state which he would not have tolerated previously. Months later, while his law firm was still seeking his legal advice concerning matters familiar to him for over thirty years, he first came to the attention of physicians when, after an episode of incontinence following an overdose of laxatives, he became agitated and incoherent and was found on examination to have a clear dementia syndrome. Patient "C" presented after calling the police on numerous occasions complaining that she had been robbed and heard people talking about her outside her apartment door. She was found to have a dementia syndrome with vivid auditory hallucinations. Patient "D" presented because of delusions of jealousy which resulted in a physical attack on his wife. He had otherwise been apathetic, sitting at home watching television until this episode brought his dementia syndrome to the attention of physicians. Patient "E" was brought to the hospital when he signed away numerous stocks and bonds without recalling the transactions. This was the first sign of trouble. Symptoms of these patients could suggest a number of possible diagnoses including schizophrenia.

*Phenomenology.* In contrast to the delirious patient, the patient with dementia syndrome is fully alert. Although he characteristically will be unable to grasp fully the nature of his total situation, he will not be drowsy or even inattentive. Thus, he can be responsive to interested and friendly conversation and can be angered by neglect and restraint. The retention of the social graces can mask the extent of the patient's intellectual deterioration as seen in patient "L" who was a polite and dapper, elderly man who asked a visitor to let him out of his hospital ward and to direct him to the front door. On arriving at the front door, he politely, with hat in hand, asked at the information desk whether he could check out of his hotel.

The tools of thinking are affected. These patients cannot quickly perceive (Bleuler, 1924) and remember. They are unable to sustain a performance i.e., they cannot concentrate. Speech and writing are frequently affected. In some patients language is sparse and unproductive but words are correctly used. In others, speech is fluent but words are incorrectly formed and used. Reasoning and judging are also impaired and often thinking is experienced as difficult by these patients. In addition to these fundamental cognitive problems, patients with a dementia syndrome suffer from other experiences which further interfere with their remaining capacity.

Disturbances of mood frequently impair thinking. Short-lived recurrent disturbances related to task failure called catastrophic reactions, (Goldstein, 1952) are distressing and illustrated by patient "G." Patient "G" was a man who never liked or trusted physicians. He cooperated for several questions being asked him as part of a mental status examination, but when he was asked to perform a three stage command, his face flushed, he quickly rose from his chair and ran from the room shouting that he did not have to answer these questions and that he wanted to leave. Thereafter he pulled the doorknobs on successive doors trying to find his way out of the building. On a later trial he was able to follow a one stage command with no such reaction. More sustained moods of melancholy or elation can occur often with accompanying changes in self-attitude and with "somatic" signs of anorexia, insomnia and motor disturbances of agitation and retardation. Patient "L" frequently awoke in the morning in great distress, crying that he had lost all of his money and could not pay his bills. By afternoon, however, he was pleasant and cheerful. Delusions and hallucinations are common as noted in the Presentation. Perseveration, as fully described by Allison, of thought, speech and movement, often resembling a catatonic motor perseveration is common. On the other hand, true obsessions and compulsions are found only occasionally in these patients. Patients' cognitive remnants are further impaired by the change in interest and energy they experience, often considered a change in personality. Patients will sit for hours staring at the wall. Others need to be encouraged to listen to music, previously a life long passion. Some patients experience the feeling that there is no reason to remember since nothing is important.

The patient's insight or lack of it is puzzling and unpredictable. Certain patients with dementia syndrome usually mild, are acutely aware of their cognitive difficulty and will suffer from this knowledge. Others experience their thinking as being perfectly normal when in fact they are totally unable to make use of past experiences in order to modify their current behavior.

Accompanying these morbid experiences and faulty performances may be pathological somatic signs such as diffuse or focal abnormalities of reflexes, pathological reflexes such as sucking and grasping, or an abnormal electro-encephalogram. These abnormalities will depend on the location of the pathological change.

The etiology and pathology of the dementia syndrome is sought first in the history and development of symptoms, and second by examination of the patient for the physical and laboratory signs that may accompany the syndrome. The history of sudden appearance of signs with subsequent improvement over days would suggest a vascular or demyelinative pathology. A progressive course of deterioration of weeks and months frequently with hemiparesis is suggestive of a brain tumor, abscess or subdural hematoma. Gradual appearance of jargon aphasia with apraxia and agnosia suggest a loss of cortical neurons perhaps associated with Alzheimer's plaques and neurofibrillary tangles. However, a progressive course may also be associated with signs of apathy, akinesia and postural defects which would suggest a subcortical pathology as is found in hydrocephalus or Parkinsonism or in some cases of affective disorder in the elderly (McHugh, 1964). A worsening syndrome can also be accompanied by the somatic and neurological signs of pellagra, pernicious anemia, hypothyroidism and syphilis. Thus, the course of the dementia syndrome can be seen to reveal the etiology and pathology. It can be sudden, insidious, acute or chronic. The reversibility of the dementia syndrome will also depend on the causal agent. In some cases the fundamental symptoms of disorientation and failure to recall can be completely reversed as in the case of hydrocephalus after shunting. However, even in those cases in which the cognitive defect is irreversible, many of the interfering symptoms can be reversible. Since reversibility does not distinguish dementia from delirium, this feature should not be used as a defining characteristic of the syndrome.

## TREATMENT

We concur with Goldstein (1952) that the treatment of patients with psychiatric syndromes associated with brain changes is the same in principle as the treatment of any other psychiatric patient. Three methods of treatment must be considered in each case: 1) The applicability of rational treatment based on the knowledge of etiology; 2) the application of empirical treatments i.e., the application of remedies demonstrated by experience and experiment to be efficacious for particular classes of patients regardless of etiology; and 3) Empathic treatment or the application of techniques of management derived from an empathetic understanding of the individual and his reaction to his circumstances.

The recognition of the major classes of dementia syndrome or delirium allows the physician to be alert for rational treatment modalities based on etiology. For the delirious group he tries to remove the toxic and metabolic causal agent. This will entail a careful study of the cardio-respiratory, hepatogastro-intestinal, renal and endocrine systems. For the dementia syndrome he will study the nervous system for pathological processes leading to neuronal loss, demyelination or structural displacement by tumors or spinal fluid. Furthermore, he can rationally treat complicating conditions caused by infection particularly pneumonia, as well as symptoms of heart failure, anemia and nutritional deficiencies such as niacin, vitamin B-12, and thiamine. Even minor disturbances produced by these conditions can seriously affect the mental state of patients with some other central nervous system disease. This was recognized by Kraepelin who considered nutritional support to be a prime factor in the treatment of delirium and dementia.

Many patients with delirium and dementia can be helped by the application of those empirically discovered remedies available to the modern psychiatrist. Recognition of the class of patient determined by a clustering of the morbid experiences present is necessary for the application of the appropriate empirical treatment. Thus patients with mood disorders which are constant and accompanied by a change in attitude and somatic signs can be relieved by antidepressant medication, tricyclics or monoamine oxidase inhibitors or electroconvulsive therapy, if depressed, or by lithium or Haldol if elated. Prolonged moods of agitation or excitement without accompanying changes in attitude or somatic signs can be relieved by phenothiazines. Likewise, delusional and hallucinatory states accompanying dementia or delirium can be relieved by phenothiazines. All drugs should be used in small dosages in these patients and the mental state should be carefully monitored for signs of increasing drowsiness and intellectual impairment, since these treatments are themselves capable of inducing a delirious state.

Since the foundation of the principles of empathic treatment are derived from an understanding of a particular individual in a particular place, the application of those principles will be to an extent limited to a particular patient. However, principles derived from empathic understanding which were found to be helpful on our wards at the Westchester Division of the New York Hospital, in large part were also found to be helpful by Dr. Post in London. For this reason we feel that they might also be helpful for other physicians treating these patients.

Since patients with delirium or dementia suffer from a variety of bewildering experiences in the best circumstances, it seemed plausible that a strange impersonal and ever changing environment would make them even more upset. Furthermore, it seemed that a friendly, homelike, regular and routine environment would make him more comfortable and hence easier to manage. For these reasons inferred from an empathic understanding of the way these patients feel, a particular milieu was designed. Patients are housed in private bedrooms with as many of their personal belongings as possible. Floors are carpeted and hall furniture is provided with comfortable chairs, sofas and adequate lighting. The patients eat in a small dining room, sitting at the same table with the same fellow patients each meal. A regular daily schedule is followed which provides activity between meals. Patients are continually informed of the schedule as well as to the day, date and place. An empathic understanding of the particular patient and his family is also helpful. Appreciating the content of the patient's symptoms such as his financial or particular family concerns can lead to planning and reassurance which bring comfort. The appreciation of the burden of illness on family members can aid social workers in aftercare planning for these patients. A great strength of the empathic method is in promoting interest and a helping attitude on the part of the staff, and cooperation on the part of the patient. Treatment of patients in this way will require the same number of staff, including doctors, nurses and social workers as required for the general psychiatric population.

In summary, diagnosis and hence treatment based on the form of the mental experiences allows one to group patients into classes of disorder from which rational treatment based on etiology can be applied as well as empirically discovered treatments found to help particular clusters of symptoms. Psychological appreciation derived from a study of the patient's particular experience leads to a program of individual treatment for the specific patient and his family.

This approach to treatment which recognizes the patient's conscious mental experience first and then applies the appropriate modes of treatment has enabled us to encourage nurses, social workers and psychiatric residents to care for these patients who have been previously unsuccessfully treated in the usual general hospital setting before coming to our unit.

## REFERENCES

Allison, R.S. *Senile Brain,* Arnold Ltd., 1962.

Bleuler, E. *Textbook of psychiatry,* authorized English edition, New York: MacMillan Co., 1924.

Curran, D. and Wolff, H.   Nature of delirium and allied states. *Archives Neurology and Psychiatry.* **33**: 1175 (1935).

DSM II, APA, 1968.

Engel, C. and Romano, J.  Delirium I EEG data. *Archives Neurology and Psychiatry.* **51**: 356 (1944).

Goldstein, K.   The effect of brain damage on the personality in psychiatry, p. 245, Vol. 15, 1952.

Jaspers, K.  *General psychopathology.*  Chicago:  University of Chicago Press, 1963.

Kraepelin, E. *Lectures on clinical psychiatry.*  New Jersey:  Hafner Publishing Co., 1968.

Lipowski, Z.  Delirium, clouding of consciousness and confusion. *Journal of Nervous and Mental Disease.* **145**: 227 (1967).

McHugh, P.R.  Occult hydrocephalus.  *Quarterly Journal of Medicine.* **33**: 277 (1964).

Posner, J.B.  Delirium and exogenous metabolic brain disease. In:  Beeson, P.B. and McDermott, W. (Eds.), *Cecil-Loeb Textbook of Medicine,* 13th Edition, p. 88, Philadelphia:  W.B. Sanders Co., 1971.

Post, F.  *The clinical psychiatry of late life.*  New York: Pergamon Press, 1965.

# 13 Geriatrics

## Alan D. Whanger
## and
## Ewald W. Busse

## INTRODUCTION

### Definition of Terms

The science of aging called *gerontology* includes the study of aging and all of its aspects — biological, psychological, and sociological. *Gero* is derived from the Greek and means old man or pertaining to old age. *Geriatrics* (old plus cure) is a more restricted term applied to the biomedical aspects of gerontology. Psychiatry is a combination of Greek derivation meaning mind-healing. Consequently, the term *geriatric psychiatry* is in some ways redundant in meaning, and for this reason there are those who prefer the term *geropsychiatry* which translated means old age mind-healing. Geropsychiatry is concerned with the mental disorders that occur in late adult life, particularly those which are predominant after the age of 65. In addition, geropsychiatry is concerned with the mental problems of late life including alterations of memory, decision-making, perceiving and interpreting feelings and behavior. In geriatrics, the term *senescence* is often utilized to identify those declines in efficiency of function that accompany the passage of time; that is, the inevitable changes that occur during the aging processes. *Senility,* or senile changes, refers to pathological changes that are acquired from infection, trauma, disease or a hostile environment.

### Population Trends in Geriatrics

In 1970, 9.9% of the population of the United States was 65 and over. One hundred years before, that is, in 1870, only 2.9% was 65 years and over. Over a period of 100 years, the actual number of elderly Americans increased from 1.2 million to approximately 20 million. Projections as to the number of elderly people living in the year 2000 can be made relatively easily, as all such persons are already alive. There will be 28.8 million older Americans by the year 2000 (Brotman, 1973).

In order to plan for the mental health needs of the elderly population, one must consider the median age of the population. It is predicted that life expectancy will advance to 73.7 years. Obviously, this means that unless preventative or therapeutic techniques are found, the physician and psychiatrist will be confronted with a sizable number of elderly people suffering from mental disorders. Furthermore, it is important for the physician to remember that although the usual age of retirement is 65 years, the majority of persons between the ages of 65 and 75 are in relatively good health. Those 75 years and over are restricted in their activities because of illness about 12 days more per year than those age 65 to 74. Of those 75 and over, 23.7% are unable to carry on major activities as opposed to 9.7% of those between 65 and 74 years of age (Busse, 1969).

## Extent of Psychiatric Disorders in the Elderly

There is considerable difficulty in determining the extent of various psychiatric disorders in the older population. This, of course, is determined both by the peculiarities of the groups studied as well as by the diagnostic criteria used. Traditionally, most of the care for psychiatric disorders in the elderly was carried out in state mental hospitals, but this represented a very skewed population. Kramer, Taube and Starr (1968) have analyzed the rates of various disorders among the institutionalized elderly. It must be kept in mind, however, that less than 1% of all those over age 65 are in some type of mental institution. Of these, about half were admitted for disorders arising in old age, while many others had been admitted previously for various functional psychoses, particularly schizophrenia, and had simply grown old in the institution. Approximately an additional 3% of the American population over age 65 are in other types of institutions, such as nursing homes, chronic disease hospitals, and homes for the aged (Redick, Kramer and Taube, 1973); and a guess would be that probably one-half of these would have some significant psychiatric disorder. Several community surveys have indicated that 5 to 6% of the elderly living in the community are either psychotic or severely impaired psychiatrically. An additional 15 to 20% of the population has moderate to severe psychopathology. Of a study of 222 community living elderly volunteers in the first longitudinal study at the Duke University Center for the Study of Aging and Human Development, only 89 (40%) were considered psychiatrically normal; 56 were psychoneurotic, of whom 25 had severe neurotic reactions; 21 demonstrated relatively mild non-psychotic organic changes; 42 had combined non-psychotic and neurotic symptoms; and 14 presented evidence of psychosis. Of the 25 persons with severe neuroses, 16 had marked hypochondriasis and 12 had depressive disorders (Busse,

Dovenmuehle and Brown, 1960). A study of state hospitals in North Carolina indicated that of those admitted for the first time after age 65, 70% had a diagnosis of acute or chronic brain syndrome, 9% had functional psychoses, 8% had various personality disorders, and 7% had neuroses (Whanger, 1971). There has been a tendency for the elderly to receive little or no care specifically for their emotional problems until the situation became so severe that they required institutionalization. Until recently, only about 2% of all those attending various psychiatric outpatient facilities were over age 65. The situation was described by the Committee on Aging of the Group for the Advancement of Psychiatry, which stated that the elderly suffer disproportionately from our "non-system of non-care" characterized by insufficient financing for both health and sickness and by fragmented delivery of services (Group for the Advancement of Psychiatry, 1970). Fortunately, in recent years an increasing interest in, and study of, the psychiatric disorders of older persons has begun changing the former pessimistic outlook of psychiatrists and other therapists, and has enabled some to overcome their reluctance to work with older patients, which trait Comfort (1967) labeled "Gerontophobia."

Of those admitted to private psychiatric facilities, the incidence of functional disorders is much higher. Statistics show that the elderly in this group had incidences of about 16% schizophrenia, 19% other functional psychoses, 13% neurotic disorders, and about 42% organic brain syndromes. Older people with alcoholism make up probably 5 to 10% of admissions of those over age 65 (Redick, Kramer and Taube, 1973).

## PROBLEMS AND FACTORS AFFECTING TREATMENT METHODS IN THE ELDERLY

### Concurrent Physical and Mental Illness

The assessment of psychopathology in older persons is complicated by the frequent concurrent presence of physical diseases, multiple psychiatric disorders, socioeconomic factors, and by the all too common tendency to ascribe any problem in an older person to "hardening of the arteries." These factors may either discourage therapists from working with the elderly in the first place or else may inhibit searching for other factors in the total problem. After age 65, 79% of all people have at least one chronic physical disorder, although only 2.3% are bedfast (Busse, 1972). An additional 11% have difficulty venturing out of a restricted environment, however. Kahn, Goldfarb, Pollack, and Gerber (1960) point out the obvious risks such individuals have from isolation, diminution of social contacts, and loss of intellectual stimulation contributing to their decline in mental capacities. Another frequent problem is the admission of an older person to an inappropriate hospital service. This problem was studied in England by Kidd (1962 a and b) who rated patients on their relative degree of psychiatric and medical disabilities and needs. He showed that 69% of those admitted on the geriatric medical service were mentally ill, while 43% of those admitted to mental hospitals had significant physical illness. He felt that 34% of those admitted to a medical service should have been admitted to a psychiatric service, while 24% of those admitted to psychiatric facilities should have been on a medical service. The consequences of these misplacements were increased mortality, disorientation, incontinence, impaired communication, and morbidity. The ability of the hospital staffs to deal with such inappropriate admissions was impaired by their being neither trained nor equipped to handle the particular type of problem. Other studies show a high incidence of mixed illness as well. Langley and Simpson (1970) found that 63% of geriatric medical patients had mental illness, and 65% of the geropsychiatric patients had physical illness. In order to try to solve this problem by correctly diagnosing and assessing mental disorder in the elderly, the British have recommended the establishment of "psychogeriatric assessment units" jointly staffed by psychiatrists and geriatricians (Arie, 1971; Department of Health and Social Security, 1970). Only recently have such facilities become available in a few areas in the United States, however.

### Altered Psychological Responses

A number of physiological changes that occur with aging affect the use of various drugs. As pointed out by Bender (1971), the factors influencing the effective levels of a drug include the absorption from the site of administration, the distribution within the person, the rate at which it is metabolized, and the rate of excretion. Changes may occur within the intestinal tract which impair absorption of various substances such as fats, thiamine, iron, and glucose. There may be a decrease in the number of absorptive cells in the mucosa, a deficiency of transport enzymes, or a decrease in blood supply. Once in the organism, the distribution is modified by peripheral circulation, membrane permeability, and tissue composition, all of which may be altered in the elderly. The replacement of various functional tissues by fat may prolong and alter the effects of drugs which are preferentially absorbed by fat. The decreased renal blood flow and glomerular filtration rate in the elderly may considerably delay the excretion of various drugs. Other drugs which are excreted through the biliary and gastro-intestinal (GI) system may show alterations secondary to impairment in these systems. Drug metabolism occurs primarily in the liver where microsomal enzymes may show variable decreases with age, with resultant higher plasma and tissue levels. As Fann (1973) points out, absorption remains generally nearer normal limits than elimination, thus causing drugs to remain in the body for longer periods and causing the aged person to be more sensitive to many drugs.

The effectiveness of a drug also depends on the interaction with the receptor sites. With age there is a diminution in the number of functional cells in the many organs and tissues which may result in either greater or lessened sensitivity to various drugs. The homeostatic mechanisms are frequently impaired also, as pointed out by Saleman, Shader, and Pearlman (1970), with a decrease in intestinal motility, cardiac output, tone of peripheral blood vessels, mass of peripheral and central neural tissue, renal excretion, and sympathetic-parasympathetic autonomic balance.

## Polypharmacology

Being subject to multiple system pathology, the elderly are very likely to have multiple drugs prescribed . This can be further compounded by a tendency of some for considerable self-medication. A study of physicians' prescribing habits showed each hospitalized medicare patient to be receiving an average of 10 prescription medications (Fann, 1973). Approximately 200,000,000 prescriptions for psychotropic drugs are written by non-psychiatrists annually in the United States. A study by Learoyd (1972) found that in Australia 16% of psychogeriatric admissions were directly attributable to the ill effects of psychotropic drugs. In Scotland, a community survey of geriatric patients showed a mean of 3 prescription drugs each, with 32% receiving various barbiturates. These investigators (Gibson and O'Hare, 1968) felt that 3 seemed to be the maximum number of drugs for a reasonably alert elderly person to manage. Lamy and Kitler (1971) wisely point out that care should be exercised so that the most important disease is given primary consideration, as otherwise toxicity may well be induced from a multiplicity of drugs.

## Medication Habits of the Elderly

Older people vary considerably in their practice of drug taking. Some see taking medication as a sign of weakness and will resist taking any medication. At the other extreme are those who seek to find a cure for the discomforts of their minds and bodies by a constant search for, and consumption of, a variety of medications. Two common problems are the retention of a medicine cabinet full of old prescriptions which may be taken indiscriminately, and of visits to two or more doctors simultaneously with failure to inform the second doctor what the first is prescribing. In their study of old people at home, Gibson and O'Hare (1968) felt that about one-third of the patients had administered drugs incorrectly. In many cases an older person may be unable to read the label on a prescription. The elderly are prone to take medicine only when they think it is necessary and many fail to get prescribed refills. In addition, economic factors may cause the older person to fail to purchase prescribed medicine (Lamy and Kitler, 1971).

## Diet and Nutrition

Less than optimal nutrition is very common among the elderly, especially those in the lower socioeconomic groups. The recent national nutrition survey showed that about 40% of the elderly poor were consuming diets with inadequate levels of vitamin A, thiamine, riboflavin, or vitamin C (Coursin, 1970). Our recent survey of elderly patients admitted to state psychiatric hospitals indicated inadequate diets in 71%, and found low or deficient folic acid levels in over one-third (Whanger and Wang, 1974). Nutritional deficiencies are almost always multiple in the elderly, and they will frequently affect absorption of various substances and their utilization in the organism. This complex and still only partially understood problem is discussed by Roe (1968).

## TYPES OF TREATMENT IN GERIATRIC MENTAL DISORDERS

### Introduction

In this section we will deal basically with the treatment of functional psychiatric disorders, and refer the reader to Chapter 12 by McHugh and Folstein regarding organic brain syndromes. Of course some overlap will be inevitable, as we will mention some aspects of treatment unique to the elderly. In this section we will refer to drugs by their generic name followed by their most commonly used American brand name for easier identification. This implies no endorsement of a particular trade product.

In the burgeoning recent literature of various treatment methods and drugs there has been a considerable amount of discrepancy. Those in the medical field for some time have seen many highly touted new remedies flash meteor-like across the therapeutic skies only to fade from view in one to two years time. Many of these probably illustrate the Hawthorne principle in that any activity in the environs of many geriatric patients would result in improvement whether or not the preparation or procedure had positive merit. Herein two or more references will be cited for most treatment modalities; and although they may disagree, they may serve as sources of reference for the interested practitioner.

Almost any of the psychiatric disorders seen in younger people may also be found in older persons. There does tend to be a narrower spectrum of disorders predominating in this age group, however. These include the organic brain syndromes, both acute and chronic, affective disorders, hypochondriacal states, anxiety states, paranoid reactions and alcoholism (Butler and Lewis, 1973; Busse and Pfeiffer, 1973; Post, 1965; Stotsky, 1968). The drug treatment of the major disease areas will be looked at first, and then some of the other types of therapy that may be adjunctive in several types of disorders will be discussed. In addition, we shall add comments from our own experience in treating psychiatric disorders in the elderly.

### General Principles of Drug Use in the Elderly

Several factors should be kept in mind when using drugs in older patients. The classic reference for these is the text by Freeman (1963). The frequent simultaneous presence of several physical and mental disorders often necessitates the use of various psychopharmaceuticals to alter specific target symptoms (Lifshitz and Kline, 1963). Obviously, adequate diagnostic assessment is crucial for optimal drug usage. Hollister (1969; 1973) points out that much of the drug therapy is toward symptomatic relief. There are enormous variations in the responsiveness of the elderly to medications, and the safest course generally is to start with low dosages and build up gradually. Variations in the homeostatic mechanisms in older patients cause side effects to be frequent and severe. Various therapists will have different drug experiences and preferences, but it is generally better to know and use a few drugs well, than many poorly.

## Depression

There are many different clinical manifestations of depression in the elderly which may determine to some extent the type of drugs or approach to a particular patient. Some of these variations are pointed out by Lippincott (1968) and Post (1966). Depressions are often "masked" in that the usual affective component is little in evidence, and there may only be a variety of neurotic complaints or a single biological concomitant such as sleep disturbance or interest loss. Depressions may cause the elderly individual to become so perplexed or withdrawn that he may appear to have an organic brain syndrome, which has sometimes been referred to as pseudo-dementia. In addition to the many external factors which may contribute to the onset of depressive feelings, recent studies by Robinson and his group (Robinson, Nies, Davis, Bunney, Davis, Colburn, Bourne, Shaw and Coppen, 1972) have shown increasing levels of monamine oxidase in the brains of the elderly, perhaps providing a biochemical explanation for the frequency of this illness. Logically the monoamine oxidase inhibitors will therefore seem appropriate antidepressants in the elderly. Indeed, as Lifshitz and Kline (1963) enumerated, several of the monoamine oxidase inhibitors were used with fair success, although several have subsequently been withdrawn from the market because of severe side effects. The MAOI's tend to be somewhat less effective in the elderly, and the risks of severe side effects such as hypertensive crises make them far less attractive. The A.M.A. Council on Drugs (1971, pp. 247-265) states that Isocarboxazid (Marplan), Nialamide (Niamid), and Phenelzine Sulfate (Nardil) should be used only with caution in the elderly. Tranylcypromine Sulfate (Parnate Sulfate) is contraindicated in any patient who is over age 60 or who has suspected cerebrovascular defect, according to the *Physician's Desk Reference* (PDR) (1973, pp. 1320-1321) because of greater likelihood of paradoxical hypertension. Some, such as Gander (1966) and Schuckit and his group (Schuckit, Robins and Feighner, 1971) have used the MAOI's in combination with the tricyclic antidepressants, with supposedly good results in some previously refractory cases, and with no greater incidence of side effects than with a single drug. Very few of their patients were in the older age range, and no particular comment was made about them. Theoretically the MAOI's and tricyclics would supplement each other's action in relieving depression, but in both the *A.M.A. Drug Evaluation* (1971, pp. 257–265) and the PDR (1973, p. 1499) the combined use is stated to be contraindicated because of possible severe atropine-like reactions, hypertensive crises, and circulatory collapse. Many drugs containing sympathomimetic substances and foods containing large amounts of tyramine, such as aged cheeses, wine, and yeasts, may cause severe reactions with the MAOI's. As it is difficult to closely monitor and control what an older person is likely to be ingesting, we generally consider that electro-convulsive therapy is probably safer for most elderly than the presently available MAOI's.

The other major group of drugs for treating depression are the dibenzazepine derivatives or the tricyclic compounds. They tend to potentiate the action of the adrenergic compounds, such as the catecholamines. Our experience coincides with that of Butler and Lewis (1973, pp. 247–248) in that the two most popular of this group of drugs in the elderly are amitriptyline (Elavil) and imipramine (Tofranil). The side effects of these drugs are mainly their anticholinergic effects, which Horwitz (1968) has used as prognostic guides to the use of the drugs. He felt that the three physiological responses most closely paralleling clinical improvement are urinary hesitancy, visual blurring, and postural hypotension. He had a small number of elderly in his studies with apparent satsifactory results, although we are concerned about dropping blood pressure significantly in this age group. Horwitz observed some increasing resistance to antidepressant drugs in severely and chronically ill patients, and occasionally maintained patients up to seven years on drugs to avoid relapses. The other lesser side effects, such as dry mouth, tremor, and sweating were of little prognostic significance, but often moderately disabling.

Among the elderly, a variety of depressive symptom clusters can be found, as described by Dovenmuehle and Verwoerdt (1963) and Wilson (1967). It is important to recognize unhappiness and normal grief reactions as being physiological and rarely requiring any drug therapy. Depressions of a retarded or apathetic type with many of the biological concomitants, such as marked psychomotor slowing and sleep or appetite disturbances, are seen. For these, we feel that imipramine (Tofranil) is probably the drug of choice. We tend to be somewhat more conservative than many, such as Agate (1970) or Lifshitz and Kline (1970), in that we usually begin with 10 mg t.i.d. (three times a day), upping the dose slowly at three-day intervals if there are no serious side effects nor improvement in the patient. In most cases, about 75 to 100 mg daily will be adequate, although some elderly will give a good response to no more than 30 mg daily. Hamilton (1968) and Agate (1970), for example, used up to 300 mg daily, although we have only occasionally found it necessary to go above a total daily dose of 150 mg. Recent studies, such as those of Hussain and Chaudhry (1973) have indicated the desirability of giving tricyclic antidepressants in a single daily dose, but we feel that it is generally preferable to give these drugs to the elderly in two or three daily divided doses, with the largest being at bedtime in order to reduce the side effects.

There is a variable period of delay of days to weeks before the tricyclic antidepressant drugs begin to become effective in relieving the patient's symptoms. Several methods of enhancing the rate of action have been tried. One of these has been the addition of L-triiodothyronine (Cytomel) in 25 mcg daily doses for the first two weeks, as described by the groups of Coppen, Whybrow, Noguera, Maggs and Prange (1972); Prange, Wilson, Rabon and Lipton (1969); and Whybrow, Coppen, Prange, Noguera and Bailey (1972). Wheatley (1972) found the same enhancement with amitriptyline. Most of the patients studied under these regimens were under age 65, and no specific comments on this combination in the elderly was made. It was noted that women responded better on the combination than men, and that there seemed to be a reduction of side effects of imipramine (Coppen, Whybrow, Noguera, Maggs and Prange, 1972). In view of the potential cardio-toxic effects of both the thyroid and the tricyclic preparations, we have been reluctant to utilize this combination in the elderly, but further study should be done. We have frequently used methylphenidate (Ritalin) as an adjunct to imipramine, as it has been noted that in addition to its mild euphoric properties, methylphenidate inhibits the liver enzymes degrading the tricyclics and so enhances their effectiveness. This is ordinarily in the dosage of 5 mg of methylphenidate after breakfast and lunch (in order to avoid an anorexiant effect) for the first week of therapy only. Two other psychostimulant drugs have been used for depression; namely, pipradol (Meratran or Alertonic) as described by Fabing (1955) and Kleemeier, Rich and Justiss (1956) and deanol acetamidobenzoate (Deaner) as described by Green (1965), but we have not found them particularly helpful. The amphetamines (such as Benzedrine, Dexedrine, or Methedrine) have been used some for depression (Sargent and Slater, 1963), but we feel that they are rarely indicated in the elderly even though they may be tolerated fairly well for short periods.

Agitated Depression

Another type of depression which is fairly common in the elderly is the agitated or excited type in which restlessness and anxiety are prominent. Roth (1964) notes that amitriptyline (Elavil) has a greater tranquilizing effect and is less likely to aggravate tension. The dosage schedule is similar to imipramine, as we usually start at 10 mg t.i.d. and then increase it as described by Feigenbaum (1973) at three-day intervals in a stepwise pattern such as 25 mg b.i.d.; to 25 mg q.A.M. and 50 mg q.h.s.; to 25 mg q.A.M. and 75 mg q.h.s.; to 50 mg q.A.M. and 100 mg q.h.s. *Another tricyclic, doxepin (Sinequan), has both antidepressant and antianxiety properties, and can be used in dosage similar to Elavil, however, we have noted that it does tend to sedate some elderly quite heavily. Our approach with antidepressants is to give a trial of a drug for three

*t.i.d. (three times a day)
 b.i.d. (twice a day)
 q.A.M. (each morning)
 q.h.s. (at bedtime)

weeks at full, reasonable dosage before deciding that the drug is ineffective, as we agree with Butler and Lewis (1973), who note that most patients who are going to respond do so in the first two weeks. Webb (1971) observes that patients may respond to one antidepressant but not to another, and so he feels it is perfectly good practice to switch tricyclics after one has failed. Our usual approach is to use one antidepressant well, and if that fails then to use ECT unless there are strong contraindications to it or the patient refuses. If the antidepressant works well, we usually continue if for at least three months beyond the point of good clinical improvement to reduce the likelihood of early relapse. Occasionally an elderly person has a chronic or frequently recurring depression which may be best treated by staying on an antidepressant for long periods.

The side effects of the tricyclic antidepressants are well delineated by Kalinowsky and Hippius (1969), who note side effects for imipramine such as hypotension, palpitations, constipation, perspiration, flushing, and a fine tremor; while amitriptyline has more anticholinergic effects such as dryness of the mouth. Both can produce electrocardiographic changes as well as arrhythmias, as noted by Salzman, Shader and Pearlman (1970). A common problem when starting with high doses in men with some prostatic hypertrophy is urinary retention.

When there is mixed symptomatology present, the therapeutic results with the antidepressants are not as good. Straker and Roth (1960) felt that imipramine was not effective in the depressive moods associated with organic brain syndromes, but this has not been our experience. The varying success rates with the antidepressants will depend on the nature of the patient group, the dosage of the drug, and the criteria for improvement. The "endogenous" type of depression will usually respond better, but our overall experience agrees closely with that of Kalinowsky and Hippius (1969) that about 70 to 75% will be significantly helped; although as noted subsequently, we tend to use other therapies along with the drugs. There are several other tricyclic antidepressants, such as desipramine (Pertofrane), nortriptyline (Aventyl), and protriptyline (Vivactil) but there is less experience with the elderly with these, and no present indications that they have any particular advantages.

Psychotic Depression

When delusions or severe agitation are a dominant part of the clinical picture of a depression, the addition of a major tranquilizer such as haloperidol (Haldol) or thioridazine (Mellaril) in small doses to the tricyclic antidepressant may be of help. Overall and his group (Overall, Hollister, Meyer, Kimball and Shelton, 1964), noted that thioridazine itself is effective in treating agitated depressions, although we do not ordinarily rely on it exclusively. Among the phenothiazines, thioridazine is probably best for this purpose as it does not aggravate depression, as chlorpromazine (Thorazine) will occasionally do in the elderly.

Another rather common syndrome seen in the aged is a mixture of depression and considerable paranoid ideation (Post, 1966b; Whanger, 1973b), but this seems to be basically an affective disorder. The symptoms may respond to either an antipsychotic or an antidepressant agent alone, but we agree with Stotsky (1973) that the simultaneous administration of two agents usually gives better results. Mixtures such as amitriptyline and perphenazine (Trilafon) are made in single tablets of varying strengths (Triavil), but we prefer the greater flexibility of mixing our own. In treating the mixed depressive-paranoid syndromes, we frequently use a tricyclic antidepressant in the appropriate dose plus 2 mg of trifluoperazine (Stelazine) twice daily. A variety of these drug combinations were noted in clinical use by Fracchia, Sheppard and Merlis (1973), but were used more commonly in female patients.

## Hypochondriasis

The excessive and anxious preoccupation with the malfunctioning of one's own body, or hypochondriasis, is a frequent problem especially among elderly women. The total approach to this problem has been detailed by Busse (1954), and Pfeiffer (Busse and Pfeiffer 1973, pp. 130–135), but this type of complaining may also represent an early or masked depression (Agate, 1970; Post 1965) which may respond better to the use of antidepressants.

## Manic-Depressive Disorders

The classical manic-depressive disorders continue into late life, but as noted by Stotsky (1973), are more often of the depressed type, with retardation, apprehension, and sometimes delusions. A manic reaction occurring for the first time late in life may be an early indicator of an organic brain syndrome. In addition, the antidepressants may occasionally contribute to a swing from a depressed phase into a manic one. Lithium carbonate (e.g., Lithane) has considerably improved the treatment of manic-depressive disease, with the hypomanic states and bipolar depressions responding best to lithium. Its use is limited by its increased toxicity in the elderly (Van der Velde, 1971) because of their decreased renal function, frequent electrolyte imbalance (often iatrogenic sodium depletion from diuretics), and marked sensitivity to side effects. These toxic reactions include nausea, ataxia, tremor, confusion, dystonia, diarrhea, muscular weakness, and twitching. We usually prefer to start lithium in older patients in the hospital, and agree with Butler and Lewis (1973) that the dose should be low. Usually we start at 300 mg daily and increase it at 300 mg increments every three days. Often a marked reduction in the manic excitement occurs by the third or fourth day, even while the serum lithium levels may be no higher than 0.7 mEq/L. We have found it well to try to hold the serum lithium level (morning fasting specimen) no higher than 1.0 to 1.4 mEq/L. Once stabilized, it should be checked probably monthly, on an outpatient basis, and a "drug holiday" as suggested by

Rice (1956) once weekly may reduce toxicity. Lithium may be of some help in prophylaxis of cyclic depression, although there has not been much experience with this in the elderly yet. We have found that mania in the elderly may respond rather well to the antipsychotic drugs, especially chlorpromazine (Thorazine) or haloperidol (Haldol). In several cases we have given haloperidol up to 5 mg twice daily for two or three days, and then have dropped the dose rapidly as the mania subsided in order to reduce the severity of extrapyramidal side effects. Should the drugs not work satisfactorily, ECT is quite effective in treating this disorder in the elderly.

### Emotional Lability

Excessive emotional lability, most often sudden outbursts of crying or anger, is a common problem among the elderly with organic brain syndromes. Lawson and MacLeod (1969) report both imipramine and amitriptyline at dosages of about 25 mg t.i.d. were effective in treating this distressing symptom.

### The Psychoses and the Major Tranquilizers

In the elderly, a variety of functional psychoses are fairly common, either as a carryover from early life of such a disease as schizophrenia, or else arising for the first time in the later years. Different psychotic symptoms may accompany a mild or moderate organic disorder as well. The advent of the group of drugs called the major tranquilizers has revolutionized the outlook of the elderly with psychotic disorders. These antipsychotic agents can be grouped into four major categories. The first are the rauwolfia alkaloids which have been used for both hypertension and mental disorders. They can be used for symptoms of anxiety, agitation, and inappropriate aggressiveness (Lifshitz and Kline, 1970). As Hollister (1973) notes, reserpine has now lapsed into virtual disuse as an antipsychotic agent. It is still fairly often used as an antihypertensive agent in the elderly; and severe depressions, appearing like the endogenous type, are occasionally seen secondary to its use (Kalinowsky & Hippius, 1969). Many cases of mild or insignificant hypertension are treated in older patients with significant side effects.
    The largest group of the antipsychotic agents are the phenothiazine drugs, which are divided into three classes according to the various side chains on the molecules. Each class has different clinical characteristics of importance in their use and dosage in the elderly, as described by Hollister (1973) and Stotsky (1968). The dimethylaminopropyl or aliphatic group is represented by chlorpromazine (Thorazine) and is noted for its sedative and hypotensive properties and low incidence of extrapyramidal effects. It is the standard of strength by which the other phenothiazines are compared. In older patients, we use chlorpromazine primarily in schizophrenia and only occasionally in mania or acute agitation not controlled by other preparations. Birkett and Boltuch (1972) reported an open trial of its use in mixed geriatric-psychiatric patients, with mild improvement

and comparatively little side effects other than tremor at daily doses from 50 to 200 mg. For agitation we usually give 25 mg I.M., but then watch the patient for hypotension.

The piperidine group is represented by thiroidazine (Mellaril), which has several features that are of help in the elderly: it is less sedative, it seems to have some antidepressant properties, it is often effective in moderately excessive emotional response, and the incidence of extrapyramidal disorders is fairly low. In spite of the very low incidence of side effects reported by Ahmed (1968) and Tsuang and his group (Tsuang, Lu, Stotsky and Cole, 1971), we have found the drug's main drawback to be a fairly substantial incidence of hypotension found in many debilitated and institutionalized elderly. As even a single large dose may produce postural hypotension lasting a week or more, we start at a very low dose, such as 10 mg b.i.d. and increase it slowly at 3-day intervals if necessary, checking the supine and standing blood pressures regularly during this time. We seldom use more than 75 mg daily, with the larger or total dose given at bedtime, although some elderly may tolerate up to 300 mg daily. The third class of the pheno-thiazines is the piperazine group represented by trifluoperazine (Stelazine), perphenazine (Trilafon), and fluphenazine (Prolixin). These are potent at low dosage and rarely cause problems with hypotension, but their use in the elderly is severely limited by the high incidence of extrapyramidal symptoms, to which the elderly, and especially brain damaged females (Fann, 1973), are particularly sensitive.

Another group of the major tranquilizers are the thioxanthenes. One of these is thiothixene (Navane) which can be of some help in withdrawn, apathetic schizo-phrenics, but otherwise has little use in the elderly. Chlorprothixene (Taractan) is somewhat similar to chlorpromazine, but seems to have less hypotensive and sed-ative effects. Smith and Barron (1965) recommended its use in disturbed geriatric patients, but we consider it primarily as an alternative drug in geriatric therapy.

The butyrophenones are the last group of the antipsychotic agents, of which haloperidol (Haldol) is the only representative available in America. Tsuang and his group (1971) felt that haloperidol was quite similar to thioridazine in both efficacy and side effects, although we find it useful as it has potent antipsychotic and calming properties, convenient dosage forms including injection and tasteless drops, and little effect on the cardiovascular system. Haloperidol has a high incidence of extrapyramidal complications if used on a regular basis at a dosage higher than 2 mg daily. The lack of effectiveness reported by Tewfik and his group (Tewfik, Jain, Harcup, and Magowan, 1970) may have represented the restlessness or akathisia which may result, although the more frequent problem we see is muscular rigidity.

Schizophrenia

Schizophrenia is found rather often in the elderly in state hospitals or in  boarding homes, where they may have lived for many years.  While most have had schizophrenia all of their adult lives, late life schizophrenia is occasionally seen and responds rather well to treatment.

Therapy of elderly schizophrenic patients is not much different than that of younger people with the same disease, and many seem to need and tolerate rather large doses of antipsychotic drugs. As Hollister (1970) points out, there are not substantial differences between the antipsychotic properties of all of the phenothiazine drugs, and there is not much rationale for the use of more than one at a time. Chlorpromazine (Thorazine) is probably best for chronic schizophrenia, as indicated by Wolff (1963). It can be given in doses from 400 to 800 mg daily if necessary to keep symptoms under control. Barton and Hurst (1966) point out the common problem of elderly psychotic individuals being left on large doses of phenothiazines long after the acute phase of the psychosis has subsided. These drugs have many and severe side effects in the elderly when used over long periods, as reported by Hamilton (1966) and Salzman, Shader and Pearlman (1970). The most common side effects are the parkinsonism and akathisias which develop in about 50%. Hypotension has been mentioned. Another major problem is the tardive dyskinesias, as described by Fann, Davis, Wilson and Lake (1973), which may be persistent. Periodic reduction of dosage or "drug holidays," such as over weekends, helps to reduce the total amount of drug given, and thus likely reduces the long-term adverse effects. Many elderly with active schizophrenia will have a relapse of symptoms about 6 to 12 weeks following the discontinuation of their phenothiazine. Among those taking long-term phenothiazines, a number will show periodic loss of drug control, with either increased or decreased sensitivity to the drug, often at about 6- to 12-month intervals. This may necessitate discontinuing the drug, adjusting the dosage, or else shifting to a different drug. It is with these individuals, perhaps, that the lesser known phenothiazines can be most helpful as alternative medications.

## Paranoid Syndromes

Paranoid symptoms, delusions and states are quite common in the elderly (Davidson, 1964; Post, 1966b; Whanger, 1973b). They can be especially distressing as they usually involve the family and neighbors of the patient. An increased incidence is found in those who are hard of hearing, as noted by Houston and Royse (1954). The best treatment is often a combination of reducing the threatening environment (often by hospitalization), psychotherapeutic intervention, and antipsychotic drugs (Busse and Pfeiffer, 1973, pp. 126–130). We have found the most useful drugs to be either haloperidol (Haldol), often in a 2 mg or less daily dosage, or trifluoperazine (Stelazine) in dosage of 4 to 7 mg daily. At these levels side effects are infrequent. It is helpful to continue on these drugs for three months or more after the older person returns home to help ease the readjustment, but some will need to stay on them for protracted periods.

## Neuroses and the Minor Tranquilizers

The symptoms of tension, "nerves," and anxiety are rather common in older people, although their response may differ from those of young people (Eisdorfer, Powell, Silverman, and Bogdonoff, 1965). There is no real indication to treat the symptoms with drugs, unless minor psychotherapeutic support or environmental manipulation have failed, and the symptoms are unduly prolonged, excessively painful, disabling, or aggravating other conditions. The antianxiety drugs include primarily central nervous system depressants, which in moderate dosages tend to have a sedative effect, and the group of drugs usually referred to as the minor tranquilizers. The sedative drugs would include the barbiturates, ethyl alcohol, bromides, paraldehyde, narcotics and several preparations which are ordinarily used as hypnotics (A.M.A., 1971, pp. 213-229), and which act primarily on cortical functions. The barbiturates have been rather widely used, and are advocated by some such as McDonald, Mowbray, and Wilson (1970). We tend to agree with Dawson-Butterworth (1970) that the barbiturates are not generally indicated in geriatric patients because of their dulling of cortical function, the variable excretion rate, the potential for addiction and withdrawal symptoms, and the interference with various enzyme systems. We generally avoid the use of the bromides, narcotics, and paraldehyde for similar reasons.

The minor tranquilizers act primarily on the various subcortical systems, and tend to have a less sedating effect. There are three basic groups of the minor tranquilizers, one being the substituted diols, including meprobamate (Equanil) and tybamate (Tybatran). Meprobamate has been used fairly often with the elderly, as characterized by Kozlowski (1961) and Lifshitz and Kline (1970), in dosages of 200 mg b.i.d. or t.i.d. In interesting studies of pharmacological load tests as predictors of drug response in geriatric patients, Lehmann (Lehmann and Ban, 1968; Lehmann, 1972) found that meprobamate caused drowsiness and reduced levels of spontaneous activity. While meprobamate does give good relief in some patients, we do not give it frequently as it tends toward easy habituation and can have severe withdrawal symptoms. The second group, the benzodiazepine derivatives, are the minor tranquilizers most used, with chlordiazepoxide (Librium) as the best known one. While it is effective with anxiety in the elderly in doses such as 5 mg b.i.d., it shares a problem with meprobamate in that it is moderately sedative and produces a type of reaction that causes many patients to specifically ask for it and become habituated to it. A related drug, diazepam (Valium) is one that we have found more useful in the elderly, as it causes less sedation and has some skeletal muscle relaxant properties. It should be started at levels of 2 mg b.i.d. and increased slowly as necessary. Its main drawback is that it causes ataxia fairly frequently. Diazepam is useful in that it seems to help mild depression accompanying anxiety in elderly women. Another related drug is oxazepam (Serax), which does not seem to have any particular advantage over the other two in the aged.

The diphenylmethane derivatives make up the third group of minor tranquilizers whose principal member used in the United States is hydroxyzine (Atarax or Vistaril). We use this only occasionally with older patients, and then more as an alternate drug than because it has any marked advantages. It can be used in dosages of 50 or 100 mg or as a PRN medication for agitation, but it seems to have little effect on some people, and may produce rather prolonged sedation in others. Our general rule of thumb with these drugs is to start the elderly on a dose of about one-third of the usual adult dose, and then to increase it slowly only as needed. Where possible, it is better to give a short course of drugs rather than to continue them indefinitely.

Also effective in anxiety are some of the major tranquilizers, especially thioridazine (Mellaril) in doses of 10 mg b.i.d. or trifluoperazine (Stelazine) in doses of 2 mg b.i.d. The minor tranquilizers should not be used as the only therapy when psychotic symptoms are present, as they seldom help, and often cause a further loss of control and thus paradoxical agitation. Occasionally we have used diazepam in doses of 2 mg t.i.d. in association with haloperidol or trifluoperazine in order to augment their effect without raising their dosage to the point where antiparkinson drugs would be needed. Drugs used generally as hypnotics can relieve anxiety when used in small sedative doses, but we have found this seldom necessary in the elderly.

### Hypnotics

A common problem among the elderly with a variety of psychiatric disorders is disturbance of sleep. Frequently the person will get his days and nights mixed up, and the nocturnal restlessness often quickly exhausts the caretakers, the family, and the patient. There are physiological variations in sleep in old age as noted by Kahn and Fisher (1969) in that it takes longer to go to sleep, stage 4 deep sleep almost disappears, and the frequent awakenings occur. A sleep disturbance should be assessed before hypnotics are prescribed freely, as there may be such problems as early congestive heart failure, anxiety, depression, pain, excessive use of stimulants (such as coffee in the evenings), or habituation to drugs. Previous studies have shown that from 7 to 10% of community-living people over age 60 were using hypnotics regularly (Busse, Barnes, Silverman, Thaler, and Frost, 1955), and a recent unpublished survey of ours of mildly to moderately psychiatrically impaired community-living elderly showed that 25% were taking sleeping pills at that time. A number of the hypnotics can cause habituation in 2 or 3 weeks of use. Restoration of a normal sleep pattern will greatly facilitate care of the patient. Such simple, safe measures as adequate exercise during the day, a quiet, comfortable bed, and a drink of warm milk at bedtime should not be overlooked. Antidepressants or antianxiety agents should be used if indicated, but the major tranquilizers should not be used to facilitate sleep without other indications for their use as well. There are considerable variations in experiences with barbiturates as hypnotics. Stotsky and group (Stotsky, Cole, Tang, and Gahn, 1971) felt that sodium butabarbital in a dose of 50 mg q.h.s. was a very helpful agent, and Pattison and Allen (1972) reported that pentobarbital 100 mg q.h.s. was satisfactory. Exton-Smith, Hodkinson, and Cromie (1963) reported that sodium amobarbital at a 200 mg dosage had an unpleasant "hangover", and Dawson-Butterworth (1970) considers this an "absolute contraindication" to barbiturates in the elderly. We tend to use barbiturates quite rarely, especially because of the confusion and unsteadiness in the mornings. Our preferred preparation is chloral hydrate, in doses of one-half or one gram at bedtime, which can be repeated once during the night with little trouble. Should the older person awake during the night, he is usually fairly clear-headed, but can go back to sleep readily. There is an infrequent paradoxical excitement reaction, as noted by Kramer (1966), or a hangover. For most the capsule form is preferable as it covers the unpleasant taste and reduces the likelihood of gastric irritation somewhat, but liquid and suppository forms are available if needed. There is a tablet form of chloralbetaine (Beta-Chlor) which is supposedly equivalent to chloral hydrate, which could be crushed. Should chloral hydrate not be satisfactory, then we usually use flurazepam (Dalmane) in doses of 15 mg at bedtime. A variety of other non-barbiturate hypnotics are available, including ethchlorvynol (Placidyl), glutethimide (Doriden), methaqualone (Quaalude), methyprylon (Noludar), and paraldehyde; but they seem to be more variable in their effectiveness in the elderly, and have a higher rate of side effects. The antihistamine promethazine (Phenergan) has a marked sedative effect, and 25 mg at bedtime may promote sleep in the elderly, although often with some hangover.

Two common problems arise in geriatric sleep disturbances. One is that some pain may be present, as from arthritis, which is not helped at all by the hypnotic. The addition of an analgesic such as aspirin or acetaminophen (Tylenol) at bedtime may help improve the sleep pattern considerably. Another problem, especially in institutions, is that the elderly are often bedded down about 7:00 P.M. and are then expected to sleep through to morning. Naturally some are going to awaken about 3:00 or 4:00 A.M., having had a full night's sleep. The nurse, however, very often gives a hypnotic then to get the person quiet and back to sleep. The more obvious solution of course would be to let the older people stay up until 10:00 or 11:00 P.M.

The sedative side effects of other drugs such as antidepressants or tranquilizers can often be used to advantage by giving them at bedtime, rather than using hypnotics. Diphenhydramine (Benadryl) can be helpful in drug induced parkinsonism, and 25 mg at bedtime may serve both this and a sedative function.

## Anti-Parkinson Agents

The elderly are especially prone to develop parkinsonism either as a primary disease or else secondarily to various psychotropic agents. Various dystonias, dyskinesias or akathisias (motor restlessness) are common also. The issue of whether to use an anti-Parkinson agent comes up. In accordance with Davis, Fann, El-Yousef and Jamowsky (1973) we do not use them routinely nor prophylactically in the elderly, as their anticholinergic side effects of constipation, dry mouth, increased intraocular tension, or urinary retention are troublesome, and acute brain syndromes or other psychoses may occur secondary to their use. When extrapyramidal signs appear, we would rather reduce the dosage of the causative drug, but if this is not possible, then we add an agent. Diphenhydramine (Benadryl) is often the drug of first choice in the elderly although its effects are mild (A.M.A. *Drug Evaluations*, 1971). A dose of 25 mg at bedtime may be started, and then later upped to 50 mg or even 75 mg if necessary. It is often helpful in conjunction with another agent. Probably the best other drug to use initially or early with the aged is trihexyphenidyl (Artane), starting with 1.0 mg in the mornings (it may cause insomnia) and increasing it at 1.0 mg increments as necessary at three-day intervals. Should other agents be needed, the following are acceptable, noted with their starting dose: biperiden (Akineton) at 1.0 mg b.i.d.; procyclidine (Kemadrin) at 2 mg t.i.d.; or benztropine mesylate (Cogentin) at 1.0 mg daily. As suggested by Orlov, Kasparian, DiMascio, and Cole (1971) the anti-Parkinson agent should be stopped in a month to see if the symptoms recur, as they will not in most cases.

## Alcohol

Alcohol is a two-edged sword among the elderly. It was called "the nurse of old age" by Galen, who observed its tranquilizing, somnificant, analgesic, euphorient, and social qualities. Several authors have commented on the value of a glass of beer, or 2 to 4 ounces of wine in the late afternoon in a social setting in geriatric institutions for improving the morale, the communication, and the sleep patterns among older patients (Kastenbaum and Slater, 1964; Leake and Silverman, 1967). Volpe and Kastenbaum (1967) noted marked improvement of behavior including ambulation and continence within two months of the introduction of beer therapy on a ward of elderly mental patients, with a marked drop in the amounts of other psychotropic drugs used. In an interesting experiment, Chien (1971) compared the effects of beer, thioridazine, and a pub milieu, and found the beer therapy to be the most effective with older institutionalized patients. It has been used as a tonic, as an appetite stimulant, and as a hypnotic. The elderly may have the common problem of keeping the dose down to therapeutic levels however, and many have a considerably decreased tolerance for alcohol. As Leake and Silverman (1967) note, alcohol may potentiate the effects of many other psychoactive drugs, and may increase the side effects, confusion, and especially the unsteadiness in older persons.

## Alcoholism

Alcoholism is seen with moderate frequency in the elderly, with Simon, Epstein, and Reynolds (1968) noting a 28% incidence of serious drinking problems in their San Francisco psychiatric screening project, and Gaitz and Baer (1971) noting a 44% incidence in patients over age 60 coming into their screening ward. The mean life span of 65.7 years they observed in alcoholics with organic brain syndromes may account for the incidence of only about 15% of alcoholism in the patients age 65 plus admitted to North Carolina hospitals (Whanger, 1971), although variations will occur with different cultural settings. These cases usually fall into the groups of those who have survived a lifelong pattern of heavy drinking and those who start their drinking late in life. The long-term drinkers differ little from younger alcoholics except that they tend to get more malnutrition and brain damage. The reader is referred to the chapter on alcoholism, but the following are some of the specific problems and approaches to the geriatric alcoholic. It often takes about three weeks to get over the effects of severe binges. For withdrawal from alcoholic bout, we usually use diazepam (Valium) in an initial dose of 5 mg I.M. and then 5 mg t.i.d. or q.i.d.* for 5 days orally, and then reduce this to 2.5 mg q.i.d. for an additional 5 days. Chlordiazepoxide (Librium) can certainly be used, but it may cause rather marked sedation. We have not yet had an elderly alcoholic develop delirium tremens if the diazepam was begun before the symptoms started. As nutritional deficiencies are usually present, we always use oral and parenteral multiple vitamin preparations in treatment. Concommitant physical problems should always be looked for, especially pneumonia and subdural hematomas. Because of the possible severe effects of ingestion of even a small amount of alcohol, we have never used disulfiram (Antabuse) as an aid in reducing the temptation to drink in the elderly.

Among those developing alcoholism late in life, many are seeking relief from a clinical depression. Following the acute withdrawal period (about 7 to 10 days), the person should be examined for depression, which may be of the "masked" type. Should it be present, then it should be treated with long-term tricyclic antidepressants in addition to other supportive and rehabilitative therapies.

Thyroid

While some of the normal changes occurring with aging resemble those of hypothyroidism, including a decrease in basal metabolic rate, most of the endocrine glands of the elderly function adequately, and do not hold "the answer" to the problem of aging. Thyroid malfunction, however, often manifests itself as psychiatric disturbance in the elderly. Lloyd (1967) found that hypothyroidism occurred in 1.7% of all admissions to a geriatric unit. Whybrow and his group (Whybrow, Prange and Treadway, 1969) noted depression and impairment of cognitive function in hypothyroidism, and a high level of anxiety as well as intellectual disturbance. As Agate (1970) observes, the clinical appearance of the elderly with hypothyroidism may be easily attributed to be "just old age." We almost routinely check the T3 and T4 levels in the elderly with organic brain changes, depression, or marked anxiety and agitation. While abnormalities are infrequent, they do respond well to hormone replacement or glandular suppression. Pomeranze and King (1966) point out that irreversible brain damage may

*q.i.d. (four times a day).

result from a long-neglected hypothyroid state. Thyroid preparations must be used with caution in the elderly, as they are quite sensitive to them, especially with the onset of cardiac arrhythmias. This is best done under close medical observation by such increments as suggested by Agate (1970) or Rodstein (1971). Some work, such as that reported by Wren (1971), has indicated that physiological thyroid therapy may reduce the severity and complications of atherosclerosis. A hypometabolic syndrome has been postulated, characterized by fatigue, nonspecific mental symptoms, a low basal metabolic rate, and slow angle reflex time, but how this fits in with aging changes is still not clear (Levin, 1960; Prange and Lipton, 1972).

Sex Hormones

While we do not know all the exact roles that hormones play in the aging process and the psychiatric complications thereof, we are aware of the changes in physical appearance and function, and other effects on emotions that may go along with the decrease in sex hormones, especially in women. In an interesting paper on the sex hormone influence on the aging process, Masters (1957) reported that such basic mental processes as memory for recent events, capacity for definitive thinking, and the ability to absorb new material, which were presumably lost on a senile basis, showed a significant improvement with long range sex steroid support. The improvement may continue up to a year, and the earlier the hormone support was initiated, the better the ultimate result. Suffice it to say, there are differences of opinion about sex hormones, and a review such as that by Rose (1972), especially about the psychiatric aspects, is recommended. Some, such as Kupperman (1963), recommend a continuing regimen of estrogen therapy in the older woman to retard aging changes. Others report improvement in various emotional symptoms such as depression, insomnia, irritability and general well being which were noted in up to 50% of patients (Kaufman, 1967; Tramont, 1966). Various methods of administration are used, but the common ones are conjugated estrogens − (Premarin) 1.25 mg daily for three weeks out of four cyclically, or one of the many combinations of estrogen and androgen, again used orally cyclically three weeks out of four. There are many geriatric preparations available, some of which are undesirable (A.M.A., 1971, pp. 301−308). Schleyer-Saunders (1971) reports very favorable results with the implantation of long-lasting pellets. The prophylactic use of androgen steroids in males does not appear warranted at this time (Lifschitz and Kline, 1970; Rose, 1972). A recent study by Lehmann (1972) however, indicated that a significant number of elderly with a variety of psychiatric disturbances were helped by combining the androgen fluoxymesterone (Halotestin), 10 mg. orally daily for 12 weeks with either nicotinic acid (100 mg t.i.d. or more) or with moderate doses of thioridizine (Mellaril) such as 25 mg t.i.d. The combination of two drugs gave better results than any single one, or all three together.

Specific sexual dysfunctions occur in the elderly, who are often still sexually active, or would like to be (Pfeiffer, 1969; Verwoerdt, Pfeiffer and Wang, 1969). Use of oral, parenteral, or topical estrogens may be of help to the woman in maintaining functional genital capacity, and impotence in the older male may respond to medication (Jakobovits, 1970). For a fuller understanding of this problem and its general management, the reader is referred to Rubin (1965) or Pfeiffer (1969).

## SOMATIC THERAPIES IN GERIATRIC MENTAL DISORDERS

### Electric Convulsive Therapy

The indications for, and general management of, electric shock are similar in the aged and in younger persons, as covered in the chapter dealing with convulsive therapy. Prout, Allen and Hamilton (1956) give a good review of the early reluctance to utilize ECT in the aged, which was gradually overcome by experience. Ordinarily we give a three-week trial of an antidepressant before using ECT, unless there is danger of suicide, marked negativism, or history of previous drug failure. As Kalinowsky and Hippius (1969) point out, the elderly, especially women, with organic brain changes may benefit from ECT if depressive affect is present. On a few occasions when deep uncertainty existed about whether a particular person had a depressive pseudo-dementia, we have used 2 or 3 ECTs as a diagnostic test. The older person should have a thorough physical examination and work up prior to ECT, although with adequate muscle relaxation and oxygenation, the risk is only mildly increased over a young person. Occasionally we have not used a barbiturate anesthetic in the geropsychiatric patient, feeling that this increases the apnea rate somewhat. The person may complain of awareness of the procedure, but we feel it is safer, especially if there are less than optimal facilities for resuscitation. The response to ECT in the elderly is often rapid, with the depressed person showing marked improvement after 2 or 3 ECTs. Ordinarily we do not use a routine number of treatments, as others suggest (Feigenbaum, 1973), but rather the general rule of good improvement, plus two for consolidation of gains. This will usually mean 5 or 6 ECTs. Some will relapse quickly and need 2 or 3 more, however. Lowenbach (1973) makes some helpful observations, such as, the convulsive threshold of the aged brain is higher − therefore an initial application of 150 volts is used to assure a full seizure. He also suggests the use of 60 mg of succinylcholine (Anectine) when osteoporosis is present, and that cyanosis be avoided by allowing no longer than 40 seconds of apnea to persist without respirating the patient. After the first two or three treatments, we usually space them about three days apart in the elderly to avoid excessive confusion, which, while not harmful in the long run, may make immediate management of the patient more difficult. Frequently we reinstitute an antidepressant drug immediately following ECT, and continue it for two or three months, which may help reduce the relapse rate while the person readjusts to life outside of the hospital.

Vitamins and Nutrients

A variety of depletion or deficiency states exist in the impaired elderly, which compounds their problems to varying degrees. Brain dysfunction and impairment are known to occur in deficiencies of thiamine, niacin, ascorbic acid, folacin, and vitamin B/12 (Exton-Smith and Scott, 1968; Milner, 1963; Mitra, 1971; Shulman, 1967; Whanger, 1973a). The classical deficiency syndromes are infrequently seen now, but many have suggested subclinical deficiency states, although this is often hard to prove. Brin (Brin, Dibble, Peel, McMullen, Bourquin and Chen, 1965) postulates five stages in the development of vitamin deficiencies, the middle one of which is the psychological stage with loss of appetite and body weight, general malaise, and irritability. It is likely that a vicious cycle often develops in a psychiatric disorder, which leads to loss of appetite or neglect of eating habits, which leads to multiple mild deficiencies, which contribute to malaise, which makes the person emotionally worse. The elderly are especially subject to factors which may contribute to low vitamin levels such as alterations in absorption and distribution of nutrients, depletion of various metabolic systems, poor eating habits, and multiple diseases (Whanger, 1973a). Should a specific vitamin deficiency exist, replacement may result in considerable improvement in mental functioning, as reported by Shulman (1967) in patients with pernicious anemia and by Mitra (1971) in patients with confused states. More often, in less specific states there may be little improvement, as noted by Kral and his group (Kral, Solyom, Enesco and Ledwidge, 1970), or it may take months to become evident (Taylor, 1968). Pennington (1966) found the response to psychotropic drugs in a wide variety of conditions to be enhanced with a vitamin supplement. Some of our studies (Whanger and Wang, 1974 a and b) suggest that the replacement of only part of the vitamins which may be deficient may cause some neurologic impairment, and it is known that using folic acid in the face of a vitamin B/12 deficiency (in pernicious anemia, anyway) may cause worsening of neurological problems. We tend to be more liberal than many in the use of vitamin supplements in the elderly, feeling that the potential benefits and reduction of excess disability considerably outweigh any remotely possible complication of their use. Ordinarily, if a patient shows signs of malnutrition or has a history of poor diet habits, we put him on a therapeutic multiple vitamin and mineral preparation for two weeks in addition to a nourishing diet. A person with severe malnutrition may get parenteral multiple vitamin injections for two days, after pernicious anemia is ruled out. Afterward the person is put on a daily maintenance multivitamin preparation of about the deca-vitamin composition. Miracles are not to be expected, but considerably more research needs to be done in this field.

Psychosurgery

The enthusiasm for surgical procedures on various tracts of the brain to modify behavior has waned in recent years, but Knight (1966) considers the severely depressed elderly as good candidates for a "stereotactic tractotomy" of the substantia innominata using implantation of radioactive yttrium seeds.  He reported no mortality and good results.  Post, Rees and Schurr (1968) reported the favorable effect of bimedial leucotomies for depression of the aged; and Thorpe (1958) reported that 96% of elderly with prefrontal leucotomies showed considerable improvement with affective disorders.

## MODES OF PSYCHOTHERAPY

### Individual Psychotherapy

The development of interest in, and techniques for, individual psychotherapy for older persons has been slow.  Part of this has been due to the influence of Freud who felt that psychoanalysis would be a failure in treating the elderly both because so much time would be required that the end of the cure would be reached at a period of life in which "much importance is no longer attached to nervous health" (Freud, 1959a, p. 245), and because "older people are no longer educable" (Freud, 1959b, p. 258).  This pessimistic view is still prevalent in that a recent survey of 30 psychoanalytically-oriented psychiatrists in private practice showed that none of them were treating any patients over age 60 (Weintraub and Aronson, 1968).  As previously cited, the elderly usually make up only 2 or 3 percent of all the patients seen at most psychiatric outpatient clinics, in spite of the high incidence of neurotic disorders.  Other therapists have found that old age is a phase of life and not a disease, and that it has its own problems, needs, and goals.

   Jung dealt with many older persons, and realized the importance of reassessment of values and introspection in his studies of the life cycle (Jung, 1933, pp. 95-114).  Erikson felt that the particular task of old age was the development and maintenance of a sense of "ego integrity" (Erikson, 1959). The existential problems have been studied by some, such as Tournier (1972).  Common phenomena among the elderly are reminiscence and life review, and the therapist should not cut this short, feeling that this sort of talk is just indicative of brain disease or childishness.  Many elderly are greatly helped by an opportunity to talk over losses, grief, and feelings about death with someone who is neither frightened by such topics nor compelled to give the person antidepressant drugs and fail to hear him out.  Meerlo (1961) and a number of analysts, such as Alexander and Grotjahn, have suggested modifications in the psychotherapeutic approach to the elderly, which are well summarized in the review of Rechtschaffen (1959).  Basically the modifications are:  the therapist must be more active, environmental manipulation may be desirable, some educational techniques may be used, resistance and transference are handled gently, and the therapy is tapered but rarely terminated.  Hypochondriasis is rather common in the elderly, and may be a manifestation of a depression, anxiety, or a psycho-physiological reaction.  Experience has shown that this can often be mitigated by the therapist if he will listen carefully and uncritically to the patient, use some mild medication such as an anti-anxiety agent, and over several weekly visits gently guide the patient into areas of emotional conflict.    The hypochondriacal defenses should not be breached directly to the patient or his family (Busse, 1954).    Goldfarb (Goldfarb and Turner, 1953) developed a method of brief psychotherapy which is particularly helpful with the brain impaired elderly person who is frightened and looking for a strong parent-figure.    The therapist accepts and fosters this role, giving the patient the feeling of having this powerful person in his possession. Two sessions of 15 minutes of this emotionally gratifying therapy are held the first week; and then the person is seen briefly at infrequent intervals for an indefinite period. Even in less organic patients, Wolff (1970) found the self-esteem of many elderly to be quite low, and so ego supportive individual therapy was most frequently helpful.

## Hypnosis

There are few reports in the literature on the use of hypnosis in the elderly, and then it is usually for suppression of symptoms.    Brennan and Knight (1943) reported an interesting case in which prolonged hypnoanalysis was used in resolving a hysterical psychosis in a 71-year-old woman.    Our experience has been that older people are generally not as good subjects as the young and that it is harder to get good states of relaxation.

## Behavior Modification Therapy

While various behavior modification techniques are increasingly popular in psychiatry, there are few reports of its specific use in older patients.    Even in the rather severely organically  impaired, Ankus and Quarrington (1972) report that behavior is modifiable by a reinforcement appropriate to the individual, such as money.    Positive reinforcement techniques used in small group settings of elderly patients were recently described by Birjandi and Sclafani (1973).    Of course, as suggested by Lindsley (1964), some of the principles of behavior modification therapies are inherent in many of the other treatment modalities used with geropsychiatric patients.

## Group Therapies

Within recent years there has been a marked upswing in the use of various group therapies with psychogeriatric patients.    The first specific use was reported by Silver (1950) working with senile psychotics, and Linden (1953) soon followed with some rather sophisticated programs.    More recently Goldfarb (1972) reviewed his work and that of others, and Klein, LeShan, and Furman (1965) reported many techniques and goals.    Wolff (1970) observed that within three months, results from group therapy with institutionalized elderly included better ward adjustment and orientation, increased communication and activity, more appropriate sex role adjustment, favorable group identification, reduced anxiety and feelings of isolation, and sustained improvement which helped subsequent adjustment outside of the hospital. Of course, the type of group therapy should be geared to the problems, needs, and goals of the particular patient. Some generalizations about groups for the elderly are that they should be sexually mixed; should have at least two therapists, generally a female and a male, and that there should be some homogeneity regarding the mental capacities, the needs, and the problems. The therapists should be warm, positive, and fairly active. The following are some types of group therapy that we and others have found helpful with elderly patients.

1. *Reality orientation.* This is a technique developed by Folsom (1968) for working with organically impaired and confused patients, in which the instructor has a group of about six with whom he meets daily for about 30 minutes. He repeatedly goes over current and personal information with each, such as the place, the date, the weather, the menu, and events. More complex information, such as time-telling, reading, and object manipulation are added as the person improves. Correct responses are immediately rewarded verbally by recognition and praise. This is reinforced by sign boards in prominent spots with similar orienting information, and by the staff who address the patients by name and inform them of events that are about to take place.

2. *Remotivation groups.* This program has been developed by the American Psychiatric Association (1965) to provide a structured framework for reaching and motivating very regressed and apathetic patients. The therapist uses non-threatening material — such as history, poetry, or nature study — in small groups in attempting to reach healthy and intact areas of the person's experiences and memory in hopes of interesting and involving him in the real present world.

3. *Grooming and homemaker groups.* These skills have often deteriorated in older hospitalized patients, and groups to help regain them may considerably enhance the self-esteem, especially of the women.

4. *Inspiration and religious groups.* These groups can provide support, oppotunity for participation, enhancement of values, and inspiration and hope for many elderly patients.

5. *Patient government.* Involving patients in discussions and decisions regarding their own care can have a positive value in increasing their self-esteem and responsibility and in making institutions more humane.

6. *Conjoint and family therapy groups.* Family and marital disorders are frequent in geropsychiatry, and satisfactory resolution often requires a variety of interventions with the spouse and relatives, as described by

Spark and Brody (1970) and Grauer, Betts, and Birnbom (1973). We have had some groups of members of unrelated families who have had similar problems.

7. *Pre-discharge groups.* In particular, those elderly who have been hospitalized for a long period have many problems and uncertainties about returning to the community. An opportunity not only to talk these over with those in a like situation, but to take part in such activities as shopping or visiting boarding homes or agencies prior to discharge tends to smooth the transition and adjustment to a more normal existence, as indicated by Nevruz and Hrushka (1969).

8. *Discussion and socialization groups.* Groups which are primarily to talk over matters of interest and to have fellowship, provide a considerable amount of support to those taking part, both in institutions and out. Butler (1973) describes some interesting age-integrated, "life crisis" groups which deal with the vicissitudes of the life cycle.

## Recreation Therapy

Recreation for the aged psychiatric patient should consist of more than television and bingo — it should provide for the restoration or preservation of creative functions of a person in addition to simply having fun. Physical activities such as walking, bowling, dancing, and rhythmical exercises are important, as are sedentary activities such as games, reading, and parties. Merrill (1967) and Davis (1967) give suggestions for programs.

## Music Therapy

Music is a pleasant therapeutic activity for many older psychiatric patients, providing socialization, renewal of happy memories, and some exercise in coordination if a rhythm section is added. Even among very demented patients, hymns and religious songs often seem well remembered and quite meaningful. Boxberger and Cotter (1968) reported that music therapy in psychogeriatric patients results in a decrease in the level of undesirable patient noise, a reduction in aggressiveness, more appropriate behavior, and less reaction to hallucinations.

## Occupational Therapy

The various rehabilitation therapies may be handled in different ways in institutions caring for the mentally impaired. The occupational therapist is able to provide assessment of functional physical capacities, and provide appropriate constructive activities to enhance capabilities and self-esteem, as Fish (1971) and Finkelstein, Rosenberg and Grauer (1971) detail.

## Milieu Therapy

Following the development of the idea of the therapeutic community by Maxwell Jones (1953), the concept that the social milieu itself can be utilized as a treatment modality has spread. One of the first to apply this to the elderly psychiatric patients was Gottesman (1967) who observed that the traditional mental hospital tended to make people worse by letting their ego skills deteriorate because no demands were made on them, and no new skills were taught. His theory is that treatment should offer a structured series of meaningful demands, and that the patient should be helped to learn to function in the various roles of normal society that he would meet outside of the hospital. Others such as Risdorfer (1970), Goldstein (1971), and Grauer (1971) have applied the techniques of milieu therapy often with good results, but with some difficulties.

Bok (1971) analyzed some of the main problems of milieu treatment of the older mental patient, noting some of them to be a lack of patient potential for change; difficulty with the staff in changing to newer modes of attitude and action; problems in the mental hospital itself of chronic shortages of personnel, funds, and flexibility; and finally, deficiencies in the community alternative which made staying in the hospital more desirable than getting out.

## Partial Hospitalization

Part-time hospitalization has provided a helpful transition from the state hospital to the community for many mental patients. For elderly patients this usually means treatment at the center during the day and return home at night. This serves to support a person in the community by giving part-time relief to the family and continuing care for the patient, as described by Bosin (1965). There are still unfortunately few such geropsychiatric centers, but Berger and Berger (1971) have described the establishment of a private partial hospitalization unit.

## RESULTS OF TREATMENT

It is difficult to give very precise results of psychiatric treatment in geriatric patients because of the wide varieties in pathology and the multiple factors in illness. In general, the affective disorders and acute brain syndromes do rather well, the thought disorders do fairly well, and the chronic brain syndromes do not do very well. The therapeutic hopelessness that has afflicted many in dealing with the elderly psychiatric patient is certainly not justified, as evidenced by such studies as those of Davis (1967), Gottesman (1967), Manson and Hall (1961), and Risdorfer (1970). We need to assess our patients accurately so as to know their problems and potentials as well as possible, so that we can set goals which are neither so low as to fail to challenge either the patient or the therapist, nor so high as to frustrate most of the attempts of the patient. We as therapists must learn to accept that slowing the rate of decline in some or providing comfort and support in the face of approaching death for others may be valid and successful therapy.

## CONTROVERSIAL ISSUES IN GEROPSYCHIATRY

### Rejuvenation

The mere prolongation of life can be a detriment rather than an asset if there is just the unpleasant experience of increasing pain and disability. The fear of increasing mental and physical defects with advancing age and the hope of maintaining youthful vigor and appearance have been of vital importance to both men and women for centuries. This has been a fertile field for hucksters and enthusiasts over the centuries, and the search for the Fountain of Youth goes on, as entertainingly described by McGrady (1968). In recent years, more conventional scientists have entered this field attempting to prevent, delay, or reverse the aging processes. Some of the procedures are of substantially unproved value, but isolated scientific reports and glowing lay reports continue to raise speculation and hopes. Among these are the lamb embryo tissue cell therapy of Niehans, placenta extracts, antireticular cytotoxic serum of Bogomolets, and royal jelly. Chebotarev (1972) recently published positive results with these in Russia.

### Gerovital GH³

For many years in Romania, Aslan has been using a modified 2% procaine preparation for a wide variety of disorders in the elderly, reporting improvements in depression, sense of well-being, and memory and mental functioning (Aslan, 1962). Others have reported some successes, such as Abrams, Tobin, Gorden, Pechtel, and Kilkevitch (1965). Recent studies indicate that Gerovital GH³ may be a selective, reversible monoamine oxidase inhibitor, possibly accounting for its use in depression. Several studies to evaluate this are presently underway in the United States.

### Vitamins

In addition to the previously described uses for vitamins in elderly psychiatric patients, there is great fad potential in vitamins. Most nutritional product stores carry a line of books and pamphlets promising remarkable results for all kinds of preparations. The current fad is the use of Vitamin E, with the barely disguised promise of restoring sexual vigor, among other things (Trotter, 1972). There may be a kernal of truth for the value of Vitamin E, assuming that the free radical theory of aging has merit (Busse, 1973). Vitamin E has antioxident properties and as such is capable of scavenging free radicals. Other antioxidants are undergoing study presently as well.

Oxygen Therapy

The use of oxygen under increased pressure (hyperbaria) was reported by Jacobs and her group (Jacobs, Winter, Alvis and Small, 1969) to be of help in restoring cognitive function in the elderly with organic brain syndrome, although Goldfarb and his group (Goldfarb, Hochstadt, Jacobson and Weinstein, 1972) reported no effective results. More recently Fraiberg (1973) reported improvement in mental functioning and behavior in a varied group of geropsychiatric patients breathing 100% oxygen under normal atmospheric pressure. Results from hyperbaric oxygenation studies at the Duke University Center for the Study of Aging reported by Davis, G., Thompson, L. and Heyman, A. at the meeting of the American Academy of Neurology in 1973, indicated that when control subjects were used for comparison no significant value to the treatment was found.

## NEEDS AND GOALS

In order to more effectively treat the psychiatric disorders found in old age several needs and goals will have to be met. On the part of the scientists, better understanding of the processes of aging and mental disorders is needed. On the part of educators, an increased ability to convey the content and feeling of geriatric care to a wide variety of students needs to be developed. On the part of therapists, a greater empathy and involvement with those afflicted by various problems of later life are crucial. On the part of those in the aging process themselves, a zest for living life as fully as possible in its spheres of work, play, love, and spirit must be sought. On the part of society as a whole, a change from those attitudes and actions which tend to isolate, oppress, and dehumanize the elderly is needed, both to relieve the excessive burden on the individual, and to move as we can toward a greater reverence for all of life.

## REFERENCES

Abrams, A., Tobin, S.S., Gordon, P., Pechtel, C. and Kilkevitch, A. The effects of a European procaine preparation in an aged population. I. Psychological effects. *Journal of Gerontology.* **20**: 139–143 (1965).

Agate, J. Mental disorder in the elderly. *The Practice of Geriatrics,* (2nd ed.), pp. 357–384. Charles C. Thomas, Springfield, Ill., 1970.

Ahmed, A. Thioridazine in the management of geriatric patients. *Journal American Geriatric Society.* **16** (8): 945–947 (1968).

*A.M.A. Drug Evaluations.* American Medical Association Council on Drugs (1st ed.), pp. 247–265. American Medical Association, Chicago, 1971.

Ankus, M. and Quarrington, B. Operant behavior in the memory-disordered. *Journal of Gerontology.* **27**: 500–510 (1972).

Arie, J. Morale and the planning of psychogeriatric services. *British Medical Journal.* **3**: 166–170 (1971).

Aslan, A. The therapeutics of old age – The action of procaine. In: Blumenthal, H.T. (Ed.), *Medical and Clinical Aspects of Aging*, 4: 272–292. Columbia University Press, New York and London, 1962.

Barton, R. and Hurst, L. Unnecessary use of tranquilizers in elderly patients. *British Journal of Psychiatry.* 112: 989–990 (1966).

Bender, A.D. Drug therapy in the aged. Clinical aspects of aging. In: Chinn, A.B. (Ed.), *Working with Older People*, pp. 308–318. U.S. Department of Health, Education and Welfare, Public Health Service Publication No. 1459, Washington, D.C., 1971.

Berger, M.D. and Berger, L., Jr. An innovative program for a private psychogeriatric day center. *Journal American Geriatric Society.* 19: 332–336 (1971).

Birjandi, P.F. and Sclafani, M.J. An interdisciplinary team approach to geriatric patient care. *Hospital and Community Psychiatry.* 24 (11): 777–778 (1973).

Birkett, D.P. and Boltuch, B. Chlorpromazine in geriatric psychiatry. *Journal American Geriatric Society.* 20 (8): 403–406 (1972).

Bok, M. Some problems in milieu treatment of the chronic older mental patient. *Gerontologist.* 11: 141–147 (1971).

Boxberger, R. and Cotter, V.W. Music therapy for geriatric patients. In: Gaston, E.T. (Ed.), *Music in Therapy*, pp. 269–290. Macmillan, New York, 1968.

Brennan, M. and Knight, R.P. Hypnotherapy for mental illness in the aged. *Bulletin of the Menninger Clinic.* 7: 188–198 (1943).

Brin, M., Dibble, M.V., Peel, A., McMullen, E., Bourquin, A. and Chen, N. Some preliminary findings on the nutritional status of the aged in Onondaga County, New York. *American Journal of Clinical Nutrition.* 17: 204–258 (1965).

Brotman, H.B. Who are the aging? In: Busse, E.W. and Pfeiffer, E. (Eds.), *Mental Illness in Late Life*, pp. 21–39. American Psychiatric Association, Washington, D.C., 1973.

Busse, E.W. The treatment of hypochondriasis. *Tri-State Medical Journal.* 2: 7–12 (1954).

Busse, E.W., Barnes, R.H., Silverman, A.J., Thaler, M. and Frost, L.L. Studies of the processes of aging, and the strengths and weaknesses of psychic functioning in the aged. *American Journal of Psychiatry.* 111(12): 896–901 (1955).

Busse, E.W., Dovenmuehle, R.H. and Brown, R.G. Psychoneurotic Reactions of the aged. *Geriatrics.* 15: 97–105 (1960).

Busse, E.W. The Modern Challenge of Threescore and Ten. *Journal American Geriatric Society.* 17: 887–893 (1969).

Busse, E.W. The geriatric patient and the nursing home. *North Carolina Medical Journal.* 33: 218–222 (1972).

Busse, E.W. What exactly is the free radical theory of aging? In: Busse, E.W. and Pfeiffer, E. (Eds.), *Mental Illness in Later Life*, p. 241. American Psychiatric Association, Washington, D.C., 1973.

Busse, E.W. and Pfeiffer, E. (Eds.). *Mental illness in Later Life*. American Psychiatric Association, Washington, D.C., 1973.

Butler, R.N. and Lewis, M.I. *Aging and Mental Health: Positive Psychosocial Approaches*. The C.V. Mosby Company, St. Louis, 1973.

Chebotarev, D.F. Biological active agents ("geriatrics") in prevention and treatment of premature aging. In: Chebotarev, D.F. (Ed.), *The Main Problems of Soviet Gerontology*. International Congress of Gerontology, Kiev, 1972.

Chien, C.P. Psychiatric treatment for geriatric patients: "Pub or drug?" *American Journal of Psychiatry*. **127** (2): 1070–1074 (1971).

Comfort, A. On gerontophobia. *Medical Opinion Review*, pp. 30–37 (September 1967).

Coppen, A., Whybrow, P.C., Noguera, R., Maggs, R. and Prange, A.J., Jr. The comparative antidepressant value of L-tryptophan and imipramine with and without attempted potentiation by liothyronine. *Archives of General Psychiatry*. **26**: 234–241 (1972).

Cosin, L. The role of the geriatric day hospital. Paper of *British Council for Rehabilitation of the Disabled*. International Seminar, 1965.

Coursin, D.B. The National Nutrition Survey in the United States. *International Journal Vitamin Research*. **40**: 541–544 (1970).

Davidson, R. Paranoid symptoms in organic disease. *Gerontologia Clinica*. **6**: 93–100 (1964).

Davis, J.M., Fann, W.E., El-Yousef, M.K. and Janowsky, D.S. Clinical problems in treating the aged with psychotropic drugs. In: Eisdorfer, C. and Fann, W.E. (Eds.), *Psychopharmacology and Aging*, pp. 111–125. Plenum Press, New York, 1973.

Davis, R.W. Acitvity therapy in a geriatric setting. *Journal of American Geriatric Society*. **15** (5): 1144–1152 (1967).

Dawson-Butterworth, K. The chemopsychotherapeutics of geriatric sedation. *Journal of American Geriatrics Society*. **17**: (2): 97–114 (1970).

Department of Health and Social Security, *Psychogeriatric Assessment Units*. Circular HM (70) 11. H.M.S.O., London, 1970.

Dovenmuehle, R.H. and Verwoerdt, A. Physical illness and depressive symptomatology. II. Factors of length and severity of illness and frequency of hospitalizations. *Journal of Gerontology*. **18**: 260–266 (1963).

Eisdorfer, C., Powell, A.H., Silverman, G. and Bogdonoff, M.D. The characteristics of lipid mobilization and peripheral disposition in aged individuals. *Journal of Gerontology*. **20**: 511–514 (1965).

Erikson, E.H. Identity and the life cycle. *Psychological Issues*. **1**: 101–164 (1959).

Exton-Smith, A.N., Hodkinson, H.M. and Cromie, B.W. Controlled comparison of four sedative drugs in elderly patients. *British Medical Journal*. **2** (2): 1037–1040 (1963).

Exton-Smith, A.N. and Scott, D.L. (Eds.). *Vitamins in the Elderly*. John Wright and Sons, Ltd., Bristol, 1968.

Fabing, H.D. Clinical experience with Meratran. *Diseases of the Nervous System*. **16**: 10–15 (1955).

Fann, W.E. Interactions of psychotropic drugs in the elderly. *Postgraduate Medicine*. **53** (3): 182–186 (1973).

Fann, W.E., Davis, J.M., Wilson, I.C. and Lake, C.R. Attempts at pharmacologic management of tardive dyskinesia. In: Eisdorfer, C. and Fann, W.E. (Eds.), *Psychopharmacology and Aging*, pp. 89–96. Plenum Press, New York 1973.

Feigenbaum, E.M. Ambulatory treatment of the elderly. In: Busse, E.W. and Pfeiffer, E. (Eds.), *Mental Illness in Late Life,* pp. 153–166. American Psychiatric Association, Washington, D.C., 1973.

Finkelstein, M., Rosenberg, G. and Grauer, H. Therapeutic value of arts and crafts in a geriatric hospital. *Journal of American Geriatric Society.* **19** (4): 341–350 (1971).

Fish, H.U. *Activities Program for Senior Citizens.* Parker Publishing Co., Inc., West Nyack, N.Y., 1971.

Folsom, J.C. Reality orientation for the elderly mental patient. *Journal of Geriatric Psychiatry.* **1**: 291–307 (1968).

Fracchia, J., Sheppard, C. and Merlis, S. Treatment patterns in psychiatry: Relationships to symptom features and aging. *Journal American Geriatric Society.* **21** (3): 234–138 (1973).

Fraiberg, P.L. Oxygen inhalation in the control of psychogeriatric symptoms in patients with long-term illness. *Journal of American Geriatric Society.* **21**: 321–324 (1973).

Freeman, J.T. *Clinical Principles and Drugs in the Aging.* Charles C. Thomas, Springfield, Illinois, 1963.

Freud, S. Sexuality in the aetiology of the neuroses. In: *Collected Papers, Vol. I,* pp. 220–248. Basic Books, New York, 1959a.

Freud, S. On psychotherapy. In: *Collected Papers, Vol I,* pp. 249–263. Basic Books, New York, 1959b.

Gaitz, C.M. and Baer, P.E. Characteristics of elderly patients with alcoholism. *Archives of General Psychiatry.* **24**: 272–278 (1971).

Gander, D.R. The clinical value of monoamine oxidase inhibitors and tricyclic antidepressants in combination. In: Garattini, S. and Dukes, M.N.G. (Eds.), *Antidepressant Drugs,* pp. 336–343. Excerpta Medical International Congress Series 122, Excerpta Medica Foundation, Milan, 1966.

Gibson, I.I.J.M. and O'Hare, M.M. Prescription of drugs for old people at home. *Gerontologia Clinica.* **10**: 271–280 (1968).

Goldfarb, A.I. and Turner, H. Psychotherapy of aged persons. II. Utilization and effectiveness of "brief" therapy. *American Journal of Psychiatry.* **109**: 916–921 (1953).

Goldfarb, A.I. Group therapy with the old and aged. In: Kaplan, H.I. and Sadock, B.I. (Eds.), *Group Treatment of Mental Illness, Modern Group Book VI,* pp. 113–131. E.P. Dutton and Company, New York, 1972.

Goldfarb, A.I., Hochstadt, W.J., Jacobson, J.H. and Weinstein, E.A. Hyperbaric oxygen treatment of organic brain syndromes in aged persons. *Journal of Gerontology.* **27**: 212–217 (1972).

Goldstein, S. A critical appraisal of milieu therapy in a geriatric day hospital. *Journal of American Geriatric Society.* **19** (8): 693–699 (1971).

Gottesman, L.E. The response of long-hospitalized aged psychiatric patients to milieu treatment. *Gerontologist.* **7**: 47–48 (1967).

Grauer, H. Institutions for the aged – therapeutic communities? *Journal of American Geriatric Society.* **19** (8): 687–692 (1971).

Grauer, H., Betts, D. and Birnbom, F. Welfare emotions and family therapy in geriatrics. *Journal of American Geriatric Society.* **21** (1): 21–24 (1973).

Green, I. Experiences in the management of geriatric patients with chronic brain syndrome. *American Journal of Psychiatry*. **122** (1): 586–589 (1965).

Group for the Advancement of Psychiatry. *Toward a Public Policy on Mental Health Care of the Elderly*, Report No. 79, New York, 1970.

Hamilton, J.A. Psychiatric aspects. In: Cowdry, E.V. (Ed.), *The Care of the Geriatric Patient* (3rd ed.) pp. 113–129. The C.V. Mosby Company, St. Louis, 1968.

Hamilton, L.D. Aged brain and the phenothiazines, *Geriatrics*. **21**: 131–138 (1966).

Hollister, L.E. Clinical use of psychotherapeutic drugs: current status. *Clinical Pharmacology and Therapeutics*. **10** (2): 170–198 (1969).

Hollister, L.E. Choice of antipsychotic drugs. *American Journal of Psychiatry*. **127** (2): 186–190 (1970).

Hollister, L.E. *Clinical Use of Psychotherapeutic Drugs*. Charles C. Thomas, Springfield, Illinois, 1973.

Horwitz, W.S. Physiologic responses as prognostic guides in the use of antidepressant drugs. *American Journal of Psychiatry*. **125** (1): 60–68 (1968).

Houston, R. and Royse, A.B. Relationship between deafness and psychotic illness. *Journal of Mental Science*. **100**: 990–993 (1954).

Hoyer, W.J. Application of operant techniques to the modification of elderly behavior. *The Gerontologist*. **13**: 18–22 (1973).

Hussain, M.Z. and Chaudhry, Z.A. Single versus divided daily dose of trimipramine in the treatment of depressive illness. *American Journal of Psychiatry*. **130** (10): 1142–1144 (1973).

Jacobs, E.A., Winter, P.M., Alvis, H.A. and Small, S.M. Hyperoxygenation effect on cognitive functioning in the aged. *New England Journal of Medicine*. **281**: 753–757 (1969).

Jakobovits, T. The treatment of impotence with methyltestosterone thyroid. *Fertility and Sterility*. **21** (1): 32–35 (1970).

Jones, M. *The Therapeutic Community*. Basic Books, New York, 1953.

Jung, C.G. *Modern Man in Search of a Soul*. Harcourt, Brace and World, New York, 1933.

Kahn, E. and Fisher, C. The sleep characteristics of the normal aged male. *Journal of Nervous and Mental Disease*. **148**: 477–494 (1969).

Kahn, R.L., Goldfarb, A.L., Pollack, M. and Gerber, I.E. The relationship of mental and physical status in institutionalized aged persons. *American Journal of Psychiatry*. **11**: 120–124 (1960).

Kalinowsky, L.B. and Hippius, H. *Pharmacological, Convulsive and Other Somatic Treatments in Psychiatry*. Grune & Stratton, New York, 1969.

Kastenbaum, R. and Slater, P.E. Effects of wine on the interpersonal behavior of geriatric patients: An exploratory study. In: Kastenbaum, R. (Ed.), *New Thoughts on Old Age*, pp. 191–204. Springer Publishing Company, Inc., New York, 1964.

Kaufman, S.A. Limited relationship of maturation index to estrogen therapy for menopausal symptoms. *Obstetrics and Gynecology*. **30**: 399–407 (1967).

Kidd, C.B. Criteria for admission of the elderly to geriatric and psychiatric units. *Journal of Mental Science*. **108**: 68–74 (1962a).

Kidd, C.B. Misplacement of the elderly in hospital. *British Medical Journal*. **2**: 1491–1495 (1962b).

Kleemeier, R.W., Rich, T.A. and Justiss, W. The clinical effects of Alpha- (2-piperidyl) benzhydrol hydrochloride (Meratran) on psychomotor performance in a group of aged males. *Journal of Gerontology*. **11**: 165–170 (1956).

Klein, W.H., Le Shan, E.J. and Furman, S.S. *Promoting Mental Health of Older People Through Group Methods*. Manhattan Society for Mental Health, New York, 1965.

Knight, G. Intractable psychoneurosis in the elderly and infirm: treatment by stereotactic tractottomy. *British Journal of Geriatric Practice*. **3**: 7(1966).

Kozlowski, V.L. Meprobamate-promazine therapy for aged psychiatric patients with chronic brain syndrome associated with arteriosclerosis. *Journal of American Geriatric Society*. **9**: 376–380 (1961).

Kral, V.A., Solyom, L., Enesco, H. and Ledwidge, B. Relationship of vitamin B12 and folic acid to memory function. *Biological Psychiatry*. **2**: 19–26 (1970).

Kramer, C.H. Dangers of chloral hydrate. *Professional Nursing Home*. August, 1966.

Kramer, M., Taube, C. and Starr, S. Patterns of use of psychiatric facilities by the aged: current status, trends, and implications. In: Simon, A. and Epstein, L., (Eds.), *Aging in Modern Society*. American Psychiatric Association, Washington, D.C., 1968.

Kupperman, H.S. *Human Endocrinology*. **2**: 426. F.A. Davis Company, Philadelphia, 1963.

Lamy, P.P. and Kitler, M.E. Drugs and the geriatric patient. *Journal of American Geriatric Society*. **19** (1): 23–33 (1971).

Langley, G.E. and Simpson, J.H. Misplacement of the elderly in geriatric and psychiatric hospitals. *Gerontologia Clinica*. **12**: 149–163 (1970).

Lawson, I.R. and MacLeod, R.D.M. The use of imipramine ("Tofranil") and other psychotropic drugs in organic emotionalism. *British Journal of Psychiatry*. **115** (1): 281–285 (1969).

Leake, C.D. and Silverman, M. The clinical use of wine in geriatrics. *Geriatrics*. **22** (1): 175–180 (1967).

Learoyd, B.M. Psychotropic drugs and the elderly patient. *Medical Journal of Australia*. **1**: 1131–1133 (1972).

Lehmann, H.E. and Ban, T.A. Pharmacological load tests as predictors of pharmacotherapeutic response in geriatric patients. In: Wittenborn, J.R., Solomon, C. and May, P.R.A. (Eds.), *Psychopharmacology and the Individual Patient*, pp. 32–54. Raven Press, New York 1968.

Lehmann, H.E. Psychopharmacological aspects of geriatric medicine. In: Gaitz, C.M. (Ed.), *Aging and the Brain*, pp. 193–208. Plenum Press, New York, 1972.

Levin, M.E. Metabolic insufficiency. *Journal of Clinical Endocrinology and Metabolism*. **20**: 106–115 (1960).

Lifshitz, K. and Kline, N.S. Psychopharmacology of the aged. In: Freeman, J.T. (Ed.), *Clinical Principles and Drugs in the Aging*. Charles, C. Thomas, Springfield, Illinois, 1963.

Lifshitz, K. and Kline, N.S. Psychopharmacology in Geriatrics. In: Clark, W.E. and Del Giudice, J. (Eds.), *Principles of Psychopharmacology*, pp. 695–705. Academic Press, New York and London, 1970.

Linden, M.E.    Group psychotherapy with institutionalized senile women. II. Study in gerontologic human relations. *International Journal of Group Psychotherapy*. **3**: 150–170 (1953).

Lindsley, O.R.    Geriatric behavior prosthetics. In: Kastenbaum, R. (Ed.), *New Thoughts on Old Age*, pp. 41–60. Springer Publishing, New York, 1964.

Lippincott, R.C.    Depressive illness: identification and treatment in the elderly. *Geriatrics*. **23** (2): 149–152 (1968).

Lloyd, W.H.    Some clinical features of hyper- and hypo-thyroidism in the elderly. *Gerontologia Clinica*. **9**: 337–346 (1967).

Lowenbach, H.    How well does electroshock treatment work in depression in the elderly? How safe is it, and how can it be given? In: Busse, E.W. and Pfeiffer, E. (Eds.), *Mental Illness in Late Life*, pp. 246–248. American Psychiatric Association, Washington, D.C., 1973.

Manson, M.P. and Hall, L.    Accelerating the therapeutic discharge rate for geriatric-psychiatric patients. *Journal of American Geriatric Society*. **9**: 294–303 (1961).

Masters, W.H.    Sex steroid influence on the aging process. *American Journal of Obstetrics and Gynecology*. **74**: 733–746 (1957).

McDonald, C., Mowbray, R.M. and Wilson, J.M.O.    A sequential trial of amylobarbitone sodium used as sedation for confused female psychogeriatric patients. *Gerontologia Clinica*. **12**: 335–338 (1970).

McGrady, P.M., Jr.    *The Youth Doctors*. Coward-McCann, Inc., New York, 1968.

Meerlo, J.A.M.    Modes of Psychotherapy in the aged. *Journal of American Geriatric Society*. **9**: 225–234 (1961).

Merrill, T.    *Activities for the aged and infirm*. Charles C. Thomas, Springfield, Illinois, 1967.

Milner, G.    Ascorbic acid in chronic psychiatric patients – a controlled trial. *British Journal of Psychiatry*. **109**: 294–299 (1963).

Mitra, M.L.    Confusional states in relation to vitamin deficiencies in the elderly. *Journal of American Geriatric Society*. **19** (6): 536–545 (1971).

Nevruz, N. and Hrushka, M.    The influence of unstructured and structured group psychotherapy with geriatric patients on their decision to leave the hospital. *International Journal of Group Psychotherapy*. **19**: 72–78 (1969).

Orlov, P., Kasparian, G., Di Mascio, A. and Cole, J.O.    Withdrawal of anti-Parkinson drugs. *Archives of General Psychiatry*. **25**: 410–412 (1971).

Overall, J.E., Hollister, L.E., Meyer, F., Kimbell, I. and Shelton, J.    Imipramine and thioridazine in depressed and schizophrenic patients. *Journal of American Medical Association*. **189**: 605–608 (1964).

Pattison, J.H. and Allen, R.P.    Comparison of the hypnotic effectiveness of secobarbital, pentobarbital, methyprylon and ethchlorvynol. *Journal of American Geriatric Society*. **20** (8): 398–402 (1972).

Pennington, V.M.    Enhancement of psychotropic drugs by a vitamin supplement. *Psychosomatics*. **7**: 115–120 (1966).

Pfeiffer, E.    Geriatric sex behavior. *Medical Aspects of Human Sexuality*. **3** (7): 19–28 (1969).

*Physician's Desk Reference* (27th ed.).    Medical Economics Company, Oradel, New Jersey, 1973.

Pomeranze, J. and King, E.J.   Psychosis as first sign of thyroid dysfunction. *Geriatrics.* **21** (1):  211–212 (1966).

Post, F.   *The clinical psychiatry of late life.* Pergamon Press, London, 1965.

Post, F.   Somatic and psychic factors in the treatment of elderly psychiatric patients. *Journal of Psychosomatic Research.* **10:**  13–19 (1966a).

Post, F.   *Persistent persecutory states of the elderly.* Pergamon Press, Oxford, 1966b.

Post, F., Rees, W.L. and Schurr, P.H.   An evaluation of bimedial leucotomy. *British Journal of Psychiatry.* **114:**  1223–1246 (1968).

Prange, A.J., Jr., Wilson, I.C., Rabon, A.M. and Lipton, M.A.   Enhancement of imipramine antidepressant activity by thyroid hormone. *American Journal of Psychiatry.* **126** (4):  457–469 (1969).

Prange, A.J., Jr. and Lipton, M.A.   Hormones and behavior:  some principles and findings.  In:  Shader, R.I. (Ed.), *Psychiatric Complications of Medical Drugs,* pp. 213–249. Raven Press, New York, 1972.

Prout, C.T., Allen, E.B. and Hamilton, D.M.   The use of electric shock therapy in older patients.  In: Kaplan, O.J. (Ed.), *Mental Disorders in Later Life* (2nd ed.), pp. 446–459. Stanford University Press, Stanford, California, 1956.

Rechtschaffen, A.   Psychotherapy with geriatric patients: a review of the literature. *Gerontology.* **14:**  73–84 (1959).

Redick, R.W., Kramer, M. and Taube, C.A.   Epidemiology of mental illness and utilization of psychiatric facilities among older persons. In: Busse, E.W. and Pfeiffer, E. (Eds.), *Mental Illness in Later Life,* pp. 199–231. American Psychiatric Association, Washington, D.C., 1973.

*Remotivation Kit.*   American Psychiatric Association, Washington, D.C., 1965.

Rice, D.   The use of lithium salts in the treatment of manic states. *Journal of Mental Science.* **102:**  604–611 (1956).

Risdorfer, E.N.   Review of results in a geriatric intensive treatment unit: some prospects.   *Journal of American Geriatric Society.*   **18:**   47–55 (1970).

Robinson, D.W., Nies, A., Davis, J.N., Bunney, W.E., Davis, J.M., Colburn, R.W., Bourne, H.R., Shaw, D.M. and Coppen, A.J.   Aging, monoamines, and mono-amine-oxidase levels. *Lancet.* **1** (1):  290–291 (1972).

Rodstein, M.   Heart disease in the aged.  In: Rossman, I. (Ed.), *Clinical Geriatrics,* pp. 143–163. J.B. Lippincott Company, Philadelphia, 1971.

Roe, D.A.   Dietary interrelationships.  In: Wohl, M.G. and Goodhart, R.S. (Eds.), *Modern Nutrition in Health and Disease* (4th ed.), pp. 436–449.  Lea and Feberger, Philadelphia, 1968.

Rose, R.M.   The psychological effects of androgens and estrogens – review. In:  Shader, R.I. (Ed.), *Psychiatric Complications of Medical Drugs,* pp. 251–293. Raven Press, New York, 1972.

Roth, M.J.   Prophylaxis and early diagnosis and treatment of mental illness in late life.  In: Anderson, W.F. and Isaacs, B. (Eds.), *Current Achievements in Geriatrics,* pp. 155–170. Cassell, London, 1964.

Rubin, I.   *Sexual Life After Sixty.* Basic Books, New York, 1965.

Salzman, C., Shader, R.I. and Pearlman, M.   Psychopharmacology and the elderly. In:  Shader, R.I. and Di Mascio, A. (Eds.), *Psychotropic Drug Side Effects,* pp. 261–279. Williams and Wilkins Company, Baltimore, 1970.

Sargent, W. and Slater, E. *An Introduction to Physical Methods of Treatment in Psychiatry.* E. & S. Livingstone, Ltd., Edinburgh, 1963.

Schleyer-Saunders, E.   Results of hormone implants in the treatment of the climacteric. *Journal of American Geriatric Society.* **19** (2):  114–121 (1971).

Schuckit, M., Robins, E. and Feighner, J.   Tricyclic antidepressants and mono-amine oxidase inhibitors. *Archives of General Psychiatry.* **24**:  509–514 (1971).

Shulman, R.   Psychiatric aspects of pernicious anemia: a prospective controlled investigation. *British Medical Journal.* **3**:  266–270 (1967).

Silver, A.   Group psychotherapy with senile psychiatric patients. *Geriatrics.* **5**: 147–150 (1950).

Simon, A., Epstein, L.J. and Reynolds, L.   Alcoholism in the geriatric mentally ill. *Geriatrics.* **23** (2):  125–131 (1968).

Smith, J.A. and Barron, A.R.   The use of chlorprothixene in the disturbed geriatric patient. *American Journal of Psychiatry.* **122**:  213–214 (1965).

Spark, G.M. and Brody, E.M.   The aged are family members. *Family Processes.* **9** (2):  195–210 (1970).

Stotsky, B.A.   *The Elderly Patient.* Grune & Stratton, New York, 1968.

Stotsky, B.A.   Psychoses in the elderly. In: Eisdorfer, C. and Fann, W.E. (Ed.), *Psychopharmacology and Aging,* pp. 193–203. Plenum Press, New York, 1973.

Stotsky, B.A., Cole, J.O., Tang, Y.T. and Gahm, I.G.   Sodium butabarbital (Butisol Sodium) as an hypnotic agent for aged psychiatric patients with sleep disorders. *Journal of American Geriatric Society.* **19** (10):  860–870 (1971).

Straker, M. and Roth, E.M.   Use of imipramine (Tofranil) in the aged chronically ill. *Canadian Medical Association Journal.* **82**:  362–364 (1960).

Taylor, G.F.   A clinical survey of elderly people from a nutritional standpoint. In: Exton-Smith, and Scott, D.L. (Eds.), *Vitamins in the Elderly,* pp. 51–56. John Wright & Sons, Bristol, 1968.

Tewfik, G.I., Jain, F.K., Harcup, M. and Magowan, S.   Effectiveness of various tranquilizers in the management of senile restlessness. *Gerontologia Clinica.* **12**:  351–359 (1970).

Thorpe, F.T.   An evaluation of prefrontal leucotomy in the affective disorders of old age: a follow-up study. *Journal of Mental Science.* **104**:  403–410 (1958).

Tournier, P. *Learn To Grow Old.* Harper & Row, 1972.

Tramont, C.B.   Cyclic hormone therapy. *Geriatrics.* **21** (2):  212–215 (1966).

Trotter, R.J.   Vitamin E, who needs it? *Science News.* **101** (3):  44–45 (1972).

Tsuang, M.M., Lu, L.M., Stotsky, B.A. and Cole, J.O.   Haloperidol versus thioridazine for hospitalized psychogeriatric patients:  double-blind study. *Journal of American Geriatric Society.* **19** (7):  593–600 (1971).

Van Der Velde, C.D.   Toxicity of lithium carbonate in elderly patients. *American Journal of Psychiatry.* **127** (2):  1075–1077 (1971).

Verwoerdt, A., Pfeiffer, E. and Wang, H.S.   Sexual behavior in senescence. II.  Patterns of sexual activity and interest. *Geriatrics.* **24**:  137–154 (1969).

Volpe, A. and Kastenbaum, R.   Beer and TLC. *American Journal of Nursing.* **67**: 100–103 (1967).

Webb, W.L., Jr.   The use of psychopharmacological drugs in the aged. *Geriatrics.* **26**: (1):  95–103 (1971).

Weintraub, W. and Aronson, H. A survey of patients in classical psychoanalysis: some vital statistics. *Journal of Nervous and Mental Diseases.* **146**: 98-102 (1968).

Whanger, A.D. Geriatric mental health in north carolina. *North Carolina Journal of Mental Health.* **5**: 43-49 (1971).

Whanger, A.D. Vitamins and vigor at 65 plus. *Postgraduate Medicine.* **53**: 167-172 (1973a).

Whanger, A.D. Paranoid syndromes of the senium. In: Eisdorfer, C. and Fann, W.E. (Eds.), *Psychopharmacology and Aging,* pp. 203-211. Plenum Publishing Corporation, New York, 1973b.

Whanger, A.D. and Wang, H.S. Vitamin B12 deficiency in normal aged and elderly psychiatric patients. In: Palmore, E. (Ed.), *Normal Aging, II.* Duke University Press, Durham, N.C., 1974a.

Whanger, A.D. and Wang, H.S. Clinical correlates of the vibratory sense in elderly psychiatric patients. *Journal of Gerontology.* **29**: 39-45 (1974b).

Wheatley, D. Potentiation of amitriptyline by thyroid hormone. *Archives of General Psychiatry.* **26**: 229-233 (1972).

Whitehead, J.A. and Chohan, M.M. Paraphrenia and pernicious anemia. *Geriatrics.* **27**: 148-158 (1972).

Whybrow, P.C., Prange, A.J., Jr. and Treadway, C.R. Mental changes accompanying thyroid gland dysfunction. *Archives of General Psychiatry.* **20**: 48-63 (1969).

Whybrow, P.C., Coppen, A., Prange, A.J., Jr., Noguera, R. and Bailey, J.E. Thyroid function and the response to liothyronine in depression. *Archives of General Psychiatry.* **26**: 242-245 (1972).

Wilson, W.P. Depression diagnosis, treatment with drugs. *Texas Medicine.* **63** (11): 64-70 (1967).

Wolff, K. *Geriatric Psychiatry.* Charles C. Thomas, Springfield, Illinois, 1963.

Wolff, K. *The emotional rehabilitation of the geriatric patient.* Charles C. Thomas, Springfield, Illinois, 1970.

Wren, J.C. Symptomatic atherosclerosis: prevention or modification by treatment with desiccated thyroid. *Journal of American Geriatric Society.* **19** (1): 7-22 (1971).

# 14 Treatment of Schizophrenia

## Benjamin B. Wolman

THEORETICAL CONSIDERATIONS

The choice of treatment method is largely determined by the therapist's view of the nature of the disease or disorder. As long as physicians believed that hysteria was caused by a uterus (hysteros) wandering inside a female body, surgery was the chosen therapeutic method. In 1882, Dr. Pean surgically removed an ovary in order to cure hysteria. According to Charcot, "it is to the ovary and to the ovary alone that one has to look for the source of the fixed iliac pain of hysteric" (1887-1888, vol 1, p. 339).

There are, probably, more theories of schizophrenia than of any other mental disorder. Accordingly, practitioners, whether they are psychiatrists or clinical psychologists, have a variety of methods to choose from. Usually, the practitioners who believe that schizophrenia is an organic mental disorder prefer to use physicochemical methods, while those who believe in a psychogenic origin of schizophrenia prefer psychotherapy.

But the controversy does not end at the crossroads between the somatic and nonsomatic factors. Students of schizophrenia represent a rainbow of theoretical colors, with all the possible combinations thereof. Those who believe in a genetic etiology of schizophrenia greatly differ from those who trace schizophrenia to a variety of biochemical determinants. Moreover, those who believe in a psychosocial etiology of schizophrenia do not necessarily exclude the possibility of a combination of genetic and environmental factors, or an interplay of biochemical predisposing causes with precipitating experiential factors.

This chapter does not intend to do justice to all the various theories and their offshoots. Nor do I plan to describe all the diversities of treatment methods. My intention is to describe briefly some of the theoretical approaches and treatment techniques, and to describe in detail my own interpretation and treatment technique.

## Statistical Indicators

According to *Mental Health Statistics,* published by the National Institute of Mental Health (1971), there were 1,269,000 admissions to inpatient services in the U.S. in one year, and 27% of these were schizophrenics, as compared to 22.5% depressives, 21% drug and alcohol addicts, and 6% with brain damage, tumors, etc. However, schizophrenics make up about 50% of all inpatients in mental hospitals at any given time (Rosenthal, 1970), which indicates a lower rate of discharge and, probably, a lower level of therapeutic success.

## Etiological Studies: Genetics

One may try various methods to fight the symptoms of a physical disease or a mental (behavioral) disorder, but there is a great advantage in knowing the causes of the problem and developing a rational therapeutic strategy directly aimed at counteracting the noxious causes. Scores of research workers have spent their lifetime trying to unravel the enigma of schizophrenia without, so far, being able to arrive at a generally accepted etiological theory.

A great many workers believe that schizophrenia is an inherited disorder. According to Kallmann's findings (1946, 1948, 1953), children with one schizophrenic parent have a 16.4% probability of developing schizophrenia, while children with two schizophrenic parents have a 68.1% probability. More impressive are the data obtained by comparison of fraternal and identical twins. Where one fraternal twin has developed schizophrenia, there is a 16.4% probability that the other will develop it also; in identical twins the chances are 86.2%. In Kallmann's study of 691 twins, dizygotic twins have shown concordance with schizophrenia in 14.7% of the cases, as compared to 77.6 to 81.5% in monozygotic twins. The higher of the latter percentages applies to twins who have been together for five years prior to breakdown. Thus, according to Kallmann, "inheritance of schizophrenia follows a biological genetic pattern" (1946, p. 318).

Moreover, Kallmann believed the outcome of schizophrenia to be "the result of intricate interaction of varying genetic and environmental influences."

A summary of Kallmann's studies of expectancy of schizophrenia is represented below (Kallmann, 1962):

|  | % |
| --- | --- |
| One-egg twins | 86.20 |
| Two-egg twins | 14.50 |
| Siblings | 14.20 |
| Half siblings | 7.10 |
| General population | 0.85 |

Altshuler (1957) confirmed Kallmann's findings and stressed the fact that expectancy rates for relatives of schizophrenics are much higher than for the general population. Vorster (1960) found 17% incidence of schizophrenia in two-egg twins, as compared with 70% incidence of schizophrenia in one-egg twins.

The idea of recessive heredity was strongly criticized by Böök (1960) and Slater (1953, 1958). Since the corrected risk figures of schizophrenia "do not differ to a significant degree between parents, siblings, and children with one or no affected parent" (Böök, 1960, p. 29), the hypothesis of a recessive heredity becomes untenable. Also Gregory (1960) noticed that the incidence of schizophrenia in various classes of relatives does not follow a simple dominant or simple recessive pattern.

Böök hypothesized that schizophrenia could be caused by gene differences expressed in homozygotes in a recessive and, occasionally, in heterozygotes in a dominant manner. This hypothesis is based on the concept of "reduced penetrance," i.e., on the assumption that the presence of a genetic factor may not affect the person carrying it. Garrone (1962) applied the penetrance hypothesis to a study of the Geneva population and maintained that schizophrenia was inherited in a simple recessive mode with 67% of homozygous penetrance.

Loretta Bender (1956) believes schizophrenia to be a process of dysmaturation and arrest of development on the embryonic level, determined by genetic factors. Resultingly, the child is born with a sort of primitive *plasticity.* The entire neurological system bears witness to the organic lag of development. The infant's sleep, respiration, blood circulation, muscular tone, and metabolic processes are disturbed. The trauma of birth activates certain defense mechanisms which develop in the well-known behavioral patterns of schizophrenia. Thus schizophrenia is a sort of *encephalopathy.*

Fish (1959) reported that a child diagnosed at the age of five and one-half years as schizophrenic had shown neurological and physiological disturbances as early as one month of age. However, Goldfarb (1961) found no significant differences in physical appearance between normal and schizophrenic children. Also Eisenberg (1957) questioned the anatomical evidence of Bender's theory of encephalopathy. On the other hand, Bergman and Escalona (1949) reported unusual sensitivity in infants later diagnosed as psychotic.

Roth (1957) remarked that "no simple genetic hypothesis accords with all the facts." Rosenthal (1960), while in favor of a genetic interpretation of schizophrenia, stated that the question of what is actually inherited would remain unclear "until the specific metabolic error can be located or the specific patterns of influence defined or established."

Jackson (1960) has critically examined the literature pertaining to genetics in schizophrenia. Schizophrenia apparently does not follow the rules of dominant heredity; were schizophrenia a product of recessive heredity, as Kallmann maintains, the rate of expectancy for monozygotic twins should be 100%; it would also be 100% for children of two schizophrenic parents. Since Kallmann's rates are substantially lower, the hypothesis of recessive heredity is also excluded (Jackson, 1960, p. 46).

The research concerning morbidity risk for schizophrenia in children of two schizophrenic parents is an important contribution to the study of genetic factors. Rosenthal (1970), after analysis of six relevant studies, concluded:

Since an unqualified theory of recessiveness or dominance predicts an incidence of 100 or 75 percent, respectively, the risk figure obtained, like all others in this section, falls below expectancy for either theory . . . . we had noted that the morbidity-risk estimate for the children of one schizophrenic parent was 9.7 percent. Thus, the risk when both parents are schizophrenic increases about fourfold. An increase is predicted by genetic theory, but not one of this particular magnitude. An increase would also be predicted by environmentalist theories that stress the contribution to schizophrenia made by rearing in a psychosis-ridden or turbulent home (pp. 116–117).

Apparently, at the present time it is rather difficult to assess the role of genetic factors in schizophrenia.

### Biochemical Determinants

Several research workers, among them Hoagland (1952) and Reiss (1954), maintain that hormonal disbalance is the cause of schizophrenia. There has been a wide range of disagreement among the workers as to whether it was thyroid or adrenaline or some other endocrine disorder that served as a cause. M. Bleuler (1954), H. Freeman (1958), and others stated, however, that at that time no connection had been established between schizophrenia and endocrine factors.

According to Hendrickson (1952, p. 10), schizophrenia is "an organic abnormality of the nervous system, really a complex and subtle type of neurological disorder." However, most detailed research in brain activity (Davidson, 1960; Hyden, 1961) has not reached the point where one could safely say schizophrenic behavior *is* caused by a smaller amount of RNA in the ganglion cells, as compared with normal.

Kety (1960) expressed serious doubts as to whether "a generalized defect in energy metabolism . . . could be responsible for the highly specialized features of schizophrenia." Also Böök (1960, p. 32) found the toxicity data rather controversial. Richter (1957), in a review of his own studies as well as of research conducted by others, concluded that no evidence was found of free aminos or any specific toxic compounds or abnormal metabolites in the blood of schizophrenics.

Heath and associates reported on several occasions that a psychosis-inducing gamma globulin fraction in the sera of schizophrenic patients, designated *taraxein,* was demonstrable by passive transfer in volunteer non-psychotic recipients and in rhesus monkeys. In a paper published in 1968, Heath and Krupp stated that "the presence of taraxein in the sera of schizophrenic patients is specifically related to acute psychotic episodes and that serum fractions of patients with psychotic diseases other than schizophrenia produced negative results."

However, Heath's experimental results could not be consistently replicated in other laboratories. His theoretical conclusions based on his own observations are therefore open to doubt.

Kety (1960) reported that injection of taraxein caused symptoms resembling schizophrenia, but that there is no evidence that taraxein causes schizophrenia. Furthermore, there is no evidence supporting the amino acid metabolism hypothesis. "The chromatographic search for supportive evidence is interesting and valuable," wrote Kety, but "the preliminary indications of differences that are characteristic of even a segment of the disease rather than artifactual or incidental has not yet been obtained" (1960, p. 127). For instance, the presence of phenolic acids in the urine of schizophrenics has been, according to the study of T.D. Mann and E.H. Lambrosse, "better correlated with the ingestion of this beverage (coffee) than with schizophrenia" (Kety, 1960). Kline (1958) pointed out that the alleged link between biochemical aberrations and psychosis is often a product of the peculiar food intake of institutionalized patients.

Several research workers experimented with injecting schizophrenic serum into animals and human subjects. Walaszek (1960) injected schizophrenic serum into rabbits. The hypothalamic adrenaline level rose to three to five times the normal level in a period of four to eight days. Bishop (1963) found that the injection of schizophrenic serum into rats considerably affected learning and retention processes. German (1963) found significant differences in the reaction of rats to the injection of human normal and schizophrenic serum. However, a comparative study of blood serum of schizophrenic and non-schizophrenic children failed to discover significant differences concerning optical density and slope and lag time (Aprison and Drew, 1958).

Woolley's hypothesis (1958) with regard to the role played by the serotonin enzyme has been tested in the so-called "model psychosis." Yet Kety (1960) and others report failure to find significant differences between normal controls and schizophrenics.

## Somato-psychic or Psychosomatic?

Human behavior, normal as well as abnormal, has traditionally been related to two distinct factors, namely mind and body. Some contemporary students of human life try to bypass this division or simply ignore it. The fact remains, however, that brain waves are not human thoughts and an act of artistic creativity is not a biochemical reaction.

These two aspects of human life remain as far apart today as they have been for millennia, and no pseudo-sophistication could do away with the complexity of the mind-body problem.

Yet there is a good deal of interaction between the two. A decision to take a walk puts one's muscles and joints into action, and an upset stomach influences one's thoughts and feelings. Apparently, nature frequently crosses this mind-body bridge, but science lags behind in interpreting this *causal* psycho-soma or soma-psyche relationship.

Practicing therapists are fully aware of the fact that some mental (or, one may call them, behavioral) disorders start with damage to the physicochemical functions of the human organism, while other disorders start with damage to one's self-esteem or other psychological determinants. The fact that chemotherapy and psychotherapy can both favorably affect the course of a mental disorder could serve as a proof that human behavior is susceptible to attack from either angle, soma or psyche.

There is, however, clearly a greater chance of making the treatment effective if it is directed toward the causes of a disorder rather than toward their effects. Thus, should schizophrenia be proven to be primarily of an organic origin, the therapists should give priority to physicochemical treatment methods. Should, however, schizophrenia be a sociogenic or sociopsychogenic disorder and its physical symptoms be of a psychosomatic nature, the therapists should prefer the use of psychotherapeutic methods. In either case, there is no reason for exclusion of alternative routes, for apparently schizophrenia can be alleviated, if not cured, by more than one treatment method.

Arieti (1955), Shattock (1950), Doust (1952), and others observed several pathological phenomena in schizophrenics, including cyanosis or bluing of the feet and hands caused by venous stasis, and other defects of the vasomotor system, such as a decrease in systemic blood pressure, decrease in the volume of flow of blood, and a tendency to vasoconstriction. Yet Kety and his associates (1948) could not find significant differences between the oxygen consumption and the flow of blood in the brains of schizophrenics and those of normal controls. There was no evidence for a cerebral anoxemia; yet the disturbances in the circulatory system of schizophrenics are well-established facts.

According to Arieti, vasoconstriction in schizophrenics is a compensatory mechanism that prevents dissipation of bodily heat. The bizarre postures of catatonics activate antigravity vasoconstrictor mechanisms. "Without these mechanisms, edema due to blood stasis would be very frequent" (Arieti, 1955, p. 395).

Several physiological peculiarities have been observed in schizophrenics, such as little reactivity to stimuli; reduced sensitivity to pain, combined with an increased fear of anticipated pain; strong inclination to skin diseases; frequent colds and an increased sensitivity to colds; sharpening of olfactory sensitivity; lowered body temperature, etc. (Arieti, 1955; Bleuler, 1950; Buck, *et al.,* 1950; Wolman, 1957, 1964; and others).

However, the research that points to the etiologic organicity of schizophrenia has been conducted on chronic schizophrenics, most of them in their middle or old age. For instance Brambilla *et al.* (1967) in a study of 72 chronic schizophrenics aged 14-53 found that endocrine glands are impaired, and that the severity of the glandular impairment corresponds to the severity and the age of onset of the disorder. Most striking pathology was found in hebephrenics with onset at puberty. The results obtained with schizophrenics whose manifest disorder was recent were rather negative. Especially striking are the negative results obtained by Aprison and Drew (1958) and Fourbye et al. (1966) in regard to children. These results indicate that *biochemical symptoms follow psychological* (behavioral) symptoms, suggesting that in schizophrenia the psychological changes are the *cause* and not the results of somatic changes.

For instance, a study by Becket and associates of carbohydrate metabolism in schizophrenia offers further support to the sociopsychosomatic theory. Becket et al. (1963) found that premorbid social isolation and diminished heterosexual drive were related to biochemical abnormalities. Specifically the mother of the schizophrenic patient was a "shielding, protecting person who did not allow her son to experience the ordinary stimulation and challenges of childhood . . . . A hypothesis is presented suggesting that a certain amount of stimulation in early life is necessary for the proper maturation of the energy-producing metabolic system."

Practically all empirical findings speak in favor of such a causal chain. There is no doubt that many (but not all) adult schizophrenics and some children with severe cases of schizophrenia develop somatic symptoms. There is little evidence that schizophrenic behavior is a result of these biochemical afflictions, for many individuals with metabolic troubles ascribed to schizophrenia never become schizophrenic. There is, however, substantial, though by no means conclusive, evidence that *schizophrenia can produce all these biochemical disorders.*

There is no doubt that emotional stress may cause biochemical changes, especially in the adrenocortical and thyroid systems, as well as in the production of epinephrine and norepinephrine. These changes are not a cause but an *effect* of emotional stress.

The hypothesis of somatic symptoms resulting from hypocathexis of bodily organs completes the *sociopsychosomatic* theory. My observations have led me to believe that noxious *environmental* (social) factors cause an imbalance in *interindividual cathexes.* This imbalance produces a severe disbalance in the *intraindividual* cathexes of libido and destrudo; this, in turn, introduces a disorder in the personality structure (psychological factors). The personality disorder causes somatic changes, either through a transformation of deficiency in mental energy into organic deficiencies or through the process of conditioning (Wolman, 1966, 1967).

Research in conditioning reported by Buck et al. (1950), Bykov (1957), Gantt (1958), Ivanov-Smolensky (1954), Lynn (1963), Malis (1961), and others distinctly points to such a possibility. Psychologically induced changes in heartbeat, rate of metabolism, circulation of blood, or respiration are not limited to Charcot's hysterics. They are common to all human beings, including schizophrenics, and can be produced by conditioning or cathexis or both. In schizophrenia these processes follow the direction of a "downward adjustment."

The magnitude of the general metabolism can be changed through conditioning by word signals. The sound of a metronome and the command, "Get ready for the experiment," caused in experimental subjects a marked increase in oxygen consumption and pulmonary ventilation. In one experiment, "a man who remained quietly lying on a couch showed an increase in metabolism when suggested that he had just completed some very hard muscular work" (Bykov, 1957, p. 179). In another experiment the rate of metabolism went up in a subject who imagined that he was working.

In terms of the sociopsychosomatic theory, schizophrenia is an impoverishment of one's own resources and a struggle for survival, caused by a morbid hypervectorialism. This state of mind may correspond to cerebrospinal hypertension, for *sociopsychological stimuli cause somatic changes.*

Analgesias are another example of the same issue. E. Bleuler wrote in 1911: "Even in well oriented patients one may often observe the presence of a complete *analgesia* which includes the deeper parts of the body as well as the skin. The patients intentionally or unintentionally incur quite serious injuries, pluck out an eye, sit down on a hot stove and receive severe gluteal burns," etc. (Bleuler, 1950, p. 57).

Analgesias can be produced by conditioning (Bykov, 1957, p. 342) and/or by a low self-cathexis. The decline in self-cathexis makes the schizophrenic less capable of loving and protecting himself, but in face of real danger, schizophrenics may display a self-defensive reaction. Severely deteriorated cases, however, with their lowest sensitivity to pain, may fall victim to any danger.

Severely deteriorated schizophrenics appear insensitive when the flame of a candle is passed rapidly over the skin. They may sit near the radiator, and, if they are not moved, they may continue to stay there even when, as a result of close contact, they are burned. They "seem to have lost the sensation of taste. When they are given bitter radishes or teaspoons of sugar, salt, pepper, or quinine, they do not show any pleasant or unpleasant reaction" (Arieti, 1955, pp. 373-374).

This is the *schizophrenic paradox:* real life is sacrificed for a pseudo protection of life. The schizophrenic feels he has to give away his life to protect those upon whom his survival depends. His lavish hypercathexis of his "protectors" leads to his own impoverishment and eventual death (Wolman, 1966).

A radical decline in pain sensation, whether interpreted as conditioning or lack of self-cathexis, destroys the individual's ability to protect his own life.

Arieti (1955, p. 392) believes that the following four changes usually take place in the cardiovascular system of schizpohrenics: (1) a decrease in the size of the heart, (2) a decrease in the volume of blood flow, (3) a decrease in systematic blood pressure, and (4) an exaggerated tendency to vasoconstriction and a resulting diminished blood supply. Arieti believes that all these are psychosomatic products of schizophrenia.

Theories of Schizophrenia

Initially Freud related schizophrenia to an early repression of libido. However, in 1907 he shifted the emphasis from sexual traumata to more general concepts of libido development.

In 1908, Abraham hypothesized that schizophrenia was caused by a regression of libido from object relationship into the autoerotic stage. According to the Freud-Abraham timetable, mental disorders are a product of fixation and/or regression. More severe disorders are a product of earlier fixations.

"The psychosexual characteristics of dementia praecox is the return of the patient to autoeroticism, and the symptoms of this illness are a form of autoerotic activity," wrote Abraham in 1908. "The autoeroticism is the source not only of delusions of persecution but of megalomania" (Abraham, 1955, pp. 74-75. "The psychosexual constitution of dementia praecox is based, therefore, on an inhibition in development." It is "an abnormal fixation to an erotogenic zone – a typical autoerotic phenomenon" (ibid., p. 77). In dementia praecox "a person who has never passed out of the primary stage of his psychosexual development is thrown back more and more into the autoerotic stage as the disease progresses" (ibid., p. 78).

Freud (in 1911 and 1912) accepted Abraham's ideas regarding the pathogenesis of schizophrenia and saw in schizophrenia a struggle between the regression of libido and its withdrawal from object relations and its efforts to recapture or restore the object relations.

According to Freud, the way people go through developmental phases depends upon interactional patterns. Whether a child will pass safely through an oral or anal stage or remain fixated or regress eventually depends on the amount and quality of satisfaction and frustration received by the child in the *interaction* with his close environment. According to Freud, "owing to the general tendency to variation in biological processes it must necessarily happen that not all these preparatory phases will be passed through and completely outgrown with the same degree of success; some parts of the function will be permanently arrested." The development can be "disturbed and altered by current impressions from without" (Freud, 1949, pp. 297 ff.).

These "impressions from without" have been studied by H.S. Sullivan. Sullivan pointed to peculiarities in the personalities of parents of schizophrenics and related the origins of schizophrenia to a state of panic disastrous to the patient's self-esteem. Parent-child relationships that prevent the establishment of the "self-esteem," and especially panic states producing dissociation (the not-me feeling), have been perceived by Sullivan as causes of schizophrenia (Sullivan, 1947, 1953).

Several workers began to study the peculiar parent-child relationship. Whether these relationships caused schizophrenia as interpreted by a Freudian withdrawal of libido or Sullivanian dissociation or any other theory, the nature of these relationships became a major topic in research in schizophrenia.

Research workers failed to find any definite pathology in the parents of schizophrenics. One worker (Alanen, 1958) found 10% of the parents of schizophrenics to be disturbed and slightly over 5% of them schizophrenic. I have found (Wolman, 1957, 1961, 1964) about 40% of fathers and 50% of mothers of schizophrenics displaying a great variety of pathological conditions, but it was impossible to state that schizophrenia in offspring is caused by any particular mental type of parents.

Lidz and his associates (1957, 1968, 1960; Lidz, 1963, 1973) found a lack of mutual understanding and cooperation between the parents of schizophrenics.

> We realized soon, that the intrapsychic disturbances of the mothers were not nearly as relevant to what happened to one or more children in the family (especially to the child who became schizophrenic) as was the fact that these women were paired with husbands who would either acquiesce to the many irrational and bizarre notions of how the family should be run or who would constantly battle with and undermine an already anxious and insecure mother (Fleck, 1960, p. 335).

Similar findings have been reported by Wolman (1957, 1961), Lu (1961, 1962), and many others.

The reported data differ in detail, but they show an almost uniform pattern of interaction. Thus, a sociopsychological theory has been proposed that links all the data into one coherent system (Wolman, 1966, 1970, 1973).

Three types of social relationship, depending upon the objectives of the participants, have been distinguished. Whenever an individual enters a relationship with the objective of receiving, it is an *instrumental* type, for the partner or partners are used for the satisfaction of the individual's needs. The infant-mother relationship is the prototype of instrumentalism. The infant is weak, the mother is strong; the infant must receive, yet cannot give. Whenever an individual enters a relationship with the objective of satisfying his own needs and also the needs of others, it is *mutual* relationship. Friendship and marriage represent mutualism. Sexual intercourse is probably the prototype of mutualism. Whenever an individual's objective is to satisfy the needs of others, it is a *vectorial* relationship. Parenthood is the prototype of vectorialism; parents are strong, infants are weak; parents give love and support and protect their children.

Normal adults are capable of interacting in all three ways. In business they are instrumental; in friendship and marriage, mutual; and in parenthood and in their ideals, vectorial.

In normal families, parents are perceived by their children as strong and friendly adults who relate to each other in a *mutual*, give and get manner and have a *vectorial* attitude toward the child, irrespective of what the child may be or do. Parental love is unconditional; the smaller and weaker the child, the more vectorial the parental attitude.

The intrafamilial relationship that produces schizophrenia does not fall into the usual descriptive categories of rejection, overprotection, overindulgence, etc.

The schizogenic family relationship represents a *reversal of social positions* and, resultingly, causes in the mind of the child who will become schizophrenic a *confusion in social roles of age, sex, family position, etc.*

Mother confuses the child by presenting herself as a martyr. She appears to be strong, for she controls the entire family and imposes her will on all in the household. She does it in a protective-hostile manner with the child: she tells the child that he is weak, sick, stupid, or ugly and that she must protect him and do things for him. Yet she presents herself as a self-sacrificing, suffering, almost dying person.

She cannot tolerate any independence, any growth of the child, any success not brought about by mother. These mothers are possessive, control their children's lives, and demand from the child an unlimited love, gratitude, and self-sacrifice for the self-sacrificing tyrant-martyr mother (see Davis, 1961; Foudraine, 1961; Lu, 1961, 1962; Weakland, 1960; Wolman, 1961, 1965; and many others).

The future schizophrenic starts his life in the same way as any other child. He is helpless and depends upon aid from outside. His attitude is instrumental, as he depends upon "narcissistic supplies." Soon he cannot fail to realize that there is something wrong with his parents. The child lives under the threat of loss of his martyr-type mother and nonparticipant baby-father. All schizophrenics, as Sullivan amply observed (1953), are panic-stricken. The child begins to worry about his parents and takes on a premature and much too costly protective hypervectorial attitude toward them. In order to survive, he must protect his protectors. *Vectoriasis praecox* (the new name for schizophrenia) sometimes comes very early and uses up the child's mental resources (Wolman, 1957, 1958, 1959b, 1961, 1962, 1965).

Certainly no woman could destroy her child without the active or tacit approval of her husband, and all fathers of schizophrenics participate in the development of schizophrenia in offspring. The father-mother relationship causes the woman to demand from the child what she failed to get from her husband. When the "mutual" interparental relationship fails, chances are that mother will develop an instrumental, exploitative attitude toward the child.

The fathers trigger the tragic involvement. They expect the child to give them what they failed to get from their wives. Most of these fathers are seductive to children of both sexes, spreading confusion with regard to age and sex identification. Some of them fight against their own wives and children. Many schizophrenic families live under father's tyranny in terror.

Schizophrenia has been thus interpreted as an *escape for survival.* It is a process of downward adjustment in an irrational struggle to stay alive. The schizophrenic withdraws from social contacts, avoids emotional involvement, and regresses into a lower level of intellectual functioning, as if acting on in unconscious belief that this is the only way to survive.

## Symptomatological Issues

E. Bleuler's initial distinction between deteriorating and recovering cases gave rise to a division of schizophrenia into process and reactive types. Kant (1948) believed the malignant *process schizophrenia* to be characterized by a gradual decline in activity, dullness, autism, ideas of reference, and thought disturbances. Oscillation between excitement and stuporous depression, and periods of almost normal functioning alternating with states of confusion are characteristics of the benign *reactive schizophrenia.*

Chase and Silverman (1943) studied recovery rates in Metrazol and insulin shock therapy. Pyknic body type, acute onset, short duration of severe symptoms, premorbid good adjustment, and extrovert personality type have been related to a good prognosis. Asthenic body type, apathy, introversion, insidious onset of severe symptoms, dissociation, and awareness of personality disintegration, have been related to poor prognosis. The Metrazol and insulin shock therapies have produced satisfactory results in the good-prognostic cases only. Apparently all these cases belong to the reactive type.

Kantor, Wallner, and Winder (1953) mention that reactive schizophrenics have good premorbid adjustment, good physical health, adequate adjustment at home and in school, extroversion, no somatic delusions, etc. The process schizophrenics have a prolonged history of maladjustment, poor physical health, difficulties at home and in school, abnormal family relationships, insidious onset of psychosis, somatic delusions, etc. However, Rorschach tests administered to patients diagnosed as process and reactive schizophrenics failed to prove psychosis in most of the process schizophrenics. Thus, serious doubts have been voiced as to whether the so-called process schizophrenics are schizophrenics (Herron, 1962) and, if so, whether the distinction of two types is justified. King (1954) found, according to the above-mentioned Kantor *et al.,* that reactive schizophrenics reacted to mecholyl with a substantially greater drop in blood pressure than the process schizophrenics. Research conducted by Zuckerman and Gross (1959) contradicted King's findings.

Brackbill and Fine (1956) and many others hypothesized that the process schizophrenia is related to organic factors. No definite evidence has been adduced. Arieti (1955), Wolman (1957), and other workers did not find clear indications for a reactive versus process distinction. On the other hand, Herron (1962) has stated that it is possible to demonstrate differences between these two groups. Phillips (1953), Garmezy and Rodnick (1959), and others believed that such a distinction had some prognostic value; however, the premorbid history of each patient is determined to a great extent by his environment, and eventually Garmezy (1965) and Offord and Cross (1969) arrived at the conclusion that the process and reactive types represent two gradual levels rather than two distinct clinical types.

Division of symptoms related to ego strength has been proposed (Wolman, 1958, 1964). The *ego-protective* symptoms indicate the struggle of the ego to retain the control over the unconscious impulses. All "defense mechanisms" and varieties of neurotic symptoms belong to this category. The preschizophrenic has been called pseudoneurotic by Hoch and Polatin (1949); most probably he is a schizo-type neurotic before he becomes a schizophrenic psychotic. The main ego-protective symptom of this hypervectorial or preschizophrenic neurotic is the overmobilization of the ego, reflected in his constricted, introverted, high-strung, tense personality. The preschizophrenic neurotic is overconscientious, moralistic, and dogmatic. He often develops phobias, obsessive-compulsive behavior, and partial withdrawal from social contacts. All these *ego-protective* symptoms may postpone and even prevent psychotic breakdown.

Therefore, one can present schizophrenia and related disorders in a continuum using sociopsychological determinants as the uniting factor. According to the aforementioned sociopsychomatic theory, schizophrenia, in a broad sense of the word, starts with the peculiar disbalance of libido cathexes. Precocious object hypercathexis and resulting self-hypocathexis, or, in terms of overt social behavior, a precocious hypervectorialism, is the core of the group of schizothymic or hypervectorial disorders.

One may distinguish five *levels* of mental disorders; namely, neurosis, character neurosis, latent psychosis, manifest psychosis, and dementive stage. In hypervectorial or schizo-type disorders the neurotic step includes phobic, neurasthenic, and obsessive-compulsive patterns. The schizoid character neurosis corresponds to what is usually called the schizoid personality. The next step in schizophrenic deterioration is latent schizophrenia. Next comes manifest schizophrenia, called *vectoriasis praecox*. The manifest psychotic level may come in four syndromes; namely, the paranoid, catatonic, hebephrenic, and simple deterioration. The last, dementive level is the end of decline and a complete collapse of personality structure. All five levels represent an ever-growing disbalance of cathexes of sexual and hostile impulses. The decline of the controlling force of the ego is the most significant determinant of each level. As long as the ego exercises control, it is neurosis. When the ego comes to terms with the symptoms, it is character neurosis. When the ego is on the verge of collapse, it is latent psychosis. When the ego fails, it is manifest psychosis, or the full-blown schizophrenia in one of its four syndromes.

The first syndrome roughly corresponds to what has usually been described as *paranoid schizophrenia* and is characterized by the ego losing contact with reality and leaving it to the superego. In the second syndrome, the *catatonic*, the superego takes over control also of the motor apparatus. In the *hebephrenic* syndrome the ego yields to the id; the superego is defeated and the id takes over. In the *simple deterioration* syndrome there is a process of losing life itself.

## PHYSICOCHEMICAL TREATMENT TECHNIQUES*

The treatment of schizophrenia is no less enigmatic than the disorder itself. The same technique may produce favorable results in one case and fail lamentably in another. Even well trained and experienced practitioners cannot tell for sure whether they will be successful with a new schizophrenic patient, and every therapist can tell about unpredictable successes and failures. Sometimes poorly trained and inexperienced beginners can produce miracles, and in some instances schizophrenics considerably improve without being exposed to systematic treatment. Moreover, different techniques based on diametrically opposed theories may produce satisfactory results. Apparently, any therapeutic process is an interactional process, that is, a *psychosocial field*, and the prognosis seems to be considerably influenced by who interacts with whom and how.

## ECT AND ICT

Experts throughout the world seem to concur that the older methods of physical treatment (ECT and ICT) still have value in treating severely disturbed patients. Remy, in his article in the *Biological Treatment of Mental Illness* (1966), emphasizes ICT's long-lasting effects. Dramatic reversal in patients' behavior was also demonstrated with ICT by Dunlop (1966), particularly in patients who had made little progress with the psychotropic drugs.

The most important addition to ICT technique has been the introduction of Glucagon by Braun and Parker (1959), which was further developed by Dussik *et al.* (1961, 1966), and Ramirez *et al.* (1966), and others. Glucagon serves two functions: (1) it facilitates insulin-induced hypoglycemia, and (2) it is the most effective and simplest way to terminate a coma (this, however, is used only in rare cases).

Alexander (1953) emphasized that success with ICT depends upon adequate depth and duration of treatment. He believed that a full course of insulin therapy should include sixty deep comas and that the effect of ICT is enhanced by the periodic use of ECT.

ECT and ICT have taken a back seat to the antipsychotic drugs in the research literature, as the dearth of studies soon will show. Smith *et al.* (1967) compared the effects of ECT and chlorpromazine with chlorpromazine alone and discovered that the combination of the two treatments was more effective than the drug alone. Markowe *et al.* (1967) studied the effect of insulin shock and chlorpromazine on 100 previously untreated schizophrenics. A ten-year follow-up study revealed no difference between those treated with insulin shock and those given chlorpromazine: 25% of both groups remained psychotic, while 45% showed no or few symptoms. ICT was used on 24 male and 18 female schizophrenics over a five-year period (Felipa-Rejas *et al.*, 1968). The findings encourage early application of ICT to hebephrenics and catatonics. Psychotherapy and ergo-

---

*In the preparation of this part of the chapter, I was assisted by Ms. Linda Pasternak, Doctoral Candidate in Clinical Psychology, Long Island University.

therapy were also considered helpful. Two Belgian psychiatrists (Luyssaert and Pierloot, 1969) have reviewed the history of insulin therapy. These doctors believe that one of the most active principles in insulin shock treatment is regression, which enables the patient to be more open to psychotherapy. Weinstein and Fischer (1971), like Smith *et al.,* maintain that the real benefit of ECT is its dual synergism with antipsychotic drugs, particularly in lifting cases off plateaus and in consolidating the patient's gains and avoiding relapses.

### Psychosurgery

Despite the fact that lobotomy is an unpredictable method that causes irreversible results, psychosurgery seems to have returned to favor, and it is still occasionally in use. Vaernet and Madsen (1970) treated 12 persons who either had personality disorders or who were schizophrenic by bilateral stereotaxic electrocoagulation of the amygdala. In 11 of the subjects the surgery resulted in either the disappearance of or marked reduction in aggression. In 2 subjects with a history of self-mutilation, symptoms disappeared after an additional basofrontal tractotomy. Kelly *et al.* (1972) reported that varieties of psychosurgery produced improvement in 70% of 78 patients. The best short-term prognosis was with depression and anxiety, while 50% improvement was obtained with obsessional neurosis, schizophrenia, and personality disorders.

### Chemotherapy

Most antipsychotic drugs are shown to be more effective than placebos. Several studies have compared reserpine with chlorpromazine (Davis, 1965). Twelve of these studies showed chlorpromazine to be more effective than reserpine; the other 14 found the two drugs to be about equivalent in effect. No studies demonstrated reserpine to be more effective than chlorpromazine. In fact, in the carefully controlled V.A. study comparing reserpine to the widely used phenothiazines (Lasky, 1962), reserpine was shown to be less effective than the phenothiazines in reducing excitement withdrawal and agitated depression. The evidence indicates that the antipsychotic drugs produce improvement, but it is not clear whether the improvement is significant and lasting.

The NIMH Pharmacology Research Branch (1967, 1968) reported that two-thirds of phenothiazine-treated patients showed much improvement, while only one-fourth of placebo-treated patients were comparably improved. Half of the placebo patients were unchanged or worse, whereas only one-tenth of the phenothiazine patients had such poor results. The best effects are obtained when the drugs are taken consistently for a long enough period to allow them to achieve maximum effect. Data from the NIMH Collaborative Study II (1968) indicate that patients make gains from the beginning of treatment to 26 weeks.

Several studies show that when phenothiazines are withdrawn, psychotic symptomatology re-emerges (Freeman, 1962; Clark *et al.*, 1967; Majerrison *et al,* 1964; and others). In addition, such symptoms as nausea, vomiting, increased sebaceous secretion, tension, restlessness, and physical complaints occur

(Simpson *et al.*, 1965). Simpson *et al.* have suggested that some of the side effects may also be attributed to withdrawal from anti-Parkinsonian medication which is often given in conjunction with phenothiazines.

One issue which clinicians are debating is whether a combination of drugs is better than a single psychotropic drug. Michaux, Kurland, and Agallianos (1966) compared various drug combinations and found that no combination of drugs showed superiority to chlorpromazine alone. Chlorpromazine seems most effective in dealing with the core symptoms of schizophrenia, especially in the reduction of schizophrenic disorganization.

Trifluoperazine and chlorpromazine were found to be equal to insulin coma therapy. Chlorpromazine was found to be equal to or more effective than ECT. Experience suggests that combining ECT with antipsychotic drugs can be useful. Also sociopsychological therapies in combination with drug treatment seem to be highly effective in facilitating return to the community for chronic patients (Greenblatt, 1965).

The NIMH Collaborative Studies I and II (1967, 1968) found that certain phenothiazines were better predictors of successful treatment of specific disorders than others. Bellak and Loeb (1969) maintain that the difference between a specific phenothiazine and a nonspecific one is as great as the difference between phenothiazine therapy and a placebo.

Some psychiatrists believe that the phenothiazines are merely sedatives and that they dull the patients' sensibilities.

The antipsychotic drugs probably have a beneficial effect on schizophrenic thought. The NIMH Psychopharmacological Study (1968) showed that there was marked improvement (with a high I.Q. group) in the patients' ability to abstract with a concomitant decrease in the amount of concrete thinking, and that the patients did not evidence as much bizarre, circumstantial, and inappropriate responses as before treatment. There is evidence that phenothiazines reduce schizophrenic thought disorders.

Comparing phenothiazines with barbiturates, Irwin (1966) found that the phenothiazines decrease motor activity, exploratory behavior, and responses to environmental stimuli; barbiturates tend to increase motor activity, exploratory behavior, and responses to environmental stimuli, and to act as disinhibiting agents.

Stupenchenko (1969) compared the effect of psychotropic drugs on schizophrenics with hereditary involvement and those whose condition was more easily attributable to exogenous factors. He discovered that the psychotropic drugs are more effective with those schizophrenics in whom heredity plays a part and least effective with catatonics.

Prien *et al.* (1971) tried to identify which sub-groups of schizophrenics had a sufficiently low probability of relapse to warrant discontinuation of medication. Relapse was found to be linked to the dosage of medication the patient received before being put on placebo (the higher the dosage the higher the probability of relapse). Results suggest that the large majority of schizophrenics who have been hospitalized for more than 15 years and are receiving low dosages can remain off drugs for six months without serious side effects.

Polak and Laycob (1972) described the treatment of acute schizophrenics in which patients were rapidly tranquilized by titrating dosages until they reached a tranquilized end point within six hours. The dosage was adjusted daily and chemotherapy was integrated with intensive social systems intervention centered on the patient's real life setting.

The NIMH Study (1968) compared high dosage and low dosage treatments using chlorpromazine. The study indicated that high dosage produced significantly more side effects and was significantly more effecitve with patients under 40 who had been hospitalized for less than 10 years. Chlorpromazine has been shown to raise serum cholesterol levels consistently and significantly. Prior to therapy with chlorpromazine, cholesterol seemed inversely related to symptoms of pathology. Following therapy, however, there appeared to be no relationship between cholesterol level and behavior. Goldberg et al. (1970) evaluated prolixin and found that prolixin enanthate is significantly superior to oral phenothiazine in drug reluctant patients, particularly in paranoid cases and those living at home who would otherwise require hospitalization. Trifluoperazine and trifluperidol were compared by Schiele et al. (1969). The comparison indicated that subjects treated with trifluoperazine showed greater improvement and fewer side effects than those treated with trifluperidol.

Two psychotropic drugs have received more attention than others, namely haloperidol and fluphenazine, from which prolixin is derived. Towler and Wick (1967) treated 59 patients with haloperidol. Of this number 45 improved but 26 required further treatment. Chronic schizophrenics with paranoid reactions showed the most significant response. Side effects occurred in one-third of the patients, but they were easily controlled. Lucky and Schiele (1967) compared the effects of haloperidol and trifluoperazine using 26 schizophrenic patients, 13 of whom took both drugs. Of the 13, only 9 completed the three-month trial. According to the authors, only 2 of the patients improved with haloperidol. There was a high incidence of extrapyramidal reactions, development of weakness, drowsiness, and depression which necessitated withdrawing haloperidol from three subjects. It was posited that the drug may be useful for chronic paranoids.

Studies dealing with fluphenazine seem to agree that the drug is most effective for chronic schizophrenic patients. Lowther (1969) concluded that fluphenazine is quite effective for maintenance therapy with chronic patients. DeAlarcon and Carney (1969) found that with slow-release intramuscular fluphenazine injections, 16 patients suffered severe depressive episodes. In five cases, the drug was thought to be responsible for suicide. The authors recommended that patients on fluphenazine be carefully supervised. The research of Itil et al., (1971) on the effect of fluphenazine on the full-night sleep process of 11 chronic schizophrenics suggests that the length of REM periods and the number of REM cycles increased significantly during fluphenazine treatment. When subjects were divided into therapy resistant and therapy responsive groups, responsive patients were found to have an augmentation of awakening states which may imply that the improvement obtained with fluphenazine may be related to its "stimulatory" effect.

Some new phenothiazine derivatives as well as other antipsychotic drugs have come to the fore. Butaperazine (NIMH, 1967), corphenazine (Havenson, 1967), metronidazole (Holden et al., 1968), thiothixene (Sterlin et al., 1970), and mepiprazol (Goncalves, 1972) seem to produce significant changes in patients, particularly chronic ones. Other recent drugs such as oxypertine and lyogen are in more experimental stages and have stirred some controversy. SKF 16336 seems comparable to chlorpromazine in eradicating schizophrenic thought disorder, but it is less potent (DeVito et al., 1969). It is considered to be more effective in combating the depressive mood disorders of schizo-affective schizophrenics. Chanoit et al. (1969) treated 102 schizophrenics with thioproperazine and have indicated that it is highly effective with hebephrenics and young patients with short hospitalizations. Seventy percent of the chronic patients were judged improved. Ezhkov (1968) used triperidol in the treatment of 84 schizophrenic patients. He noted that in small doses triperidol was a stimulant, in higher doses a sedative. Ezhkov recommended it for (1) nuclear schizophrenics with polymorphic symptomatology, (2) simple and nuclear paranoid schizophrenics, (3) the termination of manic states, and (4) the treatment of periodic schizophrenia.

It should be mentioned that the antipsychotic drugs often produce adverse side effects. These side effects are relatively mild, however, and frequently "adapt out" with continued drug treatment. There seems to be some controversy as to which drug produces the most severe side effects (V.A. Cooperative Study, 1960; Adelson and Epstein, 1962; Lasky et al., 1962), but no conclusive evidence has turned up to prove any significant differences.

## PSYCHOTHERAPY

The aim of any psychotherapy is to cure the patient. I have suggested four criteria for considering a case cured: (1) reasonably realistic perception of oneself and others (cognitive functions), (2) emotional responses appropriate to the stimuli (emotional balance), (3) ability to relate to other people, and (4) achievements commensurate with one's innate abilities and external opportunities.

Classic psychoanalysis is not the choice treatment of schizophrenia. The reclining position and the psychoanalyst's spare comments are likely to increase anxiety in the patient and facilitate regression. Even Freudians, such as Bychowski (1952), Brody and Redlich (1952), Eissler (1947, 1952), Federn (1952), Knight (1953), Rosen (1947, 1953), and Wolman (1959a) deviate from Freud's techniques when they treat schizophrenics. Thus the gulf between Freudians and non-Freudians like Sullivan (1947, 1962), Fromm-Reichmann (1950, 1952, 1959), and Arieti (1955) has been reduced. Today, both groups emphasize face-to-face relations as essential for a successful treatment.

Melanie Klein and her school interpret unconscious processes in treating schizophrenia (Pichon-Riviere, 1952; Rosenfeld, 1953; Winnicot, 1955). But Eissler (1952, p. 143), in discussing Rosen's direct interpretation, says that "another set of interpretations might have achieved a similar result." An evaluation of Rosen's methods did not prove that his interpretations were specifically helpful (English, 1961).

The fact that poorly trained and even untrained individuals have been successful in treating schizophrenia while some prominent psychotherapists, among them psychoanalysts have failed, sheds bright light on the problem. An orthodox psychoanalyst may give the impression of being impersonal and not interested, and his silence may be regarded by the schizophrenic as a sign of hostility.

But when a kind, friendly person shows interest in a schizophrenic and displays a profound desire to help him, this is a giving, vectorial attitude that helps the patient improve the balance of libido cathexes. A visit by an old friend who comes to the hospital and shows consideration and affection may do miracles and cause remission (cf. Bleuler, 1919). The fact that Freudian, Adlerian, Jungian, Sullivanian, and Horneyan psychotherapists can be successful in the treatment of schizophrenia indicates that differences between their theories are *insignificant* for the treatment. What is significant is common to all successful therapists, whatever their theoretical differences and irrespective of the method of their interpretations. Federn relied mostly on environmental help, Rosen applied "direct" interpretation of the unconscious, Fromm-Reichmann avoided interpretation, and Schwing mothered the patients. Yet, despite the highly diverse theoretical assumptions and notwithstanding the differences in the techniques and personalities of the therapists, the *interaction was basically the same in all known cases of successful treatment of schizophrenia.* In all these cases the therapist was perceived as a *strong* and *friendly* person, and his attitude was one of a *genuine vectorialism.*

A few excerpts from the writings of successful psychotherapists will illustrate this point. One may agree or disagree, for instance, with Schwing's interpretations of what was going on in the minds of her patients. But it is an undeniable fact that she has been a devoted, giving person. One cannot read her book without being moved by the humanitarian approach to her patients, as described below:

> I went to the patient. She was lying there with a burning face, swollen eyes, and parched lips . . . . The nurse interrupted me and warned: "You must not open the lattice, or in five minutes you and the rest of us will be killed!" . . . I felt unsure of myself. Could I influence a patient who should only rage or turn completely away from the world? . . . "I am sad," I said gently, "but nevertheless I will try to be very near you." . . . I obtained a chair and placed it close to the bed. I inquired sympathetically if the strait-jacket made her hot and uncomfortable and if she were not miserable lying that way. I suggested that perhaps she would like something to drink . . . . "There is much sadness in you!" I continued, "I would like

to be able to help you, may I try?" Two big tears indicated that her armor of negativism had been pierced . . . (Schwing, 1954, pp. 34–35).

A kind, giving, vectorial attitude also permeated K.R. Eissler's work with schizophrenics (Eissler, 1952). To Eissler the patient's disorder was a challenge that the therapist had to master. The patient must feel how important he is to the omnipotent and benevolent therapist.

A similar approach was applied by Arieti. Arieti wrote, "At the very beginning of treatment, when the patient's suspiciousness and distrust are very pronounced, he should leave the session with the feeling that he has been given something, not with the feeling that something, even diagnostic information, has been taken from him. The patient must feel that a benevolent, sincere effort is being made to reach him with no demand being made on him" (Arieti, 1955, p. 439).

It is easier to be the all-giving parent for a short while than to continue giving. The psychotherapist, being human himself, can only keep giving up to the point at which his own emotional resources begin to dwindle. While the therapist's personality will be discussed later, it is worthwhile to mention here that psychotherapy with schizophrenics is a serious drain on the psychotherapist's emotional resources. Hill noticed the danger of regression in the psychotherapist himself. "It is not likely that the regression will go so far as to suggest schizophrenia, but it is most likely that it will frequently extend to the level at which the physician finds himself acting in a childish fashion, indulging in wish-fulfillment and in efforts to dominate. He finds himself resenting helplessness, responding with anger and guilt and with all sorts of defenses against these unpleasant states" (Hill, 1955, p. 193). The therapist is likely to try to escape these feelings "by a resort to the defense of omnipotent fantasy."

In a review of psychotherapeutic techniques, Redlich (Brody and Redlich, 1952, p. 30) stated that there was a very broad similarity between the new psychoanalytic techniques as developed by Eissler (1947), Federn (1952), Ferenczi (1926), Fromm-Reichmann (1950), Knight (1946), and Schwing (1954) and "the eternal common-sense methods of love and patience. However, no generally accepted theory accounts for the vast differences of approach in the psychotherapeutic process with schizophrenics, varying from rather different, ego-supporting approaches to the direct id interpretations, from rigorous manipulation of the patient to marked passivity of the therapist."

Such a general theory is here proposed. My theoretical frame of reference is a modified Freudian model. Sullivan's emphasis on interpersonal relations has been invaluable, and the need to include interindividual relations dictated some modifications in Freud's theory. A new theoretical construct, "interindividual cathexis," revises Freud's pleasure and pain theory, and a new interpretation of the role of hate and destructive impulses in mental disorders is offered.

Interaction patterns are divided into instrumental (take), mutual (give and take), and vectorial (give) types of interaction. In normal families, the relationship of parent-to-parent is mutual, parent-to-child vectorial, and child-to-parent instrumental.

In families with schizophrenic offspring, the parent-parent relationship is hostile-instrumental; the mother's attitude toward the child is pseudo-vectorial, but actually exploitative-instrumental; and the father-child relationship is frankly instrumental, in a seductive or competitive fashion. The preschizophrenic child is forced to hypercathect his libido in his parents instead of having his parents worry about him. The reversal of social roles turns the child into a "protector of his protectors."

These abnormal interactional patterns represent a dysbalance in interindividual cathexes. A child, normally a "taker" (instrumental), is forced into precocious giving (hypervectorial). Hence, *vectoriasis praecox* is the proposed name for schizophrenia.

The normal reaction of a child to this emotional extortion should be hatred. But the avenues of hate are blocked. Mother convinces the child that she protects him, and the child begins to hate himself for having hostile feelings toward his self-sacrificing mother.

Schizophrenia develops as a paradoxical reaction of an organism that abandons its own protection to protect those who should protect it. The dysbalance of interindividual cathexes leads to a severe dysbalance in intraindividual cathexes of libido and destrudo.

These psychological changes affect the nervous system, endocrine, and other organic processes. Somatic symptoms of schizophrenia are psychosomatic (Arieti, 1955).

The main aim of the interactional psychotherapy process is the reversal of libido cathexes with a resultant reorganization of personality structure. Many psychotherapists who otherwise differ from each other have *a vectorial, unconditionally giving attitude. It is a helping, giving attitude irrespective of the friendly or hostile reactions of the one who receives (just as good parents love good and bad children alike).*

This is more than "common-sense love and patience." A successful psychotherapy is a distinct interactional pattern aiming at the restoration of an intraindividual balance of cathexes and a realistic perception of life. A detailed description of the interactional rules follows.

## Rules of Therapeutic Interaction

1. The first rule is *unconditional support,* protecting the patient's self-esteem by siding with him, by accepting him as an individual, by treating him in a dignified and respectful manner. A genuinely friendly attitude and atmosphere are a *conditio sine qua non.* The therapist must encourage adult (never regressive) pleasure procuring activities. An unreserved yet rational support is necessary to counteract the process of regression and downward adjustment.

2. The second rule is *ego-therapy*. The main aim of interactional psycho-therapy is to strengthen the patient's ego. In neurosis the ego is struggling against undue pressures from within; the *ego-protective*, neurotic symptoms bear witness to the struggle. In psychosis the ego has lost the battle and psychotic, *ego-deficiency* symptoms develop, such as loss of reality testing (delusions and hallucinations), loss of control over unconscious impulses, deterioration of motor coordination, etc.

Ego-therapy means the strengthening and reestablishment of the defeated ego. Thus, the therapist must never become part of the irrational transactions of the psychotic mind, be they delusions, hallucinations, or anything else. He must never offer support to erroneous perceptions of reality, and he must not interpret unconscious motivation processes if this interpretation may weaken the patient's ego.

Control of instinctual impulses is one of the most severe issues in schizophrenia. A catatonic patient in remission described this inner struggle: "I want to be strong to be able to control myself and here I am again doing terrible things."

A gifted latent schizophrenic woman said once: "I can't do what I want to do. I feel like expressing my feelings with quick motions of the brush over the canvas, but something holds me back and I paint silly little houses that I detest. I would like to let myself go in non-objective art, but something tells me it must be a composition, a plan. Maybe I am afraid to let myself go, for I may do something wrong. So I sit for hours, as if paralyzed, afraid to move . . . "

Inability to make decisions and restraint of motor freedom are typical for the schizophrenic. This conflict between the desire to "let go" and the fear of one's own impulses may, in some cases, lead to catatonic mutism and stupor. One could not therefore encourage the young painter to follow her need for a free expression, for it would have inevitably led to a panic state and perhaps even to a catatonic episode. Nor would it be wise to encourage self-restraint that would produce an unbearable tension. Thus, the best method was to foster self-esteem; with her increasing self-confidence the painter was less afraid to express her feelings on canvas. She began to believe in herself, despite her past experiences.

3. *"One step up"* is the third rule. It implies support of less dangerous symptoms against more dangerous ones, never forgetting that the ultimate goal is to strengthen the patient's ego. When the patient seems to be giving up life, even simple pleasures should be used a a lure.

Schizophrenia is a regression for survival. The psychotherapeutic vectorial interaction makes it unnecessary to lose mind in order to survive. It calls the patient back to life, to growth, to joy, to normal self-protection and self-esteem.

4. The fourth rule is *pragmatic flexibility of interaction*. When the failing ego is unable to control outbursts of unconscious impulses, the patient's moralistic superego must be supported instead. In hebephrenia, the ego has lost the battle to the id; thus, it may be advisable to strengthen the super-ego in order to prevent further deterioration. The therapist may, therefore, take a stern and demanding attitude and support whatever moral or religious convictions the patient has. When the failing ego cannot control incestuous or homosexual or destructive

impulses, the therapist may decide that he must, so to speak, "take over" and check the flood. It is, however, a temporary device for the supremacy of the ego and not of the superego is the therapeutic objective.

5. The fifth rule is *individualization.* I have supervised psychotherapists for many years, and quite often a young therapist has asked me:

"And what would *you* have done in this case?" My answer is always the same: "Psychotherapy is an interaction and depends upon the two interacting individuals. There are rules, but each therapist applies them differently depending upon who is the *therapist* and who is the *patient.* Your job is to understand *your* patient. He is not the same, even if he seems to be, as any of the 'cases' described by the masters. In fact, he is not a 'case' at all. He is a definite individual, an unhappy and disturbed human being. Try to understand him, and at the same time try to understand yourself. Your patient is a withdrawn, or an irritable, or hallucinating, or a hostile individual. Can you take that? Can you face that much of an emotional demand? Please don't try to be what you are not. You cannot treat him the way Sullivan, or Fromm-Reichmann, or Schwing, or Rosen did. But if you understand your patient, and are aware of *your* limitations and resources, and are genuinely interested in the patient, the chances are that you will be a successful psychiatrist."

6. The sixth rule is *reality testing.* The problem of interpretation and insight cannot be answered by a flat "yes" or "no."

For example, a 30-year-old paranoid patient told me once that his beloved girlfriend, who lived 1000 miles away, had disguised herself and came to a restaurant as a waitress. He blamed himself for not chasing her; he felt she must be angry with him for he had deserted her. But in the evening she had returned to the restaurant; this time her hair was dyed so that he would not recognize her. The patient wanted to approach her, but she disappeared.

The patient said he expected me to "side with him" or he would be "through" with treatment. It was obvious that disagreement would have been perceived by the patient as rejection and would have caused further deterioration and possibly an outburst of violence. Yet an acceptance of the patient's delusion could have served no therapeutic purpose.

I started to test reality with the help of the patient. I asked him about his girlfriend. He told me that she had married two years before and was living in the south, about 1000 miles away from New York. His sister had written him that the young lady had recently had a baby. Gradually the patient himself began to doubt whether the two waitresses were one person. The patient remarked, "How could she work in a restaurant if she has a baby? But it was a striking similarity, wasn't it, doc?" At this point I felt that there was a good opportunity to strengthen his reality testing. I admitted that some people strikingly resemble others and all of us may err. My comment was welcome and the patient smiled with obvious relief. He said, "So, after all, I am not completely crazy. This girl looked exactly like my girlfriend. It was just a little mistake."

In the past the patient had had visual and auditory hallucinations. He was often ridiculed, ostracized, and insulted. His parents had never missed an opportunity to call him crazy or a lunatic. An overt disapproval of his delusions and hallucinations, and even efforts to undermine them by rational reasoning were doomed to failure. A too early interpretation might have caused, in this case, deeper regression and withdrawal.

A realistic attitude on the part of the therapist helps the patient to keep contact with reality. One patient I had, insisted on his "right" to call my home whenever he pleased, at any time of the day or night, whenever he felt upset. I told him that if he did that, I would discontinue my work with him. He accused me of being selfish and inconsiderate. I calmly replied that I needed rest and sleep; otherwise I would not be able to help anyone. If someone asks more than I can do, I must refuse.

7. The seventh rule is *parsimony of interpretation.* The question is not whether to interpret but *when, how,* and *how much.* I give priority to certain types of unconscious material, namely to those that threaten to disrupt the functioning of the ego. A profound guilt feeling is often the most urgent issue and must be interpreted. If such an interpretation alleviates guilt feelings and reduces suicidal tendencies, it is a sound therapeutic step.

I have, as a rule, avoided interpretations unless firmly convinced of their therapeutic usefulness at a given moment. In some cases the last phase of psychotherapy was conducted on more or less psychoanalytic lines, bringing deep insights through interpretation of unconscious phenomena. In most cases interpretations were given by the patients themselves.

8. The eighth rule is *realistic management of transference.* In his deep transference the schizophrenic expects love, forgiveness, and care from the therapist. Many schizophrenic patients wish to be fed, dressed, supported, and taken care of by the therapist, who represents the dream-parent. Some patients develop an infantile, symbiotic attachment and call the therapist at any time of day or night, just as a baby would call its mother. Most patients develop powerful hetero- or homosexual desires toward their therapists, reflecting incestuous involvement with their parents, and try to act on them here and now. To accept the patient on his terms means to share his psychosis, but to reject him may cause further aggravation and regression.

The maintaining of a *vectorial professional attitude* is a *conditio sine qua non* for a successful treatment. The eventual emotional maturity of the patient will make future protection and guidance superfluous. Psychotherapy is an interaction that aims at being terminated. Once a satisfactory level of cure is attained, the doctor-patient relationship must be dissolved.

A thorough cure is impossible without a resolution of the oedipal entanglements, but this must be postponed until the patient's ego has gained adequate strength. In some cases, this ideal solution may be unattainable, and it may be advisable not to analyze the incestuous impulses but rather to repress them. In many cases it may not be advisable to analyze transference at all. The strength of the patient's ego is the chief determinant of how far one may go in interpretation.

9. The ninth rule requires a firm *control of counter-transference.* Any transgression of the vectorial attitude on the part of the therapist is a violation of professional ethics. The therapist must like the patient, but this libido cathexis must be vectorial and aim-inhibited. The therapist's love for the patient must be de-sexualized, and he must never ask anything of the patient except the agreed-upon fee.

Any intimacy between doctor and patient is a severe violation of professional ethics and of the psychotherapeutic interaction. It may confuse the patient and bring back memories of inecestuous parents who, instead of caring for the child, demanded the child's love.

10. The tenth rule calls for *rational handling of hostility.* A patient's acting-out of hostile impulses may be catastrophic to his environment, as well as damaging to his weak ego. Thus, violence must be banned, repressed, and kept under iron control. When patients describe their fights, I do not condemn them, for this would increase their guilt feelings and weaken their egos. But permissiveness on my part would be even more harmful. Whenever the superego has lost control, permissiveness would mean an invitation to license, freedom to the id, and further deterioration of the ego.

### The Concept of Cure

The therapist's ideas concerning cure may adversely affect his therapeutic judgment and his work. Ideally, one should bring one's patients to a state of balanced behavior as described in the first chapter of this handbook. Specifically, this implies adequate cognitive functioning, emotional balance, social adjustment, and achievements commensurate to one's abilities and environmental possibilities.

Such an ideal solution is rarely possible. No human being lives in a vacuum, and a "cured" schizophrenic has to cope with more hardships than a person who never was a schizophrenic. In cases of hospitalization, the return to open society may be traumatic; but even an ambulatory schizophrenic faces a social environment which may harbor prejudice against him and is quite often alienated by his former bizarre behavior. Moreover, the emotional scars may heal reasonably well, but they can rarely, if ever, completely disappear.

Over-ambitious therapists may expect the impossible. I have had an opportunity to see patients discharged from hospitals and/or from private practice who pretended to be more healthy than they really were, just in order not to disappoint their doctors. Some of them continued for a while to function in open society, until overwhelming anxieties caused a second or third psychotic breakdown. Relapses occur not only in post-shock cases but also after prolonged psychotherapeutic treatment, and certainly it is most frequent following chemotherapy.

My policy has been one of cautious empiricism according to the previously described principle of "one step up." When I deal with a catatonic schizophrenic or any other form of manifest schizophrenia, I am often satisfied if I can bring the patient to the state of a schizoid character neurosis. Quite often, any further work would be detrimental to the patient's health. An effort to reconstruct a poorly built house may end up in a total collapse, and on several occasions I have treated patients who were thrown into abysmal psychotic states by too-ambitious colleagues.

I once had a case of an hallucinating, suicidal, paranoid schizophrenic who intented to murder her boyfriend, her sister, and everyone else. It took a great deal of work to bring her to a state of schizoid character neurosis. In this state her hostility was channeled into bigotry (she is an ardent church-goer); she hates Protestants, Jews, and almost everyone else, but she holds a good job and gets along reasonably well in her home environment.

Whenever I discharge a post-schizophrenic patient, I use the following figure of speech. "Suppose you had a broken leg. We fixed it, and now you can walk around and do whatever you please. I would not advise, however, that you take part in the Olympics — in other words, avoid too much emotional challenge. On rainy and stormy days you may feel some pain; please call me and come in for a check-up. I believe you will never need a second surgery — that is, prolonged psychotherapy — but an occasional check-up is advisable. Even though things go well for you, please call me once in a while.

## REFERENCES

Abraham, K. *Selected papers on psychoanalysis.* New York: Basic Books, 1955.

Alanen, Y.O. The mothers of schizophrenic patients. *Acta Psychiatrica et Neurologica Scandinavia.* **33**, Supp. 724, (1958).

Alexander, L. *Treatment of mental disorder.* Philadelphia: Saunders, 1953.

Altshuler, K.Z. Genetic elements in schizophrenia. *Eugenics Quarterly.* **4**: 92–98 (1957).

Aprison, M.H. and Drew, A.L. N, N-Dimethyl phenylenediamine oxidation by serum from schizophrenic children. *Science.* **127**: 57–58 (1958).

Arieti, S. *Interpretation of schizophrenia.* New York: Brunner, 1955.

Becket, P.G.S., Senf, R., Frohman, C.E. and Gottlieb, S. Energy production and premorbid history in schizophrenia. *Archives of General Psychiatry.* **8** (2): 155–162 (1963).

Bellak, L. and Loeb, L. *The schizophrenic syndrome.* New York: Grune & Stratton, 1969.

Bender, L. Schizophrenia in childhood: Its recognition, description, and treatment. *American Journal of Orthopsychiatry.* **26**: 499–506 (1956).

Bergman, P. and Escalona, S.K.   Unusual sensitivities in very young children. *The Psychoanalytic Study of the Child.* **3-4**: 333-352 (1949).

Bishop, M.P.   Effects of plasma from schizophrenic subjects upon learning and retention in the rat. In: Heath, R.G. (Ed.), *Serological fractions in schizophrenia.* New York: Harper & Row, 1963.

Bleuler, E.   *Das autistisch-undisziplinierte Denken in der Medizin und seine Uberwindung.* Berlin: Springer, 1919.

Bleuler, E.   *Dementia praecox or the group of schizophrenias.* New York: International Universities Press, 1950.

Bleuler, M.   *Endokrinologische Psychiatrie.* Stuttgart: Thieme, 1954.

Böök, J.A.   Genetical aspects of schizophrenic psychoses. In: Jackson, D.D. (Ed.), *The etiology of schizophrenia.* New York: Basic Books, 1960.

Brackbill, G. and Fine, H.   Schizophrenia and central nervous system pathology. *Journal of Abnormal and Social Psychology.* **52**: 310-313 (1956).

Brambilla, F., *et al.*   Endocrinology in chronic schizophrenia. *Diseases of the Nervous System.* **28** (11): 745-748 (1967).

Braun, M. and Parker, M.   The use of Glucagon in the termination of therapeutic insulin coma. *American Journal of Psychiatry.* **115**: 814-820 (1959).

Brody, E.B. and Redlich, F.C. (Eds.)   *Psychotherapy with schizophrenics: A symposium.* New York: International Universities Press, 1952.

Buck, C.W., *et al.*   Temperature regulation in schizophrenia. *American Medical Association Archives in Neurology and Psychiatry.* **64**: 828-842 (1950).

Bychowski, G.   *Psychotherapy of psychosis.* New York: Grune & Stratton, 1952.

Bykov, K.   *The cerebral cortex and the inner organs.* New York: Chemical Publishing, 1957.

Chanoit, P., *et al.*   L'utilisation de la thiopropérazine dans la schizophrenie. *Encephale.* **58** (2): 112-157 (1969).

Charcot, J.M.   *Leçons sur les maladies sur le système nerveux,* 2 vols. Paris: 1887-1888.

Chase, L.S. and Silverman, S.   Prognosis in schizophrenia. *Journal of Nervous and Mental Diseases.* **98**: 464-473 (1943).

Clark, M.L., *et al.*   Chlorpromazine in women with chronic schizophrenia: The effect on cholesterol levels and cholesterol on behavior. *Psychosomatic Medicine.* **29** (6): 634-642 (1967).

Davidson, J.N.   *The biochemistry of the nucleic acids.* New York. Wiley, 1960.

Davis, D.R.   The family triangle in schizophrenia. *British Journal of Medical Psychology.* **34**: 53-63 (1965).

De Vito, R.A., *et al.*   SKF 16336 versus schizophrenia. *Diseases of the Nervous System.* **30**: (6): 405-406 (1969).

Doust, J.W.I.   Spectroscopic and photoelectric oximetry in schizophrenia and other psychiatric states. *Journal of Mental Science.* **98**: 143-160 (1952).

Dunlop, E.   Concomitant use of insulin therapy and pharmacology. In: Rinkel, M. (Ed.), *Biological treatment of mental illness,* pp. 800-807. New York: Farrar, Straus & Giroux, 1966.

Dussik, K.T., *et al.* Increased control of insulin coma by prior administration of Glucagon: A preliminary communication. *American Journal of Psychiatry.* **118**: (July): 66-69 (1961).

Dussik,K.T., *et al.* Serial Glucagon tests in schizophrenics. In: Rinkel, M. (Ed.), *Biological treatment of mental illness,* pp. 837–847. New York: Farrar, Strauss & Giroux, 1966.

Eisenberg, L. The fathers of autistic children. *American Journal of Orthopsychiatry.* 27: 715–724 (1957).

Eissler, K.R. Dementia praecox therapy – psychiatric ward management of the acute schizophrenic patient. *Journal of Nervous and Mental Diseases.* 105: 397–402 (1947).

Eissler, K.R. Remarks on the psychoanalysis of schizophrenia. In: Brody, E.B. and Redlich, F.C. (Eds.), *Psychotherapy with schizophrenics.* New York: International Universities Press, 1952.

English, O.S., *et al. Direct analysis and schizophrenia.* New York: Grune & Stratton, 1961.

Ezhkov, A.A. The treatment of schizophrenia with Triperidol. *Zhurnal Neuropatologii i Psikhiatrii.* 68 (9): 1394–1400 (1968).

Federn, P. *Ego psychology and the psychoses.* New York: Basic Books, 1952.

Felipa-Rejas, E., *et al.* La cure d'insuline: Evaluation d'une technique psychothérapique. *Annales Medico-Psychologiques.* 2 (5): 647–663 (1968).

Ferenczi, S. *Further contributions to the theory and technique of psychoanalysis.* London: Hogarth Press, 1926.

Fish, B. Longitudinal observations of biological deviations in the schizophrenic infant. *American Journal of Psychiatry.* 116: 25–31 (1959).

Fleck, S. Family dynamics and origin of schizophrenia. *Psychosomatic Medicine.* 22: 333–344 (1960).

Foudraine, J. Schizophrenia and the family: A survey of the literature 1956-1960 on the etiology of schizophrenia. *Acta Psychotherapeutica et Psychosomatica.* 9: 82–110 (1961).

Fourbye, A., *et al.* Failure to detect 3, 4-dimethoxyphenylethylamine in the urine of psychotic children. *Acta Psychiatrica Scandinavia.* 42, Supp. 191. (1966).

Freeman, H. Physiological studies. In: Bellak, L. (Ed.), *Schizophrenia: A review of the syndrome.* New York: Logos, 1958.

Freeman, P. Treatment of chronic schizophrenia in a day center. *Archives of General Psychiatry.* 7: 259–265 (1962).

Freud, S. *An outline of psychoanalysis.* New York: Norton, 1949.

Fromm-Reichmann, F. *Principles of intensive psychotherapy.* Chicago: University of Chicago Press, 1950.

Fromm-Reichmann, F. Some aspects of psychoanalytic psychotherapy with schizophrenics. In: Brody, E.B. and Redlich, F.C. (Eds.), *Psychotherapy with schizophrenics.* New York: International Universities Press, 1952.

Fromm-Reichmann, F. *Psychoanalysis and psychotherapy.* Chicago: University of Chicago Press, 1959.

Gantt, W.H. *Physiological basis of psychiatry.* Springfield, Illinois: Charles C. Thomas, 1958.

Garmezy, N. Process and reactive schizophrenia: Some conceptions and issues. In: Katz, M.M. *et al.* (Eds.), *Classifications in psychiatry and psychopathology.* Washington, D.C.: U.S. Government Printing Office, 1965.

Garmezy, N., and Rodnick, E.H.   Premorbid adjustment and performance in schizophrenia.   *Journal of Nervous and Mental Diseases.*   **129**:   450–466 (1959).

Garrone, G.   Statistical genetic study of schizophrenia in the Geneva population between 1901–1950.   *Journal of Genetic Psychology.*   89–219 (1962).

German, G.A.   Effects of serum from schizophrenics on evoked cortical potential in the rat.   *British Journal of Psychiatry.*   1,09:   616–623 (1963).

Goldberg, S.C., *et al.*   A clinical evaluation of prolixin enanthate.   *Psychosomatics.*   **11**   (3):   173–177 (1970).

Goldfarb, W.   *Childhood schizophrenia.*   Cambridge, Mass.:   Harvard University Press, 1961.

Goncalves, N.   Clinical effects of mepiprazol on hospitalized chronic schizophrenics.   *Psychopharmacologia.*   **25** (3):   281–290 (1972).

Greenblatt, M.   (Ed.)   *Drug and social therapy in chronic schizophrenia.*   Springfield, Illinois:   Charles C. Thomas, 1965.

Gregory, I.   Genetic factors in schizophrenia.   *American Journal of Psychiatry.*   **116**:   961–972 (1960).

Havenson, I.   Corphenazine in the intensive care of chronically ill psychotics.   *International Journal of Neuropsychiatry.*   **3** (4):   332–336 (1967).

Heath, R.G. and Krupp, I.M.   Schizophrenia as a specific biologic disease.   *American Journal of Psychiatry.*   **124**:   1019–1027 (1968).

Hendrickson, W.J.   Etiology in childhood schizophrenia:   An evaluation of current views.   *Nervous Child.*   **10**:   9–18 (1952).

Herron, W.G.   The process-reactive classification of schizophrenia.   *Psychological Bulletin.*   **59**:   329 (1962).

Hill, L.B.   *Psychotherapeutic intervention in schizophrenia.*   Chicago:   University Chicago Press, 1955.

Hoagland, H.   Metabolic and physiologic disturbances in the psychoses.   In:   Cobb, S.S. (Ed.), *The biology of mental health and disease.*   New York:   Hoeber, 1952.

Hoch, P.H. and Polatin, P.   Pseudoneurotic forms of schizophrenia.   *Psychiatric Quarterly.*   **23**:   248 (1949).

Holden, I., *et al.*   The effects of metronidazole on schizophrenic psychopathology.   *Journal of Clinical Pharmacology and Journal of New Drugs.*   **8** (5):   333–341 (1968).

Hyden, H.   Satellite cells in the nervous system.   *Scientific American.*   **205** (6):   62–70 (1961).

Itil, T., *et al.*   Effects of fluphenazine hydrochloride on digital computer sleep prints of schizophrenic patients.   *Diseases of the Nervous System.*   **32** (11):   751–758 (1971).

Ivanov-Smolensky, A.G.   *Essays on the patho-physiology of higher nervous activity.*   Moscow:   Foreign Language Publishers, 1954.

Jackson, D.D. (Ed.)   *The etiology of schizophrenia.*   New York:   Basic Books, 1960.

Kallmann, F.J.   Genetic theory of schizophrenia:   Analysis of 691 twin index families.   *American Journal of Psychiatry.*   **103**:   309–322 (1946).

Kallmann, F.J.   Genetics in relation to mental disorders.   *Journal of Mental Science.*   **94**:   250 (1948).

Kallmann, F.J. *Heredity in health and mental disorders.* New York: Norton, 1953.

Kallmann, F.J. (Ed.)   *Expanding goals of genetics in psychiatry.* New York: Grune & Stratton, 1962.

Kant, O.   Clinical investigation of simple schizophrenia. *Psychiatric Quarterly.* 22: 141 (1948).

Kantor, R., *et al.* Process and reactive schizophrenia. *Journal of Consulting Psychology.* 17: 157–162 (1953).

Kety, S.S.   Recent biochemical theories of schizophrenia. In: Jackson, D.D. (Ed.), *The etiology of schizophrenia.* New York: Basic Books, 1960.

Kety, S.S., *et al.*   Cerebral blood flow and metabolism in schizophrenia: Effects of barbiturate seminarcosis, insulin coma. *American Journal of Psychiatry.* 104: 765–770 (1948).

King, H.E. *Psychomotor aspects of mental disease.* Cambridge, Massachusetts: Harvard University Press, 1954.

Kline, N.S.   Non-chemical factors and chemical theories of mental disease. In: Rinkel, M. and Denber, H.C.B. (Eds.), *Chemical concepts of psychosis.* New York: McDowell, 1958.

Knight, R.P. Psychotherapy of an adolescent catatonic schizophrenic with mutism. *Psychiatry.* 9: 323 (1946).

Knight, R.P.   Management and psychotherapy of the borderline schizophrenic patient. *Bulletin of the Menninger Clinic.* 17: 139 (1953).

Lidz, T. *The family and human adaptation.* New York: International Universities Press, 1963.

Lidz, T. *The origin and treatment of schizophrenic disorders.* New York: Basic Books, 1973.

Lidz, T., *et al.*   The intrafamilial environment of schizophrenic patients: II. Marital schism and marital skew. *American Journal of Psychiatry.* 114: 241–248 (1957).

Lidz, T., *et al.*   The intrafamilial environment of the schizophrenic patient: IV. Parental personalities and family interaction. *American Journal of Orthopsychiatry.* 28: 764–776 (1958).

Lidz, T. and Fleck, S.   Schizophrenia, human interaction and the role of the family. In: Jackson, D.D. (Ed.), *The etiology of schizophrenia.* New York: Basic Books, 1960.

Lowther, J.   The effect of fluphenazine enanthate on chronic and relapsing schizophrenia. *British Journal of Psychiatry.* 115 (523): 691–692 (1969).

Lu, Y.C. Mother-child role relations in schizophrenia. *Psychiatry.* 24: 133–142 (1961).

Lu, Y.C.   Contradictory parental expectations in schizophrenia. *Archives of General Psychiatry.* 6: 219–234 (1962).

Lucky, W.T. and Schiele, B. A comparison of haloperidol and trifluoperazine in a double blind controlled study on chronic schizophrenic patients. *Diseases of the Nervous System.* 28 (3): 181–186 (1967).

Luyssaert, W. and Pierloot, R.   Insulinotherapie et schizophrenie. *Acta Neurologica et Psychiatrica Belgica.* 69 (5): 315–335 (1969).

Lynn, R.   Russian theory and research in schizophrenia. *Psychological Bulletin.* 60: 486–498 (1963).

Malis, G.A. *Research on the etiology of schizophrenia.* New York: Consultants Bureau, 1961.

Markowe, M., *et al.* Insulin and chlorpromazine in schizophrenia: A ten year comparative survey. *British Journal of Psychiatry.* 113 (503): 1101–1106 (1967).

National Institute of Mental Health Psychopharmacology Research Branch. Differences in the clinical effects of three phenothiazines in "acute" schizophrenia. *Diseases of the Nervous System.* 28 (6): 369–383 (1967).

National Institute of Mental Health. High dose chlorpromazine therapy in schizophrenia: Report of the National Institute of Mental Health Psychopharmacology Research Branch Collaborative Study Group. *Archives of General Psychiatry.* 18 (4): 482–495 (1968).

National Institute of Mental Health. *Mental health statistics.* Washington, D.C.: U.S. Government Printing Office, 1971.

Offord, D.R. and Cross, L.A. Behavior antecedents of schizophrenia: A review. *Archives of General Psychiatry.* 21: 267–283 (1969).

Phillips, L. Case history data and progress in schizophrenia. *Journal of Nervous and Mental Diseases.* 117: 515-535 (1953).

Pichon-Riviere, de E. Quelques observations sur le transfere de patients psychotiques. *Review Française de Psychanalyse.* 16: 254–262 (1952).

Polak, P. and Laycob, L. Rapid tranquilization. *American Journal of Psychiatry.* 128 (5): 640–643 (1972).

Prien, R.F., *et al.* Discontinuation of chemotherapy for chronic schizophrenics. *Hospital and Community Psychiatry.* 22 (1): 4–7 (1971).

Ramirez, E., *et al.* Glucagon in terminating insulin coma: Clinical and biochemical aspects. In: Rinkel, M. (Ed.), *Biological treatment of mental illness,* pp. 694–714. New York: Farrar, Straus & Giroux, 1966.

Reiss, M. Correlations between changes in mental states and thyroid activity after different forms of treatment. *Journal of Mental Science.* 100: 687–703 (1954).

Remy, M. Lasting value of insulin shock treatment. In: Rinkel, M. (Ed.), *Biological treatment of mental illness,* pp. 793–799. New York: Farrar, Straus & Giroux, 1966.

Richter, D. (Ed.) *Schizophrenia: Somatic aspects.* New York: Macmillan, 1957.

Rosen, J.N. The treatment of schizophrenic psychosis by direct analytic therapy. *Psychiatric Quarterly.* 21: 117–119 (1947).

Rosen, J.N. *Direct analysis.* New York: Grune & Stratton, 1953.

Rosenfeld, H. Considerations regarding the psychoanalytic approach to acute and chronic schizophrenia. *International Journal of Psychoanalysis.* 35: 153 (1953).

Rosenthal, D. Confusion of identity and the frequency of schizophrenia in twins. *Archives of General Psychiatry.* 3: 297–304 (1960).

Rosenthal, D. *Genetic theory and abnormal behavior.* New York: McGraw-Hill, 1970.

Roth, M. Interaction of genetic and environmental factors in the causation of schizophrenia. In: Richter, D. (Ed.), *Schizophrenia: Somatic aspects.* New York: Macmillan, 1957.

Schiele, B.C., *et al.* A double-bind comparison of trifluperidol and trifluoperazine in acute schizophrenic patients. *Comprehensive Psychiatry.* **10** (5): 355–360 (1969).

Schwing, G. *A way to the soul of the mentally ill.* New York: International Universities Press, 1954.

Shattock, M.F. The somatic manifestations of schizophrenia: A clinical study of their significance. *Journal of Mental Science.* **96**: 32 (1950).

Slater, E. Psychotic and neurotic illnesses in twins. In: Medical Research Council, *Special report no. 278.* London: H.M. Stationery Office, 1953.

Slater, E. The monogenic theory of schizophrenia. *Acta Genetica.* **8**: 50–56 (1958).

Smith, K., *et al.* ECT and chlorpromazine compared in the treatment of schizophrenia. *Journal of Nervous and Mental Diseases.* **144** (4): 284–290 (1967).

Sterlin, C., *et al.* The place of thiothixene in treatment of schizophrenic patients. *Canadian Psychiatric Association Journal.* **15** (1): 3–14 (1970).

Stupenchenko, M.V. Clinico-statistical analysis of the results of treating with psychotropic agents schizophrenics whose psychosis follows a continuous progradient course. *Zhurnal Neuropatologii i Psikhiatrii.* **69** (3): 428–431 (1969).

Sullivan, H.S. *Conceptions of modern psychiatry.* Washington, D.C.: W.A. White, 1947.

Sullivan, H.S. *The interpersonal theory of psychiatry.* New York: Norton, 1953.

Sullivan, H.S. *Schizophrenia as a human process.* New York: Norton, 1962.

Towler, M.L. and Wick, P.H. Treatment of acute exacerbations in chronic schizophrenic patients. *International Journal of Neuropsychiatry.* **3**: 61–67 (1967).

Vaernet, K. and Madsen, A. Stereotaxic amygdalotomy and basofrontal tractotomy in psychotics with aggressive behavior. *Journal of Neurology, Neurosurgery and Psychiatry.* **33** (6): 858–863 (1970).

Vorster, D. An investigation into the part played by organic factors in childhood schizophrenia. *Journal of Mental Science.* **106**: 494–522 (1960).

Walaszek, E.J. Brain neurohormones and cortical epinephrine pressor responses as affected by schizophrenic serum. *International Review of Neurobiology.* **2**: 137 (1960).

Weakland, J.H. The double-bind hypothesis of schizophrenia and three party interaction. In: Jackson, D.D. (Ed.), *The etiology of schizophrenia.* New York: Basic Books, 1960.

Weinstein, M. and Fischer, A. Combined treatment with ECT and antipsychotic drugs in schizophrenia. *Diseases of the Nervous System.* **32** (12): 801–808 (1971).

Winnicot, D.W. Regression et repli. *Revue Française de Psychanalyse.* **19**: 323–330 (1955).

Wolman, B.B. Explorations in latent schizophrenia. *American Journal of Psychotherapy.* **11**: 560–588 (1957).

Wolman, B.B. The deterioration of the ego in schizophrenia. Paper presented at Eastern Psychological Association, 1958.

Wolman, B.B.  Psychotherapy with latent schizophrenics. *American Journal of Psychotherapy.* **13:** 343–359 (1959a).

Wolman, B.B.  Continuum hypothesis in neurosis and psychosis and the classification of the mental disorder.  Paper presented at Eastern Psychological Association, 1959b.

Wolman, B.B.  The fathers of schizophrenic patients. *Acta Psychotherapeutica et Psychosomatica.* **9:** 193–210 (1961).

Wolman, B.B.  Research in etiology of schizophrenia.  Paper presented at Eastern Psychological Association, 1962.

Wolman, B.B.  Non-participant observation on a closed ward. *Acta Psychotherapeutica et Psychosomatica.* **12:** 61–71 (1964).

Wolman, B.B.  Family dynamics and schizophrenia. *Journal of Health and Human Behavior,* 1965.

Wolman, B.B. *Vectoriasis praecox or the group of schizophrenias.* Springfield, Illinois:  Charles C. Thomas, 1966.

Wolman, B.B. The socio-psycho-somatic theory of schizophrenia. *Psychotherapy and Psychosomatics.* **15:** 373–387 (1967).

Wolman, B.B. *Children without childhood.* New York:  Grune & Stratton, 1970.

Wolman, B.B. *Call no man normal.* New York: International Universities Press, 1973.

Woolley, D.W.  Serotonin in mental disorders. *Research Publications of the Association for Nervous and Mental Disease.* **36:** 381–400 (1958).

# 15 Treatment of Depressive Disorders*

## Dean Schuyler

## INTRODUCTION

Depression has been recognized as a human problem from the beginning of recorded time. The Old Testament, the writings of Homer (?9 B.C.) and Plutarch (2 A.D.) and, more recently, descriptive accounts of "melancholy" attest to the age of the concept.

Attempts to understand depression have led to the production of analogous syndromes in dogs (Seligman, 1974) and monkeys (Harlow and Suomi, 1971).

The landmark observations of Spitz (1946) recorded depression in human infants separated from a mothering figure. Depressive disorders in older children have been documented and classified by Anthony (1967) and Cytryn (1972).

Comprehensive descriptions of the signs and symptoms of depression have been compiled by Beck (1967). Case histories abound, even in popular writings (Freeman, 1969).

Despite the wealth of available descriptive phenomenology, approaches to treatment have lagged behind. It was not until 1938, when electroconvulsive therapy was introduced, that a definitive treatment for depression was available. ECT was initially prescribed for the treatment of schizophrenia and was not recommended for depression until the 1940s.

In 1957, the first antidepressant drug (imipramine) was made available. Over the years since then, a rapidly acting and predictably effective drug therapy has still not emerged.

Lithium carbonate, first successfully employed in the acute treatment of mania (Cade, 1949), has been progressively reported as useful in decreasing the frequency and intensity of manic and depressive episodes and may even have

---

* This material represents the views of the author and not necessarily those of NIMH or DHEW.

value in the treatment of some acutely depressed patients. Although it may represent a major breakthrough in the treatment of *some* patients, it is thought by no means to represent a panacea for the depressive disorders.

What have been the obstacles to discovering an adequate treatment for depression? First, the term "depression" has come to encompass a broad range of entities, clearly heterogeneous despite some similarities. The depressive spectrum (Schuyler, 1974) includes a *feeling state* familiar to most individuals, a *grief reaction* experienced by many persons and a *neurotic depressive reaction* to stress, in addition to *severe, medical depressive illness.* The milder forms of depression comprise perhaps 75% of the population seen by clinicians with a diagnosis of depression (Secunda, Katz, Friedman and Schuyler, 1973). Classification and clear separation of these entities has by no means been achieved. This "nosology" problem has had a major retarding influence on the development of effective treatment.

Second, the etiology of depression is still unknown. Promising leads of the last decade, for example, the Catecholamine Hypothesis (Schildkraut, 1965), remain unproven. The search for chemical clues in the periphery (blood and urine) has largely given way to more central approaches (cerebrospinal fluid). The classification muddle mitigates against the collection of a homogenous patient sample which might yield etiological answers. The initial optimism related to the notion of increases in brain biogenic amines in mania and decreases in depression has given way to considerations of ratios and relationships of differing amines (e.g., norepinephrine and serotonin) at receptor sites. The problem is not a simple one and has not yet been resolved.

This chapter will concentrate on the severe, "medical" depressions. Although they may represent only one-quarter of the total, they are the most disabling and paradoxically, the most responsive to treatment. Even within this group, sub-classification is critical for proper therapy. The need to differentiate severe depression from schizophrenia and to rule out underlying medical conditions responsible for the illness as well as organic brain disease is equally critical.

## MAGNITUDE OF THE PROBLEM

In 1971 (latest available figures; Biometry Branch, NIMH) the depressive disorders accounted for 275,555 hospital admissions for psychiatric care in the United States. This represented 22.5% of the total, second only to schizophrenia (27%) and surpassing that for alcoholism (15.8%). There is no available breakdown of admissions by subtype of depression, however, it seems a reasonable assumption that the vast majority represented severe depressive illness.

Unlike most categories of emotional illness, the depressive disorders may be fatal. Suicide was the eleventh leading cause of death in the United States (1972), claiming 24,280 *recorded* deaths. This figure is widely believed to be an underestimate because of unstandardized judgments and unpredictable recording practices in the different municipalities. A more accurate estimate is 50,000 suicidal deaths per year.  Suicide is the fifth leading cause of death (1972) among the most potentially productive members of our society (ages 25–44).  Depressive illness has been diagnosed retrospectively in as much as 80% of reported samples of hospital patients who die by suicide (Flood and Seager, 1968).  In a review of 21 follow-up studies of depression, Robins and Guze (1972) concluded that suicide accounted for 13–17% of the eventual causes of death.

## MAKING THE DIAGNOSIS OF SEVERE AFFECTIVE ILLNESS

The general medical dictum that an accurate diagnosis must precede treatment need not be labored here.  Once the common symptoms and signs of depression (see Table 15-1) have been recognized in a patient, guidelines are necessary before prescribing treatment.  In general, each classification of depression identifies a subtype called: "endogenous," "vital," "retarded" or "empty." It is these clinical pictures which conform to medically serious depression.

TABLE 15-1  COMMON SIGNS AND SYMPTOMS OF DEPRESSION.

| Emotional Changes | Physical Changes |
|---|---|
| sadness | sleep disorder |
| guilt | eating disorder |
| anxiety | constipation |
| anger | menstrual irregularity |
| diurnal mood variation | impotence/frigidity |
| | weight loss |
| | weakness |
| | easy fatigability |
| | pain, unexplained origin |
| | diminished sexual "drive" |

| Behavioral Changes | Cognitive Changes |
|---|---|
| crying | negative self-concept |
| withdrawal | negative view of the world |
| retardation | negative expectations for the future |
| agitation | self-blame |
| hallucinations | self-criticism |
| | indecisiveness |
| | helplessness |
| | hopelessness |
| | worthlessness |
| | delusions (of guilt, sin, worthlessness) |

The most widely employed label, so-called "endogenous depression," may have psychotic symptoms of hallucinations or delusions, or may not.  Much has been made of the absence of a clear precipitating event in these patients. Obtaining this historical fact, however, may have more to do with the clinical interviewing ability of the examiner than with the illness of the patient (Alarcon and Covi, 1972). The other defining characteristic of the endogenous depression has been the presence of vegetative (physical) symptoms. Even more reliable, however, may be the criteria determined by Mendels and Cochrane (1968) in their review of the literature on endogenous depression (see Table 15-2).

### TABLE 15-2  CRITERIA FOR A DIAGNOSIS OF ENDOGENOUS DEPRESSION.*

1. psychomotor retardation or agitation
2. distinct quality to depressed mood (eg., different from the feeling one has following the death of a loved one)
3. lack of reactivity (response) to environmental changes
4. loss of interest in usual activities or decreased sexual drive
5. poor appetite
6. weight loss
7. early morning awakening
8. self reproach or inappropriate guilt
9. suicidal behavior

*Mendels and Cochrane, 1968.

An additional screening method for identifying the severe, medical form of depression frequently employed by researchers is known as the *Feighner* (Feighner, Robins, Guze, Woodruff, Winokur and Munoz, 1972) *criteria* (see Table 15-3).

### TABLE 15-3  FEIGHNER CRITERIA FOR A DIAGNOSIS OF MAJOR DEPRESSIVE ILLNESS.*

At least 5 of the following 8 symptoms for "definite" and 4 for "probable."

1. poor appetite or weight loss (2 lb per week or 10 lb or more for the past year when dieting) or increased appetite or weight gain
2. sleep difficulty or sleeping too much
3. loss of energy, fatigability or tiredness
4. psychomotor agitation or retardation
5. loss of interest in usual activities, or decrease in sexual drive
6. feelings of self-reproach or excessive or inappropriate guilt (either may be delusional)
7. complaints of, or evidence of, diminished ability to think or concentrate, such as slow thinking or mixed up thoughts
8. recurrent thoughts of death or suicide, including thoughts of wishing to be dead

*Feighner *et al.,* 1972.

A consideration of these two sets of criteria should draw a picture for the clinician of severe depression. Most often these patients are incapacitated; cannot work, derive no pleasure from their lives, interact nonproductively with others, if at all. Psychomotor retardation or agitation (evident in posture, speech and gait) is often striking. Although *involutional melancholia* may not exist as a separate entity, the features of agitation, insomnia, pathological guilt, paranoid ideation and somatic preoccupation or delusions have been identified with depression occurring in this life period. (Mendels, 1970).

The ideal situation, of course, would be to identify the characteristics of those patients who respond to the typical treatment for severe depression and develop a classification based upon treatment response. We have not yet attained this ideal state.

## CLASSIFICATION OF SEVERE DEPRESSIVE ILLNESS

Once the clinician has determined that the patient meets the criteria for severe depression, some additional historical data may help in the determination of a prognosis and the prescription of treatment. The classification problem has been reviewed in detail elsewhere (see Schuyler, 1974). The most clinically useful nosology can be derived from the work of Winokur (1973).

TABLE 15-4  CLASSIFICATION OF DEPRESSIVE ILLNESS.*

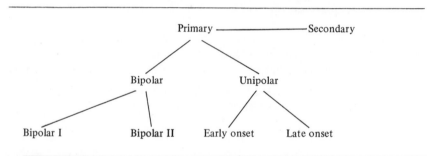

*Modified from Winokur, 1973.

The initial distinction between Primary and Secondary Depression (see Table 15-4) related to *chronology* of occurrence. In Primary Depressive Illness, the first appearance of a manic or depressive episode must *predate* any other major psychiatric illness in that patient. If the criteria for any of the following diagnoses were met before the occurrence of depressive illness, a diagnosis of Secondary Depression is made: schizophrenia, anxiety neurosis, phobic neurosis, obsessive-compulsive neurosis, hysteria, antisocial personality, alcoholism, drug dependence, homosexuality, or a physical illness leading to major changes in living conditions or one associated with psychological symptoms (Robins and Guze, 1972). That Secondary Depression is fundamentally different from Primary has not been established. Specific treatment recommendations do not yet follow from this dichotomy. It may, however, facilitate communication and eventually have implications for treatment.

The second distinction separates those patients who have had an episode of mania (bipolar) from those with recurrent depressions without mania (unipolar). The existing nosology of "manic-depression reaction" resulted in blurring the distinction between recurrent depressions, cyclic mania and depression. Criteria for the diagnosis of a manic episode appear in Table 15-5.

### TABLE 15-5  CRITERIA FOR A DIAGNOSIS OF MANIA.

1. persistent elevation of mood
2. increased social, sexual or physical activity
3. pressured speech
4. flight of ideas
5. grandiosity (may be delusional)
6. diminished sleep time
7. hallucinations or delusions may be present

In recent years, there has been a tendency to expand the category of manic-depression to include more patients. Perhaps this represents an attempt to compensate for the suggestion that, in America, schizophrenia is over-diagnosed and manic-depressive illness is missed, or classified elsewhere (Zubin and Fleiss, 1971). Perhaps the introduction of a major new drug treatment (lithium carbonate) offering renewed hope for bipolar depressives has led to a loosening of the criteria for this diagnosis. In any case, bipolar I patients represent the classical manic-depressive illness category. Bipolar II patients may have had a *hypomanic* episode (without history of mania), or even merely a family history of mania to qualify for the diagnosis (Winokur and Reich, 1970). In addition, the current (1968) edition of the *Diagnostic and Statistical Manual* lists manic-depression as a "reaction" rather than as an "illness." This may reflect, in part, an awareness that manic and depressive episodes need not have psychotic symptoms to conform to the diagnosis. Winokur (1973) has summarized the differences he has noted in unipolar and bipolar depression (see Table 15-6). This dichotomy may reflect significant genetic differences and may eventually suggest different modes of treatment.

### TABLE 15-6  DIFFERENCES BETWEEN BIPOLAR AND UNIPOLAR DEPRESSION.*

|  | Bipolar | Unipolar |
|---|---|---|
| 1. presence of mania in proband | yes | no |
| 2. median age of onset in proband | 28 | 36 |
| 3. six or more episodes | 57% | 18% |
| 4. affective illness in parent | 52% | 26% |
| 5. families with two generations of affective illness | 54% | 32% |
| 6. affective illness in parents or extended family | 63% | 36% |
| 7. bipolar illness in first degree relatives | 10.8% | 0.35% |

*Modified from Winokur, 1973

Unipolar depression has been subclassified by age of onset into early (before age 40) and late (after age 40) onset (see Table 15-4). The former has been called *depressive spectrum disease.* The prototype patient is female, with a high family incidence of depression but also of alcoholism and sociopathy (Winokur, 1973). The late onset *(pure depressive disease)* prototype is male, with a low family incidence of depression and practically no family incidence of alcoholism and sociopathy. Once again, these findings may reflect genetic differences as well as eventual treatment implications.

## DIFFERENTIAL DIAGNOSTIC CONSIDERATIONS

Once the clinician has established that the criteria for a severe depressive illness are present, care must be taken to exclude similar conditions which are treated differently.

Hallucinations and delusions, the secondary symptoms of *schizophrenia,* may occur in depression as well. Their character, however, often reflects the lowered self-esteem of the depressive (e.g., self-deprecatory delusions). The psychomotor retardation of the depressive may be so pronounced as to warrant the description of "depressive stupor": a virtually motionless patient who neither speaks, eats nor moves about. This may be confused with the catatonic form of schizophrenia. Although the cognitive distortions seen in depression (see Beck, 1973) may be pre-eminent, the classical signs of a thought disorder in schizophrenia (including autism, ambivalence, a disorder of attention and an associational defect) should aid in a differential diagnosis.

In some types of schizophrenia, however, the affective component is predominant. These cases have been diagnosed *Schizophrenia, Schizo-affective type.* It is currently unclear whether they more closely resemble schizophrenia or the primary affective disorders. (Cohen, Allen, Pollin and Hrubec, 1972).

Organic brain disease of any cause, may present with severe depression (Castelnuovo-Tedesco, 1961). Differential factors can generally be identified with careful attention to the examination of the sensorium: orientation, memory, judgment and insight.

General medical illnesses which may be associated with depression include: infectious diseases (hepatitis, mononucleosis, rheumatic fever, tuberculosis); psychosomatic illnesses (ulcerative colitis, asthma, rheumatoid arthritis); anemias; malignancies; endocrine illnesses (thyroid disease, hypoglycemia). It is now commonly taught that carcinoma of the tail of the pancreas, generally silent with late onset of symptoms, may present with depression as its sole initial manifestation (Yaskin, 1931).

## THE PRESCRIPTION OF TREATMENT

### Hospitalization

Although some patients with severe, medical depression can be treated effectively on an outpatient basis, hospitalization is frequently an important consideration. A major indication for hospitalization of the depressed patient is a significant risk of suicidal behavior.

It has been widely publicized that many patients who commit suicide do so after recent contact with a physician (Robins, Murphy, Wilkinson, Gassner and Kayes, 1959). This statement implies that the physician, in some cases, might not have been aware of the suicidal intent of the patient. For many clinicians, the confrontation with suicide (self-inflicted death) may be a difficult and painful one. Mastering the anxiety provoked and accepting the challenge of the suicidal patient would be aided by some guidelines for assessing suicidal risk.

An important first step in the evaluation of suicide potential can be taken by *asking the patient* about suicidal ideas. Concern about "suggesting the possibility of suicide to an unknowing individual" has been laid to rest by recent clinical commentary. It is essential to ask the depressed patient about suicidal thoughts whether he volunteers their presence or not. A common reaction of the patient is relief at the opportunity to share his thought. Constant preoccupation with suicidal ideas is clearly more dangerous than occasional thoughts of death.

If suicidal thoughts are acknowledged, the clinician must inquire, in order, about a suicidal *plan, access* to the lethal materials necessary to carry out such a plan, and any *past history* of suicidal behavior or contact with such behavior in significant others (Schuyler, 1974b).

The next step entails an inquiry into the patient's *motivation* for considering suicide. It has been suggested (Schuyler, 1972) that suicidal intent may reflect a complexity of motivations varying from a wish to escape an intolerable internal (intrapsychic) or external situation, to a desire to affect the behavior of a significant other through suicidal behavior or suicidal death. Often elements of surcease, or cessation ("I don't want to die, just to sleep for a while and have everything stop"), are intermixed with instrumental wishes to influence someone else.

A consideration of motivation often leads logically to an evaluation of the patient's social resources. When no significant other is available to the patient, the risk of sucidal thoughts being translated into action is increased. When a significant other has ignored previous signals of distress, suicide potential is enhanced. When the patient is being evaluated subsequent to suicidal behavior, a measure of motivation may be obtained by asking the structured questions associated with the *Suicide Intent Scale* (Schuyler and Beck, 1972; Beck, Schuyler and Herman, 1974) or the *Risk-Rescue Rating* (Weisman and Wordon, 1972).

A discussion of the likely consequences of his or her suicidal behavior completes the evaluation and may serve a therapeutic function as well. ("What will happen to you when you die? What effect will your death have on significant others?").

The presence of continuous suicidal thoughts in the absence of any social resources or the presence of a suicidal plan (especially with access to the means for carrying it out) generally indicates the need for hospitalization. Even when suicide is not an immediate concern, some patients with severe depression may have regressed to the extent that they cannot care for their personal needs at home. In others, a pathological interaction between the patient and a family member may require interruption. (Mendels, 1970). When ECT is prescribed or when administration of antidepressant medication may entail the risk of severe side reactions, hospitalization may be indicated. Considering the degree of incapacitation inherent in severe depression, a surprising number of patients have been treated successfully on an outpatient basis.

## Psychotherapy

The severely depressed patient is rarely a candidate for other than supportive psychotherapy during the acute episode (Jacobsen, 1971). Such therapy entails: (1) an *explanation* to the patient and family of the nature of the illness (Campbell, 1953); (2) unconditional *acceptance* of the patient despite his or her rejecting posture toward the therapist (Wilson, 1955); (3) encouraging an attitude of *understanding, hope and appropriate planning* for the future (Kraines, 1957); (4) anticipation of the *risk of suicide* with appropriate intervention (Regan, 1965); (5) provision of a *structured daily program,* if necessary (Beck, 1967).

## Drug Therapy

In the ideal situation, the reader would be referred, at this time, to the section on classification of severe depression. For each mutually exclusive subtype of depression described, there would be a drug with proven efficacy, clearly superior over numerous trials to placebo and other relevant drugs. A brief description of administration, side reactions and contraindications would suffice to guide the practitioner in selecting the right drug for the right patient. This section would be short, concise and definitive.

Unfortunately, this section will neither be short nor definitive. Rather it will attempt to illuminate a rather muddled picture consistent with our current state of knowledge.

A necessary backdrop to a presentation of drug efficacy in depression is as follows: *Depression, even in its most severe form, is generally a self-limited disease which will run its course and terminate without treatment within 6 months to one year.* About 10% of severe depressions have been reported to have a chronic, unremitting course (Robins and Guze, 1972). The rationale for treatment, in most cases, is to relieve the intense suffering depression brings to its victim and to diminish the probability of a suicidal outcome. Although drug therapy has demonstrated equivocal worth in the treatment of the milder, neurotic, reactive forms of depression; its success in the severe, medical depressions has been notable.

A second preliminary note relates to the nature of the research findings to be presented in this section. The earliest "drug studies" were generally done in heterogeneous samples of depressed patients. The validity of their findings is subject to real question. Many studies did not have a matched control group with random assignment of subjects to active drug or placebo. The phenomenon of spontaneous improvement (e.g., the illness "running its course") could account for the findings reported. Many of the studies were not "double-blind" – that is, either the investigator or the subjects or both were aware of the nature of the tablet being administered. Since many of the antidepressant drugs possess readily identifiable side effects (e.g., dry mouth or sedation), the double-blind aspect of the study is compromised unless the placebo produces similar effects. Orne (1962) has demonstrated the power of the subject's awareness of the "demand characteristics" in an experiment to be a potential major determinant of outcome.

The utilization of a "drug-free wash-out" period prior to beginning the study is a necessary condition for evaluating the efficacy of a drug under study (Ainslie, Jones and Stiefel, 1965). Finally, many studies have compromised their value by administering insufficient dosage of medication for inadequate periods of time (Davis, 1965). A careful investigation into the usefulness of a drug is, therefore, a difficult and demanding procedure.

Mindful of these limitations, let us now examine the evidence which has accrued from the investigation of drug therapy for severe depression. There are three classes of drugs proposed for the treatment of depression which seem to possess clinical relevance: the tricyclics, the monoamine oxidase inhibitors, and lithium carbonate. A heterogeneous group of other drugs with peripheral or as yet unproven indications for depressive illness will be examined together at the end of this section.

## THE TRICYCLIC COMPOUNDS

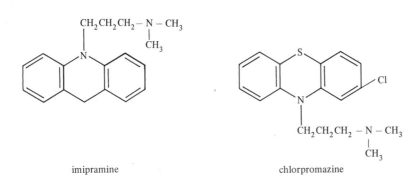

imipramine                                          chlorpromazine

Fig. 15-1. Tricyclic antidepressants and phenothiazines: structural resemblance.

The tricyclic antidepressants were originally suggested for the treatment of schizophrenia. Their structural resemblance to the phenothiazines lent support to this claim. Their name was derived from the common structural presence of three contiguous benzene rings (see Fig. 15-1). Kuhn (1958) is credited with introducing imipramine hydrochloride (Tofranil ®, Presamine ®, Imavate ®, SK-Pramine ® ) as an antidepressant drug. Six drugs in this group have received attention: imipramine and desipramine (a demethylated derivative); amitriptyline and nortriptyline (a demethylated derivative); protriptyline and doxepin. Their chemical structures and trade names are illustrated in Fig. 15-2.

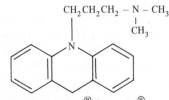

imipramine (Tofranil®, Presamine®, Imavate®, SK-Pramine®)

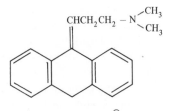

amitriptyline (Elavil®)

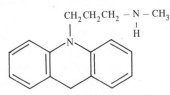

desipramine (Norpramin®, Pertofrane® )

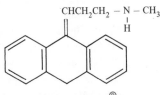

nortriptyline (Aventyl® )

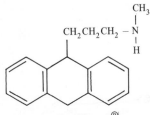

protriptyline (Vivactil®)

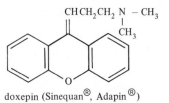

doxepin (Sinequan®, Adapin®)

Fig. 15-2.   The tricyclic antidepressants.

## Controlled Studies

In reporting the results of drug studies, consideration will be limited to inpatient material. The assumption will be made that outpatient samples, in general, have a larger representation of milder, neurotic depressives. Beck (1973) has reviewed the controlled studies in which imipramine has been compared with placebo on inpatient depressives. A finding of superiority in his review indicates a statistically significant difference in the improvement of patients on either imipramine or placebo at a 5% level of confidence. Out of 43 studies meeting his criteria for inclusion, imipramine was superior in inpatient depressives in 26 (62%) and placebo was superior in 16 (38%). Other tricyclics have been investigated in far fewer controlled studies (see Table 15-7) with less striking results. These figures suggest a substantial superiority of imipramine over placebo in the samples studied.

TABLE 15-7  CONTROLLED STUDIES OF
TRICYCLIC DRUGS VS. PLACEBO*.

| Drug studied | Superior to placebo | Inferior to placebo |
|---|---|---|
| imipramine | 26 | 16 |
| desipramine | 3 | 2 |
| amitriptyline | 7 | 4 |
| nortriptyline | 4 | 3 |
| protriptyline | 1 | 0 |
| doxepin | 1 | 0 |

*Modified from Beck, 1973.

In comparisons matching amitriptyline vs. imipramine in inpatients, 5 out of 10 favored the former, and in 4 out of 10 there was no difference (Beck, 1973). Comparison of desipramine vs. imipramine was stimulated by initial claims of more rapid onset of action for desipramine (Klerman and Cole, 1965). In 9 of 11 reported studies (Beck, 1973), there was no difference in the effectiveness of the two drugs; in 2 studies, imipramine was superior. Five reports were inconsistent with a more rapid effect for desipramine. Comparative studies of imipramine vs. other tricyclics (nortriptyline, doxepin) were few and showed no difference (Beck, 1973).

Investigations of the effectiveness of amitriptyline vs. other tricyclics in depressed inpatients revealed few significant differences. Comparisons of derivatives of imipramine with those of amitriptyline likewise showed no difference. (Beck, 1973).

Choosing a Tricyclic Drug

The choice of which tricyclic for which patient, therefore, rests more with anecdotal experience and prior history of patient response than it does with the results of controlled investigations. The initial consideration relates to the factors which mitigate against tricyclic use in some patients (see Table 15-8). In addition, caution is indicated with pregnancy (use only when potential benefits outweigh possible hazards), seizure disorders (may lower seizure threshold), and in those receiving guanethidine or similar agents (Lewis, 1973). If the patient has a history of favorable response to a particular tricyclic drug, this is generally the medication to start with.

The tricyclic group can be roughly divided in terms of degree of sedation (see Table 15-9).  In the anxious or agitated depressive, mild accompanying

## TABLE 15-8  FACTORS AGAINST TRICYCLIC USE*.

1. cardiovascular disease
2. thrombophlebitis
3. hyperthyroidism
4. history of glaucoma or increased intraocular pressure
5. history of urinary retention
6. concurrent use of an MAO-inhibitor (FDA recommends 2-week discontinuation of MAOI prior to prescription of a tricyclic)

*Adapted from Lewis, 1973.

## TABLE 15-9  SEDATIVE QUALITIES OF TRICYCLIC DRUGS*.

| Sedative | Non-sedative | Activating |
|---|---|---|
| amitriptyline | imipramine | protriptyline |
| nortriptyline | desipramine | |
| doxepin | | |

*Modifed from Kline, 1969.

sedation may be useful. In the withdrawn, retarded depressive, a non-sedative or activating drug would be a better choice. In the treatment of outpatients with severe depression, the patient's occupation, need to drive a car, suicide potential and lack of others to supervise his drug taking may all mitigate against the choice of a sedating drug (Kline, 1969). Finally, the patient's capacity to tolerate the mild side effects of the drug may be a critical determinant of drug choice (see Table 15-10). Many of the milder side effects are due to the anticholinergic actions of the drug. Serious side effects reported in 0.5-1% of patients studied include: leukopenia, leukocytosis, jaundice, agranulocytosis. Hypotension (5%) and tachycardia (5%) are slightly more common. Pulmonary emboli, myocardial

## TABLE 15-10  COMMON SIDE EFFECTS OF TRICYCLIC DRUGS*.

1. dry mouth
2. visual distortions
3. nausea, vomiting, constipation, diarrhea
4. sweating
5. drowsiness
6. mild tremor of upper extremities
7. skin rash

*Adapted from Beck, 1973.

infarction, and congestive heart failure are rare. For both mild and serious side effects, it is unclear whether the reactions observed were due solely to the effect of the drug or related to the patient's past history and predisposition (Beck, 1973). A careful review of the medical management of side reactions can be found in either Beck (1973) or Kline (1969).

## Procedure of Administration

Once the clinician has decided to prescribe a tricyclic antidepressant and chosen a particular compound, considerations of dose and strategy are next. The initial dose recommended for a patient of average weight in the 15-60-year age range is 25 mg three times a day (Kline, 1969). An exception in the tricyclic group is protriptyline (Vivactyl) for which the recommended initial dose is 5 mg three times a day. These are only general guidelines, however, and individual variation in response to these drugs is not uncommon. For the patient whose weight is well above average, an initial dose of 25 mg four times a day may be indicated (for protriptyline, 5 mg four times a day). For the older patient or one with markedly reduced weight, an initial twice a day dosage might be better tolerated. The availability of 10 mg tablets of imipramine, amitriptyline, nortriptyline and doxepin offers even more flexibility of dosage.

Once the patient's tolerance (no idiosyncratic reaction, no disabling side effects) has been established, the dosage is generally increased to the average therapeutic level within two weeks (50 mg, three times a day; 10 mg of protriptyline, three times a day). Further increase of dose (to 100 mg, three times a day; 20 mg of protriptyline three times a day) has been suggested by Kline (1969) when a four-week plateau has been reached without satisfactory response. An alternative course, after four weeks without response, is the substitution of another tricyclic drug for the original choice.

## Maintenance Therapy

After clinical improvement has been manifested for several weeks (the exact time period has not been established), dosage may be reduced to a maintenance level. Suggested maintenance dose levels vary for the five tricyclics from 25-50 mg once per day. For protriptyline, 5-10 mg once per day is the equivalent dosage. It is suggested that maintenance therapy be continued for 3-6 months "to minimize the probability of relapse" (Beck, 1973). There are clinicians who maintain depressed patients on maintenance medication for at least one year after clinical recovery.

## New Developments

The discontinuation of medication by an outpatient due to annoying side effects (chiefly too much sedation to perform usual activities) has been identified as a management problem in the treatment of depression. A new preparation (imipramine pamoate) has been marketed (Trimipramine ®, Tofranil-PM ®) in 75 mg and 150 mg capsules for the purpose of providing single nightly dosage administration in the treatment of depression. One study (Goldberg and Nathan, 1972) found no significant difference between 75 mg imipramine pamoate nightly vs. 75 mg imipramine hydrochloride in three divided doses. A second comparison (Mendels and Di Giacomo, 1973) of imipramine hydrochloride, 50 mg three times daily vs. 150 mg of imipramine pamoate at bedtime had similar findings. A third study, employing doses up to 200 mg per day (Huzzain and Chaudhry, 1973) found similar therapeutic efficacy, a diminution of complaints about side effects and more regular drug consumption. For some patients, the loss of flexibility inherent in a single dose preparation may mitigate against use of this drug. For others, however, the possibility of avoiding side effects which might otherwise lead to discontinuation of chemotherapy may represent a major advance.

A clear relationship between subtype of depressive illness and response to a specific antidepressant drug has not yet been established (Kline, 1969). One approach, related to the psychodynamic issues relevant to the patient's depression, has been suggested by Alexander, Berkeley and Cohen (1972). Another, based upon depressive subtypes derived from factor analysis (anxious, hostile, and retarded depression) had significant numbers of neurotic and "schizophrenic depressions" in their sample (Raskin, Schulterbrandt, Reatig, Crook and Odle, 1974). Still another examined the effect of amitriptyline upon different subtypes of outpatients in a mixed diagnostic sample (Paykel, 1972). The relevance of these reports to severe, medical depression is unclear at this time.

More relevant, perhaps, are two studies (Maas, Fawcett and Dekirmenjian, 1972; Schildkraut, Draskoczy, Gershon, Reich and Grab, 1972) which have correlated drug response with a biochemical metabolite found in the urine (MHPG). This metabolite (3-methexy, 4-hydroxy phenylglycol) is one endproduct of the breakdown of norepinephrine in the brain. The catecholamine hypothesis of depression (Schildkraut, 1965) attributes etiological significance to this metabolic pathway. Although the biochemical antidepressant effect of the tricyclic drugs remains unknown, it is thought that by blocking the re-uptake of norepinephrine by nerve cells, the level of the biogenic amine is increased. In the first study (Maas *et al.*, 1972); those patients who responded best to imipramine had *low* levels of MHPG in their urine prior to treatment. In the second study (Schildkraut *et al.*, 1972), patients with *high* levels of MHPG prior to treatment responded well to amitriptyline. Future work in this area may have important implications for the development of a biochemical parameter to indicate drug choice in the treatment of severe depression.

## THE MONOAMINE OXIDASE INHIBITORS

There are no reliable estimates available to document antidepressant drug prescriptions in the United States. When such an investigation is accomplished it is likely to reach two conclusions: (1) More tricyclics than MAO-inhibitors are prescribed for depression in the U.S.: (2) However, more MAO-inhibitors than one would predict are being prescribed.

The initial drug in this class, *iproniazid,* was being used in the treatment of tuberculosis in 1955. When some patients noted euphoria as a side effect, its potential as an antidepressant drug was suggested.

In 1957, the MAO-inhibitors were introduced for the treatment of severe depressive illness. No differential indication separated this class of drugs from the tricyclics. They have been labeled "psychic energizers."

In practice, the prescription and approval of many drugs in this class has been retarded by the so-called "cheese reaction" in which there is an apparent interaction between certain foods and the drug. This will be considered in more detail in the section on side reactions.

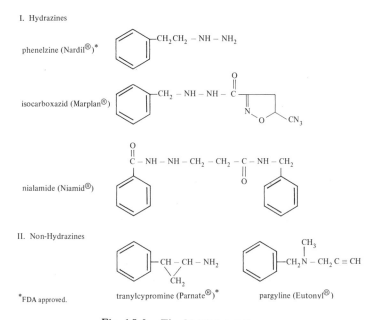

Fig. 15-3 The MAO-Inhibitors.

The MAO-inhibitors are thought to exert an antidepressant effect by inhibiting the function of the enzyme *monoamine oxidase,* necessary for biochemical degradation in the catecholamine pathway, effectively increasing the level of biogenic amines in the brain. Structurally, there are two subgroups of drugs marketed in this class — the hydrazines (e.g., phenelzine) and the non-hydrazines (e.g., tranylcypromine). Chemical structures and trade names of the MAO-inhibitors are illustrated in Fig. 15-3. Currently, only phenelzine (Nardil ®) of the hydrazines and tranylcypromine (Parnate ® ) are approved for use in this country by the Food and Drug Administration.

### Controlled Studies

Phenelzine has been reported to be superior to placebo in 6 out of 10 studies; tranylcypromine in 3 out of 4 studies (Beck, 1973). In comparison with imipramine, there was no significant difference in 17 studies; in 9 others, imipramine was superior.

### TABLE 15-11  DOSE SCHEDULE FOR MAO-INHIBITORS.

|  | initial dose (twice a day) | therapeutic dose (twice a day) | maximal dose (twice a day) | maintenance dose (twice a day) |
|---|---|---|---|---|
| phenelzine (Nardil ®) | 15 mg | 30 mg | 45 mg | 15 mg |
| tranylcypromine (Parnate ® ) | 10 mg | 20 mg | 30 mg | 10 mg |

### Procedure of Administration

Recommended initial, therapeutic and maintenance dosage for phenelzine and tranylcypromine are presented in Table 15-11. Sensitivity to food-drug interactions may be greatest immediately after administration (Kline, 1969). If true, this would be an important determinant for dose scheduling. The FDA recommends a two-week time lapse between the discontinuation of a tricyclic and the starting of an MAO-inhibitor. Kline (1969) has found 5-7 days to be "usually sufficient."

### Side Effects

The MAO-inhibitors are contraindicated in patients with cardiovascular or cerebrovascular disorders, pheochromocytoma, liver disease or history of headaches (Beck, 1973). The FDA cautions against their use in conjunction with other MAO-inhibitors, with tricyclics (see later), or with sympathomimetic drugs. A list of foods to be avoided should be presented to the patient (preferably in writing) at the time of prescription. These include: alcohol, cheeses, pickled herring, chianti, beer, wines, yeast extract, chicken liver, pods of broad beans, canned figs. The avoidance of these foods is justified by the report of severe (sometimes fatal) hypertensive crises precipitated by the interaction of tyramine (in these foods) with the drug.

The patient must be cautioned to avoid incompatible medications while being treated with an MAO-inhibitor such as:  phenylephrine (Neo-synephrine ® ), sedatives (especially with tranylcypromine, opiates, meperidine (Demerol ® ), cocaine, procaine (and related preparations), anti-hypertensive agents, anesthetics (especially ether, scopolamine or atropine, and especially with tranylcypromine), antihistamines (especially with tranylcypromine), diuretics (especially with tranylcypromine), dopa, dopamine or tryptophan, anti-parkinsonian agents, over-the-counter drugs for colds, hay fever, weight reduction and sympathomimetics (including amphetamines).

MAO-inhibitors can artificially depress blood sugar levels. They may diminish anginal pain in cardiac patients and remove this indicator of possible impending illness. Patients should be cautioned to restrict their activity in accordance with cardiovascular capacity (Kline, 1969) rather than "how they feel" while on MAO-inhibitors. A detailed discussion of the management of serious side reactions and personal experience with management of patients on MAO-inhibitors can be found in Kline's (1969) monograph.

Combination Therapy

The FDA specifically cautions against the use of combination treatment with tricyclics and MAO-inhibitors prescribed concurrently. Recent reports, however, challenge this dictum (Schuckit, Robins and Feighner, 1971; Ray, 1973). They suggest that combination therapy is safe and often useful, especially in cases refractory to treatment with either drug alone. Kline (1969) cites the legal risk involved in the use of this therapeutic combination, then notes that: "the physician who has exhausted other therapeutic measures must consider whether the needs of the patient or his own added legal safety should be given priority. Officially, to legally administer such a combination would require the filing of an Investigation of New Drug (IND) application with the Food and Drug Administration" (Kline, 1969).

It is apparent that, in many places outside the U.S., utilization of MAO-inhibitors is more widespread than in our country. Given the multitude of reported side reactions, regardless of their frequency, many clinicians approach the possibility of employing MAO-inhibitors with caution, and only after failure with several tricyclics. Further research is needed to clarify this picture.

LITHIUM CARBONATE

In 1949, lithium carbonate was reported by Cade to be useful in the treatment of acute mania. Its efficacy for mania has been confirmed by several investigators (Schou, Juel-Nielsen, Stromgren and Voldly, 1954; Gershon and Yuwiller, 1960; Maggs, 1963). A recent study (Prien, Caffey, Klett, 1972) found chlorpromazine (Thorazine ® ) more effective in highly active manic patients, while lithium was preferable in less active mania.

More recently, lithium carbonate has been proposed as an effective anti-depressant in some severely depressed patients. This claim, although muted, has been met with reservation on the part of clinicians and researchers alike. This reaction derives logically from the past medical history of lithium use. There were numerous unsubstantiated claims of its efficacy in the treatment of gout, epilepsy and insomnia (Kline, 1969) in the late nineteenth and early twentieth centuries. In 1949, lithium chloride was proposed as a salt substitute in patients on restricted sodium diets, with disastrous consequences. The accumulation of toxic doses of lithium in these patients led to many, at first, unexplained deaths. This experience led to an extreme reluctance to investigate the drug further and probably retarded the realization of its potential as a mood stabilizer in bipolar depressives (Kline, 1969).

The efficacy of lithium carbonate in severe depression is far from established. Early studies either found no such effect (Cade, 1949), or reported some success using lithium with or without additional treatment in uncontrolled studies (Hartigan, 1963). Dyson and Mendels (1968) and Nahunek, Svestka and Redova (1970) reported additional uncontrolled observations suggesting the value of lithium as an antidepressant.

In the first reported controlled trial, Fieve, Platman and Plutchick (1968) compared lithium with imipramine in hospitalized depressed patients. They attributed to lithium "a mild antidepressant effect." Goodwin, Murphy and Bunney (1969) found lithium effective in the treatment of selected bipolar depressed patients. Stokes, Shamoian Stoll and Patton (1971) found no significant difference between treatment of depressive episodes with lithium or placebo. By contrast, Mendels, Secunda and Dyson (1972) found lithium equivalent in efficacy to desipramine with selected depressed patients. Finally, Johnson (1974) reported improvement in a small number of unipolar depressed patients treated with lithium.

The status of lithium as a treatment for acute depression remains experimental. If it indeed is effective, it is unclear from the literature which subtype of depressive illness is more likely to respond. Further study in a well-described sample under double-blind conditions with placebo and antidepressant control groups is required.

When the course of a severe depressive illness is to include only one episode in a patient's lifetime, treatment with a tricyclic antidepressant or electroconvulsive therapy may be said to effect a "cure." When a patient is followed up for several decades, however, it becomes apparent that recurrent illness is the likely course for a majority of the sample. (Robins and Guze, 1972). For these individuals, treatment can be better understood as producing a remission in a relapsing illness. In the manic-depressive (bipolar) patient, perhaps better studied than its unipolar counterpart, even intermorbid periods cannot be characterized as "normal." The needs of these patients, therefore, often go beyond the capabilities of acute treatment and extend to maintenance therapy. For some, psychotherapy is a useful adjunct to the treatment of acute mania and acute depression. For many, the prospect of uninhibited highs and severely withdrawn lows dictates a life of chaos and sorely strained relationships.

For these reasons, the claims being made for the efficacy of lithium carbonate as a mood stabilizing ("preventive") medication deserve a careful reading by the clinician treating bipolar depression. There is a growing literature to support the usefulness of prophylactic lithium therapy. Its major advocate, Dr. Mogens Schou, has co-authored more than 60 papers on the drug (Kline, 1969).

Early studies were largely anecdotal or uncontrolled. They compared a patient's course prior to lithium treatment (viewed in retrospect) with a subsequent period on lithium maintenance. Studies by Angst, Weis and Grof (1970), Baastrup (1964), Baastrup and Schou (1967), Hartigan (1963) and Hullin, McDonald and Allsopp (1972) suggested that fewer affective epsiodes occurred during the lithium treatment period. By contrast, Stancer, Furlong and Godse (1970) found no evidence of a prophylactic effect for lithium. The methodology of these studies was severely criticized by Blackwell (1969), Saran (1969) and an Editorial in *Lancet* (1969). Saran suggested that the findings attributed to lithium might instead reflect the natural history of manic-depressive illness.

By 1970, controlled investigations (lithium vs. placebo) began to appear in the literature. Baastrup, Poulsen, Schou, Thomsen and Amdisen (1970) discontinued a follow-up study after 5 months because 21 patients on placebo had relapsed although none on lithium had. This study included both bipolar and unipolar patients. The second major controlled study was that of Coppen, Noguera, Bailey, Burns, Swani, Hare, Gardner and Maggs (1972). The results, in a mixed unipolar and bipolar sample, strongly suggest a prophylactic lithium effect. However, the interpretation may be confounded by the vast number of subjects receiving supplemental (largely tricyclic antidepressant) medication (14 out of 28 on lithium; 35 of 37 on placebo).

The third major controlled investigation was the VA-NIMH study. In part I (Prien, Caffey and Klett, 1973) 205 bipolar patients, hospitalized for the treatment of mania, were discharged on lithium or placebo maintenance therapy. The prophylactic effect demonstrated was impressive for future manic episodes, less so for depression. In part II (Prien, Klett and Caffy, 1973), 122 unipolar and bipolar patients hospitalized for depression were discharged on lithium, imipramine or placebo. For the bipolar group, there were significantly fewer affective episodes with lithium treatment. There was a relatively high incidence of subsequent manic episodes in the imipramine group. For the unipolar depressives, imipramine and lithium were equally good and each was almost twice as good as placebo in "preventing" depression. Additional reports supporting the prophylactic claim for lithium are by Mendlewicz, Fieve and Stallone (1973) and Stallone, Shelley, Mendlewicz and Fieve (1973). Cundall, Brooks and Murray (1972), Hullin, McDonald and Allsopp (1972); and Melia (1970) however, found no statistical difference between lithium and placebo treated patients. Mendlewicz *et al.* (1973) and Stallone *et al.* (1973) each report that a family history of mania may indicate the likelihood of a positive response to lithium prophylaxis.

In summary, for bipolar patients, lithium maintenance seemed to be associated with less intense and less lengthy (but not always less frequent) affective episodes. For unipolars, the less toxic imipramine seemed to do as well as lithium. There is the need for more lithium vs. tricyclic studies, especially with unipolar patients. The combination of lithium and a tricyclic drug has not been adequately studied. Lithium has not been systematically compared with tricyclic drugs other than imipramine (e.g., amitriptyline). It is not clear how long the clinician must wait before expecting a "lithium" effect — some investigators have suggested a 15–24 month observation period. The early course of lithium maintenance may be marked by more affective episodes than are seen later on. In a study of "lithium carbonate prophylaxis failures," Dunner and Fieve (1974) found a disproportionate representation of "rapid cyclers" (at least four affective episodes per year). Davis (1973) finds good experimental validation of lithium prophylaxis in bipolars; but notes that it is "unclear whether lithium or imipramine is the better prophylactic for unipolar patients."

Although the depressed state may lend itself to creativity for a select few, the majority of severely depressed persons intensely want relief. For some bipolar depressives, however, periods of hypomania (and even mania) have been considered to be a basic facet of their personality. They may refuse prophylactic lithium therapy (which may diminish or terminate the cyclic experience of these mood states) or discontinue an ongoing program of therapy (Polatin, 1972). Others may deny the chronic, relapsing nature of their bipolar illness by refusing to accept treatment when they are well (Polatin and Fieve, 1971).

The impact of lithium carbonate on the severe depressive illnesses can no longer be overlooked. As a research tool, it may help illuminate the etiology of severe depression. (Secunda *et al.*, 1973). It is felt that the lithium ion may alter the transport of electrolytes and/or biogenic amines across cell membranes (Blinder, 1972; Mendels and Frazer, 1973; Glen and Reading, 1973). As a clinical tool, it may offer relief from the acute suffering of mania and depression and may have a prophylactic effect on a major psychiatric disorder (Fieve, 1970).

Treating a patient with lithium carbonate offers the clinician both the need and the opportunity to acquaint himself with the use of laboratory facilities and to deal with the issue of obtaining blood samples from his patient. A serum lithium level is readily obtainable from many medical laboratories. The narrow margin of safety between therapeutic levels of lithium carbonate and toxic levels makes serum determination a necessity.

The initial dose of lithium is generally one 300 mg capsule (Eskalith ®, Lithane ®, Lithonate ®) three times a day. The dose is increased in 300 mg increments until a serum level of 1.0–1.5 mEq/L is reached in the treatment of acute mania. Approximately 1,800 mg/day is usually necessary to reach this serum level, but there is considerable individual variation. Guidelines for the treatment of acute depression are not yet available. Although the FDA has approved the use of lithium only in acute mania thus far, revision to include prophylactic treatment of at least bipolar depressive illness is anticipated in the near future. For prophylactic treatment, 300 mg three times a day is the starting dose; increments of 300 mg following serum determination is the usual course of therapy. A serum level of 0.8–1.2 mEq/L is generally regarded as therapeutic, although again there is individual variability.

## Contraindications and Precautions

Lithium is not recommended for patients with significant cardiovascular or renal disease or evidence of brain damage (Lewis, 1973). A physical examination including laboratory studies of electrolytes and blood urea nitrogen, urinalysis and electrocardiogram (at the minimum) should precede lithium therapy (Beck, 1973). Effects of lithium on mother and fetus during pregnancy are not known. Effects on children under twelve are likewise unstudied. Interaction of lithium and oral contraceptives is unknown.

Lithium tolerance increases during mania, often necessitating larger doses to maintain desired serum levels. Lithium reduces sodium reabsorption by the kidney, therefore there is a need to be sensitive to changes in diet, fluid balance and especially electrolyte changes. Protracted sweating and diarrhea or intercurrent infection may tip an unsuspecting patient into toxic reactions.

### TABLE 15-12  TOXIC REACTIONS TO LITHIUM.

1.  Neuromuscular: *
    tremor, muscle hyperirritability, ataxia, choreo-athetotic movements, hyperactive DTRs

2.  Central nervous system:
    blackouts, seizures, slurred speech, dizziness, vertigo, urinary and fecal incontinence, somnolence, psychomotor retardation, restlessness, confusion, stupor, coma

3.  Cardiovascular:
    arrhythmia, hypotension, shock

4.  Gastrointestinal:
    anorexia, nausea, vomiting, diarrhea

5.  Genito-urinary:
    albuminaria, oliguria, polyuria, glycosuria

6.  Skin:
    drying and thinning of hair, anesthesia of skin

7.  Autonomic nervous system:
    blurred vision, dry mouth

8.  Thyroid abnormalities

9.  EEG changes

10.  EKG changes

11.  Leucocytosis

12.  Organic brain syndrome

*1–7 are generally thought to be dose related

## Side Effects and Toxic Reactions

Common side effects include fine tremor of hand or mouth, increased thirst and transient, mild nausea. A variety of toxic reactions have been described (see Table 15-12). Thyroid abnormalities (particularly hypothyroidism) have been reported (Candy, 1972; Shopsin, Shenkman, Blum and Hollander, 1973). Diabetes insipidus may occur, is unresponsive to Pitressin but is reversible with discontinuation of lithium (Gershon, 1973, personal communication). An intermittent elevated white blood count may confound the usefulness of this measure in an intercurrent infection (O'Connell, 1970).

Acute overdosage may produce somnolence, confusion, seizures, restlessness, stupor and coma. Treatment consists of hydration, infusion of sodium, potassium and glucose. Diuretics and/or dialysis may be indicated for some patients. Several case examples have been reported (Schou, Amdisen, Trap-Jensen, 1968; Gaind and Saran, 1970).

The value of plasma-lithium monitoring cannot be overestimated. Clinical experience has documented chronic underdosage (Fry and Marks, 1971) as well as impending toxicity in some unmonitored patients.

## OTHER DRUG THERAPIES

It is common practice in the management of the severely agitated or anxious depressed patient to supplement antidepressant drug therapy with a tranquilizer. This may be accomplished by prescribing a phenothiazine (e.g., perphenazine, trifluoperazine, thioridazine) in addition to the tricyclic agent. One such combination (perphenazine and amitriptyline) has been marketed (Triavil ®, Etrafron ®) in a variety of dose combinations (2-10, 2-25; 4-10; 4-25) as a single pill. The addition of a tranquilizer offers several potential benefits in selected, appropriate patients. Where insomnia is a problem, the anti-anxiety effect may add to the sedative side effect of either tranquilizer or antidepressant to make sleep more likely. The tranquilizing effect should be manifest before the accompanying antidepressant effect, demonstrating to some patients that they are "getting better." One chemical preparation (doxepin) claims both an early anti-anxiety effect and a later onset antidepressant action.

In May, 1972, a stir was created by the appearance of a report of a brief antidepressant effect for *thyrotropin-releasing hormone* on humans (Prange, Wilson, et al. 1972). This effect has been replicated by Kastin, Schalch, Ehrensing and Anderson (1972). By implication, this finding underlines the relevance of the hypothalamus to the affective disorders. Due to the transient nature of the antidepressant effect, it has little current clinical value; perhaps considerable research significance.

An earlier finding, that the addition of 25μg of *thyroid hormone (T3)* to imipramine enhanced clinical response, may be more immediately relevant to the clinician (Wilson, Prange, McClane, Rabon, Lipton, 1970). It was noted later

(Secunda *et al.,* 1973) that the beneficial effects of this combination seemed confined to women. Thyroid-stimulating hormone (TSH) may exert a similar effect (Prange, 1973, personal communication). This exciting research approach appears to have begun with a peripheral chemical (T3) and progressively focused back (TSH-TRH) to central neurological structures. Its eventual etiological significance may be of lasting importance.

Other compounds under investigation for their efficacy include L-*tryptophan* (a serotonin precursor) in mania (Prange, Wilson, Lynn, Alltop, Stikeleather, 1974) and depression (Coppen and Noguera, 1970) and L-*dopa* (useful in the treatment of parkinsonism) in depression (Bunney, Murphy, Brodie, Keith and Goodwin, 1970).

## ELECTROCONVULSIVE THERAPY

A review of the efficacy of and indications for ECT must begin with a consideration of the negative feelings with which it is often associated in the minds of clinicians, laymen and prospective patients. An advocate and leader in the field of research in convulsive therapy, Fink (1973) begins a recent editorial comment in *Biological Psychiatry* with an appropriate quote from Goethe: "Names are but noise and smoke, obscuring heavenly light." The offensive labels of "shock" and "shock therapy" are being abandoned by many investigators, convinced that a beneficial treatment has been withheld from some patients because of the clinician's (or patient's, or family's) aversion to its use.

The induction of a convulsion in the treatment of a mental disorder was attempted as early as 1785 (Beck, 1973). In 1933, Meduna used camphor to produce a seizure, and later (1935) Metrazol. In 1938, in Italy, Cerletti and Bini introduced the technique of electrically-induced seizures. Kalinowski first used this procedure in the U.S. in 1940. As with the antidepressant drugs, the initial indication for ECT was in the treatment of schizophrenia. In the early 1940s, severe depression replaced schizophrenia as the major indication for this treatment. Until the introduction of the psychoactive drugs, ECT was the most common method of treatment for hospitalized depressives (Mendels, 1970).

The availability of a less dramatic and potentially beneficial "tablet treatment" retarded the use of convulsive therapy. The public mind, dominated by early reports of grand mal seizures, unmodified by muscle relaxants and anesthesia, refused (in many cases) to consent to this form of treatment. Consequently, research into the effects and efficacy of ECT diminished.

In the late 1960s and early 1970s, there has been a resurgence of interest and activity in convulsive therapy. Modifications of the technique of administration have made it a more benign treatment intervention. Comparative studies have suggested its effectiveness, in some cases its superiority to antidepressant medication. Outpatient administration has become a reality for some patients. The addition of maintenance antidepressant therapy may eliminate the problem of early relapse mitigating against its use.

The physiological effects of ECT have been summarized by Holmberg (1963). When unmodified by muscle relaxants, there is a grand mal seizure, preceded by a jerk indicative of cortical stimulation. After a brief latent period, tonic and clonic convulsions follow. The EEG indicates generalized spike, and spike and wave activity. There is a brief period of electrical silence, followed by a return of the usual pattern. Blood $pCO_2$ is increased; $pO_2$ is decreased. Anoxia, increased heart rate and fluctuations in blood pressure occur due to the excitation of the autonomic nervous system. Blood sugar is increased for several hours; BUN, (blood urea nitrogen), potassium, calcium, phosphorus, and steroids increase in the blood (Beck, 1973). Impairment of memory (from forgetting names and dates to severe confusion) is a disturbing side effect but invariably reversible within a month of termination of treatment (Cronholm and Molander, 1964).

## Procedure of Administration

Woodruff et al., (1968) recommend the following procedure. In most hospital settings, a cart is wheeled into the patient's room, with medication, syringes, oxygen apparatus and a box-like generator contained upon it. Electrodes are placed on the temporal areas of each side of the head (only on the non-dominant side in unilateral ECT — see later). The patient is given 1 mg of atropine subcutaneously 30-60 minutes prior to treatment. (This counteracts irregularity of heart rate and increases in bronchial and salivary secretions otherwise seen.) Methohexital (a short-acting barbiturate anesthetic) is injected intravenously (50 mg of a 5% solution) in a 5-second period. Immediately following, through the same intravenous needle, succinylcholine (0.5 mg per kg) is administered over 1-2 seconds. After an interval of 50 seconds, electric current is passed (70-130 volts) over a 0.1-0.5 second period. A tonic phase convulsion (finger twitches may be the only observable indicator in a modified convulsion) persists for 10 seconds. A clonic phase convulsion follows for 30-40 seconds. Following the clonic phase, respiration is induced for three excursions of the thorax by means of a bellows and oxygen mask (Winokur, Clayton and Reich, 1969). Additional artificial respiration may be needed until spontaneous respirations are visible. Within 20 minutes, the patient can generally be served breakfast with amnesia for the treatment period but otherwise without sequellae of the procedure. The majority of patients who respond to ECT do so after 6-8 treatments administered at the rate of 3 per week (Mendels, 1970).

## Treatment Efficacy

Reports of improvement rates for heterogenous groups of depressed patients have varied from 40-100% (Beck, 1973). In an early study, Huston and Locher (1948) found an 88% recovery rate in patients treated with ECT contrasted with a 79% rate in a group hospitalized before the introduction of ECT. Bond and Morris (1954) found similarly equivalent recovery rates when they followed their patients for 5 years. However, in both studies, the duration of illness was markedly shortened for the ECT group. (9 months vs 15 months; 2.3 months vs. 4.5 months). The involutional (mid-life) depressives in Bond and Morris's study had twice the recovery rate (56%-27%) of controls and a markedly shorter duration of illness (2 months vs. 12 months).

More recent comparative ECT-drug studies have clearly demonstrated the efficacy of ECT for severe depression (Bruce, Crone, Fitzpatrick, Frewin, Gillis, Lascelles, Levene and Mersky, 1960; Greenblatt, Grosser and Wechsler, 1964; McDonald, Perkins, Merjerrison and Podilsky, 1966).

A more difficult clinical question is whether to prescribe ECT or antidepressant medication for the severely depressed patient. The risk of the procedure for the patient is probably less with drug therapy, however, ECT with today's modifications is a safe treatment (Beck, 1973). The onset of effect with convulsive therapy is usually more rapid than the onset of antidepressant drug effect. This may be an important consideration in the severely regressed or acutely suicidal patient. The relapse rate is thought to be greater following ECT, however, subsequent maintenance antidepressant therapy may eliminate this phenomenon. In some settings, ECT may necessitate hospitalization while drug therapy could be conducted on an outpatient basis. Finally, the apprehension of patient and/or family (and clinician) about ECT may lead to a decision favoring drug therapy. Especially when the patient has proven resistant or hypersensitive to drug therapy in the past, these objections might well be overcome.

TABLE 15-13   PREDICTORS OF RESPONSE TO
CONVULSIVE THERAPY.*

Presence of:
1. history of previous favorable response to ECT
2. early morning awakening
3. psychomotor retardation
4. family history of depression

Absence of:
5. neurotic traits in childhood
6. neurotic traits in adulthood
7. inadequate personality
8. hypochondriasis
9. hysterical attitude toward the current illness

*Adapted from Mendels, 1967.

An attempt has been made to specify those characteristics of depressive illness that seem most responsive to treatment with convulsive therapy. Mendels (1967) has found that the characteristics usually associated with "endogenous depression predict a favorable response in many cases (see Table 15-13). A recent

paper by Folstein, Folstein and McHugh (1973) identified the following characteristics in a mixed sample of patients receiving ECT as predictors of positive
response (regardless of diagnosis): family history of mood disorder, suicide,
symptoms of hopelessness, worthlessness or guilt.

## Precautions and Contraindications

The only absolute contraindication to convulsive therapy is brain tumor. The
sudden increase in intracerebral pressure during the treatment may result in
fatality or spread of the tumor (Freedman and Kaplan, 1967). Many patients
with myocardial disease and even recent coronary occulsions have been treated
successfully with ECT (Freedman and Kaplan, 1967) with a modification of
pretreatment anesthesia (replace barbiturates with a subconvulsive stimulus). In
the cardiac patient, however, the benefit of relief of agitation related to the
depressive illness must outweigh the risk inherent in undergoing treatment. A
recent report by Ballenger (1973) describes the successful treatment with
ECT of a manic patient who had a cardiac pacemaker.   Conditions predisposing to hemorrhage which were contraindications in unmodified ECT
are rarely problems with today's techniques (e.g., peptic ulcer, subdural
hematoma, aortic aneurysm).   Since intraocular pressure *decreases* in ECT,
glaucoma is not a contraindication.   Succinylcholine, however, may increase
intraocular pressure so pretreatment of glaucoma patients with eserine is
necessary.

## Unilateral Convulsive Therapy

Perhaps the most important recent modification of the procedure of administering ECT involves the placement of unilateral electrodes over the non-dominant
temporal area instead of bilateral placement. This approach has diminished or
eliminated the complaint of confusion and memory loss (Abrams, 1972). Some
investigators feel that unilateral ECT may be less potent and require additional
treatments than the bilateral form (Karliner, 1972). Others (D'Elia, 1970) feel
that unilateral ECT should replace the bilateral form. Abrams, Volavka, Roubicek,
Dornbush and Fink (1970), and Karliner (1972) agree that after initial treatment
with bilateral ECT, a switch to unilateral placement should reduce side effects
without diminution of efficacy.

## Mechanism of Action

A sequential accounting of the various effects of convulsive therapy has successfully narrowed the search to understand how ECT works. The use of muscle
relaxants without compromising therapeutic benefit indicates that the motor
convulsion is not the major event (Cherkin, 1974). The success of unilateral ECT
(without memory impairment) indicates that this side effect is nonessential
(Zornetzer, 1974).   Flurothyl (Indoklon) inhalation-induced convulsions are

effective – therefore, electric current is not a necessary feature (Small, 1974). Studies of multiple seizures under forced oxygenation (MECT) produced no more rapid results than every-other-day treatment (Blachly and Gowing, 1966). These findings have made the central biochemical changes in the brain, related to cerebral proteins and/or biogenic amines, the major focus of the inquiry.

Contradictory findings in this area indicate that final answers are not yet available (Kety, 1974). ECT increases turnover of both norepinephrine and and serotonin (Schildkraut and Draskoczy, 1974). It has proven effective in some cases of mania as well as depression. The time course of its effect seems uninfluenced by changes in number of seizures delivered or method. Therefore, central changes accumulating over many days may prove to be the etiology of the effectiveness of convulsive therapy. This research may help illuminate the etiology of the affective disorders as a by-product of seeking to understand the mechanism of action of convulsive therapy. A comprehensive account of research to date has been recently published (Fink, Kety and McGaugh, 1974).

## REFERENCES

Abrams, R. Recent clinical studies of ECT. *Seminars in Psychiatry.* **4** (1): 3–12 (1972).

Abrams, R., Volavka, J., Roubicek, J., Dornbush, R. and Fink, M. Lateralized EEG changes after unilateral and bilateral ECT. *Dis. Nerv. Syst.* **31** (Supp.): 29–33 (1970).

Ainslie, J.D., Jones, M.B. and Stiefels, J.R. Practical drug evaluation method: imipramine in depressed outpatients. *Arch. Gen. Psychiat.* **12**: 368–373 (1965).

Alarcon, R.D. and Covi, L. The precipitating event in depression: Some methodological considerations. *J. Nerv. Ment. Dis.* **155**: 379–391 (1972).

Alexander, L., Berkeley, A.W. and Cohen, S.L. Which anti-depressant for which patient? *Psychosomatics.* **13** (1): 49–56 (1972).

American Psychiatric Association. *Diagnostic and Statistical Manual of Mental Disorders (2nd ed.).* Washington: A.P.A. Pub., 1968.

Angst, J., Weis, P. and Grof, P. Lithium prophylaxis in recurrent affective disorders. *Brit. J. Psychiat.* **116**: 604–614 (1970).

Anthony, E.J. Psychoneurotic disorders. In: Freedman, A.M. and Kaplan, H.G. (Eds.), *Comprehensive Textbook of Psychiatry,* pp. 1387–1406. Baltimore: Williams & Wilkens Co., 1967.

Baastrup, P.C. The use of lithium in manic depressive psychosis. *Comprehensive Psychiat.* **5**: 396–408 (1964).

Baastrup, P.C., Poulsen, J.C., Schou, M., Thomsen, J. and Amdisen, A. Prophylactic lithium: Double-blind discontinuation in manic-depressive and recurrent depressive disorders. *Lancet.* **1**: 326–330 (1970).

Baastrup, P.C. and Schou, M. Lithium as a propylactic agent against recurrent depressions and manic-depressive psychosis. *Arch. Gen. Psychiat.* **16**: 162–172 (1967).

386    DEAN SCHUYLER

Ballenger, J.C. Electroconvulsive therapy and cardiac pacemakers. *Psychosomat. Med.* **14**: 233–234 (1973).

Beck, A.T. *Depression: Clinical, experimental and theoretical aspects.* New York: Harper & Row, 1967.

Beck, A.T. *The Diagnosis and Management of Depression,* pp. 19–24. Philadelphia: University of Pennsylvania Press, 1973.

Beck, A.T., Schuyler, D. and Herman, I. Development of Suicide Intent Scales. In: Beck, A.T., Resnik, H.L. and Lettieri, D.J. (Eds.), *The Prediction of Suicide.* Bowie, Md: Charles Press, 1974.

Blachly, P., Gowing, D. Multiple monitored electroconvulsive treatment. *Comprehensive Psychiat.* **7**: 100–109 (1966).

Blackwell, B. Lithium: Prophylactic or panacea. *Intern. Drug Therapy Newsletter.* .**4**: 29–36 (1969).

Blinder, M.G. The use of lithium carbonate. *Behavioral Neuropsychiat.* **4**: 22–24 (1972).

Bond, E.D. and Morris, H.H. Results of treatment in psychoses – with a control series: III. Manic depressive reactions. *Amer. J. Psychiat.* **110**: 881–887 (1954).

Bruce, E.M., Crone, N., Fitzpatrick, G., Frewin, S.J., Gillis, A., Lascelles, C.F., Levene, C.J. and Mersky, H. A comparative trial of ECT and Tofranil. *Amer. J. Psychiat.* **117**: 76 (1960).

Bunney, W.E., Murphy, D.L., Brodie, H., Keith, H. and Goodwin, F.K. *L*-Dopa in depressed patients. *Lancet.* **1**: 352 (1970).

Cade, J.P.J., Lithium salts in the treatment of psychotic excitement. *Med. J.* of *Australia.* **2**: 349–55 (1949).

Campbell, J.D. *Manic-Depressive Disease.* Philadelphia: Lippincott, 1953.

Candy, J. Severe hypothyroidism – an early complication of lithium therapy. *Brit. Med. J.* **5821**: 277 (1972).

Castelnuovo-Tedesco, P. *Depressions in Patients with Physical Disease.* Cranbury, N.J.: Wallace Laboratories, 1961.

Cherkin, A. Effects of Flurothyl (Indoklon) upon memory in the chick. In: Fink, M., Kety, S. and McGaugh, J.L. (Eds.), *Psychobiology of Convulsive Therapy.* Washington; V.H. Winston & Sons, 1974.

Cohen, S.M., Allen, M.G., Pollin, W. and Hrubec, Z. Relationship of schizoaffective psychosis to manic-depressive psychosis and schizophrenia. *Arch. Gen. Psychiat.* **26**: 539–545 (1972).

Coppen, A. and Noguera, R. *L*-tryptophan in depression. *Lancet.* **2**: 1111 (1970).

Coppen, A., Noguera, R., Bailey, J., Burns, B.H., Swani, M.S., Hare, E.H. Gardner, R. and Maggs, R. Prophylactic lithium in affective disorders. *Lancet.* **2**: 275–279 (1972).

Cronholm, B. and Molander, L. Memory disturbances after electro-convulsive therapy: 5. Conditions one month after a series of treatments. *Acta Psychiat. Scand.* **40**: 211–216 (1964).

Cundall, R.L., Brooks, P.W. and Murray, L.G. Controlled evaluation of lithium prophylaxis in affective disorders. *Psychological Medicine.* **3**: 308–311 (1972).

Cytryn, L. and McKnew, D.H. Proposed classification of childhood depression. *Amer. J. Psychiat.* **129**: 149–155 (1972).

Davis, J.  Efficacy of tranquilizing drugs and anti-depressant drugs. *Arch. Gen. Psychiat.* **13**: 552–572 (1965).

Davis, J.  Special Report on Depression: A Panel. Presented at the annual meeting of the A.P.A., Honolulu, Hawaii, May, 1973.

D'Elia, G.  *Unilateral Electroconvulsive Therapy.* Copenhagen: Munksgaard, 1970.

Dunner, D.L. and Fieve, R.R.  Clinical factors in lithium carbonate prophylaxis failure. *Arch. Gen. Psychiat.* **30**: 229–233 (1974).

Dyson, W.L. and Mendels, J.  Lithium and depression. *Current Therap. Res.* **10**: 601–608 (1968).

Editorial. *Lancet.* **1**: 709–710 (1969).

Feighner, J., Robins, E., Guze, S.B., Woodruff, R.A., Winokur, G. and Munoz, R.  Diagnostic criteria for use in psychiatric research. *Arch. Gen. Psychiat.* **26**: 57–68 (1972).

Fieve, R.R.  Clinical controversies and theoretical mode of action of lithium carbonate. *Intern. Pharmacopsychia.* **5**: 107–118 (1970).

Fieve, R.R., Platman, S.R. and Plutchick, R.R.  The use of lithium in affective disorders. *Amer. J. Psychiat.* **125**: 487–498 (1968).

Fink, M.  "How shocking is 'shock therapy.' " *Biol. Psychiat.* **7 (2)**: 79–80 (1973).

Fink, M., Kety, S.S. and McGaugh, J.L.  *Psychobiology of Convulsive Therapy.* Washington: V.H. Winston & Sons, 1974.

Flood, R. and Seager, C.  A restrospective examination of psychiatric case records of patients who subsequently commit suicide. *Brit. J. Psychiat.* **114**: 443–450 (1968).

Folstein, M., Folstein, S. and McHugh, P.R.  Clinical predictors of improvement after electroconvulsive therapy of patients with schizophrenia, neurotic reactions and affective disorders. *Biol. Psychiat.* **7** (2): 147–152 (1973).

Freedman, A.M. and Kaplan, H.I. (Eds.). *Comprehensive Textbook of Psychiatry.* Baltimore: Williams & Wilkens, 1967.

Freeman, L.  *The Cry of Love.* Toronto: The MacMillan Co., 1969.

Fry, D.E. and Marks, V.  "Value of plasma – Lithium Monitoring." *Lancet.* **7705**: 886–888 (1971).

Gaind, R. and Saran, B.M.  Acute lithium poisoning. *Postgrad. Med.* **46**: 629–631 (1970).

Gershon, S. and Yuwiller, A.  Lithium ion: A specific psychopharmacological approach to the treatment of mania. *J. Neuropsychiat.* **1**: 229–241 (1960).

Glen, A.I.M. and Reading, H.W.  Regulatory action of lithium in manic depressive illness. *Lancet.* **2**: 1239–1241 (1973).

Goldberg, H.L. and Nathan, L.  A double-blind study of Tofranil pamoate vs. Tofranil hydrochloride. *Psychosomatics.* **13** (2): 131–134 (1972).

Goodwin, F.K., Murphy, D.L. and Bunney, W.E.  Lithium carbonate treatment in depression and mania. *Arch. Gen. Psychiat.* **21**: 486–496 (1969).

Greenblatt, M., Grosser, G.H. and Wechsler, H.  Differential response of hospitalized depressed patients to somatic therapy. *Amer. J. Psychiat.* **120**: 935–943 (1964).

Harlow, H.F. and Suomi, S.J.   Production of depressive behaviors in young monkeys. *J. of Autism and Childhood Schizophrenia.* **1** (3):   246–255 (1971).

Hartigan, G.P.   The use of lithium salts in affective disorders. *Brit. J. Psychiat.* **109**: 810–814 (1963).

Holmberg, G.   Biological aspects of convulsive therapy. *Intern. Rev. Neurobiol.* **5**: 389–412 (1963).

Hullin, R.P., McDonald, R. and Allsopp, M.N.   Propylactic lithium in recurrent affective disorders. *Lancet.* **1**: 1044–1046 (1972).

Huston, P.E. and Locher, L.M.   Manic-depressive psychosis:   course when treated with electric shock. *Arch. Neurol. & Psychiat.* **60**: 37–48 (1948).

Huzzain, M.Z. and Chaudhry, Z.A.   Single vs. divided daily dose of Trimipramine in the treatment of depressive illness. *Amer. J. Psychiat.* **130**: 1142–1144 (1973).

Jacobsen, E.   *Depression : Comparative studies of normal, neurotic and psychotic conditions.* New York: International Universities Press, 1971.

Johnson, G.   Anti-depressant effect of lithium. *Comprehensive Psychiat.* **15** (1): 43–47 (1974).

Karliner, W.   Present status of unilateral shock treatments. *Behavioral Neuropsychiat.* **4** (10):   2–4 (1972).

Kastin, A.J., Schalch, D.S., Ehrensing, R.H. and Anderson, M.S.   Improvement in mental depression with decreased thyrotropin response after administration of thyrotropin-releasing hormone. *Lancet.* **2**: 740–742 (1972).

Kety, S.   Biochemical and neurochemical effects of electroconvulsive shock. In: Fink, M., Kety, S.S. and McGaugh, J.L. (Eds.), *Psychobiology of Convulsive Therapy.* Washington: V.H. Winston & Sons, 1974.

Klerman, G.L. and Cole, J.O.   Clinical pharmacology of imipramine and related anti-depressant compounds. *Pharmacology Review.* **17**: 101–141 (1965).

Kline, N.S.   *Depression: Its Diagnosis and Treatment.* Basel: S.Karger, 1969.

Kraines, S.H.   *Mental Depressions and Their Treatment.* New York: Macmillan, 1957.

Kuhn, R.   The treatment of depressive states with G-22355 (imipramine hydrochloride). *Amer. J. Psychiat.* **115**: 459–464 (1958).

Lewis, A.J. (Ed.)   *Modern Drug Encyclopedia, Twelfth edition.* New York: The Dun-Donnelley Pub. Co., 1973.

Maas, J.W., Fawcett, J.A. and Dekirmenjian, H.   Catecholamine metabolism depressive illness and drug response. *Arch. Gen. Psychiat.* **26** (3): 252–262 (1972).

Maggs, R.   Treatment of manic illness with lithium carbonate. *Brit. J. Psychiat.* **109**: 56–65 (1963).

Mc Donald, I.M., Perkins, M., Merjerrison, G. and Podilsky, M.   A controlled comparison of amitriptyline and electroconvulsive therapy in the treatment of depression. *Amer. J. Psychiat.* **122**: 1427–1431 (1966).

Melia, P.I.   Prophylactic lithium:   A double-blind trial in recurrent affective disorders. *Brit. J. Psychiat.* **116**: 621–624 (1970).

Mendels, J.   The prediction of response to electroconvulsive therapy. *Amer. J. Psychiat.* **124**: 153–159 (1967).

Mendels, J. *Concepts of Depression*, pp. 29–33. New York: John Wiley & Sons, 1970.

Mendels, J. and Cochrane, C. The nosology of depression: The endogenous-reactive concept. *Amer. J. Psychiat.* **124** (Supp.): 1–11 (1968).

Mendels, J. and DiGiacomo, J. The treatment of depression with a single daily dose of imipramine pamoate. *Amer. J. Psychiat.* **130**: 1022–1024 (1974).

Mendels, J. and Frazer, A. Intracellular lithium concentration and clinical response: Towards a membrane theory of depression. *J. Psychiat. Research.* **10**: 9–18 (1973).

Mendels, J., Secunda, S. and Dyson, W. A controlled study of the antidepressant effects of lithium carbonate. *Arch. Gen. Psychiat.* **26**: 154–157 (1972).

Mendlewicz, J., Fieve, R.R. and Stallone, F. Relationship between the effectiveness of lithium therapy and family history. *Amer. J. Psychiat.* **130**: 1011–1013 (1973).

Nahunek, K., Svestka, J. and Redova, A. Lithium's position among antidepressants in the treatment of acute endogenous and involutional depressions. *International Pharmacopsychiat.* **5**: 249–257 (1970).

O'Connell, R.A. Leukocytosis during lithium carbonate treatment. *International Pharmacopsychiat.* **4**: 30–34 (1970).

Orne, M. On the social psychology of the psychological experiment. *American Psychologist.* **17** (11): 776–783 (1962).

Paykel, I.S. Depressive typologies and response to amitriptyline. *Brit. J. Psychiat.* **120**: 147–156 (1972).

Polatin, P. Lithium carbonate prophylaxis in affective disorders (Clinical versus research applications). *Dis. Nerv. Syst.* **33** (7): 472–475 (1972).

Polatin, P. and Fieve, R.R. Patient rejection of lithium carbonate prophylaxis. *J. Amer. Med. Assoc.* **218** (6): 864–866 (1971).

Prange, A.J., Wilson, I.C., Lara, P.O., Alltop, L.B. and Breese, G.R. Effects of thyrotropin-releasing hormone in depression. *Lancet.* **2**: 999–1002 (1972).

Prange, A.J., Wilson, I.C., Lynn, C.W., Alltop, L.B. and Stikeleather, R.A. *L*-tryptophan in mania. *Arch. Gen. Psychiat.* **30**: 56–62 (1974).

Prien, R.F., Caffey, E.M. and Klett, C.J. Comparison of lithium carbonate and chlorpromazine in the treatment of mania. *Arch. Gen. Psychiat.* **26**: 146–153 (1972).

Prien, R.F., Caffey, E.M. and Klett, C.J. Prophylactic efficacy of lithium carbonate in manic-depressive illness. *Arch. Gen. Psychiat.* **28**: 337–341 (1973).

Prien, R.F., Klett, C.J. and Caffey, E.M. A comparison of lithium carbonate and imipramine in the prevention of affective episodes in recurrent affective illness. *Arch. Gen. Psychiat.* **29**: 420–425 (1973).

Ray, I. Combinations of anti-depressant drugs in the treatment of depressive illness. *Can. Psychiat. Assoc. J.* **18**: 399–402 (1973).

Raskin, A., Schulterbrandt, J.G., Reatig, N., Crook, T.A. and Odle, D. Depression subtypes and response to phenelzine, diazepam and a placebo. *Arch. Gen. Psychiat.* **30**: 66–75 (1974).

Regan, P.F. Brief psychotherapy of depression. *Amer. J. Psychiat.* **122**: 28–32 (1965).

Robins, E. and Guze, S.B.  Classification of affective disorders:  The Primary-Secondary; the Endogenous-Reactive, and the Neurotic-Psychotic concepts. In:  Williams, T.A., Katz, M.M., Shield, J.A. (Eds.), *Recent Advances in the Psychobiology of the Depressive Illnesses,* pp. 283–293. Washington: USGPO, 1972, DHEW Pub. No. (HSM) 70–9053.

Robins, E., Murphy, G.E., Wilkinson, R.H., Gassner, S. and Kayes, J. Some clinical considerations in the prevention of suicide based on a study of 134 successful suicides. *Amer. J. Pub. Health.* **49**: 888–899 (1959).

Saran, B.M. Lithium. *Lancet.* **7607**: 1208–1209 (1969).

Schildkraut, J.J.  The catecholamine hypothesis of the affective disorders:  A review of supporting evidence. *Amer. J. Psychiat.* **122**: 509–522 (1965).

Schildkraut, J. J. and Draskoczy, P.  Effects of ECT on catecholamine metabolism:  basic and clinical studies. In:  Fink, M., Kety, S.S. and McGaugh, J.L. (Eds.), *Psychobiology of Convulsive Therapy.* Washington:  V.H. Winston & Sons, 1974.

Schildkraut, J.J., Draskoczy, P.R., Gershon, E.S., Reich, P and Grab, E.L. Catecholamine metabolism in affective disorders – IV. *J. Psychiat. Res.* **9** (3): 173–185 (1972).

Schou, M., Amdisen, A. and Trap-Jensen, J. Lithium poisoning. *Amer. J. Psychiat.* **125** (4): 520–527 (1968).

Schou, M., Juel–Nielsen, N., Stromgren, E. and Voldby, H. The treatment of manic psychoses by the administration of lithium salts. *J Neurol. Neurosurg. Psychiat.* **17**: 250–260 (1954).

Schuckit, M., Robins, E. and Feighner, J.  Tricyclic anti-depressants and monoamine oxidase inhibitors. *Arch. Gen. Psychiat.* **24 (6)**: 509–574 (1971).

Schuyler, D. Suicidal motivation: Measurement and meaning. *St. Bartholmew's Hospital Journal.* **76**: 23–26 (1972).

Schuyler, D. The Depressive Spectrum. New York: Jason Aronson, Inc., 1974a.

Schuyler, D. The evaluation of the suicidal patient. In: Novello, J.R., (Ed.) *Practical Handbook of Psychiatry.* Springfield: Charles C. Thomas, 1974b.

Schuyler, D. and Beck, A.T. The assessment of suicidal intent. In: Litman, R., (Ed.), *Proceedings of the VIth International Congress for Suicide Prevention.* Ann Arbor: Edwards Brothers, 1972.

Secunda, S.K., Katz, M.M., Friedman, R.J. and Schuyler, D. *Special Report: 1973:  The Depressive Disorders.* Washington: U.S.G.P.O., 1973. DHEW Pub. No. (HSM) 73–9157.

Seligman, M.E.P. Depression and learned helplessness. In: Friedman, R.J. and Katz, M.M. (Eds.), *The Psychology of Depression: Contemporary Theory and Research.* Washington: V.H. Winston & Sons, 1974.

Shopsin, B., Shenkman, L., Blum, M. and Hollander, C.S. Iodine and lithium induced hypothyroidism. *Amer. J. Med.* **55**: 695–699 (1973).

Small, I.F. Inhalant convulsive therapy. In: Fink, M., Kety, S.S. and McGaugh, J.L. *Psychobiology of Convulsive Therapy.* Washington; V.H. Winston & Sons, 1974.

Spitz, R.A. Anaclitic depression. *Psychoanalytic Study of the Child.* **2**: 313–342 (1946).

Stallone, F., Shelley, E., Mendlewicz, J. and Fieve, R.R. The use of lithium in affective disorders, III: A double blind study of prophylaxis in bipolar illness. *Amer. J. Psychiat.* **130**: 1006–1010 (1973).

Stancer, H.C., Furlong, F.W. and Godse, D.D.   A longitudinal investigation of lithium as a prophylactic agent for recurrent depressions.   *Can. Psychiat. Assoc. J.*   **15:**   29–40 (1970).

Stokes, P.E., Shamoian, C.A., Stoll, P.M. and Patton, M.J.   Efficacy of lithium as acute treatment of manic-depressive illness. *Lancet.* **1:** 1319–1325 (1971).

Weisman, A.D. and Worden, J.W.   Risk-rescue rating in suicide assessment. *Arch. Gen. Psychiat.* **26:** 553–560 (1972).

Wilson, D.C.   Dynamics and psychotherapy of depression. *J. Amer. Med. Assoc.* **158:** 151–153 (1955).

Wilson, E.C., Prange, A.J., McClane, T.K., Rabon, A.M. and Lipton, M.A. Thyroid hormone enhancement of imipramine in non-retarded depressions. *New Engl. J. Med.* **19:** 1063–1067 (1970).

Winokur, G.   The types of affective illness. *J. Nerv. Ment. Dis.* **156** (2): 82–95 (1973).

Winokur, G., Clayton, P.J. and Reich, T. *Manic Depressive Illness.* St. Louis: C.V. Mosby Co., 1969.

Winokur, G. and Reich, T.   Two genetic factors in manic-depressive disease. *Comprehensive Psychiat.* **11:** 93–99 (1970).

Woodruff, R.A., Pitts, F.N. and McClure, J.N. The drug modification of ECT: I. Methohexital, thiopental and pre-oxygenation. *Arch. Gen. Psychiat.* **18:** 605–611 (1968).

Yaskin, J.C.   Nervous symptoms as earliest manifestations of carcinoma of the pancreas. *J. Amer. Med. Assoc.* **96:** 1664–1668 (1931).

Zornetzer, S.   Retrograde amnesia and brain seizures in rodents: electrophysiological and neuroanatomical analyses. In: Fink, M., Kety, S.S. and McGaugh, J.L. (Eds.), *Psychobiology of Convulsive Therapy.* Washington: V.H. Winston & Sons, 1974.

Zubin, J. and Fleiss, J.   Current biometric approaches to depression. In: Fieve, R.F. (Ed.), *Depression in the 70's,* pp. 7–19. Princeton: Excerpta Medica, 1971.

# 16 The Treatment of Neuroses and Borderline Cases

## Richard D. Chessick

Two basic assumptions will be made about the reader of this chapter. The first is that he is familiar with the standard textbook symptom-based descriptions of the neuroses, and also at least superficially aware of the various and confusing descriptions of borderline cases. For those who wish to review these syndromes, Freedman and Kaplan (1975) present adequate descriptions of the classical neurotic syndromes; Grinker *et al.* (1968) and Chessick (1974a) present clinical descriptions of the borderline patient. At the same time, it is clear that confusion reigns in the nosology as evidenced by the shift in the classification from DSM-I to DSM-II*; the reader, if he has been trained several years ago, must familiarize himself with this shift in nosology. The present chapter will refer to the current nosology (DSM-II) although in my opinion it represents a step backwards from understanding the neurotic disorders, because it eliminates the important dynamic concept of emotional illness as a reaction.

The second major assumption is that the reader is familiar with the basic definitions and techniques of intensive psychotherapy as have been presented in detail, for example, in texts by DeWald (1971), Chessick (1969, 1971, 1974), and in papers by Strupp (1969, 1970, 1972). There is not space in this chapter to discuss in detail the essence of intensive psychotherapy as it applies to the treatment of the neuroses and borderline cases, and since I have discussed this elsewhere in the references already cited, it will be assumed that the reader is reasonably familiar with the definitions, basic concepts, and also the current controversies in the field. If the reader is not familiar with this literature it would

*American Psychiatric Association Diagnostic and Statistical Manual of Mental Disorders, Second Edition (II).*

be in his best interest to stop at this point and study the references cited before attempting to wade into highly controversial issues discussed in the present chapter.

## ADMIXTURE OF OPINIONS

No better summary of the problems covered in this chapter and slogan to characterize what is happening in the treatment of the neuroses and borderline cases can be found than the title to Grinker's (1964) brief paper: "Psychiatry Rides Madly in All Directions." He writes

> The public today holds an admixture of opinions. As magical helpers of nature's curative powers who know so much about the unknowable, who can interpret a glance, a gesture, a slipped word, or a phrase to mean so much, we are endowed with all the powers of the idealized or supernatural father. The press exemplifies this attitude by insisting on obtaining and even printing our comments off the cuff on any and all facets of life and even behavior. . . . The professional view held by psychiatrists is today mixed and confused. Psychoanalysis, for which many have sacrificed so much, has not become the therapeutic answer; it seems to be mired in a theoretical rut vigilantly guarded by the orthodox and, except for relatively few examples, prevented from commingling with science. The great breakthrough promised by the modern psychosomatic approach, with its concepts of specificity of psychological etiology of degenerative diseases, has succumbed to the hard facts of multiple causation and critical phases of development. Small wonder that with these disappointments a fertile soil has been created for new therapies − pharmacological, psychological, and social − each one rapidly exploited as a panacea.

This situation has been described by Abrams (1969) as the new eclecticism. This author considers it "a refreshing departure" that dynamic psychotherapy is not always recommended as the treatment of choice for every disorder. We now have the enormous advances of pharmacotherapy, electric shock therapy, the behavior therapies, hypnosis and suggestion techniques, and group techniques such as psychodrama, role-playing, couple or family therapy, sensitivity or T-group training, and milieu therapy, as additions to our treatment procedures. Abrams does recognize that "The dangers of this proposed technical eclecticism are many: dilettantism, superficiality, dehumanization."

Even within the field of psychotherapy itself many "innovations" have been proposed and brought together (see for example, Goldman and Milman (1972)). Among these are such intriguingly entitled procedures as rational-emotive psychotherapy, bioenergetic analysis, Gestalt therapy, multiple therapy, and less esoterically titled proposals such as crisis therapy, existential therapy, hypnotic therapy, the use of videotape playback and many other conceptualizations. Some of these vastly wander away from and others deliberately deny many of the basic concepts and premises of psychoanalytically-informed psychotherapy.

An important and extremely controversial subgroup of the therapeutic techniques used in the treatment of the neuroses and borderline cases today are the behavior therapies, accompanied by an impressive array of scientific-sounding terminologies and statistics. There are as many varieties of behavior therapy proposed as there are varieties of psychotherapies — as summarized for example, by Kanfer and Phillips (1966). Quite significantly their paper has a subtitle: "A Panacea for All Ills or a Passing Fancy?" Whether or not the behavior therapies really simply represent another example of manipulation of the patient in a positive transference as basically suggested by Marmor (1971), it is certainly clear that, as he insists

> In the final analysis, the technique of therapy that we choose to employ must depend on what aspect of man's complex psychic functioning we address ourselves to. If we choose to focus on the patient's overt symptoms or behavior patterns, some kind of behavior therapy may well be the treatment of choice. On the other hand, if the core of his problems rests in symbolic distortions of perception, cognition, affect or subtle disturbances in interpersonal relationships, the source and nature of which he may be totally unaware, then the more elaborate re-educational process of dynamic psychotherapy may be necessary.

## THE PSYCHOTHERAPIST

To put this another and perhaps a simpler way, the basic decision about what form of therapy to use in the treatment of neuroses and borderline cases depends at least in part on the personality of the psychotherapist, on his philosophy of life, attitude toward people, and his beliefs about the nature and etiology of emotional disorder which are largely a function of his personality. Perhaps the most dramatic description of what is going on in this controversial field today is provided by Kubie's (1971) discussion of the retreat from patients. Kubie explains that an important factor in the choice of how to manage and treat emotional disorders is what he calls "maturity" as a psychiatrist. This maturity is a result of the meeting of three rivers in life:

> The individual has first to work his way out of many of the conflicts which he buried in early life and which tie him to his own childhood. In one way or another. . . an evolving series of therapeutic experiences must occur if man is to escape bondage to his own past in order to win his freedom and to grow toward maturity as a human being. Secondly, maturity requires that he must have accepted such adult responsibilities as marriage and parenthood. It is in coping with these that he will encounter and master the problems which confront every adult as he emerges from youth. Emotional maturity of this kind is a necessary prerequisite for dealing with the problems of others from a mature basis . . . (Third) Not reading, not diligent study, not psychological aptitude can supplant the experiences of sus-

tained relationships with patients as they fall ill and fall well again. Nothing can take the place of being a participant-observer of these fluctuating changes over weeks, months, and even years.

Kubie reviews a variety of reasons for the current "flight from patients," or more precisely for the current tendency to avoid involving patients with one's self in long-term intensive psychoanalytically-informed psychotherapy. What it boils down to is the tremendous demands that are made on the psychological structure of the therapist by the prolonged experience of doing a lot of intensive psychotherapy, for surely psychotherapeutic involvement imposes complex emotional stresses on all therapists, and especially on the novice.  As Kubie points out, "Every patient who is undergoing psychotherapy of any kind requires high investments of feeling and time: *time* because change and growing up take time and *feeling* because of the therapist's inescapable, mixed identifications with the patient, subtly masked though these may be . . . when we treat someone else we are also treating or at least defending ourselves.  This takes a great deal out of the therapist at any age, but especially when he is young."

The constant battering from the patients, their frequent overt or masked primitive demands, and the continuous exposure to the hostility from the patient and patient's family, wears down the older therapist and tends to produce depression.  Kubie calls this phenomenon "the late age drop-out" from clinical work. These "drop-outs" often turn bitterly against their early activities and mislead younger men into following suit.  Kubie makes it clear that the score of a few complete successes, many partial successes, and some partial failures and complete failures, can breed depression and anger so that "A long life devoted to therapy in psychiatry may lead even the skillful, experienced, and successful among us to an ill-defined sense of mourning and a weariness of the spirit."

All these pressures tend to influence the young psychiatrist or the resident in psychiatry to retreat from work with the individual patients and to work with groups or families.  Such a retreat often involves turning prematurely to teaching, research, or administration of community services.  This seduction of the young therapist away from psychotherapy before he has developed the ability to deal with interaction between his own emotional problems and those of his individual patients, may cause irreparable harm to the future of psychiatry.

All psychiatrists today are under enormous social pressure.  The sources of this pressure are manifold.  The practitioners of group therapy, behavior therapies, community psychiatry, and statistical research as well as the so-called directive and organic psychiatrists described by Hollingshead and Redlich (1958) exert a powerful pressure on the psychotherapist toward ostracism, loneliness, and isolation from his colleagues.   Derogatory references often describe intensive psychotherapy as a religion, a mystic faith, or sheer quackery, and especially attacking it as a non-scientific technique which cannot provide the standard statistical proofs of its efficacy.   Therefore the practitioners of intensive psychoanalytically-informed psychotherapy become second class citizens in the psychiatric and medical profession. They often react to such pressures with separatist tendencies, abandoning the white coat and the ordinary professional medical journals and forming groups, seminars, and publications of their own.

In addition to this, every possible pressure from the rest of the medical profession is constantly present. There is an almost total lack of understanding of long-term psychotherapy among many in the medical profession itself. This is especially manifest in the insistence of the nonpsychiatrist physician that patients show fast-fast-fast results in a few sessions, in a continual derogation of the long-term psychotherapist in jokes and comments made among nonpsychiatrist physicians, and in a constant resentment of the psychotherapist who cannot take one patient after another on referral because he can only see so many patients in long-term therapy and there is very little turn-over. Perhaps the most lethal of all criticisms is the direct expression of opinions by respected nonpsychiatrist physicians to their patients, accusing analytically-oriented psychotherapists of at best being foolish and incompetent and at worst as being seducers and exploiters of their patients.

## SOCIOCULTURAL FACTORS

As if this is not enough, society itself has become increasingly inimical to a concentration on the unfolding of the individual. Kepecs (1968) explains that the style of psychoanalysis, once a revolutionary movement, has now become relatively conservative. "Much of its value system and orientation is in conflict with aims and aspects of contemporary society and of contemporary American psychiatry ... Its style, characterized by leisurely introspection and study of the function of the human mind and by minute self-conscious observations of the details of human interactions and transactions, is in many ways not compatible with current social circumstances. And adaptation to many social needs and pressures is probably not compatible with psychoanalysis."

One of the greatest psychoanalytic psychotherapists, Franz Alexander (1964) in the last paper before his recent death reminds us that

> The psychoanalyst who still holds on to the original goal, to understand each person on the basis of his highly specific life history, which may resemble grossly others in the same group, but which is still different, is looked upon by many as having an antiquated 19th century orientation. Mass civilization is not concerned with the unique person. . . . Psychoanalysis and psychotherapy in general are among the few still existing remedies against the relentlessly progressing levelization of industrial societies which tend to reduce the individual person to becoming an indistinguishable member of the faceless masses.

This trend, which was already apparent to Alexander in the early 1960s has continued with a vengeance into the early 1970s. Applebaum (1972) for example, explains how political, social and technological forces, with greater or lesser regard for scientific considerations, have lately impinged upon individual long-term psychotherapy. The goals of such forces include the delivery of health care on as wide a numerical or economic basis as possible, the use of community resources rather than private practice ones, and the discovery of new means of treatment with which to achieve these goals. "Often these objectives are accompanied by skepticism as to the extent that insight into unconscious influence on behavior results in beneficially changed behavior. . . . In these contexts, the term 'long term treatment' is often used invidiously to suggest that it is old fashioned and wasteful as well as ineffective."

At this point the reader of this chapter will have to make up his own mind. This controversy is far from resolved. My opinion is that intensive psychoanalytically-informed psychotherapy remains at this time still the most effective procedure available for both the understanding of and the amelioration or cure of the neuroses and borderline cases, and at the same time it affords one of the few opportunities left in our modern day civilization for the full unfolding of the individual's potential for reason, love, and creative work. Thus on philosophical, humanistic, and theoretical psychiatric grounds as well as from the vantage point of almost 20 years of clinical experience in the practice of outpatient and office intensive psychotherapy with the neuroses and borderline patients, I still choose to stand against the enormous pressures that have been described above toward abandoning intensive psychotherapy as our fundamental therapeutic technique. This does *not* imply that the whole variety of new treatment techniques which have been developed in the past 25 years are useless or irrelevant, but it does relegate them to a secondary role at least for the time being. In proceeding to review the neuroses and borderline cases, I will attempt to show, when appropriate, what the role of these secondary techniques might be.

## PSYCHOANALYTIC CONCEPTS

If one accepts that a basic psychoanalytic orientation is necessary to understand and treat the neuroses and borderline cases effectively then it is clear that no treatment of these disorders can be sensible without a thorough understanding of the psychodynamics and psychopathology of each individual patient. This cannot be provided by a chapter of this nature, but certain basic principles in approaching the psychodynamics of neuroses and borderline cases could be outlined. The pioneer attempt to establish a rational nosology based on understanding rather than symptom description was made by Freud, whose initial classification was very limited in that it was designed to separate the psychoneuroses which had definable content from the "actual neuroses" in which anxiety resulted from a transformation of more or less mechanically blocked libido (1962a).

Sadow (1969) points out that currently this system appears crude since today we rarely concern ourselves with Freud's concept of the actual neuroses. "However, it is at the same time an historically interesting idea because Freud separated structured from primitive and relatively unstructured disease entities." This problem in the nosology of the neuroses is still with us as any one who studies DSM-I and DSM-II will quickly discover. A typical modern psycho-analytically-informed approach to the neuroses and borderline cases however is provided by Sadow, who attempts to classify these disorders not in terms of symptomatology but in terms of the functioning of the ego. He thinks of the ego axis as a developmental continuum and describes the borderline patient, for example, as not being characterized by any specific defense or ego defect but in terms of the range of movement along the ego axis. Thus the psychotic patient is unable to function even briefly at more structuralized levels of ego function-ing, whereas the borderline patient shifts back and forth, which means that al-though much of his behavior is characterized by prestructuralized object relations, he frequently proves capable of rather highly developed functions as well. Sadow likes to place this group of disturbances developmentally as related to the period of the transitional object.

Similarly, in the field of the transference neuroses, as they were originally described by Freud, the level of structuralization has grown to far greater propor-tions and the range of ego states available is very large. In the neuroses, when regression takes place, recovery is generally prompt, complete, and relatively independent of external intervention.

The point of all this, whether one agrees or disagrees about Sadow's particular depiction of the ego axis, is that important decisions regarding treatment method and goals may be made more reasonably if the ego pathology is recognized. To offer one's self to the patient as a long-term, stable potential object is the general plan of the treatment. The therapist experiences the patient's frustra-tions and gratifications with him so that an eventual separation becomes possible. "The goal is to help stabilize the ego by way of identification with the therapist so that the more flexible defenses become possible." Thus as one moves from the borderline area of ego functioning to the area of transference neuroses the emphasis shifts from stabilization and building of ego structure to interpretation of unconscious motivations in order to really free up the ego for conflict free functioning.

In order for the latter to occur, a workable transference neurosis has to develop in the therapy (Chessick, 1969, 1974). This in turn is a function of the state of ego development and the position along the ego axis in which the patient happens to be living at any given time in the treatment.

It is therefore obviously incumbent upon the therapist at all times to assess as accurately as possible the state of ego functioning of the patient and to minister to the patient in a way that is appropriate and compatible with the patient's ego state. A number of guidelines for the assessment of a patient's ego functioning are offered by DeWald (1971). Thus if one accepts the intensive psychotherapy orientation in the treatment of the neuroses and borderline cases, one works primarily from assessment of ego states rather than from nosological classifications that have been developed on the basis of predominant symptomatology. It is obvious that the capacity to assess a patient's fluctuating ego states requires far more training and demands mandatory intensive psychotherapy of the therapist, whereas symptomatic descriptions are more easily observable and can be rated and assessed in a whole variety of statistical ways and rating procedures.

## CLASSIFICATORY SYSTEM

From the point of view of clinical experience, the neuroses and borderline cases may be divided into four groups. The first of these groups contains the DSM-II diagnostic entities anxiety neurosis, hysterical neuroses (including hysterical neurosis, conversion type and hysterical neurosis, dissociative type), and phobic neurosis, as well as perhaps the depersonalization neurosis. In my experience these disorders rarely present in pure form and we usually encounter a mixture of symptomatology.

The second group would be the depressive neuroses and the neurasthenic neuroses which often overlie a more basic emotional disorder of one kind or another (I will discuss this in detail below). The third group following DSM-II is obsessive compulsive neurosis, which frequently shades off into either the borderline case, the paranoid personality, or frank schizophrenic disorder. This shading off has been discussed in an outstanding characterization by the world's foremost expert on the subject, Harry Stack Sullivan (1956), and cannot be covered in detail in this chapter.

Finally, we have the fourth group DSM-II hypochondriacal neurosis which is a common feature of the borderline case and will be discussed with it, although the hypochondriacal neurosis is a frequent accompaniment of paranoid and schizophrenic disorders also. There is no place in DSM-II for the borderline case as I have described it in previous publications (Chessick, 1969, 1974a). The closest we get to it is the category of schizophrenia, latent type, where in my opinion, it does not belong. As stated at the beginning of this chapter, no attempt will be made to describe in detail the clinical pictures of any of these disorders and it is assumed that the reader is already familiar with them.

## ANXIETY NEUROSIS

Let me now review the therapeutic strategies for each of these clinical groups. The kind of treatment presented to a patient complaining of anxiety must be completely dependent on the clinical assessment of the cause of the anxiety. Thus the ordinary appearance of anxiety or panic states very frequently is *not* and should not be diagnosed as an anxiety neurosis, and requires crisis intervention, supportive treatment, and psychopharmacologic therapy. Similarly, acute schizophrenic panics or serious adjustment reactions are best treated in a brief and eclectic fashion. The clinician must be clear when he is dealing with an anxiety neurosis and when he is not, and this is usually not too difficult to discern if a *careful history* is obtained.

In one form of the anxiety neurosis, the patient suffers chronically from acute flareups of anxiety — and he is well acquainted with this fact, has insight that his mental functioning is disturbed, and is aware that the flareups subside pretty much regardless of what form of support is offered. In another form, the patient suffers from chronic "free floating" anxiety, which does not cause the patient to deteriorate in terms of its intensity or associated disintegration of function, but in which he maintains a constant high level of anxiety or tension associated with practically anything. The best diagnosis of anxiety neurosis is made from the patient's own description and opinion of what is going on. In the chronic anxiety neurosis, whether it be characterized by occasional flareups or free floating anxiety, there are usually deep-seated problems in ego functioning and very frequently phobic reactions, conversion reactions, and dissociative reactions are resorted to when the anxiety becomes too overwhelming.

The techniques of support and modifying stress as well as medication and deconditioning may be used in these disorders if it is felt that the patient is not a suitable candidate for intensive psychotherapy, but the treatment of choice if this has been a chronic condition is intensive psychotherapy, and these patients often respond well to it. In the area of treatment of the anxiety states, Dyrud (1971) has attempted to indicate the overlap between the behavior therapies and psychoanalytically-oriented psychotherapy. He quotes Freud's famous dictum "Anyone who wants to make a living from the treatment of nervous patients must clearly be able to do something to help them."

From time to time in clinical experience one is fooled by a patient with a chronic anxiety neurosis which proves to be absolutely refractory to intensive psychotherapy, although the acute flareups can be ameliorated by many varieties of supportive psychopharmacologic or behavior techniques. Usually such patients turn out to be schizophrenic or borderline cases who have been inaccurately assessed in terms of their ego states. The anxiety neurosis in these cases protects the patient from further decompensation.

## HYSTERIAS

In a similar fashion, the conversion and dissociative disorders have been treated by an infinite variety of techniques. Most of these techniques achieve symptomatic relief, for example in the use of hypnosis or pentothal by intravenous drip to encourage abreaction and subsequent relief of symptoms. But often even as Freud's pioneering studies in hysteria (Freud and Breuer, 1962) indicate, the patients come up with new symptoms often almost as fast as the old symptoms are removed (although this has been challenged by some proponents of behavioral therapy). The psychodynamic understanding of the conversion hysterias and the hysterical character are one of the most confused areas in all psychiatric and psychoanalytic theory. For example, Lazare (1971) writes: "The historical development of psychoanalytic theory, therefore, has made its current concept of the hysterical character confusing to many general psychiatrists. As a consequence (and for other reasons), analysts and nonanalysts rarely acknowledge each other in the literature, even when discussing the same subject."

Lazare presents a fine review of the concept of the hysterical character in the literature and moves into a discussion of the so-called healthy hysteric in contrast to the sicker patient who shows more infantile manifestations and responds much more poorly to intensive uncovering psychotherapy. Again we are left fundamentally with the necessity to assess ego function. Thus it is not uncommon for the sick hysteric to experience considerable subjective relief and show dramatic objective changes following a relatively brief period of ego supportive psychotherapy. The important factor is to determine whether the patient can tolerate intensive psychotherapy or whether we must limit our goals and use supportive measures – or, as has been recently suggested by Kass (1972), a behavioral group treatment of hospitalized patients with hysteria with little attention to the basic psychodynamic factors and focus primarily on the strengthening executive ego functions "on the assumption that the patient might then be in an advantageous position on his own to perform those integrative, synthetic ego functions with regard to his experience and his biological endowment."

Unfortunately it is often clinically very difficult to delineate those patients with hysterical neuroses who will best respond to intensive psychotherapy and those who will not. The first step, especially in the dissociative disorders, is a very careful physical and psychological examination because a variety of organic medical disorders can produce the typical symptomatology of both the conversion and dissociative types of hysterical neuroses. It is a tragedy for the patient when these organic disorders are missed. I believe that whenever possible patients with hysterical neuroses should receive a trial of intensive psychotherapy for at least six or eight months with no fixed date chosen for making any decisions about further treatment, because the tendency in such patients to simply stall around and cling to their symptoms is very great.

After six or eight months the experienced clinician can usually judge if any progress is being made toward the development of a transference and the uncovering of significant material. If not it is perhaps best to recommend to the patient that procedures be instituted to afford specific symptomatic relief, In a great many such cases, the patients have already undergone a whole variety of procedures for symptomatic relief and they know what helps and what does not. Sometimes it is necessary to continue in primarily a supportive manner in order to help the patient adjust to the limitations in their ego function.

In the trial of psychotherapy it is very important for the therapist to try to assess carefully the potentials of the patient. If it seems that the potential exists for the formation of a workable transference neurosis, formal psychoanalysis is the treatment of choice. If, on the other hand, the patient shows no capacity to respond to uncovering treatment and little if anything can be done about the secondary gain, the therapeutic goals should be modified and kept as realistic as possible. It is equally as tragic to come across a patient with a hysterical neurosis who has had many years of formal psychoanalysis with several psychoanalysts with no improvement as it is to find a patient with a hysterical neurosis who has never had a reasonable chance to work in intensive psychotherapy with anybody.

## PHOBIAS

The phobic neurosis is of course the classic disorder to which the behavioral techniques have been applied, and a pure phobic neurosis is rare in clinical therapeutic practice. When one encounters a pure or almost pure phobic neurosis especially in children it is probably best to use brief psychotherapy, environmental manipulation and in the case of adults, reassurance, group therapy, drugs, and the behavioral therapies. As a matter of fact, Agras *et al.,* (1972) provide evidence in a five-year follow-up of 30 phobics that even untreated phobia tends to improve. Children's phobias usually improve quickly, if they do not mask serious underlying psychopathology. In the study of this group 100% showed improvement or recovery at the end of five years. Exposure to the feared object or situation seems to be the basic mechanism that brings about recovery in these cases, especially in the context of a supportive relationship in which the therapist lends his authority to a realistic evaluation of the circumstances and assures the patient that no harm will come to him.

Frazer and Carr (in Freedman and Kaplan, 1975) indicate that "Even with classical psychoanalysis designed to accomplish major personality change it has been found that the phobia usually will not disappear simply by uncovering the original situation that led to its formation. Freud himself saw a necessity for the modification of psychoanalysis in the treatment of phobias, stressing the need for the psychoanalyst to intervene and insist that patients attempt to brave the anxiety-provoking situation. . . . 'and to struggle with their anxiety while they make the attempt'." In the context of a relationship with a guiding supportive figure, the patient is encouraged at the appropriate state of transference into desensitization experiences, whether they are so labeled or not. These authors also point out, and I agree from clinical experience, that although a high degree of optimism is possible in the treatment of phobias, a certain small percentage appear quite resistive to therapeutic endeavors. This usually turns out again to be a misappraisal of ego functioning with the hidden presence of an underlying borderline or schizophrenic disorder.

It is important in discussing those cases of anxiety neurosis, hysterical neurosis, and phobic neurosis which do not respond to intensive psychotherapy to make it clear that the diagnosis of an underlying borderline schizophrenic disorder should not be based on the lack of response, but should be made at the beginning in the initial assessment of the patient by careful attention to what Knight has described as microscopic signs (1954). The astute clinician will most of the time be able to spot the presence of an underlying schizophrenia or a borderline case especially if it is possible to obtain a good history. One cannot sufficiently stress the importance of taking a thorough history and a careful psychological examination of every patient at the beginning of every treatment.

## DEPRESSIONS

The treatment of choice, once an accurate diagnosis of depressive *neurosis* has been made, is psychotherapy. Careful distinction between a depressive neurosis and other disorders such as involutional melancholia, manic depressive illness, and psychotic depressive disorders is absolutely mandatory and as a matter of fact the patient's life may depend on it. The first responsibility of the psychotherapist in the treatment of the depressive disorders is the assessment of suicide risk. In those cases where it is judged that a serious suicide risk is present, precautions for the prevention of suicide must take precedence over everything else. In my clinical experience, if a depressive neurosis has been accurately diagnosed and if the patient is being seen frequently enough and the lines of communication and contact between the patient and therapist are carefully preserved, the suicide risk is minimal. However, there is always a certain suicide risk in dealing with a depressive neurosis and this is a serious stress on the psychotherapist. Only those therapists who are willing to assume such a risk should work with depressed patients. It is necessary to assess carefully the suicidal problem because it is extremely disruptive to a psychotherapy for a patient to be going in and out of the hospital in revolving door fashion every time he threatens suicide.

Davies (1964) reminds us, "Depressive illness is colored into almost innumerable shades by the personality and character of the individual in whom the disease occurs." Chodoff (1972) has attempted to review the enduring personality patterns that influence clinical depression and possibly predispose certain individuals to episodes of depressive illness. The situation at present is seriously compromised by methodological inadequacies. In my clinical experience, the depressive neurosis is frequently a secondary formation that appears when other forms of either neurotic defenses or characterologic defenses have failed to deal with the situation. Therefore, the therapist should be prepared that as the depression lifts he will be dealing with a more basic underlying psychologic disorder.

It is extremely important for the clinician to realize that the lifting of a depression in a depressive neurosis is not a cure and that a long period of psychotherapeutic work is ahead. Unfortunately it is exactly at this point that the patient considers leaving treatment because he feels better and it is incumbent on the therapist to confront the patient with evidence of the underlying disorder in order to stimulate the patient's motivation to really work through the basic problem. This is frequently possible, because the patient already has some experience with the therapist, and since there has been improvement the transference at this point is often positive; on the basis of this the patient may proceed. One of the finest summaries of suggestions for treating the depressed patient that I have seen is presented by Levin (1965), and the reader is referred to this paper for details of the psychotherapy of the depressed patient.

The question of whether to use psychopharmacological agents in the treatment of the depressive *neurosis* remains unsettled; definitely such patients ordinarily do not respond to electric shock treatment. In my experience, it is rarely necessary to give patients with depressive neurosis mood elevating drugs, and often when it is done the patient bitterly complains of side effects. The experience of my colleagues has not always been the same and the practicing therapist will have to experiment around to decide for himself.

I am personally inclined not to use drugs in the treatment of the psychoneuroses beyond occasionally the minor tranquilizers or soporifics, because if the treatment is an intensive psychotherapy then an enormous magical power is attributed to the therapist and at times the treatment disintegrates around the issue of attempting to get the therapist to give more gratification in terms of medication. On the other hand, a patient who is suffering intensely from insomnia or from anxiety deserves the relief that medication can give if it is judiciously and carefully controlled. In my experience in supervising neophyte therapists, the vast majority of medication that is handed out to neurotic patients and borderline cases is in order to allay the anxiety of the therapist.

## OBSESSIVE-COMPULSIVE NEUROSES

Whereas patients with the depressive neurosis have an excellent response rate to psychotherapy, the treatment of obsessive-compulsive disorders remains one of the thorniest and — if the reader will pardon the irony — stubborn and obstreperous problems in psychiatry. The decision about whether to use psychotherapy in the obsessive-compulsive neurosis is especially important, because many such patients quickly permit the therapy to degenerate into an endless obsessional debate, which leads to frustration for both the therapist and the patient. The utmost sensitivity is necessary on the part of the therapist to judge when the patient is really capable of insight into what the therapist and patient are experiencing in the treatment. If there are precipitating events and some evidence of good relationships with others, and the patient is not utterly paralyzed by the obsessive-compulsive neurosis, then psychotherapy has possibilities. On the other end of the spectrum there are patients who are so severely paralyzed with obsessive-compulsive neurosis that leukotomy has been recommended. There is evidence that leukotomy can lessen the intensity of the disorder.

To get the flavor of the treatment of the obsessive-compulsive neuroses I have already suggested reading Sullivan (1956) and I also recommend Freud's famous case of the Rat-Man (1962b). The psychotherapy of such disorders is invariably extremely long and difficult. Behavior therapy has been tried with some claims of symptomatic relief; at present there are no drugs or other somatic therapies that are useful in the treatment of this disorder.

In my experience, the obsessive-compulsive disorder is a step backward on the ego axis and often shades off into schizophrenia; therefore the patient is actually vigorously protecting himself against a schizophrenic breakdown by clinging to a severe obsessive-compulsive neurosis. For this reason the inner sense of protection causes the patient to stubbornly maintain a neurotic position in order to prevent disaster. Only those psychotherapists should work with the obsessive-compulsive neuroses, who are willing to endure over a long period of time, the very special kind of sticky relationship that takes place between the patient and the therapist in the treatment of such disorders. This has been described by Sullivan as the fly-paper pattern of interpersonal relations. Certainly therapists who need to see rapid changes should stay away from the treatment of such patients. At present, the treatment of choice, especially if the disorder has not been long standing, is formal psychoanalysis. Of all the entities discussed in this chapter the chronic long standing conversion hysteria and obsessive-compulsive neurosis, especially if the symptoms are of a fixed nature, are the most refractory to any form of treatment.

## BORDERLINE CASES

I turn finally to a discussion of the treatment of borderline cases. By this time it should be clear that a continuum exists between the various neurotic disorders and the borderline case and that the same considerations of the assessment of ego function upon which a rational psychotherapeutic plan is developed apply to all. Although the borderline case may be fragile and may have a vulnerable personality organization, ". . . borderline regression can be understood as decompensation and defense, as regressive flight from more advanced tasks, and as enfeebled, deviant infantile adaptation. . . . Selective assessment of the regressed, distorted and intact ego functions is of fundamental importance in both diagnosis and treatment" (Blum, 1972).

One of the most common mistakes in the treatment of the neuroses is to mistake a borderline case for a classical neurosis as a result of an inadequate history and psychological examination. There are as many varieties of recommendations for the treatment of the borderline patient as there are for the neuroses and general agreement is found only on a few basic issues.

Ordinary encouragment or supportive therapy produces either no effect or a dramatic remission soon followed by a relapse into the same or new symptoms accompanied by the angry demand for more magic — especially if the supportive therapy primarily has been the administration of various psychopharmacological agents for symptomatic relief. These patients abuse the dosage instructions and the side effects produced complicate the picture tremendously; they may even collect medication from various physicians and make suicide attempts with them.

It is also generally agreed that the rapid shifts up and down the ego axis with all the excitement, storm, and panic this causes the patient and those around him, usually accompanied by either missing appointments, failure to pay the bill, or spending session after session in talking about symptoms and constantly introducing new problems, soon make the physician and the patient frustrated and discouraged. Typically there occurs an increasing exasperation on the part of the therapist as well as a developing barrage of complaints about the treatment from the patient which often leads to an impasse and a referral either for chronic hospitalization or to another form of treatment. A variety of ways are employed by psychotherapists to get rid of these patients.

## FOUR APPROACHES

As I have previously written (1974a), four types of psychotherapy have been recommended for these patients. The first of these is an authoritative and directive approach with much psychological shoving of the patient to "get him moving." This is a total push type of treatment often used for schizophrenics and deals mainly with the symptoms; so unless interminable contact is maintained with the patient, relapse is to be expected especially when life stress arises. If this approach is made to work it is certainly quicker and cheaper than long-term intensive psychotherapy.

At the other end of the spectrum is formal psychoanalysis argued to be the treatment of choice, for example, by Boyer and Giovacchini (1967; Giovacchini, 1972). Most psychotherapists reject this approach out of clinical experience in which many borderline patients show a complete intolerance to the formal psychoanalytic situation, reacting with suicidal attempts, transitory psychosis, or dramatic and chaotic symptoms and acting out that finally interrupt the treatment.

The third approach attempts to combine supportive psychotherapy with providing a direct "correct emotional experience" for the patient, which essentially amounts to giving direct gratification to the patient. This can range from minor gratifications such as taking the patient's hand to actually holding, rocking, feeding, and having sexual intercourse with the patient. I have discussed the great dangers of direct primary process interchange with patients in other publications (1969, 1971, 1974) and it is unnecessary to review that here.

The treatment that is coming to be most generally accepted for the borderline patient is what has been called psychoanalytically-oriented psychotherapy or psychoanalysis with parameters — the latter a controversial term. The most complete and thorough review of psychoanalysis with parameters has been presented in a series of papers by Kernberg (1967, 1968, 1971, and in Giovacchini, 1972). These are excellent but very difficult papers and require considerable knowledge on the part of the reader. In Wilson's summary (1971), Kernberg advises interpretation of the predominantly negative transference in the here and now, limit setting to block acting out, and noninterpretation of the less primitive aspects of the positive transference to strengthen the therapeutic alliance. "Consistent transference interpretations of the primitive defensive operations which rigidly protect the borderline patient's weak ego can result in the resumption of ego growth. Clarification of interpretations to cope with the patient's distortions are an important component of Kernberg's interpretative approach."

My publications referred to above have presented a similar approach for the analytically-oriented psychotherapist. The psychotherapy of the borderline case is very difficult and long, but is quite rewarding for both the therapist and the patient. The borderline case is being seen with increasing frequency in the offices of psychotherapists. In fact, at present the borderline patient already constitutes a very substantial increment of patients seeking psychotherapy.

In the neuroses it is certainly possible to argue that somatic, or behavioral, or group therapies form a feasible alternative in the therapeutic armamentarium. At least they do harm a relatively small percentage of the time — perhaps no more often than psychotherapy. In the borderline cases, especially the psycho-pharmacological and often the group approaches — especially if conducted by amateurs — may do serious harm. Although these patients tend to decompensate far less than was originally thought, and are not so fragile in the sense that they can easily become schizophrenic for a long period of time, they *are* impulsive and may be precipitated by the use of psychopharmacologic agents or intensive or marathon group or encounter maneuvers into actions that may be destructive or even fatal for them. Here again the essence of the choice of treatment for the neuroses and the borderline cases rests on a careful diagnostic evaluation of the patient by an alert and well-trained clinician with as thorough as possible an understanding of himself.

## REFERENCES

Abrams, G. The new eclecticism. *Archives of General Psychiatry.* **20**: 514–523 (1969).

Alexander, F. Social significance of psychoanalysis and psychotherapy. *Archives of General Psychiatry.* **11**: 235–244 (1964).

Agras, W., *et al.* The natural history of phobia. *Archives of General Psychiatry.* **26**: 315–317 (1972).

Applebaum, S. How long is long term psychotherapy? *Bulletin of the Menninger Clinic.* **36**: 651–655 (1972).

Blum, H. Borderline regression. *International Journal of Psychoanalytic Psychotherapy.* **1**: 46–60 (1972).

Boyer, L. and Giovacchini, P. *Psychoanalytic Treatment of Characterological and Schizophrenic Disorders.* New York: Science House, 1967.

Chessick, R.D. *How Psychotherapy Heals.* New York: Science House, 1969.

Chessick, R.D. *Why Psychotherapists Fail.* New York: Science House, 1971.

Chessick, R.D. *The Technique and Practice of Intensive Psychotherapy.* New York: Jason Aronson, 1974.

Chessick, R.D.: The Borderline Patient. In: Arieti, S., (Ed.), *The American Handbook of Psychiatry,* Second edition. New York: Basic Books, 1974a.

Chodoff, T. The depressive personality. *Archives of General Psychiatry.* **27**: 666–667 (1972).

Davies, E. Some varieties of depression and their treatment. In: Davies, E. (Ed.), *Depression.* London: Cambridge University Press, 1964.

De Wald, P. *Psychotherapy,* Second edition. New York: Basic Books, 1971.

Dyrud, J. Treatment of anxiety states. *Archives of General Psychiatry.* **25**: 298–305 (1971).

Freedman, A. and Kaplan, H. *Comprehensive Textbook of Psychiatry*, Second edition. Baltimore: The Williams and Wilkins Co., 1975.

Freud, S. and Breuer, J. Studies on Hysteria. *Standard Edition of the Complete Psychological Works of Sigmund Freud,* Vo. 2. London: Hogarth Press, 1962.

Freud, S. Early Psychoanalytic Publications. *Standard Edition of the Complete Psychological Works of Sigmund Freud, Vol. 3,* London: Hogarth Press, 1962a.

Freud, S. Little Hans and the Rat-Man. *Standard Edition of the Complete Psychological Works of Sigmund Freud, Vol. 10.* London: Hogarth Press, 1962b.

Giovaccini, P. (Ed.) *Tactics and Techniques in Psychoanalytic Therapy.* New York: Science House, 1972.

Goldman, G. and Milman, D. *Innovations in Psychotherapy.* Springfield, Ill.: Charles C. Thomas, 1972.

Grinker, R. Psychiatry rides madly in all directions. *Archives of General Psychiatry.* **10**: 228–237 (1964).

Grinker, R., *et al.* *The Borderline Syndrome.* New York: Basic Books, 1968.

Hollingshead, A. and Redlich, F. *Social Class and Mental Illness.* New York: John Wiley and Sons, 1958.

Kanfer, F. and Phillips, J. Behavior therapy. *Archives of General Psychiatry.* **15**: 114–128 (1966).

Kass, D. Behavioral group treatment of hysteria. *Archives of General Psychiatry.* **26**: 42–50 (1972).

Kepecs, J. Psychoanalysis today. *Archives of General Psychiatry.* **18**: 161–167 (1968).

Kernberg, O. Borderline personality organization. *Journal of the American Psychoanalytic Association.* **15**: 641–685 (1967).

Kernberg, O. The treatment of patients with borderline personality organization. *International Journal of Psychoanalysis.* **49**: 600–619 (1968).

Kernberg, O. Prognostic considerations regarding borderline personality organization. *Journal of the American Psychoanalytic Association.* **19**: 595–635 (1971).

Knight, R.P. *Psychoanalytic Psychiatry and Psychology.* New York: International Universities Press, 1954.

Kubie, L. The retreat from patients. *Archives of General Psychiatry.* **24**: 98–106 (1971).

Lazare, A. The hysterical character in psychoanalytic theory. *Archives of General Psychiatry.* **25**: 131–137 (1971).

Levin, S. Some suggestions for treating the depressed patient. *Psychoanalytic Quarterly.* **34**: 37–65 (1965).

Marmor, J. Dynamic psychotherapy and behavior therapy. *Archives of General Psychiatry.* **24**: 22–28 (1971).

Sadow, L. Ego axis in psychopathology. *Archives of General Psychiatry.* **21**: 15–24 (1969).

Strupp, H. Toward a specification of teaching and learning in psychotherapy. *Archives of General Psychiatry.* **21**: 203–212 (1969).

Strupp, H. Specific versus non-specific factors in psychotherapy and the problem of control. *Archives of General Psychiatry.* **23**: 393–401 (1970).

Strupp, H. On the technology of psychotherapy. *Archives of General Psychiatry.* **26**: 270–278 (1972).

Sullivan, H.S. *Clinical Studies in Psychiatry.* New York: W.W. Norton and Co., 1956.

Wilson, C. On the limits of the effectiveness of psychoanalysis. *Journal of the American Psychoanalytic Association.* **19**: 552–564 (1971).

# 17 The Treatment of Antisocial Behavior

## Sanford Goldstone

We do not possess a causal therapy of the psychopathies; medicinal or organotherapeutic attempts are in their earliest stages. Final therapy setting out from the basis of intimate knowledge of the personality has always to strive toward a psychagogic effect. We are still unable and perhaps always will remain unable to change the constitutional structure of the psychopathic personalities but we can educate many of them to understand themselves, to come to terms with themselves, and to set themselves genuine goals which they may reach in spite of their psychopathic peculiarities. (Kahn, 1931)[1]

This began as a straightforward clinical discussion of the treatment of anti-social behavior by the mental health professions. Unfortunately, the eclectic eyes of this practitioner have become sufficiently clouded by simultaneously rewarding and frustrating experiences that the straightforward and the clinical were at first difficult, and at last impossible, to produce. What seems to have emerged is an essay derived from these experiences tied to prevailing ideas and knowledge about antisocial conduct from the standpoint of the clinician and behavioral scientist. Unless we limit our discussion of antisocial behavior to the few exotic actions that apparently respond to aversive conditioning, or unless we exaggerate the dangers to society of the consequences of those mental diseases

[1]This chapter is dedicated to Eugen Kahn, my teacher and colleague from 1955 to 1967. His many hours of patient discussion with a slowly developing young psychologist initiated an enduring interest in deviant personalities and their social consequences. It is too bad that Professor Kahn is not here to author this presentation since his wisdom, experience and perspective would have yielded a substantially greater contribution.

that can be treated chemically, there are no successful therapeutic handles upon this problem; confinement treats the effects, not the behavior. Such a limitation of the scope of discussion about antisocial behavior would be as unrealistic as a more general discourse accompanied by exaggerated treatment claims and hopes. Hence, these clouded eclectic eyes will present a clouded eclectic picture leaving little more than the plea for increased clarity of thinking and the challenge of accumulating additional knowledge for the behavioral scientist and clinician. It is too early in the development of our professions to hope, let alone claim, but it is not too early to continue our slow beginning.

## INTRODUCTION

Although almost half a century has elapsed since Kahn (1931) published his *Psychopathic Personalities*[2], the summary of his views regarding treatment cited at the outset continues to represent the state of the art and science. Clinicians preceding Kahn as well as his contemporaries wrote prolifically about the "enemies of society" and in general shared his view about the limitations of the mental sciences in delivering relief to and from those deviant people who behaved antisocially. Our generation of mental health professionals in this last half of the twentieth century cannot point with the pride of noticeable progress to new discovery and greater control in the treatment of antisocial behavior, and if I could return and report 100 years from now, nothing would surprise me more than the happy discovery that things had changed; nothing would be more pleasing than to learn that this change had transpired with significant contribution from behavioral and clinical scientists.

Contemporary clinicians, while quarreling about etiology and technique are in general agreement about outcome. Antisocial behaviors of individuals and groups may be products of complex interacting endogenous and exogenous forces that are legion, but our scientific and clinical knowledge of these forces and our capacity to measure and control them are limited.

Perhaps this discussion of antisocial behavior and its treatment should be presented by an enthusiastic supporter of a therapeutic tool, a theory, an area of psychologic, biologic, or social research accompanied by the conviction of certain and significant success in some not too distant tomorrow. To suggest at the outset that we have not progressed noticeably during this golden century of the mental and social sciences may be viewed as destructively pessimistic and discouraging; to voice skepticism about probable future progress deriving predominantly from the mental sciences may be seen as cynical. To date we have had no shortage of technique, theory, social movement, and research sparks that promised progress and success with fanfare and failed the test of time and laboratory. Clinical realism about problems as complex as man and his nature

---

[2]This book was published first in 1928 as part of Oswald Bumke's *Hanbuch der Geisteskrankheiten.*

is neither discouraging nor pessimistic. Realism permits perspective and encourages the mental sciences to offer limited and modest assistance in coming to grips with antisocial behavior along with all others concerned with man's nature, suffering, healing, and survival. No single profession or discipline has earned the status of primacy in the search for knowledge about antisocial behavior, and none has a successful treatment. All in concert require their part in this effort to reduce man's action against man but none alone represents cause and promotes cure. Hence, it is a prime thesis of this presentation that antisocial behavior is *never* a psychiatric disease or illness, *never* a personality disorder, *never* a mental health problem alone; antisocial behavior may be symptomatic of disease or impaired health but is never a natural consequence of illness. This position eliminates the promise by mental health workers that treatment will eliminate or significantly reduce antisocial behavior, and may avoid pointless arguments between professions and persuasions which assign blame for the frustrating outcome of sincere and active efforts. Antisocial behavior as symptomatic of both normal and deviant people is part of the subject matter of the behavioral sciences, but does one treat the antisocial behavior directly?[3]

This presentation will review representative ideas about antisocial behavior and its treatment from a clinical and behavioral science point of view through the eyes of an observer who feels that the effort and struggle are worthwhile with possible progress impeded predominantly by prevailing mythologies and a failure to develop a rational approach to a science and philosophy of personality that is both clinically functional and logically sound. Such an approach may be feasible by combining the structural properties of *personality* (e.g., impulse, character, etc.) as seen by the clinician with those related areas of behavioral research (e.g., arousal, learning, etc.)

Antisocial behavior, its diagnosis or assessment and its treatment will be examined from the standpoint of the mental health professions. The frames of reference of psychiatry, clinical psychology, and social work have enough in common to be grouped together; these professions are linked to the clinico-scientific point of view which generally excludes moral judgment and public policy, and the focus will be upon individual functioning. The professions that represent man's morality, justice, and codes of conduct as well as the disciplines devoted to the study of society, culture, large groups and the nature of our species have a larger stake in the understanding and modification of antisocial behavior, but they will not be included here. These other professions ultimately define behavior as antisocial, not the mental health workers. Antisocial behavior will be considered here in a general sense as unacceptable conduct usually in violation of values, statutes and codes that reflect pervasive public policy (e.g., homicide, assault, theft, property destruction) and specific community standards (e.g., pornography, public drunkenness). Some antisocial behaviors are invariant, and consistent from time-to-time and place-to-place, while others are culturally

[3]Except with physical and chemical confinement.

judged and involve wider variations with time and content. Discussion will exclude (1) antisocial behavior which is a product of psychosis or where, for any reason, the individual is exempt from criminal responsibility,[4] (2) group behavior such as ghetto and student riots, (3) victimless behavior with consenting adults, and (4) the very infrequent or single antisocial act by an individual whose life-style is predominantly acceptable. In short, we are back by any name, to those *psychopathic personalities* which are presumed to increase vulnerability to antisocial behavior. Kahn's (1931) book will be used as a basic clinical resource since it describes graphically the varieties of the psychopathic personalities that we all see, and its non-theoretical orientation and age removes it from the battleground of contemporary controversy. Since Kahn's work is not generally known, his ideas will be summarized briefly as a tribute to this psychiatrist-scholar, and as a reflection of my point of view regarding the structure of personality and its deviations. The Kahn schema for personality structure and organization provides a classification schema with clinical merit, and permits the construction of delicate bridges to the theoretician and researcher who study the *psychopath.*[5] Other clinical references with merit (Cleckley, 1964; Craft, 1965; Maughs, 1941; McCord & McCord, 1964) warrant additional study for those who wish both historical perspective and comparison among ideas and experiences. A recent volume by Hare (1970) represents an excellent and detailed review of contemporary clinical, theoretical, and scientific work in this field, and the *Comprehensive Textbook of Psychiatry* (Freedman and Kaplan, 1967) reflects the views of a sufficient number of clinicians to reflect consensus among workers about etiology, diagnosis and the discouraging therapeutic picture.

This discussion will proceed from (1) a presentation of general issues, to (2) a summary of Kahn's views about the structure of personality and its capacity for deviation, to (3) a brief review of contemporary theory and research about *the psychopath,* concluding with (4) additional comment about hopeful possibilities and risky pitfalls confronting the mental health professions as they join the other professions in the treatment and control of antisocial behavior.

---

[4]We do not wish to complicate the picture further by incorporating that confusing interface between the mental sciences and law, *the insanity defense.*

[5]Schneider disliked the ambiguity associated with the term *psychopathy,* pointing out that it had been used previously in a more inclusive sense for all psychopathological phenomena; he preferred *deviate personalities* which were seen as "variations, deviations from the vaguely conceived but ill-defined, average of human personalities, deviations upwards or downwards, toward the more or toward the less, abnormal personalities in the most literal sense." This use of the *average man* is similar to the legal community standard based upon the *reasonable man* and emphasizes the cultural basis for defining the middle ground of psychopathic antisocial behavior. There are no absolute boundaries between the normal and the psychopathic, only fluid transitions. "In one point in history and environment much may be considered psychopathic which in another time or another locality or among other races were or are considered in no sense outside the pale of the normal" (Kahn, 1931).

## ISSUES

A rational treatment is based upon a scientific approach to etiology, and an objective, empirical evaluation of outcome, not upon fashionable technique, social pressure, mythology, or evangelical zeal. At the very most we can hope for reasonable knowledge of origin and cause, and the therapy a rational product of etiology; at the very least, our techniques and outcomes should stand the empirical tests of clinical research to be retained as substantially true and effective. Hence, we must come to grips with fundamental issues which have received clinical comment, but are not dealt with via reason, rigor and clarity.

Rational diagnosis should precede rational treatment. *Who* are those psychopathic personalities[6] that behave antisocially? Is there a rational taxonomy with reliable and valid properties that can define useful classes? Upon which available frame of reference shall a functional schema be based? The most obvious and traditional point of departure has been to view the psychopathic personalities who behave antisocially from the standpoint of *disease,* a view rejected by Kahn and Schneider who emphatically refused to consider psychopathy from the standpoint of disease, preferring to see it as characterologic (Schneider) or personality (Kahn) variations. The psychopath differs quantitatively *(deviate)* not qualitatively *(disease)* from a norm. Although one rarely encounters the notion of psychopathy as disease at this juncture the implication of this position lingers on. While a diagnostic tag need not imply disease, it is difficult for the diagnostician to ignore tradition. An inspection of the relevant elements of the *Diagnostic and Statistical Manual of the American Psychiatric Association* (1952, 1968), an accepted classification schema for mental disease, reveals apparent contradiction, vagueness, and underscores this dilemma. Although labels pertaining to the psychoses, neuroses and brain syndromes change slightly from time to time, these modifications have been small reflecting conceptual, clinical and scientific progress. Relative consistency of these pathologies persists across time, and generations of professions, and they appear to be quite resistent to social pressure and change. However, this is not the case with the personality disorders. The 1952 *Manual* subcategory *sociopathic personality disturbance* was eliminated in 1968; three subtypes, *sexual deviation, alcoholism,* and *drug dependence* are now listed separately, while the *dyssocial reaction* is no longer viewed as a primary psychiatric disorder. Only the *antisocial personality* remains.

This term is reserved for individuals who are basically unsocialized and whose behavior pattern brings them repeatedly into conflict with society. They are incapable of significant loyalty to individuals, groups, or social

---

[6]The label *psychopathic personality* is used here to represent any and all deviation, excesses, or insufficiencies of personality structure and function without psychotic, neurotic, or organic origin whether or not accompanied by antisocial behavior. However, the term *psychopathic* is retained to reflect a clinical or mental health orientation to the problem of deviant behavior as opposed to sinful or criminal; antisocial behavior is viewed as symptomatic of personality pathology.

values. They are grossly selfish, callous, irresponsible, impulsive, and unable to feel guilt or to learn from experience and punishment. Frustration tolerance is low. They tend to blame others or offer plausible rationalizations for their behavior. A mere history of repeated legal or social offenses is not sufficient to justify this diagnosis. (1968)

The description is clear, but as a diagnosis based upon a medical or mental health frame of reference it is absurd. First, it does not describe personality; it is a description of "enemies of society" and community irritants. Second, it defines a moral and social, not personality disorder. Finally, the concluding caveat[7] reveals the greatest measure of contradiction. The *mere history* should be a prime basis for any diagnosis, if there exists in fact an *antisocial personality*. Perhaps it would be more useful to speak of antisocial behavior as symptomatic of other disorders of personality, mental disease, and social deviance. The diagnosis, *antisocial personality* as a mental disorder does not conform to a rational diagnostic schema.

It is interesting to note that the personality disorders are so subject to social and cultural pressures that they may be voted in or out of existence as witnessed by the 1973-1974 decision of the American Psychiatric Association which eliminated homosexuality from the *Manual*.[8]

In rejecting the disease model as the basis for rational diagnostic and therapeutic schemata, other scientific and theoretic frames of reference that have been employed to study psychopathic personalities should be emphasized. Do the problems posed by antisocial behavior have any place in the scientific and clinical domains of the mental sciences? Can any aspect of antisocial behavior be understood and perhaps controlled with the conceptual and clinical tools of the behavioral sciences?

Antisocial behavior has been viewed as a learning disability subject to specific training procedures; as an insufficiency of arousal and stimulus deprivation requiring a continued infusion of motivational and affective supplies. It has been viewed from the standpoint of deviant memory, attention, or information processing; as a product of toxic families due to loss, separation, rejection, brutality, uncertainty, or defective genes; and as a structural or functional disorder of the brain. These distinctions are heuristically useful, and have been valuable in the scientific study of psychopathic personalities and antisocial behavior. Each provides a solid bedrock of tradition and technique for studying different aspects of life touching all strata from the molecular to the social. However, when concerned with a functional disorder of man's relation to man involving violations

---

[7]The caveat is useful when testimony involving exculpation or diminished criminal responsibility is an issue since it permits the expert witness to accept a life-style of antisocial behavior without the diagnosis of antisocial personality.

[8] At the time of this writing members of the Association have requested a new ballot because of unfair election practices.

of social codes of conduct, no approach that reduces the system to simple biologic and psychologic elements can provide more than a partial picture of the substrate. Although this writer accepts the scientific necessity for studying personality and social behavior via biologic and psychologic research, these segments do not pool spontaneously to recreate the total person interacting with a dynamic environment. The clinical and social engineer must organize both scientific and descriptive data into a picture of human-world struggles and compromises. Antisocial behavior must be viewed as a disorder of design and function of the total personality interacting with an equally complex social environment. When we refer to a psychopathic personality who behaves antisocially we speak of a purposive human with a unique personality subject to description and classification interacting with a purposive social environment equally subject to description and classification. The very concepts of *antisocial* and *personality* cannot be rendered meaningful if one excludes purpose and if one does not tackle the whole personality, the whole environment and the entirety of the interaction. It is likely that the psychopathic personalities *are* learning disabilities, *and* disorders of insufficient arousal or stimulation, *and* deviate information processing, *and* products of family experiences, *and* defective genes, *and* brain dysfunction. It is at once each and all of these combined and yet none separately. Just as one cannot describe the visual essence of a sunset to a congenitally blind person via the physical properties of the stimuli, so the antisocial behavior can be neither described nor classified by any system that is less than holistic. Hence, a compromise may be required in proposing a diagnostic and theoretical frame of reference; to be rational and functional it must be holistic and teleological which reduces the potential for direct scientific inquiry. At the same time it is possible for the elements of a holistic approach to personality to be studied scientifically and be integrated into the corpus of knowledge about the whole. It may be useful to analyze scientifically a Rembrandt in terms of chromatic or chemical characteristics of the pigment; knowledge about the painter and painting is obtained although it does not define the nature of artistic truth and beauty which is less subject to laboratory study.

It would seem that the state of the art, the state of the science and the overpowering complexity of the problem might lead to the discouraging conclusion that the mental sciences have little if anything to contribute to a complex problem area. While understanding and knowledge is limited with treatment and control even less developed, we should continue to progress in our understanding of parts and pursue the ultimate challenge of the whole.

Kahn (1931) considered this challenge. As a psychiatrist he concerned himself with the whole and offered three definitions of psychopathic personalities. *First,* the causal or scientific definition: "By psychopathic personalities we understand those personalities which are characterized by quantitative peculiarities in the impulse, temperament, or character strata." This definition highlights his three-tiered approach to personality structure. Each tier (i.e., impulse, temperament, character) is clinically useful and at the same time subject to scientific study but the personality is the pooled state of all three strata. Since this definition defines statically the individual psychology of the person, it is incomplete functionally. Hence, the *second* teleological definition: "By psychopathic personalities we understand personalities whose unified goal striving activity is impaired by quantitative deviations in the ego and foreign valuation leading to the establishment of pseudovalues and the striving toward pseudogoals." This definition emphasizing purpose and philosophy describes general directions, fate, and destiny. Both combine in the *third* causal-teleological and, hence, clinical definition providing a holistic approach to the nature of man: "By psychopathic personalities we understand those discordant personalities which on the causal side are characterized by quantitative peculiarities in the impulse, temperament, or character strata, and in their unified goal striving activity are impaired by quantitative deviations in the ego and foreign valuations." This complex definition has both scientific and functional merit, viewing the personality as an integration of its biological, psychological and social properties with a will, a purpose and a destiny. Any lesser definition which attempts to cope with psychopathy and **antisocial behavior** represents an oversimplification. No one can take such complicated stuff as man's personality, man's social behavior and man's nature, and explain them in terms of any single frame of reference. Psychopathic antisocial behavior is at once biologic and social, a product of constitution and heredity and experience.

## KAHN'S PSYCHOPATHIC PERSONALITIES

As a psychiatrist, Kahn's *personality* had to be potentially normal or deviate in its structural properties and in organization permitting the portrayal of the plethora of styles and sizes encountered by the clinician. He wanted building blocks and architecture that were clinically and scientifically useful. The structure consisted of three interacting properties, *impulse, temperament* and *character* pooled in harmonious or non-harmonious, concordant or discordant equilibrium. Each property was assessed separately in quality and magnitude, and the organized whole **portrayed** as the total personality in preparing a diagnostic formulation. Each property represents a researchable area for the behavioral scientist. As with Freud, the *personality* begins with impulses which are instinctual vital urges toward biologic need gratification dedicated to self and species preservation and development. Strong impulse is dominant in young children who proceed developmentally toward more voluntary (character) and compassionate (temperament) processes. Impulse is aimless "raw" arousal with intensity its only dimension, and with it begins the normal dynamic personality and the deviate personality with unmoving weak impulse or less controlled powerful urge. It is the *impulse* property of personality that is most closely and obviously linked to antisocial behavior, and it is this property that requires careful diagnostic attention and therapeutic control. From impulse develops the affective component of personality, *temperament* with both arousal intensity and quality (e.g., happy, or unhappy). The final dimension, *character* is the organizer, regulator, and steerage for the personality; it is the final cause and image of the personality perpetuating its aims, attitudes and purposes. It is the *character* that regulates interaction between the whole personality and the environment. *Impulse* and *temperament* are in constant contact with the environment but *character* controls the interaction between total personality and environment. The concordant personality involves harmony of impulse, temperament and character with all processes moving with minimal friction. No *impulse, temperament* or *character* component alone necessarily produces a psychopathic personality, only a system out of balance.

The reader is urged to study Kahn's (1931) book for more complete details of his views about the development and structure of personality and those deviations that increase the likelihood of antisocial behavior. It is of particular interest to note his meticulous clinical appraisal of *impulse, temperament,* and *character* as the basis for accounting for history and predicting course. Specifically, his graphic portrayal of clinically useful types and classes highlights the numerous qualitative and quantitative varieties of personality that emerge from the harmonious and the discordant pooling of impulse, temperament and character. There is no singular *psychopath* that reflects a simple and specific personality stereotype as outlined in the diagnosis *antisocial personality*. Indeed, the neuroses for Kahn were variations on the psychopathic theme involving anxiety and conflict; borderline states were also in this category involving extremes of poor adaptation, inadequacy, and incompetence.

Kahn describes 16 clinically useful classes of psychopathic personalities, adding three to Schneider's list: the nervous, the anxious, the sensitive, the compulsive, the excitable, the hyperthymic, the depressive, the moody, the affectively cold, the weak-willed, the impulsive, the sexually perverse, the hysterical, the fantastic, the cranks, and the eccentric. This was a pragmatic typology with all classes vulnerable to antisocial behavior, although some more than others. These classes of deviate personalities were developed conceptually from a predominant disorder of impulse alone, or temperament alone, or character alone, or the discordant balance among properties. From the standpoint of impulse one views normal development toward increased control from a charged, restless and tense state to voluntary directed behavior. The often noted relationship between psychological and biological immaturity on the one hand and deviate personality on the other may be associated with maturational lag of impulse controls. Very few psychopathic personalities derive alone from impulse of excessive intensity but more often from discordant balance between the regulating character and impulse producing in adults and more frequently in children stealing, fire-setting, wandering, sexual acting-out, and assault. The psychopaths weak in impulse with low vitality are commonly seen but rarely are antisocial.

From the standpoint of temperament alone, personalities may deviate from affective excess (e.g., vivacious, excitable, explosive, irritable, cheerful, etc.), insufficiency (e.g., phlegmatic, torpid, shallow, etc.) or instability and lability. Again, temperament alone rarely produces antisocial behavior.

It is from the standpoint of character alone that we being to approach the problem of antisocial behavior, since without disorder or deviance here, no such conduct is likely. Character is the combined attitudes and goals of the personality; it regulates and directs; it is the purposive component of personality; it is portrayed in the ego and is formed through contact with the environment. Kahn stresses five aspects of character important in the development of psychopathic personalities: (1) the excessive concern for ego or environment, (2) the over- or under-evaluation of ego, (3) the under- or over-evaluation of the foreign or non-ego, (4) the ability to establish goals and values, and (5) the negative effect of environment on the personality. There are two types of ego over-evaluation, the *active* autist who denies the environment, exaggerates ego strength and sees himself as conqueror of the enemy world, and the egocentric whose grandiosity is a protest against weakness. There are two types of ego under-evaluation, the *passive autist* whose weakness produces a yearning for the non-ego and a life on a protected island, and the *ego-searcher* whose style is devotion, sacrifice and self-surrender. These excesses and insufficiencies of *impulse, temperment,* and *character* combine to yield the predominant, non-adaptive, disordered, tormented and tormenting personalities, some especially disposed to antisocial behavior. Kahn described several such combinations: The passive *asocial personality weak in impulse* who is driven by the environment and because of poorly directed steerage is without goal or purpose producing potential parasites who are often habitually petty criminals. The *cold, affectively shallow passive autist weak in impulse* and *active autist strong in impulse* correspond to Kraepelin's antisocial psychopaths and Schneider's affectless morally blind and insane. The disorder is in the affect, not cognition. They are indifferent to the feelings of others without shame and remorse.

The *passive, cold autists, weak in impulse* show both affective torpidity and poverty and a lack of psychic activity. They are typically lazy and have no earnest endeavor and no interest. They are passively asocial and contribute largely to the ranks of the petty criminal. Although weak in impulse they are capable of sudden, explosive, ruthless animal urges but crumble in the face of strength.

The *active, cold autists, strong in impulse* show a poverty of affect and powerful urge to do battle with an enemy society. They are agile, mobile and autistically euphoric, at war with the environment as "picked troops of professional criminals"(Heindl*).They are ruthless, unyielding, tyrannical personalities, with leadership ability. Circumstances may allow them to be great pioneers and leaders but their courage, coldness and denial of the outside world leave them without pity and potential criminals at war with society. As for prognosis, they are uneducable and untreatable due to an absence of affective resonance.

The *hysterical psychopathic personality* as a role playing theatrical may

* Cited in Kahn (1931).

contribute fraud, swindling and quackery as well as some eccentric cranks. Their natural bearing is pose and lack of genuineness. Most are shallow in affect and egocentric in character.

These complex types have one thing in common, a relative lack of affective resonance which is seen as the basis for their poor prognosis. Regardless of theoretic persuasion or mode of practice, shallow affect and poor motivation reduce educability and the potential for behavior change.

## CONTEMPORARY VIEWS

It would appear that the clinician can view antisocial behavior from the stand-point of disordered personality structure and organization. The diagnosis should emphasize impulse strength, temperament quality and magnitude, and character strength and direction with the total personality portrayed as an image of the integration and balance among these properties. Those psychopathic personalities most vulnerable or disposed to antisocial behavior have in common shallow, nonresonant emotion which reduces compassion, motivation, and the capacity for reinforcement of social learning. The *active,* alienated grandiose narcissist, and the *passive,* "as-if" narcissist searching for self in the reflected appraisals of others provide the characterologically determined leaders and followers. Finally, those affectively shallow and characterologically narcissistic people strong in impulse yield the more dangerous, potentially explosive, and persistent threats to society; those shallow narcissists weak in impulse may be troublesome but usually in a more petty less frightening fashion. The various combinations of quality and intensity of these properties of personality produce the various kinds of people most likely to do violence to prevailing social norms.

If we are to pursue treatment beyond confinement or detention in hospitals and prisons, there must be valid ideas and knowledge about impulse control, shallow effect, and character formation. Let us touch briefly on the state of the science.[9]

First we will deal with impulse, a fundamentally biologic concept studied physiologically through autonomic and cortical responsiveness and their corre-lations with impulse control. Writers and researchers have viewed this problem of impulse control from the standpoint of maturational retardation, reduced cortical arousal, and related excessive need for stimulation.

A second approach to the psychopathic personalities is through studies of learn-ing and learning deficiency as a possible product of reduced affective resonance.

The final and most popular area of study emphasizes character formation as a product of experience through family impact and socialization. Antisocial behavior derives from attitudes, values and behavioral styles conditioned by unfortunate family and social experiences such as deprivation, separation, rejec-tion, and discord during the critical years of personality development. The

[9]Hare (1970) has written a more complete review.

social and family impact hypothesis may derive its popularity from simplicity since blame is clear, and because it offers hope since prevention is possible. The impulse-arousal and shallow affect-learning hypotheses require complex research and provide less immediate hope for modification or prevention, the locus of blame is less clear, and they do not lend themselves to exploitation as rational foundations for social reform movements.

Impulse-Arousal Approach

The studies of cortical correlates (e.g., Bay-Rakal, 1965; Ellingson, 1954, Knott, *et al.*, 1953; Kurland, *et al.*, 1963; Schwade and Geiger, 1956; Hill and Watterson, 1942) which point to the kinds of EEG tracings frequently found in normal or minimal brain dysfunction children (e.g., excessive slow activity, 14 and 6 positive spikes, etc.) add credence to the *maturational retardation* hypothesis. Such characteristic psychopathic behavior as narcissism, impulsiveness, and reduced ability to delay gratification also point to maturational retardation. If psychopathy is related to slow cortical maturation, incidence should decrease with age. It has been suggested (e.g., Gibbens, *et al.*, 1955; Robins, 1966) that psychopaths with abnormal EEGs tend to outgrow both EEG and behavioral abnormality; also, psychopaths tend to become less antisocial with age. The slower recovery rate by both psychopaths and schizophrenics (Shagass and Schwartz, 1962) suggests reduced cortical excitability, which could relate to attenuation of sensory input magnitude, particularly input with disturbing consequences.

Early autonomic studies were equivocal or nondifferentiating, but a recent study by Hare (1968a) using Cleckley's (1964) strict criteria showed that psychopaths had lower levels of resting skin conductance and less nonspecific GSR (Galvanic Skin Response) activity indicating under-arousal. These results require cautious interpretation but in general when positive results appear, autonomic under-arousal and under-activity occur. Stimulation provides guidance and regulatory cues based upon effective information processing and prior learning. Stimuli also increase the level of activation or arousal, which is the physiological and psychological state of the organism proceeding from sleep through awareness to excitement. A prevailing view is that psychopathy is related to a lower state of cortical arousal and to a chronic need for stimulation as with Petrie (1967) who divides extremes of sensory modulation into reducers and augmenters. Studies (Hare, 1968b; Schoenherr, 1964) suggest a higher shock detection threshold in psychopaths; and psychopaths who are not anxious had higher pain tolerance thresholds than anxious nonpsychopathic delinquents. This important research is in an embryonic stage, but in general psychopathy appears related to a tendency to attenuate sensory input. If so, cues essential for social functioning may be too subtle and too weak; if near or below threshold, they may be ineffective. In an attempt to maintain optimum arousal the psychopath may seek more intense stimulation or exciting, arousing stimulation. In scanning the environment for exciting stimulation he may miss or ignore many social cues for the guidance and regulation of behavior.

This area of research is exciting and continues to provide essential clues about the nature of the psychopathic personality who behaves antisocially. It would seem that the psychopath compensates for low arousal and stimulus deprivation through high input intensity requirements.

The understanding of impulse-arousal through continued research may provide therapeutic handles for this part of the problem of antisocial behavior, but except for chemical and physical confinement, *no treatment modality is suggested that has worked.*

### Shallow Affect-Learning Approach

The students of human learning focus upon psychopathy as a product of a specific kind of learning experience or deficiency in the ability to learn certain kinds of behavior. Eysenck (1964) views the psychopath as an extrovert with a nervous system predisposed to the rapid development of cortical inhibition. He acquires conditioned responses slowly and extinguishes them rapidly and this learning defect is viewed as a constitutional predisposition. In general, psychopaths do not develop conditioned fear responses readily; they learn responses poorly that are motivated by fear and reinforced by fear reduction (e.g., Lykken, 1955; Schacter and Latane, 1964; Schoenherr, 1964; Schmauk, 1968). Also, they tend to be less influenced by the relationship between past events and consequences of present behavior.

The behavior therapists have reported successful extinction of some sexual deviations (e.g., Barlow, *et al.,* 1969; Callahan and Leitenberg, 1973; Feldman, *et al.,* 1968; Fookes, 1969) but aversive conditioning models require the presence of fear and its reduction and, hence, the psychopath is not viewed as an appropriate candidate for this kind of therapy. Occasional dramatic claims for results in the office and on the cell block notwithstanding, it is generally accepted that *behavior therapy does not work* in correcting the learning defects of psychopathic personalities who behave antisocially.

### Socialization-Character Formation Approach

The most popular and persistent view of all proposes to explain the psychopathic personalities and their antisocial behaviors on the basis of life-styles produced by social conditions and disturbed family relationships. This approach is both appealing and tempting because (1) it is simple and easily understood, (2) it assigns blame and permits the endorsement and support of personal prejudices in the name of science and health, (3) it provides a rational basis for social pressure and reform. Hence, this hypothesis has wide acceptance, blaming specific social conditions (e.g., poverty) and family friction (e.g., separation) for the development and formation of character patterns and life-styles that are psychopathic[10] and antisocial.   Proponents inevitably accept predominant environmental causation.  Blame is assigned to very specific social and family factors and, with minimal evidence, social reform and family styles are recommended as preventive treatment.  This places the mental sciences in the center of potential mythology which attains truth value by appeal, assertion, and fiat. The need for social reform and intact families should not be supported without fact through mental health mythology.

The prevailing generalization that psychopathic personalities are produced by specific and nonspecific disturbances in family and social conditions has been supported by research and survey using retrospective methodology (e.g., Greer, 1964; Gregory, 1958) which is subject to substantial error and should be used to search for, not test hypotheses.  Hence, these studies carry little more weight than the clinical convictions of Kahn (1931) and Cleckley (1964) who viewed family conditions as minor contributing and potentiating factors.  The proponents of social and family causation cannot account rationally for the fact that most people survive deplorable family and social conditions without developing a psychopathic personality accompanied by antisocial behavior.

Importance of experience in character development and formation is an issue of such fundamental importance for the mental health professions that it cannot be sustained by a prevailing mythology.  Epidemiologic research methods are appropriate in the determination of the effects of specific early social and family factors in the understanding of subsequent disordered personalities and antisocial behavior.  Two such studies are worthy of mention since they offer useful facts.

The first by Robins (1966) and co-workers represents a landmark in social research about the conditions associated with the development of the psychopathic personalities and antisocial behavior.   About 30 years after children appeared in a psychiatric clinic, they were studied in terms of their adult social and psychiatric characteristics; the sample included more than 500 patients and 100 healthy controls. The childhood predictors of adult psychopathic personality emphasizing antisocial behavior were enumerated and a profile drawn.  The most important discoveries pertained to family background.  While most of those who developed antisocial, psychopathic personalities came from low socioeconomic homes, the father emerged as the most significant figure.  Fathers of psychopaths were more likely to have a history of antisocial or irresponsible behavior. Robin's work emphasizes the lack of available discipline and the presence of marital discord rather than parental loss or separation as predictors of adult psychopathic behavior.

The second study by Rutter (1971) and his co-workers on family factors and antisocial behavior found no significant long-term effects of permanent or

---

[10] Again, we are not referring to group behavior of obvious social origin such as campus and ghetto riots. Our psychopaths who behave antisocially have a nonharmonious balance of the personality factors *impulse, temperament,* and *character* producing a nonspecific behavioral disposition or vulnerability.

transient parent-child separation when considered in combination with parental discord and disharmony. Again, loss or separation was secondary to prevailing conditions prior to loss or separation.

The importance of social factors and parent-child relationships in personality development and character formation has been established. However, absolute positions that assert family and social causation of antisocial behavior are without foundation.

Robins and Rutter have provided the most substantial evidence to date about the relative importance of loss and separation on the one hand, and discord and disharmony on the other, yet the broken home myth remains. More research on the process of socialization and character formation will provide the facts necessary for a science of preventive intervention. However, *no treatment method based upon disordered character formation from disturbed social and family conditions has worked* in the modification or prevention of psychopathic personalities who behave antisocially.

## COMMENTS ON TREATMENT

A realistic appraisal of clinical and scientific progress through 1974 demands the reaffirmation of Kahn's (1931) comment of more than four decades ago that was used to open this chapter. We still *do not possess a causal therapy* of the psychopathic personalities and efforts at biologic and psychologic intervention at the levels of treatment and prevention remain *in their earliest stages.* Therapeutic programs must emerge from *intimate knowledge of the personality* based upon combined psychological and educational procedures. While we are *still unable and perhaps always will remain unable to change the constitutional structure of the psychopathic personalities,* hope lies in increasing our capacity to *educate many of them to understand themselves, to come to terms with themselves, and to set themselves genuine goals which they may reach in spite of their psychopathic personalities.*

Unfortunately those combinations of strong or weak impulse, shallow emotion, and self-centered grandiose or impressionable characters most vulnerable to a life-style emphasizing antisocial behavior provide few assets that would permit the education and adaptation of these psychopathic personalities.

Again, mental health workers must emphasize knowledge of personality and its interaction with experience. When antisocial behavior is involved these professionals must join forces with other concerned disciplines. We have prime responsibility for learning to modify personality functioning, but we are one among many in the treatment of antisocial behavior. As suggested earlier, antisocial behavior and its reduction is not the province of the mental and behavioral sciences -- the study of biologic, psychologic, and social influences upon personality development and formation represents our domain.

Without credible exception, students of these antisocial psychopathic personalities continue to report poor results (e.g., Cleckley, 1964; McCord and McCord,

1964; Hare, 1970) with psychologic, biologic, and social therapies. Modest successes have been reported in authoritarian, highly disciplined and structured correctional settings (Arendsen Hein, 1959; Sturup, 1964) but these findings may be, in part, a product of the suggestion that the severity of antisocial behavior decreases spontaneously with age (Hare, 1970; Robins, 1966). Patterson (1966) has summarized possible bases for poor treatment results: *First,* psychotherapies assume the presence of pain and discomfort as motivating forces for change. Unfortunately, the antisocial psychopathic personality rarely experiences sufficient distress and does not recognize the wrongness of the conduct. *Second,* data suggests a defect in time orientation with a predominant focus upon the here and now, depriving the antisocial psychopath of an opportunity to profit from a past, and predict with concern the consequences in the future. *Three,* and, of fundamental importance, is the therapeutic requirement of an affective relationship with sufficient depth to provide a setting for corrective emotional experience. The shallow temperament precludes all but an intellectual therapeutic experience without personal, compassionate involvement. *Finally,* Patterson suggests that the pessimism of the therapist concerning the effectiveness of treatment for this group of people may produce a self-fulfilling prophesy.

Considering these difficulties and the complexity of the problem, Thorne (1959) delivered a prescription based upon Kahn's notion that the antisocial psychopathic personality might become more effective by educating him to the fact that the behavior is defeating, and extending time perspective from present orientation into the future through total command and control over reward and punishment. Thorne's model requires the mobilization of family, friends and the entire community in controlling reinforcement and modifying life-style. This theoretical model requires the following for successful treatment: The therapist must control all finances as formal trustee; family and friends must never rescue the antisocial psychopath from the consequences of his behavior; the therapist must be strict and persistent in setting limits and establishing controls; the therapist must never rescue from or stand in the way of legal and social consequences; the therapist must respond only to effective social action and not to verbal promises and commitments; the antisocial psychopath must be faced repeatedly with the self-defeating nature of his behavior; and, the therapist must be alert for reinforcing incentives which will promote more socially effective behavior, even if it requires bribery with the money he controls. In 1959, Thorne placed a conservative annual price-tag on this therapy at $15,000, and the effort and feasibility were highlighted. Indeed, the dollar cost would be much greater at this time but insignificant compared with the turmoil, chaos and exhaustion imposed upon family, friends, and therapist. The Thorne prescription may be viewed as a satiric effort to demonstrate the cost in time, money, effort, people, and community resources required to provide a treatment program with questionable likelihood of success. Even if the Herculean therapist and family, and Utopian community were located, Thorne's hope for locating effective reinforcing incentives and extending time perspective may represent an unrealistic dream.   Needless to say, the Thorne prescription has not received a fair test.

Frustration tends to lead to the hope that some biologic magic is lurking offshore that will permit a chemical, surgical or genetic engineering solution to this problem; the tides do not seem favorable for fulfillment from these sources.

What we can do is very modest, but does represent a contribution.   We can't treat antisocial behavior or change the psychopathic personality who behaves antisocially.   We can offer a useful appraisal of personality as a whole and assess its distinct properties.   We can provide clinical opinions regarding vulnerabilities and dispositions, and speculate about outcome in general and in relation to specific circumstances.   I have accepted the role as supporting service to other agencies directly responsible for antisocial behavior, consulting about the nature of the individual, his psychopathology and personality with recommendations about biologic, psychologic, and social intervention that might reduce the probability of destructive conduct.

## CONCLUSIONS

Economists are now regrouping behind their drawing boards after a disastrous decade of enthusiastic prediction and treatment; theories and methods were promoted and tried with a mildly arrogant certitude for success (Greene, 1974). No approach or point of view has produced change in what appears to have been the economic destiny of our times.   The state of the science was insufficiently developed and too narrow for the complexity of man's economic nature to yield an art or technology that could alter significantly history's course.

The mental sciences are also given to promises, and our failures have been predominantly due to premature excessive and enthusiastic commitment, and the inability to deliver.   Nowhere is this more evident than with the management and treatment of antisocial behavior.   As with the economists, we are now witnessing an erosion of public trust and professional confidence.

It has been the thesis of this discussion that the mental health professions and behavioral sciences have no treatment for the antisocial behaviors of psychopathic personalities.   However, these disciplines can contribute to the understanding of personality structure and function, thereby defining and classifying people who are most vulnerable and disposed to behaving antisocially.   The point of view offered by the mental health professions adds another useful dimension to the complex matrix of disciplines concerned with man's relationships.   A science and technology based upon the nature of our species utilizing the methodology of ethology (Tinbergen, 1968) must provide fundamental data on characteristics given by evolution, their function, and their modifiability.   Are homicide and theft mere extensions of man's natural hunting, aggressive and predatory instincts becoming deviant only through an interaction of unfortunate personal characteristics and social circumstances?   Can the properties of a psychopathic personality be harnessed through education and opportunity to reduce the likelihood of antisocial behavior? Can we learn to predict early enough in the formation of personality to modify direction prior to the development of the antisocial style? It is fair to state that the disposition for psychopathic antisocial behavior has roots in the development and formation of personality, but the antisocial life-style is conditioned by experience and circumstances. To date the mental health professions have not produced effective tools for prevention or treatment at the stage of development or at the interface with society. It is not discouraging to stipulate our ignorance, and to acknowledge slow progress early in man's most complex professional sport — *knowing himself.* We are still in the process of learning from deviance about man's nature, and are not yet ready to apply knowledge toward effective control.

Excessive promises and social pressures combined with a bit of narcissistic self-deception have placed the mental health professions in danger of becoming an instrument of public policy. In the name of diagnosis and treatment, people are often confined, detained, and medicated because of presumed dangerousness from mental illness and emotional disorder. These decisions, made by health professionals, represent a form of preventive detention using health facilities as arms of the Criminal Law, and provide convenient but abused resources for those responsible for the administration of justice.

This essay did not yield much useful information about the treatment of antisocial behavior for the health professional. Yet the health "mentality" is seen as quite useful in providing a supporting service to those responsible for representing public policy which defines and controls antisocial behavior.

> Since in psychopaths not everything is psychopathic it is possible to bring many of them to turn more and more toward their non-psychopathic *Anlagen,* and on this basis to deal successfully with their inner difficulties, at least to a certain degree. In such attempts it is expedient to call the psychopaths' attention to the fact that even *psychopathy lays responsibility on the individual. Psychopathy means not only aberration and difficulty but also differentiation and capacity for suffering.* The physician, however, and the psychotherapist in particular, may be confirmed by this insight in that which fundamentally every man owes to every other; respect for his fellowman. (Kahn, 1931)

## REFERENCES

Arendsen, Hein, G. Group therapy with criminal psychopaths. *Acta Psychotherap.* (Suppl.). 7: 6–16 (1959).

Barlow, D.H., Leitenberg, H. and Agras, W.S. Experimental control of sexual deviation through manipulation of the noxious scene in covert sensitization. *J. Abnorm. Psychol.* 74: 597–601 (1969).

Bay-Rakal, S. The significance of EEG abnormality in behavior problem children. *Can. Psychiat. Assoc. J.* 10: 387–391 (1965).

Callahan, E.J. and Leitenberg, H.   Aversion therapy for sexual deviation:   Contingent shock and covert sensitization.   *J. Abnorm. Psychol.*   **81**:   60–73 (1973).

Cleckley, H.   *The mask of sanity,* (4th edition).   St. Louis: Mosby, 1964.

Craft, M.J.   *Ten studies into psychopathic personality.*   Bristol: John Wright, 1965.

*Diagnostic and statistical manual of mental disorders,* (first and second editions).   Washington, D.C.: American Psychiatric Association, 1952, 1968.

Ellingson, R.J.   Incidence of EEG abnormality among patients with mental disorders of apparently nonorganic origin:    a criminal review.   *Amer. J. Psychiat.*, 1954, **111**:   263–275 (1954).

Eysenck, H.J.   *Crime and personality.*   London:  Methuen, 1964.

Feldman, M.P., MacCulloch, M.J. and MacCulloch, M.L.   The aversion therapy treatment of a heterogeneous group of five cases of sexual deviation.   *Acta Psychiat. Scand.*   **44**:  113–123 (1968).

Fookes, B.H.   Some experiences in the use of aversion therapy in male homosexuality, exhibitionism, and fetishism-transvestism.   *Brit. J. Psychiat.* **115**: 339–341 (1969).

Freedman, A. and Kaplan, *Comprehensive textbook of psychiatry.*   Baltimore: Williams & Wilkins, 1967.

Gibbens, T.C.N., Pond, D.A. and Stafford-Clark, D.   A follow-up study of criminal psychopaths.   *Brit. J. Delinq.*   **5**:   126–136 (1955).

Greene, W.   Economists in recession.   *N.Y. Times Magazine.*   May 12, 1974.

Greer, S.   Study of parental loss in neurotics and sociopaths.   *Arch. Gen. Psychiat.*   **11**:   177–180 (1964).

Gregory, I.   Studies of parental deprivation in psychiatric patients.   *Amer. J. Psychiat.*   **115**:   432–442 (1958).

Hare, R.D.   Psychopathy, autonomic functioning, and the orienting response.   *J. Abnorm. Psychol.*, (Mono. Suppl.).   **73** (No. 3, Part 2):   1–24 (1968a).

Hare, R.D.   Detection threshold for electric shock in psychopaths.   *J. Abnorm. Psychol.*   **73**:   268–272 (1968b).

Hare, R.D.   *Psychopathy:   theory and research.*   New York:   John Wiley, 1970.

Hill, D. and Watterson, D.   Electroencephalographic studies of the psychopathic personality.   *J. Neurol. Psychiat.*   **5**:   47–64 (1942).

Kahn, E.   *Psychopathic personalities.*   New Haven:   Yale University Press, 1931.

Knott, J.R., Platt, E.B., Ashby, M.C. and Gottlieb, J.S.   A familiar evaluation of the electroencephalogram of patients with primary behavior disorder and psychopathic personality.   *EEG Clin. Neurophysiol.*   **5**:   363–370 (1953).

Kurland, H.D., Yeager, C.T. and Arthur, R.J.   Psychophysiologic aspects of severe behavior disorders.   *Arch. Gen. Psychiat.*   **8**:   599–604 (1963).

Lykken, D.T.   A study of anxiety in the sociopathic personality.   Doctoral Dissertation, University of Minnesota, 1955.

Maughs, S.B.   Concept of psychopathy and psychopathic personality:   its evolution and historic development.   *J. Crim. Psychopath.*   **2**:   329–356 (1941).

McCord, W. and McCord, J. *The psychopath: an essay on the criminal mind.* New York: Van Nostrand Reinhold, 1964.

Patterson, C.H. Theories of counseling and psychopathy. New York: Harper & Row, 1966.

Petrie, A. *Individuality in pain and suffering.* Chicago: University of Chicago Press, 1967.

Robins, L.N. *Deviant children grown up.* Baltimore: Williams & Wilkins, 1966.

Rutter, M. Parent-child separation: psychological effects on the children. *J. Child Psychol. & Psychiat.* **12**: 233–260 (1971).

Schachter, S. and Latane, B. Crime, cognition and the autonomic nervous system. In: Jones, M.R. (Ed.), *Nebraska symposium on motivation.* Lincoln: University of Nebraska Press, 1964.

Schmauk, F. A study of the relationship between kinds of punishment, autonomic arousal, subjective anxiety and avoidance learning in the primary sociopath. Doctoral Dissertation, Temple University, 1968.

Schoenherr, J.C. Avoidance of noxious stimulation in psychopathic personality. Doctoral Dissertation, University of California, Los Angeles, 1964.

Schwade, E.D. and Geiger, S.G. Abnormal electroencephalographic findings in severe behavior disorders. *Diseases Nervous System* **17**: 307–317 (1965).

Shagass, C. and Schwartz, M. Observations on somatosensory cortical reactivity in personality disorders. *J. Nervous Mental Disease.* **135**: 44–51 (1962).

Sturup, G.K. The treatment of chronic criminals. *Bull. Menninger Clin.* **28**: 229–243 (1964).

Thorne, F.C. The etiology of sociopathic reactions. *Amer. J. Psychotherapy.* **13**: 319–330 (1959).

Tinbergen, N. War and peace in animals and man: an ethologists approach to the biology of aggression. *Science.* **160**: 1410–1418 (1968).

# 18 The Treatment of Drug Addiction

## James W. Dykens and G. Donald Niswander

Of the many individual, family and community problems confronting the professional dealing with mental disorder, none presents a greater challenge than drug addiction. Its prevalence is widespread and its incidence difficult to measure (Lavenhar, 1973). Unrest, peaking to panic in the community, has led to much heated opinion in approaching the problem but little effective concerted social action in reaching a solution. Legislation and law enforcement approaches have targeted upon the sources of drug supply, the drug traffic and control of the addict all with questionable success. Increasingly, there is a turning toward the physician, psychologist, psychiatrist, social worker and behavior scientist to assist in managing the problem. As this occurs, the comprehensive mental health worker is confronting a myriad of conceptual models and techniques each of which may be drawn upon to deal with the individual addict and with addiction as a social issue.

It is intended here to scan issues from the psychological, social, developmental, behavioral, and medical models which are pertinent for management of the individual addict as well as for participation of the therapist in broader social and preventive programs. While a primary concern in the treatment of the addict centers about somatic crises such as those related to detoxification, it is hoped that this scan of related issues will assist the therapist in planning and packaging a comprehensive treatment program for the addict.

The first cluster of issues concerns the social backdrop of the addict. The drug subculture made the scene in the ambiance of the 1960s in which there was increased awareness of the self and of the social milieu. Opening up of the mind for greater self understanding and activism for social change occurred. The movements toward civil rights, dealing with poverty, alienation, poor housing, environmental pollution, sexism and racism emerged. Rationalism gave way to the expression of feelings and action. Reinforcement occurred in literature, art forms, including films and acid rock music, and street violence. The street walker was joined by the street user, the street pusher, the nomadic alcoholic street sleeper — and the street worker. Meanwhile, in the homes lining city streets as well as suburban and rural roads, the American adult public was ingesting psychotrophic medicine by the ton to deal with its anxieties, depressions and emotional crises. Double messages and double binds between the generations led to dissatisfaction and alienation — and in some instances, tragic deaths by overdosage. The increased use of mind-expanding drugs helped perhaps to fertilize the field of chemical addiction.

Through identification with his primary group, the addict found a common language and support from peers against what was perceived to be a Janus-faced family and establishment. Through habituation, the addict became increasingly isolated with social breakdown, anomie, isolation and psychosocial regression. Criminal behavior associated with the seeking of drug supplies or abandonment of the search through suicide has confounded the social problem.

A number of very significant issues in treatment of the addict are clustered within the family situation. A concept of useful value to clinicians for understanding the addict's family comes from the work of Johnson and Szurek, (1952) which is pertinent to all acting out behavior. This model holds that the genesis of acting out behavior in the child arises from unconscious wishes and impulses in the parent which are expressed vicariously through the child. Clinical experience, as pointed out by Seldin, (1972) supports the idea that until and unless the family is considered in understanding and managing the addict, little progress is likely to be made. Parental inconsistency and communication disorders in the family may place the addicted member in a double bind. A commonly found family situation is a mother who alternates between over-protection and active rejection which generates a basic ambivalence about supplies. The absent, distant, or passive father is unavailable for rescue operations through identification for the male or for helping the female separate from a domineering mother. For the married addict, the marriage itself may emerge as the main target for therapy. Through displacement from the primal family, the spouse may symbolically stand for the parent and vicariously gain gratification through the addict's addiction. It is to be noted, also, that within the street culture are also figures who symbolically may represent family members. Thus, the pusher-supplier, the police-authority, and the security-guaranteeing jail, can both cause and express suffering reminiscences for the addict.

Family crises relating to developmental or accidental life change events described by Caplan (1964) are of signal importance in the management of the drug addict. Of special importance, here, is the idea that in dealing with the drug addict, the therapist not get caught up entirely in the patient's crisis coping mechanism and deal with the symptomatic responses to crisis only, but that he assists the addict to come to grips with the crisis-cause and his unsuccessful problem solving attempts. In treating the addict, while it may not be practicable to tackle problems within a resilient character armor, it is feasible to detail out a life change event which has brought the addict to the treatment situation. In approaching the addict-in-crisis, the therapist may profitably detail out the elements of the psychosocial crisis as carefully as he details out the detoxification procedure. While the addict appears to move in his life-style, from one supply crisis to another, with constant yearning for need-satisfaction, there always is the straw which breaks the camel's back. An understanding of such a crisis situation can lead to greater understanding of the addict, especially of his perception of family role or its extension into his peer group.

A number of psychosocial and intrapsychic factors are to be considered in treatment of the addict. The oral-narcissistic and regressive dynamic pattern is a consistent finding in the addict. In considering the oral nature of acting out, Altman (1957) reinforces the belief that oral needs are characterized by their urgency and their lack or capacity for gaining satisfaction from substitutes. While it is possible to provide the orally impulsive character with food for thought, it is not possible to substitute thought for food. Through the substitute feeding needle, the addict seeks satisfaction which never really comes. Thinking before acting is not part of his life-style.

Oceanic feelings of bliss in the addicted state represent both a physiological and psychological escape from the helpless and hopeless feelings of depression. It is of major importance that in detoxifying the addict, the therapist be aware of clinical depression which may emerge as the drug is withdrawn. Substitute supplies are necessary through supporting interpersonal relationships from staff. The psychosocial dynamics of depression are those of the loss. In detoxification, the addict must work through the loss of his drug. In order to prevent recidivism, it is to be noted that feelings of loss occur when he makes voluntary renunciation as well as when something is "taken away." Thus, in helping the addict to remain drug free, his feelings of loss in letting go of the drug require working through.

In treating and managing the addict, the need to understand him as a person, nearly goes without saying. Understanding, in a comprehensive sense, is facilitated by consideration of Erikson's work (1963). Especially relevant in dealing with the addict is Erikson's elaboration of the oral phase of psycho-sexual development into the first incorporative mode of behavior associated with "getting" and the second incorporative mode, associated with "taking." Depending on the mode or style of behavior developed through prior psycho-social transactions between mother and child, the infant learns a basic pattern of trusting or distrusting. In the addict this nuclear concept appears to be unsolved. In failing to establish a point of orientation in the trust-distrust behavior continuum, the addict swings between the extremes of gullible self-deceit to massive distrust of a nonsupplying milieu. His manipulation and acting out against treatment, as well as society, require that treatment programs create the expectation of trust and, at the same time, do not get caught in the confidence game the addict may try to play.

Finally, in managing the addict the therapist may consider the addict's use of the repetition compulsion in his addiction. Further regression into the use of early defenses such as denial and projection may require active management in order to deal with the meaning of his addictive behavior.

In the total management and treatment of the drug addict, a broad spectrum of somatic issues must be considered. Prior to attempts to bring a comprehensive mental health approach to the treatment of the drug addict and the management of addiction as a social problem, the fields of medicine and law collaborated for control of drug use and dispensing.

Brecher (1972) has presented some of the most comprehensive overviews about the drug problem in general; several chapters of this book deal with drug addiction. The reader is reminded that the drug and addiction literature is so vast that difficulty is encountered in keeping abreast of it; one quarterly review publication from the National Institute of Mental Health recently contained 246 references about the problem (1973).

Recognition of the problem of drug addiction has come under the scrutiny of the medical profession in the United States only in the past 20 years. Since the early 1960s, the problem was seen as existing (at endemic proportions) only in metropolitan areas. After 1965, awareness of the problem began to seep from metropolitan-urban areas into urban-rural areas in this country. At first drug addiction was identified with ghettos in New York, Chicago, and San Francisco. Lately, it has been generally seen as affecting all social groups, low, medium or high, according to one's classification of social and ethnic groups.

Although prevalency probably continues to be the highest in metropolitan areas, the clinician profitably remembers that vague, strange and erratic behavior in an individual in a small community may be an expression of drug addiction or drug-abuse, not necessarily caused by narcotic addictive substances.

Narcotic compounds are to be focused upon here. Suggestions for treatment and rehabilitation will be recommended for the opiates and their derivatives. Mention will be made about barbiturate addiction.

It is particularly interesting from a historical point of view, that addiction has become a medical highlight in the mid-twentieth century. Prior to this, it was generally concluded by medical, sociological and criminal historians that the use of these addictive substances dated back several thousands of years. In the Middle Ages and in the Far East, the effect of opium was akin to godly and religious states of being, just as the affliction of certain physical disorders was recognized as something special from the gods and idols which the early tribal and ethnic groups worshipped or feared. Examples of these throughout early medical history are epilepsy, consumption, and mental illness. Goulding (1972) states that, medically, opium was the "keystone of medications for thousands of years." In more recent years, the increased use of opium became recognized as a social-cultural problem. In fact, the Chinese Emperor, Yung Cheng, in 1829, attempted to prohibit the use of opium, because "he identified its excessive consumption with the misery, crime and evil" (1972) that was considered so rampant among his people who indulged in using the substance.

In the early nineteenth century, morphine had been extracted from crude opium. By the time of the Civil War in this country in the 1860s, the hypodermic syringe had been invented, and many Northern and Southern troops became addicted when they were given morphine over extended periods for analgesic purposes. "Soldiers Disease" was the term used to describe the disorder, even though it had its beginning as a medical treatment for injuries suffered during combat.

It was not until 1914 that the Congress of the United States enacted the Harrison Act, a law designed to control the interstate traffic of opiates, marijuana, and cocaine. This law has been amended in more recent years for stricter regulations on the sale of narcotics, barbiturates and other harmful drugs; it was administered by the Bureau of Narcotics and Dangerous Drugs, operating out of the Department of Justice. In 1973, the Drug Enforcement Administration (DEA) was established in the Department of Justice, combining several scattered Federal agencies for drug regulations, control, and enforcement.

Until 1964, drug addiction and drug habituation were defined separately, at which time the World Health Organization Expert Committee made the following distinction: that the two terms be defined as a state arising from continuous and repeated administration of a drug, but, to specify the drug type, such as morphine, cocaine, and barbiturates.

The current extent of the overall drug problem in this country is actually indeterminable. Statisticians generally agree that prevalence rates of drug addiction, whatever the source, are unreliable and inaccurate. The estimates of the multiple thousands of addicts in a city like New York only reflect the actual known addicts to the authorities. It does not include the additional probably thousands of other addicts who can procure and maintain their habit, and never actually come into the hands of authorities for criminal behavior, as is almost universal with the first group.

The same is true in the urban-rural areas where there are known addicts, but where there is no accounting of the hidden addict. Failure to recognize, or even deny the problem by citizens and law enforcement persons is widespread.

Today, drug addiction can be considered a disease of neglect just as venereal disease, tuberculosis, and poliomyelitis, are examples of past physical disorders, neglected when knowledge was lacking and research difficult and meager. Wursmer (1972) has called the problem of drug addiction the "nemesis of psychiatry." He concludes that "the enormousness of emotional problems dwarfs our skills more than our knowledge; we understand far more than we can actually influence," and he compares this with the problem of infectious diseases before antibiotics.

This expresses the desperate need for research and study to better apply our skills in treating drug addiction.

Throughout history, every culture appears to have had mind changing substances. In early years these were derived mostly from plants. More recently, synthetic substances, manmade in either recognized reliable pharmaceutical laboratories, or in the "garage-laboratory operations" for the street suppliers and pushers, became drug sources. In respect to the drug addicts' relationship with the latter group, Jaffe (1970) estimates that the addict spends more time, money and energy obtaining drugs from illegal sources, than he does for any other activity.

Because addiction and problems caused by it are widespread, there is great need for concentrated research, treatment studies and rehabilitation models to meet the problem head-on in the next few years. Those working in the addiction area in the past decade recognize that cutting and prohibiting the drug supply are not the answer. This approach leads only to more illicit drugs, and to the creation of greater social problems, involving not only individuals, but their families, employers, and peers. The complexity of causes and effects of addiction require a multiply faceted problem solving approach. America has apparently forgotten what it learned during the alcohol prohibition days in the late twenties.

The treatment of drug addiction embraces many interrelated concepts of therapy, leading hopefully toward total rehabilitation of the individual with the problem. Approaches for treatment of the addict are very controversial. Results of various treatment programs are very unreliable, unclear, and at times misleading, just as is the clear estimation of the incidence of prevalence of drug addiction problems.

Earlier treatment programs, prior to 1959 and sponsored mostly by Federal funds, were largely phased out because of the high rate of treatment failure. The majority of patients returned to the drug scene upon release from the treatment facility. Early programs including those under the Public Health Service, had a "cold-turkey," "lock-up" orientation and, in general, offered little in the way of psychotherapy, activity therapies, recreation, job training and other rehabilitation programs. "Conning" was rampant.

This is in contrast to present day concepts of treatment which are gradually emerging from multidisciplinary study and research. Whether a program emphasizing psychotherapy, encounter groups, drug substitutes, religion or other modalities of reaching people with problems, the clinician is faced with the task of finding out which program package best fits his patient's needs. In fact, the worker in the drug field finds that he must use all the patience and ingenuity he can muster in trying to find exactly where his patient will receive the greatest benefit. The worker also must tolerate an angry addict's various verbal abuses, threats, acting out behavior, and other situations in testing the limits of the therapeutic relationship, before meaningful rapport with the patient is made. At times the worker changes his professional "cloak." He finds that meeting the addict in a common environment and territory, *his* street; speaking the language, *his* "jargon," and empathizing with *his* human struggles, *his* feelings; will more quickly establish therapeutic rapport.

Dogmatically assuming that any one particular treatment may be tailored for all addicts is not to realize the addict as an individual who requires a wide variety of treatment approaches.

Especially early in the course of treatment there is a tendency for the patient to manipulate, connive and plainly "con" the therapist. An interesting article on the "conning" procedures by addicts is by Levine and Stephens (1971). They discuss games the addict plays, the rewards of the games and finally, some therapeutic guidelines in dealing with them. While addicts will yield to a therapeutic relationship and give up this type of behavior, reversion to old habits is always possible, particularly when new situations of stress and strain are encountered. However, once an addict has been successfully treated, a reverting to previous behavior patterns can be handled and dissolved, usually more easily, if the therapist makes himself available at times of future emergencies. Under such circumstances the drug addict is no different from the chronic alcoholic, who once having overcome his problem, resorts to his old habits under a new life crisis.

The treatment of the drug addict often centers around several medically and psychiatrically-oriented approaches toward rehabilitation.

Frequently associated with an addiction problem are physical disorders which result from the living style of the addict. Often he has become completely numb and unconcerned about his physical health. His nutritional state commonly is poor. His living conditions result in exposure to diseases and disorders through his contacts with peers. Thus, respiratory disorders, vitamin deficiencies, various neurologic disturbances and venereal disease are often seen. A major problem in the addict is jaundice and other liver disturbances, usually associated with some type of hepatitis, resulting from "shooting-up" with dirty equipment. Many addicts give a history of multiple episodes of jaundice and liver tenderness. Nelson (1971) thoroughly discusses several important points for the initial treatment of the addict and covers the multitude of physical disorders encountered.

When an addict presents himself for treatment, therefore, the first item of importance is the recording of a complete medical and social history. A complete physical examination with attention to neurologic signs is necessary. Laboratory studies include urinalysis, complete blood count, serology, blood tests, and liver function tests to establish a baseline physiological data screen for the patient. It is especially recommended that liver transaminase studies (SGOT and SGPT) be made to determine evidence of liver damage. In addition, a blood urea nitrogen level is desirable to establish a basic renal function screen. A fasting blood sugar test as a further endocrine screen for the patient is useful. An x-ray of the chest is desirable for uncovering latent respiratory disease.

A modified type of classical mental status examination should be done. It is necessary to ascertain and record orientation, mood, presence of thought disorder, and mental aberrations, such as hallucinations, and delusions. Many addicts are found to use projective defenses, or to have paranoid-colored thought content. Both patients and experienced drug workers are aware of this.

These data establish the basic medically-oriented treatment program for the new addict. If there is a question of psychosis or organic brain disease, psychological testing is indicated early in the treatment program. When not initially indicated, these studies can assist the therapist in finding some of the patient's underlying problems, including those in establishing a therapeutic interpersonal relationship.

Complete early studies are costly in time and money, but necessary in developing a plan for treatment and future care.

Initially, the problem of withdrawal from the narcotic substance takes precedence over all other treatment. In emergency conditions the medical workup is accomplished during and after the withdrawal period. Nelson also has pertinent remarks and recommendations about withdrawal treatment for various addictive compounds (1971).

A rather drastic, less medically accepted, method of withdrawal is "cold-turkey:" letting the patient experience symptoms of withdrawal without administering any medication to lessen and soften the painful experience of the sudden cut off from a drug supply. In using this technique, within 18–24 hours the patient becomes tremulous, experiences chills, develops sniffles, abdominal cramps and vague aches and pains in the bones of the long extremities, the joints and the spinal column. Gradually the syndrome worsens with disturbed emotional states. These are characterized by crying, writhing and yelling, and usually associated with hallucinations. Other symptoms, not unlike those seen in the withdrawal syndromes from alcoholism and other known addictive agents, are not uncommon. This state can persist for 24–96 hours after which it gradually burns out. The therapist is commonly left with a frightened, suspicious and sometimes, borderline psychotic patient. The height of the "cold-turkey" method presents a medical emergency, with such problems as convulsions, vomiting, aspiration, pulmonary edema, cardiac failure and urinary retention. While not common, these complications may occur. The treatment team must be prepared to cope with them.

A more scientific, therapeutic and humanistic approach of detoxification during the withdrawal phase is that of drug substitution. The drug of choice for detoxification is methadone. For detoxification purposes, Jaffe (1970) reports the following equivalents for the opiates commonly used by drug addicts: 1 mg of methadone for 2 mg heroin; 1 mg of methadone for 4 mg of morphine. Occasionally, the addict substitutes hydromorphone for heroin or morphine when he cannot obtain the latter − 1 mg of methadone is used for 0.5 mg of hydromorphone for detoxification.

For withdrawal, it is recommended generally that methadone be administered initially in a single oral dosage of 15–30 mg. This may be repeated when withdrawal symptoms recur. Usually after 36 hours a stabilizing dose is established (Jaffe, 1970). This dosage 10–40 mg, is then administered orally once daily. It is recommended that this dosage be reduced 5 mg daily, until the methadone is discontinued. Some mild abstinence symptoms can occur a few days after completing the detoxification schedule.

This type of rapid detoxification is recommended to prevent withdrawal symptoms. A slower detoxification process may lead the patient to become addicted to methadone. The amount of drug taken by an addict is rarely known to the clinician or addict. Therefore, great care is necessary in withdrawal programs. The administration of doses of methadone in these small amounts in the first 24–36 hours is especially recommended.

Dole and Nyswander (1965) introduced methadone as a treatment for heroin addiction. They found that methadone, in adequate dosages, relieves narcotic hunger and blocks euphoric effects when heroin is injected by the addict. Methadone is prescribed daily for the addict. The amount of methadone varies, but a small dosage usually of 60–100 mg is adequate to gain the desired effects.

Candidates for the Methadone Maintenance Program must be carefully selected by clinicians who view the problems of the addict in a comprehensive fashion. It is generally accepted that the presence of an overt psychotic, regressed patient is a contraindication.

Patients on methadone maintenance are able to work, to support themselves and families, and to contribute to society.

It is to be noted that Methadone Maintenance Programs are carefully controlled by the Federal Government through the Drug Enforcement Administration. Patients must be referred to licensed programs for treatment.

More recently, Raynes and Patch (1973) reported a different approach to the problem of detoxification. They compared a group of addicts who self-determine the reduction schedule of methadone. This was accomplished in an outpatient hospital setting, which provided psychotherapy and other activities such as day care. They reported twice the success in this group of patients compared to a control group of hospitalized addicts, whose medication was doctor-controlled on a regular basis. Psychosocial support is also cited in the effective employment of this new method of detoxification.

During detoxification, the patient is treated medically according to symptoms. It has been found that prescribing psychotropic substances during the withdrawal period can cause untoward reactions. Jarvik (1970) cites that phenothiazines have been shown to increase the sedative effects of morphine; monoamine oxidase inhibitors are suspected to interfere with the "detoxification mechanisms for other drugs." There is also some question about the use of dibenzazepine derivatives with some drugs of abuse.

Controversy exists concerning the setting for detoxification. Some advocate that detoxification be done in the hospital. Others believe that detoxification should be done on an outpatient basis, providing that the same medical, social and psychological services are available as are afforded the inpatient.

An essential adjunct to any treatment program for the drug addict is urine monitoring. Sensitive laboratory methods have been developed for detecting almost all the substances drug addicts and abusers use, (opiates, barbiturates, amphetamines). Random urine sampling is a definitive method to determine whether a patient is drug free. A "clean" urine also has psychological implications in the management of the addict.

The occurrence of narcotic overdosage is a major community problem. The management of the overdosed addict presents an acute medical emergency. It requires special training for ambulance rescue workers and hospital emergency room personnel. Whether the cause of overdosage is accidental or otherwise, certain medical principles are of importance in treating this emergency situation.

Under no circumstances, should other central nervous system depressant agents be administered to a questionable or known overdose victim. This includes not only narcotic agents, but also barbiturate compounds.

In the early management of overdosage, it is essential that the patient's airway be kept open and unobstructed. Emergency measures, such as continual mouth-to-mouth resuscitation may be required until oxygen can be administered.

Symptomatic treatment is recommended for any other complications occurring during the acute overdosage phase.

In established opiate overdosage, levallorphan is recommended as the drug of choice to antagonize the depressant effect of the opiate. One milligram of level-lorphan injected intravenously reacts quickly. The unconscious state from opiate can be completely reversed; the patient becomes rapidly conscious, sits up, breathes normally and talks with those about him. One-half milligram doses of this medication can be repeated if signs of drowsiness and respiratory depression return at 15-20 minute intervals for 3-4 dosages.

Today the clinician is more frequently encountering the person addicted to more than one drug. The poly-addict is usually an older individual. His source of supply is likely the legal prescriptions from his own or other physicians. The multi-addict may visit offices of several physicians, whom he "cons" in his compulsive search for drugs.

Poly-addiction may involve combinations of opiates, barbiturates and synthetic substances, often complicated by the excessive use of alcohol. Withdrawal and treatment are difficult in such patients and should only be managed in hospital settings which provide emergency medical procedures

Psychotherapy in some form is often part of the treatment program for the drug addict. The choice and type of psychotherapy program must be carefully selected and tailored to meet the individual's need.

Individual therapy geared toward in-depth insight should be in the hands of the experienced psychotherapist, who has a sympathetic awareness of all the psycho-social problems of the drug addict.

Many addicts require an eclectic therapist, especially one who is skilled in crisis intervention, as well as adeptness in listening and offering reassurance.

The usefulness of group concepts and methods in managing addiction, requires the eclectic therapist to be skilled as well, in this approach. Addicted patients have a common identification with strong peer ties which facilitates group solidarity. Again, the therapist is cautioned about manipulative tendencies of his patients, even in a group situation; he must constantly be alerted to testing trust in the group experience.

The concept of the therapeutic community for the treatment of the addict has met with a great deal of success in various programs throughout the country. Some of these are Marathon House, Odyssey House, Daytop Village, Phoenix House, Synanon and others. These "self-help" programs often are conducted and managed by former addicts who are "graduates" of a therapeutic community. In such a community, a group lives together, shares daily responsibilities for residential living, and at the same time, works through conflicts by various psychotherapeutic and corrective emotional experience. Many self-help programs rely on traditional professional guidance and consultation, together with peer management and leadership. Other programs depend entirely on techniques developed and carried out by ex-addicts and the peer group. In both approaches, individual, group and encounter techniques are used, following an orientation to the therapeutic community setting. The addict starts and advances to higher levels as he is able to assume more self-responsibilities. Most addicts complete a therapeutic community program in a 15–24 month period.

In view of the global aspects of drug addiction, the reader is reminded again that a wide variety of coping methods may be applied in helping the addict. Such approaches include mysticism, yoga and transcendental meditation. While these methods may not rest easy with scientific tradition, they may offer constructive strength to the addict's attempts to cope and grow.

Seldin, as previously cited, has carefully reviewed the literature on the family of the addict. He believes that in planning treatment programs, involvement of the addict's family is necessary as part of the total therapeutic process. This kind of involvement is rewarding for the addict, the family and the therapist. Family participation in treatment is, however, made difficult by geographic or psychologic distance.

An additional chemotherapeutic approach for the drug addict is through the use of the opiate antagonist. Cyclazocine is the antagonist most commonly used although it is still in an experimental phase of study and its use has not been officially recognized and recommended. This antagonist blocks the effects of the opiates in the central nervous system. A maintenance dosage level of 4 mg orally, daily, is recommended, starting at a dosage of 1 mg daily, which is gradually increased to 4 mg over a 10-day period.

Brecher (1972) points out two major disadvantages for drug antagonists when compared to methadone. Firstly, he indicates antagonists "do not assuage the post-addiction syndrome – the anxiety, depression, and craving . . ." for heroin. Secondly, since the antagonist is not an addicting substance, the patient can stop taking the medication at any point in his treatment and return to heroin.

Brecher clearly points out the advantages of methadone maintenance over the use of the narcotic antagonist as well as of the use of legalized heroin or morphine maintenance.

Holland (1971) discusses the possible role of two narcotic antagonists — cyclazocine and naloxane — only to conclude that neither is the solution to the problem of drug addiction. In comparing methadone and cyclazocine therapy, he points out the most favorable overall emotional and psychological response the patient has to methadone.

Next to alcohol, the most common addictive agent in this country is the prescribed barbiturate. A person is usually considered addicted to a barbiturate substance if he has taken the medication in amounts of 400 mg or more for over a month. Such a patient remains ambulatory and often is able to maintain most of his normal social pattern.

The withdrawal period from barbiturate addiction requires close and careful medical management. In a program for withdrawal from barbiturates, pentobarbital is presently the drug substitute of choice. As recommended by Jaffe (1970) it should be administered at a dosage level to produce a mild secondary intoxication with tremulousness, slurred speech, ataxia and drowsiness. This dosage level should be maintained 24 hours, and then gradually decreased 50-100 mg daily until it is discontinued. If withdrawal signs return while pentobarbital is being withdrawn, further reduction should be discontinued for 1-2 days and then the withdrawal procedure again continued.

In considering treatment of the drug addict, it is necessary in every instance to understand the addict as a total person. A coordinated and comprehensive program for the individual addict is required. Problems brought by the addict as an individual will require an organized treatment program which involves somatic, psychological and social factors.

## REFERENCES

Altman, L.L. On the oral nature of acting-out. *Journal of the American Psychoanalytic Association.* **5**: 648–662 (1957).

Brecher, E.M. *Licit and Illicit Drugs.* Boston: Little, Brown & Company, 1972.

Caplan, G. *Principles of Preventive Psychiatry.* New York: Basic Books, 1964.

Dole, V.P. and Nyswander, M. A medical treatment for diacetyl morphine (heroin) addiction: A clinical trial with methadone hydrochloride. *Journal of the American Medical Association.* **63**: 646–650 (1965).

Erikson, E. *Childhood and Society (2nd ed.).* New York: W.W. Norton & Co., 1963.

Goulding, R. Drug Addiction. In: *Encyclopedia Brittanica,* pp. 702–706. Chicago: Encyclopedia Brittanica, Limited, 1972.

Holland, A.L. Narcotic antagonists: New Methods to treat heroin addiction. *Science.* **173**: 503–506 (1971).

Jaffe, J.H. Drug addiction and abuse. In: *Encyclopedia Americana,* pp. 414–418. New York: Americana Corporation, 1970.

Jaffe, J.H., Drug addiction and drug abuse. In: Goodman, L.S. and Gilman, A. (Eds.), *The Pharmacological Basis of Therapeutics,* pp. 276–313. New York: The Macmillan Company, 1970.

Jarvik, M.D. Drugs used in the treatment of psychiatric disorders. In: Goodman, L.S. and Gilman, A. (Eds.), *The Pharmacological Basis of Therapeutics,* pp. 151–203. New York: The Macmillan Company, 1970.

Johnson, A.L. and Szurek, S. The genesis of antisocial acting-out in children and adults. *The Psychoanalytic Quarterly.* **21**: 323–343 (1952).

Lavenhar, M.A. The drug abuse numbers game. *American Journal of Public Health.* **63** (9): 807–809 (1973).

Levine, S. and Stephens, R. Games addicts play. *The Psychiatric Quarterly.* **45**: 582–592 (1971).

National Institute of Mental Health. *Drug Abuse Awareness System.* National Clearing House for Drug Abuse Information. **2**: 1 (1973).

Nelson, A.S. Medical management of drug addiction. *Arizona Medicine.* (December, 1971).

Raynes, E.D. and Patch, V.D. An improved detoxification technique for heroin addicts. *Archives of General Psychiatry.* **29**: 417–419 (1973).

Seldin, N. The family of the addict: A review of the literature. *The International Journal of the Addictions.* **7**: 97–107 (1972).

Wursmer, L. Drug abuse: Nemesis of psychiatry. *International Journal of Psychiatry.* **10** (4): 94–107 (1972).

# 19 Alcoholism

## Morris E. Chafetz

There are many definitions of alcoholism. A widely quoted definition is used by the World Health Organization and states that "alcoholism is a chronic behavioral disorder manifested by repeated drinking of alcoholic beverages in excess of the dietary and social uses of the community and to an extent that interferes with the drinker's health or his social or economic function."

This definition is less than satisfactory because it is descriptive and symptomatic, rather than etiological. The physiological, psychological and social phenomena it embraces are integrated at varying levels, leading to qualification and often forcing the observer to act more as a moralist than as a scientist. The definition also implies a greater concern with group deviance than with individual discomfort, signifying that much destruction must occur before difficulties can be noted.

I believe instead that alcoholism is a chronic behavioral disorder manifested by an undue preoccupation with alcohol and its use to the detriment of physical, emotional and social function. In light of this thinking, the approach, understanding, therapy and evaluation of the alcoholic is holistic, although relief of specific symptoms may be of primary importance at a given moment (Chafetz, 1967a).

The patient in a state of acute alcohol intoxication is in pretty sad shape, and his appearance and manner are not conducive to sympathy. The intoxicated patient often is anxious and has little control over his body's actions. He may be obnoxiously demanding, even belligerent. He may be dressed sloppily and his hair may be uncombed. His red eyes stare out from a blotchy face; his mouth is dry; his breath reeks of ethanol. Frequently, his skin is clammy and cold. Just as common as these physical signs are his expressions of guilt. This is different from the guilt we psychiatrists usually see because it is accompanied by overt evidence that "I have been a bad person," which is the way both he and society look at alcoholic bouts serious enough to require medical attention. Complicating this sorry state may be various physiological, traumatic or psychological symptoms, such as pneumonia or head injuries.

An alcoholic patient is often greeted with displeasure and disgust. Hospital emergency room staffs usually look on him as a troublesome intruder. Unless he has a major surgical or medical complication, the alcoholic commonly is given a cursory examination, summarily treated, and sent away (Chafetz, 1967b).

To treat only the patient's acute intoxication and to ignore the need for rehabilitation is the poorest form of "half-practice", and the height of therapeutic folly. I believe that being concerned only with the acute state of alcoholism accomplishes little beyond temporary relief for the patient and provides the potential for generous multiplication of the physical, psychological and social problems of alcoholism.

Drug therapy can be employed both for relieving the acute bout of alcoholism and as a valuable adjunct in a rehabilitation program. It must be remembered throughout that therapy always should be individually tailored to meet each patient's needs.

Another important point should also be emphasized: No matter what the pharmacological action of a drug, its total effectiveness cannot be evaluated without knowing how, where, when and by whom the drug is given and in what manner countervailing forces to its effect are present in the therapeutic situation.

## ACUTE ALCOHOLIC INTOXICATION

1. Patients who do not require hospitalization may be treated with a minor tranquilizer such as chlordiazepoxide (Librium), 10 to 25 mg four times per day for one to three days, or with hydroxyzine (Vistaril). In elderly alcoholic people, the least possible effective dose should be used and precaution is advised in suicidal patients. Because of their addiction potential, Librium and Vistaril should be used judiciously in treating alcoholics. They should not be used on a prolonged basis in these patients.

Syncope, drowsiness, ataxia and confusion are reported side effects of chlordiazepoxide. Also associated with its use have been skin eruptions, idiopathic jaundice, menstrual irregularities, extrapyramidal symptoms and nausea.

In agitated alcoholic states, chlordiazepoxide has been found to significantly alleviate agitation. A dose of 100 mg intravenously also eliminates gross, generalized tremors when these are present as the sole manifestation of alcoholic withdrawal. Librium appears to be more effective when the alcoholic state is uncomplicated by a major psychiatric disease.

Hydroxyzine (Vistaril) is useful in eliminating anxiety, tension, agitation, apprehension and confusion without impairing mental alertness. Oral dosage varies with individual requirements and ranges from 25 mg three times daily to

100 mg four times a day.

Drowsiness may accompany its use, and dryness of the mouth may occur when higher doses are used.

For rapid calming of the patient, hydroxyzine may be given intramuscularly 50-100 mg and repeated every 4-6 hours as required.

2. There has been recent interest in the use of propranolol (Inderal) as a possible "sobering pill." However, in a recent double-blind, crossover study with propranolol and a placebo, Dr. Ernest P. Noble and co-workers at the University of California, Irvine, found that, contrary to early reports that the drug counteracts the effects of alcohol, the effect was, in fact, the opposite (Noble *et al.*, 1973). In most tests, propranolol showed significant synergistic effects with alcohol. Thus these findings preclude propranolol's use as a "sobering up pill," and also point to the possible danger of alcohol ingestion by patients who have been prescribed the drug for treatment of arrhythmias.

3. Since alcohol acts as a diuretic, it has been common practice to administer electrolytes intravenously (Knott and Beard, 1970). However, it has been shown that alcohol acts as a diuretic only when its blood concentration is rising and stops when high levels are reached. In fact, the chronic alcoholic may be overhydrated, rather than in a state of dehydration. Therefore, fluid replacement should not automatically be started in the patient in withdrawal. If the patient has severe malnutrition, vomiting or diarrhea, replacement may be necessary.

4. Diphenylhydantoin (Dilantin) is useful in treating the convulsions that patients in withdrawal may experience. Patients  may be started on 0.1 g (1 1/2 grains) three times daily, and the dose adjusted upward according to response.

Common side effects include nystagmus, dizziness, muscular incoordination, insomnia, diplopia, transient nervousness, motor twitchings, headache, nausea, vomiting and constipation. Hypersensitivity reactions manifested by rash and fever also occur. Most disappear with reduction in dosage. Prolonged convulsions may be treated with diazepam administered intravenously.

5. In addition, treatment of the acutely intoxicated individual should include adequate diet and vitamin supplements, proper nursing care, and medical management of other complications commonly associated with acute and chronic alcoholism.

## REHABILITATION

Most treatment facilities stop their efforts on behalf of alcoholics when recovery from the acute state has occurred. As we showed when I was director of the Massachusetts General Hosptial's Alcohol Clinic and Acute Psychiatric Service, the acute stage of alcoholic intoxication may be the crucial event in initiating a rehabilitative program for sufferers from alcoholism. I again emphasize that: *Any and all rehabilitative endeavors must be tailored to the individual needs of the patient and his resources.* This requires a thorough evaluation of him physically, emotionally and socially. Drug treatment in the rehabilitation of the alcoholic must be combined with a total effort in the patient's behalf. It is senseless to believe that merely pushing some pills at a patient will produce an effective therapeutic response.

To use drugs effectively, the physician must first have established some sort of relationship with the patient. A practitioner who permits himself only a nodding acquaintance with his patient had better not try his hand at rehabilitating alcoholic persons. Interest, concern, respect and a desire to understand, rather than to judge, are requisites of effective treatment.

It must be remembered that alcohol is a drug which the person uses in abundant doses as a form of self-medication. If the physician merely offers him another drug in an impersonal way, the chances of his misusing the new drug are increased. Tailoring medication to the patient in itself implies the necessity of learning something about the person, which is the cornerstone of beginning relations.

There are many different reasons why people have alcoholic problems. Depression is common to most alcoholic patients. The pain of aloneness and hopelessness that most alcoholics suffer is intense enough to demand relief at any cost. Reason and moralism cannot deal with what the person must contend with within himself. To the patient, alcohol seems the only solace. Many alcoholics are aware that, for some, alcohol only intensifies depression, but they cannot give it up because there is no substitute. Since our goal of rehabilitation is to lessen or abolish the need for alcohol, drugs which combat depression are one part of total treatment. If the patient has symptomatic depression after he has dried out, antidepressants should be used.

1. The antidepressant imipramine (Tofranil) is a useful adjuvant. The drug's action appears to be specific to depressive states and its effect has been characterized as depressolytic, rather than stimulatory. Dosage range is usually 100-150 mg daily, most often administered orally. One hundred fifty milligrams is common as the average daily dose. Signs of improvement or response to the medication may be measured by a number of criteria: disappearance of psychomotor inhibition, disappearance of feelings of hopelessness and helplessness and lessening of self-destructive attitudes. Patients often will report that with relief of depression their desire for alcohol also diminishes. Imipramine also works by lessening feelings of guilt. Furthermore, the alleviation of depression turns the person from a preoccupation with his inner self to outer directedness, offering the potential for reaching the patient with other rehabilitative methods. The amenability of the patient, whose intense depression has been lessened, to respond to other measures is important. For some patients, symptom control may be all that can be hoped for, while for others a drug-free life may be well within reach.

Dryness of the mouth, slight tremor of the extremities, dizziness and blurred vision, pruritus and dermatitis, nausea and vomiting have been reported with imipramine. However, they are relatively infrequent and are usually readily controlled by lowering dosage. Rare cases of hypotension, exacerbation of eczema and ulcerative colitis have been reported.

While imipramine usually is effective in treatment of depression associated with alcoholism, there is a certain delay before therapeutic effectiveness is noted. The drug should be maintained for about three months with gradual weaning over ten days to prevent complications. Some investigators feel that prolonged maintenance may be indicated depending upon the expected course of the depression.

Clinical experience at the Massachusetts General Hospital showed that imipramine is effective in lowering the intensity of the depression commonly found among alcoholic persons.

2. Amitriptyline hydrochloride (Elavil) is also useful in treating depression. Like imipramine, amitriptyline's principal effect is a blocking of the re-uptake of norepinephrine at synapses within the central nervous system. It provides more of a sedative effect than does imipramine.

The usual daily dose is 100–150 mg. The expected response to therapeutic doses of both these drugs may require about three weeks, and the drug should be continued for two to three months after depression is alleviated. Amitriptyline usually is stopped after a maximum of six months as tolerances can be reached over long periods. In the event of relapse, reinstitution of the drug is possible.

Side effects are mild with amitriptyline. Drowsiness, dizziness, nausea, excitement, hypotension, tremulousness, weakness, headache, anorexia, perspiration and lack of coordination have been reported. In rare instances, dermatitis and peripheral neuropathy occur. High doses may bring acute psychotic reactions, temporary confusion and disturbed concentration. Tachycardia, urinary retention, constipation and dry mouth sometimes appear. Since the side effects appear to be an extension of the pharmacological activity of the drug, reduction of dosage will usually control them.

Use of amitriptyline is contraindicated for patients with glaucoma and urinary retention. Because of unpredictable potentiation effects, patients who have been receiving other antidepressants — especially those in the amine inhibitor group — should be allowed two weeks before amitriptyline is introduced, and even then it should be done cautiously and gradually.

In the use of antidepressant medication, the physician should be on guard for suicidal possibilities. In addition, since these drugs alter the electrocardiogram and may produce arrhythmias, especially with overdose, they should be used with caution in heart patients. The use of any drug in the treatment of alcoholism without the careful interest and observation of an interested physician may be the source of a fatal therapeutic encounter when *only* symptom removal is the goal.

3. Trifluoperazine (Stelazine) and/or chlorpromazine (Thorazine) is useful in treating thought disturbances and psychotic disorganization which may be associated with alcoholism. One to two milligrams of trifluoperazine twice a day and/or 25 to 50 mg of chlorpromazine three times a day may be prescribed.

Hypotensive responses, jaundice, dermatitis, agranulocytosis, dryness of the mouth, constipation and extrapyramidal symptoms have been reported as side effects of these drugs. They should be stopped immediately if jaundice or agranulocytosis appears. Dermatological complications can usually be counteracted by the administration of an antihistaminic drug, such as diphenhydramine hydrochloride (Benadryl), 50 mg three times a day or by switching to another phenothiazine. The antihistaminic may be given concurrently without interfering with the therapeutic effects of trifluoperazine and chlorpromazine. Reduction of dosage or the addition of an anticholinergic substance, such as benztropine (Cogentin) or trihexphenidyl hydrochloride (Artane) will usually control the other side effects. The possibility of a coexisting depression must also be borne in mind.

## DETERRENCE

No discussion of drugs in the treatment of alcoholism would be complete without reference to drugs designed to deter drinking. These drugs have given much hope to those who worship at the altar of simple answers to complex problems, but on the whole they have been disappointing. However, when they are placed in proper perspective, their aid in the total treatment of the alcoholic problem can be marked.

Most experience, as well as most hope, rests with disulfiram [bis (diethylthiocarbamyl) disulfide], popularly known as Antabuse. Under ordinary circumstances, this substance is relatively inert in the body, but when alcohol is drunk, it interferes with its metabolism.

In an individual who has taken disulfiram, a toxic reaction begins moments after ingestion of alcohol. A rapidly deepening, lobster-red color develops from the head downward and spreads over the face, sclerae, upper limbs and chest. The intense redness is accompanied by a sensation of heat and the rising crescendo of a pounding headache, by feelings of constriction in the neck and an irritation of throat and trachea resulting in spasms of coughing. All of this unpleasantness is accompanied by a sudden steep rise in blood pressure for about 30 minutes to a point of maximum intensity. This is followed by a precipitous drop of blood pressure, the onset of nausea and the replacement of redness by pallor. If enough alcohol has been taken, nausea turns to violent vomiting. Breathing is difficult and gasping, precordial pain simulating a coronary attack is present; and a sense of uneasiness and fear of dying develops — so terrifying that many a patient has wished for what he feared. After the severe discomfort has lasted for two to four hours, the patient falls to sleep, ending the discomfort as well as the alcohol-disulfiram reaction.

Dizziness, head pressure, blurred vision, air hunger, palpitations, numbness of the hands and feet, and insomnia also have been reported.

Side effects to disulfiram alone have been minimal. Some patients complain of fatigue or impotence. Others occasionally develop mild dermatitis, malaise, headache or gastric distress, and a few have a characteristic "garlic odor" to the breath. Some therapists caution against use in the patient with incipient psychosis, severe coronary disorder, cirrhosis of the liver, kidney disease, diabetes, pregnancy, asthma and epilepsy; but most practitioners who are confident of their relationship and understanding of the individual have used disulfiram with people in these categories with caution and without harm.

One 500 mg tablet of disulfiram is administered daily upon arising for five days, starting 24 hours after the last drink, and then half a tablet (250 mg) daily is used as a maintenance dose. I suggest routinizing the taking of disulfiram, preferably upon awakening. This eliminates a day of decision making about drinking. Some practitioners maintain patients on 125 mg daily (1/4 of a tablet), but our experience at Massachusetts General Hospital showed this to be an unsatisfactory maintenance dose. Patients who are maintained on the large dose of 500 mg daily develop symptoms of polyneuritis. Patients who discontinue disulfiram are advised to wait at least four days, and preferably for one week, before resuming their alcohol intake.

## TREATING THE DISULFIRAM-ALCOHOL REACTION

1. Place the patient in shock position and provide generous amounts of ascorbic acid intravenously.

2. Electrolytic balance can be maintained by dextrose and saline infusions and plasma and oxygen provided where indicated.

3. Antihistamine medication is useful intramuscularly or intravenously.

When disulfiram was introduced, it was believed that an "experience session" with the drug and alcohol would certainly "cure" the alcoholic person's desire for drink. Person after person was hustled off to the hospital, begun on disulfiram, and then given his half ounce of whiskey. However, in time, and after some deaths from cardiac and respiratory failure, it was judged an unnecessary and perhaps cruel experience for patients. Consequently, now the treating physician only describes the consequences and the occasional patient who tests out his disbelief does not usually require additional evidence.

Generally, those who have evaluated disulfiram's effectiveness have stressed its usefulness as ancillary to a total program of rehabilitation.

## ALCOHOLISM: A CHRONIC DISEASE

There is no one single magic cure for alcoholism. Problems of alcoholism, like most behavioral disorders, are long-standing and chronic. To expect, as do many physicians, that the alcoholic patient should never relapse is as unrealistic as to expect the diabetic never to go out of control. Response to treatment should be judged on a multiple scale of altered drinking patterns and evidence of improved social, physical and emotional function, rather than against the single criterion of being alcohol-free.

# REFERENCES

Chafetz, M.E.  Addictions.  III:  alcoholism.  In:  *Comprehensive Textbook of Psychiatry.*  Baltimore, Md.:  Williams & Wilkins Co., 1967a.

Chafetz, M.E.  Drugs in the treatment of alcoholism.  *Medical Clinics of North America,* **51**:  5 (1967b).

Knott, D.H. and Beard, J.D.  Diagnosis and therapy of acute withdrawal from alcohol.  *Current Psychiatric Therapies,* **10** (1970).

Noble, E.P., Parker, E., Alkana, R., Cohen, H. and Birch, H.  Propranololethanol interaction in man.  Paper presented at 1973 Federation of American Societies for Experimental Biology, Atlantic City, New Jersey.

# 20 Treatment of Psychosomatic Disorders

## R. A. Ramsay, E. D. Wittkower and H. Warnes

## INTRODUCTION

### Historical Considerations

The marriage between medicine and psychology over the centuries has been a stormy one, marked by frequent separations, charges of infidelity to certain hallowed principles by both partners, and zealous attempts at marital counseling by eclectic interdisciplinary therapists. A comprehensive account of the historical development of the field of psychosomatic medicine would require a full chapter. For elaboration on the following brief account, the reader is referred to other writings on the subject (Alexander, 1950, 1962; Alexander and Selesnick, 1966; Margetts, 1954; Kaplan and Kaplan, 1956; Wittkower and Dudek, 1973).

The attempt to understand the complex interrelationships of psychological and biological events has had its greatest expression only in the present century, although other periods in history have seen naturalistic (including biological) events attributed to psychological phenomena. For example, several early civilizations explained thunder and lightning as representing the ire of the gods, and falling "prey" to a crippling illness could be similarly viewed. Bribing or placating the gods became a way of influencing them by psychological means. Early man was unaware of the laws of physics or biology, but had an intuitive understanding of psychology. There was an awareness of primitive emotions within himself, and many phenomena of nature were explained by attributing human-like motivation to them.

The general area of interest covered by the term "psychosomatic," coined in 1818 by Heinroth, is intimately associated with the mind-body dichotomy whose psychological and philosophical implications have been debated since antiquity. In a recent discussion of the history of the mind-body relationship, Wittkower and Dudek (1973) have traced its early origins in Greek, Egyptian, Chaldean and Indian medicine, then through the periods of Hippocrates (460–375 B.C.) and Galen (131–201 A.D.), both of whom made important observations on the soma-psyche relationship. Cicero in Rome showed some reaction against the concentration on purely physical explanations of illness: "Why should the art of curing and preserving the body be so much sought after and why should the medicine of the mind be so neglected?"

In the Dark Ages the search for naturalistic explanations was overwhelmed by a surge of primitive religious and metaphysical preoccupation which stifled progress for a dozen centuries. Later, with the Renaissance, science gradually gained the upper hand, naturalism replacing demonology. The first signs of this trend occurred in the thirteenth century but no significant impact was discernible until the seventeenth century. As in other natural sciences, there followed rapidly major discoveries in anatomy and physiology which had the effect of demystifying the somatic processes – and this delivery of natural phenomena from demonology, or the deanimation of nature, was a prodigious milestone. The conceptualization of phenomena being explainable on the basis of concrete, physical, measurable entities captivated men's imagination, no less so in the areas of medicine and biology than in other scientific disciplines. It was tempting to hypothesize that explanations for all phenomena would be found in physics and chemistry. The role of the doctor came to be viewed mechanistically: he was seen as a skilled repairman of breakdowns in the human organism, conceived of as a complex physicochemical apparatus.

The results of such an approach were in general favorable and contributed to the many advances in modern medicine. There was another effect, however, which although unintended, seemed to delay the understanding and development of medical psychology. Identification of all non-naturalistic explanations as demonological retarded the acceptance of psychological phenomena which were generally frowned upon as nonphysical and hence unscientific and suspect. It was considered a sign of muddleheadedness for a scientist to be wasting valuable time on psychological phenomena. Thus the latter were largely neglected although occasional greats did record some of their relevant observations, as early as the seventeenth century. For example, Sydenham boldly stated that hysterical hemiplegia may proceed from some "violent commotion of the mind," and William Harvey, famous for his description of the circulatory system, commented: "Every affection of the mind that is attended with either pain or pleasure, hope or fear, is the cause of an agitation whose influence extends to the heart." Many of Harvey's writings were lost when a mob burned them for his Loyalist leanings; he was certainly one of the fathers of the modern psychosomatic era.

The early nineteenth century was the era of the so-called "romantic psychiatrists." They expressed disillusionment with scientific rationalism, calling for a more inward-looking approach. Reil in 1803 produced the first systematic treatise on psychotherapy, and clearly recognized the mutual interaction between psychological and physical events in the organism. His program for investigation in this direction fell on deaf ears in the scientific community.

Heinroth, in addition to his contribution of the term "psychosomatic," introduced the idea of internal conflict as a basis of mental disease, being the forerunner of Freud in this regard. Carus spoke of unconscious processes, but gave this a very wide meaning, being practically equivalent with the whole life process, both organic and mental. He held an extreme viewpoint that the unconscious animates all physiological processes, hence all organic illnesses are rooted in the unconscious mind.

Alexander (1962) claims that the views of these men never received acceptance because they discovered no method to investigate and substantiate their views. Thus interest in psychosomatic relationships cooled for 50 years until the beginning of dynamic psychiatry.

In general, the psychiatrists of this era, anxious to be accepted as a "legitimate" branch of medicine, collaborated with their colleagues in medicine to explain disturbances of the mind on the basis of anatomy and physiology, and then treat with similar methods — physical, chemical and surgical.

Freud, who was unaware of the early "romantic psychiatrists," made a greater impact because of the development of an operational tool to investigate psychological events and to gain access to repressed unconscious material in the therapeutic situation. He provided the means for empirical study of the unconscious and for gauging its influence upon overt behavior and physiological processes. Subsequent use of this method was a significant factor in the rise of interest, over the past 40 years, in psychosomatic interrelationships, although Freud himself did not contribute to the study of psychosomatic phenomena, apart from his paper on visual disturbances (Freud, 1910).

Modern Conceptual Models

There has been an enormous growth of interest in psychosomatic interrelationships in the past half century, and the contributions to the field have been representative of a wide variety of disciplines and theoretical orientations. The authors are aware that full justice cannot be given in this chapter to these many contributions, and we urge the reader to consult the references suggested in the following brief outline.

Psychoanalytic theory, as developed first by Freud, was enthusiastically embraced by some early workers, and many subsequent conceptual models show its strong influence. Ferenczi (1926) was one of the first to apply the psychoanalytic model to explain vegetative disturbances. Fenichel (1945) discussed psychosomatic disorders in relation to neurotic disturbance, and Melanie Klein (1948) considered that pregenital conversion could occur as an organ neurosis. Garma (1950) postulated that physiological regression was implicated in the pathogenesis of gastric ulcer. Groddeck, a physician, working first in the 1920s, is considered by many as the father of psychosomatic medicine insofar as he saw psyche and soma not as separate entities but as facets of one whole. His treatment of psychosomatic disorders ranged from massage, hydrotherapy and rest, to psychoanalytic interpretations and dream analysis (Groddeck, 1926).

Two influential psychoanalytic investigators, Franz Alexander and Flanders Dunbar, were closely associated with the early concepts of specificity in psychosomatic disorders, and combined analytic understanding with the fight-flight model of Cannon. Dunbar (1938, 1943) attempted to correlate personality profiles with specific psychosomatic illness whereas Alexander and his group believed that the specificity involved underlying intrapsychic conflicts rather than personality descriptions (Alexander, 1939, 1950; Alexander, French and Pollack, 1968).

Grinker (1953) provided an understanding of psychosomatic mechanisms in terms of his developmental field theory. Wolff and his group emphasized cultural as well as biological and physical stress in the production of disease (Wolff, 1950, 1953; Hinkle and Wolff, 1957) and Rahe and co-worker studied disease in relation to life events (Rahe, McKean and Arthur, 1967; Rahe and Arthur, 1968; Rahe, 1972; Holmes and Rahe, 1968). There have been notable contributions from the Rochester school along similar lines, including the study of object loss in the precipitation of psychosomatic disease, and the concepts of helplessness and hopelessness as they relate to disease onset and outcome (Engel, 1962, 1967; Engel and Schmale, 1967; Schmale and Engel, 1967; Schmale, 1972; Greene and Swisher, 1969).

Ruesch (1948) outlined the significance of the communicative aspects of psychosomatic illness and described the infantile personality prevailing in psychosomatic patients. Kubie (1943, 1953, 1965) worked out a complicated and comprehensive theory of psychosomatic disease which incorporates the research results of both experimental biology and psychoanalysis.

Sociopsychological and sociocultural models are represented by such writings as those of Halliday (1943, 1948), Mead (1947), Pflanz, Rosenstein and von Uexkul (1956), Waitzkin and Stoeckle (1972), and Wittkower (1973). This review is unable to do justice to the many contributions to the field by workers outside of North America, but it should be noted that many countries now have active psychosomatic societies, notably France, Germany, Great Britain and Japan (Wittkower, Cleghorn, Lipowski, Peterfy and Solyom, 1969).

Other important general contributions in the field include the publications of Weiss and English (1943), Wittkower and Cleghorn (1954), Lief, H.I., Lief, V.F. and Lief, N.R. (1963), Lipowski (1967a and b, 1968) and Hill (1970). The theoretical formulations of the Paris group of psychoanalysts, as represented by Marty and de M'Uzan (1963), also deserve mention. Finally, the fundamental conceptualizations of Cannon (1915, 1939) and Selye (1946, 1956) have been vital in the understanding of psychosomatic relationships, and the contributions of Pavlov and his followers in the field of corticovisceral medicine should not be forgotten. A comparison and synthesis of the psychosomatic and corticovisceral approaches is provided by Wittkower and Solyom (1967).

## Definition and Discussion of Terms

In view of the manifold contexts in which the word "psychosomatic" is used, it is necessary to make explicit the understanding of the various terms as they are used in this chapter. "Psychosomatic" and "somatopsychic" are complementary terms, both of which imply the existence of two theoretically separable classes of phenomena, the psychic and the somatic. This distinction has heuristic value in scientific investigation and the conceptualization of intra-organismic relationships, and for these purposes, as Lipowski (1968, p. 396) points out, may remain "neutral with regard to metaphysical questions concerning the nature of the mental and the physical." The sequential arrangement of the components in each word is at times taken literally in terms of causality, namely, "psychosomatic" implying the effect of psychic factors on somatic processes, and "somatopsychic" suggesting the opposite. Much unproductive effort has been expended on attempting to define these relationships causally; what is needed is a means of expressing the essential interrelationship and feedback characteristics of these systems, e.g.,

$$\left( \begin{array}{c} \text{psyche} \\ \text{soma} \end{array} \right)$$

In this chapter "psychosomatic," unless otherwise qualified, will denote the general concept of this interrelationship. It should be noted that further extension of the term to include social aspects has some logical support (Wittkower and Dudek, 1973) but has the disadvantage of further dilution of an already over-extended concept.

The "psychosomatic movement" was in part a reaction to the distorted understanding of soma and psyche interrelationships, an unfortunate and persistent inheritance from the "scientific era" beginning 300 years ago. Its initial thrust was thus reformist in nature, calling for a change in medical practice so as to take into consideration the patient as a person. The reformist zeal was in due course augmented by the application of the same scientific method to the study of various psychosomatic problems.

A milestone in this regard in North America was the founding of the American Psychosomatic Society, and its journal, *Psychosomatic Medicine,* in 1939. In the first issue of this journal, the editors in their introductory statement (*Psychosomatic Medicine,* 1939, p. 3) suggested as the object of psychosomatic medicine "to study in their interrelation the psychological and physiological aspects of all normal and abnormal bodily functions and thus to integrate somatic therapy and psychotherapy." This may appear too narrow a conceptualization, particularly with regard to psychological forms of therapy, but it reflected the limited therapeutic possibilities of that era. As discussed by Wittkower and Lipowski (1966), the early emphasis on intensive clinico-biographical studies shifted over the next 25 years to basic psychophysiologic research. Partly as a response to this trend toward "molecularization" in the original journal, new publications have appeared which provide a form for clinically-oriented studies and theoretical articles in the field. Most notable of these are *Psychosomatics,* appearing first in

1959, as the organ of the Academy of Psychosomatic Medicine, and *Psychiatry in Medicine,* first published in 1970.

A brief consideration is necessary of the conditions subsumed under the term "psychosomatic disorders" or "psychosomatic illnesses." In the 1930s a group of seven illnesses were considered as "classical" syndromes, and consisted of bronchial asthma, rheumatoid arthritis, ulcerative colitis, essential hypertension, neurodermatitis, thyrotoxicosis, and peptic ulcer. In relation to these illnesses, the underlying hypothesis was that recurrent or chronic emotional stress has a cumulative physiological effect and eventually may produce, in certain susceptible individuals, reversible or irreversible organic dysfunction. Early data were derived primarily from the intensive psychoanalytic studies of these disorders, in case reports by Bartemeier, Weiss, French, Ferenczi, Wittkower, Reich, Alexander, Sperling, Margolin, Kaufman and others.

As principles obtained in the study of the "holy seven" began to have obvious wider applicability, more and more previously considered pure "medical" illnesses (e.g., diabetes mellitus, migraine, coronary artery disease) have gained acceptance (perhaps more in psychiatry than in medicine) as having significant psychic components in terms of etiology, pathogenesis and course. Classification of these disorders came to be conceived in terms of organ systems under the American system, namely: "Psychophysiological autonomic and visceral disorders" (DSM II, 1968). The use of this term was in part an attempt to overcome the increasingly ambiguous meaning of the term "psychosomatic." There is no universal agreement on the membership of these categories, and the same clinical syndrome (e.g., bronchial asthma) may have different loadings of somatic and psychic factors in different patients. Conceptually as well, the term "psychophysiologic autonomic and visceral disorder" provided a means of separating these organic disorders from those illustrating the use of psychological defense mechanisms in the simulation of such organic-like conditions as paralysis, anesthesia, and pain — namely, conversion hysteria or hysterical neurosis, conversion type.

The term "psychosomatics" is of more recent use, and is most prominently applied to the name of an important journal in the field, as noted above. We would agree with Lipowski (1968) that this term is preferable in some ways to "psychosomatic medicine" which connotes a preoccupation with disease, thus excluding the study of psyche-soma interrelationships in non-disease states. Employed as an adjective, "psychosomatic" is frequently used in medical circles to mean "psychogenic," often with a pejorative connotation.

In the wider frame of reference, Hambling (1965) defines an illness as psychosomatic when it (1) begins at a time of crisis in the patient's life, (2) shows a time correlation with situations provoking stress in the patient, and (3) clears up when the situation changes for the better or the patient learns to adapt to it without undue tension.

Thus the range of application of the term "psychosomatic" varies from those who consider it should apply only to phenomenologically-defined "psychophysiological autonomic and visceral disorders" of the current classification, to those who would include in the term all phenomena, ranging from atomic physics, at one pole, to cultural and climatic factors, at the other, insofar as they bear any relation to the human organism in health and disease.

To illustrate the expansion of the meaning of the term "psychosomatic medicine," particularly in North America, Lipowski (1968) considers the term to encompass three large areas: a science embodying research and theory, a method of approach to health and disease, and the consulting activities of psychiatrists with other physicians. The European understanding of the term remains much closer to the "holy seven" pole, and there has been some criticism of the North American trend as representing a "dilution" of the original conceptualization which implied that illnesses such as bronchial asthma and peptic ulcer differ in kind with regard to mechanism from a purely psychiatric disorder on the one hand and a purely organic disease on the other. It is unfortunate that semantic wrangling should impede progress in the field.

## Areas for Consideration in this Chapter

The concept of treatment as applied to psychosomatic medicine is thus seen to be dependent on the use of the word. A comprehensive view of the term requires a comprehensive statement of treatment which, traced to its logical limit, would include the holistic approach to management of all illness, including such areas as the doctor-patient relationship, psychologic sequelae of acute and chronic illness, intensive care units, psychological preparation for surgery, dialysis, patient-ward staff interaction, and so on. Such a comprehensive review would require a book in itself. This chapter will consider one aspect of this complex field, namely, a liberal interpretation of the so-called psychophysiologic autonomic and visceral disorders. These are defined explicitly in DSM II (1968, p. 46) as follows:

> This group of disorders is characterized by physical symptoms that are caused by emotional factors and involve a single organ system, usually under autonomic nervous system innervation. The physiological changes involved are those that normally accompany certain emotional states, but in these disorders the changes are more intense and sustained. The individual may not be consciously aware of his emotional state. If there is an additional psychiatric disorder, it should be diagnosed separately, whether or not it is presumed to contribute to the physical disorder. The specific physical disorder should be named and classified in one of the following categories.

These categories are further specified in the Manual, for example: Psychophysiological skin disorder, e.g., atopic dermatitis, psychophysiological gastrointestinal disorder, e.g., peptic ulcer.

The particular nature of these conditions has rendered them of interest in their own right. It is also correct to say that they have offered a great challenge to the psychiatrist in terms of treatment. Until recently they have been treated largely in medical settings, with occasional psychiatric involvement. Traditional forms of treatment employed in the more purely psychiatric disorders have not been uniformly successful in the psychophysiological disorders. However, in discussing management of this group, some of the comments will inevitably apply to a broader field, as the concepts involved are often general and not bound necessarily to specific diagnostic categories.

It is perhaps relevant to list some of the other terms which have been used, particularly in the psychoanalytic literature, to refer to this group of disorders. Thus, for example, Alexander speaks of "vegetative neurosis," Fenichel of "organ neurosis," Adler of "organ inferiority," and Reich of muscular "armor," referring both to character defense and muscular hypertonus.

### Approach to Treatment of These Disorders

Psychosomatic treatments can be said to have a conceptual frame based on:

(1) inherited or early acquired (through illness or conditioning) organ or system vulnerability;

(2) chronic emotional arousal leading to damaging effects in a specific organ system;

(3) psychological patterns of conflict and defense formed in early life;

(4) sustained emotional arousal on response to stress, the degree and duration of arousal depending both on the nature of the stress and the individual's perception of it;

(5) precipitating life situations;

(6) psychosomatic self-regulations; and

(7) socio-cultural factors pertaining to the stresses characteristic of a given society.

In planning treatment the therapist may search for the constitutional-biological basis of the disorder in order to bring about change or search for a postulated personality pattern which may allow prediction of a particular clinical syndrome (e.g., the coronary prone personality of Friedman and Rosenman (1971)), or he may attempt to modify the sources of stress and conflict, both internal and external, and the reaction of the patient to them.

When exposed to stress the psychosomatic patient does not heed his alarm-feelings and affects in contrast to the psychoneurotic patient. Bastiaans (1969) points out that alarm-feelings (anxiety, guilt or shame) are warded off because they are considered to be childish or infantile. In his effort to be in control of his emotional life he has lost touch with his body warning signals and spontaneous emotions. Aggression is a particularly difficult affect for these patients to cope with directly, and sado-masochistic regulation of aggression is not uncommon. Although large quantities of aggression are invested in the psychosomatic symptom-formation, its uncovering has not led to significant results, and can have undesirable effects if used indiscriminately (Lowy, 1970).

Wolf, Pfeiffer, Ripley, Winter and Wolff (1948) wrote in their study on hypertensives:

they ... displayed a taste for dealing with problems by action ... mobilized for combat . . . under a facade which was often affable and easy-going, they were tense, wary and suspicious . . . displayed a strong need to conform and keep peace . . . in brief, our hypertensive subjects, often gentle, poised and apparently easy-going, were filled with aggressive drive which was tightly restrained by a need to please (p. 1070).

Hinkle and Wolff (1958) linked disease onset with heightened life stress in certain individuals:

The great majority of the clusters of illness episodes that occur in the lives of the members of every group occurred at times when they perceived their life situations to be unsatisfying, threatening, overdemanding and productive of conflict, and they could make no satisfactory adaptation to these situations (p. 1382).

Lipowski (1973) has proposed four major categories of subjectively meaningful stress which may be consciously or unconsciously perceived; these are threat, loss, gain and insignificance.

The decrease of known psychosocial stress and the protective effect in reducing the risk of psychosomatic illness of a cohesive, mutually supportive social group with strong family and community ties (which lessens the impact of loss, grief and trauma) has obvious implications in the total therapeutic approach to psychosomatic illnesses (Wolf, 1971). It is, however, important to point out that stress arising out of a life situation is quite specific for the individual in the sense that he perceives it to have a special meaning for him. In this regard, a promotion may be a reason for joy or a severe stress according to the psychological meaning of the event. Put another way, the critical psychic stresses may not be related to the objective magnitude of external pressures or demands, but rather to the exacerbation of key but unconscious conflicts which the patient with psychophysiologic disorders characteristically attempts to solve by modifying the external world.

## SOME GENERAL CONSIDERATIONS

Since the great majority of patients with psychophysiological disorders are both seen initially and treated principally by non-psychiatric physicians — general practitioners, internists, dermatologists, surgeons and gynecologists — it is important first to conceptualize what happens at this level in relation to this group of patients. An important first qualification is that the degree of psyche and soma implicated in any disorder in this category can vary considerably from one patient to another. Thus, in the common condition of bronchial asthma, one finds those patients in whom immunological factors predominate, in contrast to others where demonstrable allergic components are lacking and the relationship of attacks to psychosocial stimuli is undoubted. It is for this reason, among others, that overgeneralization about either somatic or psychic components in the category as a whole is unwarranted.

As noted above, patients with these disorders, presenting as they do with physical symptoms of mild to severe degree, routinely make their first contact with a primary physician or hospital clinic. In most cases there is an obvious need for treatment of the somatic component of the illness, e.g., the severe bronchospasm in bronchial asthma, the bloody diarrhea in ulcerative colitis, or the extreme undernutrition in anorexia nervosa. At times medical or surgical intervention is life-saving, and only after the urgent somatic component has been brought under control is there consideration given to the importance of psychological variables in the pathogenesis of the patient's illness.

It should be noted that there is a wide variation in medical circles concerning the relevance or practical importance of emotional variables generally, including in the psychophysiological disorders. The tendency often in medical practice is to delete the "psycho-" from the term and to consider these illnesses purely in terms of pathological anatomy and physiological dysfunction. It is by far the rule rather than the exception that reports concerning these disorders in the medical and surgical literature omit any reference to psychosocial variables in the discussion of etiology, onset, clinical course, treatment and prognosis. At times there are vague references to "emotional upset," "family problems" or "stress." In general these variables are not considered as particularly worthy of special attention, or the attention granted them may be more in terms of lip service. This is not just an academic point, as in the authors' experience, attention to or neglect of psychological factors in a particular patient may well affect the outcome of the illness, especially in those patients showing the characteristics of helplessness or hopelessness (Schmale and Engel, 1967).

The general practitioner or other primary-care physician has to make a decision, based on the complaints of the patient, his behavior, or the nature of the disorder, whether an exploration of the patient's emotional life is indicated. He may carry out such an examination himself or may refer the patient to a psychiatrist or psychologist. It is common experience that psychosomatic patients, more than other groups, often resent being examined psychiatrically, and can accept the discreet enquiries of an interested and empathetic family physician more readily than abrupt or unprepared referral to a "shrink."

As a result of the exploration of the patient's emotional life or irrespective of it, the physician decides what treatment procedures to adopt. He may come to the conclusion that the patient's symptoms can be adequately controlled by specific medication, e.g., steroids in bronchial asthma, or that surgery is indicated, e.g., colectomy in fulminant ulcerative colitis.

In addition to such specific measures directed against the somatic component of the illness, practitioners who acknowledge the psychosocial aspects of illness have an opportunity to assess the patient psychologically and provide important supportive measures. According to Horder (1965), the crucial steps involve helping the patient to talk, identifying the psychopathology, and recognizing external stresses and internal conflicts likely to explain the particular psychosomatic symptom. General practitioners rely on supportive psychotherapy, open and friendly discussion, continuous availability, involvement in and awareness of the patient's family and community (often for many years or even two generations), home visits, advice, sympathy, reassurance and covert or overt paternalistic (or maternalistic) gratification of the patient's needs. It is also useful to keep in mind that the symbolic meaning of medical treatment or how it is administered may have profound psychological significance. For example, the milk diet prescribed for ulcer patients represents at times direct gratification of infantile needs, and dermatological agents may work better if applied by the wife or mother of the patient.

Environmental manipulation can at times be extremely useful. A striking example of this is the removal of an asthmatic child from his home environment, referred to as "parentectomy" by Peshkin in 1930, recently reviewed by Robinson (1972). Sainsbury (1965) comments that often the modification of environmental preciptating stresses or attitudes of family members is a better treatment than trying to treat the patient himself. The ready availability of various psychotropic drugs has to some extent simplified the management of these patients in the general practice setting, with success in their use being dependent upon the practitioner's skill in correctly labeling associated disturbances of affect and prescribing appropriate drugs for their control. In acute stages of many of these disorders, general supportive measures, including the use of drugs, constitute appropriate attention to the psychic components. Confrontation with sources of unconscious conflict is rarely indicated and may be dangerous in the acute patient whose defenses are being greatly strained.

## Psychosomatic Symptoms, Syndrome Shifts and Psychosis

Mention should be made in this regard of the known interrelationships of some psychophysiologic disorders with one another, and of the not infrequent alternation of some of these illnesses with psychotic breakdown.

It is not unusual to observe a cluster of illnesses in the same patient: for instance, the combination of migraine headaches and spastic colitis; of asthma, eczema and vasomotor rhinitis; or of hypertension, diabetes and coronary occlusion. A shift of symptoms may occur in such clusters. Van der Valk (1965) reported on a form of syndrome shift in patients who developed hypochondria and depression after a gastrectomy for peptic ulcer. Kral (1951) noted syndrome suppression or dramatic improvement of psychosomatic illnesses during the war in concentration camps.

Clusters of illnesses are also seen within a family, with each member having at times a particular disorder, for example, eczema, asthma, enuresis and stammering. At certain times of crisis there may be a shift of involvement from one to another member, with concomitant change in symptom patterns in the family (Van der Valk, 1965).

The literature contains several examples of psychosis alternating with psychosomatic disorder. Among these is that of Yeh (1958) who described such an inverse relationship between urticaria and psychosis. Sperling (1955) has written on the psychoanalytic aspects of the relationship between psychosis and psychosomatic illness, as well as commenting on the relationship between acting out behavior and psychosomatic symptoms (Sperling, 1968). Seitz (1953) reported that three patients whose psychocutaneous disorders cleared up with brief psychotherapy appeared to have been converted at least temporarily into antisocial character disorders.

In his review of available literature, Pedder (1969) noted the relative infrequency of psychosomatic disorders among psychotic patients. There were 8 schizophrenics among 126 psychosomatic cases compared with 16 schizophrenics among the controls. The difference was not significant yet in clinical practice it is not infrequent to observe cases of syndrome shift: asthma replaced by severe depression; schizophrenia replaced by ulcero-colitis; severe dermatitis followed by psychosis; rheumatoid arthritis shifting into a depression or a paranoid psychosis. In the study of Pedder (1969), he also found associations between phobic reactions and patients who had asthma or peptic ulcer.

The practical implication of these findings is that one should be cautious in the application of an interpretive analytic approach to psychosomatic patients. This has been stressed by Marty and de M'Uzan (1963) and by Sifneos (1972). Macalpine (1952) regards the classical psychoanalytic approach as unsuitable for these disorders but we feel such a view is unnecessarily pessimistic as we have seen, along with others (Weinstock, 1962), spectacular recoveries from ulcerative colitis, for example, in response to a psychoanalytic approach.

The apprehension that abrupt symptom removal will be replaced by other physical or by psychological symptoms is not consistently justified. For example, follow-up studies on the psychological response to colectomy in 41 patients suffering from ulcerative colitis (Druss, O'Connor, Prudden and Stern, 1968), and the effective handling of 38 cases of neurodermatitis with brief psychotherapy (Schoenberg and Carr, 1963) showed that in both instances there was no significant symptom substitution or other serious consequence.

The emphasis in treatment should be flexible; in some cases psychodynamic exploration is justified, in others, abrupt symptom removal, for example, by surgery, is indicated; in still others, gratification of dependency needs (for example, bed rest, holidays) might be suggested while in others supportive psychotherapy or autogenic training and biofeedback might be the treatment of choice. These approaches are not mutually exclusive.

Referral

For a variety of reasons the primary physician may decide to refer his psychosomatic patient for specialized assessment and/or treatment by a professional with specific expertise in the management of psychological problems. Some of these might be:

1. General psychological assessment of the problem, with suggestions to the practitioner regarding management (for example, environmental manipulation, psychotropic drugs, focus for supportive psychotherapy). Such practitioners usually are familiar with some of the writings in the psychosomatic area.

2. Failure of the patient to respond to intensive medical treatment.

3. Emergence of overt neurotic, psychotic or behavioral pathology during or following resolution of the acute somatic symptomatology. The motive for referral in some cases may be to obtain assistance, in others to get rid of a troublesome patient.

4. A wish on the part of the physician and/or the patient for the latter to obtain psychological help concurrently with the required medical management.

A referral to the psychiatrist is often felt by the patient as a rejection, and, in this regard, how the primary physician presents it to him may have important consequences. Such remarks as "I can't find anything wrong with you – it must be in your mind," or "perhaps the psychiatrist will have more luck with you" may seriously affect the patient's receptivity to a psychological approach.

The conjoint management of psychophysiologic patients requires close collaboration on the part of the physician and the mental health professional, particularly if the psychological treatment consists of dynamic psychotherapy. The exacerbation of somatic symptoms which often occurs in response to the emergence of emotionally-charged areas during psychotherapy may lead the physician to intervene in a manner incompatible with the psychotherapeutic approach. In addition, in such collaborative treatment care must be taken that the physician not provide an alternative outlet for catharsis or offer psychotherapy of his own. It is also relevent to note that if the physician has a skeptical, or perhaps even antagonistic, attitude concerning the efforts of the mental health worker, the patient's awareness of this will work to the detriment of the treatment.

On the other hand, the role of the physician should not be underestimated by the mental health professional, and patients suffering from serious or life-threatening exacerbations of symptoms should always be referred back to the physician or surgeon for appropriate management. A close working relationship, involving frequent communication and agreed-upon division of responsibility, is the most effective way to ensure effective conjoint management of psychosomatic disorders.

In commenting on the kind of supportive psychotherapy useful in the conjoint management of ulcerative colitis patients, Freyberger (1973) outlines four basic technical principles: (1) stabilization of the defense formation by the creating and/or strengthening of object relationships; (2) careful concern for a positive transference; (3) offering of good advice; and (4) constant availability of internist and psychosomaticist. As positive outcomes of this approach Freyberger mentions the lengthening of remissions between relapses of colitis, the shortening of actual relapses, the mitigation of psychic suffering and the advancement of social rehabilitation.

## FORMS OF TREATMENT

An attempt will now be made to outline in greater detail the current state of specific treatment procedures for the psychophysiologic group of disorders. Some of these have applicability within the context of the practitioner-patient relationship (e.g., psychopharmacology, hypnosis), whereas others are more closely associated with treatment by various mental health professionals (for example, psychoanalytically-oriented psychotherapy, group and family psychotherapy, and behavior therapy). It is possible that some of the latter techniques may eventually be performed by skilled general practitioners having interest and training in their application.

The following treatment modalities will be discussed:

> Psychoanalysis and Psychotherapy
> Psychopharmacology
> Behavior Therapy
> Group Therapy
> Family Therapy
> Hypnosis
> Autogenic Therapy

An exhaustive coverage of the field is impossible within the confines of space, but examples illustrative of trends in the field will be provided, with an emphasis on recent literature. Finally, one specific psychophysiological disorder — namely, bronchial asthma, will be discussed separately in terms of the various kinds of psychologically-oriented treatment currently available or under investigation. As the focus of the volume is on treatment, little space will be devoted to detailed theoretical considerations which are readily available elsewhere.

### Psychoanalysis and Psychotherapy

Psychosomatic illnesses were first treated by psychoanalysts and psychoanalytically oriented therapists over 40 years ago. However, systematic presentations of the techniques of psychotherapy in these disorders did not appear until 1943 when Dunbar's *Psychosomatic Diagnosis* and Weiss and English's *Psychosomatic Medicine* were both published. Subsequently Alexander and French provided another comprehensive volume entitled: *Studies in Psychosomatic Medicine: An Approach to the Cause and Treatment of Vegetative Disturbances.* Important reviews of this field were produced by Sperling (1952), F. Deutsch (1953), Margolin (1954), DeM'Uzan (1959) and Kaufman (1964). Others who have attempted to systematize the various psychotherapeutic principles in psychosomatic medicine include Mueller-Hegemann (1959), Kleinsorge and Klumbies

(1959), Stokvis (1960), Meyer (1965), Hopkins and Wolff (1965), Kaplan (1967), Cain (1971) and Brautigam and Christian (1973).

As noted earlier in this chapter, psychoanalytic interest in the psychosomatic disorders began not with Freud but with some of the second generation of analysts in the late 1920s. The application of developing analytic techniques to the study of these illnesses provided a detailed understanding of the complex dynamic psychosomatic relationships in individual patients. Considerable information was also gathered concerning the precipitation of physical symptoms by psychologically stressful events and the nature of the characterological defenses in these patients.

The intensely interesting findings from these studies, the claims of many apparent therapeutic successes, and the enthusiasm characteristic of the early investigators raised great expectations that psychotherapy based on analytic principles would become of primary significance in the everyday treatment of these conditions. With the passage of time and the acquisition of further experience, psychoanalysts and psychoanalytically-oriented psychotherapists have adjusted earlier expectations to a more realistic level, consonant with a fuller understanding of certain difficulties and at times potential hazards of exploratory therapy in psychosomatic patients. Additionally, the time required and monetary outlay involved in such intensive therapy remains an unfortunate barrier to its general application in suitable patients. The knowledge gleaned from analytic study and experience however, has provided much useful information directly applicable to the overall psychological management of patients with these disorders. Weiss and English (1957) have noted: "Between simple reassurance at one end of the scale and adequate psychoanalysis at the other, there are all degrees of psychotherapy which can be applied depending on the degree of illness and the circumstances of the patient" (p. 13).

Physiological dysfunctions characterized by these disorders are related to early oral-anal fixations, and there has usually been a severe disturbance in the mother-child relationship dating from the pre-genital period. Dunbar (1959) pointed out both the importance of pre-verbal communication patterns between mother and child in these disorders, and also the tendency of some mothers to rely almost entirely on physical communication focused on organ function in relation to their children. Psychological defense mechanisms of massive repression, denial and reaction formation contribute to peculiar forms of object relations and transference reactions. Arousal of the autonomic nervous system and hypertonus of the musculo-skeletal system are characteristic also, as emphasized particularly by Reich (1961).

Individuals with a psychosomatic disorder present particular challenges to even the most skilled psychotherapist. In most cases these patients believe that their problems are strictly medical, confined to a simple matter of bodily dysfunction. Along with this characteristic, Bastiaans (1969) emphasizes a complementary feature: these individuals insist they are normal and mentally healthy, and they want to be in control of themselves, even in difficult stress situations. He notes that this attitude of wanting to show themselves as normal to the outsider is one of their most effective mechanisms of defense. One result of this defense is a poor awareness of their emotions generally, particularly unpleasant affects such as anxiety, sadness, guilt and shame. Denial of these affects, general inhibition of libidinal and aggressive impulses, and a striking poverty of fantasy life (Marty and de M'Uzan, 1963; Nemiah and Sifneos, 1970) provide psychotherapeutic challenges unlike those in most psychoneurotic patients. A statement by Weiss and English (1957, p. 111) is particularly applicable to these disorders: " .... resistance to psychotherapy causes many patients to make trials in every other direction and to suffer considerably before they will attempt a treatment which calls for a scrutiny of their emotions and their relations to other human beings."

Given the difficulty of psychotherapeutic management, certain considerations are essential in the optimal use of this form of treatment. 1) Intervention is more beneficial in initial phases of the illness before irreversible tissue damage occurs. 2) As the gravity of the same illness varies from patient to patient, the type or degree of psychotherapeutic intervention should be individualized. 3) There are risks in conducting an exploratory psychotherapy where a psychotic potential is suspected. 4) On the other hand, there are risks of another kind implicit in the evolution of the illness, and psychotherapeutic intervention may in some situations be crucial. 5) At times active environmental manipulation, such as separation of the patient from a strongly noxious home atmosphere, must be effected before psychotherapy can be undertaken.

Stokvis (1960) reported that, in his experience, only a small minority of psychosomatic patients are suitable candidates for classical psychoanalytic treatment. Sifneos (1972) suggests that the majority of psychosomatic patients do not fulfill the criteria for psychodynamic psychotherapy, which requires a degree of psychological sophistication, an ability to verbalize, an awareness of emotions, a capability to express them and a motivation for self-examination. He found that some patients get worse with such therapy. The authors are of the opinion that such estimates are unnecessarily pessimistic, and that many patients, using a dynamic approach with appropriate modifications depending on diagnosis, stage of illness, and ego capacity, may be greatly helped. As an example:

A 50-year-old executive presented with severe and unremitting angina pectoris precipitated during a highly stressful and guilt-ridden period of his life. Due to the gravity of his condition he was forced to give up a demanding managerial position and a mistress who was becoming a source of guilt and embarrassment. For three years his anginal attacks, brought on by emotional unheavals, sexual intercourse out of wedlock, stressful dreams and conflicts at work, were not substantially relieved, even by a combination of propanolol, isosorbide dinitrate, and diazepam during the third year. The addition of psychoanalytically-oriented psychotherapy made him aware of his self-directed aggression and he was free of symptoms after a further eight months.

Each patient selected for psychotherapy should be followed conjointly by the general practitioner or the internist in order to monitor any somatic changes. During psychotherapy, the therapist should carefully gauge external and internal stresses, muscular tension, character "armor" which prevents expression of affect, the therapist-patient relationship, and the overall clinical state so as to determine which direction the psychotherapy should take. It may be useful to recommend autogenic training (Luthe and Schultz, II, 1969) in individuals who are highly obsessional and who derive great pleasure from independent performance. In other patients, a type of relaxation therapy may be indicated as described, for example, by Ajuriaguerra and Garcia-Badaracco (1953). Relaxation is combined by these authors with psychodynamic formulation and psychoanalytically-oriented interpretations. However, as with orthodox psychoanalysis, the various relaxation therapies should be judiciously prescribed because of their potentially releasing effect on a latent psychosis or at times their aggravating effect on the psychosomatic symptom.

A highly specialized psychoanalytically-oriented approach referred to as "anaclitic therapy" has been applied in some psychosomatic patients by Margolin (1954), who describes techniques leading to profound physiological and psychological regression, associated with remission of symptoms. After this first phase of treatment the patient is next helped in the restoration of his ego functions, following which a more lengthy character analysis is undertaken. Although effective, this treatment is extremely demanding on the therapist's time and emotional resources.

Criteria for the application of psychotherapy have been given by Dunbar (1943). They are: (1) a relatively uncrystallized symptom-neurotic picture; (2) reasonably good adjustment prior to the episode of illness; (3) a strong ego; (4) an ability within a few sessions to recognize the relationships between the somatic disorder and the emotional difficulty; and (5) a capacity for establishment of interpersonal rapport with the therapist.

Two articles providing more detailed discussion of the role of psychotherapy in psychosomatic disorders are those of Chalke (1965) and Stevens (1972).

*Therapeutic Results and Follow-up Studies.* In a preliminary report of treatment in a psychosomatic clinic Ripley, Wolf and Wolff (1948) examined and followed 889 patients suffering chiefly from bronchial asthma, hypertension, vasomotor rhinitis, migraine, urticaria, hypoglycemia, dermatitis, peptic ulcer, mucous colitis, ulcerative colitis, and phenomena of muscle tension. An attempt was made to explain to the patient what had been happening to him, in order that perplexity might be replaced by a grasp of the dynamics at work in his illness. The past experiences and reactions were integrated with the present in order to increase insight into his life adaptation. Thirteen principal approaches were used, as follows:

| | |
|---|---:|
| Reassurance and emotional support | 309 |
| Free expression of conflicts and feelings | 304 |
| Advice regarding attitudes, habits and activities | 173 |
| Explanation of psychophysiologic processes | 140 |
| Symptomatic drug therapy | 123 |
| Intravenous use of "sodium amytal" | 112 |
| Ruling out neoplastic and infectious disease | 112 |
| Dealing with other members of the family. | 101 |
| Development of insight | 99 |
| Analysis of emotional development | 91 |
| Attempts to modify situation | 71 |
| Dream analysis | 52 |
| Help from Social Service Department | 39 |

The following features were good prognostic indicators: (1) recognition of failure of present patterns of adjustment and desire for help; (2) confidence in and ability to cooperate with the physician; (3) flexibility of personality structure; (4) disorder of recent origin; (5) long intervals between attacks; (6) capacity and willingness to assume responsibility in treatment; (7) past record of constructive interpersonal relationships; (8) past record of ability to derive satisfaction from occupation, religion, sports, lodges and other activities; and (9) willingness of the family to cooperate.

An average of only 9 hours per patient was expended and no one received more than 84 hours of clinic time during the two-year follow-up. There were basic lasting improvements in one out of five (19%) and at least symptomatic improvement in more than half of the group treated. The authors concluded that the most powerful therapeutic force stemmed from the ability of the physician and the clinic to inculcate in the patient faith in himself and his capacity to recognize and deal constructively with his problem.

Samples of outcome studies will be presented for two psychosomatic disorders ulcerative colitis and peptic ulcer.

Ulcerative colitis has been the subject of considerable study in relation to psychotherapy. General principles have been discussed by Groen and Bastiaans (1951) and West (1961). Daniels, O'Connor, Karush, Moses, Flood and Lepore (1962), in a follow-up study of 57 selected patients who had had definite ulcerative colitis and who underwent psychoanalytically-oriented psychotherapy, state that the psychiatric diagnosis proved to be a most reliable variable in prognosis for both mental and physical states. Out of 48 living patients, 4 had excellent responses to psychotherapy, 27 had good responses, 6 had moderate ones, 8 had no significant changes, and 3 had poor responses.

Karush, Daniels, O'Connor and Stern (1969), reporting on 30 patients with chronic ulcerative colitis, found that the outcome of psychotherapy was correlated with factors arising from the psychotherapeutic situation. They noticed that individuated patients did well with interpretation and abreaction whereas symbiotic patients did better with support, suggestion and graded abreaction.

The fit between the patient's dependency needs and style of expressing them and the therapist's responsiveness to them was particularly important to the outcome. Therapist's interest, empathy, and optimism when combined with his patient's hopefulness produced the highest improvement rate (p. 201).

Follow-up findings indicated that the longer the duration of treatment, the better were the results. Of 18 patients who were treated for a year or less, 10 (56%) were physically improved. Of 12 patients who were treated for 1–3 years or more, 10 (83%) were physically improved. Four patients were treated for less than 6 months; of these, 3 (75%) remained unimproved.

Weinstock (1962) reported on 28 cases of ulcerative colitis, treated by 20 analysts; 14 cases were treated with classical psychoanalytic techniques and the other half were treated with psychoanalytically-oriented psychotherapy. Treatment lasted from 1 1/2 to 5 years and the patients were again evaluated 9 years later. Twenty-two patients (nearly 80%) were symptom-free for periods ranging from 3 to 18 years (median 9 years) and 6 patients were considered therapeutic failures. Members of this last group were chronically ill (5 to 12 years) prior to the beginning of therapy. The majority of cases that did well were those that came to treatment after hospitalization and in an ambulatory state with mild or few symptoms even though the interval between onset of the disease and the beginning of psychiatric treatment averaged 5 years.

Freyberger (1970) reported the outcome of psychotherapy and medical treatment in 65 patients with ulcerative colitis or proctosigmoiditis followed up for several years: in 67.6% a complete remission was attained; in 15.4% a moderate improvement occurred and in 16.9% no improvement was noticed. From this last group 4 patients had a successful colostomy and 5 patients died.

The assessment of treatment efficacy is very difficult in peptic ulcer, a usually chronic psychosomatic disorder characterized by exacerbations and remissions. This difficulty applies as much to medical as to psychological components of treatment. As Nemiah (1971) points out, ulcer patients usually improve rapidly after admission to hospital, regardless of the severity of their symptoms, and this has generally been explained on the basis of the hospitalization experience representing a direct gratification of dependency needs. Several controlled studies, including that of Backman, Kalliola and Ostling (1960), demonstrate the equal effectiveness of placebo as compared with standard medical regimens in the alleviation of symptoms.

With regard to assessing the effectiveness of exploratory psychotherapy or psychoanalysis in peptic ulcer, Nemiah (1971) indicates the necessity of long-term follow-up with a control sample, as any individual exacerbation can be expected to clear up almost regardless of what treatment is given. Such a rigorous study has not yet been done, and there is relatively little in the literature concerning intensive treatment and follow-up. Alexander and French (1946, 1948) as well as Stine and Ivy (1952) report initial improvement with psycho-analysis, but a high incidence of later recurrence of symptoms. One unique study suggesting the potential value of the psychoanalytic approach is that of Orgel (1958) who reported treatment of a mixed population of 15 gastric and duodenal ulcer patients. Five of these patients who dropped out of treatment continued to have ulcer symptoms, but all 10 patients who completed analysis and were followed up from 10 to 22 years were completely free of symptoms and consid-ered cured.

As noted in the section on behavior therapy, there is increasing scientific evidence that a learning of involuntary and glandular responses takes place during life and that autonomic functions can be influenced through the training tech-niques of relaxation, Yoga, autogenic training and biofeedback training. The view is sometimes expressed that, in comparison with classical psychotherapy, such other methods may be faster and more effective in inducing beneficial psychophysiological changes. A more comprehensive outlook is that psycho-therapy is not incompatible with the psychophysiological methods, and it is probable that combined approaches will offer the best results. Also, it is important to mention that these psychophysiological methods are to some extent dependent on psychotherapeutic principles, such as a good therapist-patient relationship.

Psychopharmacology

The discovery of potent psychoactive drugs during the past two decades has given rise to the new discipline of psychopharmacology and has revolutionized the treatment of several categories of mental illness, especially the psychoses (functional and organic) and the psychoneuroses. Judging by the huge quan-tities of tranquilizers and mood-elevating drugs prescribed annually by doctors in both family and specialist practice, the psychoactive drugs have also found acceptance (perhaps overacceptance) for use in a variety of patients in whom "psychosomatic" or "somatopsychic" factors are operating. In contrast to the now voluminous literature on psychopharmacological treatment of the neuroses and psychoses, published studies of the use of psychoactive drugs in the classical psychosomatic disorders particularly are relatively few. In the medical and surgical literature generally, psychoactive drugs are considered adjunctive to the treatment of these conditions, or they are not considered at all. Drugs are of course widely used in these disorders, but are directed more at the somatic or physiological rather than the psychological component. A greater involvement by psychopharmacologists in medical practice generally will lead, in all proba-bility, to the development of greater precision in the use of psychoactive agents in these conditions. As examples of the problems encountered, medical practi-tioners frequently give doses which are too small, do not allow sufficient time to assess the efficacy of antidepressants before dismissing them as useless, and do not make appropriate associations between relapse of symptoms and premature discontinuation of the drug.

Animal experiments have provided some data on the effect of various psychoactive drugs on "psychosomatic" processes. For example, one study (Bonfils and Dubrasquet, 1969) found that imipramine administered to rats provided very efficient protection against the development of restraint-produced stomach ulceration. Chlorpromazine, thioridizine and thioproperazine also provided some protection, whereas reserpine increased the frequency of ulcers. In another study by Birnbaum (1969) diazepam was found to have a pronounced inhibitory action upon gastric secretion and motility in rats, the stress being unusual optic or acoustic stimulation. Birnbaum also reports similar effects in humans in which the use of diazepam led to decreased gastric secretion and relief of pain. As this occurs even in patients who have undergone vagotomy, the effects are probably not via vagal pathways.

Marino (1969) has suggested a model for the psychosomatic evaluation of psychotropic drugs. Using the cardiovascular system as an example, he describes three types of effects of psychotropic drugs: (1) somatic effects: side effects independent of psychotropic activity result from direct action on the heart and blood vessels or are mediated through cardiovascular neuro-regulation. Somatic effects may influence both psychogenic and nonpsychogenic cardiovascular diseases; (2) somatopsychic effects: result from action on the psychic repercussions of psychogenic and nonpsychogenic cardiovascular diseases; (3) psychosomatic effects: result from action on the psychogenic factor which determines, precipitates or contributes to the development of cardiovascular diseases. For example, in essential hypertension amitriptyline is very useful, especially in early stages. It has hypotensive, tranquilizing and antidepressant effects which may antagonize respectively the somatic, somatopsychic and psychosomatic components of the disease. Marino reports a study of 29 patients with essential hypertension and depression-anxiety syndrome who were treated with amitriptyline in a dose of 25–60 mg orally daily for 2 to 6 months, in a double-blind crossover experiment. All the treated patients improved significantly after the treatment, from both the psychological and cardioangiologic points of view. Marino claims that the main point is to choose specific drugs in the treatment of psychosomatic disorders, keeping in mind these three categories of effect.

As a general rule in psychosomatic disorders, according to Sanger (1964), the more evident the psychic involvement, the better the results obtained by adding psychoactive drugs to the regimen.

The common association of depression with various psychosomatic disorders or symptoms has led to extensive prescription of tricyclic antidepressant drugs in such cases. Some early studies reported on the beneficial action of imipramine in chronic psychosomatic illnesses such as rheumatoid arthritis (Scherbel, 1958) and asthmatic bronchitis (Evans, 1960). A good summary of the general effect of imipramine on the depressive components of medical disorders was provided by Kaplan, Kravetz and Ross (1961).

A more recent study (Kashiwagi, McClure and Wetzel, 1972) reported that, in 100 patients with vascular, tension, or "combined" headaches, 47 were found with a history of depression. These were treated with 75–150 mg per day of amitriptyline. In 65.6% of patients both headache and depression responded, in 13.8% only depression responded, in 3.5% only headache responded, and in 17.2% neither headache nor depression responded. In another mixed sample of vascular and tension headaches it was found that doxepin hydrochloride was superior to either amitriptyline or diazepam in relief of headache (Okasha, Ghaleb and Sadek, 1973). The authors attribute the superiority of doxepin to its claimed triple action, namely, anxiolytic, antidepressant and central muscle relaxant.

A survey of the use of psychoactive drugs in post-myocardial infarction patients was reported by Greenblatt and Shader (1971). Of 253 patients investigated, 88% received daytime sedation while hospitalized. Of these prescriptions 60% were for phenobarbital, 30% for chlordiazepoxide, and 6% for meprobamate. Despite the greater use of phenobarbital, the authors consider that it has an uncertain value in the relief of anxiety, produces central nervous system depression, has a narrow margin of safety, is more likely to produce habituation, and antagonizes warfarin-type anticoagulants. They recommend the use of benzodiazepine tranquilizers such as chlordiazepoxide or diazepam. Considering antidepressant agents, phenothiazine tranquilizers and propanolol, Greenblatt and Shader share the common belief that the risks associated with the use of these drugs in acute myocardial infarction patients are considerable and should be weighed carefully before they are administered.

Some data is available with regard to the use of psychotropic drugs in rheumatoid arthritis. A double-blind crossover study (Vince and Kremer, 1973) comparing the use of diazepam versus placebo found no significant improvement in pain, morning stiffness or general well-being. It should be noted, however, that the total period of study was only two weeks, with the crossover occurring after one week, and the dose of diazepam fixed at 5 mg three times a day. A previous study by Scott (1969) showed, on the other hand, that imipramine, when given concurrently with analgesic drugs to patients with rheumatoid arthritis, lessened pain and improved function as compared with placebo, thus confirming an earlier report by Scherbel (1958).

An uncontrolled study of 97 patients with various gastrointestinal disorders suggested a good response to amitriptyline, particularly in cases of spastic colitis and duodenal ulcer (Diamond, 1964), but the absence of a control group makes the findings less certain. Similar objections can be raised to a study (Brandsma, 1970) of the effectiveness of medazepam (a benzodiazepine derivative) in a group of 57 patients consisting of a mixture of psychophysiologic reactions, organic conditions with strong emotional overlay, and psychoneurotic reactions with vague somatic symptoms. Results were reported as favorable in 49 patients, of whom 14 were completely relieved of their presenting symptoms. Krakowski (1966) reported on the superior results of chemotherapy in the management of

49 children and adolescents showing various chronic and severe psychosomatic gastrointestinal disorders, refractory to previous methods of pediatric therapy. No clear specificity of action was noted in the drugs used which were amitriptyline and opipramol. Overall satisfactory improvement (good or excellent) was 43% with psychotherapy alone, 75% with chemotherapy alone and 54% with both.

Imipramine has been reported effective in alleviating the pain in peptic ulcer (Varay, Berthelot, Billiottet, Viterbo and Graf, 1960). A recent article (Monges and Salducci, 1973) reports on the compound sulpiride which shows promise in the treatment of peptic ulcer. Its action on diencephalic structures produces rapid control of physical symptoms of pain and vomiting, and radiological clearing of the ulcer in 15–21 days. Of additional interest is the observation that concurrent improvements occur in the psychological realm, also related to central action. The patients appear much more relaxed, especially those in whom the acute illness was precipitated or exacerbated by obvious psychic factors.

In a double-blind, placebo-controlled study of four dermatoses (atopic dermatitis, seborrheic dermatoses, psoriasis and hyperhidrosis), Lester, Wittkower, Kalz and Azima (1962) studied the effectiveness of four phrenotropic drugs: chlorpromazine, imipramine, meprobamate and chlordiazepoxide. Among other findings they noted a good correlation of improvement between the dermatological variables, rash and itching, and the psychiatric variables, tension-anxiety and depression. Both chlorpromazine and imipramine had a marked effect on itching, and symptoms of depression, although of a neurotic-reactive nature, responded in 65% of the patients treated with imipramine. About 50% of the patients showed improvement in the cutaneous symptoms of the dermatoses studied, whereas the response to placebo did not exceed 30%.

Medansky (1971) reported a double-blind study of placebo and two psychotropic drugs, Librium (chlordiazepoxide and Etrafon (perphenazine 2 mg and amitriptyline 10 mg)) in what he calls the "collaborative group" of dermatoses — those in which organic causes and emotional factors collaborate in different degrees to produce the skin disorders (neurodermatitis, psoriasis, acne, warts herpes simplex, alopecia areata). Over a four-week period the placebo proved more effective than the psychotropic agents, and the author suggests that the interest and attitude of the physician may be a more crucial factor than the drug.

The possible value of the $\beta$-adrenergic blocking agent propanolol in migraine headaches is suggested by two double-blind studies, one of which (Weber and Reinmuth, 1972) reported that 79% of patients treated for migraine responded better to propanolol than to placebo. A later study (Malvea, Gwon and Graham, 1973) investigated its usefulness in the prophylaxis of this disorder, as compared with placebo. Of 29 patients, propanolol was more effective than placebo in 16 patients and placebo judged more effective in 8 patients, with 5 expressing no preference. Results were considered not to be dramatic, but it is concluded that in some patients it appears to be very effective and thus potentially useful.

The management of anorexia nervosa, one of the most difficult therapeutic challenges in psychosomatic medicine, has been simplified in some cases by the administration of at times, massive doses of chlorpromazine (Crisp, 1966; Browning and Miller, 1968) along with other measures. In other cases where depressive elements are prominent, Kuhn (1969) recommends the use of antidepressant drugs in the hospital, pointing out that the patient may not take the drug if at home.

## Behavior Therapy

*Theoretical Aspects.*   Behavior therapy or behavior modification represents a variety of treatment models which have as their common factor a basis in learning theory; in particular, those aspects of learning theory dealing with the principles of classical and operant conditioning. In the context of this chapter, the term "behavior" is taken to include manifestations of autonomic or involuntary muscle functioning, and "behavior therapy" thus encompasses techniques in the early stage of development, known generally under the heading of biofeedback control. A detailed description of behavior therapy is found elsewhere in this volume, and we shall consider only those aspects of this treatment approach which have been found applicable to the psychosomatic group of diseases.

Important in the consideration of the behavioral model of some psychosomatic conditions are various studies related to autonomic functioning. For example, the work of Lacey's group suggests that there are marked individual differences, developing early in life, in the patterns of autonomic reactivity to stress (Lacey, J.I., Kagan, Lacey, B.L. and Moss, 1963). Other investigators (Malmo, Shagass and Davis, 1950; Hahn and Clark, 1967) have provided evidence of a relationship between the patient's patterns of autonomic reactivity and the particular psychosomatic symptoms he develops.

Chesser and Meyer (1970) outline some difficulties in accepting a purely behavioral paradigm concerning classical psychosomatic conditions. For example, if recurrent migraine headaches are considered a conditioned emotional response, why does it not become extinguished? They refer to recent work by Eysenck (1968) which suggests that aversive classical and instrumental conditioning can lead to the acquisition of responses which show great resistance to extinction and may actually increase in the absence of further exposure to the unconditioned stimulus. Another important question concerning the application of the behavioral model is whether short-term reactions to stressful stimuli can be equated with sustained aberrations of physiological parameters associated in many cases with structural damage. Chesser and Meyer (1970) refer to some experimental support for this involving peptic ulceration in monkeys and rats and sustained hypertension in dogs, rats and mice. The same authors provide a theoretical formulation of how certain autonomic components of unconditioned responses, by means of the sequential operation of classical and operant conditioning principles, may develop into stable conditioned responses in genetically predisposed individuals.

As discussed in detail by Kimmel (1967), the traditional view that autonomic activity is subject to classical conditioning but not to operant conditioning may have to be re-evaluated in the light of recent findings. Early interest in this question was reflected by a series of articles over a decade ago concerning the conscious control of autonomic functions among practitioners of Yoga (Wenger and Bagchi, 1961; Wenger, Bagchi and Anand, 1961; Anand, Chhina and Singh, 1961). Although they noted changes in heart rate brought about by conscious effort, this and other easily measured autonomic responses are known to be affected by skeletal responses such as breathing and tensing of the diaphragm. Thus it is possible that, instead of directly learning a visceral response, the subject has learned a skeletal response, the performance of which causes the visceral change being recorded (Miller, 1969).

Davidson and Krippner (1972) summarized recent animal studies in this area. Many fascinating experiments investigated such questions as operant control of salivation in thirsty dogs (Miller and Carmona, 1967), heart rate conditioning in curarized rats (Trowill, 1967), and blood pressure and heart rate responses in monkeys (Plumlee, 1969; Benson, Herd, Morse and Kelleher, 1969; Engel and Gottlieb, 1970). Davidson and Krippner conclude that, taken as a whole, the animal studies suggest that with training, an organism can learn to control any bodily function for which one can obtain a means of recognition. Katkin and Murray (1968) point out the difficulty of extrapolating from animal experiments to human experiments on autonomic conditioning in which the influence of nonautonomic factors is not ruled out. Some of the objections raised by these authors were answered by Crider, Schwartz and Shnidman (1969).

Turning to data on humans, considerable evidence has been accumulated concerning the conditioning of cardiovascular parameters. One group of experiments showed the feasibility of controlling systolic blood pressure (Shapiro, Tursky, Gershon and Stern, 1969; Miller, Di Cara, Solomon, Weiss and Dworkin, 1970). More recent studies (Shapiro, Schwartz and Tursky, 1972; Schwartz, 1972) have investigated the relationship of heart rate to both systolic and diastolic pressure, finding a closer integration of the heart rate with the diastolic than the systolic pressure. Another experiment (Shapiro, Tursky and Schwartz, 1970) demonstrated that humans are capable of learning operantly conditioned discriminations between blood pressure and heart rate. Teplitz (1971) points out that this is a necessary precondition for any therapeutic application of operant conditioning of blood pressure because it indicates that learned changes in blood pressure can be specific and independent of other responses. Teplitz (1971) cautions that studies of short-term blood pressure regulation in normal, normotensive animals and humans may not accurately resemble the situation in subjects with early labile, or late stable, essential hypertension.

Davidson and Krippner (1972) point out that the application of such techniques would have many advantages over such traditionally oriented practices as chemotherapy in hypertension. Drug effects are usually quite general, often with serious or inconvenient side effects. Biofeedback as an example of behavior modification, can, on the other hand, be quite specific in its effects and this specificity has been demonstrated in humans (Engel and Hansen, 1966; Shapiro, Tursky and Schwartz, 1970).

A further possible application of behavioral techniques to cardiovascular abnormalities involves the area of cardiac arrhythmias. One study reports the successful control of premature ventricular contractions in some patients (Weiss and Engel, 1973). A more recent study (Bleecker and Engel, 1973) showed the possibility of patients with atrial fibrillation learning to control their ventricular rate.

*Biofeedback.* Biofeedback training combines the elements of automatic conditioning and the concept of control of the process utilizing a feedback apparatus during the initial training period. In the biofeedback paradigm as outlined by Davidson and Krippner (1972), the organism is placed in a closed feedback loop in which information concerning one or more of his bodily processes is continually made known to him. When the organism possesses this type of information about a bodily process it is possible for him to learn to control this function. In animals reinforcement can be provided, for example, by electrical stimulation of the pleasure center of the brain or by escape from electric shock. In humans a variety of reinforcers have been used, such as the approval of the experimenter or the production of behavior which is self-reinforcing; for example, the removal of symptoms or the production of a pleasurable state of consciousness associated with alpha rhythm on the electroencephalogram.

The conditionability of alpha rhythm has been known since the early studies of Jasper and Shagass (1941) and Mulholland and Runnals (1962a and b). Fuller investigation, including the first assessment of the associated subjective state, was carried out in a series of studies by Kamiya (1962, 1967, 1968, 1969). The possibility of individuals being able to induce a state of altered consciousness which may render them less aware of the presence of chronic pain is currently under investigation by Melzack and co-workers (personal communication), following upon a study showing the beneficial effect of alpha induction on the prevention (but not alleviation) of severe headaches in one patient (Gannon and Sternbach, 1971). Mechanisms involved in alpha are discussed in papers by Peper (1971) and Lynch and Paskewitz (1971).

A good example of the applicability of the biofeedback paradigm to psychosomatic symptoms was a study demonstrating feedback control of the frontalis muscle in patients with tension headaches (Budzynski, Stoyva and Adler, 1970). In this study it was found that biofeedback training reduced both the patient's subjective experience of headache and the EMG potential recorded from the frontalis. Significantly, changes noted in the laboratory were transferred to everyday life. After completing the training period the patients reported (1) a heightened awareness of maladaptive rising tension, (2) an increasing ability to reduce such tension, and    (3) a decreasing tendency to overreact to stress.

Davidson and Krippner (1972) suggest there are important implications of biofeedback training in that the person is able to use his volition or will to control physiological processes, and they suggest this might contribute to a greater integration of personality and an individual who is capable of resisting certain cultural biases and forms of societal conditioning as outlined by Maslow (1962). The aspect of patient involvement or control may have important implications also in relation to the fact that many patients with psychosomatic disorders experience great anxiety when exposed to traditional psychiatric therapies (for example, psychotherapy or drugs) which may be interpreted as threatening or unwelcome control by another person or agent. The possibility of establishing personal control as part of the therapeutic process may make psycho-logically-oriented treatment more acceptable than it has been in the past with this group of patients.

*Applications of Behavior Therapy in Psychosomatic Conditions.* In the psycho-somatic area, behavior therapy has so far had its greatest application in bronchial asthma, obesity and anorexia nervosa. Bronchial asthma will be discussed in detail later in this chapter.

The first report of a patient with anorexia nervosa treated by selective positive reinforcement of weight gain was by Bachrach, Erwin and Mohr (1965). In a later study of two patients with this disorder, Leitenberg, Agras and Thomson (1968) reported that simple ignoring of physical complaints was effective in eliminating their expression, but that this extinction procedure was insufficient to reinstate a normal eating pattern. However, selective positive reinforcement of progressive gains in weight and amount eaten gradually restored caloric intake and weight to the desired levels. Positive reinforcement included verbal praise and extension of tangible privileges desired by the patient.

Increasing sophistication in the techniques of behavioral analysis has provided new opportunities for positive reinforcement of desired eating patterns. Of great importance was the recognition that the hyperactivity so often associated with anorexia nervosa could be restricted, and that opportunity for physical activity could be made contingent upon weight gain. The use of this approach and its impressive success in leading to rapid restoration of weight was reported in a study by Blinder, Freeman and Stunkard (1970). Subsequent investigation revealed that other suitable contingencies might be devised if hyperactivity was not employable. For example, Stunkard (1972) reported one case where a patient complaining of the sedative effects of chlorpromazine was informed that reduc-tion of dose would be contingent upon weight gain. As a result the patient gained an average of 6 pounds per week despite the consequent radical decrease in chlorpromazine dosage.

The apparent ease in re-establishing weight by behavioral means points to this method as a useful and important innovation in the treatment of anorexia nervosa. As a cautionary note, however, this technique alone may be insufficient to ensure the maintenance of the weight gain or the alteration of other often severe psychopathological manifestations in these patients. Moldofsky (1973) has reported on two subsequent relapses among five cases successfully treated using behavioral techniques.

Obesity, as probably the most common of the psychosomatic disorders, has been the subject of intensive recent study concerning the possibility of its treatment by behavioral techniques. An early paper by Ferster, Nurnberger and Levitt (1962) presented a detailed behavioral analysis of eating and means of control. Stunkard (1972) outlined a modified program, used by his group, based on four basic principles: (1) description of the behavior to be controlled; (2) modification and control of the discriminatory stimuli governing eating; (3) development of techniques to control the act of eating; and (4) prompt reinforcement of behaviors that delay or control eating. A full description of behavioral methodology as applied to obesity is provided by Stuart and Davis (1972).

The last decade has seen a considerable refinement and elaboration of the behavioral techniques applied to obesity. An uncontrolled trial lasting one year resulted in a completion rate of 80%, with 6 out of 10 patients losing more than 30 pounds (Stuart, 1967). This method involved individual sessions, with both patient and therapist participating in the setting up of the behavioral program.

Following a cogent discussion of overeating behavior as it relates to learning theory, Harris (1969) reports a controlled study of obese college students which emphasized the development of individual programs, absence of prohibitions, gradual rather than dramatic losses, and group reinforcement. There was a mean weight loss of 8.5 pounds for the experimental group as against a 3.6 pound gain for the control group over four months.

A well-controlled study published by Wollersheim (1970) compared a control group awaiting treatment to three other groups of obese patients under the following experimental conditions: (1) "focal" (behavioral) treatment, (2) non-specific treatment, and (3) social pressure TOPS (Take Off Pounds Sensibly) attendance. Here, the focal group changed more than the other three, reaching statistically significant results in three of six factors, namely, "emotional and uncontrolled overeating," "eating in isolation," and "between-meal eating." At the time of eight-week follow-up the superior results in the "focal" group were maintained and there was no evidence of symptom substitution.

Hagen (1969) showed that the use of a manual describing behavioral treatment principles could be used by obese patients for effective weight loss, even in the absence of a therapist. Another study showed the superiority of behavioral techniques over traditional supportive psychotherapy and dietary control (Penick, Filion, Fox and Stunkard, 1971). These principles have found application in a variety of specialized situations; for example, among obese chronic schizophrenics (Harmatz and Lapuc, 1968).

A different theoretical approach, namely, aversive conditioning, was used in a study on obese patients by Foreyt and Kennedy (1971). These workers employed noxious odors as unconditioned stimuli and their initial results were good, although a 48-week follow-up showed that most of the experimental subjects had regained a portion of the lost weight.   Janda and Rimm (1972), using the aversive technique of covert sensitization, found that subjects who experienced the most intense subjective discomfort to imagined aversive scenes showed a much greater mean weight loss than those reporting only slight discomfort.

Stunkard (1972) points out that behavioral techniques provide the possibility of exercising great creativity by both therapist and patient, and that obese patients have great demands placed upon them between sessions, thus emphasizing their own responsibility in the treatment process.

Apart from the eating disorders, other applications of behavior therapy to psychosomatic conditions have included the treatment of spasmodic torticollis (Agras and Marshall, 1965; Brierley, 1967; Meares, 1973) and neurodermatitis (Walton, 1960b; Allen and Harris, 1966; Ratliff and Stein, 1968). There is a recent case report of successful treatment of a reflex trigeminal nerve blepharospasm by behavior modification (Haidar and Clancy, 1973). Behavior therapy has been used successfully to control nervous diarrhea and vomiting (Cohen and Reed, 1968) and has also been described as useful in the control of temporal lobe epilepsy (Efron, 1957). Mitchell (1969, 1971) has performed some interesting experiments using behavior therapy in migraine.  In the 1971 study, he has shown that combined desensitization, involving applied relaxation, desensitization and assertive therapy, was superior to applied relaxation or to no treatment in the reduction of migraine attacks.  He produced the quite striking figure of 89.5% improvement in the number of attacks by the combined treatment group as compared with control subjects who had no treatment.  An interesting combination of techniques referred to as "autogenic feedback training" has recently been found effective in controlling many migraine headaches (Sargent, Green and Walters, 1973).   The treatment model consists of the learning of autonomic vascular control such that voluntarily increased blood flow to one hand results in recovery from the migraine attack.

A recent case report (Corson, Bouchard, et al., 1973) outlines the employment of conditioning principles in the treatment of severe perspiration experienced as part of an anxiety response to social situations in a 20-year-old man. Following instruction in progressive relaxation the patient was presented with a cognitive strategy allowing him gradually to gain instrumental control of sweating over a 10-week period.  Follow-up for 15 months has revealed no recurrence of the symptom or symptom substitution.

Behavior therapy has, within a few years, established itself as an innovative and promising treatment modality for psychosomatic disorders.  It is too early to assess its long term effects and some recent reports (e.g., Moldofsky, 1973) have introduced a cautionary note concerning the use of behavioral modification unsupplemented by attention to underlying conflicts.

Group Therapy

The first reported use of group psychotherapy was to help patients deal with their reactions to tuberculosis (Pratt, 1906). Since that time group therapy has developed in many directions, with application to a wide variety of problems. Recent texts which give a general view of current trends in this area are those of Yalom (1970), Kaplan and Sadock (1971), and Solomon and Berzon (1972). Stein (1971) claims, in describing the applicability of group psychotherapy to psychosomatic conditions, that the factors that limit the effectiveness of individual psychotherapy in the treatment of these disorders are specific indications for the use of group psychotherapy. He conceives of the following defects in patients with psychosomatic illness: (1) a tendency to have object relationships of intense symbiotic type; (2) very poor tolerance of separation, object loss, or any frustrating experience; (3) an ego that is weak and buffeted by intense emotional reactions and the restrictions of a punitive, archaic superego; (4) affective responses that are excessive and intense, and expressed through autonomic and somatic channels with blocking of outward expression; (5) difficulties in establishing contact with the therapist – the primitive type of transference that does develop stems from the passive, symbiotic type of object relationships used by these patients.

Stein claims that the group process provides features which facilitate a psychotherapeutic relationship so difficult to establish in these patients with individual psychotherapy. For example, the intensity of the transference is lessened because of the presence of a number of members. In addition, the transference is split, since it is directed toward other members of the group as well as toward the therapist. These factors help rigid psychosomatic patients cope with overly intense reactions stemming from their passive symbiotic relationships, and also provide opportunities to examine the nature of their interactions and to develop new kinds of relationships.

Stein believes that rigid superego attitudes are dealt with better, through the sharing of guilt and the use of various kinds of spokesmen. Group processes also help psychosomatic patients to express feelings through speaking, shouting, weeping, etc., something they were previously unable to do. Opportunities for increased interpersonal contact in the group, and the group's realistic nature help to lessen isolation and strengthen contact with reality, leading to more effective ego functioning. The nature of the ties in the group, especially identifications, help the members to supply each other with a great deal of emotional support.

Other authors who have reviewed the use of group psychotherapy in psychosomatic disorders in various settings include Deutsch and Lippman (1964) and Enke (1968).

*Clinical Studies in Psychosomatic Disorders.* An interesting early use of group therapy in the psychosomatic area consisted of the treatment of 32 patients with peptic ulcer through an intensive group experience aimed primarily at improving ego functions (Chappell, Stefano, Rogerson and Pike, 1936–37). At the end of six weeks they reported dramatically superior results for the acute phase of the ulcer as compared with a control group, but at the end of three years only 10 had remained free of symptoms. In another study of peptic ulcer patients (Fortin and Abse, 1956), a number of university students with this illness were treated in a group. It was found that the treatment first heightened the patients' dependency needs and led to angry outbursts as a result of the frustration of these unreal expectations from the therapist. Later, these feelings were worked through in the group interaction and all the patients were said to have registered improvement in their ulcer symptoms. Garma (1973) attests to the usefulness of group psychoanalysis in the treatment of peptic ulcer patients.

Many reports are cited by Stein (1971) of favorable outcome using group therapy in obese patients. Among the most impressive of these is a study by Mees and Keutzer, (1967) of a group of obese women obtaining benefit from short-term group therapy. However, other authors have expressed doubts about its use for all obese patients (Holt and Winick, 1961). One study suggested that group therapy did not help obese patients lose weight, but it did have a beneficial effect on their emotional stability (Slawson, 1965). A variety of lay groups utilizing group support for weight reduction have been as successful in this goal as many "professional" methods. One such group – TOPS (Take Off Pounds Sensibly) is discussed by Toch (1965).

More recently very promising results have been obtained by the use of various forms of group therapy or group support combined with behavior modification techniques; for example, a study by Jordon and Levitz (1973). Other illustrations of such investigations are outlined in the section on Behavior Therapy in this chapter.

The use of group therapy in hospitalized hypertension patients tended to raise blood pressure more than individual therapy (Titchener, Sheldon and Ross, 1959). The treatment of dermatoses such as neurodermatitis or atopic eczema has met with some success using group therapy, according to Milberg (1956) and Shoemaker, Guy and McLaughlin (1955). One study claims its value in the treatment of migraine headaches (Cooper and Katz, 1956).

Stein (1971) has reported on many years' personal experience in developing group techniques for psychosomatic patients. Initially, he noticed that chronic psychosomatic patients formed small groups spontaneously in the waiting room; the relationships seemed to be useful and supportive for them. Accordingly, he organized subsequent group therapy experiences with menopausal patients and with mixed groups of psychosomatic patients, including such varied conditions as ulcerative colitis, bronchial asthma, peptic ulcer and neurodermatitis. All of these patients had rigid, constricted personalities and all had negative attitudes toward individual psychotherapy. Stein claims that group sessions helped them to find support for their feelings and to overcome their guilt in expressing some of these feelings.

Stein describes in detail a group psychotherapy experience with a group of female patients who had had ileostomies for ulcerative colitis. It is a good illustration of how the group may operate to help such patients convert their somatic responses to conflict into more purely affective modalities, for example, anger, shouting and weeping.

It is somewhat difficult to assess the results that Stein obtained in various conditions, although it appears that many patients obtained some benefit. Criteria for improvement are not explicitly stated, but assessment was based on the performance of a clinical psychiatric examination.

Yalom (1970) mentions that training, professional background and theoretical orientation are important variables in the approach to group therapy of psychosomatic conditions. Thus, these patients are seen as anathemas to some therapists and interesting challenges to others. As well as various other diagnostic categories, Slavson (1955) considers that what he calls hypochondriacal patients are poor candidates for intensive outpatient groups.

The use of group therapy in bronchial asthma will be noted in the final section.

## Family Therapy

Partly as a result of the presence of somatic symptoms and demonstrable organ pathology, and partly from the traditional psychiatric emphasis on the individual and his internal field, the principal approaches to treatment of psychosomatic patients have focused on individual-oriented modalities. The development over the past 20 years of varieties of family group therapy has offered the opportunity to consider the psychosomatic patient within a broader frame of reference. Until recently, little has appeared in the literature concerning the applicability of family treatment to this group of disorders. Two extensive reviews of the literature on outcome studies of family therapy (Riskin and Faunce, 1972; Wells, Dilkes and Trivelli, 1972), based on several hundred references, contain virtually nothing about psychosomatic patients treated by this method.

A recent review of the literature concerning the family perspective of psychosomatic factors in illness is provided by Grolnick (1972). In that paper, "psychosomatic" has the broad meaning of psychological factors in somatic processes. It thus includes psychophysiological disorders but is not restricted to that category. Grolnick usefully reviews various models including individual intrapsychic and stress responsive conceptualization, diadic relationships (mother-child and object loss), married couples, and families. He considers the earliest attempt to introduce the concepts of family dynamics into psychosomatic medicine to have been by Richardson (1948) whose book had such chapter headings as "The Family as the Unit of Illness," "Psychosomatic Medicine and the Family Pattern," "The Family Equilibrium," and "The Family as a Unit of Treatment." The emphasis was on clinical data and the theoretical outlook included psychoanalytic concepts and general systems theory.

Grolnick (1972) points out that there is in fact no body of knowledge as yet regarding the applications of family therapy to psychosomatic disorders. He refers to Witkin's studies of "psychological differentiation" (Witkin, 1962, 1965) and its significance in relation to various forms of psychopathology. Psychosomatic patients in which the field dependency parameter has been investigated (ulcer, obesity, childhood asthma, diabetes, functional cardiac disorders) have all been found, according to Witkin, to be field dependent or at a low level of psychological differentiation as are people who somatize their psychological program generally and those with deep-seated dependency problems. Witkin feels that treatment can improve integration and adaptation at a particular level of differentiation but that the level of differentiation is immutable. He believes that less-differentiated patients are less suitable for and less attracted to individual psychotherapy, and that an active, structured form of family therapy is suited to the field-dependent psychosomatic patient for several reasons:

1. The effort is directed at altering the field (family) upon which they are so dependent and to which they react.

2. These patients elicit more patient-therapist interactions in therapy, and family treatment provides a greater range of interaction than individual treatment.

3. They are more likely to accept the suggestions which are often given in family therapy.

4. This model can be used to treat many patients who would not likely engage in other forms of treatment.

Grolnick (1972) points out that the family functions as a system in relation to the physically ill member and that an outbreak of illness has an active feedback with the family system. It may either stabilize the situation into a pattern of chronic illness, or feedback may further unsettle the family equilibrium, resulting in psychosomatic outbreaks or other dysfunctions in other members. Goldberg (1958) and Rosenbaum (1963) have thrown interesting light on the important family influences in considering the psychosomatic patient. Meissner (1966) has dealt with the issue of threatened or actual loss of an important family member as well as other disruptions in the family which may act as a precipitating factor in psychosomatic illnesses such as ulcerative colitis. Looff (1970) considers family therapy as a kind of workshop in which to train the psychosomatic patient and his family in the awareness of significant affects, in order to avoid their being short-circuited into somatic dysfunction.

There are some cautionary notes regarding the use of family therapy for psychosomatic patients. Ackerman (1966) for example considers the vulnerability to "critical psychosomatic breakdown" as a relative contraindication to family therapy, but on the other hand lists "psychosomatic crisis" as one area where family therapy can be useful.

Grolnick (1972, p. 478), in commenting on objections raised to the use of family therapy in psychosomatic disorders, points out that "the risk of psychosomatic breakdown in IP (the identified patient) or another family member is only one of a number of unfavorable outcomes such as alcoholism, violence, delinquent acts, accidents, and psychotic episodes, to which these families are prone and which brings them to the attention of the therapist in the first place." He does agree that it is important for the family therapist to collaborate closely with the family physician.

There is a very complete exposition of the treatment of an anorectic 14-year-old girl, using the structural approach to family therapy, by Aponte and Hoffman (1973). The therapist ingeniously served lunch to the family during the initial interview and derived a great deal of information about the symptom of anorexia and its use as the only means of control by the patient.

The technique of therapeutically induced family crisis (Minuchin and Barcai, 1969) has been found promising in the management of anorexia nervosa. Barcai (1971) outlines specific strategies which neutralize the continuous struggle over food and thus allow (or force) the family to work on other individual or family problems. Behavioral techniques have also been found useful in conjunction with family therapy. Barcai (1971) reports one case where the patient was allowed to stay out of hospital with her family only as long as she continued to gain weight as an outpatient.

One case history has been published (Vosburg, 1972) claiming the successful use of conjoint couple therapy in the treatment of a patient with migraine headaches.

## Hypnosis

A British Medical Association (1955, p. 191) subcommittee report described hypnosis as follows:

A temporary condition of altered attention in the subject which may be induced by another person and in which a variety of phenomena may appear spontaneously or in response to verbal or other stimuli. These phenomena include alterations in consciousness and memory, increased susceptibility to suggestion, and a production in the subject of responses and ideas unfamiliar to him in his usual state of mind. Further, phenomena such as anesthesia, paralysis and rigidity of muscles, and vasomotor changes can be produced and removed in the hypnotic state.

As noted by Kroger (1963), the mechanism through which these various phenomena are effected remains a matter for speculation, and purely psychological hypotheses are being supplemented by attempted explanation in terms of brain physiology.

A good historical account of hypnosis is given by Barrucand (1969) who traces the development of this phenomenon for two centuries between 1769 and 1969. In a recent review of the subject Peterfy (1973) comments that the controversy regarding the use of hypnosis as a therapeutic tool is almost unmatched in the annals of medicine. Although known since antiquity, hypnosis has come up for scientific study only recently, and its applicability as a therapeutic device in medicine and psychiatry has been hampered by general skepticism within the medical profession, based largely on the theatricality of some of its practitioners, both medical and lay. As Peterfy (1973) notes, only in 1955 did the British Medical Association report its approval of hypnosis as a mode of treatment. In 1958 the American Medical Association recommended that hypnosis be taught in medical schools and postgraduate training centers.

Merskey (1971), in a recent appraisal of hypnosis, notes that in general it is not used much in psychiatry. Where it is, claims have been made for its value during childbirth and in psychosomatic conditions, such as warts and bronchial asthma. This writer points out that warts respond to other kinds of suggestion while asthma benefits most in respect to the patient's reports of subjective well-being but very much less with regard to physical indices like vital capacity, as noted in the study of Maher-Loughnan (1970).

Merskey supplies a comment which reflects his own view, based on recent literature discussions concerning the nature of hypnosis by Barber (1969) and others:

> Hypnosis is a manoeuver in which the subject and the hypnotist have an implicit agreement that certain events (e.g., paralysis, hallucination, amnesias) will occur, either during a special procedure or later, in accordance with the hypnotist's instructions. Both try hard to put this agreement into effect and adopt appropriate behavioral rules and the subject uses mechanisms of denial to report on the events in accordance with the implicit agreement. This situation is used to implement various motives whether therapeutic or otherwise, on the part of both participants. There is no trance state, no detectable cerebral physiological change, and only such peripheral physiological responses as may be produced equally by non-hypnotic suggestion or other emotional changes (p. 579).

Apart from the problems of definition and the controversy still unresolved concerning the nature of the hypnotic state (Ulett, Akpinar and Itil, 1972), there is a considerable difference of opinion regarding the therapeutic usefulness of hypnosis in a variety of conditions, including the psychosomatic disorders.

Black (1965) points out that both hypnosis and psychosomatic disorders are ill-defined, and he claims, based on his own experience, that only 5% of the British population is capable of a deep trance, which he defines as a subject spontaneously amnesic for the period of hypnotic trance and capable of being psychologically regressed to childhood states. About 35% can achieve medium trance, which means they are easily hypnotized but are neither amnesic or regressible. Referring to the remaining 60%, he claims they will form "a positive transference as a result of my efforts to hypnotize them, and I shall then be forced to see them weekly for the rest of my life" (p. 63). He claims this is a most serious objection to the use of hypnosis for anything. Despite his reservations, Black considers that hypnosis has been useful for the relief of sciatic and low back pain, and headaches. He also found it useful as adjunctive therapy in peptic ulcer, ulcerative colitis and hysterical conversion states.

An article by St. Amand (1972) gives one view of the role of hypnotherapy in clinical medicine. He claims that the proper use of hypnosis is not dangerous but rather it is the misuse that is dangerous. Hypnosis is adjunctive to conventional treatment having a facilitatory and accelerating effect. In answer to the frequently expressed criticism that hypnosis involves only the alleviation of symptoms, St. Amand points out that most of medicine involves the alleviation of symptoms. He points out that if the patient has a strong, perhaps unrecognized need for the symptoms the suggestion will not be accepted. As a positive feature he notes that teaching the patient self-hypnosis forces him to take an active role in the treatment, thus shifting the responsibility of getting well to the patient where it properly belongs and reducing his dependency on the therapist. In a cautionary note, St. Amand says that hypnotherapy is not a panacea for all patients, and that enthusiasm for the method should not replace good clinical judgment. Like Black (1965) and Erikson (1965), St. Amand has found hypnotherapy useful in the relief of chronic pain syndromes.

*Specific Applications in Psychosomatic Disorders.* Moody (1953) evaluated the effect of hypnotic as compared with conventional therapy on two well-matched groups of duodenal ulcer patients. Although the group treated by hypnotherapy alone showed greater clinical improvement, the long-term effects are uncertain. Raginsky (1959) stresses the need for an understanding of psychodynamics before undertaking the treatment of peptic ulcer by hypnosis. He gives examples of cases where too energetic removal of the symptom through hypnotherapy was followed by serious behavior problems.

The application of hypnotic procedures to ulcerative colitis should be approached even more cautiously because of the possibility of precipitating a latent psychosis, as experienced workers in the field have emphasized (Raginsky, 1959; Ambrose and Newbold, 1968). A recent report by Byrne (1973) points out that, using the recent revelations concerning the modifiability of autonomic functions, he has successfully employed hypnosis to suggest to two patients with the irritable bowel syndrome that they can control their symptoms.

Headaches involving muscle tension have been relieved by hypnotic suggestions directed at relaxation of the involved muscles rather than by direct symptom removal (Simons, Day, Goodell and Wolff, 1943). Vascular headaches of migraine type have also been treated with hypnotic techniques. In a study by Harding (1965), 90 consecutive cases of refractory migraine headaches were treated with the hypnotherapeutic technique of symptom removal. Of these, 34 experienced complete relief for periods of up to 8 years, 29 patients reported 25-75% reduction in the frequency, duration or intensity of the migraine episodes and 27 either reported failures or were lost to follow-up. Favorable results with hypnotherapy in this condition were also reported by Horan (1953).

Hypnosis in the treatment of warts has been described recently by Surman, Gottlieb, Hackett and Silverberg (1973). They give a historical review of the treatment of warts by hypnosis beginning with the study by Bloch (1927). They

also refer to a study by Asher (1956) which showed cure dependent on susceptibility to hypnosis. The patients capable of a deep trance had a 65% cure rate
while those who could not be hypnotized at all had a 0% cure rate. Similar
results were presented by Ullman and Dudek (1960). An interesting study by
Sinclair-Gieben and Chalmers (1959) showed that hypnosis could effect cure of
warts on one side of the body and not on the other with the appropriate
suggestion. The results of this study were partially challenged by several writers
including Tenzel and Taylor (1969). In the study by Surman, Gottlieb, Hackett
and Silverberg (1973), 17 experimental patients with bilateral common warts
were hypnotized weekly for five sessions and were told that the warts would
disappear on one side only. They were reexamined three months from the time
of the first hypnotic session. Seven patients who were untreated were similarly
examined. 53% of the experimental group improved and no improvement was
noted among the controls. This study does not support the hypothesis that
hypnosis can influence lesions selectively; however, it appears that hypnosis
produces a general effect on host response to the etiologic virus.

Further information on the use of hypnotherapy in skin and allergic diseases
is provided in a book by Scott (1960), and a recent general reference text on
hypnotherapy has been written by Cheek and LeCron (1968).

## Autogenic Therapy

Autogenic training is the basic therapeutic method of a group of psychophysiologically oriented autogenic approaches which constitute "Autogenic Therapy." In contrast to other medically or psychologically oriented
forms of treatment, the methods of autogenic therapy approach and
involve mental and bodily functions simultaneously. (Schultz and Luthe,
1969, p. 1)

The collection of techniques thus referred to had its origins in Germany around
the turn of the century, arising from a series of experiments on sleep and hypnosis carried out by the psychophysiologically oriented neuropathologist Oskar
Vogt (Vogt, 1897) and his collaborator Korbinian Brodmann (Brodmann, 1902).
Vogt noted the capacity of certain intelligent hypnotic subjects to induce a kind of
auto-hypnotic state for short periods. Feelings of heaviness and warmth during
the induction phase were associated with the beneficial effects of relief of
fatigue, tension, and some specific symptoms such as headache. These self-
directed mental exercises were termed "prophylactic rest-autohypnoses" (Schultz
and Luthe, 1969) and were considered of therapeutic value by Vogt and
Brodmann.

A Berlin psychiatrist and neurologist, J.H. Schultz, was interested in developing techniques which would reduce or eliminate what he considered such
unfavorable aspects of hypnotherapy as the passivity of the patient and his
dependence on the therapist (Schultz, 1963). His own studies elaborated the

earlier findings of Vogt and Brodmann and he developed a series of six standard formulas or exercises in which the patient is asked to concentrate on achieving heaviness and warmth in the extremities, regulation of cardiac activity and respiration, abdominal warmth, and cooling of the forehead. Essentially, this "autogenic training" is said to promote a psychophysiological shift to a specific state, the "autogenic state," which facilitates and mobilizes brain-directed processes of self-normalization (Luthe, 1973). The shift to this state is enhanced by the reduction of afferent stimuli, both exteroceptive and proprioceptive, and minimization of efferent activity. Specific horizontal or sitting postures are employed, and the mental activity involves what is termed "passive" concentration. Schultz and Luthe (1969, p. 17) write: " . . . the regular practice of passive concentration or autogenic formulas is associated with a variety of functional changes which, from a psychophysiological point of view, are diametrically opposed to the effects of stress." The patient is largely responsible for carrying out his own treatment once the standard exercises have been learned. Frequency of exercises is usually three times daily, each time for a period of 10–15 minutes.

Additional techniques have been developed for special circumstances or diagnoses. "Meditative exercises" represent a focus on certain mental activities, as compared with the physiological focus of the standard exercises to which they may be added for advanced trainees. Two techniques subsumed under the term "autogenic modification" are "organ-specific exercises," designed to meet the pathophysiologic requirements of certain disorders such as bronchial asthma, and "intentional formulae," used to influence more specifically certain mental functions and behavior deviations. These techniques supplement or are combined with the standard exercises.

Finally, advanced methods have evolved which appear "to enhance the therapeutic effects of autogenic training by giving the brain better opportunity to elaborate or release according to its own self-curative principles . . . (Luthe, 1970, p. 2)." The related techniques known as "autogenic abreaction" and "autogenic verbalization," which cannot be further described here, constitute the last category, "autogenic neutralization."

The concept of the body as an efficient homeostatic or self-curative mechanism is a central theme throughout the writings on autogenic therapy, and the various therapeutic exercises are claimed principally to facilitate these natural processes by the modification of psychophysiological factors inhibiting their operation. This treatment modality can be combined with psychotherapy and has obvious links with hypnosis, and, more recently, biofeedback techniques (Sargent, Green and Walters, 1973). Its use has been widespread in continental Europe and in Japan and its copious literature has been mainly in non-English-language journals, accounting for its relative lack of recognition in North America.

*Application to Psychosomatic Disorders.* Luthe and Schultz (1969) cite several dozen studies which claim to demonstrate the benefit of adding autogenic training to the standard medical regimen for peptic ulcer. Use of the fifth standard exercise ("My solar plexus is warm") is said to be contraindicated in this condition, as passive concentration on warmth in the abdominal area produced hypermotility of peristalsis, significant increase in blood flow in the gastric mucosa and augmentation of gastric acidity. On the other hand, emphasis on the fifth exercise has been found useful in biliary dyskinesia (Kleinsorge, 1959; Salfield and Reverchon, 1964), where bile flow mechanics are said to be improved due to relief of muscular spasm and pain in the region.

The value of autogenic therapy in ulcerative colitis has been described in many articles, among them that of Schaeffer (1966). In a mixed-severity sample of 32 patients, 23 were reported as cured and 6 as significantly improved, in most cases without the use of medication. Based on observation periods lasting up to 12 years, Schaeffer concludes that autogenic training stabilizes and normalizes disturbances of relevant autonomic functions, reduces progressively the frequency and severity of relapses, and eliminates or reduces the need for medication.

Several varieties of functional cardiovascular disorders have been treated by this method, among them paroxysmal tachycardia (Bobon, Breulet, Degossely and Dongier, 1966). Ischemic heart disease has also been investigated, and autogenic therapy is claimed to be useful prophylactically in the so-called coronary-prone individual, operating through such mechanisms as better adjustment of blood pressure, of cardiac activity, of coronary and peripheral circulation, buffering and reduction of psychological stress, and lowering of serum cholesterol (Hellerstein, 1964). In the patient with a clinical picture of angina pectoris or myocardial infarction, close attention to medical management is mandatory, and Luthe and Schultz (1969) emphasize the need for individual tailoring of the autogenic program, at the same time affirming the efficacy of the method. Reported increase in coronary blood flow, as indicated by a normalization of ischemic changes on the electrocardiogram (Kleinsorge, 1954), and lowering of blood cholesterol levels (Luthe, 1965), may be important variables.

Another important application is in the management of essential hypertension, where reduction of both systolic and diastolic elevations have been reported by, among many others, Klumbies and Eberhardt (1966). Peripheral vascular diseases of various types have also benefited from the increased blood flow effected by autogenic methods (Luthe and Schultz, 1969).

Very recent work has combined ingeniously the technique of autogenic training with the rapidly-developing biofeedback aspect of behavior therapy to produce a new therapeutic modality called autogenic feedback training. This method has been found useful in the treatment of migraine headaches in the early stages (Sargent, Green and Walters, 1973), as noted previously in the behavior therapy section of this chapter.

Many other psychosomatically conceived disorders, including migraine, tuberculosis, diabetes mellitus, thyrotoxicosis, rheumatoid arthritis, functional urinary and sexual disorders, dysmenorrhea, and certain dermatoses are reported to benefit from autogenic methods, applied solely or in conjunction with other treatments.  Space limitations prevent further discussion, but the interested reader is referred to a series of volumes on the subject, edited by Luthe (Schultz and Luthe, 1969; Luthe and Schultz, II, III, 1969; Luthe, IV, V, 1970; VI, 1973). Applications to bronchial asthma will be noted in the final section of this chapter.

## TREATMENT OF BRONCHIAL ASTHMA AS A PARADIGM OF PSYCHOSOMATIC DISORDER

Bronchial asthma is a respiratory affliction which has been known in the medical literature for over two thousand years but the etiology and pathogenesis of which have come under close study only in the past century.  A widely accepted definition of this condition is as follows: "Asthma is a disease characterized by an increased responsiveness of the trachea and bronchi to various stimuli and manifested by a widespread narrowing of the airways that changes in severity either spontaneously or as a result of therapy" (American Thoracic Society, 1962).  This is an open definition which does not mention specific cause and is consonant with the psychosomatic concept in that it implies the possibility of multifactorial genesis and interaction.  A recent review of current concepts of asthma usefully summarizes the epidemiology, immunology, pathogenesis and biochemistry of this condition (Beall, Heiner, Tashkin and Whipp, 1973). Contemporary medical treatment is outlined in a discussion by Fink and Sosman (1973).

There have been various attempts to classify asthma patients according to the predominant etiological factor, that is, whether principally allergic or psychogenic.  Such attempts have met with limited success and produced contradictory findings (McDermott and Cobb, 1939; Rees, 1956).  A well-designed study by Dekker, Barendregt and De Vries (1961) investigated neuroticism scores in two groups of patients: an "alergic" group consisting of patients in whom attacks of asthma could be provoked by the inhalation of nebulized allergens, and a "non-allergic" group composed of patients who either showed no positive skin reactions or in whom all positive skin reactions were followed by a negative inhalation test. No significant differences were found between the neuroticism scores of these two groups.  A possible objection to any conclusions drawn from such a study is that "neuroticism" may in some cases act as a predisposing or precipitating factor, whereas in others it may represent a somatopsychic response to an anxiety-producing, potentially life-threatening symptom.

Following early descriptions of the psychodynamic aspects of asthma, especially the classic monograph by French and Alexander (1941), there have been a large number of studies investigating the contribution of psychological factors in this disorder.  Among areas covered in the literature, as noted by Pinkerton and Weaver (1970), are personality characteristics and behavior patterns of the patient, association of asthma with psychiatric illness generally, precipitation of attacks by emotional factors, relationship of asthma to psychosis, electroencephalographic abnormalities of allergic diseases, and allergic aspects of behavior disorders. Comprehensive literature reviews of the psychological aspects of asthma include those of Leigh (1953), Wittkower and White (1959), Wright (1965), Leigh and Marley (1967), and Kelly and Zeller (1969). Interesting accounts concerning the potency of psychological factors in asthma are reported increasingly in the literature, an example of which is a study by Luparello, Leist, Lourie and Sweet (1970) which showed how appropriate suggestion could significantly modify or even reverse the pharmacological effect on airway reactivity of administered bronchodilators or bronchoconstrictors in asthmatic subjects.

### Referral Pattern

Asthma represents one of the most important of the psychosomatic disorders, and will be discussed in some detail from the standpoint of modern psychological treatment available.

Typically, the patient presents to a family physician's office or to the emergency room of a hospital during a first asthmatic attack which may be mild or severe, or after having experienced several attacks. In general, the somatic component becomes the focus of treatment, and the administration of a bronchodilator or, in more serious attacks, epinephrine or steroids, terminates the attack. The next step usually consists of referral to an allergist who may carry out immunological investigations and make recommendations concerning allergen removal or desensitization. If infection is present in the chest, it is treated with antibiotics. A regimen consisting of preventive measures and drug treatment of attacks when they occur is developed, and this may be simple or complicated, depending upon the severity of the illness.

It is the usual experience that only as a last resort will a bronchial asthma patient be referred to a mental health professional for consultation or treatment. If he is, the type of psychological treatment he receives is based largely on the particular training and orientation of the therapist.

The extent to which different degrees of attention will be paid to somatic and psychological components, respectively, depends on several factors:

1. the true proportions and interrelationships of these components in the individual patient;

2. the attitude of the patient — one can see extremes from insistence on a purely somatic etiology with rejection of psychological factors to an overemphasis on the latter and disregard of at times life-threatening physical aspects;

3. the orientation of the physician — there is a wide spectrum of attitudes in this regard, with origins rooted in personality, medical school and residency training, previous experience with such patients, and the outcome of previous psychiatric referral of such patients.

The following methods are reflections of various theoretical approaches to the problem, and have all met with some degree of success. They will each be briefly discussed as they apply to bronchial asthma.

Psychoanalysis and Psychotherapy

Many psychodynamic formulations about asthma have been advanced. Authors mentioned in the introduction to this section should be consulted for full details. Concerning the personality and conflicts of asthma patients, Wittkower and Engels (1965, p. 149) comment:

> . . . it is now generally held that behavior and appearances vary widely, but that underlying a variety of superficial manifestations there is generally a deep-seated emotional insecurity and an intense need for a parental love and protection. Fear of losing support, goodwill and love, however, it may be manifested, is an outstanding feature of the premorbid personality of asthmatics.

Knapp and Nemetz (1960) studied several hundred acute asthmatic attacks and postulated that stress, emotional arousal and failing defenses activated unconscious conflicts in which destructive urges and affects are inhibited by guilt and fear, while primitive longings and urges to take in, retain and eliminate through the respiratory apparatus, are accentuated.

A very early survey by Pollnow, Wittkower and Petow (1929) reported on the treatment of 43 asthmatics by 18 authors who used psychotherapeutic methods ranging from waking suggestion and sedative hypnosis to psychoanalysis. Twenty-three of these were reported as "cured" of their asthma and a further 18 had relapses after previously successful treatment. Wilson (1941) reported on the psychoanalytic treatment of 7 patients with hay fever, several of whom had other allergic manifestation, including bronchial asthma.

In their later monograph, French and Alexander (1941) provided a theoretical formulation concerning the emotional background of asthma attacks as well as data outlining results of psychoanalytically-oriented treatment in a series of patients. Briefly stated, they theorized that asthmatic attacks tend to be precipitated by situations threatening to separate the patient from some maternal figure. Although the feared separation may involve actual physical removal, more frequently it concerns the danger of alienation from the parental figure due to some temptation – sexual, aggressive or otherwise – to which the patient is exposed. In such a situation the asthma attacks may represent a suppressed cry whose direct expression is considered as forbidden.

Concerning their outcome study, French and Alexander (1941) reported on 16 adults, followed up for from 3 months to 4 years. Of the total, 6 broke off treatment and 6 were still in analysis at the time of publication. Eight were considered free of symptoms, 5 were much improved, and 3 were unchanged. Of 11 children treated, 3 only were symptom-free, 3 were improved and 4 were unchanged. The maximum follow-up was for 20 months and in 9 cases treatment was interrupted. There were no further follow-up studies after 1941 from the Alexander group.

Billings (1947) treated 13 patients with asthma. Reporting on results, he claimed: 1 patient well after 5 years, 2 greatly improved after 2 years, 3 improved after 2 or 3 years, 2 unimproved after 2 years. Of 5 patients who could not be followed up, 4 were improved or slightly improved and 1 unimproved on discharge. A similar study by O'Neill (1952) of 20 cases (13 adults and 7 children) observed from a few months to more than 3 years suggested great improvement in 9, reduction of attacks in 7, and no change in the remaining 4 patients.

Bastiaans and Groen (1955), reporting on their experience using psychoanlaytically-oriented psychotherapy, claim that cure, defined as a situation in which patients can be discharged and stay well without further treatment, has been achieved in only a few cases. In their sample many of the successes do well only as long as they maintain some connection with the therapist. This may involve regular therapy, an occasional phone call, or simple assurance of availability if required. They refer to the many difficulties associated with assessing the outcome of psychotherapy, but are of the opinion that their results are so much better than those of routine medical treatment that further efforts seem justified.

The same authors, commenting on some of the phenomena they have encountered during the course of therapy, mention that the therapist should be prepared for unexpected improvement after a few sessions. This initial success, say Bastiaans and Groen, is due in part to removal of the patient from the "asthmatogenic" environment, as well as a new feeling of security in the therapeutic situation. However, symptoms inevitably return as repressed conflicts come to the surface and the patient realizes that even the therapist is not going to be the completely submissive parent he had hoped to find. Another common finding is that asthmatic attacks developing during therapy sessions may serve as an indicator of resistance to the emergence of conflict-laden material. Miller and Baruch (1953) have reported their use of psychotherapy during acute attacks of asthma.

Returning to outcome studies, Weiss (1959) reported on a highly allergic patient suffering at various times in her life from bronchial asthma, seasonal hay fever, allergic rhinitis, urticaria and contact dermatitis who had been free of symptoms for eight years after psychoanalysis.

In the treatment of allergic children, Falliers (1969) reported three fundamental changes associated with the manifest alleviation of symptoms following psychotherapy of any type: (1) a modification of physiologic function, such as hormonal homeostasis or autonomic reactivity; (2) a reduction in the range of triggering stimuli as, for example, the removal of a child from a tense family situation, or treatment of the family to reduce tensions, or teaching the child to modify his anxiety; and (3) a sufficient alteration in the patient's attitude toward the disease, which results in a reduction of what might be considered "secondary symptoms."

A study by Purcell, Bernstein and Bukantz (1961) divided asthmatic children into two groups based on the response of their asthmatic symptomatology to separation from the parental home.   The rapidly-remitting group (Group I) became dramatically symptom-free and remained so without medication.   The steroid-dependent group (Group II) required continuous corticosteroid treatment for symptom control.   Comparison of the groups showed that Group I had significantly later onset of asthma and more neurotic symptoms than Group II. Also, the parents of the first group, as measured by attitude tests, were found to be more hostile and rejecting in relation to child-rearing and family relationships than their Group II counterparts.

The original studies of Peshkin (1930) concerning "parentectomy" for 25 intractably severe asthmatic children reported great improvement in 23 subjects, the period of separation varying from two months to over one year.   In a control group of 16 who did not leave home no improvement occurred.   The use of temporary separation, combined with intensive and comprehensive institutional treatment, has since proven of considerable value in the rehabilitation of asthmatic children.   Related to this, Peshkin (1960) has established the value of investigative psychotherapy in easing the return of these children to their homes.

At times it may be productive to focus therapeutic attention not only on the asthmatic child, but on one or both parents as well.   Miller and Baruch (1960) report on their use of individual psychotherapy in parents of allergic children.

Dennis and Hirt (1965) suggest that no techniques of psychotherapy have been developed which seem exclusively appropriate for asthmatics. These authors outline a variety of characterological defects among many asthmatics and point out that these defects complicate the psychotherapeutic process.   In addition, they believe that asthmatics function best in a highly predictable environment, requiring external control to lessen their anxiety.

Leigh and Marley (1967), in reviewing the published outcome studies on psychotherapy in bronchial asthma, find themselves unable to come to definite conclusions. They summarize: "The lack of adequate controls or of sufficient follow-up renders much of the work quoted as of little more than anecdotal value. There still exists the need for a well-controlled study of the effect of individual psychotherapy in bronchial asthma" (p. 108).

Psychopharmacology

As Pinkerton and Weaver (1970, p. 100) point out, the aim of therapy in bronchial asthma is "to stabilize the labile bronchus." In the medical armamentarium the traditional bronchodilators such as aminophylline and isoprotorenol were joined about two decades ago by the corticosteroids and more recently by agents such as disodium cromoglycate (Jones and Blackhall, 1970) which are thought to act by local interference with the antigen-antibody reaction which initiates bronchospasm.   As could be expected, relief of bronchospasm by these agents leads in itself to an improvement in the psychological state, especially by removal of the anxiety secondary to the threat to such a vital organ system.

There are several references in the literature to the usefulness of employing tranquilizers as adjunctive treatment combined with other measures. Crocket (1960) suggested that chlorpromazine was the most satisfactory tranquilizer in asthma, particularly in the presence of severe distress. Meprobamate, although a good sedative, had little effect on the asthma itself. Chlordiazepoxide, in a double-blind study (McGovern, Ozkaragoz, Barkin *et al.*, 1960),was found useful in reducing emotional patterns and allergic symptoms in 45 of 50 allergic children treated with it.

A controlled study by Fox (1958) found that the combination of the minor tranquilizer hydroxyzine with the corticosteroid prednisolone offered several advantages over the latter alone in the short-term symptomatic treatment of bronchial asthma and other allergic disorders. This was substantiated in an independent report by Santos and Unger (1960).

Sanger (1962) reported on the usefulness of various ataractic drugs in the management of bronchial asthma, also mentioning that phenobarbital was found satisfactory in many instances. Of the antidepressant drugs, he claimed the tricyclics, especially amitriptyline, were more effective than monoamine oxidase inhibitors. Sanger felt that psychotropic drugs are useful adjunctive therapy but not a substitute for adequate allergic management. Meares, Mills and Horvath (1971) claimed beneficial results with the use of amitriptyline in asthma, suggesting its effect is probably due not to an antidepressant action, but to antagonism of bronchoconstrictor substances.

## Behavior Therapy

Turnbull (1962) put forward a detailed and sophisticated theoretical model to account for the pathogenic factors in asthma which are learned. He postulated that asthma-like responses may first occur as unconditioned responses to allergens and then become conditioned responses to neutral stimuli by the ordinary process of classical conditioning. Several clinical examples are given including asthmatic attacks precipitated by exposure to symbolic cues such as photographs of scenes which originally seemed to precipitate attacks. This could be an example of stimulus generalization. It seems that asthma-like behavior or respiratory changes can be induced by emotionally disturbing material, allergens, or aversive stimuli and can then be conditioned to previously neutral stimuli, A second learning process suggested by Turnbull involves the shaping that can occur in operant conditioning. If crying or other respiratory responses emitted by the child are not effectively rewarded, for example, by comfort and attention from mother, he is likely to perform slightly different responses to obtain reinforcement and asthmatic breathing may become a more effective method of obtaining reward. If this occurs asthmatic breathing may become a frequent operant response emitted both to obtain positive reward or anxiety reduction. Operant conditioning could therefore account for the development of asthma behavior in subjects in whom allergic stimuli do not elicit asthma.

Other early writers on the concept of bronchial asthma as a conditioned response include Jaspers (1948) and Franks and Leigh (1959). Moore (1965) presents a theoretical model, modified after Osgood's mediation hypothesis (Osgood, 1953) to explain the production of conditioned bronchospasm with the factors facilitating and defacilitating the response.

Using Wolpe's (1958) technique of reciprocal inhibition, Walton (1960a) was the first to apply learning theory to the treatment of a case of bronchial asthma. In this treatment the unadaptive conditioned reflex of bronchospasm was extinguished by conditioning an incompatible response, namely, relaxation, to the conditioned stimulus.  The patient was at first deconditioned to fantasy situations far removed from the causative stimulus, and then getting gradually nearer to it.  Theoretically, then, whenever the conditioned stimulus presents, the response is relaxation instead of bronchospasm. Another early case report by Cooper (1964) produced good results in a 24-year-old asthmatic woman. Following a program of inpatient desensitization the patient was followed up by boosters on an outpatient basis and Cooper considered this a feasible program which might have great applicability in the treatment of chronic asthmatics. Moore (1965), in a controlled study, confirmed his hypothesis that reciprocal inhibition is the crucial factor in the production of improvement in both the subjective feeling of the patient and in the respiratory function.

Wohl (1971) has written on the applicability of behavior modification to the study and treatment of childhood asthma. In discussing the aspect of operant conditioning, he comments that it probably occurs more in those individuals with a stronger psychological component to their asthma, but theoretically the same factors could act powerfully even in those cases more clearly of an allergic nature.

The rapidly developing area of biofeedback has very recently been applied to asthma in a study by Davis, Saunders, Creer and Chai (1973). They note that the application of this technique to asthma is a logical development considering recent work showing the ability of asthmatics to learn to monitor and control their attacks (Budzynski and Stoyva, 1969). In this study the authors include 24 subjects in two age groups: the first 6–10, and the second 11–15. One half of each age group was considered severe (on steroids) and one half not severe (no steroids). There were three groups of 8 children each and in experimental group I the children received modified Jacobsonian relaxation training assisted by biofeedback.  The second experimental group received relaxation training without feedback, whereas the third group served as a control and was provided with assorted reading material and told to relax. The biofeedback was provided by the use of a specially designed apparatus which enabled the subjects to "hear" their muscle tension, while being provided with the opportunity to manipulate it.  In the present study the latter was accomplished by instructing the subject to try to lower the tone that he heard.  By a gradual shaping procedure, the sensitivity level of the machine was increased as a given subject improved in his ability to relax.  The PEFR (Peak Expiratory Flow Rate) was measured three times daily. The study took 3 weeks in all, including a baseline period of 8 days, a treatment period of 5 days, and a post-treatment assessment period requiring 8 days. Medication schedules were held constant throughout the experiment. In the findings a significant difference was found between the treatment groups of non-severe asthmatics. These children showed, over 5 biofeedback facilitated relaxation sessions, a reduction in airway resistance that was significantly greater than that evidenced by the control group. The subjects with relaxation training only also improved, but not as much. No significant differences were found between the treatment conditions of the severe, that is, the steroid dependent subjects. This obviously has important implications for treatment. There are no clear-cut explanations for the differences noted between the severe and the non-severe subjects although the severe group was found to show extreme response variability. It was noted that the PEFR readings in the post-treatment weeks were not significantly different. Thus the improvement occurred during treatment but was not maintained in the post-treatment period. The authors point out that further work is needed to evaluate the possibility of more sustained improvement.

## Group Therapy

As noted previously, group therapy has been applied to the psychological management of several psychosomatic disorders, among them bronchial asthma. Stein (1971) mentions that most studies of its application in this condition report some benefit. In reporting on the study of a group whose members were all asthmatic, Clapham and Sclare (1958) found that identification occurring with other group members allowed these patients to overcome an initial guardedness and to move on to produce affect-laden material with resultant improvement.

Reed (1962) describes the use of group psychotherapy as part of a comprehensive treatment approach in 125 patients who had suffered from asthma for at least five years and whose response to medical management had been unsatisfactory. He reports significant reduction in morbidity, attributing this to "the breaking of the pathologic dependence upon the hospital or emergency room and the parenteral injection which is acquired by most patients with severe asthma" (p. 825).

Groen and Pelser (1960) report the results of a therapeutic trial with 18 male and 15 female asthma patients who were treated with group psychotherapy combined, if necessary, with ACTH and symptomatic therapy over a period of four and two years, respectively. Comparison with control groups treated symptomatically showed considerable benefit from the combined approach as judged by patients, spouses, and group leaders. Psychological testing of these patients by Barendregt (1957) showed statistically significant changes on the Rorschach responses as compared with control subjects receiving symptomatic therapy.

Two studies have demonstrated the value of group psychotherapy for the parents (Abramson and Peshkin, 1960) or the mothers (Wohl, 1963), respectively, of children with severe bronchial asthma. Reckless (1971) outlines his interesting experience with mixed groups of neurotic and psychosomatic patients, and describes a complicated combination of group interaction, group analytic and behavior modification techniques. Although imaginative, this is a difficult study from which to draw definite conclusions.

## Family Therapy

The authors are unaware of any specific published studies on the use of family group therapy as a specific psychological treatment for bronchial asthma, although its appropriateness has been suggested for this condition (Szyrynski, 1964).

## Hypnosis and Suggestion

The controversy over the nature and therapeutic benefit of hypnotic suggestion is reflected in the literature on the use of this technique in bronchial asthma. Houghton (1967) reports his experience, claiming that an auto-hypnotic trance lasting 15 minutes can be used to avert impending asthmatic attacks. Frequent reinforcement of the method is necessary, and treatment may extend to a year or more. Houghton claims the procedure is usefully employed at bedtime to induce relaxation and reduce the frequency of nocturnal attacks. He reports disappointing results in patients who have been previously maintained on steroids for long periods, have developed superimposed chronic bronchitis, or have underlying psychosis. Marchesi (1949) and Van Pelt (1949) have both reported favorably on the use of hypnosis in asthma and Raginsky (1959) is in agreement, although cautioning against a too rapid removal of symptoms. Several authors stress the benefits of employing hypnosis judiciously to facilitate the progress of psychotherapy in asthmatic subjects.

There are relatively few well-controlled studies on the use of hypnosis in asthma. Most reported trials have lacked objective measurement of the degree of airway obstruction, and some studies rely principally on the patient's own report of his clinical state.

A study by Maher-Loughman, Macdonald, Mason and Fry (1962) reported that patients treated with hypnosis and auto-hypnosis showed significantly greater improvement than noted in a matched control group. A later study (British Tuberculosis Association, 1968) compared 127 subjects who were given hypnosis monthly and practiced auto-hypnosis daily, with 125 control subjects who were prescribed a specially devised set of breathing exercises aimed at progressive relaxation. Assessment by independent physicians after one year found the asthma to be "much better" in 59% of the hypnosis group and 43% of the control group. Physicians with previous experience of hypnosis obtained significantly better results than those without such experience.

This study was criticized by Freedman (1968) who claimed that the patient's subjective assessment of wheezing, one of the variables examined, was quite unreliable when he was under the influence of post-hypnotic suggestion. He points out that the only objective tests undertaken, monthly recording of forced expiratory volume and vital capacity, showed no difference between the treated and control groups. His conclusion is that hypnosis may be just a euphoriant. This compares with a point made by Edwards (1960) that even in the absence of a physiological benefit as reflected in improved ventilatory function, hypnosis sometimes conferred a lack of awareness of the disability, and he suggested that this alone was therapeutically useful.

Clarke (1970) has shown significant mean decreases in FEV (Forced Expiratory Volume) of 19.8% after hypnotic suggestion of an attack of asthma alone and 22.4% after the simultaneous suggestions of fear, anger, and attack of asthma and cough. Although this and another study (Smith, Colebatch and Clarke, 1970) provided evidence that hypnotic suggestion could be used to modify pulmonary resistance, other studies have demonstrated that suggestion alone, in the absence of hypnosis, can produce such changes (Dekker and Groen, 1956; Luparello, Lyons, Bleecker and McFadden, 1968). Moore (1965) makes the point that the therapeutic effect of hypnosis is analogous to that of deep relaxation but that additional benefits might be conferred by techniques of suggestion or reciprocal inhibition given under hypnosis.

## Autogenic Therapy

Luthe and Schultz (1969) indicate that the autogenic approach in the treatment of bronchial asthma is based on three factors: (a) certain nonspecific modifications of central nervous system activities, as reflected by certain changes of diencephalic coordination and changes in behavior, (b) localized organ-specific changes of a neuromuscular and circulatory nature, and (c) the patient's experience that he himself can deal effectively with the asthmatic attacks without the necessity for drugs. The treatment program involves a combination of standard exercises and organ-specific approaches designed to meet a number of the physiological and psychodynamic implications of the disease. Luthe and Schultz have found small groups useful in introducing asthmatic patients to the initial stages of autogenic training.

Schultz (1928) was the first to apply this method to bronchial asthma, and more recent studies (Schenk, 1958; Kleinsorge and Lazarus, 1966) have reported cure or significant improvement in approximately two-third of patients treated, with follow-up for up to seven years. Schenk (1958) noted marked improvement of anxiety and paroxysms after about 11 days of heaviness and warmth training, and dependency on drugs fell sharply within two weeks.

There are some limitations reported in applying the method to asthmatic children, particularly those below the age of nine who usually have difficulty maintaining passive concentration effectively (Luthe and Schultz, 1969). Dorlochter (1949) has found it useful with children to practice the first few exercises under hypnosis, emphasizing colorful pictorial illustrations of the heaviness formula.

### Bronchial Asthma — Case Report

It may be appropriate to conclude this chapter with an illustrative case history which highlights some of the points made.

Miss X was a 20-year-old female suffering from bronchial asthma since the age of 13. She was referred by a general practitioner who had noticed that her parents' divorce and the onset of puberty precipitated her bronchial asthma and that the recurrence of attacks was closely associated with various emotional upheavals such as loss of a job, an abortion, disappointment with her first boyfriend and situations of tension which she could not master.

The asthma seemed to represent an attempt to bring her separated parents back together; to express distress over a lost oneness with a rejecting mother, and to gain attention and express her frustration. During therapeutic sessions, when angry, she attempted to suppress this feeling, often thus triggering off respiratory distress and even frank asthmatic attacks. In a dream her mother was criticizing her choice of carpets. The patient listened and was afraid of displeasing her. In an angry voice, the mother directed her second husband to change them and they bought "the ugliest and cheapest carpets." The patient at that moment protested but her mother wouldn't "listen to a word I said." "Then I woke up suffocating — I could hardly catch my breath." The day residue was the fact that the patient, who was no longer living at her mother's, had bought a couple of carpets. During an asthma attack in the session she tried to recapture the dream by looking at the carpets and felt a distinct fear and later guilt at having spent money on such expensive carpets. At that moment she heard her mother's voice as if in her dream yelling at her: "Are your friends and your carpets more important: Don't you love me enough?" The patient realized the struggle for and against a symbiotic need toward her mother, started to cry, and the asthma attack was interrupted. The patient has a facade of going her own way, yet: "I want to say please don't go. I don't want to be alone but I don't let myself."

She was being followed concomitantly by the general practitioner during the course of psychotherapy. Periodically it became necessary during therapy to call the physician because of aggravation of her symptoms and to monitor closely the effect of corticosteroids or sympathomimetic drugs upon her mentation and emotional state.

She gradually became aware of how she could induce her asthma attacks. "I will make myself so sick that father will realize and come back to me." At 13 her parents came together to see her and she was so happy that all symptoms vanished during an attack. Her need for affection and attention, her anger and resentment at her mother were expressed during an attack in the following manner: "It was *not* to hurt mother, I just wanted to have her for myself." One time her mother became angry at her during an attack and told her that it was all her fault and that she should be able to stop it, which frightened the patient. The incipient attack was suddenly aborted. Her mother used to ridicule her tears and ended up "paying more attention to my asthma than to my sobbing."

During therapy she brought up many issues: fantasized aggression against her mother or her deserting father; feelings of worthlessness and helplessness for having submitted to an abortion, or for being at the mercy of a rejecting mother; feelings of guilt and self-pity, and conflict over the need to dominate and control others like mother did; and a masochistic need to be rejected and criticized to preserve the symbiotic bind with an overpowering mother. Her need for love was so tremendous that during the course of therapy she excelled so as to live up to what she felt would please the therapist. Going to college, finding another job, getting married and bringing dreams were an expression of her transference reaction and helped her to overcome her psychological invalidism and destructive mother fixation. Fear of loss of love, fear of closeness and, at the same time, a wish to incorporate (or inhale) the therapist became triggering factors of asthma during several sessions. For a long period she spoke of wishing to be a psychiatrist and under the therapist's instigation interpreted to herself what she wanted to hear from me and her mother. Her independence and pride were defenses against a demanding and exacting need for dependency and closeness. During that phase she wanted to undergo hypnosis to stop her asthma once and for all. Her need for an idealized, nurturing symbiosis with a good mother was interpreted.

The therapist became gradually her lost father who protected her from the regressive, overprotective, infantilizing and punitive influence of a guilt-ridden and overcontrolling mother. Her need for steroids decreased, the attacks became less frequent and allergies that formerly had precipitated an attack no longer did so. The principal gains in therapy surrounded the acquisition of a real identity separate from her mother and the adequate grieving of her losses.

## REFERENCES

Abramson, H.A. and Peshkin, M.M. Psychosomatic group therapy with parents of children with intractable asthma. *Annals of Allergy.* 18: 87–91 (1960).

Ackerman, N. Family psychotherapy: some areas of controversy. *Comprehensive Psychiatry.* 7: 375–388 (1966).

Agras, S. and Marshall, C. The application of negative practice to spasmodic torticollis. *American Journal of Psychiatry.* 122: 579–582 (1965).

Ajuriaguerra, J. and Garcia-Badaracco, J. Les therapeutiques de relaxation en medecine psychosomatique. *La Presse Medicale.* 61: 316–320 (1953).

Alexander, F. Emotional factors in essential hypertension. *Psychosomatic Medicine.* 1: 173–179 (1939).

Alexander, F. *Psychosomatic medicine: its principles and applications.* New York: Norton, 1950.

Alexander, F. The development of psychosomatic medicine. *Psychosomatic Medicine.* 24: 13–24 (1962).

Alexander, F. and French, T.M. *Psychoanalytic therapy.* New York: Ronald Press, 1946.

Alexander, F. and French, T.M. *Studies in psychosomatic medicine.* New York: Ronald Press, 1948.

Alexander, F., French, T.M. and Pollack, G.H. (Eds.) *Psychosomatic specificity. Vol. 1. Experimental study and results.* Chicago: University of Chicago Press, 1968.

Alexander, F.G. and Selesnick, S.T. *The history of psychiatry.* New York: Harper & Row, 1966.

Allen, K.E. and Harris, F.R. Elimination of a child's excessive scratching by training the mother in reinforcement procedures. *Behavior Research and Therapy.* 4: 79–84 (1966).

Ambrose, G. and Newbold, G. *A handbook of medical hypnosis* (2nd ed.). London: Balliere, Tindall & Cassell, 1968.

American Thoracic Society. Chronic bronchitis, asthma and pulmonary emphysema. A statement by the Committee on Diagnostic Standards for Nontubercular Respiratory Diseases. *American Review of Respiratory Diseases.* 85: 762–768 (1962).

Anand, B.K., Chhina, G.S. and Singh, B. Some aspects of electroencephalographic studies in Yogis. *Electroencephalography and Clinical Neurophysiology.* 13: 452–456 (1961).

Aponte, H. and Hoffman, L. The open door: a structural approach to a family with an anorectic child. *Family Process.* 12: 1–44 (1973).

Asher, R. Respectable hypnosis. *British Medical Journal.* 1: 309–313 (1956).

Bachrach, A.J., Erwin, W. and Mohr, J.P. The control of eating behavior in an anorexic by operant conditioning techniques. In: Ullmann, L.P. and Krasner, L. (Eds.). *Case studies in behavior modification,* pp. 153–163. New York: Holt, Rinehart & Winston, 1965.

Backman, H.; Kalliola, H. and Ostling, G. Placebo effect in peptic ulcer and other gastrointestinal disorders. *Gastroenterologia* (Basel). 94: 11–20 (1960).

Barber, T.X. *A scientific approach to hypnosis.* New York: Van Nostrand Reinhold, 1969.

Barcai, A. Family therapy in the treatment of anorexia nervosa. *American Journal of Psychiatry.* 128: 286–290 (1971).

Barendregt, J.T. A psychological investigation of the effect of group psychotherapy in patients with bronchial asthma. *Journal of Psychosomatic Research.* 2: 115–119 (1957).

Barrucand, D. L'hypnose de 1769 a 1969. *Encephale.* 58: 447–470 (1969).

Bastiaans, J. The role of aggression in the genesis of psychosomatic disease. *Journal of Psychosomatic Research.* 13: 307–314 (1969).

Bastiaans, J. and Groen, J. Psychogenesis and psychotherapy of bronchial asthma. In: O'Neil, D. (Ed.), *Modern trends in psychosomatic medicine,* pp. 242–268. London: Butterworth & Co., 1955.

Beall, G.N., Heiner, D.C., Tashkin, D.P. and Whipp, B.J.   Asthma:   new ideas about an old disease. *Annals of Internal Medicine.* 78:   405–419 (1973).

Benson, H., Herd, A.J., Morse, W.H. and Kelleher, R.T.   Behavioral induction of arterial hypertension and its reversal. *American Journal of Physiology.* 217: 30–34 (1969).

Billings, E.G.   Dynamic and therapeutic features of 17 cases of so-called psychogenic asthma. *Rocky Mountain Medical Journal.* 44:   197–199 (1947).

Birnbaum, D.   The influence of psychotropic drugs on gastrointestinal function: experimental and clinical data.   In:   Pletscher, A. and Marino, A. (Eds.), *Psychotropic drugs in internal medicine,* pp. 101–108.   Amsterdam:   Excerpta Medica Foundation, 1969.

Black, S.   The use of hypnosis in the treatment of psychosomatic disorders. In: Hopkins, P. and Wolff, H.H. (Eds.), *Principles of treatments of psychosomatic disorders,* pp. 59–68.   Oxford:   Pergamon, 1965.

Bleecker, E.R. and Engel, B.T.   Learned control of ventricular rate in patients with atrial fibrillation. *Psychosomatic Medicine.* 35:   161–175 (1973).

Blinder, B.J., Freeman, D.M.A. and Stunkard, A.J.   Behavior therapy of anorexia nervosa:   effectiveness of activity as a reinforcer of weight gain. *American Journal of Psychiatry.* 126:   1093–1098 (1970).

Bloch, B.   Uber die heilung der warzen durch suggestion. *Klinische Wochenschrift.* 6:   2271–2275 (1927).

Bobon, J., Breulet, M., Degossely, M. and Dongier, M.   Le training autogene dans les maladies et les dysfonctions cardiovasculaires.   In:   Lopez Ibor, J.J.(Ed.), *IV World Congress of Psychiatry,* Madrid, 1966.   International Congress Series, No. 117, 44. Amsterdam:   Exerpta Medica Foundation, 1966.

Bonfils, S. and Dubrasquet, M.   Psychotropic drugs in experimental peptic ulcer induced by psychological stress.   In:   Pletscher, A. and Marino, A. (Eds.), *Psychotropic drugs in internal medicine,* pp. 80–94.   Amsterdam:   Excerpta Medica Foundation, 1969.

Brandsma, M.   Preliminary experience with medazepam (nobrium) in the management of psychophysiologic reactions. *Psychosomatics.* 11:   197– 200 (1970).

Brautigam, W. and Christian, P. *Psychosomatische Medizin.*   Stuttgart:   George Thieme, Verlag, 1973.

Brierley, H.   The treatment of hysterical spasmodic torticollis by behavior therapy. *Behavior Research and Therapy.* 5:   139–142 (1967).

British Medical Association.   Medical use of hypnotism.   Report of a subcommittee appointed by the Psychological Medicine Group Committee of the British Medical Association. *British Medical Journal Supplement.* 1:   190–193 (1955).

British Tuberculosis Association.   Hypnosis for asthma – a controlled trial.   A report to the Research Committee of the British Tuberculosis Association. *British Medical Journal.* 4: 71–76 (1968).

Brodmann, K.   Zur Methodik der hypnotischen Behandlung. *Zeitschrift fur Hypnotismus, Psychotherapie, Psychophysiologie und Psychopathologie Forschungen.* 10:   314–375 (1902).

Browning, C.H. and Miller, S.I.   Anorexia nervosa: a study in prognosis and management. *American Journal of Psychiatry.* 124:   1128–1132 (1968).

Budzynski, T.H. and Stoyva, J.M.   An instrument for producing deep muscle relaxation by means of analog information feedback. *Journal of Applied Behavior Analysis.* 2: 231–237 (1969).

Budzynski, T.H., Stoyva, J.M. and Adler, C.  Feedback-induced muscle relaxation: application to tension headache. *Journal of Behavior Therapy and Experimental Psychiatry.* 1: 205–211 (1970).

Byrne, S.  Hypnosis and the irritable bowel: case histories, methods and speculation. *The American Journal of Clinical Hypnosis.* 15: 263–272 (1973).

Cain, J.  *Le Symptôme psychosomatique.* Toulouse: Privat, 1971.

Cannon, W.B.  *Bodily changes in pain, hunger, fear and rage.*  New York: Appleton, 1915.

Cannon, W.B.  *The wisdom of the body* (2nd ed.).  New York: Norton, 1939.

Chalke, F.C.R.  Effect of psychotherapy for psychosomatic disorders. *Psychosomatics.* 6: 125–131 (1965).

Chappell, M.N., Stefano, J.J., Rogerson, J.S. and Pike, F.H.  The value of group psychological procedures in the treatment of peptic ulcer. *American Journal of Digestive Diseases.* 3: 813–817 (1936–1937).

Cheek, D.B. and Le Cron, L.M.  *Clinical hypnotherapy.*  New York: Grune & Stratton, 1968.

Chesser, E. and Meyer, V.  Behavior therapy and psychosomatic illness.  In: Hill, O.W. (Ed.), *Modern trends in psychosomatic medicine.* 2: 262–277. London: Butterworths, 1970.

Clapham, H. and Sclare, A.  Group psychotherapy with asthmatic patients. *International Journal of Group Psychotherapy.* 8: 44–54 (1958).

Clarke, P.S.  Effects of emotion and cough on airways obstruction in asthma. *Medical Journal of Australia.* 1: 535–537 (1970).

Cohen, S.I. and Reed, J.L.  The treatment of "nervous diarrhoea" and other conditioned autonomic disorders by desensitization.  *British Journal of Psychiatry.* 114: 1275–1280 (1968).

Cooper, A.J.  A case of bronchial asthma treated by behavior therapy. *Behavior Research and Therapy.* 1: 351–356 (1964).

Cooper, M. and Katz, J.  The treatment of migraine and tension headache with group psychotherapy. *International Journal of Group Psychotherapy.* 6: 266–271 (1956).

Corson, J.A., Bouchard, C., Scherer, M.W., Amit, Z., Hisey, L.G., Cleghorn, R.A. and Golden, M. Instrumental control of autonomic responses with the use of a cognitive strategy. A case report. *Canadian Psychiatric Association Journal.* 18: 21–24 (1973).

Crider, A., Schwartz, G.E. and Shnidman, S.  On the criteria for instrumental autonomic conditioning:   a reply to Katkin and Murray. *Psychological Bulletin.* 71: 455–461 (1969).

Crisp, A.H.  A treatment regime for anorexia nervosa. *British Journal of Psychiatry.* 112: 505–512 (1966).

Crocket, J.A.  Experiences with tranquillising drugs in asthma. *Acta Allergologica.* Suppl. VII: 355–359 (1960).

DSM II.  *Diagnostic and statistical manual of mental disorders* (2nd ed.), American Psychiatric Association.  Washington: APA Publications, 1968.

Daniels, G.E., O'Connor, J.F., Karush, A., Moses, L., Flood, C.A. and Lepore, M. Three decades in the observation and treatment of ulcerative colitis. *Psychosomatic Medicine.* **24**: 85–93 (1962).

Davidson, R. and Krippner, S. Biofeedback research: the data and their implications. In: Stoyva, J., Barber, T.X., DiCara, L.V., Kamiya, J., Miller, N.E. and Shapiro, D. (Eds.), *Biofeedback and self-control 1971*, pp. 3–34. Chicago: Aldine-Atherton, 1972.

Davis, M.H., Saunders, D.R., Creer, T.L. and Chai, H. Relaxation training facilitated by biofeedback apparatus as a supplemental treatment in bronchial asthma. *Journal of Psychosomatic Research.* **17**: 121–128 (1973).

Dekker, E., Barendregt, J.T. and De Vries, K. Allergy and neurosis in asthma. In: Jores, A. and Freyberger, H. (Eds.), *Advances in psychosomatic medicine,* pp. 235–240. New York: Brunner, 1961.

Dekker, E. and Groen, J. Reproducible psychogenic attacks of asthma. *Journal of Psychosomatic Research.* **1**: 58–67 (1956).

de M'Uzan, M. Therapeutique psychosomatique. *Encyclopedie Medico-Chirurgicale, Psychiatrie,* 11 37492 A10, X-1959, 1–6.

Dennis, M. and Hirt, M. Treatment of the asthmatic patient. In: Hirt, M. (Ed.), *Psychological and allergic aspects of asthma,* pp. 296–320. Springfield: Charles C. Thomas, 1965.

Deutsch, A.L. and Lippman, A. Group psychotherapy for patients with psychosomatic illness. *Psychosomatics.* **5**: 14–20 (1964).

Deutsch, F. (Ed.) *The psychosomatic concept in psychoanalysis.* New York: International Universities Press, 1953.

Diamond, S. Amitriptyline in the treatment of gastrointestinal disorders. *Psychosomatics.* **5**: 221–224 (1964).

Dorlochter, Fr. Probleme beider Behandlung kindlichen Bronchial-asthma mit autogenem Training. *Mschr. Kinderheilk.* **97**: 208–212 (1949).

Druss, R.G., O'Connor, J.F., Prudden, J.F. and Stern, L.O. Psychologic response to colectomy. *Archives of General Psychiatry.* **18**: 53–59 (1968).

Dunbar, F. *Emotions and bodily changes.* New York: Columbia University Press, 1938.

Dunbar, F. *Psychosomatic diagnosis.* New York: Hoeber, 1943.

Dunbar, F. *Psychiatry in the medical specialities.* New York: McGraw-Hill, 1959.

Edwards, G. Hypnotic treatment of asthma. Real and illusory results. *British Medical Journal.* **2**: 492–497 (1960).

Efron, R. The conditioned inhibition of uncinate fits. *Brain.* **80**: 251–262 (1957).

Engel, B.T. and Gottlieb, S.H. Differential operant conditioning of heart rate in the restrained monkey. *Journal of Comparative and Physiological Psychology.* **73**: 217–225 (1970).

Engel, B.T. and Hansen, S.P. Operant conditioning of heart rate slowing. *Psychophysiology.* **3**: 176–187 (1966).

Engel, G.L. *Psychological development in health and disease.* Philadelphia: Saunders, 1962.

Engel, G.L. Psychological factors and ulcerative colitis. Correspondence. *British Medical Journal.* **4**: 56 (1967).

Engel, G.L. and Schmale, A.H.   Psychoanalytic theory of somatic disorder: conversion, specificity and the disease onset situation. *Journal of the American Psychoanalytic Association.* **15**: 334–365 (1967).

Enke, H.   Somatization and group psychotherapy.   *Psychiat. Neurol. Med. Psychol.* **20**: 4 (1968).

Erickson, M.H.   An introduction to the study and application of hypnosis for pain control.   In:   Lassner, J. (Ed.), *Hypnosis and psychosomatic medicine,* pp. 83–90. Berlin:   Springer Verlag, 1965.

Evans, W.L.   Clinical experience with phenelzine in psychosomatic and psychophysiologic disorders. *New York State Journal of Medicine,* **60**:   865–868 (1960).

Eysenck, H.J.   A theory of the incubation of anxiety/fear responses. *Behavior Research and Therapy.* **6**: 309–321 (1968).

Falliers, C.J. Psychosomatic study and treatment of asthmatic children. *Pediatric Clinics of North America.* **16**:   271–286 (1969).

Fenichel, O. *The psychoanalytic theory of neurosis.* New York:   Norton, 1945.

Ferenczi, S.   *Further contributions to the theory and technique of psychoanalysis.* London:   Hogarth, 1926.

Ferster, C.B., Nurnberger, J.I. and Levitt, E.B. The control of eating. *Journal of Mathetics.* **1**: 87–109 (1962).

Fink, J.N. and Sosman, A.J. Therapy of bronchial asthma. *Medical Clinics of North America.* **57**: 801–808 (1973).

Foreyt, J.P. and Kennedy, W.A.   Treatment of overweight by aversion therapy. *Behavior Research and Therapy.* **9**: 29–34 (1971).

Fortin, J. and Abse, D.   Group psychotherapy with peptic ulcer: a preliminary report. *International Journal of Group Psychotherapy.* **6**: 383–391 (1956).

Fox, J.L.   Use of a tranquilizing agent (hydroxyzine) with prednisolone in the control of allergic disorders. *Annals of Allergy.* **16**:   674–677 (1958).

Franks, C.M. and Leigh, D. The theoretical and experimental application of a conditioning model to a consideration of bronchial asthma in man. *Journal of Psychosomatic Research.* **4**: 88–98 (1959).

Freedman, B.J. Hypnosis for asthma. Correspondence. *British Medical Journal.* **4**: 329 (1968).

French, T.M. and Alexander, R.   *Psychogenic factors in bronchial asthma.* Psychosomatic Medicine, Monograph IV.   Washington:   National Research Council, 1941.

Freud, S.   The psycho-analytic view of psychogenic disturbance of vision.   In: Strachey, J. (Ed.), *The standard edition of the complete psychological works of Sigmund Freud, Vol. 11,* pp. 209–218.   London:   Hogarth Press, 1955.

Freyberger, H.   The doctor/patient relationship in ulcerative colitis. *Psychotherapy and Psychosomatics.* **18**: 80–89 (1970).

Freyberger, H.   *Supportive psychotherapy in the medical clinic.*   Paper presented at the Second Congress of the International College of Psychosomatic Medicine in Amsterdam, June 21, 1973.

Friedman, M. and Rosenman, R.H.   Type A behavior pattern:   its association with coronary heart disease. *Annals of Clinical Research.* **3**:   300–312 (1971).

Gannon, L. and Sternbach, R.A.   Alpha enhancement as a treatment for pain: a case study. *Journal of Behavior Therapy and Experimental Psychiatry.* **2**: 209–213 (1971).

Garma, A. On the pathogenesis of gastric ulcer. *International Journal of Psychoanalysis.* **31**: 53–72 (1950).

Garma, A. Group psychoanalysis in patients with peptic ulcer. *Internationale Zeitschrift fur Psychiatrie und Psychoanalyse.* 6 Jahrgang, 1 Heft, 1973.

Goldberg, E.M. *Family influences and psychosomatic illness.* London: Tavistock Publications, 1958.

Greenblatt, D.J. and Shader, R.I. Psychopharmacologic management of anxiety in the cardiac patient. *Psychiatry in Medicine.* **2**: 55–56 (1971).

Greene, W.A. and Swisher, S.N. Psychological and somatic variables associated with the development and course of monozygotic twins discordant for leukemia. *Annals of the New York Academy of Science.* **164**: 394–408 (1969).

Grinker, R.R. *Psychosomatic research.* New York: Norton, 1953.

Groddeck, G. Traumarbeit und arbeit des organischen symptoms. *Internationale Zeitschrift fur Psychoanalyse.* **12**: 504–512 (1926).

Groen, J.J. Treatment of bronchial asthma by a combination of A.C.T.H. and psychotherapy. *Acta Allergologica.* Suppl. III: 21–48 (1953).

Groen, J. and Bastiaans, J. Psychotherapy of ulcerative colitis. *Gastroenterology.* **17**: 344–352 (1951).

Groen, J. and Pelser, H. Experiences with, and results of, group psychotherapy in patients with bronchial asthma. *Journal of Psychosomatic Research.* **4**: 191–205 (1960).

Grolnick, L. A family perspective of psychosomatic factors in illness: a review of the literature. *Family Process.* **11**: 457–486 (1972).

Hagen, R.L. *Group therapy versus bibliotherapy in weight reduction.* Thesis, University of Illinois, Champaign, 1969.

Hahn, H.W. and Clark, J.A. Psychophysiological reactivity of asthmatic children. *Psychosomatic Medicine.* **29**: 526–536 (1967).

Haidar, A. and Clancy, J. Case report of successful treatment of a reflex trigeminal nerve blepharospasm by behavior modification. *American Journal of Ophthalmology.* **75**: 148–149 (1973).

Halliday, J.L. Concept of a psychosomatic affection. *Lancet.* **2**: 692–696 (1943).

Halliday, J.L. *Psychosocial medicine. A study of the sick society.* New York: Norton, 1948.

Hambling, J. The psychosomatic patient. In: Wisdom, J.O. and Wolff, H. (Eds.), *The role of psychosomatic disorders in adult life,* pp. 53–62. Oxford: Pergamon, 1965.

Harding, C.H. Hypnosis in the treatment of migraine. In: Lassner, J. (Ed.), *Hypnosis and psychosomatic medicine,* pp. 131–134. Berlin: Springer-Verlag, 1965.

Harmatz, M.G. and Lapuc, P. Behavior modification of overeating in a psychiatric population. *Journal of Consulting and Clinical Psychology.* **32**: 583–587 (1968).

Harris, M.B. Self-directed program for weight control: a pilot study. *Journal of Abnormal Psychology.* **74**: 263–270 (1969).

Hellerstein, H.K. Reconditioning and the prevention of heart disease. *Modern Medicine of Canada.* **19 (10)**: 161–181 (1964).

Hill, O.W. (Ed.)   *Modern trends in psychosomatic medicine,* 2:   London: Butterworths, 1970.

Hinkle, L.E. and Wolff, H.G.   The nature of man's adaptation to his total environment and the relation of this to illness. *A.M.A. Archives of Internal Medicine.* **99**: 442–460 (1957).

Hinkle, L.E. and Wolff, H.G.  Ecologic investigations of the relationship between illness, life experiences and social environment. *Annals of Internal Medicine.* **49**:1373–1388 (1958).

Holmes, T.H. and Rahe, R.H.   The social readjustment rating scale. *Journal of Psychosomatic Research.* **11**: 213–218 (1968).

Holt, H. and Winick, C.  Group psychotherapy with obese women. *Archives of General Psychiatry.* **5**: 156–168 (1961).

Hopkins, P. and Wolff, H.H. (Eds.)   *Principles of treatments of psychosomatic disorders.* Oxford: Pergamon, 1965.

Horan, J.S. Hypnosis and recorded suggestion in the treatment of migraine: case report. *International Journal of Clinical and Experimental Hypnosis.*   **1**: 7–10 (1953).

Horder, J.P. The approach of the general practitioner. In:  Hopkins, P. and Wolff, H.H. (Eds), *Principles of treatments of psychosomatic disorders,* pp. 103–109. Oxford: Pergamon, 1965.

Houghton, L.E.  Hypnosis and auto-hypnosis in the treatment of asthma. In: Lassner, J. (Ed.), *Hypnosis and psychosomatic medicine,* pp. 157–159. Berlin: Springer-Verlag, 1967.

Janda, L.H. and Rimm, D.C.  Covert sensitization in the treatment of obesity. *Journal of Abnormal Psychology.* **80**: 37–42 (1972).

Jasper, H. and Shagass, C.  Conditioning occipital alpha rhythm in man. *Journal of Experimental Psychology.* **28**: 373–388 (1941).

Jaspers, K.   *Allgemeine Psychopatholgie* (4th ed.).  Berlin:  Springer-Verlag, 1948.

Jones, R.S. and Blackhall, M.I.  The role of disodium cromoglycate ("Intal") in the treatment of childhood asthma. *Archives of Diseases of Childhood.* **45**: 49–53 (1970).

Jordan, H.A. and Levitz, L.S.   Behavior modification in a self-help group. *Journal of the American Dietetic Association.* **62**: 27–29 (1973).

Kamiya, J.  *Conditioned discrimination of the EEG alpha rhythm in humans.* Paper presented at the meeting of the Western Psychological Association, San Francisco, April, 1962.

Kamiya, J.  EEG operant conditioning and the study of states of consciousness. In:  Freedman, D.X. (Chm.), *Laboratory studies of altered psychological states.*   Symposium at the American Psychological Association Meeting, Washington, D.C., September 4, 1967.

Kamiya, J.  Conscious control of brain waves. *Psychology Today.* **1**: 57–60 (1968).

Kamiya, J.  Operant control of the EEG alpha rhythm and some of its reported effects on consciousness. In: Tart, C.T. (Ed.), *Altered states of consciousness.* New York: John Wiley & Sons, 1969.

Kaplan, H.I. and Kaplan, H.S. An historical survey of psychosomatic medicine. *Journal of Nervous and Mental Disease.* **124**: 546–568 (1956).

Kaplan, H.I. and Sadock, B.J. (Eds.) *Comprehensive group psychotherapy.* Baltimore: Williams & Wilkins, 1971.

Kaplan, H.S. Treatment of psychophysiological disorders. In: Freedman, A.M. and Kaplan, H.I. (Eds.), *Comprehensive textbook of psychiatry,* pp. 1113–1119. Baltimore: Williams & Wilkins, 1967.

Kaplan, S.M., Kravetz, R.S. and Ross, W.D. The effects of imipramine on the depressive components of medical disorders. *Proceedings of 3rd World Congree of Psychiatry,* Montreal. **2**: 1362–1367 (1961).

Karush, A., Daniels, G.E., O'Connor, J.F. and Stern, L.O. The response to psychotherapy in chronic ulcerative colitis. II. Factors arising from the therapeutic situation. *Psychosomatic Medicine.* **31**: 201–226 (1969).

Kashiwagi, T., McClure, J., Jr. and Wetzel, R.D. Headache and psychiatric disorder. *Diseases of the Nervous System.* **33**: 659–663 (1972).

Katkin, E.S. and Murray, E.M. Instrumental conditioning of autonomically mediated behavior: theoretical and methodolgocial issues. *Psychological Bulletin.* **70**: 52–68 (1968).

Kaufman, M.R. (Ed.) *Evaluation of psychosomatic concepts.* New York: International Universities Press, 1964.

Kelly, E. and Zeller, B. Asthma and the psychiatrist. *Journal of Psychosomatic Research.* **13**: 377–395 (1969).

Kimmel, H.D. Instrumental conditioning of autonomically mediated behavior. *Psychological Bulletin.* **67**: 337–345 (1967).

Klein M. *Contributions to psychoanalysis.* London : Hogarth, 1948.

Kleinsorge, H. Gezieltes gruppentraining bei organfunktionsstorungen. *Zeitschrift fur Psychotherapie und Medizinische Psychologie.* **4**: 184–193 (1954).

Kleinsorge, H. Psychodiagnostik und psychotherapie bei funktionellen organerkrankungen. In: Hesse, P.G. (Ed.), *Beitrage zur modernen Therapie,* pp. 231–238. Jena: VEB Fischer-Verlag, 1959.

Kleinsorge, H. and Klumbies, G. *Psychotherapie in Klinik und Praxis.* Munchen and Berlin: Urban und Schwarzenberg, 1959.

Kleinsorge, H. and Lazarus, P. Erster Bericht uber die Hochseeklimakur mit MS. "Volkerfreundschaft." *Allergie und Asthma.* **12**: 220–225 (1966).

Klumbies, G. and Eberhardt, G. Results of autogenic training in the treatment of hypertension. In: Lopez Ibor, J.J. (Ed.), *IV World Congress of Psychiatry,* Madrid, 1966. International Congress Series, No. 117, 46–47, Amsterdam: Excerpta Medica Foundation, 1966.

Knapp, P.H. and Nemetz, S.J. Acute bronchial asthma. *Psychosomatic Medicine.* **22**: 42–56 (1960).

Krakowski, A.J. Treatment of psychosomatic gastrointestinal reactions in children. *Diseases of the Nervous System.* **27**: 403–408 (1966).

Kral, V.A. Psychiatric observations under severe chronic stress. *American Journal of Psychiatry.* **108**: 185–192 (1951).

Kroger, W.S. *Clinical and experimental hypnosis in medicine, dentistry and psychology.* Philadelphia, Lippincott, 1963.

Kubie, L.S. *The basis of a classification of disorders from the psychosomatic viewpoint.* Paper presented at the Joint Meeting of the Section of Neurology of the New York Academy of Medicine and the New York Neurological Society, New York, 1943.

Kubie, L.S. The central representation of the symbolic process in psychosomatic disorders. *Psychosomatic Medicine.* **15**: 1-7 (1953).

Kubie, L.S. The struggle between preconscious insights and psychonoxious rewards in psychotherapy. *American Journal of Psychotherapy.* **19**: 365–371 (1965).

Kuhn, R. Psychopathology, pharmacotherapy and psychotherapy of anorexia nervosa. In: Pletscher, A. and Marino, A. (Eds.), *Psychotropic drugs in internal medicine,* pp. 74–79. International Congress Series No. 182, Amsterdam: Excerpta Medica Foundation, 1969.

Lacey, J.I., Kagan, J., Lacey, B.L. and Moss, H.A. The visceral level. Situational determinates and behavioral correlates of autonomic response patterns. In: Knapp, P.H. (Ed.), *Expression of the emotions in man.* New York: International Universities Press, 1963.

Leigh, D. Asthma and the psychiatrist. A critical review. *International Archives of Allergy.* **4**: 227-246 (1953).

Leigh, D. and Marley, E. *Bronchial asthma: a genetic, population and psychiatric study.* Oxford: Pergamon, 1967.

Leitenberg, H., Agras, W.S. and Thomson, L.E. A sequential analysis of the effect of selective positive reinforcement in modifying anorexia nervosa. *Behavior Research and Therapy.* **6**: 211–218 (1968).

Lester, E.P., Wittkower, E.D., Kalz, F. and Azima, H. Phrenotropic drugs in psychosomatic disorders (skin). *American Journal of Psychiatry.* **119**: 136–143 (1962).

Lief, H.I., Lief, V.R. and Lief, N.R. *The psychological basis of medical practice.* New York: Hoeber Medical Division, Harper & Row, 1963.

Lipowski, Z.J. Review of consultation psychiatry and psychosomatic medicine. I. General principles. *Psychosomatic Medicine.* **29**: 153-171 (1967a).

Lipowski, Z.J. Review of consultation psychiatry and psychosomatic medicine. II. Clinical aspects. *Psychosomatic Medicine.* **29**: 201-224 (1967b).

Lipowski, Z.J. Review of consultation psychiatry and psychosomatic medicine. III. Theoretical issues. *Psychosomatic Medicine.* **30**: 395-422 (1968).

Lipowski, Z.J. Psychosomatic medicine in a changing society: some current trends in theory and research. *Comprehensive Psychiatry.* **14**: 203-215 (1973).

Looff, D.H. Psychophysiologic and conversion reactions in children. Selective incidence in verbal and non-verbal families. *Journal of the American Academy of Child Psychiatry.* **9**: 318-331 (1970).

Lowy, F.H. The abuse of abreaction. An unhappy legacy of Freud's cathartic method. *Canadian Psychiatric Association Journal.* **15**: 557-565 (1970).

Luparello, T.J., Leist, N., Lourie, C.H. and Sweet, P. The interaction of psychologic stimuli and pharamacologic agents on airway reactivity in asthmatic subjects. *Psychosomatic Medicine.* **32**: 509-513 (1970).

Luparello, T., Lyons, H.A., Bleecker, E.R. and McFadden, E.R. Influences of suggestion on airway reactivity in asthmatic subjects. *Psychosomatic Medicine.* **30**: 819–825 (1968).

Luthe, W. Lowering of serum cholesterol during autogenic therapy. In: Luthe, W. (Ed.), *International edition: Autogenic training. Correlationes Psychosomaticae,* pp. 88–91. New York and London: Grune & Stratton, 1965.

Luthe, W. *Autogenic therapy. IV. Research and theory.* New York and London: Grune & Stratton, 1970.

Luthe, W. *Autogenic therapy. V. Dynamics of autogenic neutralization.* New York and London: Grune & Stratton, 1970.

Luthe, W. *Autogenic therapy. VI. Treatment with autogenic neutralization.* New York and London: Grune & Stratton, 1973.

Luthe, W. and Schultz, J.H. *Autogenic therapy. II. Medical applications.* New York and London: Grune & Stratton, 1969.

Lynch, J.J. and Paskewitz, D.A. On the mechanisms of the feedback control of human brain wave activity. *Journal of Nervous and Mental Disease.* **153**: 205–217 (1971).

Macalpine, I. Psychosomatic symptom formation. *Lancet.* **1**: 278–282 (1952).

Maher-Loughnan, G.P. Hypnosis and autohypnosis for the treatment of asthma. *International Journal of Clinical and Experimental Hypnosis.* **18**: 1–14 (1970).

Maher-Loughnan, G.P., Macdonald, N., Mason, A.A. and Fry, L. Controlled trial of hypnosis in the symptomatic treatment of asthma. *British Medical Journal.* **2**: 371–376 (1962).

Malmo, R.B., Shagass, C. and Davis, J.F. Symptom specificity and bodily reactions during psychiatric interview. *Psychosomatic Medicine.* **12**: 362–375 (1950).

Malvea, B.P., Gwon, N. and Graham, J.R. Propanolol prophylaxis of migraine. *Headache.* **12**: 163–167 (1973).

Marchesi, C. The hypnotic treatment of bronchial asthma. *British Journal of Medical Hypnosis.* **1**: 14–19 (1949).

Margetts, E.L. Historical notes on psychosomatic medicine. In: Wittkower, E.D. and Cleghorn, R.A. (Eds.), *Recent developments in psychosomatic medicine,* pp. 41–68. Philadelphia and Montreal: J.B. Lippincott, 1954.

Margolin, S.G. Psychotherapeutic principles in psychosomatic practice. In: Wittkower, E.D. and Cleghorn, R.A. (Eds.), *Recent developments in psychosomatic medicine,* pp. 134–153. Philadelphia and Montreal: J.P. Lippincott, 1954.

Marino, A. Pharmacology and psychosomatic medicine: the experimental and clinical approach to a psychosomatic evaluation of psychotropic drugs. In: Pletscher, A. and Marino, A. (Eds.), *Psychotropic drugs in internal medicine,* pp. 47–56. Amsterdam: Excerpta Medica Foundation, 1969.

Marty, P. and de M'Uzan, M. La "pensee operatoire." *Revue Francaise de Psychoanalyse.* **27**: Suppl. 1345 (1963).

Maslow, A.H. *Towards a psychology of being.* New York: Van Nostrand Reinhold, 1962.

McDermott, N.T. and Cobb, S. A psychiatric survey of fifty cases of bronchial asthma. *Psychosomatic Medicine.* **1**: 203–244 (1939).

McGovern, J.P., Ozkaragoz, K., Barkin, G., *et al.* Studies of chlordiazepoxide in various allergic diseases. *Annals of Allergy.* **18:** 1193–1199 (1960).

Mead, M. The concept of culture and the psychosomatic approach. *Psychiatry.* **10:** 57–76 (1947).

Meares, R.A. Behavior therapy and spasmodic torticollis. *Archives of General Psychiatry.* **28:** 104–107 (1973).

Meares, R.A., Mills, J.E. and Horvath, T.B. Amitriptyline and asthma. *Medical Journal of Australia.* **2:** 25–28 (1971).

Medansky, R.S. Emotion and skin: a double-blind evaluation of psychotropic agents. *Psychosomatics.* **12:** 326–329 (1971).

Mees, H.L. and Keutzer, C.S. Short term group psychotherapy with obese women. A pilot project. *Northwest Medicine.* **66:** 548–550 (1967).

Meissner, W.W. Family dynamics and psychosomatic processes. *Family Process.* **5:** 142–161 (1966).

Melzack, R. Personal Communication, 1973.

Merskey, H. An appraisal of hypnosis. *Postgraduate Medical Journal.* **47:** 572–580 (1971).

Meyer, B.C. Aspects de la psychotherapie en medecine psychosomatique. *Revue Francaise de Psychoanalyse.* **19:** 357–380 (1965).

Milberg, I.L. Group psychotherapy in the treatment of some neurodermatoses. *International Journal of Group Psychotherapy.* **6:** 53–60 (1956).

Miller, H. and Baruch, D.W. Psychotherapy in acute attacks of bronchial asthma. *Annals of Allergy.* **11:** 438–444 (1953).

Miller, H. and Baruch, D.W. Psychotherapy of parents of allergic children. *Annals of Allergy.* **18:** 990–997 (1960).

Miller, N.E. Psychosomatic effects of specific types of training. *Annals of the New York Academy of Sciences.* **159:** 1025–1040 (1969).

Miller, N.E. and Carmona, A. Modification of a visceral response, salivation in thirsty dogs, by instrumental training with water reward. *Journal of Comparative and physiological Psychology.* **63:** 1–6 (1967).

Miller, N.E., DiCara, L.V., Solomon, H., Weiss, J.M. and Dworkin, B. Learned modifications of autonomic functions: a review and some new data. *Circulation Research.* **26–7** (Suppl. 1): 3–11 (1970).

Minuchin, S. and Barcai, A. Therapeutically induced family crisis. In: Masserman, J. (Ed.), *Science and psychoanalysis, Vol. 14: Childhood and adolescence,* pp. 199–205. New York: Grune & Stratton, 1969.

Mitchell, K.R. The treatment of migraine: an exploratory application of time limited therapy. *Technology.* **14:** 50–55 (1969).

Mitchell, K.R. A psychological approach to the treatment of migraine. *British Journal of Psychiatry.* **119:** 533–534 (1971).

Moldofsky, H. Symposium on obesity, 1973 Annual Scientific Meeting, Ontario Medical Association. Reported in *Canadian Medical Association Journal.* **108:** 1552 (1973).

Monges, H. and Salducci, J. Influence des psychotropes sur l'evolution de la maladie ulcereuse. *Semaine des Hopitaux de Paris (Therapeutique), 1973,* **49:** 153–155.

Moody, H. *British Journal of Medical Hypnosis.* **5:** 23 (1953).

Moore, N.  Behavior therapy in bronchial asthma:  a controlled study. *Journal of Psychosomatic Research.* **9**:  257–276 (1965).

Mueller-Hegemann, D.  *Psychotherapie Ved Verlag Volk und Gesundheit.*  Berlin: 1959.

Mulholland, T. and Runnals, S.  A stimulus-brain feedback system for evaluation of alertness. *Journal of Psychology.* **54**:  69–83 (1962a).

Mulholland, T. and Runnals, S.  Evaluation of attention and alertness with a stimulus-brain feedback loop.  *Electroencephalography and Clinical Neurophysiology.* **14**:  847–852 (1962b).

Nemiah, J.C.  The psychological management and treatment of patients with peptic ulcer.   In:  Weiner,  H.  (Ed.), *Advances in psychosomatic medicine. Vol. 6: Duodenal ulcer,* pp. 169–185. Basel: Karger, 1971.

Nemiah, J.C. and Sifneos, P.E.  Affect and fantasy in patients with psychosomatic disorders.   In:   Hill, O.W.  (Ed.),  *Modern trend in psychosomatic medicine,* **2**:  26–34.  London:  Butterworths, 1970.

O'Connor, J.F.  A comprehensive approach to the treatment of ulcerative colitis. In:  Hill, O.W. (Ed.), *Modern trends in psychosomatic medicine,* **2**:  172–188. London: Butterworths, 1970.

Okasha, A., Ghaleb, H.A. and Sadek, A.  A double-blind trial for the clinical management of psychogenic headache. *British Journal of Psychiatry.* **122**: 181–183 (1973).

O'Neill, D.  Asthma as a stress reaction: its diagnosis and treatment.  *The Practitioner.* **169**:  273–280 (1952).

Orgel, S.Z.  Effect of psychoanalysis on the course of peptic ulcer. *Psychosomatic Medicine.* **20**:  117–123 (1958).

Osgood, C.E.  *Method and theory in experimental psychology.*  Oxford:  Oxford University Press, 1953.

Pedder, J.R.  Psychosomatic disorder and psychosis. *Journal of Psychosomatic Research.* **13**:  339–346 (1969).

Penick, S.B., Filion, R., Fox, S. and Stunkard, A.J.  Behavior modification in the treatment of obesity. *Psychosomatic Medicine.* **33**:  49–55 (1971).

Peper, E.  Reduction of efferent motor commands during alpha feedback as a facilitator of EEG alpha and a precondition for changes in consciousness. *Kybernetik.* **9**:  226–231 (1971).

Peshkin, M.M.  Asthma in children. IX. Role of environment in the treatment of a selected group of cases: a plea for a "home" as a restorative measure. *American Journal of Diseases of Children.* **39**:  774–781 (1930).

Peshkin, M.M.  Management of the institutionalized child with intractable asthma. *Annals of Allergy.* **18**:  75–79 (1960).

Peterfy, G.  The present status of hypnosis. *Canadian Medical Association Journal.* **109**:  397–407 (1973).

Pflanz, M.E., Rosenstein, E. and von Uexkul, Th.  Socio-psychological aspects of peptic ulcer. *Journal of Psychosomatic Research.* **1**:  68–74 (1956).

Pinkerton, P. and Weaver, C.M.  Childhood asthma. In: Hill, O.W. (Ed.), *Modern trends in psychosomatic medicine,* **2**:  81–104.  London: Butterworths, 1970.

Plumlee, L.A.  Operant conditioning of increases in blood pressure. *Psychophysiology.* **6**:  283–290 (1969).

Pollnow, H., Wittkower, E.D. and Petow, H.   Beitrage zur Klinik des Asthma bronchiale und verwandter Zustande.   IV. Zur Psychotherapie des Asthma bronchiale.   *Zeitschrift fur Klinische Medizin.*   **110:**   701–721 (1929).

Pratt, J.H.   The home sanitorium treatment of consumption.   *Johns Hopkins Hospital Bulletin.*   **17:**   140 (1906).

*Psychosomatic Medicine.*   **1:**   3–5.   Editorial. Introductory Statement. (1939).

Purcell, K., Bernstein, ·L. and Bukantz, S.C.   A preliminary comparison of rapidly remitting and persistently "steroid-dependent" asthmatic children.   *Psychosomatic Medicine.*   **23:**   305–310 (1961).

Raginsky, B.B. Hypnosis in internal medicine and general practice. In: Schneck, J.M. (Ed.), *Hypnosis in modern medicine,* 2nd ed., pp. 29–99.   Springfield: Charles C. Thomas, 1959.

Rahe, R.H.   Subjects' recent life changes and their near-future illness susceptibility.   In: Lipowski, Z.J. (Ed.), *Advances in psychosomatic medicine. Vol. 8: Psychosocial aspects of physical illness,* pp. 2–19.   Basel:   Karger, 1972.

Rahe, R.H. and Arthur, R.J.   Life change patterns surrounding illness experience.   *Journal of Psychosomatic Research.*   **11:**   341–345 (1968).

Rahe, R.H., McKean, J.D. and Arthur, R.J.   A longitudinal study of life-change and illness patterns.   *Journal of Psychosomatic Research.*   **10:**   355–366 (1967).

Ratliff, R.G. and Stein, N.H.   Treatment of neurodermatitis by behavior therapy: a case study.   *Behavior Research and Therapy.*   **6:**   397–399 (1968).

Reckless, J.B.   A behavioral treatment of bronchial asthma in modified group therapy.   *Psychosomatics.*   **12:**   168–173 (1971).

Reed, J.W.   Group therapy with asthmatic patients.   *Geriatrics.*   **17:**   823–838 (1962).

Rees, L.   Physical and emotional factors in bronchial asthma.   *Journal of Psychosomatic Research.*   **1:**   98–114 (1956).

Reich, W.   *The function of the orgasm.*   New York: Panther, 1961.

Richardson, H.B.   *Patients have families.*   New York:   Commonwealth Fund, 1948.

Ripley, H.S., Wolf, S. and Wolff, H.G.   Treatment in a psychosomatic clinic.   *Journal of the American Medical Association.*   **138:**   949–951 (1948).

Riskin, J.M. and Faunce, E.E.   An evaluative review of family interaction research.   *Family Process.*   **11:**   365–455 (1972).

Robinson, G.   The story of parentectomy.   *Journal of Asthma Research.*   **9:**   199–205 (1972).

Rosenbaum, M.   Treatment of psychosomatic disorders.   In: Lief, H.I., Lief, V.R. and Lief, N.R. (Eds.), *The psychological basis of medical practice,* pp. 501–509.   New York: Hoeber Medical Division, Harper & Row, 1963.

Ruesch, J.   The infantile personality — the core problem of psychosomatic medicine.   *Psychosomatic Medicine.*   **10:**   134–144 (1948).

Sainsbury, P.   Influencing the environment.   In: Hopkins, P and Wolff, H.H. (Eds.), *Principles of treatments of psychosomatic disorders,* pp. 71–77.   New York: Pergamon, 1965.

St. Amand, A.E.   The role of hypnotherapy in clinical medicine.   *Medical Clinics of North America.*   **56:**   687–692 (1972).

Salfield, D.J. and Reverchon, F. Relaxation et medecine generale. In: Aboulker, P., Chertok, L. and Sapir, M. (Eds.), *La relaxation (Reeducation psychotoninque). Aspects theoriques et practiques* (3rd ed.), pp. 181-201. Paris: Expansion Scientifique Francaise, 1964.

Sanger, M.D. The use of tranquilizers and antidepressants in allergy. *Annals of Allergy.* **20**: 705-709 (1962).

Sanger, M.D. Psychosomatic factors in the etiology of allergic diseases. *Annals of Allergy.* **22**: 418-422 (1964).

Santos, I.M.H. and Unger, L. Hydroxyzine (Atarax) in allergic diseases. *Annals of Allergy.* **18**: 172-178 (1960).

Sargent, J.D., Green, E.E. and Walters, E.D. Preliminary report on the use of autogenic feedback training in the treatment of migraine and tension headaches. *Psychosomatic Medicine.* **35**: 129-135 (1973).

Schaeffer, G. Ergebnisse des autogenen Trainings bei der Colitis ulcerosa. In: Lopez Ibor, J.J. (Ed.), *IV World Congress of Psychiatry,* Madrid, 1966, International Congress Series, No. 117,48. Amsterdam: Excerpta Medica Foundation, 1966.

Schenk, Th. Das autogene Training in der Behandlung von Asthmakranken. *Psychotherapie.* **3**: 148-150 (1958).

Scherbel, A.L. The effect of marsilid in patients having rheumatoid arthritis; the theoretical causal role of certain amine oxidases. *Journal of Clinical and Experimental Psychopathology.* **19**: 118-122 (1958).

Schmale, A.H. Giving up as a final common pathway to changes in health. In: Lipowski, Z.J. (Ed.), *Advances in psychosomatic medicine. Vol. 8: Psychosocial aspects of physical illness,* pp. 20-40. Basel: Karger, 1972.

Schmale, A.H. and Engel, G.L. The giving up – given up complex illustrated on film. *Archives of General Psychiatry.* **17**: 135-145 (1967).

Schoenberg, B. and Carr, A.C. An investigation of criteria for brief psychotherapy of neurodermatitis. *Psychosomatic Medicine.* **25**: 253-263 (1963).

Schultz, J.H. Die Psychotherapie des Asthma bronchiale. *Deutsch. Med. Wschr.* **54**: 964-965 (1928).

Schultz, J.H. Die Bedeutung der organismischen Verfahren in der Psychiatrie. *Arztl. Praxis.* **15**: 525-526 (1963).

Schultz, J.H. and Luthe, W. *Autogenic therapy. I. Autogenic methods.* New York and London: Grune & Stratton, 1969.

Schwartz, G.E. Voluntary control of human cardiovascular integration and differentiation through feedback and reward. *Science.* **175**: 90-93 (1972).

Scott, M.J. *Hypnosis in skin and allergic diseases.* Springfield, Ill.: Charles C. Thomas, 1960.

Scott, W.A.M. The relief of pain with an antidepressant in arthritis. *The Practitioner.* **202**: 802-807 (1969).

Seitz, P.F.D. Dynamically-oriented brief psychotherapy: psychocutaneous excoriation syndromes. *Psychosomatic Medicine.* **15**: 200-242 (1953).

Selye, H. The general adaptation syndrome and the diseases of adaptation. *Journal of Clinical Endocrinology.* **6**: 117-230 (1946).

Selye, H. *The stress of life.* New York: McGraw-Hill, 1956.

Shapiro, D., Schwartz, G.E. and Tursky, B. Control of diastolic blood pressure in man by feedback and reinforcement. *Psychophysiology.* **9**: 296-304 (1972).

Shapiro, D., Tursky, B., Gershon, E. and Stern, M.   Effects of feedback and reinforcement on the control of human systolic blood pressure. *Science.* **163**: 588–590 (1969).

Shapiro, D., Tursky, B. and Schwartz, G.E.   Differentiation of heart rate and systolic blood pressure in man by operant conditioning. *Psychosomatic Medicine.* **32**: 417–423 (1970).

Shoemaker, R.J., Guy, W.B. and McLaughlin, J.T.   Usefulness of group therapy in management of atopic eczema. *Pennsylvania Medical Journal.* **58**: 603–609 (1955).

Sifneos, P.E.   Is dynamic psychotherapy contraindicated for a large number of patients with psychosomatic diseases?   *Psychotherapy and Psychosomatics.* **21**: 133–136 (1972).

Simons, D.J., Day, E., Goodell, H. and Wolff, H.G.   Experimental studies on headaches: muscles of the scalp and neck as sources of pain. *Research Publications. Association for Research in Nervous and Mental Disease.* **23**: 228–244 (1943).

Sinclair-Gieben, A.H.C. and Chalmers, D.   Evaluation of treatment of warts by hypnosis. *Lancet.* **2**: 480–482 (1959).

Slavson, S.R.   Criteria for selection and rejection of patients for various kinds of group therapy. *International Journal of Group Psychotherapy.* **5**: 3–30 (1955).

Slawson, P.F.   Group psychotherapy with obese women. *Psychosomatics.* **6**: 206–209 (1965).

Smith, M.M., Colebatch, H.J.H. and Clarke, P.S.   Increase and decrease in pulmonary resistance with hypnotic suggestion in asthma. *American Review of Respiratory Disease.* **102**: 236–242 (1970).

Solomon, L.N. and Berzon, B. (Eds.), *New Perspectives on encounter groups.* San Francisco: Jossey-Bass, Inc., 1972.

Sperling, M.   Psychotherapeutic techniques in psychosomatic medicine. In: Bychowski, G. and Despert, J.L. (Eds.), *Specialized techniques in psychotherapy,* pp. 279–301. New York: Basic Books, 1952.

Sperling, M.   Psychosis and psychosomatic illness. *International Journal of Psycho-Analysis.* **36**: 320–327 (1955).

Sperling, M.   Acting out behaviour and psychosomatic symptoms: clinical and theoretical aspects. *International Journal of Psycho-Analysis.* **49**: 250–253 (1968).

Stein, A.   Group therapy with psychosomatically ill patients. In: Kaplan, H.I. and Sadock, B.J. (Eds.), *Comprehensive group psychotherapy,* pp. 581–601. Baltimore: Williams & Wilkins, 1971.

Stevens, A.   The role of psychotherapy in psychosomatic disorders. *Behavioral Neuropsychiatry.* **4**: 2–5 (1972).

Stine, L.A. and Ivy, A.C.   The effect of psychoanalysis on the course of peptic ulcer:   a preliminary report. *Gastroenterology.* **21**:   185–211 (1952).

Stokvis, B.   Possibilities et limitations de la relaxation dans la medecine psychosomatique.   *Revue de Medecine Psychosomatique.* **2**:   142–147 (1960).

Stuart, R.B.   Behavioral control of overeating. *Behavior Research and Therapy.* **5**: 357–365 (1967).

Stuart, R.B. and Davis, G.   *Slim chance in a fat world: behavioral control of obesity.*   Champaign, Ill.: Research Press, 1972.

Stunkard, A. New therapies for the eating disorders. Behavior modification of obesity and anorexia nervosa. *Archives of General Psychiatry.* 26: 391–398 (1972).

Surman, O.S., Gottlieb, S.K., Hackett, T.P. and Silverberg, E.L. Hypnosis in the treatment of warts. *Archives of General Psychiatry.* 28: 439–441 (1973).

Szyrynski, V. Psychotherapy with families of allergic patients. *Annals of Allergy.* 22: 165–172 (1964).

Tenzel, J.H. and Taylor, R.L. An evaluation of hypnosis and suggestion as treatment for warts. *Psychosomatics.* 10: 252–257 (1969).

Teplitz, T.A. Operant conditioning of blood pressure: a critical review and some psychosomatic considerations. *Communications in Behavioral Biology.* 6: 197–202 (1971).

Titchener, J.L., Sheldon, M.B. and Ross, W.D. Changes in blood pressure of hypertensive patients with and without group psychotherapy. *Journal of Psychosomatic Research.* 4: 10–12 (1959).

Toch, H. *The social psychology of social movements.* New York: Bobbs-Merrill, 1965.

Trowill, J. Instrumental conditioning of the heart rate in the curarized rat. *Journal of Comparative and Physiological Psychology.* 63: 7–11 (1967).

Turnbull, J.W. Asthma conceived as a learned response. *Journal of Psychosomatic Research.* 6: 59–70 (1962).

Ulett, G.A., Akpinar, S. and Itil, T.M. Hypnosis: physiological, pharmacological reality. *American Journal of Psychiatry.* 128: 799–805 (1972).

Ullman, M. and Dudek, S. On the psyche and warts. II. Hypnotic suggestion and warts. *Psychosomatic Medicine.* 22: 68–76 (1960).

Van der Valk, J.M. Clusters of illnesses and syndrome shifts as observed in clinical practice. In: Wisdom, J.O. and Wolff, H. (Eds.), *The role of psychosomatic disorders in adult life,* pp. 3–9. Oxford: Pergamon, 1965.

Van Pelt, S.J. Hypnotherapy in medical practice. *British Journal of Medical Hypnosis.* 1: 8–13 (1949).

Varay, A., Berthelot, J., Billiottet, J., Viterbo, G. and Graf, B. Action de L'imipramine dans les affections gastro-duodenales. Premiers resultats. *Bulletins et Memoires de la Societe Medical des Hopitaux de Paris.* 76: 228–239 (1960).

Vince, J.D. and Kremer, D. Double-blind trial of diazepam in rheumatoid arthritis. *The Practitioner.* 210: 264–267 (1973).

Vogt, O. Die Zielvorstellung der Suggestion. *Ztsch. f. Hypnotismus, Psychotherap., Psychophysiolog. u. Psychopatholog. Forschg.* 5: 332–342 (1897).

Vosburg, R. Conjoint therapy of migraine: a case report. *Psychosomatics.* 13: 61–63 (1972).

Waitzkin, H. and Stoeckle, J.D. The communication of information about illness. In: Lipowski, Z.J. (Ed.), *Advances in psychosomatic medicine. Vol. 8: Psychosocial aspects of physical illness,* pp. 180–215. Basel: Karger, 1972.

Walton, D. The application of learning theory to the treatment of a case of bronchial asthma. In: Eysenck, H.J. (Ed.), *Behavior therapy and the neuroses,* pp. 188–189. New York: Pergamon Press, 1960a.

Walton, D. The application of learning theory to treatment of a case of neuro-dermatitis. In: Eysenck, H.J. (Ed.), *Behavior therapy and the neuroses,* pp. 272–274. New York: Pergamon Press, 1960b.

Weber, R.B. and Reinmuth, O.M. The treatment of migraine with propanolol. *Neurology.* **22**: 366–369 (1972).

Weinstock, H.J. Successful treatment of ulcerative colitis by psychoanalysts. *Journal of Psychosomatic Research.* **6**: 243–249 (1962).

Weiss, E. Emotional factors in allergy with special reference to asthma. *International Archives of Allergy and Applied Immunology.* **14**: 148–161 (1959).

Weiss, E. and English, O.S. *Psychosomatic medicine. The clinical application of psychopathology to general medical problems.* Philadelphia: Saunders, 1943.

Weiss, E. and English, O.S. *Psychosomatic medicine. A clinical study of psycho-physiologic reactions* (3rd ed.). Philadelphia and London: W.B. Saunders, 1957.

Weiss, T. and Engel, B.T. Operant conditioning of heart rate in patients with premature ventricular contractions. *Psychosomatic Medicine.* **33**: 301–321 (1971).

Wells, R.A., Dilkes, T.C. and Trivelli, N. The results of family therapy: a critical review of the literature. *Family Process.* **11**: 189–207 (1972).

Wenger, M.A. and Bagchi, B.K. Studies of autonomic functions in practitioners of yoga in India. *Behavioral Science.* **6**: 312–323 (1961).

Wenger, M.A., Bagchi, B.K. and Anand, B.K. Experiments in India on "voluntary" control of the heart and pulse. *Circulation.* **24**: 1319–1325 (1961).

West, R. The place and recognition of emotional factors in the etiology and treatment of chronic non-specific colitis. In: Jores, A. and Freyberger, H. (Eds.), *Advances in psychosomatic medicine,* pp. 270–280. New York: Brunner, 1961.

Wilson, G.W. A study of structural and instinctual conflicts in cases of hay fever. *Psychosomatic Medicine.* **3**: 51–65 (1941).

Witkin, H.A. *Psychological differentiation; studies of development.* New York: John Wiley & Sons, 1962.

Witkin, H.A. Psychological differentiation and forms of pathology. *Journal of Abnormal Psychology.* **70**: 317–336 (1965).

Wittkower, E.D. Transcultural psychosomatics. In: *Proceedings of the 2nd International Congress of Psychosomatic Medicine.* Amsterdam, 1973 (in press).

Wittkower, E.D., Cleghorn, J.M., Lipowski, Z.J., Peterfy, G. and Solyom, L. A global survey of psychosomatic medicine. *International Journal of Psychiatry.* **7**: 499–516 (1969).

Wittkower, E.D. and Cleghorn, R.A. (Eds.) *Recent developments in psychosomatic medicine.* London: Pitman, 1954.

Wittkower, E.D. and Dudek, S.Z. Psychosomatic medicine: the mind-body-society interaction. In: Wolman, B.B. (Ed.), *Handbook of general psychology,* pp. 242–272. Englewood Cliffs: Prentice-Hall, 1973.

Wittkower, E.D. and Engels, W.D. Psyche and Allergy. In: Hirt, M.L. (Ed.), *Psychological and allergic aspects of asthma,* pp. 143–171. Springfield: Charles C. Thomas, 1965.

Wittkower, E.D. and Lipowski, Z.J. Recent developments in psychosomatic medicine. *Psychosomatic Medicine.* **28**: 722–737 (1966).

Wittkower, E.D. and Solyom, L. Models of mind-body interaction. *International Journal of Psychiatry.* **4**: 225–233 (1967).

Wittkower, E.D. and White, K.L. Psychophysiologic aspects of respiratory disorders. In: Arieti, S. (Ed.), *American handbook of psychiatry, Vol. I, pp.* 690–707. New York: Basic Books, 1959.

Wohl, T. The role of group psychotherapy for mothers in a rehabilitative approach to juvenile intractable asthma. *Mental Hygiene.* **47**: 150–155 (1963).

Wohl, T.H. Behavior modification: its application to study and treatment of childhood asthma. *Journal of Asthma Research.* **9**: 41–45 (1971).

Wolf, S. Psychosocial forces in myocardial infarction and sudden death. In: Levi, L. (Ed.), *Society, stress and disease: the psychosocial environment and psychosomatic diseases,* pp. 324–330. London: Oxford University Press, 1971.

Wolf, S., Pfeiffer, J.B., Ripley, H.S., Winter, O.S. and Wolff, H.G. Hypertension as a reaction pattern to stress. *Annals of Internal Medicine.* **29**: 1056–1076 (1948).

Wolff, H.G. Life stress and bodily disease – a formulation. In: Wolff, H.G. and Itase, C.C. (Eds.), *Life stress and bodily disease.* Baltimore: Williams and Wilkins, 1950.

Wolff, H.G. *Stress and disease.* Springfield: Charles C. Thomas, 1953.

Wollersheim, J.P. The effectiveness of group therapy based upon learning principles in the treatment of overweight women. *Journal of Abnormal Psychology.* **76**: 462–474 (1970).

Wolpe, J. *Psychotherapy by reciprocal inhibition.* Stanford: Stanford University Press, 1958.

Wright, G.L.T. Asthma and the emotions: aetiology and treatment. *Medical Journal of Australia.* **1**: 961–967 (1965).

Yalom, I.D. (Ed.) *The theory and practice of group psychotherapy.* New York: Basic Books, 1970.

Yeh, E.K. Recurrent urticaria alternating with psychosis. *Psychosomatic Medicine.* **20**: 373–378 (1958).

# Author Index

# Subject Index